STUDIES IN CHRISTIAN HISTORY AND THOUGHT

"An Educated Clergy"

Scottish Theological Education and Training in the Kirk and Secession, 1560-1850

STUDIES IN CHRISTIAN HISTORY AND THOUGHT

A full listing of titles in this series
appears at the end of this book

STUDIES IN CHRISTIAN HISTORY AND THOUGHT

"An Educated Clergy"

Scottish Theological Education and Training in the Kirk and Secession, 1560-1850

Jack C. Whytock

Foreword by A. T. B. McGowan

WIPF & STOCK · Eugene, Oregon

Wipf and Stock Publishers
199 W 8th Ave, Suite 3
Eugene, OR 97401

"An Educated Clergy"
Scottish Theological Education and Training in the Kirk and Secession, 1560–1850
By Whytock, Jack C.
Copyright©2007 Paternoster
ISBN 13: 978-1-55635-664-3
ISBN 10: 1-55635-664-1
Publication date 1/8/2008

This Edition Published by Wipf and Stock Publishers by arrangement with Paternoster

Series Preface

This series complements the specialist series of *Studies in Evangelical History and Thought* and *Studies in Baptist History and Thought* for which Paternoster is becoming increasingly well known by offering works that cover the wider field of Christian history and thought. It encompasses accounts of Christian witness at various periods, studies of individual Christians and movements, and works which concern the relations of church and society through history, and the history of Christian thought.

The series includes monographs, revised dissertations and theses, and collections of papers by individuals and groups. As well as 'free standing' volumes, works on particular running themes are being commissioned; authors will be engaged for these from around the world and from a variety of Christian traditions.

A high academic standard combined with lively writing will commend the volumes in this series both to scholars and to a wider readership.

Series Editors

Alan P. F. Sell, Visiting Professor at Acadia University Divinity College, Nova Scotia, Canada

David Bebbington, Professor of History, University of Stirling, Stirling, Scotland, UK

Clyde Binfield, Professor Associate in History, University of Sheffield, UK

Gerald Bray, Anglican Professor of Divinity, Beeson Divinity School, Samford University, Birmingham, Alabama, USA

Grayson Carter, Associate Professor of Church History, Fuller Theological Seminary SW, Phoenix, Arizona, USA

To Nancy,

Ian, Alistair, Andrew, and Janet

μόνη θυτέον τῇ ἀληθείαι

Contents

Foreword by Andrew T. B. McGowan	xv
Preface	xix
Acknowledgements	xxv
Abbreviations	xxvii
Part One: Theological Education and Training in the Kirk	1
Chapter 1 Continental Reformed Theological Education and Training	3
Introduction	3
The Genevan Academy and the Company of Pastors	6
Heidelberg, Leiden and France	19
Summary	24
Chapter 2 Period I: 1560-1576, *The First Book of Discipline*	25
Introduction: The 1560 *First Book of Discipline*	25
The *FBD* and Schools	26
The *FBD* and Universities	27
The Exercise – A Vital Role	29
Vacant Parishes?	32
A Student	33
Summary	34
Chapter 3 Period II: 1577-1637, *Nova Erectio*	36
1577-1606 Melvillian Assertions	36
Glasgow	36
St. Mary's	37
Edinburgh	39

King's	42
Marischal	44
The Exercise and Presbyterial Involvements	47
Orkneys and Fraserburgh	48
1606-1638 Episcopal Assertions	49
Chairs of Divinity	50
Degrees	51
Theological Writings by Principals and Professors	52
Summary	54

Chapter 4 Period III: 1638-1661, Covenanter Period — **56**

Introduction	56
The Galaxy of Divines: Baillie, Dickson, Gillespie, Rutherford and Row; the Covenanter Expository Series; and Leighton	57
General Assemblies	72
The Westminster Standards	74
College and Student	77
Summary	79

Chapter 5 Period IV: 1662-1689, Episcopal Restoration — **81**

Introduction	81
Exercise/Presbytery and Diocesan Synod	82
Gilbert Burnet	85
"School of Theology"	87
Degrees	90
Summary	90

Chapter 6 Period V: 1690-1825, Revolution Settlement — **91**

Introduction	91
The General Assembly: 1690-1825	91
Subscription	91
The Exercise and Addition and the Rise of "Societies"	92
Bursars	97
Libraries in the Highlands	98
Assembly Standing Laws for Licensure of Students	100
Memoirs and Autobiographical Sketches	103
University Changes in Period V	110

Leading Scottish Educationalists	117
Pluralities	124
On the Matter of Books	126
Principal George Campbell: Lectures, Books, Student Training and The Scottish Enlightenment	132
George Hill (1750-1819)	139
Summary	142

Chapter 7 Period VI: 1826-1860, Universities' Commission — 144

Introduction	144
Royal Commission into the State of the Universities of Scotland, 1826-1830	145
The General Assembly Acts	152
Royal Commission and the Five Universities' Divinity Halls, 1826-1830	158
The Chair of Biblical Criticism and Robert Lee	162
Professors and Their Writings	164
Summary	165

Part Two: Theological Education and Training in the Secession — 167

Chapter 8 Introduction: Origins of the Secession and First Efforts for a Divinity Hall — 169

Introduction	169
Origins	169
First Efforts: William Wilson, "the face of an ox" (Perth)	172
Gleanings from the Associate Presbytery Minutes	178
Alexander Moncrieff, "the face of a lion" (Abernethy)	181
Development of a Philosophical Class/College	184
Summary	186

Chapter 9 The 1747 Breach and Two Halls — 187

Introduction	187
The Associate Hall: 1746-1767	187
Ebenezer Erskine, "the face of a man" (Stirling)	187
James Fisher, "the face of an eagle" (Glasgow)	193
John Swanston (Kinross)	198

Discontinuation of the Philosophical Class	200
The General Associate Hall: 1748-1785	201
Alexander Moncrieff (Abernethy)	201
William Moncrieff (Alloa)	201
Continuation of the Philosophical Class	204
Summary	207

Chapter 10 The Associate Divinity Hall with John Brown of Haddington (1767-1787) — 208

Introduction	208
A Biographical Sketch	208
Professor Brown	210
Brown and the Marriage of Theology and Piety	215
Brown and Practical Divinity	223
Casuistry	223
Homiletics, Catechising and Sacraments	228
Polity	233
Unto Exemplification	235
Brown and History	240
Brown and Baxter	242
Brown and Scripture	243
The Associate Divinity Library (1770)	252
The Theological Society: Kinross, Haddington, Selkirk	252
Summary	255

Chapter 11 The Associate Divinity Hall with George Lawson (1787-1820) — 257

Introduction	257
Biographical Sketch	257
Synod Actions in the Lawson Era	259
The Divinity Hall at Selkirk	260
The Professor and His Writings	264
Summary	270

Chapter 12 The General Associate Hall (1786-1820) — 272

Introduction	272
The Archibald Bruce Era	272

Biographical Sketch	272
Bruce's Vision as Theological Professor	274
Bruce's Writings	279
George Paxton	285
Biographical Sketch and the Hall	285
Writings	287
Summary	289

Chapter 13 The United Secession Divinity Hall (1821-1847) — 291

Introduction	291
John Dick: Solo Professor	291
Biographical Sketch	291
The United Divinity Hall	293
Student Petition	296
Professor Dick and His Printed Divinity Lectures	297
The Appointment of a Second Professor (1825-1833)	303
The Appointment of a Third and Fourth Professor (1834-1847)	309
John Brown: Exegetical Theology	310
Robert Balmer: Systematic Theology	318
Alexander Duncan: Pastoral Theology and Ecclesiastical History	321
Summary	324

Chapter 14 The Auld Light Divinity Halls — 327

Introduction	327
The Auld Light Burghers	327
Introduction	327
The Original Burgher Synod Divinity Hall (1799)	329
The Auld Light Antiburghers	336
Constitutional Associate Divinity Hall (1806)	336
Protesters Divinity Hall (1820)	340
Original Secession Divinity Hall (1827)/United Original Secession Divinity Hall (1842)	341
Summary	343

Part Three: Scottish Patterns and British North America   345

Chapter 15 A Case Study in Theological Education in British North America (1820-1843)   347
Introduction   347
Thomas McCulloch: Biographical Sketch, Writings and the Hall   348
   Biographical Sketch   348
   McCulloch's Writings and the Divinity Hall   352
   The Hall   359
Synod Records and Theological Education   367
Summary   379

Chapter 16 Conclusion   380

Appendices   395
Appendix A: A Listing of Theological Professors in the Scottish Universities, c.1560-1860   395
Appendix B: A Complete Listing of Theological Professors in the Secession Churches, 1733-1847   406

Bibliography   411

Index   439

FOREWORD

It gives me great pleasure to be able to contribute a foreword to this work by Dr. Jack Whytock. Having watched it grow and develop over a number of years, I am delighted that it is now to be published. It is a work of significant scholarship and fills a clear gap in the historical research of the period.

The larger portion of the work is given over to Dr. Whytock's analysis of the Seceder tradition of theological education. Those whose ecclesiastical roots lie in that tradition, as well as those with an historical interest in it, will be most in Dr. Whytock's debt. They will not only enjoy learning about their roots but will also witness the disposal of many oft repeated myths regarding the way in which theological education was carried out by their forefathers. There is also much that those of us in the Kirk can learn from his study of theological education in the Church of Scotland and in the Secession during the three hundred year period under consideration. Indeed, anyone with an interest in theological education will find this book to be rich in information and analysis.

The way in which Dr. Whytock sets the scene for his study by giving a description of the early Reformed period is very instructive. The influence of Humanism, with its emphasis on a return to original sources in their original languages, was hugely formative in the thought of Calvin and others. Reformed pastors were to be those who were able to read and study the Scriptures for themselves and would not be dependent upon the Church for a "definitive" interpretation of Scripture. This led to a strong emphasis on the importance of an educated and well-read ministry. The Genevan Company of Pastors and the subsequent Genevan Academy became a model which other Reformed churches were to follow, not least the Church of Scotland. As Dr. Whytock points out, however, there were other somewhat different traditions which also impacted on later Reformed theological education; for example, Heidelberg and Leiden. It is also interesting to note that many Scottish academics in the seventeenth and eighteenth centuries had strong links with the continental universities and spent time there, perhaps even more so than is generally the case today.

Part One of the book concerns Dr. Whytock's analysis of the Church of Scotland and is divided into six periods. This study is full of insight and helpful information. It also serves to highlight how many of the most significant

Scottish academics have been largely neglected, even in their own country. The name of John Knox is well known – although usually disparaged and mistreated by an ignorant and hostile media – but little is heard today of many others, not least the great Andrew Melville, one of the key thinkers behind the Scottish political, ecclesiastical and theological settlement. When Dr. Whytock goes on to document the Kirk's training processes over three hundred years and lists all the professors during the period, he unearths many forgotten (or almost forgotten) names. In doing so, he underlines how much work remains to be carried out in researching the area of Scottish theology.

When he comes to Part Two of the book, concerning the Seceders, Dr. Whytock is on home ground. This is a tradition he knows well. He not only provides some general historical background to the First Secession of 1733, but succeeds in explaining the complexity of the situation, noting the many factors involved. When he then goes on to analyze the theological education within the Secession churches, the surprises come thick and fast. For example, most people imagine that the training of ministers in the Secession was like the present-day training within the Free Presbyterian Church of Scotland, where there is no separate theological college as such, but where students are assigned to a tutor (or indeed several tutors, covering different subjects). It turns out that there are probably more similarities than dissimilarities between Kirk and Secession when it came to theological education and training.

In the concluding Part Three of the book, Dr. Whytock turns his attention to his native Canada and to the influence of the Seceders there. This not only demonstrates the influence of the Seceder tradition beyond Scotland but also enables Dr. Whytock to reflect on this tradition and its background. This excursus only covers a short period (1820-1843) but is rich in detail and interest.

As with any good piece of research, as he comes to the end of his work, Dr. Whytock indicates areas where further study might be carried out, and it is to be hoped that some of these suggestions will be taken up by other scholars. He also seeks to apply the research to the situation today in theological education, and he challenges us to review our current philosophy of theological education and training. In this regard there is considerable wisdom in the concluding set of questions asked by Dr. Whytock in seeking to apply the lessons learned from his historical study. For example, he points out that our modern emphasis on distance and open learning, such a key element in modern educational theory and practice, might not be as modern as we think. He notes that the balance between distance learning and residential training was something well known in the eighteenth century, as students spent perhaps as little as two months per year actually in the colleges or halls and did the remainder of their work through presbyteries or with their professors, albeit at a distance.

He also raises the question of the nature and purpose of the theological training and the implications for the professors. Are they to be primarily scholars engaged in research, doing some teaching as well, or is their primary purpose to teach and train their students for ministry? In an environment where, at least in the United Kingdom, such great emphasis is placed on the Research Assessment Exercise (RAE) and where academics often have much less time for teaching and to engage with students because of the pressure to write and publish, it is a valid question. It is one which was famously answered by John Henry Newman in his lectures *On the Idea of a University*. He argued that universities were places where knowledge was passed on to the next generation and that the professors should not spend a large amount of their time in research – that was to be left to the Royal Societies and other such bodies specifically created for the purpose. The ideal is probably somewhere between Newman on the one hand and the pressures of the RAE on the other hand!

The final question Dr. Whytock raises concerns the educational background of incoming theological students. He believes that we need to re-think this issue. What ought to be required in terms of pre-requisite and preparatory studies? In earlier days an arts degree was required before a student could begin the study of theology. This meant that certain expectations could be legitimately held regarding the new theological students. Today there are different requirements for incoming students, depending upon the denomination for which one is a candidate for ministry. The matter is also complicated by the fact that many people study theology for reasons other than preparation for the ministry, a factor unknown in the period discussed by Dr. Whytock. There is the even more significant factor that many university divinity colleges have become departments of religious studies, with theology only a sub-section of the curriculum and often with a small minority of the total number of students in the department.

As we reflect on these questions for our current practice, it is my hope and prayer that readers will be as stimulated and instructed by this work as I have been.

Andrew T. B. McGowan
Dingwall, Scotland
August 2006

PREFACE

A perception has grown that from the days of Knox, Scotland has elevated the role of education, and Scottish Presbyterianism has often been characterized by its insistence upon "an educated clergy". This book, *"An Educated Clergy"*, cannot explore all aspects of these perceptions, but the focus here will be to examine the study of divinity and the training for those preparing for the ministry within the Church of Scotland and in the Secession churches, from the time of Knox until the middle of the nineteenth century. How exactly was this enterprise carried forth? What were their priorities? What were the great continuities? What were the changes?

There appears to be a lack of historical survey of this vast enterprise of the education and training of Scottish Presbyterian ministers. Thus, *"An Educated Clergy"* seeks to provide an overall survey of the theological education and training of ministers for these two branches of Scottish Presbyterianism To my knowledge there is not one thesis or book that is an effort to examine the field in an organic manner.[1] The best survey is David Wright's article on theological education in Scotland in the *Dictionary of Scottish Church History and Theology*, yet it is limited simply by the fact that it is a dictionary article.[2]

---

[1] For the Church of Scotland there are several excellent singular volumes; however, these often focus upon one hall, group, or line of professors. By contrast, I have examined the various halls to endeavour to see the general tenor and approach. Some such singular volumes worthy of mention are the following: William Ian P. Hazlett, ed., *Traditions of Theology in Glasgow 1410-1990 A Miscellany* (Edinburgh, 1993); H. M. B. Reid, *The Divinity Professors in the University of Glasgow 1640-1903* (Glasgow, 1923); G. D. Henderson, "Aberdeen Divines: being a History of the Chair of Divinity in Kings College, Aberdeen", typescript *MS* (Historic Collections, Special Libraries and Archives, King's College, University of Aberdeen); and Henry Sefton, "St. Mary's College, St. Andrews, in the eighteenth century", *RSCHS* 24 (1991), 161-179. There are several theses on particular professors within the halls (both Kirk and Secession), as evidenced in the bibliography, but what is lacking is the overall picture of theological education.

[2] *DSCHT*, 278-285. I will follow the custom of only identifying the reference dictionary with page numbers in the footnote, rather than also including the article title and author. Stewart Mechie's three articles on the history of theological education for ministers in

However, it is most helpful as a starting point and brings a preliminary organizational structure to the topic.

Second, *"An Educated Clergy"* addresses an acute neglect of the study of the historical practices of education and training which occurred within the Secession halls and churches. This book attempts to examine the Seceders' contribution to theological education in Scotland. Ian Hamilton described the study of the Secession as the "Cinderella" of Scottish historical theological studies.[3] By Hamilton's description, the inference is made that generally there has been a neglect of serious writing on the Secession in terms of historical theology. However, serious study in any field does reveal some amazing "beauties". This certainly applies to the field of study before us. Before the emergence of the Free Church of 1843, the "Dissenting" Presbyterians had an impact in Scottish ecclesiastical life which must not be ignored.[4] Kenneth Roxburgh's recent study, *Thomas Gillespie and the Origins of the Relief Church in 18th Century Scotland*, is a most helpful work for commencing the study of the place of one branch of the Dissenting Presbyterians in Scotland's history, the Relief Presbyterians. Their patterns of theological education need to be explored and taken up by scholars.[5] Also, Dissenting Presbyterians had a vital role in the British Colonies and America. It was the Seceders who first undertook the work of theological education in British North America. Thus, it is appropriate to study the history of the contribution of the Dissenting Presbyterians to theological education in Scotland for background to this.

The key work on the history of the Seceders in theological education is P. Landreth's *The United Presbyterian Divinity Hall, in its Changes and*

Scotland since the Reformation are certainly helpful, but the desire is for much needed expansion. See Stewart Mechie, "Education for the Ministry in Scotland Since the Reformation", 1 and 2, *RSCHS* 14 (1963), 115-133; 161-178; "Education for the Ministry in Scotland Since the Reformation", 3, *RSCHS* 15 (1966), 1-20.

[3] Ian Hamilton, *The Erosion of Calvinist Orthodoxy: Seceders and Subscription in Scottish Presbyterianism*, Rutherford Studies in Historical Theology, eds. N. M. de S. Cameron, D. MacLeod and D. F. Wright (Edinburgh, 1990), iii.

[4] See David Bebbington, ed., *The Baptists in Scotland: A History* (Glasgow, 1988), 4, who wrote: "Recent research has established that religious Dissent has been much more powerful in Scotland than has often been supposed." Bebbington includes non-Church of Scotland Presbyterian bodies under Dissenters. "In the 1830's, before the Disruption created the Free Church of Scotland, 30% of worshippers in Edinburgh and 27% in Glasgow were Presbyterian Dissenters." See also David Bebbington, *Evangelicalism in Modern Britain: A History from the 1730's to the 1980's*, original 1989 (Grand Rapids, 1992), 34. Bebbington bases this upon C. G. Brown, *The Social History of Religion in Scotland since 1730* (London, 1987), 61.

[5] Kenneth B. E. Roxburgh, *Thomas Gillespie and the Origins of the Relief Church in 18th Century Scotland* (Bern, 1999).

Preface

Enlargements for 140 Years (1876). However, it is old and inadequate.[6] It contains no footnotes and virtually nothing by way of primary source material, nor does it make any attempt to contextualize what the Seceders were doing.

I am aware that many helpful studies on education within the Scottish universities have come forth recently, often in connection with the universities' anniversaries. However, they have not always reflected the type of historical work on the study of divinity that is being undertaken here.[7] Also, this book deliberately refrains from exploring the Free Church efforts at theological education or the Church of Scotland post-1850s. The recent work *Disruption to Diversity* covers this topic for the largest hall of this time period, New College, and is well beyond the scope of our study.[8] For the Seceders recent studies on the Marrow and related matters dealing with the Erskines have been helpful, but I am unaware of efforts to deal with the Seceders in relation to theological education.[9]

I hope this book will also provide an historical framework for the current practice of theological education and training within the Reformed tradition. This book does not set out to critique modern models of theological education, although some may perceive such to be the case. There are current studies which are making assessments of contemporary trends and methods of theological education. I hope this book will give needed historical perspective to this ongoing endeavour.[10]

---

[6] P. Landreth, *The United Presbyterian Divinity Hall, in its Changes and Enlargements for 140 Years* (Edinburgh, 1876).

[7] Aberdeen University has produced an extensive series of books in connection with its 500th anniversary. See the series: "Quincentennial Studies in the history of the University of Aberdeen". The same can be said for the University of Glasgow in connection with its 550th anniversary in 2001. See A. L. Brown and Michael Moss, *The University of Glasgow 1451-2001* (Edinburgh, 2001), and Michael Moss, Moira Rankin, and Lesley Richmond, comps., *Who, Where and When: the History and Constitution of the University of Glasgow* (Glasgow, 2001). All of these works will be very important for students of the history of Scottish education, but my focus in this book is to attempt to bring together in one place a survey which will allow one to see overall changes, patterns, developments, and comparisons.

[8] David F. Wright and Gary D. Badcock, eds., *Disruption to Diversity Edinburgh Divinity 1846-1996* (Edinburgh, 1996). Mention here should also include the Free Church and theological education in Glasgow and Aberdeen which would also have to be examined.

[9] David Lachman, *The Marrow Controversy* (Edinburgh, 1998); Joel Beeke, "Ebenezer and Ralph Erskine: Dissenters with a Cause (1)", *Banner of Sovereign Grace Truth* (November, 1999), 229-231; Joel Beeke, "Ebenezer and Ralph Erskine: Dissenters with a Cause (2)", *Banner of Sovereign Grace Truth* (December, 1999), 262-264.

[10] I think here of such studies done by John H. Leith, *Crisis in the Church: The Plight of Theological Education* (Louisville, 1997). See also the critical review by William S. Barker, "John H. Leith, *Crisis in the Church*" a review in *WTJ* 61 (1999), 140-143. Also, D. G. Hart and R. Albert Mohler, Jr. eds., *Theological Education in the*

I also desire that this book may help to remedy a general failure in historical studies of Canadian theological education; that is, the failure to connect colonial Canadian Presbyterian patterns to their roots in Scottish theological education. The historical context needs to be more fully appreciated and developed. To this end one case study will be examined – the first Presbyterian divinity hall in British North America, conducted under the labours of Thomas McCulloch. His work as a theological educator is sadly neglected within the study of church history in Canada. Several studies do cover McCulloch's philosophical work and thoughts on liberal education, but nothing of a significant size recognizes him in the context of a theological educator. Sheldon MacKenzie's *Gathered by the River: The Story of the West River Seminary and Theological Hall 1848-1858* deals with the time period after McCulloch and only casts a cursory glance back to him. McCulloch needs to be seen in light of the Scottish patterns, which is in part my reason for this book. McCulloch's originality was neither in method nor pattern of teaching or training; he inherited these from Scotland.

Since this latter point takes us from Scotland to the Colonies, I see a range of topics which needs to be explored beyond this book; namely, the relationship between Scotland and the colonial endeavour or mission and how Scots were involved in foreign enterprises in theological education. Indeed, of significance are not only the relationship of Scotland and "overseas"; the Scottish influences upon theological education in Ireland, Wales and England will occasionally also be pointed to in this book and will hopefully be more fully examined by others in the future. If the book will induce further research, I will be pleased. One particular area that needs to be more fully explored is the Scottish Seceders and their influence upon theological education through Seceders in Ireland.

This book is structured by division into three parts: "Part One: Theological Education and Training in the Kirk"; "Part Two: Theological Education and

---

Evangelical Tradition (Grand Rapids, 1996); Edward Farley, "The Reform of Theological Education As a Theological Task", *Theological Education* 17 (1981), 93-117; Farley's *Theologia: The Fragmentation and Unity of Theological Education* (Philadelphia, 1983); Robert Wood Lynn, "Notes Toward a History: Theological Encyclopedia and the Evolution of Protestant Seminary Education, 1808-1868", *Theological Education* 17 (1981), 118-144; Harvie M. Conn and Samuel Rowen, eds., *Missions and Theological Education in World Perspective* (Urbanus, Michigan, 1984); William D. Graham, "Training for the Future", in *Proceedings of the International Conference of Reformed Churches – African Region* (Cape Town, 1995), 70-89; and Richard A. Muller, *The Study of Theology: From Biblical Interpretation to Contemporary Formulation*, Foundations of Contemporary Interpretation, ed. Moisés Silva, vol. 7 (Grand Rapids, 1991). This list could go on for several pages. Suffice it to say that there is much current discussion on the models for theological education and training today. An additional factor is the rise of technology and its use in theological education. This book is firmly rooted in its aim to be an historical study but will hopefully as such be of value to modern discussions.

Training in the Secession"; and, "Part Three: Scottish Patterns in British North America". Parts One and Two constitute the majority of the book, and Part Three is presented as a case study to explore continuities or discontinuities with the theological education and training in Scotland by Scottish Seceders in British North America within the given time frame.

In Part One the time period, c.1560 to c.1860, needed to be surveyed within the Church of Scotland and made manageable for study. Thus, I have established six "periods" for the Kirk, for which I do not claim great originality. The general contours for these periods have been followed before, as found in well established histories. I have not endeavoured to offer an exhaustive study of the six periods in the Church of Scotland but have given an overview. Periods V and VI have added detail, as these parallel the time period of Part Two of this book. In Part Two the Secession is surveyed from 1733 to 1847. I have not structured this chronologically by periods, but rather followed the historical developments via the emergence of the various halls.

The method of research used places strong emphasis upon biographical information (mainly, but not solely, of professors), the lectures and writings of professors, the official church statements, student accounts and pedagogical forms. An attempt has been made to discover what practical training was included. Since there is such a large corpus of writing or names, in certain instances decisions have been made to focus upon the essential, majority or representative. This last statement must by necessity apply particularly to the Kirk halls.

Finally, the book focuses primarily upon theological education and not the pre-requisite arts or philosophical curriculum. References are made to the latter, but not extensively. Although our main attention is upon the formal educational setting within the halls, it is also be broadened to include the wider aspects of ministerial development or training.[11] The time period covered is c.1560 to c.1850, and these terminus dates are appropriate for a number of reasons which have been hinted at above and will be referred to throughout the book. To briefly summarize those reasons here, the first date, c.1560, is the logical point of connection to the Scottish Reformation in the 1560 *First Book of Discipline*. I conclude with c.1850 for the following three reasons: first, the Free Church contribution to theological education and training in Scotland is such a vast

---

[11] I have adopted the understanding at the outset that theological education chiefly refers to those formal studies undertaken in the divinity halls, yet there was also "informal" training done by the presbyteries through the extensive student assignments and ministerial exercises. Also, the judicatories were heavily involved in making preaching rotas for probationers, so this perhaps is best seen as "training" as opposed to the more formal theological "education". Hence this book's title reflects the formal and the informal – education and training – and upon occasion it could be argued the two blend very closely together. See, Glenn Miller's, *Piety and Intellect: The Aims and Purposes of Ante-Bellum Theological Education* (Atlanta, 1990), 12-13; and *ERF*, 363.

field it could not be adequately dealt within this book; second, 1847 was the year in which the majority of Seceders joined with the Relief Church to form the United Presbyterian Church, which, arguably speaking, represents a major development within Scottish Dissenting Presbyterianism; and third, between 1850 and 1900 there were several major changes in theological education in Scotland that would clearly constitute another distinct period.

The book ends with overall conclusions concerning what has been learned in this study of Scottish theological education and training. Differences and similarities are stated and critical philosophical movements or ideas are examined as they affect theological education and training.

Jack C. Whytock
Charlottetown, Prince Edward Island, Canada
August 2006

Acknowledgements

I am most grateful to be able to present this book as a revision of my Ph.D. thesis. It was a wonderful privilege to be able to engage in research in Scottish church history. I do not believe my thesis would have been completed without a study leave in 1998, when we lived in Ayrshire as a family for seven months. I am flooded with memories of life on the Halket as I re-read portions of this book. To the many gracious friends in Scotland who ever afforded much encouragement – I thank each of them here. Their kindness, conversations, and hospitality helped me to persevere.

On the Canadian side of the Atlantic, the first debt I owe is to my former secretary, Mrs. Margaret Plewes, who did a "yeoman's" job without ever a word of complaint. She simply stepped in where I was lacking in skill. This was followed by my present personal assistant, Christina Lehmann, who has offered me much assistance in preparing this book for publication.

Research is not possible, of course, without libraries, and at every corner I have been met with invaluable assistance. To each of the following I offer my appreciation and thanks: Glasgow University Special Collections and University Library; Edinburgh University Library; New College Library, Edinburgh; Rutherford House, Edinburgh; Scottish National Archives; Free Church College, Edinburgh; Special Collections, University of Aberdeen; Westminster College, Cambridge; Dalhousie Special Collections, Halifax; Atlantic School of Theology, Halifax; Maritime Conference Archives, Sackville; Victoria University Archives and United Church Archives, Toronto; Knox College Library, Toronto; Fisher Rare Book, Toronto; Trinity College, Toronto; University of Western Ontario, London; and Acadia University Library, Wolfville. It was a joy to meet many new friends in several of these places. I will always remember the efficiency and courtesy with which the staff in these libraries offered me assistance.

I express my gratitude to Dr. Andrew McGowan of Highland Theological College, my thesis supervisor and the writer of the Foreword for this present volume. Also, thanks is given to Dr. Nick Needham, who read portions of this book in thesis form after he went to H. T. C. and to Dr. Frances Knight of the University of Wales, Lampeter for her reading of the thesis. I am appreciative of Dr. Kenneth Stewart for his prompting that my thesis be published – you were a great inspiration. Also, thanks to the staff at Paternoster for all of their assistance.

Finally, I acknowledge the patience and assistance of my wife, Nancy, who has spent endless hours discussing Scottish theological education. To each of my four children – Ian, Alistair, Andrew, and Janet – I owe tremendous appreciation. Nancy and the children were so kind and encouraging every time I walked into a library, was away, or sat working in the dining room. Thank you. I believe this work belongs to us as a family.

J.C.W.

Abbreviations

AGACS	*Acts of the General Assembly of the Church of Scotland 1638 to 1842* (Pitcairn)
ARF	*Archiv für Reformationsgeschichte*
APS	*Acts of the Parliaments of Scotland*
BDEB	*Blackwell Dictionary of Evangelical Biography 1730-1860*
BUK	*Booke of the Universall Kirk of Scotland*
CWAB	*Collected Works of Archibald Bruce*
DSCHT	*Dictionary of Scottish Church History and Theology*
DNB	*Dictionary of National Biography* (Edited by Leslie Stephen and S. Lee)
ERF	*Encyclopedia of the Reformed Faith*
FBD	*First Book of Discipline*
FES	*Fasti Ecclesiae Scoticanae*
ODCC	*Oxford Dictionary of the Christian Church (Third Edition)*
OER	*Oxford Encyclopedia of the Reformation*
PANS	*Public Archives of Nova Scotia*
RSCHS	*Records of the Scottish Church History Society*
SBD	*Second Book of Discipline*
UP	*United Presbyterian*
WTJ	*Westminster Theological Journal*

PART ONE

Theological Education and Training in the Kirk

CHAPTER 1

Continental Reformed Theological Education and Training

Introduction

In Part One we will undertake a chronological overview of the history of theological education and training of ministers in the Reformed Church of Scotland from the Reformation to 1850, a time span of approximately three hundred years. What emerges in these three hundred years are six distinct periods of theological education, and each is looked at in succession. These six divisional periods are not absolutes by any means; however, there is sufficient data to justify organizing the material into such categories.[1] Scottish methods, curricula and approaches are introduced, which will then be reflectively compared in Part Two with the Seceders in Scotland and again in Part Three with early approaches to theological education in British North America by Scottish Seceders.

In the six periods of the history of theological education in the Church of Scotland, the first two periods clearly highlight the matter of medieval inheritance and shifts to Reformed theological education and training. Just as Richard Muller has correctly characterized Luther's reform of the theological curriculum as that of "the reshaping of the theological curriculum at Wittenburg", so this idea of reshaping can be applied to Scotland in 1560.[2] And at the core of Luther's reshaping of the theological curriculum was his

---

[1] The six periods are to aid the organization of the material studied in Part One. These are established as broad periods to present an orderly historical presentation for the theme of theological education and training. See further how a generation ago Maxwell and Burnet created certain broad periods in their studies in the area of worship: William D. Maxwell, *A History of Worship in the Church of Scotland* (London, 1955), vii, and George B. Burnet, *The Holy Communion in the Reformed Church of Scotland 1560-1960* (Edinburgh, 1960), x. Also, Burleigh's treatment as a general Church history follows the same basic contours as the six periods I have formulated. J. H. S. Burleigh, *A Church History of Scotland* (London, 1960), ix-x.

[2] Richard A. Muller, "The Era of Protestant Orthodoxy", in *Theological Education in the Evangelical Tradition*, eds. D. G. Hart and R. Albert Mohler, Jr. (Grand Rapids, 1996), 103.

"insistence on the study of Scripture in the original languages, his attacks on late medieval scholastic theology, and his demand for the liberation of theology from Aristotle...", so we will find these same points the focus for the reshaping of Scottish theological education in the first two periods.[3] The centres for theological education in 1560 were three Scottish medieval universities. That was the inheritance, but the Scottish Reformation involved the absorption of theology, liturgy, discipline and educational models from continental Europe. Each of these in its own right is worthy of investigation, but our focus is on the last – theological education. We do not propose to turn this into a study of continental influences upon Scottish theological education. Nonetheless, this must be recognized at the outset. We need to make only brief mention of certain well known facts.

In Periods I and II, comprising the *First Book of Discipline* and the Melvillian Struggle for *Nova Erectio*, continental contacts, in particular Genevan and French, were numerous but certainly not exclusive. John Knox spent time in Geneva and in France, where he came under Calvin's tutelage both directly and indirectly.[4] And Andrew Melville's time in France is critical to understanding him – the man, his theology and his educational ideals. He, too, spent time in Geneva, a regent in the Academy and a student of Hebrew and of theology under his mentor, Beza. He imbibed the continental regenting method of the time in arts and theology and returned to strive for its adoption.[5] Others like George Keith, the Earl Marischal and founder of Marischal College, studied in Geneva.[6] The list could go on, as many Scots in their *wanderjahre* toured France, Germany and Switzerland. Some have seen in the founding of Edinburgh College a pattern of the two divisions of the Geneva Academy as the

---

[3] Muller, "Era of Protestant Orthodoxy", 103.
[4] W. Stanford Reid, *Trumpeter of God* (New York, 1974), 105, 109, 130.
[5] Thomas McCrie, *The Life of Andrew Melville*, vol. 1 (Edinburgh, 1819), 17-55. While in Geneva Melville became associated with Lambert Danaeus and Beza, who both taught theology in the Academy. Danaeus was afterwards the professor of theology at the University of Leiden. A careful reading of these pages on Melville lays out the case for Continental Reformed influence very well. James Kirk's "The Influence of Calvinism on the Scottish Reformation", *RSCHS* 18 (1974), 157-179, is a most helpful survey of the influence of Continental Calvinism upon the Scottish Reformation. See also R. G. Philip, "Scottish Scholars at Geneva", *RSCHS* 6 (1938), 216-231, and Jack C. Whytock, "The Influence of Continental Models of Church Discipline on the Scottish First Book of Discipline" (unpublished M.Th. thesis, University of Glasgow, 1987).
[6] G. D. Henderson, *The Founding of Marischal College, Aberdeen* (Aberdeen, 1947), 49.

backdrop,[7] while others have recognized in the founding of Marischal College the backdrop not only of Geneva but also of Herborn.[8]

A brief excursus into some of the theological texts used in these two periods reveals the study of Calvin's *Institutes*, Beza's *Questionaes*, the Heidelberg Catechism and other continental productions as the primary texts.[9] The list for continental influence on these first two Protestant periods of Scottish education could go on here, but the point is made – the medieval and humanistic model was fused with a reform which was clearly related to the continental Protestant and Reformed approach to theological education.

Thus, before we begin Period I, we must turn briefly to the Genevan Academy and the Company of Pastors. Also, consideration will be given to Reformed theological education in Heidelberg, Leiden and France in Periods I and II. Other centres could be included, but that would take this work beyond the parameters laid down. These select European studies will accomplish the goal of viewing Scottish theological education within its European connection. Some of the literature included in the footnotes will allow for further directed study. A careful reading of James K. Cameron's article, "Some Aberdeen Students on the continent in the late sixteenth and early seventeenth centuries", goes a long way to putting facts and names to Aberdeen and the continent. This will make us more sensitive to continental contacts in all six periods and also illustrate tensions and struggles on the continent which often were not unlike the Scottish struggles. We clearly find continental influence through Dort in Period III, and Periods V and VI had much Dutch contact, whether through Leiden or Dutch writings, as well as Turretin of Geneva.[10] The conclusion is obvious: continental influence and contact were significant in the history of theological education in Scotland.

We turn now to the continent and Geneva with its emerging Academy and the Company of Pastors. The theme for educational reform begins here under the leadership of John Calvin. Such educational reform was viewed not as an option but as imperative for reform and renewal of the Church and society. W. Stanford Reid summarized it well: "Only if adequate education were given to

---

[7] Alexander Grant, *The Story of the University of Edinburgh*, vol. 1 (London, 1884), 176-178.
[8] James K. Cameron, "Some Aberdeen Students on the Continent in the late sixteenth and early seventeenth centuries", in *The Universities of Aberdeen and Europe: The First Three Centuries*, ed. Paul Dukes (Aberdeen, 1995), 60.
[9] James Young, *Life of John Welsh* (Edinburgh, 1866), 25-27; W. Ian P. Hazlett, "Ebbs and Flows of Theology in Glasgow 1451-1843", in *Traditions of Theology in Glasgow 1450–1980*, ed. Ian Hazlett (Edinburgh, 1993), 8-9.
[10] William Steven, *The History of the Scottish Church, Rotterdam* (Edinburgh, 1832), 313. "During the eighteenth century, two thousand British students, attracted by Boerhaave and other eminent teachers, were enrolled as members of the University [of Leiden]...." Though this is a very general comment, we will see it applied in terms of theology as we proceed.

the people, as well as to their leaders, could the Reformation movement be powerful to overcome the massed forces of Romanist error and political despotism."[11]

The Genevan Academy and the Company of Pastors

Before going directly to the Genevan Academy, a brief excursus needs to be made concerning the relationship of humanism to the reform movement. This relationship greatly affected the curriculum of the Genevan Academy and the education and training of ministers. It will also be seen that it was fundamental to the reform of the theological course in the Scottish universities and carried over into the Secession halls.

John Calvin's vision of education combined humanist methodology with the education of ministers for the Reformed churches. Reardon was correct when he wrote that in the fifteenth century changes in intellectual outlook mark "a point at which Renaissance and Reformation clearly interlink".[12] Humanism's slogan *ad fontes* (back to the sources) "was the return to the original sources of western European culture in classical Rome and Athens", and in theology it "meant a direct return to the title-deeds of Christianity – to the patristic writers, and supremely to the Bible, studied in the original languages".[13] A casual student of Calvin quickly discovers that his first published work was his *Commentary on 'De Clementia' of Seneca* (1532). This work was not so much a study in clemency towards Protestants in France but rather an academic

---

[11] W. Stanford Reid, "Calvin and the Founding of the Academy of Geneva", *WTJ* 18 (1955), 1. Mark A. Noll made a very similar point about Johannes Bugenhagen, who likewise "recognized the critical role that education had to play if the reform were to succeed." Mark A. Noll, "The Earliest Protestants and the Reformation of Religion", *WTJ* 43 (1980), 107. Bugenhagen's work in organizing the churches and schools of northern Germany "had only one counterpoint in the entire Reformation period – the work of John Calvin in organizing and systematizing reformed structures for church and school in Geneva and France", wrote Noll, 106.

[12] Bernard M. G. Reardon, *Religious Thought in the Reformation* (London, 1981), 14. Also, Glenn T. Miller, *Piety and Intellect: The Aims and Purposes of Anti-Bellum Theological Education* (Atlanta, 1990), 13.

[13] Alister E. McGrath, *Christian Theology: An Introduction*, 2d ed. (Oxford, 1997), 51-52. See also Alister E. McGrath, *Reformation Thought: An Introduction*, 3d ed. (Oxford, 1999), 44-45. I am using the term humanism here as it is defined in Alister E. McGrath, *Historical Theology: An Introduction to the History of Christian Thought* (Oxford, 1998), 350. "Humanism: In the strict sense of the word, an intellectual movement linked with the European Renaissance. At the heart of the movement lay, not (as the modern sense of the word might suggest) a set of secular or secularizing ideas, but a new interest in the cultural achievements of antiquity. These were seen as a major resource for the renewal of European culture and Christianity during the period of the Renaissance."

addition to Erasmus' published works of Seneca.[14] Calvin, as a student of this great Stoic author, brought to the reader's attention many more details which Erasmus had not dealt with. It is interesting to note, as Wendel draws out, that the Church Fathers often referred to the Stoics, and in particular Seneca, and thus "the humanists were only following, albeit accentuating a much earlier tendancy".[15] Calvin's *Commentary* shows his knowledge of classical antiquity in his amassing of parallel quotations from other ancient writers and also in his appeal to grammar and logic. He then transferred this method over to the Scriptures with the stress upon grammatical-historical exegesis. J. Neuerhaus' comment from 1909 still remains valid:

> Calvin, while absorbing all the elements of humanistic culture, endeavoured to use them to the service of his faith, and avoided the dangers which might have arisen from them. The Hellenistic spirit faded little by little before the Christian spirit; nevertheless, Calvin preserved to the end the reputation of an excellent humanist.[16]

A brief excursus into Calvin's *Institutes* brings a virtually united conclusion that Calvin was a close student of the Bible as well as of Luther, Bucer, and most notably of the writers of antiquity and the Church Fathers – in particular John Chrysostom and Augustine. He also knew well Medieval scholastics; for example, Anselem, Peter Lombard, Thomas Aquinas and the mystic Bernard. In exploring the *Institutes* as to sources, the classical authors and Church Fathers are well represented.[17] Thus, it would be expected that Calvin's Genevan Academy included an emphasis on classical authors, the early Church Fathers and Scripture – all *ad fontes* in the education of men for the ministry.

Calvin's exegetical method was built primarily upon the shoulders of Lorenzo Valla (1405-1457) and Desiderius Erasmus (c.1469-1536). Valla was responsible for bringing a fresh approach to New Testament study by "attempting a critical comparison between the Vulgate and the Greek original".[18] Erasmus went the next step and produced an edition of the Greek

---

[14] François Wendel, *Calvin: Origins and Development of His Religious Thought*, trans. Philip Mairet, original 1950 (Grand Rapids, 1997), 27-28.

[15] Wendel, *Calvin*, 29.

[16] J. Neuerhaus, quoted in Wendel, *Calvin*, 34.

[17] Wendel, *Calvin*, 124, 126-127. The most comprehensive volume to explore the theme of Calvin and his use of patristic literature and medieval writers is that by Anthony N. S. Lane, *John Calvin, Student of the Church Fathers* (Grand Rapids, 1999). My point is simply that Calvin did have an acquaintance with the Church Fathers, etc., and I do not need to enter a scholarly debate as to the adjectives which could be used to describe the level of Calvin's indebtedness. A cursory reading of Lane's "Bibliography of Modern Works on Calvin and the Fathers/Medievals" will quickly convince a reader of this basic point. (xi, 261-286).

[18] Reardon, *Religious Thought in the Reformation*, 16.

New Testament (1516), *Novum Instrumentum omne*, based upon ten manuscripts and their collation together with his acquaintance of patristics.[19] This Greek text of the New Testament was a tool in the hands of the Reformers for lecturing and preaching. Erasmus' text pointed out three classic translation errors in the Vulgate which challenged medieval church life and demonstrated the need for church leaders to be well trained in the biblical languages.[20]

Humanism not only stressed a return to the original sources – classical literature, Scripture or Church Fathers – but also had a love for rhetoric, both written and spoken. McGrath summarized the difference between the humanists and the Reformers: they both stressed rhetoric "but for different reasons. For the humanists, rhetoric promoted eloquence; for the reformers, it promoted the Reformation", and "rhetoric was therefore the means to the end of the propagation of the ideas of the Reformation".[21]

In summary, the development of the Genevan Academy must be seen within this humanist background. A study of this development must reveal the "interlinking" of humanism with reform. It will be seen as we proceed that classics, patristics, Scripture in Greek and Hebrew, and rhetoric were all at the heart of the Genevan Academy's agenda for the education of ministers as Calvin and others envisaged it.

However, though the Reformers were greatly indebted to humanism, we must not ignore their distinctive commitments and worldviews. Robert Pazmiño has summarized the contrasts between the two groups with the following six points:

> 1.) Whereas the Renaissance generally focused upon persons, the Reformation centered life and education upon God, evidencing a renewed consideration of persons as God's creatures with definite privileges and responsibilities.
> 2.) Whereas the Renaissance centered primarily on the elite, the Reformation included the masses of society as well.
> 3.) In the Reformation spiritual renewal was primary, whereas the Renaissance centered upon cultural and intellectual renewal. But spiritual renewal and cultural or intellectual renewal are not mutually exclusive. In Reformation thought, human reason was viewed as fallen and subject to God's revelation in Scripture, whereas

---

[19] Reardon, *Religious Thought in the Reformation*, 29. Also see, McGrath, *Christian Theology*, 52. I adopt Reardon's position that Erasmus used ten manuscripts versus McGrath's five. Parallels also in: McGrath, *Reformation Thought*, 54-55.

[20] McGrath, *Christian Theology*, 53. For further comment also see Alister E. McGrath, *The Intellectual Origins of the European Reformation* (Oxford, 1987), 122-139, 152-174, 175-190.

[21] McGrath, *Reformation Thought*, 62. A helpful article on the humanist movement is Ronald G. Witt, "The Humanist Movement", in *Handbook of European History, 1400-1600*, vol. 2, eds. Thomas A. Brady, Jr., Heiko A. Oberman and James D. Tracy (Grand Rapids/Leiden, 1995), 93-125. This article contains an extensive bibliography on humanism.

in certain Renaissance developments human reason was perceived as perfected. Given the Reformers' sensitivity to human depravity their primary source for understanding was the Bible, but biblical truths were integrated with insights gained through reason and experience.

4.) In contrast with a Reformed focus on the Bible, Renaissance thinkers primarily relied on extrabiblical classical literature.

5.) Reformers stressed the expanded use of the vernacular in disseminating knowledge in contrast with the exclusive use of classical languages by Renaissance scholars who were not necessarily committed to universal education. Nevertheless, many of the Reformers were schooled in classical studies and used classical languages in their scholarship.

6.) A final contrast might be stated in terms of the ultimate goal of education. In the Reformation knowledge was viewed in relation to the higher goal of commitment to and communion with God, whereas in the Renaissance traditional knowledge itself was a goal, largely irrespective of God's revelation.[22]

Pazmiño concluded, "Thus the Renaissance and Reformation pose the issue of the relationship between theism and humanism in the context of the very human enterprise of education which seeks to be faithful to God."[23]

The Reformation came to the city-state of Geneva with a plea for structural change earlier than in the nation of Scotland. By the late 1530s the medieval Catholic Church structure was destroyed in Geneva, creating a vacuum in the leadership of parishes and schools. This was the situation that John Calvin faced in 1541 upon his return from Strasbourg,[24] the city where Calvin had experienced much of Reformed liturgy, church order and discipline, and the school of Jacob Sturm.

Geneva in 1541 was in critical need of pastoral leadership and ministry. The *Ecclesiastical Ordinances*, adopted 20 November 1541, furnished the vision that the securing of sufficient pastors lay with the establishment of a college:

> But since it is possible to profit from such teaching only if in the first place there is instruction in the languages and humanities, and since also there is need to raise up seed for the future so that the Church is not left desolate to our children, it will

---

[22] Robert W. Pazmiño, *Foundational Issues in Christian Education: An Introduction in Evangelical Perspective*, 2d ed. (Grand Rapids, 1997), 146.

[23] Pazmiño, *Foundational Issues in Christian Education*, 147.

[24] Wm. Naphy, "The Renovation of the Ministry in Calvin's Geneva", in *The Reformation of Parishes*, ed. A. Pettegree (Manchester, 1993) 116-124. For a very general discussion on the educational philosophy of Calvin, see T. M. Moore, "Some Observations Concerning the Educational Philosophy of John Calvin", *WTJ* 46 (1984), 140-155.

be necessary to build a college for the purpose of instructing them, with a view to preparing them both for the ministry and for the civil government.[25]

Fuller details as to the nature of an educational programme to train ministers were not given in the *Ordinances* of 1541. Eighteen years passed before the formal realization of this vision with the establishment of the Geneva Academy in 1559.

This does not mean that theological education and training were absent in Geneva from 1541 to 1559. Nor does this mean that Calvin waited for a college from which to graduate men in order to fill the many pastoral vacancies in Geneva and the surrounding area. Rather, we see that by 1546 Calvin had several Reformed pastors gathered together as the "Company of Pastors" in Geneva. Also, a school for training the youth beyond the basic, elementary level was revived in 1542, although it had deplorable buildings and was in a general state of poverty.

For higher education from 1541 to 1559, there was the ongoing training of pastors. Calvin was prodigiously at work in this period lecturing mid-week with series after series as well as preaching sermons which were all models of sound biblical interpretation, exegesis, theology and the use of the original languages.[26]

Calvin's published material in this period is interesting to read, and anyone familiar with his commentaries knows that they are combinations of his lectures and written commentary. Many came to hear him lecture – former priests and monks, French and English refugees, men studying to be pastors. They all came to Calvin – "a school of the prophets". One of those who came was a Scots refugee, John Knox, and he gave us the famous quotation, "Here's the most perfect school of Christ on earth...."[27] All of the marks of a school

---

[25] *The Register of the Company of Pastors in Geneva in the Time of Calvin*, ed. and trans, P. E. Hughes (Grand Rapids, 1966), 41. For commentary, see: J. H. M. d'Aubigne, *History of the Reformation in Europe*, vol. 7 (London, 1876), 87-88.

[26] T. H. L. Parker wrote concerning Calvin's sermons and lectures: "In this, (the expository method) we may note, the sermons differ a little from the lectures, where normally each verse receives due treatment." See Parker's two excellent studies on Calvin the Preacher: T. H. L. Parker, *Calvin's Preaching* (Edinburgh, 1992), and T. H. L. Parker, *The Oracles of God: An Introduction to the Preaching of John Calvin* (London, 1947).

[27] John T. McNeill, *The History and Character of Calvinism* (New York, 1954), 192; Robert Kingdon, "Geneva and the Coming of the Wars of Religion in France, 1555-1563" (unpublished Ph.D. thesis, Columbia, 1955), 33-35; Karin Maag, "Education and Training for the Calvinist Ministry", in *The Reformation of Parishes*, ed. A. Pettegree, (Manchester, 1993), 134; W. de Greef, *The Writings of John Calvin*, trans. Lyle D. Bierma (Grand Rapids, 1993), 93-120, 238-240. De Greef traces Calvin's lecturing back to Strasbourg, where he lectured in Sturm's gymnasium. He then follows a careful dating of Calvin's published commentaries, many of which appeared in the pre-

were there, albeit without the formal title. Training for the Reformed Church meant learning the Scriptures and the crucial task of rightly dividing the word of God. This was clearly going on in Geneva prior to 1559. It is conceded that this was not a theological school in the technical sense, but as Baird reminds us, it "at least merited the appellation of a preparatory school in theology".[28] The stress was on the study of the Scriptures in their original languages, and frequent lectures in college and in church were held daily. Also, public exercises on theology were given, open to all who desired to attend.[29]

Reardon summarized Calvin's lectures on the Bible books and is helpful to quote at length here:

> Certain of the New Testament and most of the Old Testament commentaries originated as lectures delivered before often large audiences at the College de Geneve. When lecturing Calvin did not read from a script but spoke extempore; he did so slowly and in a way that made it fairly easy for his actual words to be taken down by his students, and he himself went over their work to correct any errors before sending it to press. His procedure in his Old Testament lectures was first to read the selected passage in the original tongue and then to translate it into Latin, preferring usually, despite his familiarity with the Vulgate, to make his own version. His knowledge of Hebrew has sometimes been questioned, but it would seem from the evidence of the commentaries themselves that he was proficient in the language, with a sound knowledge of its grammar and an appreciative understanding of its style. In dealing with the New Testament, his comments on which were in the main dictated privately to secretaries, he used the Latin versions of Erasmus as well as the Vulgate, though here again he would adopt his own rendering whenever it suited him. The Greek text itself was Erasmus's, which, as we have seen, the reformers generally found an indispensable tool; but he was of course a fine enough scholar in his own right not to be confined to it. After the text and translation he went on to explain the passage as a whole before going into details, but he always kept close to the text, discussing phrases and words with characteristic precision and orderliness. Finally, to make sure that the meaning had been clearly conveyed, he went over the passage once more, paraphrasing where necessary so as to underline the sense, and patiently elucidating any lingering points of difficulty, even at the cost of repetitiveness, not infrequently evident in the published text. But he was never afraid to be polemical, and his wit could be mordant.
>
> Calvin's thorough acquaintance with humanistic methods stood him in excellent stead as a biblical commentator. He had learned to respect a text as a

---

Academy period. Calvin lectured extensively on the Bible to students and ministers before 1559; for example, on Isaiah, Genesis, Psalms, and Hosea. It is uncertain how many more were taught before 1560. There were also Calvin's sermons during this time and his contributions to the weekly *Congregation* (colloquia) on Friday mornings, which were to help ministers and students.

[28] H. M. Baird, "Notes on Theological Education in the Reformed Churches of France and French Switzerland", *Presbyterian Review* 1 (1880), 86.

[29] Baird, "Notes on Theological Education", 87.

text, and realized the need for a philological approach and the importance of comparing manuscripts and authorities. His equipment was enhanced also by the extraordinary width and depth of his classical and patristic reading, his knowledge of the Fathers especially being unrivalled, perhaps, in his day. His primary aim was to ascertain the plain or literal meaning of the text on which he was working, since in his view this was the only genuine one, in contrast with the allegorism which had been so grossly overworked by early and medieval commentators alike, though he himself resorted to typology, which can become hardly less fanciful. The proper course was to endeavour to penetrate the mind of the biblical author, to fathom his intention and purpose, whereas the allegorizing of a passage, might easily invest it with a sense wholly removed from the original and so resulting in uncurbed abuse.[30]

Yet, in educating ministers there must also be training. In these early years Geneva turned to the men who came for refuge and learning to fill its vacuum of Protestant leadership. The students were employed to preach, conduct worship, catechize and to assist in schools in the Genevan parishes and in the villages around Geneva. Thus, it is no wonder that by 1546 and even more by 1554 radical changes were observable in the Genevan Church. It has been remarked that by 1554 the Company of Pastors represented a "high level of learning, expertise, and quality".[31] We can conclude that instruction and practice were taking place. Yet, this was not all that was occurring prior to 1559. In Geneva the Company of Pastors was clearly involved from an early stage in the examination process of prospective pastors. Oral examination of theology and Scripture and the hearing of sermons were critical. *The Ecclesiastical Ordinances* of 1541 state:

> The examination consists of two parts, the first of which concerns doctrine, to ascertain whether he who is to be ordained has a good and sound knowledge of Scripture, and then whether he is a fit and proper person to communicate it to people in an edifying manner... To ascertain whether he is fit to teach, it will be necessary to proceed by way of interrogation and by privately hearing him expound the teaching of the Lord. The second part concerns his life, namely whether he is of good morals and has always conducted himself without reproach. The rule of procedure to which we should adhere is very well shown by St. Paul.[32]

The other aspect of ministerial formation that should be considered in this pre-Academy period is the weekly meeting of the pastors, called variously the congregation or colloquy, for the discussion of Scripture and doctrine.

---

[30] Reardon, *Religious Thought in the Reformation*, 178-179.
[31] Naphy, "The Renovation of the Ministry in Calvin's Geneva", 124. See also the lists of professors in the Faculty of Theology: Henri Heyer, *L'Eglise de Geneve 1535-1909*, original 1909 (Niewkoop, 1974), 235-238.
[32] *The Register of the Company of Pastors*, ed. Hughes, 36.

Thus, the theological education for pastors in Geneva was not limited to lectures by Calvin. There was opportunity for practical ministerial training, whether in village churches: catechism instruction, stenography of Calvin's lectures and tutoring or training in defending the Reformed faith in preparation for hostile French settings. One can only speculate on the role the colloquy played in hermeneutics, homiletics and exegesis. It must be borne in mind that many of these things remained in place after the formal establishment of the Academy – ministerial placements, Company examinations and the colloquy.

By 1555 Calvin had gained many concessions for the Company of Pastors, and by the late 1550s the vision of 1541 for a college bore fruit as the Company of Pastors were in a position to press for the erection of a college. Of particular note leading up to Calvin's work in founding the Academy was his trip in 1557 to Strasbourg and his visit with John (Jacob) Sturm. During this visit discussion occurred concerning educational problems. It is undoubtedly significant that two years later the Geneva Academy was founded.[33]

This founding coincided with the resignation of the faculty from the academy at Lausanne due to a dispute with the civil magistrates. Several from that faculty came to join the new Geneva Academy, the most noteworthy being Theodore de Beza. The establishment of the new academy meant the reorganization of Geneva's educational system. Technically, the Academy refers to two inter-connected schools; the lower school, the *schola privata* (a lower level Latin school), and the upper school, the *schola publica*, often called the Academy.[34] According to the council registers, both actually constituted the College or Academy. The *schola privata* was divided into seven classes, beginning with class seven down through to class one for the brightest scholars,

---

[33] Reid, "Calvin and the Founding of the Academy of Geneva", 9. Various scholars have seen a real influence of Sturm upon Calvin and thus upon the Geneva Academy. This raises other very interesting questions, primarily the influence of the late medieval northern European Brethren of the Common Life. Sturm was a student of the Brethren School in Liege, as was Calvin, though less directly, while at Collège de Montaigu. This latter college had as regent Jan Standonck, who himself had been trained at Gouda under the Brethren. See further Dennis E. Tamburello, *Union With Christ: John Calvin and the Mysticism of St. Bernard* (Louisville, 1994), 16-21, 119, for a good introduction to this theme. Tamburello concludes that Sturms's educational reforms at Strasbourg were modelled upon Liege and those at Geneva upon Strasbourg. See also Kenneth Strand, "John Calvin and the Brethren of the Common Life", *Andrews University Seminary Studies* 13 (1975), 67-78, and Kenneth Strand, "John Calvin and the Brethren of the Common Life: The Role of Strasbourg", *Andrews University Seminary Studies* 15 (1977), 43-50.

[34] Miller, *Piety and Intellect*, 13. Miller asserts that Calvin called Geneva's college an "Academy", "following the Athenian example". I have found no clear reference to this elsewhere.

who were destined for the *schola publica*.[35] The lower level school was to train the students to read Greek and Latin. "Among the authors read were Virgil, Cicero, Ovid, Caesar, Isocrates, Livy, Xenophon, Polybius, Homer, Demosthenes."[36] At their opening the two schools had six hundred students and within a year the enrolment went up to nine hundred. Clearly humanities or classical writers were to be taught, yet as Ronald Wallace has correctly pointed out, "In Geneva humanistic studies were to be directed to the service of the Word of God."[37]

The *schola publica* eventually became the University of Geneva. Education was for all ages since the grammar school had to be in place in order for the upper part of the Genevan Academy to reach its true potential for local sons. The Academy quickly gained an international student body, the largest number of students coming from France.

The statutes for the Genevan Academy in 1559 list five professorships: Hebrew, Greek, arts and two for theology. With various degrees of success, professors in law and medicine were subsequently appointed.[38] Calvin and Theodore de Beza were the professors of theology and at the same time pastors of Saint Peter and Saint Matthew churches respectively.

The curriculum has been referred to as heavily influenced by Renaissance humanism. In a certain sense this is true – the study of Scripture in the original languages. Yet in another sense this interpretation has its limitations. Glenn Miller has summarized the education at the Academy as follows: "Exegesis was the nucleus of Reformed church life", and "The need for correct exegesis determined much of the early history of Reformed theological education."[39]

However, Reformed education was not limited to attending lectures or reading books. As one engages in a study of the education of ministers through the Genevan Academy, it is clear that formal instruction is only half of the

---

[35] Karen Maag, *Seminary or University? The Genevan Academy and Reformed Higher Education, 1560-1620* (Aldershot, 1995), 9.

[36] Ronald S. Wallace, *Calvin, Geneva and the Reformation* (Grand Rapids/Edinburgh, 1988), 99.

[37] Wallace, *Calvin, Geneva and the Reformation*, 100.

[38] Jeannine E. Olson, "Geneva Academy", in *OER*, vol. 2, 163-164. See also E. William Monter, *Calvin's Geneva* (New York, 1967), 111-114; Wallace, *Calvin, Geneva and the Reformation*, 98; Reid, "Calvin and the Founding of the Academy", 22-23. It is of vital importance within Periods I to III in our Scottish study to be familiar with Reid's translation into English of "The Order of the College of Geneva".

[39] Glenn Miller, "Theological Education", in *ERF*, 363. See also C. A. Briggs, *History of the Study of Theology*, vol. 2 (London,1916), 128. "Calvin discarded the Scholastic Theology, and turned to the Scriptures as alone possessed of divine authority". And it was Arminius who wrote in 1609 of Calvin: "I exhort my pupils to persue Calvin's Commentaries.... I affirm that he excels beyond comparison in the interpretation of Scripture...." Care needs to be used with Brigg's quotation. Calvin did not divorce himself completely from scholastic theology or methodology.

picture. The other half was achieved by several means. Much was gained by way of table talk and observation. In addition, many students also gained valuable experience in what we may refer to today as a variety of part-time jobs: as tutors for wealthy families by providing instruction in language, Bible and catechism; as secretaries to the leading ministers of Geneva; as stenographers; as chaplains; and as preachers in the rural parishes where there were vacancies.[40] We might well call this "pastors-in-training".

One wonders, "Why did the Reformed churches of France send their men to Geneva from 1559 to 1620?" Part of the answer lies in the fact that until the early seventeenth century France did not possess academics on a comparable scale.[41] However this answer by itself is a bit too superficial. The letters from the churches in France to the Genevan Company of Pastors speak for themselves. For example, the Church of Aubeterre sponsored Jean Boutellant to go to Geneva in 1565 and wrote:

> He is in Geneva to study and profit not only from the languages and doctrine of the Word of God, but also from the practice of doctrine and good order which can bolster ecclesiastical discipline, which is a most necessary thing.... Please have him practise in some village, so that he will be less of a novice when he comes to lead the flock in this area.

And another letter from France to the Company of Pastors stated:

> ... We would ask that he could have entry to your consistories, to learn that good order which was first born among you and then spread to the churches of France. We also ask you to use him sometime, as you do others of the same status, to preach in the villages of your area, so that by speaking in public, he may be able to train his voice and grow in confidence.[42]

The acquisition of the languages, theology and exegesis were foundational, but knowledge of church discipline (polity and censure) and preaching were also expected. It was the Company of Pastors who made the judgement as to the competence of the student in these areas. Karen Maag summarized it well: "Training for the ministry in Geneva thus remained a curious mix of the formal and informal, in which the practical expertise of the Company of Pastors played as important a role as the scholarly training provided by professors of the Academy."[43]

---

[40] Kingdon, "Geneva and the Coming of the Wars of Religion in France", 40-44.
[41] Maag, *Seminary or University?*, 192.
[42] Maag, "Education and Training for the Calvinist Ministry", 141; Maag, *Seminary or University?*, 109.
[43] Maag, "Education and Training for the Calvinist Ministry", 149; Maag, *Seminary or University?*, 44.

It must be borne in mind that the professors of the Academy were each members of the Company of Pastors. Lambert Daneau was the one exception. During part of his time as professor of theology he was not the pastor of a congregation due to his poor health.[44] Later, by the early 1600s, not all of the professors in the Academy were serving as pastors, but they were often in part-time positions in a parish, such as leaders of catechism sessions. However, this does not appear to be the case for theology professors at the Genevan Academy. They remained parish ministers for several generations – for example, the three generations of Turretins.

Returning now to the students who came to the Academy, we learn from the French correspondence that most came already acquainted with Latin, Greek and philosophy. Some letters also attest to their having successfully completed the humanities course, as in the case of one at Bourdeaux. The students were expected to attend the lectures, sermons and meetings for public examination with the Company. The format for these public examinations is noteworthy. On Saturdays between two and three o'clock, students in turn expounded a passage of Scripture, after which critical responses were given by the presiding minister and others. Also, once a month the student was required to draw up a "proposition" in advance to hand in to the professor of theology. Then on the Saturday of the propositions, the students debated them.[45]

The Genevan Academy did not grant degrees to its students, but those in theology were issued a letter of recommendation or accreditation from the Company of Pastors. Here is one such letter sent to the church of Privas for the student Jean Valeton, dated 9 December 1584, after two years of study in Geneva:

> As regards his doctrine, having heard him expound various passages of Scripture several times, and after having had him practice for a time by preaching in one of our parishes in the area, we have always found him to hold a pure and complete doctrine. He also possesses a certain ability for teaching and for making himself heard. With God's will, he will develope these skills. And as for his morals, he has always lived here in a Christian and peaceful manner, so that we can but hope that he will bear good fruit.[46]

Such accrediting letters were not given in all cases. If one was judged "too timid" or his "voice not loud enough", yet orthodox, he was recommended to pursue being a schoolmaster. This was the case of at least one theology student.[47]

---

[44] Maag, "Education and Training for the Calvinist Ministry", 149; Maag, *Seminary or University?*, 44.

[45] Gillian Lewis, "The Geneva Academy", in *Calvinism in Europe, 1540-1620*, eds. Andrew Pettegree, Alastair Duke and Gillian Lewis (Cambridge, 1996), 219.

[46] Maag, *Seminary or University?*, 122.

[47] Kingdon, "Geneva and the Coming of the Wars of Religion in France", 60 - 67.

These facts then lead to the conclusion that the Genevan Academy of this time did not function as a university. Maag writes: "The schola publica provided a half-way point, between completely practical training for future pastors, and years of higher study culminating in the granting of degrees."[48]

Beza's inaugural address on June 5, 1559, at the founding of the Academy reminded all in attendance that acquiring knowledge was not for attaining to cleverness. As Plato said, knowledge should not take one away from virtue and justice. Beza told the students that "they were not there solely for instruction, and even less for ephemeral games, as the Greeks were accustomed to in their gymnasia, but that they had for their task, to work for the glory of God, and for their duty, to become soldiers worthy of their mission".[49] This parallels very closely both the oath for the rector and the oath for the professors and regents. We quote the latter:

> I promise and swear loyally to fulfill the charge committed to me, that is, to work for the instruction of the children and auditors, to give the lectures ordained by the statutes of our Lords and superiors, and to take pains that the school may be conducted in good order. I also promise to see, as far as I possibly can (as I hope God will give me grace), that the scholars shall live peacefully, in all modesty and honesty, to the glory of God and the profit and repose of the city.[50]

It should be recognized that what Beza was saying was in keeping with what other Protestants envisaged for theological education. For example, Bullinger in his 1527 *Ratio studiorum* insisted that for true learning to occur, there must be "sound belief, true worship, piety, and reverence to the end that all good results are dedicated to the glory of God" (Muller's summary).[51] Others likewise held to this same vision. Perhaps the most exhaustive treatment on this came from the pen of Andreas Hyperius in *De theologo, seu de ratione studii theologiae*. His approach to theological education was a union of learning with the religious life or *pietas literata* and *literaturia pia*.[52] This marriage of learning and piety was the model of theological education in Geneva and for many other centres.

Throughout "The Order of the College of Geneva" we find this clear, God-centred approach to education requiring piety in the faculty and students and close relations to the church. All subscribed to the Confession of Faith of

---

[48] Maag, *Seminary or University?*, 191.
[49] Reid, "Calvin and the Founding of the Academy", 10, where Reid translates from Beza's inaugural address. Clearly the Academy under Calvin and Beza and well into the seventeenth century retained this vision. One does wonder how such a vision would be received on many college campuses today, but that is for others to debate.
[50] "The Order of the College of Geneva", in Reid, "Calvin and the Founding of the Academy", 33.
[51] Muller, "The Era of Protestant Orthodoxy", 105-107.
[52] Muller, "The Era of Protestant Orthodoxy", 107-109.

Geneva and, though Calvin did not receive as much authority for the ministers over the Academy as he desired, they certainly closely supervised the students. The Company could nominate the staff, but the city fathers made the appointment. Perhaps such relationships are parallel to Edinburgh and its Town College.

The *schola privata* was highly structured and regulated, even more than Sturm's Strasbourg gymnasium. The *schola publica* was less regulated, and those who attended were often referred to as auditors and had a freer life with less academic regulation than in the *schola privata*. The curriculum of the *schola privata* insisted upon a thorough acquaintance with Latin and French, and in lower classes, Greek. Class seven's basic text was the Latin and French Catechism for reading, spelling and pronunciation. Then followed a very classical study, ending in rigorous teaching and practice in dialectic (a form of logic). The goal in the *schola privata* was to produce a student who could read, think and express himself well.

The *schola publica* continued the study of the classics, but added arts and theology, including Hebrew. Arts centred upon rhetoric, mathematics and science (to better know the Maker). Rhetoric had a practical benefit: "The basic requirement of a minister was that he should preach and of a lawyer or civil administer that he should plead. Consequently, although this stress on advanced rhetoric may appear at first to be rather useless, in the eyes of Calvin and his disciples this was one of the most practical courses of lectures offered."[53]

Thus, these arts courses, although in one way humanistic, were centred in God, and His glory was to be manifested through all that was taught. The theological lectures of Calvin and Beza were clear expositions of the Scripture, in the grammatico-historical method, free of "fanciful" exegesis and the spiritualizing of the text. Saturday student preaching and propositions, along with the practical experience of preaching in churches, the mandatory attendance at two Lord's Day services and catechism were all part of training that accompanied the academic studies.[54]

For Calvin and Beza and their immediate heirs, all of this learning was necessary in order for a man to teach others. Reid comments, "If one were to teach, his thinking had to be clear and direct, untrammelled with conceits and mannerisms in order that even the most ignorant might comprehend the teacher's meaning."[55] The student must use everything at his disposal to study and understand the Scriptures and then to communicate them. Calvin did not disparage the vernacular tongue, but rather the students were encouraged to know French well. He did not only write in Latin but promoted his French translation in order that all might hear and read the truth.

---

[53] Reid, "Calvin and the Founding of the Academy", 15.

[54] Reid, "Calvin and the Founding of the Academy", 16; and "The Order of the College of Geneva", 32-33, 24.

[55] Reid, "Calvin and the Founding of the Academy", 19.

Calvin's comments on 1 Corinthians 1:17 are worthy for study to learn how he interprets Paul here as being opposed to a preaching that is ambitious, ostentatious and fastidious. Paul desired simplicity of the gospel presentation, not ingenious speculations. Likewise, Calvin maintained that Paul did not condemn the arts as unfavourable to piety but rather as assisting men in important purposes.[56]

The contribution of Geneva to Reformed higher education and the training of pastors for the period 1541 to 1620 is impressive. Certainly excellent theological education and training was taking place from 1541 to 1559. In fact, if one studies the voluminous amount of speaking Calvin undertook in this period, one can understand how a former priest or monk or any ministerial student would be well grounded in the Reformed faith. Also, when we take into account the mentoring, practical work experience and the collaquy, we can see how a theological "school of the prophets" was able to offer training for ministers for Geneva, France and beyond.

The establishment of the Genevan Academy strengthened and modelled what could be done in the formal training of ministers as well as augmenting the professorial number, which must be viewed in a positive light. At the same time, the clear hand of the church through the Company of Pastors was critical to the training of pastors. They were the mentors, examiners, participants and guardians of the students' pastoral preaching, etc. They were, as well, the accreditors.

Were degrees or diplomas critical to the functioning of the Academy? No. Yet there were tensions between the Company of Pastors and the magistrates in the running of the Academy, although this is not the focus of our study. What we do see from 1541 to 1620 is ministerial education and training centred around exegesis, sound doctrine, Reformed discipline and wholesome piety which was preceded by a vigorous education in Christian Renaissance learning and training. This was not going to be "an unlearned ministry" nor one which could not defend, propagate and teach the Reformed truth.

Heidelberg, Leiden and France

As was stated in the introduction, Calvin's example in teaching and the work of the Genevan Academy is critical to understanding the work of the Reformation in Scotland in 1560. However, the Genevan Academy was not a medieval university; it was a new creation. It had many parallels with the ancient universities, but it was nevertheless different. Therefore, to further provide a backdrop for Scottish theological education, we must turn now to consider other institutions of learning in continental Europe. Although reference will be found in Parts One and Two to several continental Reformed universities and

---

[56] John Calvin, *Commentary on I Corinthians*, trans. John Pringle, vol. 1 (Calvin Translation Society: Edinburgh, 1848), 73-75.

academies and their contacts with Scotland, this brief study examines the two most noteworthy, Heidelberg and Leiden. Suffice it in summary to note the names of these other continental Reformed universities: Frankfurt-on-the-Oder (1506), Marburg (which turned Reformed in 1607), Herborn (1584), and Duisburg (1655). Both Herborn and Duisburg had smaller student enrolments than the others. Nicholas Hope gives this summary statement:

> Staff of all Lutheran and Reformed university faculties were obliged to respect the symbols, or articles of faith of the local church before this gradually disappeared c.1800-50.... Until c.1750, Duisburg, Herborn and Marburg required from all staff and students observance of the Reformed articles of the faith; [eg.] Johann Stephen Putter (1725-1807), who pioneered imperial public law at Gottingen after 1747 for sixty years, was refused as a Lutheran a professorship in Reformed Marburg University.[57]

The one other key Reformed school would no doubt be that of the Academy of Utrecht, where the noted Gisbertus Voetius taught.[58] Brief reference will be made to this when necessary, but we will not make this our focus. We turn now to two famous Reformed universities on the continent, Heidelburg and Leiden, and the teaching of theology there.

The University of Heidelberg was founded in 1386 and in 1558 was reformed into a centre of German humanism. The faculty accepted the Augsburg Confession, but as new faculty members were attracted, a rift emerged between Lutheran and Reformed. Elector Frederick III accepted the Reformed faith and paved the way for the university to become the bulwark for the Reformed faith in the Palatinate in the second half of the sixteenth century.[59]

Heidelberg's approach to education and training was different from that of Geneva and the *schola publica*. Heidelberg was much more truly a university than the Genevan Academy *schola publica* and offered a wider range in fields of study, thus attracting more students. However, the involvement of the Reformed churches in Heidelberg was non-existent. The theology students at

---

[57] Nicholas Hope, *German and Scandinavian Protestantism 1700 to 1918* (Oxford, 1995), 100, 107. For a further discussion on the Reformed communities in Genevan lands see: Johann Heinrich Kurtz, *Church History*, trans. John MacPherson (New York and London, 1898), 2:379-383; 3:10-14.

[58] Joel R. Beeke, "Gisbertus Voetius: Toward a Reformed Marriage of Knowledge and Piety", in *Protestant Scholasticism*, 231, 242. "His [Voetius'] teaching also attracted many Presbyterian Scots and nonconformist English students." Also, Keith L. Sprunger, *Dutch Puritanism: A History of English and Scottish Churches of the Netherlands in the Sixteenth and Seventeenth Centuries*, Studies in the History of Christian Thought, vol. 31 (Leiden, 1922), 359.

[59] Gottfried Seebag, "Heidelberg University", in *OER*, 2:216-217.

Heidelberg did not have, as they did at Geneva, direct accountability to the Company of Pastors. Maag provides a good summary of the differences:

> The essential directing force of the church in higher education was absent in Heidelberg, and it is this lack of a role given to the church which, in the final analysis, places Heidelberg and Geneva in separate categories.... Heidelberg University predated the Reformation, and was used in Reformed periods to achieve certain aims. Unlike the schola publica, which was created in response to the educational and training needs of Calvinism, Heidelberg's university was adapted, but never permanently transformed into a Reformed centre of higher education in the later Reformation period.[60]

The way Heidelberg adapted as a university was through the creation of a college of theology within the university. Yet, it would appear that this was really more a residential unit within the university system. It was called the *Collegium Sapientiae*, where students had room and board paid for by the church, and was administered by a church council. The students matriculated in the university. Once again, there was some recognition at Heidelberg of certain limitations on the university to train ministers beyond academic preparations. Hence, the theology students were placed in their own community.

Heidelberg University, like Leiden and the French academies, was also a centre where Scots journeyed to study. John Forbes (one of the Aberdeen Doctors) studied there under Pareus, a professor of theology[61], and Pareus' commentary on the Heidelberg Catechism was popular in Scotland in subsequent generations. Thomas Boston read Pareus' commentary three or four times.

Mention needs also to be made of Leiden University because Leiden theologians were significant for Scottish divinity professors in subsequent generations. In addition, turning to another continental Reformed centre of higher education helps us to put into perspective what occurred in Scotland. Leiden University was founded in 1575 at the instigation of William of Orange and was the first university of the United Provinces. (Other Dutch universities where theological faculties were founded subsequently included Franecker in 1585, Groningen in 1612, and Utrecht in 1636.)[62] The university was not a creation of the church and thus not under her control. Serious faculty problems existed in the early years; for example, during the first twelve years there were nine different theology professors. Likewise, the number of theology students remained small, as many continued to travel to Heidelberg or Geneva to study theology. One of the theologians of the Leiden University was François DuJon, a pupil of Calvin's and author of *Opera Theologica*. Three volumes of DuJon's

---

[60] Maag, *Seminary or University?*, 170-171.
[61] Drummond, *The Kirk and the Continent*, 59.
[62] Briggs, *History of the Study of Theology*, 2:155.

Opera Theologica are listed in the contents of the Dumbarton Presbytery Library of 1705.[63]

The one event of significance at Leiden was the establishment of the collegiate system whereby the States College and the Walloon College provided ministerial training for Dutch and French theology students. These colleges were established in connection with Leiden University in 1592 and 1606 respectively.[64]

Unlike the States College, the Walloon College was very dependent upon the church and less on the university and civil authorities. It was only through the colleges that the academic was combined with practical training. This did not occur within the university. The university had professors of theology, but the colleges had their own regents. Evidently the course of study of the Walloon College lasted for four years, with arts in year one and two, Greek in year one, and Hebrew in year two with catechism. Years three and four were for theology and exegesis. Throughout the four years students conducted oral disputations and once a year were examined by the Walloon Synod.

The theological disputes of Leiden were also significant for the Scottish Church. Leiden's professors of theology included both Jacob Arminius and Francis Gomar at the same time. Gomar was opposed to Arminius and was one of the chief leaders at the Synod of Dort. In the middle of the seventeenth century, Leiden became a stronghold for scholastic Calvinism. Marck (Marckius), who taught here, figures prominently in Scottish theology.[65]

France turned first to Geneva and Lausanne for the training of its ministers, the majority being trained in Geneva. It was five students from Lausanne who were martyred for the faith in the city of Lyons in 1552. Once such persecution abated in the second half of the late sixteenth century, the French Reformed churches began to implement their own academies for ministerial training due to the tremendous need for ministers.[66] The result was that six academies were founded during period: Nimes (1561), Saumur (1598), Montauban (1598), Die (1604), Orthez (1566), and Sedan (about 1580 as a college and then in 1602 as an academy with a theological hall).[67] Thus, we see by 1600 that the French Reformed Church was not looking to Geneva as the chief seat for the theological training of its ministers.

The Huguenot academies were essentially arts colleges with a school or hall for theology attached to them. They were very much in the tradition of the *schola illustres* or *gymnasia illustria*, as the name was used in the preceding generation in Strasbourg under Sturm or Herborn, where Olevian taught.

---

[63] Briggs, *History of the Study of Theology*, 2:155.

[64] "Leiden", in *The Oxford Dictionary of the Christian Church*, 3d ed., eds. F. L. Cross and E. A. Livingstone (Oxford, 1997), 965.

[65] *ODCC*, 689-695; also Drummond, *The Kirk and the Continent*, 110.

[66] Baird, "Notes on Theological Education", 88.

[67] Briggs, *History of the Study of Theology*, 2:58-59.

Though in many ways they had features like universities, as with the Genevan Academy, they did not grant degrees. We know that Scots travelled to study or teach at the Huguenot academies in the early seventeenth century at Saumur, Sedan, Montauban, Die, Montpellier, Nimes and Loudun. Some like Robert Boyd combined a local pastorate with a position at Saumur Academy as professor of theology (*seigneur, professeur et pasteur*).[68]

In outlining some of the leading features of these French Reformed academies, Briggs and Baird tell us that in 1561 Nimes added a school of theology to what was already an ancient academy. Four professors were responsible for theology: one for Hebrew, one for Greek, one for doctrine and one for philosophy. Orthez was noted for having Viret and Daneau teaching there, and Die had the noted theologian Daniel Chamies for one year, 1607-1608. Saumur became known for the teaching of Amyraldianism after its most famous professor Amyraut. It took a different understanding of the doctrine of predestination from that of Geneva or the two French academies, Montauban and Sedan, known for their strict maintenance of orthodox Calvinism.[69] All six of these theological academies were later closed by the government in the seventeenth century, the last being Montauban which had transferred to Puy-Laurens.[70]

The French academies were all closed by 1685, and for the next one hundred years, until after the Edict of Toleration of 1787, there was virtually no Reformed theological education of ministers in France. Some went to Geneva or Holland, and an undefined number were trained by Antoine Court, who conducted a seminary in fields and caves.[71] Court describes this method as follows:

> ... Here we encamped nearly a week; this was our lecture-room.... I gave them a text of Scripture to make remarks upon. It was the first eleven verses of the fifth chapter of Saint Luke.... I propounded to them now a doctrinal point to explain, now a passage of Scripture, or a moral precept; or I gave them passages to harmonize. Here is the method I employed: As soon as I had proposed the question, I asked the youngest for his opinion, and then the others in turn until I reached the eldest. After each one had stated what he thought, I again addressed the youngest and asked him whether he had any objection to the opinions of the others and so from one to the other. When all had argued, I gave them my own judgment respecting the matter proposed. When their exercises were ready, a pole

---

[68] Drummond, *The Kirk and the Continent*, 27-28; also, Jacques Pannier, "Scots in Saumer in the Seventeenth Century", trans. W. J. Couper, *RSCHS* 5 (1935), 141; Marguerite Guignet, "Mark Duncan, Professor at Suamur,1606-1640", *RSCHS* 5 (1935), 75.
[69] Briggs, *History of the Study of Theology*, 2:158-159; Baird, "Notes on Theological Education", 88-89.
[70] Baird, "Notes on Theological Education", 89-90.
[71] Baird, "Notes on Theological Education", 90.

was placed across two forked stakes, and this, for the present occasion, served as a pulpit for preaching. When one of the candidates had resigned it, I asked all to state what they had remarked, observing the method above given.[72]

In summary, the French Reformed churches likewise demonstrated a commitment to a trained ministry. The rise of the French academies in the second half of the sixteenth century and the early seventeenth century clearly reveals this. They also show the nature of Reformed theological controversy in the early seventeenth century and the various influences upon Scotland at this time. The connection of the French academies to Scotland was virtually over by 1650, and it was never recovered to this extent again. But although this was true of the French academies, French theological literature remained important in subsequent periods in Scotland.

Summary

Reformed theological education on continental Europe took place in the existing universities as well as in the new *gymnasia* or universities. The rise of theological colleges, such as Leiden, proved an effective way of teaching theology within the university system. Yet for the latter sixteenth and early seventeenth century, the terms "university", "academy" and "college" were virtually interchangeable. As time passed, these terms grew in precision.

Continental Europe provided a storehouse of literature both for arts and theology in Scotland in the second half of the sixteenth and into the seventeenth century. Many of the names of these European writers and theologians will be introduced and discussed in Parts One and Two.

---

[72] Baird, "Notes on Theological Education", 90, quoting from a paper compiled by Charles Bois, written in 1877. See also Otto H Selles, "A Case of Hidden Identity: Antoine Court, Benedict Pictet, and Geneva's Aid to France's Desert Churches (1715-1724)", in *The Identity of Geneva: The Christian Commonwealth, 1564-1864*, eds. John B. Roney and Martin I. Klauber (Westport, CT, 1998), 93-109.

CHAPTER 2

Period I: 1560-1576, *The First Book of Discipline*

Introduction: The 1560 *First Book of Discipline*

Like John Calvin's return to Geneva in 1541, John Knox's return to Scotland in May of 1559 commenced a time of reorganization and consolidation in the Reformed faith. It would be simplistic to say that this reorganization was entirely under the leadership of Knox. Before the parallel is pressed too far with Calvin's return in 1541, it must be recalled that Knox's return to Scotland was to a nation, not a city-state.

After his return the Confession of Faith was quickly drawn up and approved by Parliament in August of 1560. This Confession is clearly in keeping with the Reformed theology of Geneva and Zurich. Also, the Protestant Lords of Scotland requested a "Book of Reformation" to be composed by the leading ministers, chief of whom was John Knox.[1] This book went through various processes of expansion and finally ended as the *First Book of Discipline* (*FBD*). The privy council and many nobles agreed to it, but not without qualifications. These qualifications and the ensuing political instability meant frustrations in implementation. However, the General Assembly did "its best", writes James Kirk, to see that the *FBD* was put into effect in the 1560s. With the exception of the Convention of Leith in 1572, its ideals remained in force until 1598 and the publishing of the *Second Book of Discipline*.[2]

Clearly for this reformation to effectively take root in Scotland, ministers needed to be trained in the theology and practice of the Reformed faith. The three interpolations from the *FBD* were of particular concern for Scottish theological education and training; namely, superintendents, schools and universities. The ninth head of the *FBD*, "For Prophesying or Interpreting of the Scriptures", is also related.

The Scottish Reformers believed that the old ways promoted spiritual darkness and superstition. Therefore, they tried to ensure that ministers were

---

[1] J. Kirk, "First Book of Discipline", *DSCHT*, 321-322; W. I. P. Hazlett, "The Scots Confession of 1560: Context, Complexion and Critique", *AFR* 78 (1987), 28-320; W. I. P. Hazlett, "Exercise or Prophesying", *DSCHT*, 31-312; A. I. Dunlop, "Exhorter, Office of", *DSCHT*, 312.
[2] Kirk, "The First Book of Discipline", *DSCHT*, 321.

duly educated, properly trained in preaching and catechizing, and rightly able to administer church polity and discipline. They were unanimous that training for the ministry was to be supervised by those who possessed a learning which resulted in sound exposition of Scripture coupled with godly living. Thus, in 1560 it was thought better to leave a parish vacant than to place an unqualified man in the parish as an ordained minister.[3]

The *FBD* was also a document realistic about the needs of the situation. It would take time to raise up Reformed ministers across the land. They therefore approved the use of readers and exhorters to help to alleviate some of this problem. The adoption of the continental exercise or colloquy was also helpful to the situation. Long-term solutions began by envisioning a natural opportunity to educate children and youth and to reform the universities, especially in the area of theology, but also in arts as preparation for theology.

The *FBD* and Schools

As in Geneva, where the education of children and youth was a "nursery" for the Reformed Academy's *schola publica*, so also in Scotland reform had to begin with the schools. The educational ideas here were not original but were borrowed from the continent: Sturm's work in Strasbourg, Calvin's in Geneva and Claud Baduel's work while resident in Geneva and then Nimes. James Cameron noted clear references in the *FBD* to Martin Bucer's *De Regno Christi*, where he outlined education from childhood to manhood.[4]

The *FBD* was not so much concerned with critiquing any existing medieval schools in Scotland but rather with the development of a "comprehensive scheme for the whole country and providing for the needs of everyone capable of benefiting from education".[5] Two years of primary schooling were envisaged

---

[3] Stewart Mechie, "Education for the Ministry in Scotland since the Reformation" *RSCHS*, 14 (1963), 115. For further comments concerning the ignorance of much of the pre-Reformation parish clergy see: W. Murison, *Sir David Lyndsay* (Cambridge, 1938), 95-96; Robert Richardinus, *Commentary on the Rule of St. Augustine*, original 1530, reprinted (Scottish History Society, Edinburgh, 1935), 28, 74, 14-149. Richardinus is valuable to show defects in medieval monasticism and some efforts for remedying abuse.

[4] *FBD*, 129, 133. Martin Bucer, *De Regno Christi*, in *Melanchthon and Bucer*, trans. W. Pauck, Library of Christian Classics, vol. 19 (London, 1969), 335-337, gives ample evidence for this: "But when the boys have learned the writings and the catechism of our religion, those paidonomoi, directors of youth education, must find out which of the boys have talents for acquiring greater learning... if some of the boys who have already learned reading, writing, and the catechism of our faith, or who even have applied themselves for some time to the learning of liberal arts, appear not to be gifted by the Lord for the reception of further academic instruction, let these be directed to other pursuits, each to that for which each seems more naturally endowed and gifted."

[5] *FBD*, 57.

followed by grammar school for "about" four years. In areas without a schoolmaster, the minister or the reader took care of the children and youth. It is also noteworthy that the *FBD* stipulated that those who were readers in church and in charge of teaching parish children were to progress within two years to be able to "exhort".[6] Thus we find, in essence, a form of "pastor-in-training" programme. The *FBD* provided for this mobility from reader to exhorter to minister: "If from reading he begin to exhort, and explain the Scriptures, then ought his stipend to be augmented, till finally he come to the honour of a Minister."[7] One example of such progression can be found in the Parish of Urquhart and Logie Wester.[8]

The *FBD* and Universities

Even from its first sentence, it is evident that the interpolation on the universities was built upon the section on the schools: "The Grammar Schoole being erected, and of the tongues (as we have said) [Latin and hopefully some Greek] next we think it necessary there be 3 Universities in this whole realm...."[9] The Reformers inherited these three medieval universities, and what follows in the *FBD* is the vision for reforming them.

St. Andrews University was dealt with first in a fairly exhaustive manner. It was reorganized, yet maintained the existing three colleges. Rather than each college teaching the same thing, each henceforth was to specialize. The first college served as the entry college to the university and was centred in arts. The third college taught Hebrew, Greek and the exposition of the Scriptures. It appears that this college was modelled upon the recently founded Geneva Academy.[10] Also, the old system of regents[11] taking students completely

---

[6] *FBD*, 130.

[7] *FBD*, 111.

[8] Wm. G. Young, *The Parish of Urquhart and Logie Wester* (n.p., 1984), 36.

[9] *FBD*, 137.

[10] *FBD*, 58, 138-141. There does appear to be some ambiguity as to how much this reorganization into three specialized colleges was enacted upon in the 1560s. For example, about 1566 George Buchanan became principal of St. Leonard's College and "As Principal of the college, Buchanan delivered occasional prelections on Theology, and at the weekly meetings of the clergy, and other learned men in the district, held for expounding the Scriptures, then styled the exercise of Prophesying, he exhibited proofs of his intimate acquaintance with the oracles of God." See, Anon, "Life of George Buchanan", in *The History of Scotland* by George Buchanan, trans. James Aikman, vol. 1 (Glasgow, 1827), xxvii. In Appendix A I have not included those who taught divinity from 1560-1579 at St. Andrews University and the three colleges due to this being a period of transition. The above illustration on Buchanan at St. Leonard's shows that he gave lectures on theology and was involved in the prophesying meeting while principal of an arts college and yet not an ordained minister. See *DSCHT*, 106-107.

through their course leading to examination and graduation was to be replaced by "specialist" readers solely responsible for certain subjects each year.

Both of the other universities, Glasgow and Aberdeen, were patterned around two colleges each – an arts college and a college for moral philosophy, Roman and statute law, Hebrew and divinity. This second college combined what the second and third colleges at St. Andrews taught. All three universities were granted freedom as to the books to be read and "all such like particular affairs" at the discretion of the masters, principals and regents. This interpolation ended with an appeal to the Lords to exercise their civil authority and responsibility for the advancement of the universities.[12]

Entrance to the three Scottish universities after 1560 was much like that of pre-1560. A student had to possess a knowledge of Latin.[13] In the post-1560 period the following evidence was required: a letter from the master of the grammar school verifying attendance and knowledge of Latin, a letter from the minister as a testimonial, and a trial in Latin competency. Likewise, to move from arts to divinity, letters of testimony were needed showing evidence of the arts classes attended. It was not specifically stated that one had to possess the M.A. degree, and there is ample evidence that many who studied arts then went on to study divinity without ever taking the M.A. degree. Perhaps one reason for this was the cost of actual graduation, which for poorer students was a substantial burden.[14]

The emphasis on maintenance of knowing Latin was variously interpreted in the church courts. The General Assembly of March 7, 1575, passed the following:

> Forsuameikle as the greatest part of the doctors, and interpretars of the Scriptures that hes travellist in the interpretation and exposition of the same, hes written and comentit in the Latine tongue, and therthrow it is thocht necessar for sic as enters into the function of the ministrie, to have understanding and knowledge of the same; Therefore, the General Assembly of the Kirk hes votit and concludit, that, frae this tyme furth, none shall be admittit in the function of one minister within the Kirk be the Bishops, Superintendants, and Commissioners of cuntries, but sic as have understanding of the Latine tongue, and are able to interpret the Commentars writte in the same language, and speak congruous Latine, except sic as, be exemption of the General Assembly of the Kirk, for their singular graces

---

[11] A regent should be viewed as a general lecturer/tutor taking a student through his entire course of studies in the arts curriculum.

[12] FBD, 154-155.

[13] There is reason to believe that many students pre-1560 did not know Latin upon their entrance to one of these three Scottish medieval universities. See Murison, *Sir David Lyndsay*, 95-96.

[14] FBD, 142-143.

and gifts of God, sall be fund also be them to use their functione without knowledge of the Latine tongue.[15]

It would appear that in the period under study there was not an absolute enslavement to the requirement that all ministers read Latin. In all likelihood these exceptions tended more for those who had been readers and exhorters. What is of particular interest is the end for which Latin was to be acquired; namely, for better biblical interpretation and exposition. The lectures in the universities were ordinarily in Latin, but in subsequent periods there was an erosion of this practice.

The curriculum for theological education envisaged in the *FBD* centred upon the Biblical languages, exegesis and divinity. As David Wright summarized it: "The Bible's domination of the curriculum is striking."[16]

The Exercise – A Vital Role

Training for the ministry in Scotland in this period was not solely in the hands of the three universities. Reference has already been made to the exercise.[17] On the continent this was variously called the prophesying, the congregation, the colloquy or the coetus.[18] The exercise played a vital role for those who were ministers coming into the Reformed Church from the priesthood or monastic orders, in one sense serving as a "continuing education programme". Likewise, it was an invaluable training tool for students for the ministry. Andrew Pettegree provided a helpful summary of the coetus in East Friesland in the 1540s and the Kirckenrat or Church Council there, describing it as a consistory or city-wide "presbytery".[19]

---

[15] *BUK*, 146.

[16] *DSCHT*, 279.

[17] The term "exercise" was used with various meanings. In a very general sense, it referred to the assigned discourses and topics given to students in the divinity hall or at the meeting of presbytery. It could be exegetical in nature or doctrinal stressing correct interpretation. The word was also employed as a general term for a form of rhetorical declamation used as a method for training and learning and would deal with context, difficult words, etc., offer a paraphrase, and include a logical division of the text. In addition, the term was used of the formal meeting of ministers, students and elders in which the chief focus was upon testing the theological development and learning of ministers and students.

[18] This does not necessarily mean that these words are all synonyms, but rather on occasion people use these words to describe a common meeting – the presbytery exercise. Technically speaking, the prophesying in à Lasco's usage was the congregation hearing a minister explain a matter; the usage likely originated in Zurich, then went to East Friesland, then to the Stranger Churches in London. See Andrew Pettegree, *Emden and the Dutch Revolt: Exile and the Development of Reformed Protestantism* (Oxford, 1992), 23-24, 33.

[19] Pettegree, *Emden and the Dutch Revolt*, 33-34.

With the passage of time, the meeting for the exercise became formally known as the presbytery when the General Assembly declared "the exercise may be judged a presbytery".[20] The presbytery of this time evidently did more than assemble to hear expositions and critiques, for we know that in 1573 each exercise received copies of the Acts of the Assembly, which certainly is evidence of combining church business with instruction. It is also true that at times censures were given for failure to hold or regularly attend the weekly exercise.[21] The authors of the *FBD* clearly borrowed from the influence of Zwingli, Calvin, à Lasco and others.[22] It was an opportunity for the most learned ministers to present the standards which were to be required. Also, it allowed opportunity for exhorters to grow in their experience. Thus, the exercise served as a way of developing orthodoxy, recruiting ministers and training them.[23] Hence, in the *FBD* the purpose of the exercise was "to the end that they themselves [ministers and exhorters] may either learn or else others may learn by them".[24] Linda Dunbar, in a recent article which works with a

---

[20] James Kirk, *Patterns of Reformation* (Edinburgh, 1989), 32-53, describes that between 1579 and 1581 the exercise "became merged with the new court of presbytery" and further, "The Genevan exercise makes it highly probable that it was the latter which acted as a serviceable prototype for Knox and the reformers." *Patterns*, 81. See also G. D. Henderson, *The Burning Bush* (Edinburgh, 1957), 53; John Knox, *The Works of John Knox*, ed. D. Laing (Edinburgh, 1846) 4:178-179; 6:294.

[21] Henderson, *The Burning Bush*, 53.

[22] Henderson, *The Burning Bush*, 47. Also, Duncan Shaw, "Zwinglian Influences on the Scottish Reformation", *RSCHS* 22 (1985), 135-136. Shaw sees the Scottish exercise as having a function similar to that of Zwingli's *Prophezei* in Zürich, from I Corinthians 14. That there were two exercises operating, the one congregationally and the other for ministers, students and elders, must also be remembered. It appears that it was really more the second exercise which operated in Scotland. See Shaw, 136: "'The Scottish reformers' concern that Biblical interpretation should remain within the control of the church rather than the universities was Zwinglian." Shaw then cites two examples from John Knox to support this claim: "I protest that nather the pulpet of Sanct Androis, nather yit of any congregatioune within the Realme, be subject to the censure of the schooles, universitie, or facultie within the same; bot only that it be reserved to God the Judge of all, and to the General assemblie gatherit within the same realme, launchfullie." [and] "Above all things preserve the Kirk from the bondage of the Universities." These quotations come from Knox, *Works*, VI, 630, 619.

[23] Janet G. MacGregor, *The Scottish Presbyterian Polity* (Edinburgh, 1926), 53-54. MacGregor fails to see that the Scottish exercise was mainly a ministerial event. In certain instances congregations may have attended, as is evidenced by the movement of the exercise from church to church. Thus, the core element of the exercise would not vary, whereas the congregational element did. See William McMillan, *The Worship of the Scottish Reformed Church, 1550-1638* (London, 1931), 368.

[24] McMillan is quoting from the *FBD* version found in Knox, *Works*, 2:244. See McMillan, *Worship of the Scottish Reformed Church*, 366.

manuscript revealing the pre-1572 Synod of Fife, confirms what has just been written in this paragraph. Dunbar wrote:

> The synod of Fife was keen to enforce a strict hierarchy in the office of reader, exhorter and minister. Corresponding to *The First Book of Discipline*, the lower offices of reader and exhorter were seen as intermediary steps undertaken by those aspiring to a full ministerial post. The synod ruled that no reader would be permitted to continue in a post for more than three years unless he demonstrated that he had gained in knowledge during that time. Through study and increased "knowledge of letteris" readers could, and should, become exhorters and, eventually, ministers. Exhorters were likewise to continue to study. Together with others "haweing ye gift to interpret" they were expected to travel up to ten miles to attend and participate in the "exercise", where, as *The First Book of Discipline* explained, they would take turns to expound on scriptural passages before the critical judgement of their brethren.[25]

The Synod of Fife directive confirms the importance of the exercise for ministerial formation and education. The directive also shows how a Synod might modify the *FBD*, which stipulated six miles to travel, whereas the Synod of Fife said up to ten miles was acceptable. Dunbar went on to state that the Synod of Fife directed that only ministers could enter the pulpit in a church building and barred readers and exhorters from standing in the pulpit.[26] The *FBD* was silent on this matter, and how prevalent such a directive was is difficult to assess here.

One specific instance can be sited to highlight the value of the exercise for the training of ministers. Peebles was in need of a minister in 1561 and John Allane, a former priest, was chosen. It was decided that he would be sent to Edinburgh to hear John Knox preach, to attend the Edinburgh Exercise, and to learn about session discipline. Obviously it was recognized that the establishment of a reformed ministry required the provision of some kind of training or mentoring in the new theology and church order.[27]

A fuller scholarly treatment of the history and origins of the exercise/presbytery is needed. It would need to examine both its instructive role and its disciplinary role. One of the best short treatments on the exercise in this period remains that of William McMillan in an appendix in his *The Worship of the Scottish Reformed Church, 1550-1638*.[28] McMillan pointed out that the name "exercise" was "transferred from the purpose of the gathering to the

---

[25] Linda J. Dunbar, "Synods and Superintendence: John Winram and Fife, 1561-1572", *RSCHS* 27 (1997), 101-102. Dunbar is referring to: St. Andrews' University Muniments, *MS* 30451, undated, fo. 4v., and *FBD*, 111, 188-991.

[26] Dunbar, "Synods and Superintendence: John Winram and Fife", 102. Dunbar is referring to: St. Andrews' University Muniments, I 30451, undated, fo. 5v.

[27] Kirk, *Patterns of Reform*, 113-114.

[28] McMillan, *Worship of the Scottish Reformed Church*, 366.

gathering itself".²⁹ That the General Assembly took the exercise seriously is evidenced by a 1577 ruling that if the two ministers who had been appointed to "prophecy and add" failed to attend, they were to be censured upon the first offence, and if it occurred again they were to be deposed.³⁰ McMillan believed that the exercise portion meant an "interpretation" by the first minister and that the addition by the second minister meant the application or the exhortation which would arise from the doctrine. The exercise was also held at the beginning of the meeting prior to the "business". Going beyond the period of the *FBD* into that of Melvillian reforms, the exercise still continued to meet for exercise and addition.³¹

Vacant Parishes?

Many books have recorded that during the 1560s a large number of parishes were destitute of Reformed ministry. Reliable studies have now shown that this was not the case, even in the Highlands, where the differences were only marginal from the rest of Scotland. Most parishes had their ministers, exhorters or readers along with the Protestant chaplains who were employed by some nobles and lairds. In charges vacant of a minister but possessing an exhorter or reader, there may have been a designation of the title reader due to the level of remuneration. Margaret Sanderson cites one possible example. Dunlop Parish had John Hamilton as the "minister" and "faithful pastor", yet in 1567 he is listed as an "Exhorter" and also from 1567-1596 as a "Reader" and then as "Minister" from 1597-1606. Sanderson suggests that this raises more the question of remuneration than ability. "...Readers who served so many post-Reformation churches may have been perfectly able to preach, with the neighbouring Minister-with-oversight being called in to dispense the communion, which was in any case infrequent."³² James Kirk refutes the opinion that there were a large number of vacancies and suggests that the interpretation should be along these lines:

> Generally, however, the real challenge facing the reformed church was not so much a problem of recruiting ministers at the Reformation, which, on the whole, was achieved without a significant lapse in time over much of the country, but one

---

[29] McMillan, *Worship of the Scottish Reformed Church*, 366-369.
[30] McMillan, *Worship of the Scottish Reformed Church*, 367.
[31] McMillan, *Worship of the Scottish Reformed Church*, 367.
[32] Margaret Sanderson, *Ayrshire and the Reformation* (East Linton, 1997) 165, 110. Sanderson shows that in 1560 in Ayrshire there were 44 parishes and in 1567, 38 of the 44 parishes were filled by a minister, exhorter or reader, 16 of which had been clearly mentioned before 1567.

of replacing the recruits of the early 1560's with a second generation of fully-fledged ministers, educated under the new regime and trained in the universities.[33]

F. D. Bardgett is in accord with Kirk, as Bardgett concludes that following Andrew Melville's return, "the kirk moved towards the *SBD* with its objective of a minister for each parish, to be achieved by abolishing the readership and reducing the number of Scotland's parishes".[34] Thus, the question of vacancies in the 1560s and 1570s must be carefully handled.

It is evident that for the 1560s the exercise played an important role in the training of leadership. We return now to examine further how the three universities were educating students for the ministry.

A Student

We learn from the standard works on the histories of the three universities that certain patterns developed. For example, principals served as professors of theology. Also, from 1560 to the late 1570s, the universities were still a mixture of the medieval order and the new reform. Lombard's *Sentences* were gone, but still there were such statutes as required celibacy of students and forbade faculty wives from living in the college buildings. All faculty and students were required to subscribe to the new Scots Confession of Faith.[35]

One of the best glimpses of the life of a student of this time comes from *The Autobiography and Diary of James Melville*. Melville was a student in arts at St. Andrews from 1569 to 1572 and then regent at Glasgow in 1574 under his uncle Andrew Melville, who was to greatly impact Reformed education in Scotland.[36] From his diary we learn that James Melville took his arts under the regency of Mr. Wilyeam Collace, St. Leonard's College. At first he could not understand the regent's speaking in Latin, but after tutoring he made great advances. The most momentous event of his first year at St. Andrew's was hearing Knox, whom Melville called a "noteable prophet and apostle", preach from Daniel. Knox visited with the students and gave them exhortations. In his

---

[33] Kirk, *Patterns*, 148. For further details see Charles Haws, *Scottish Parish Clergy at the Reformation 1540 -1574* (Scottish Record Society, Edinburgh, 1972).

[34] F. D. Bardgett, "'Four Parische Kirkis to Ane Preicheir'", *RSCHS* 22 (1986), 208. Bardgett appears to be in accord with James Kirk's, "The development of the Melvillian movements in the late sixteenth century" (unpublished Ph.D. thesis, University of Edinburgh, 1972).

[35] R. G. Cant, *The University of St. Andrews*, rev. ed. (Edinburgh, 1970), 47-51; J. D. Mackie, *The University of Glasgow 1451-1951* (Glasgow, 1954), 63; James Coutts, *A History of the University of Glasgow* (Glasgow, 1909), 49-50; J. M. Bulloch, *A History of the University of Aberdeen 1495-1860* (London, 1895); Robert S. Tait, *The Universities of Scotland* (Aberdeen, 1895).

[36] *The Autobiography and Diary of Mr. James Melville*, ed. R. Pitcairn (Edinburgh, 1842).

second year Melville wrote of the primarius (the principal) lecturing and the giving of daily prayers in the church. The primarius took the students through Samuel and Kings and Psalm singing. In his third year he obtained his Bachelor of Arts degree. His fourth year was spent learning the elements of Greek, philosophy and some law as well as how to play musical instruments and sing.[37] It appears Melville did not undertake the M.A. degree. He proceeded to Glasgow University in 1574 to study under Andrew Melville, the newly appointed principal and professor of divinity.

We learn from James' description of the herculean work-load of his uncle and all that he taught.The year after his arrival at Glasgow University, at age 19, James was appointed a regent for Greek grammar and then went on to regent in arithmetic, logic, ethics, and philosophy. It would thus appear that the old regenting system was still in place despite Andrew Melville's dislike of it. While regenting, James continued his studies in Hebrew, reading works by Beza and taking lessons in Calvin's *Institutes*, taught by Andrew Melville. During this time James spoke at the exercise and once a week he took a chapter of Scripture and gave its doctrine and made exhortation to the students and others who gathered at a nearby church. Between 1575 and 1580 he often accompanied his uncle to the General Assembly.[38]

Summary

To summarize the teaching of theology and the training of ministers in this period 1560 to the *Second Book of Discipline,* we can note the following: the Church of Scotland did supply the churches, not always with ministers but sometimes with readers and exhorters who were in local "training institutes", namely, the exercise; obviously there was some discrepancy in the knowledge of Latin grammar for those entering university; and, struggles existed in implementing the ideals of the *FBD* in theological education. For example, learning of Greek and Hebrew demanded adequate professors and regents first. The students were very young by today's standards, and often the regents themselves were very young. Records of men graduating with a B.D. degree in this period do not exist, and in all likelihood this was not important. The actual reform of the universities during the 1560s was very slow, and it appears someone like Andrew Melville was clearly needed to bring reform if the three Scottish universities were going to become effective centres of Reformed theological education.[39]

---

[37] *Autobiography... James Melville,* ed. Pitcairn, 25-48. Also see *DSCHT,* 558, for Melville's correct dates for study at St. Andrews.
[38] *Autobiography... James Melville,* ed. Pitcairn, 49. H. M. B. Reid, *The Divinity Principals in the University of Glasgow* (Glasgow, 1917), 46-47.
[39] True, the General Assembly of 1563 and 1565 ordered that all university regents must adhere to the Reformed religion or else be replaced. In the 1560s at King's, this was

virtually impossible to enforce. In fact, it appears that King's resisted the reforms of the *FBD* down to 1569, remaining basically Roman Catholic. In 1569 two regents and the principal were deprived of their positions at King's. Thus, the ensuing years revealed the on-going struggle for King's to be transformed into a Reformed college to educate Reformed ministers. See David Stevenson, *King's College, Aberdeen, 1560-1641: From Protestant Reformation to Covenanting Revolution* (Aberdeen, 1990), 7-19.

CHAPTER 3

Period II: 1577-1637, *Nova Erectio*

1577-1606 Melvillian Assertions

The second distinctive period of Scottish Reformed education at the universities commenced with the return of Andrew Melville to Scotland in 1574. Melville had studied arts at Saint Andrews, philosophy under Peter Ramus in Paris, law in Poitiers, and finally theology and church government under Theodore Beza in Geneva. In addition to his studies in Geneva, he taught humanities in the final classes of the *schola privata*. Returning to Scotland "as a man in demand" by both St. Andrews and Glasgow, he chose Glasgow.[1] Glasgow College was in a precarious situation upon his arrival, but in 1577 it was given a new foundation – *nova erectio*, clearly the vision of Melville, the educational reformer.[2] This New Foundation proved to be fundamental to Glasgow University for the ensuing years until at least 1858.

Glasgow

The *nova erectio* for Glasgow was a fusion of the medieval curriculum with modern Christian humanism. It was an arts degree that was heavily classical, yet full of deep religious piety which was thoroughly Protestant in its nature. An arts course generally took three and a half years, while for those proceeding on into theology it required four years to allow time for beginning Hebrew. The classical languages, Greek and Latin, were the mainstay of the course. Study was through lectures, reading, disputation and memorization. The regents issued a letter of promotion to each student to admit him to the next class.[3] Despite Melville's aversion to the old regenting system, it was only temporarily

---

[1] J. G. Riddell, "Divinity", in *Fortuna Domus*, ed. J. E. Neilson (Glasgow, 1952), 3. Riddell refers to Melville's new position at Glasgow, appointed by the General Assembly, as a "Doctor" to interpret Scripture. This title is close to Calvin's vision of the office of doctor.

[2] H. M. B. Reid, *The Divinity Principals in the University of Glasgow* (Glasgow, 1917), 26-36; John Durkan and James Kirk, *The University of Glasgow 1451-1577* (Glasgow, 1977), ix, 254, 270.

[3] James Coutts, *A History of the University of Glasgow* (Glasgow, 1909), 60-61.

abandoned at Glasgow. This old system meant that a regent took his students through their studies for the complete set of subjects for the M.A. The principal lectured and furnished the religious exercises, as did a regent once a week.

The first class under Melville, the regent *primus*, graduated in 1578. Those continuing in theology remained under Melville, who was both principal and professor of theology as well as minister of Govan Parish Church. Melville stressed the study of Hebrew and also some Chaldee and Syriac. He gave lectures on the Psalms and other books. Calvin's *Institutes* was his chief theological text next to the Scriptures themselves. Student life at the college remained very cloistered, with vigorous exercise in intellectual and religious knowledge. Women did not live in the college, nor it appears even visit it.[4]

Melville achieved considerable success, as is evidenced by the movement of students from St. Andrews to Glasgow due to Melville's academic reputation. At first upon his arrival, Melville basically did all the teaching. Then James Melville began regenting in mathematics, logic and moral philosophy (an attempt at specialized regenting). Thus, there was a slow progression from the old regenting system to the new specialized system.[5]

Before tracing the major developments at Glasgow following Melville and the *nova erectio* and down to 1638, we must first examine the *nova erectio* and it's impact upon the other Scottish colleges. James Kirk wrote: "The *nova erectio* was a landmark in Scottish university organization, and it was recognized as such by the other universities which sought to imitate features of the scheme. Melville had rescued Glasgow University and had raised its stature immeasurably...."[6] Melville's influence, directly and indirectly, affected the ongoing reform of St. Andrews, as is evidenced in its New Foundation, 1579, and likewise of King's College, Aberdeen, and its New Foundation, 1583.[7]

St. Mary's

One year after the New Foundation for St. Andrews, Andrew Melville went to St. Mary's College as the principal and professor of divinity. James Melville writes that he went "sear against his will" and "for reforming of the universitie and erecting a college of divinitie for the profession of learned tongues and theologie against the seminaries of Rems and Rome...."[8] St. Mary's then

---

[4] Ian Hazlett, "Ebbs and Flows of Theology in Glasgow 1451-1843", in *Traditions of Theology in Glasgow 1450-1980*, ed. Ian Hazlett (Edinburgh, 1993), 8-9.
[5] Durkan and Kirk, *The University of Glasgow*, 282.
[6] Durkan and Kirk, *The University of Glasgow*, 287-288.
[7] For the full texts of the respective New Foundations see the following: J. Durkan and J. Kirk, *The University of Glasgow*, 430-438, in Latin and English; "The New Foundation", trans. G. Patrick Edwards, in David Stevenson, *King's College, Aberdeen, 1560-1641*, (Aberdeen, 1990), 149-166.
[8] *Autobiography... James Melville*, ed. Pitcairn, 83.

became a divinity college, as had really been envisaged in the *FBD* in 1560. In the colleges of St. Leonard's and St. Salvator's, the old regenting system remained in effect, but not at St. Mary's, where specialized regents or professors were instituted. Sessions lasted for eleven months for the arts course. In theology it was considerably less, probably four to six months.

Andrew Melville, in his efforts to reorganize St. Andrews University, personally appealed to Thomas Cartwright and Walter Travers to accept chairs there in 1580. This appeal was reinforced by letters also from the chancellor, rector, dean and principal of Glasgow College. Cartwright and Travers were key leaders of the English Presbyterian movement and Melville and Cartwright had spent time together in Geneva. Likewise, Melville so highly regarded Travers' book, *Explicatio ecclesiasticae disciplinae*, a work expounding Presbyterianism, that he had a copy given to Arbuthnot, principal of King's College, Aberdeen.[9] All of this shows Melville's efforts for the *nova erectio* in the Scottish colleges and his commitment to establishing them as thorough-going Presbyterian universities.

Like at Glasgow, degrees of theology at St. Andrews were not advocated nor granted under Melville. Cant wrote of Melville that "to some extent (Melville) distrusted them as symbols of the old orders. For him, the really important thing was that candidates for the ministry should be adequately trained."[10] Some theology students evidently ended their studies with a thesis for disputation, and seven such theses survive from the Melville period. None of these give any evidence that degrees were granted.[11] St. Mary's under Melville became the leading Scottish college of theology and attracted a number of foreign students from France, the Low Countries, Scandinavia, Germany and Poland.[12]

It is insightful to look at the lives of students whenever available. One student during Melville's principalship at St. Mary's was Robert Bruce, later to be a noted Reformed minister. Bruce attended from October, 1583, until 1587. He tells of some of the methods employed in training students. Students and masters ate their meals together, during which time a student read a chapter of Scripture and then proceeded to provide commentary. Evidently Robert Bruce was timid at first to take up this task. James Melville and Robert Dury gave Bruce private tutoring in the exercise, and before long he was taking his turn at the exercise before the students and master and finally publicly in churches.[13]

---

[9] Gordon Donaldson, "Scottish Presbyterian Exiles in England, 1584-1588", *RSCHS* 14 (1960-1962), 67.

[10] Ronald G. Cant, *The University of St. Andrews*, 3d ed. (St. Andrews, 1992), 65-66.

[11] Cant, *The University of St. Andrews*, 66.

[12] Cant, *The University of St. Andrews*, 67. Reference also to J. K. Cameron, "Some students from the Netherlands at the University of St. Andrews in the late 16th and early 17th centuries", in C. G. F. de Jong and J. Van Sluis, eds., *Essays on Church History* (1991).

[13] *Sermons and Life of Mr. Robert Bruce*, comp. Robert Woodrow (Edinburgh, 1843), 6, 7.

Two other colleges were founded during this period of Melvillian reform, both with links to Melville. Edinburgh College was founded in 1583 under Robert Rollock as regent. Marischal College was founded in 1593 by the fifth Earl Marischal, influenced by the Geneva Academy and Melvillian educational ideals. We turn now to an examination of these and the reformation at King's College.

Edinburgh

Turning first to the new college of Edinburgh, we find Robert Rollock (1555-1599), who had been a regent at St. Andrews while Melville was there. Rollock, regent at the new Edinburgh college, commenced a four year arts course which he taught with the assistance of a second regent in year two. Again, the course was very classical with a stress on Latin and Greek, while Ramarian taught logic, ethics and math. Rollock personally conducted the final examinations for each student to receive the M.A. Over time this approach was modified.[14]

After the first class graduated in 1587, Rollock was made principal and professor of theology. His duties were then more concentrated on the religious well-being of the students and the training of ministers, and thus his involvement as an arts regent came to an end. However, brief comment does need to be made on his philosophical curriculum, especially concerning Ramism. Charteris tells us that Rollock read aloud from Aristotle to the students each day plus gave instruction in arithmetic, anatomy, and geography. Other works tell us he also taught from Ramus' *Dialectics*. Since much has been made of Ferme and Ramism, the connection here needs to be noted. With Rollock we notice that he did not abandon Aristotle but continued to use him alongside the works of Peter Ramus (1515-1572). In essence, Ramus had attempted to simplify the highly complex logic of the Middle Ages, which was Aristotelian in its basis. Ramus developed a model for logic whereby "one divided a subject into two parts, subdivided each of these into two, then again dichotomized each subdivision, and so on". Thus, Ramists stressed "logical analysis" or "method".[15] It is easy to see this in use in Scottish sermons of the seventeenth and eighteenth centuries.[16] Ramus' method stressed classification and "arranging concepts to make them understandable and memorable

---

[14] Alexander Grant, *The Story of the University of Edinburgh*, vol. 1 (London, 1884), 151, 20-202; Andrew Dalzel, *History* (Edinburgh, 1895), 33-334.
[15] Walter J. Ong, "Ramus, Peter", in *The Encyclopedia of Philosophy*, ed. Paul Edwards (New York, 1967), 7, 66-68.
[16] Philip Ryken, *Thomas Boston as the Preacher of the Fourfold State*, Rutherford Studies in Historical Theology, eds. David F. Wright and Donald MacLeod (Carlisle and Edinburgh, 1999), 28-34.

according to 'method', the orderly presentation of a subject".[17] Woolsey gives us the best interpretation of Rollock and Ramism:

> The evidence indicates that Rollock, like most of the other theologians in the Reformed tradition, was ready to utilize in his teaching method what he considered to be of value in the thought of Ramus, but not to follow him exclusively.[18]

We have good insight into what he taught as principal and professor of theology from the *Life of John Welsh*, one of Rollock's students, and from Rollock's *Select Works*. Welsh graduated with an M.A. in August, 1588, and in 1589 was settled at Selkirk. Thus, he technically had one year (one session) in theology; however, we know that arts and theology students attended most of the same lectures by the principal and then one group, arts or divinity, was dismissed. Rollock gave an early morning lecture each Sunday at 7:00 a.m. in East Kirk Church and one Sunday afternoon on the Heidelberg Catechism. All students, both arts and divinity, attended these along with many from the public. On Saturday mornings Rollock heard student disputations and on Saturday afternoons he took all students through Beza's *Quaestiones*. "In order to facilitate the memories of the students" he published a short analysis of Beza's *Quaestiones et Responsiones*, which was entitled *Prolegomena in primum librum Quaestiones Theodori Bezae*.[19] In addition, he delivered extensive expository lectures to the students. These expositions were later published as nine commentaries. He also published five volumes of sermons. Rollock is known as the Scottish Father of Covenant Theology, and it would be interesting to trace the influence of Beza, the Heidelberg authors and the Church Fathers on his federal theology.[20]

---

[17] Donald K. McKim, "Ramus, Peter", in *ERF*, 314. McKim states that Ramus' logic provided "an alternative to prevailing Aristotelianism and was used by Puritan theologians as an intellectual basis for their thought." This means Aristotelianism from the Middle Ages as Ramus saw it. Many were "semi-Ramists". Duncan Shaw makes this helpful assessment concerning R. S. Rait and Rait's seminal article, "Andrew Melville and the Revolt against Aristotle in Scotland", *The English Historical Review* xiv (1899), 25-60.: "The differences, however, between the logic of Aristotle and Ramus were not so great as maintained by Rait." Duncan Shaw, "Zwinglian Influences on the Scottish Reformation", *RSCHS* 22 (1985), 138.

[18] Andrew Woolsey, "Unity and Continuity in Covenantal Thought", vol. 2 (unpublished Ph.D. thesis, University of Glasgow, 1988), 257.

[19] Woolsey, "Unity and Continuity in Covenantal Thought", 2:256; *Select Works of Robert Rollock*, ed. W. M. Gunn, vol. 1 (Woodrow Society, Edinburgh, 1849), x, xiii; *DSCHT*, 726.

[20] Andrew Woolsey, "Unity and Continuity in Covenantal Thought", 2:255-258. A helpful study on the later sixteenth century development of covenant theology on the Continent amongst the Reformed is Lyle D. Bierma, *German Calvinism in the Confessional Age: The Covenant Theology of Caspar Olevianus* (Grand Rapids, 1996).

Andrew McGowan has written concerning Rollock's 1597 *Tractatus de Vocatione* that this "was the first clear Scottish exposition of covenant theology" and being "in its developed two covenant form".[21] The year prior to this, Rollock published a smaller work, *Quaestiones et Responsiones Aliquoi de Foedere Dei: deque Sacramento quod Foederis Dei sigillum est* (1596). This work made the idea of the covenant the central substance of the treatise, which was incorporated the next year in the larger *Tractatus de Vocatione*.[22] It is good to see Rollock's name being given greater prominence in recent scholarship, yet he still remains far too neglected. His influence on covenant theology has recently begun to be acknowledged, and hopefully his wider work at Edinburgh University will receive more attention as well. Andrew Woolsey wrote of Rollock:

> Rollock exercised a remarkable ministry, not only through his college work, but in the pulpit. A whole generation of notable Scottish divines were trained by him, including Charles Ferme, John Welch, John Row, David Calderwood and Robert Boyd.[23]

It would thus seem clear that more attention needs to be given to Rollock as an exegete, preacher and teacher of the Bible. It was Beza who, speaking of Rollock's commentaries on Romans and Ephesians, stated that:

> [I] take it to be spoken without flattery or partiality, that I never read or met with any thing in this kind of interpretation more pithily, elegantly, and judiciously written: so as I could not contain myself, but must needs give thanks, as I ought unto God, for this so necessary and so profitable a work.[24]

The characteristics of Rollock's principalship and professorship were as follows: expounding scripture (hence he was the first Scot to publish a commentary); teaching theology which was clearly Protestant and covenantal; conducting disputations; and displaying an overall concern about the spiritual advancement of the students.[25] Like both Melville and the Geneva Academy with their stress on arts and theology, developing a full university was not Rollock's first priority. Rather, he believed that the training of men for the ministry was his fundamental task. Although evidence that Rollock taught

---

[21] Andrew T. B. McGowan, *The Federal Theology of Thomas Boston*, Rutherford Studies in Historical Theology, eds. David F. Wright and Donald MacLeod (Carlisle and Edinburgh, 1997), 1, 4. See *Select Works of Robert Rollock*, 1:xiii, 1-288.
[22] Woolsey, "Unity and Continuity in Covenantal Thought", 2:255.
[23] Woolsey, "Unity and Continuity in Covenantal Thought", 2:255.
[24] Woolsey, "Unity and Continuity in Covenantal Thought", 2:256, quoting from, *Letters of John Johnstone c.1565-1611 and Robert Howie*, ed. J. K. Cameron (Edinburgh, 1963), 331-334.
[25] Young, *Life of John Welsh*, 25-27; *Select Works of Robert Rollock*, 1:.x, xiii; *DSCHT*, 726.

Hebrew is not found in the writings of two of his students, Welsh or Charteris, this silence is not completely conclusive. Rollock had studied Hebrew under James Melville while at St. Andrews.[26]

Concerning student life at Edinburgh, we note that it was not dissimilar from that of Glasgow St. Andrews, King's and Marischal. The bursars had their early morning duties to perform before classes. The arts regents read their lectures at dictation speed, hence they were often called "dictates". Some student notebooks of dictates in arts are preserved in Edinburgh University Library. These show the care taken in recording lectures. They appear as hand-written textbooks.[27] The principal and professors provided public lectures to the college as a whole. Recreation was allowed from two until four o'clock each afternoon under the supervision of the regents, who had given the dictates and conducted the questions in class. Saturday was the disputation day, and Sunday was devoted to several religious meetings which commenced very early, six or seven in the morning, and ended mid-afternoon. College holidays were for one month, August, and sometimes September.

Most of the students at Edinburgh in this Melvillian period were Scots, while the second largest group before 1603 were Huguenots, followed by English Presbyterians. As the seventeenth century proceeded, the Huguenots stopped coming, as they were now enrolling in their own academies that were established from the early 1600s and onward. Those who graduated with an M.A. were quite few in number in comparison to the number who actually matriculated during this Melvillian period at both Glasgow and Edinburgh. The statistics did begin to change by the Restoration period.[28]

Discipline was strict during the Melvillian and Covenanter periods. At Edinburgh College the regents carried a staff for disciplinary matters. We will see that much of this changed in the latter part of the Episcopal Period (Restoration Period) and in the days of the Revolution Settlement.[29]

King's

We know that in the late 1570s Principal Arbuthnot was in correspondence with Andrew Melville concerning educational reform at King's College, Aberdeen. King's received its New Foundation in 1582-1583, the *Nova*

---

[26] Grant, *The Story of the University of Edinburgh*, 1:213-214.

[27] D. B. Horn, *A Short History of the University of Edinburgh 1556-1889* (Edinburgh, 1967), 23-25. The reference is to a rare book in the University Library, Edinburgh. I have in my possession student dictate notebooks from a different era and place – London, England, 1860 – yet there is virtually no difference, except that the former is in Latin and the latter in English. Likewise for King's College, Aberdeen; see G. D. Henderson, *Religious Life in Seventeenth Century Scotland* (Cambridge, 1937), 122-123, 275.

[28] Horn, *History of the University of Edinburgh*, 30-31.

[29] Horn, *History of the University of Edinburgh*, 25, 31-32.

Period II: 1577-1637, Nova Erectio

Fundatis, and the guiding hand of Melville was clearly evident.[30] King's New Foundation was modelled after Glasgow's and centred the college around arts and theology. The curriculum for arts was also rooted in the classics, and the Ramist teaching of Aristotle, with logic taught in this manner. As we have seen at Glasgow, Geneva, Edinburgh and now King's, medicine and law were not prominent. The emphasis was upon acquisition of the classics and the tools of exegesis and the development of sound Reformed theology in all students. The arts course allowed for the study of such other subjects as cosmography, geography, astronomy and physiology. However, alongside this were the mandatory lectures on the Confession of Faith and attendance at religious services conducted by the regents and principal (where scripture was seriously expounded, catechism taught, and a rigorous combination offered of exegesis and polemic dogmatics in Romans and Ephesians, two key New Testament works). Thus, today we find David Stevenson, commenting on the curriculum of King's, stating that this "was primarily a seminary training ministers", much as Maag argues for Geneva Academy in an over-lapping time period.[31]

King's, like Glasgow, introduced Hebrew to final year arts students who were proceeding into theology, yet it was of an inconsistent nature in Aberdeen. It was not taught until 1564, probably then by James Lawson, regent, and only until 1572, when he left for Edinburgh as Knox's successor. It may have then ceased for a time, although one regent, Ogston, was known to have some knowledge of Hebrew.

King's was in need of a New Foundation in 1583, yet how far the actual reforms were able to be carried into full effect is somewhat disputed. Many visitations occurred before the end of the sixteenth century, but it was a period of political instability. The old regenting system remained in effect at King's, although the New Foundation did set forth that ideally the regents should specialize in their "professions". The staff remained much as at Glasgow: a principal, who was the professor of theology and a doctor at St. Machar's Church, plus four regents and a grammarian, who served also at the local grammar school.

The regents were usually either young men recently graduated with their M.A. and studying for the ministry or local ministers who combined their duties in college and church. Student life was much like at Glasgow. Poor

---

[30] Bulloch, *A History of the University of Aberdeen*, 91; Stevenson, *King's College, Aberdeen*, 29-31; Durkan and Kirk, *The University of Glasgow*, 288-289. See also *Autobiography and Diary of James Melville*, ed. Pitcairn, 53.

[31] Stevenson, *King's College, Aberdeen*, 54. Also, for other summaries of curriculum and method see Stevenson, 42-47, for the best, but also Robert S. Rait, *The Universities of Aberdeen: A History* (Aberdeen, 1895), 118-119, 254-258, and J. M. Bulloch, *A History of the University of Aberdeen, 1495-1895* (London, 1895), 78, where he describes the Ramist approach to Aristotle well: "Aristotle, though deposed, was reassessed, not ousted."

students were admitted as "bursars" – on bursaries. These helped to do menial tasks in the college, such as waking students, meal duty, janitorial tasks, or porters at the gate.[32] Bearing in mind that lectures commenced at 6:00 a.m., one can appreciate the valuable service of the bursars.

What we see is really not a move away from the ideals in the *FBD* for these New Foundations, but rather stages of development "to hasten, intensify and systematize the process already initiated by the coming of Protestantism to the colleges".[33] King's College made slow steps forward under the New Foundation, but by 1597 it was firmly on this footing.[34]

Marischal

There has been disagreement as to why Marischal College was founded in 1593 in Aberdeen, as King's was not far away and was a Protestant college. G. D. Henderson has demonstrated convincingly that King's was certainly anti-Romanist in its teaching, yet his answer as to why another college was established in Aberdeen is not adequate.[35] Kirk appears to be closer to the mark when he locates Marischal's founding within the favourable Presbyterian climate of the "Golden Act" of 1572 and suggests that this climate influenced the Earl Marischal to found his college in 1593.[36] In no way does this detract from the reason of "need", that is, the need of the time for more ministers and the need to meet the growing Jesuit threat of the Counter Reformation.

Marischal was modelled after Glasgow's New Foundation, except it was to have only three regents plus a principal/professor of theology, one who knew Hebrew and Syriac.[37] The college was granted its own charter to award degrees and moved into the buildings of the old Greyfriars. The motto of Marischal was: "Thay haif said, what say thay? Lat thame say", which for some has been interpreted as a slur against King's, as the charter's preamble does speak of the neglect currently "in the northern parts of the Kingdom of Scotland" and of "an honourable, liberal and Christian education".[38]

---

[32] Stevenson, *King's College, Aberdeen*, 58.

[33] Stevenson, *King's College, Aberdeen*, 41.

[34] Durkan and Kirk, *The University of Glasgow*, 289.

[35] G. D. Henderson, *The Founding of Marischal College*, 54. "It cannot be said that Marischal College was rendered necessary by any want of enthusiasm at King's College for the principle and practises of the Reformed Church; but the new college received the Church's encouragement and blessing as a welcome addition to the institutions necessary for the provision of an increased number of well qualified ministers to uphold and spread the established Protestant form of the Christian religion."

[36] Durkan and Kirk, *The University of Glasgow*, 289.

[37] Perhaps another underlying tension between King's and Marischal Colleges was Melville's Ramism. See Hugh Kearney, *Scholars and Gentlemen Universities and Society in Pre-Industrial Britain 1500-1700* (London,1970), 58, 89.

[38] Bulloch, *A History of the University of Aberdeen*, 94, 91.

Parallels have been seen between the High School (Academy) at Herborn, founded in 1584 by Count John VI of Nassau, and Marischal College of Aberdeen. The High School was the first Calvinist institution of its kind in Germany and "was to train preachers, teachers and civil servants in the academic atmosphere of the current Calvinism, and to prepare them for confronting the Catholic universities of the day by providing a confessionally based programme of instruction".[39] Herborn had Olevianus and Piscator as theologians and Johannes Althusius, a Ramist, as professor of jurisprudence.[40]

Again, Marischal was to have only the arts course, which also included theology. There is no mention of law or medicine. Typically, like Glasgow and King's, the college community resided together. Regents were not permitted to marry. The list of subjects is identical, and therefore it is not necessary to repeat it here. It is interesting that in the first class the regent was given six months to accustom the students to written exercises in Latin. One wonders if this was to bring about a standard of unity, a problem Rollock faced when he began the first class at Edinburgh in 1583.[41] Both Rait and Kirk maintain that Marischal did follow the new specialist regenting system. The charter clearly expected this to be the case: "It is our desire that the teachers of our Academia shall not shift about to new professorships, but shall work in the same professorships, that the youths who ascend step by step may have a teacher worthy of their studies and talents."[42]

Rait shows that this new regenting system remained in effect until 1642-1643 when the old regenting system was introduced at Marischal under the Covenanters, setting aside the Melvillian and Genevan approach.[43] Provision for bursars was again provided with similar menial tasks to do as stated before. Conversation in the college was in Greek or Latin, and no arms were to be possessed. We may make one final comment on Marischal College concerning the names applied to the college as found in the charter. Several times it is called a *"Gymnasium"* or an *"Academia"* or a *"Collegium"*, but only once is it referred to as a *"Universitas"*.[44] This is highly reminiscent of Geneva and Strasbourg as well as the charter of Edinburgh College. The stress at this time was clearly to train the youth in the true faith, and it was hoped that many would go on to enter the ministry.

The first principal of Marischal was Robert Howie (1568-c.1645), who had studied at Herborn in Hesse under Kaspar Olevianus and in Basel under J. J.

---

[39] James K. Cameron, "Some Aberdeen Students on the Continent in the Late Sixteenth and Early Seventeenth Centuries", in *The Universities of Aberdeen and Europe The First Three Centuries*, ed. Paul Dukes (Aberdeen, 1995), 60.

[40] Cameron, "Some Aberdeen Students on the Continent", 60.

[41] Bulloch, *A History of the University of Aberdeen*, 95.

[42] Rait, *The Universities of Aberdeen*, 255.

[43] Rait, *The Universities of Aberdeen*, 256.

[44] Rait, *The Universities of Aberdeen*, 262.

Grynaeus. He had remained on the continent from 1585-1591. Following his principalship at Marischal, Howie became Melville's replacement as principal at St. Mary's in 1606.[45] Robert Howie, argues Andrew Woolsey, provided an important link in the development of Robert Rollock's covenantal theology by relating the interchange to the Heidelberg theologians particularly. Howie must be considered along with Rollock as one of Scotland's earliest covenantal theologians. His seven years on the continent were critical and formative years. At Herborn he was the first Scot to study under Johannes Piscator and Kaspar Olevianus. Howie's thesis disputation at Herborn in March 1587 concerns rhetoric, logic, arithmetic, geometry, physics, ethics, economics, politics, history and law. The crown of his thesis was *Theologicae Coronidis Loco*, defending that "the Word of God is the divine testimony concerning the covenant of grace, comprehending the canonical books of either testament".[46] It would appear that John Johnston was not in agreement with this thesis and wrote back to Piscator stating that Howie asserted that all theology is the doctrine of the covenant. Olevianus and Rollock, however, were in agreement with Howie. Rollock wrote in *De Vocatione:*

> Now therefore, we are to speak of the Word, or of the Covenant of God, having first set down this ground, that all the word of God appertains to some covenant; for God speaks nothing to man without the covenant.[47]

While in Basel, Howie produced the tract *De reconciliatione hominis cum Deo, seu de humani generis redemptione*, and "with this tract he has sometimes been credited with introducing federal theology to Scotland".[48]

Woolsey draws out the parallels between the writings of Howie and Rollock on the covenantal theme. Yet he is careful to state that Rollock's covenantal theology did not come from one source only, namely, through Howie. Rollock was acquainted with a larger group of theologians, yet the picture remains that as Olevianus and Ursinus held a close theological affinity in theology, so too did Rollock and Howie.[49] Thus, during Howie's term as principal at Marischal and later as principal at St. Mary's, it can be asserted with confidence that covenant theology was being taught. McCrie wrote concerning the correspondence between Andrew Melville and his nephew that though Howie

---

[45] *DSCHT*, 415; Rait, *The Universities of Aberdeen*, 264; McCrie, *Life of Melville*, 2:278-280.

[46] Woolsey, "Unity and Continuity in Covenantal Thought", 2:259, quoting from Robert Howie, *Theses Philosophicae* (Herborn, 1587) 6 (unpaginated) *"Verbum Dei est testimonium divinum de foedere gratuito, canonicis utriusque testamenti libis comprehensum."* The English translation is that of Woolsey.

[47] Woolsey, "Unity and Continuity in Covenantal Thought", 2:259, and Rollock, *Selected Works*, 1:33-34.

[48] Cameron, "Some Aberdeen Students on the Continent", 62.

[49] Woolsey, "Unity and Continuity in Covenantal Thought" 2:261-275.

was Andrew Melville's replacement, "there is not an invidious hint thrown out against Howie". Rather, in 1610 James wrote of Howie "with high respect in a letter to his uncle".[50]

Like at the other colleges, students attended lectures and disputations, gave disputations, heard sermons, were instructed in the catechism and benefited from living together as a college community. The work of the M.A. degree was a solid footing for further theological studies, yet it must be remembered that students of theology were also expected to attend the exercise. Thus, the colleges were not the complete system of training.

The Exercise and Presbyterial Involvements

Under this Melvillian period the erection of presbyteries was effected in 1581. In St. Mary's the exercise was actually meeting within the college, affording ample opportunity for student attendance. Melville, it appears, ensured that St. Mary's during his tenure strove to be a model for theological education and training. Students, likewise, at Glasgow and Edinburgh attended the exercise.[51] By the presbytery in its embryonic stages taking over the exercise, which included the examination of ministerial candidates, the "assumption of this power by Presbyteries from 1581 was achieved with little dislocation".[52]

However, in an examination of the *Presbytery Records of Stirling, 1581-1587*, we note an absence of students in attendance. It appears that the presbyteries of Glasgow, St. Andrews, Aberdeen and Edinburgh were mainly those with theology students present. Stirling had its weekly exercise before the administration portion of the meeting, but we note that it was ministers, exhorters and readers, and schoolmasters who attended the exercise. Thus, for the out-lying presbyteries the exercise was limited to examining ministers, running a form of a "pastors continuing education programme", and maintaining doctrinal orthodoxy. It is difficult to view these presbyteries as achieving vital training of students through the exercise. The exception, however, would be where there were schoolmasters who had been teaching school before they took a church.[53]

It is important to realize that final accreditation in theology lay with the exercise/presbytery, where a series of exercises, lectures and trials were an

---

[50] McCrie, *Life of Melville* (1819), 2:280-281.
[51] Durkan and Kirk, *The University of Glasgow*, 333.
[52] James Kirk, Introduction to *Stirling Presbytery Records 1581 to 1587* (Scottish History Society, Edinburgh, 1981), xix.
[53] James Kirk, Introduction to *Stirling Presbytery Records*, xxvi - xxvii. See also the text of the presbytery records for penalties imposed of 10 or 5 shillings for missing the presbytery (21) and the assignment of the exercise texts (25), Genesis, catechism, Gospel Harmonies, etc. Discussion of commentaries also occurred, eg. Calvin, Beza, Gualteir, Musculus, etc. (and 323, index on exercise).

essential part of virtually all presbytery meetings. It appears that under Melville some theology students also disputed theses on such themes as predestination, justification, the sacraments, etc. These were printed and have been preserved. At King's, Marischal, Edinburgh and Glasgow there are no printed theses on record for the years 1577 to 1606. This does not mean that theses/disputations were not requisite, but perhaps were required in a less formal sense than at St. Mary's. Students did their disputations in all the colleges, but how this may have differed from a printed thesis is somewhat difficult to judge. Theology degrees were not given for these theses, nor for graduation in theology in general.

During the time of "Episcopal Assertions", 1606-1638, the exercise meetings continued. Sometimes commonheads were dealt with, but also quite often the exercise/presbytery did a series through a book of Scripture. For example, in August, 1620, the Presbytery of Perth had finished Romans and then commenced with 1 Corinthians. "In 1638, the Presbytery of St. Andrews, at their weekly exercise, were proceeding through the Gospel according to St. John, with an 'exercise and addition' upon each verse."[54] McMillan asserts that "the introduction of Episcopacy made no difference in the conduct of these meetings, except that in 1610 it was decided that if the Bishop was present he should moderate, and if not, then he was to appoint some person to act for him".[55] Again we find regulations for failure to attend. At Perth in 1618 a fine of ten shillings was imposed for failing to attend the exercise without reasonable excuse. It appears that efforts were made to regulate the time taken up by the exercise and addition. The Diocese/Presbytery of Dunkeld set it at one hour, with each portion taking half of this time. Upon occasion some were censured for being too long.[56]

Orkneys and Fraserburgh

Before passing from this phase of theological training, which clearly is identified with Melville and the *nova erectio*, mention must be made of two other efforts to establish more centres of higher learning in Scotland. In 1581 a proposal was made before the Scottish Parliament to establish a college in the Orkneys.[57] It appears that nothing came of this venture. In 1592 Sir Alexander Fraser proposed to create a university at Fraserburgh and obtained a charter from King James. In 1597 the Scottish Parliament was informed that the buildings had begun and provision was made for an endowment. Charles Ferme, a graduate of Rollock's first class in Edinburgh, 1587, and a regent in Edinburgh from 1590 to 1598, accepted the charge of Philorth, Fraserburgh,

---

[54] McMillan, *Worship of the Scottish Reformed Church*, 367.
[55] McMillan, *Worship of the Scottish Reformed Church*, 368.
[56] McMillan, *Worship of the Scottish Reformed Church*, 368-369.
[57] *Acts of the Parliament of Scotland*, 3:214.

and in 1600 the General Assembly appointed him the new principal.[58] Three neighbouring ministers of Crimmond, Rathen and Tyrie were appointed as regents.[59] Ferme taught until 1605, when he was imprisoned for his Presbyterian views. It is unclear if classes resumed after his restoration to his parish in 1609. He may have continued as principal until his death in 1616.[60] Ferme was the author of *Logical Analysis of the Epistle of Paul to the Romans*, wherein he applied Ramist logic to exegesis.[61]

Yet, in addition to Ramistic logic, we should also note with Ferme a consistent theme of covenantal theology. Ferme, too, saw the one covenant of grace embracing the Old Testament saints as well as the New Testament believers. Israel had the promises, which were made fully known in the gospel. Rollock conveyed his covenantal theology to Ferme, who likewise was its expounder.[62]

It is noteworthy that the General Assembly method of teaching was not dissimilar from that used at Edinburgh College or Marischal College. So little information is readily available concerning Fraserburgh that many questions remain as to how many ministers or other students were trained there. Thomas McCrie makes brief reference to its demise in his *Life of Andrew Melville*, and attributes Marischal College's founding to the demise of Fraserburgh.[63]

1606-1638 Episcopal Assertions

There are two natural divisions in this period of the *nova erectio*: the first with Andrew Melville generally present in Scotland from the first New Foundation in 1577 through to 1606, when he was banished to the Tower of London never

---

[58] *BUK*, 486. "The Generall Assemblie having considered the necessity of the said worke, and how the Laird of Phillorthe has refusit to sustaine one pastor at the said Kirk, unless he undertake both the saids charges. Therefore commands and charges the said Mr. Charles Ferme to undertake and awayte upon, alsweill the said Kirk, as to be Principal of the College of Fraserburgh." Sess. 7, Mar. 21, 1600, Montrose. See also *FES*, 6:220-221.

[59] *FES*, 6:212-213, 245. Regents: John Gordon, Crimond, also a graduate of Edinburgh; Duncan Davidson, Rathen, a former regent at Aberdeen; John Howeson, Tyrie, of whom little is known.

[60] Rait, *The Universities of Edinburgh*, 263 – 264; *DSCHT*, 318-319. Rait writes that the University of Fraserburgh ceased to exist in 1605, whereas David Wright in his article suggests that Ferme resumed classes after his release from prison in 1609. *BUK*, 3:958; *APS*, 4:14 -148.

[61] C. Ferme, *A Logical Analysis of the Epistle of Paul to the Romans*, ed. W. L. Alexander (Wodrow Society, Edinburgh, 1850); *FES*, 6:220-221; R. Lippe, *Selections from Wodrows Biographical Collections* (New Spalding Club, Aberdeen, 1890), lxxvii-lxxviv, 270-281.

[62] Woolsey, "Unity and Continuity in Covenantal Thought", 2:277-278.

[63] McCrie, *Life of Andrew Melville* (1819), 2:287.

to return to Scotland; the second from 1606 to 1638, when Episcopacy was reasserted in Scotland with various degrees of success and with acceleration as time passed. Yet the effects of the New Foundations continued to hold influence in the colleges, especially for theological education. What now follows is mention of some significant developments in theological education during this second period; we will not attempt a close portrayal here. Chief developments in this time were the establishment of Chairs of Divinity, restoration of degrees, more theological writing, and a greater consistency in the study of Hebrew.[64]

Chairs of Divinity

Both Edinburgh College and King's College received new Chairs of Divinity in 1620. The *FBD* had actually proposed a teacher of divinity in addition to the principal, yet it was not until 1620 that this was realized at King's and Edinburgh. Marischal erected a Chair of Divinity four years earlier, in 1616. The duties of the new professor of divinity in Edinburgh were to direct theology students in their reading, lecture on Tuesday and Friday from 11:00 a.m. until noon, conduct each Monday the exercise in Scots for each student, and to meet with students "privately" on Thursdays to take care that they were examining some theological *loci* in Latin by sustaining a thesis at a disputation. By "private" is meant a Latin disputation with only the theology students, not the public, present. The professor was also expected "to teach something of the Hebrew tongue".[65] These were clearly advances, provided the principal as primarius professor of theology fulfilled his task by teaching divinity, something which basically ceased in Glasgow in 1661, after which the principal was rarely involved in teaching theology. Thus, what could eventually occur was that the one professor of theology would have the teaching burden fall on him.[66] It would appear that St. Mary's continued through to 1638 to be in the best position in terms of the most teaching staff.

The impetus for the creation of these new chairs was due to unsatisfactory standards. Bishop Patrick Forbes founded the new chair at King's in 1620 due to the unsatisfactory work of Principal Rait, who taught little Hebrew. We can speculate about the Bishop's displeasure with Principal Rait, as he nonetheless awarded him a D. D. in 1620 and filled the new Chair of Divinity with his own son, John Forbes. Nonetheless, there was merit in John Forbes appointment. He was a student at Heidelberg, then at Sedan under Melville, and ordained by a Dutch classis.

At Marischal College, though a separate Chair of Divinity had been founded earlier, it must be questioned just how advantageous this chair was. In 1617

---

[64] G. D. Henderson, *Religious Life in Seventeenth Century Scotland*, 38-39.
[65] Dalzel, *History of theUniversity of Edinburgh*, 2:38-382.
[66] S. Mechie, "Education for the Ministry in Scotland Since the Reformation", 2:119.

William Forbes was in the chair. He transferred to the principalship in 1619 due to the principal's death. William Forbes was principal, a local minister and professor for a very short duration before resigning to take an Edinburgh church. The next professor of theology was Robert Baron, who combined being professor at Marischal with pastoral duties. He gave two lectures a week to the theology students. Baron felt that with such an arrangement he could take a theology student through the course in three years. He was one of the famous "Aberdeen Doctors".[67]

Degrees

The actual conferment of theological degrees ended in Scotland at the Reformation and was not resurrected until King James VI sought its restoration in an effort to secure Episcopal unity in the realm (this refers to all theological degrees including that of the Doctor of Divinity). The first two Doctor of Divinities at King's College were given in 1620. The first of these was given to Principal Rait, whose thesis was *De libero arbitrio*. The second was awarded to John Forbes, the new professor of divinity, for his thesis *De sacramentis*. It certainly appears from the records that the D.D. was not simply an honorary degree but was connected to a theological thesis. Also, in these years the theses were printed by Raban, the printer in Edinburgh. Eleven D.D.'s were given at King's from 1620 to 1635.

One unusual fact about those years is that two of the eleven men to whom D.D.'s were granted were also made Bachelors of Divinity along with the Doctor of Divinity degree. Following these B.D. awards there was a lapse of over one hundred years before a B.D. was granted again, and then only to dissenting ministers in London, England. After this it was not given again until the end of the nineteenth century.[68] Those who received the D.D. under Chancellor, Bishop Patrick Forbes, are referred to as the "Aberdeen Doctors".

The Covenanting period did not promote the D.D., as the Covenanters saw this as the "road to Rome". John Row saw the doctor as "the prelate's eldest son and heir" and, "Doctoratus is nothing else but a step to a Prelacie."[69] Thus, it is interesting to consider how Calvin, Melville and the Covenanters understood the office of doctor in the church as distinct from the degree. It would appear that King James VI's motivation was to conform Scotland more to the atmosphere of things English.

One of the first recipients of the D.D. degree from St. Andrews was William Forbes, who briefly served as principal at Marischal College.[70] Edinburgh did

---

[67] Rait, *The Universities of Aberdeen*, 266-270, 274-275.
[68] *Officers and Graduates of University and King's College, Aberdeen*, ed. Peter John Anderson (New Spalding Club, Aberdeen, 1893), 97-98, 109.
[69] John Row, *Historie*, 261, 318; McCrie, *Life of Andrew Melville* (1819), 2:451-454.
[70] G. D. Henderson, *Religious Life in Seventeenth Century Scotland*, 41.

not confer the D.D. until 1709 and then there followed a twenty year absence.[71] Glasgow, likewise, did not confer this degree in this period, yet we find the use of the term "doctor" used in 1640 to describe Mr. David Dickson's admission to the office of Professor and Doctor of Theology.[72] This is more in keeping with the Presbyterian use of the term doctor after the Reformation and into the Covenanting period. At Glasgow the Doctor of Divinity degree was not conferred until 1709, when Daniel Williams and two others received it. In 1710 Cotton Mather received the Doctor of Divinity degree.[73]

Theological Writings by Principals and Professors

Reference has already been made to the contribution of Robert Rollock by way of written works on covenant theology. Rollock also produced a *Prolegomena* for the use of divinity students as an introduction to Beza's *Book of Christian Questions*, perhaps Beza's most complete work.[74] Rollock's most voluminous writings, as have been briefly mentioned, were scripture expositions (the reader is directed to the bibliography for a full listing of these). Andrew Melville also published works during this period, many during his exile in France.

Perhaps the most famous work of the Covenanter period was written by Robert Boyd while principal of Glasgow College. His *Commentary on Ephesians* is described as "monumental in size, encyclopaedic in theological scope – as much a dogmatic thesaurus as a biblical commentary".[75] Although it was published posthumously in 1652, it demonstrates Boyd's learning and, being the contents of his class lectures in theology, shows what he would have been teaching students.[76] Boyd served as another connector to the continent as he was ordained in France in 1604 and spent many years in France teaching in Reformed academies and pastoring before his tenure at Glasgow. He later was principal and professor of theology and minister at Govan from 1615 to 1621 and then fulfilled the same positions at Greyfriars, Edinburgh for one year before his death. He has been described as one who desired an exegetical approach to theology, which was evidenced in the colleagues and pupils who gathered around him – Dickson, Blair, and Livingstone, and those who followed in this tradition, Ferguson, Nisbet, Binning and Durham, the great Covenanting expositors of the next period.[77]

---

[71] *A Catalogue of the Graduates in the Faculties of Arts, Divinity, and Law, of the University of Edinburgh* (Edinburgh, 1858), 239.

[72] *Munimenta Alme Universitatis Glasguensis*, ed. C. Innes, vol.4 (Indices) (Maitland Club, Glasgow, 1854), xcix.

[73] *Munimenta Alme Universitatis Glasguensis*, 3:304.

[74] *Select Works of Robert Rollock*, vol. 1, lxxxviii. In Latin: *Prolegomena in primum librum Qaestionum Theodori Bezae*.

[75] Hazlett, "Ebbs and Flows of Theology in Glasgow 1451-1843", 11.

[76] *DSCHT*, 92.

[77] William Campbell, "Robert Boyd of Trochrigg", *RSCHS* 12 (1954-1956), 228.

Boyd's successor at Glasgow was the controversial John Cameron, who stayed only two years and then went to France to teach. Cameron was associated with Amyraldianism. Cameron's successor was Dr. John Strang (one of the first St. Andrew's doctors, 1616). Strang's literary output as principal and professor was minimal. We note that from 1625 to 1640 the teaching of theology fell on his shoulders at Glasgow College. Again, after his death his works were published, prepared by his son-in-law, Robert Baillie, and printed in Amsterdam and Rotterdam.[78]

This leaves out one group of theologians thus far, "The Aberdeen Doctors". Their chief publications were polemics against the rising Covenanter Party. Of the six doctors, three taught theology at either King's or Marischal with the clear leader being John Forbes, first professor of divinity at King's. His *Irenicum* of 1629 argued for the lawfulness of the Five Articles of Perth and the conferring of divinity degrees.[79] His main theological work was not published until 1645, *Instructiones Historico-Theologicae* (Doctrine of the Catholic Church, Historically Considered), a work on the history of doctrine from lectures to his students. MacMillan interpreted the Aberdeen Doctors as turning more to Arminius as a champion to study. Each must be assessed on his own merits.[80] There is no doubt that they were anti-Melvillian and hence anti-Ramist. Yet their classes were also humanist and strongly exegetical. Greek and Hebrew were taught; divinity students assisted for two years as regents (up to a maximum of six years) and then went on to take a church.[81]

From 1607 to 1638, St. Mary's was in the hands of its principal, Robert Howie, a federal or covenant theologian who had studied at Herborn under Olevianus. He was principal of St. Mary's during the Episcopal years, yet he also remained principal after the re-establishment of Presbyterianism in 1638. One of his books, dedicated to Andrew Melville, is on *Predestination*. Other works included one on *Justification* (Basel, 1590).

We have already mentioned the most prolific writer at Edinburgh during this period, Rollock. The others wrote very little. Ramsay wrote Latin poetry and had taught in France at the Academy in Saumur.[82] Similarly, John Sharp, one of his successors at Edinburgh, had also spent time teaching in France. Sharp wrote some tracts, as well as *Symphonia Prophetarum et Apostolorum*, which was printed twice, in 1625 and 1629.[83]

---

[78] Reid, *Divinity Principals in the University of Glasgow*, 270, 301; *DSCHT*, 801.
[79] D. MacMillan, *The Aberdeen Doctors* (London, 1909), 45; *DSCHT*, 238.
[80] Kearney, *Scholars and Gentlemen*, 89-90. He argues that William Forbes was an Arminian but the Aberdeen Doctors, such as Baron, were Calvinist yet conservative in views concerning politics and society, not challenging the King.
[81] MacMillan, *The Aberdeen Doctors*, 43-44.
[82] *DSCHT*, 691.
[83] *DSCHT*, 769.

Summary

Upon Melville's return to Scotland in 1574, the three Scottish universities were clearly in need of someone to make the ideals of the *FBD* a reality in terms of theological education. It is realistic to term Andrew Melville "the Second Founder of Glasgow University". However, his vision was primarily with the college as an educational training centre for the church. The M.A. course was an arts degree set clearly in the atmosphere of a Reformed theology. It really needs to be seen as an M.A. in arts and theology. Stress was on the ancient languages in order to train the students to read both the classics and the Scriptures in their original languages. Syriac was taught for the reading of the older Syriac manuscripts. The revolution in teaching logic was to provide a tool for scriptural analysis. All of this was the vision of the *nova erectio*. It also meant a change in method to specialization in order to ensure proficiency and mastery in teaching.

The new curriculum was brought to bear at Glasgow, St. Andrew's, and the new colleges at Edinburgh and Aberdeen. King's College adopted much of the curriculum but not as evenly. The new regenting system worked in St. Mary's, at Glasgow for a time, in Marischal, and partially at Edinburgh in this period. At Glasgow from 1574 to 1640 the principal was solely responsible for teaching the theology class after their degree (if they took one). King's, Marischal and Edinburgh were all the same until the creation of chairs of divinity in the early seventeenth century. St. Mary's was the exception in this period with more staff. Generally the principal served a local church, although at Glasgow this was stopped in 1620. However, this did not imply a loss of church involvement but more a matter of how much one man could do. It was the responsibility of the principal to ensure that Hebrew was taught. As the period advanced, the creation of chairs of divinity were helpful, yet one wonders if in some instances the principal's involvement in teaching actually declined (as, for example, in Edinburgh).

We have seen that in the Melvillian period theological degrees were associated with episcopacy and Romanism. However, within the universities it certainly appears that academic standards in arts and theology were high. The church's role in the exercise/presbytery in the towns and cities of the colleges also acted as an accrediting agency of the education and training. The church was taking steps forward in supporting bursar students in each of the colleges by the General Assembly Act of 1616, which involved all presbyteries systematically in this programme.

The writings which were published by the principals and professors show a marked development in biblical and theological studies. The extent of the biblical commentaries and sermons produced by professors still needs to be better accessed. It was also a time when Scottish Covenantal theology was being refined, as can be seen with Ferme, Howie and chiefly Rollock. There continued to be much more contact with the continent by students studying

Period II: 1577-1637, Nova Erectio

there in Reformed universities and academies. Also, one writer suggests that in the early years of the seventeenth century, one half of the faculty in some French academies were Scots. This shows their ability, but perhaps is more reflective of the tumultuous times between Episcopacy and Presbyterianism in Scotland.[84] The by-product must have been that it kept Scottish theology infused with continental Reformed literature, debate and sources.

It is very clear that by 1600 the Reformed Church of Scotland had made strides forward in possessing a godly and learned ministry. Even the short-lived Fraserburgh University shows a commitment to train an educated clergy for Scotland. The colleges helped to do this, but so did the exercise/presbytery by helping some readers become exhorters and then ministers. W. R. Foster in *The Church Before the Covenants* shows from several scattered presbyteries in 1600 that the actual number of ministers with arts degrees had substantially increased. Even those who lacked the M.A. may have attended college, as many attended but never took the degree due to the fees to graduate. By 1638, Foster states, even in the remotest presbyteries almost all ministers had the M.A. degree.[85]

---

[84] Campbell, "Robert Boyd of Trochrigg", 222.
[85] W. R. Foster, *The Church Before the Covenants* (Edinburgh,1975), 133.

CHAPTER 4

Period III: 1638-1661, Covenanter Period

Introduction

We come now to the age of the Presbyterian ascendancy, framed on one side by the General Assembly in Glasgow, 1638, and on the other side by the ejection of Presbyterian ministers in 1662. From 1606 to 1637 Episcopalian advancements were being made in Scotland. This affected the universities and the training of ministers. Men like Andrew Melville and Robert Boyd were ejected or demitted office rather than conform to the wishes of King James VI. Such was the case with Boyd, who demitted his work as principal at Edinburgh University and minister at Greyfriars. Opposition to the rising Episcopacy and conformity to the English practices broke with the Glasgow Assembly of 1638, wherein Episcopacy was abolished, the *Book of Common Prayer* ruled unlawful, and the government of the church was settled as being presbyterian.

In this period we call "Covenanter", there was a quintet of names which stood out in the five colleges for their contributions to Scottish Presbyterianism: Samuel Rutherford, Robert Baillie, David Dickson, Patrick Gillespie and John Row. The lists in the appendices give further names during this period, but these five names rose above the others. One additional name needs to be examined for his contributions as principal and professor of divinity during the Covenanter Period, that of Robert Leighton. At the Restoration he became the Bishop of Dunblane. He must not be omitted as he held his Edinburgh University position for almost ten years during this time. Therefore, we begin by looking at the quintet of Covenanter professors followed by an examination of Leighton. In doing this we will review their writings, curriculum and other significant contributions in theological education and training. Finally, we will consider the actions of the General Assembly in this period and take a glimpse into presbytery contributions. Student life and the increase in divinity student numbers will be noted as we proceed.

The Galaxy of Divines: Baillie, Dickson, Gillespie, Rutherford and Row; the Covenanter Expository Series; and Leighton

Of the five divinity professors listed above, Samuel Rutherford's name is the most prominent. Rutherford took the M.A. at Edinburgh, graduating in 1621, and in 1623 was an arts regent in Latin while studying theology under Adam Ramsay, the first professor in the new Chair of Divinity. Rutherford remained a regent through to 1625 and then studied theology until 1627, when he settled at Anwoth.[1] He remained at Anwoth until 1636, the year he was exiled to Aberdeen. In that same year, 1636, his first work, *Exercitationes Apologeticae pro Divina Gratia*, was published in Amsterdam. He was able to return to Anwoth in 1638, and subsequently in 1639 he was asked by the General Assembly to become a professor of divinity at St. Mary's College.

Rutherford's 1636 work on divine grace was a defense against the Arminians, and it won him a reputation in many circles. It was at the publication of this work in Amsterdam that he was invited to become the divinity professor at Utrecht. John MacLeod speculates that Rutherford's invitation to Utrecht was because of his supralapsarian position, which was the same as Voetius'.[2] MacLeod carefully stated concerning Rutherford's scholastic writing: "The tendency to lay what looks like an undue burden on the absolute Sovereignty of God was one in which a daring thinker like Rutherford indulged."[3] Is this a gentle criticism of Rutherford's scholastic theology and precision? Principal Strang of Glasgow University was not a supralapsarian, and it would appear he wrote against Rutherford's high predestinationism in his work *De Providentia*. Though many supported Rutherford's scholasticism, he did have his detractors in this area of metaphysics.[4] (Strang was Baillie's father-in-law).

While at St. Andrews Rutherford frequently preached in the town or adjacent villages on Sundays and gave church lectures on Mondays. His involvement as a commissioner to the Westminster Assembly of Divines is well accorded. While at St. Mary's as professor and then also as principal in 1647, his many other writings brought him a vast reputation on the continent.[5] Invitations continued to come to join other colleges, as did invitations by churches in Scotland to become their minister.[6] His *Examen Arminianismi* was

---

[1] *Letters of Samuel Rutherford with a Sketch of his Life*, ed. Andrew Bonar, original 1664 (Edinburgh, 1984), 4-6.
[2] John MacLeod, *Scottish Theology*, 2d ed. (Edinburgh, 1946), 70.
[3] MacLeod, *Scottish Theology*,70.
[4] Walker, *Theology and Theologians of Scotland*, 18.
[5] For a good listing of Rutherford's theological works see: Thomas F. Torrance, *Scottish Theology From John Knox to John MacLeod Campbell* (Edinburgh, 1996), 123-124.
[6] It appears quite certain that Rutherford preached on occasion for Robert Blair in the Town Church, but it cannot be said that he held his appointment as professor in conjunction with being a pastor of Town Church, St. Andrews. On this detail John

a collection of lectures to students at St. Mary's which, as the title suggests, concerned the debate between Calvinists and Arminians. Walker characterized this work as an excellent theological manual.[7]

Rutherford's greatest scholastic theological work was *De Providentia*, a tome of almost seven hundred closely printed pages. Walker tells us that it abounds with references to Thomas Aquinas, John Scotus, Bradwardine and Twiss, which Walker views as possessing "a certain scholastic artificiality". It is a "maze of logical distinctions" but shows a keen mind tackling questions of a most difficult nature, such as:

> What is the nature of God's permissive will?... Is God the origin and cause of possibilities and impossibilities? Is this possible something real? Is there anything impossible save as it has its original impossibility from God?[8]

1638 to 1661 has often been referred to as a "golden era" of theological training in Scotland. Rutherford's abilities and gifts were immense as a pastor, but also as a professor of theology. There is little doubt that some of Scotland's best pastors were made professors of theology and/or principals in the various colleges of this time. Robert MacWard studied at St. Andrews and was also Rutherford's amanuensis at the Westminster Assembly in London. As a former student, he spoke with glowing praises about his mentor. MacWard commented on Rutherford's presence at St. Andrews:

> God did so signally second His servant's indefatigable pains both in teaching in the schools and preaching in the congregation, that it became forthwith a Lebanon out of which were taken cedars for building the house of the Lord through the whole land.[9]

In a quick survey of Rutherford's writings, the *Letters*, penned while in exile in Aberdeen to his parishioners scattered at Anwoth, evidence "the most remarkable series of devotional letters that the literature of the Reformed Churches can show".[10] MacLeod summarized their content as that of fervent piety, zeal, love to Christ Jesus, the response of love, all dressed in figurative language, paralleling the Song of Songs and Psalm 45, and showing raptures

---

MacLeod, *Scottish Theology* page 69 is incorrect (compare with *FES*). That Rutherford was in high demand as a preacher is very certain. He involved himself this way in church life while a professor and principal. Rutherford, however, did not technically pastor in the Town Church, but rather he took his turn in the rota of preaching there.

[7] *DSCHT*, 537-538, 735-736.
[8] Walker, *Theology and Theologians of Scotland*, 9.
[9] Iain Murray, "Ministerial Training: A Sketch of Theological Education in the 16th and 17th centuries", *Banner of Truth* 15 (1963), 20.
[10] MacLeod, *Scottish Theology*, 68.

Period III: 1638-1661, Covenanter Period 59

not unlike that of Bernard.[11] *Letters* went through one hundred editions and has remained one of the most popular Scottish devotional works.[12]

Rutherford's writings are not only of a devotional nature[13] but also include the subject of political theory, and many consider these to be some of his most significant contributions. His *Lex Rex* or *Law is King* "denied that a limitless sovereignty belonged to the King, and contended that the Crown is bestowed by the voluntary consent of the people, who are at liberty to resist a tyrant".[14] This work was in the tradition of George Buchanan's *Dejure regni apud scotos*, and it had significant influence on political theory for many in Scotland for generations, not to mention twentieth century, non-Scottish writers such as Francis A. Schaeffer.[15] Again, MacLeod, who traces a connection between Rutherford and James Renwick and Alexander Shields in the Covenanting Period, concluded that:

---

[11] MacLeod, *Scottish Theology*, 68-69. An interesting study on the nature of Rutherford's devotional writings is: C. N. Button, "Scottish Mysticism in the 17th Century, with special reference to Samuel Rutherford" (unpublished Ph.D. thesis, University of Edinburgh, 1927). Also related is: D. R. , "Union With Christ in the Theology of Samuel Rutherford" (unpublished Ph.D. thesis, University of Edinburgh, 1972).It appears that the parallel with Bernard of Clairvaux was first made by James Walker in *The Theology and Theologians of Scotland: 1560-1750*, original 1872 (Edinburgh, 1982), 13. Walker also draws parallels to Augustine's *Confessions* and Thomas à Kempis (8).

[12] John Coffey, *Politics, Religion and the British Revolutions: The Mind of Samuel Rutherford* (Cambridge, 1997), 1, 82-113. Coffey's chapter "The Puritan Pastor" is very helpful to understand the devotional aspect of Puritanism and of Rutherford in particular. An interesting comparison, I would suggest, would be to compare Samuel Rutherford's use of the Song of Songs in his *Letters* to Ralph Erskine's "Scripture Songs: Part III. A New Version of the Song of Solomon" in *The Sermons and other Practical Works of Ralph Erskine*, vol. 7 (London, 1865), 522-538. See also J. K. Cameron, "The Piety of Samuel Rutherford (c.1600-61): a neglected feature of seventeenth-century Scottish Calvinism", *Nederlands Archief voor Kerkgeschiedenis*, 65 (1985), 153-159.

[13] Other devotional works would include: Samuel Rutherford, *Trial and Triumph of Faith* (London, 1645) and *Christ Dying and Drawing Sinners to Himself* (London, 1647). Both of these works exalt Christ and set forth the life of fellowship in Him. See MacLeod's comments on these works, pages 75-78 in *Scottish Theology*.

[14] *DSCHT*, 735. This article is by Sherman Isbell. The most recent in depth study on Rutherford as a political theorist would be Coffey's chapter "The political theorist" in *Politics, Religion and the British Revolutions: The Mind of Samuel Rutherford*, 146-147.

[15] Francis A. Schaeffer, *A Christian Manifesto* in *The Complete Works of Francis A. Schaeffer A Christian Worldview*, original 1981, vol. 5 (Westchester, Illinois, 1982), 415, 431, 471-479, 489-490, 493. See also William M. Campbell, "Lex Rex and Its Author", *RSCHS* 7 (1941), 204-228.

The freedom of a constituency of responsible rational beings is not a thing to be bought or sold or sacrificed or trodden underfoot. Such lessons are not so antiquated or old-fashioned as not to be called for in these days of ours. Our old Scots Whigs were true conservatives of Divine rights and claims and not illiberal teachers of human rights and duties in the realm of civil government and citizenship.[16]

Ecclesiology and polity were generally considered standard fare in the curriculum of candidates for the ministry in Presbyterian churches. Rutherford wrote extensively in this field, so it is not too difficult to assume that he would have wanted the students at St. Andrews to know these ecclesiastical principles. His three works on this topic were: *The Peaceable Plea for Presbytery*, *The Due Right of Presbyteries*, and *The Divine Right of Church Government*. These works appear to have rivalled Rutherford's younger contemporary George Gillespie, who also wrote on these matters. Rutherford's position was that the New Testament sets forth a form of church government by elders and presbyteries, and that church discipline is in the power of the church officers, not the civil magistrate (Erastianism).[17]

The impression of Rutherford we are left with, whether at Anworth or St. Andrews, is that there was a rich combination of experimental Calvinistic theology and rigorous, theological scholasticism in his writings, lectures and sermons. This combination was likewise recognized in a recent article by Ian Hamilton.[18]

Robert Baillie held the next light to Rutherford. Even today his *Letters* and *Journals* on the Westminster Assembly of Divines provide us with valuable information. While Baillie was professor of divinity at Glasgow College, 1642-1662, he lectured on the Westminster Confession of Faith and Catechisms, along with the Canons of Dort.

Baillie graduated from Glasgow College in 1620 prior to attending the public divinity lectures of Principal Boyd on Ephesians before Boyd resigned and went to Edinburgh in 1623. Baillie's first appearance at the presbytery to conduct an exercise was in 1624, and in 1625 he became a regent at Glasgow. Presbytery records show Baillie did two exercises, one controversy and one addition, in each of the years 1624, 1625, 1628, and 1629. In 1631 Baillie was the minister of Kilwinning, remaining there until 1637.[19] Following that he was

---

[16] MacLeod, *Scottish Theology*, 73. A proper study of someone like Professor Archibald Bruce on political theory appears to me as an extension in certain respects of Samuel Rutherford's political theory.

[17] *DSCHT*, 735-736.

[18] Ian Hamilton, "Samuel Rutherford (ca 1600-1661)", *Banner of Truth* 443 and 444 (August-September, 2000), 9-18.

[19] F. N. McCoy, *Robert Baillie and the Second Scots Reformation* (Berkeley, 1974), 18-27. Hazzlett, "Ebbs and Flows of Theology in Glasgow", 14.

involved with the Glasgow Assembly of Divines. However, what concerns us here is his work teaching theology while at Glasgow.

Dickson was appointed first divinity professor in 1640; Baillie was appointed second divinity professor in 1642. Together with Principal Strang, they carried the teaching load at Glasgow. Baillie taught Hebrew, controversies and church government while Dickson handled the expository study of Scripture. The principal heard the disputations of students and lectured on the hard places of Scripture.[20] In later years Baillie added some Chaldean and Syriac to his language teaching. He wrote that at that time (that is the 1650s) there were few theology students in Glasgow, so he taught Hebrew and catechism to all the arts students. He casually commented that he found the divinity students were not applying themselves to their studies. During this time Baillie was also the minister of the low church (Tron) at the Trongate, Glasgow until 1649.[21] After that time he continued to preach at the Tron, though no longer the minister there, and was busy writing.

While at Glasgow Baillie began the writing of his *magnum opus*, which was to be a universal history of humanity, divided into epochs. Although he died before its completion, having finished up to the time of Emperor Constantine, the theology students frequently heard lectures on his chronology.[22] This work was first published in 1663 in Amsterdam, but Hazlett asserts that it was in use for fifty years after this by presbyters when they examined students in ancient, biblical and early Church history.[23]

As a doctor of the church, Baillie had three primary responsibilities in teaching: the controversies, oriental languages and chronology. He attempted to form each of his dictates into a textbook. In 1654 he published *Catechesis Elenctica Errorum*, a textbook for controversies in the form of questions and answers with proof from Scripture of the truth. Baillie viewed it as the duty of professors of theology, freed from the full task of a pastorate, to defend the truth. This textbook was one such way. He also prepared a Hebrew grammar, printed in 1650, which ends with this statement: "I shall indicate in my lectures any printer's errors or other lapses of inadventure, for it is my own students that this little work is intended."[24] Mention has already been made of his chronology, a combination of biblical history and Church history.

Baillie had immense respect for his colleague and mentor, David Dickson, to whom he dedicated one of his books. Dickson's work as professor at Glasgow and Edinburgh is especially valuable in terms of his writing and his vision to create an expositors' library for students and parish ministers. Dickson had

---

[20] McCoy, *Robert Baillie*, 87.
[21] *FES*, 3:474.
[22] *The Letters and Journals of Robert Baillie*, ed. David Laing, vol. 3 (Edinburgh, 1841), 285.
[23] Hazlett, "Ebbs and Flows of Theology in Glasgow", 12.
[24] Reid, *Divinity Professors in the University of Glasgow*, 102.

been a minister in Irvine before taking the Chair of Divinity at Glasgow in 1640.[25] While professor in Glasgow, he also "preached every Lord's Day forenoon in the High Church".[26] He very much combined the work of the pastor and doctor of the Church. We learn about the nature of this expositors' series from a preface included in the 1759 edition of James Durham's *An Exposition of the Book of Job*. (It had fallen on hard times with the Restoration, hence it was not published for over one hundred years.). The preface reads as follows:

> As there were few expositions or commentaries upon the holy Scripture in this nation, about an hundred and twenty years ago, so the most learned and eminent ministers agreed, about the year 1650, to print some plain and short expositions of the principal books in the Old and New Testament...[27]

The preface then goes on to list the expositors involved and their volumes: [28]

Author	Bible Books	Dates	Language(s)
David Dickson	Epistles	1640	(English unless specified)
	Hebrews	1637	
	Epistles of Paul, James, Peter, Jude	1645	Latin
		1659	English
	Matthew	1647	
	Psalms	1653-1654	
George Hutchison	Twelve Minor Prophets	1653, 1654, 1657	
	John	1657	
	Job	1669	
James Ferguson	Philippians and Colossians	1656	
	Galatians and Ephesians	1659	
	1 and 2 Thess.	1674, 1675	

---

[25] *DSCHT*, 248; Reid, *Divinity Professors in the University of Glasgow*, 10-11.
[26] R– W– , preface to David Dickson, *Truth's Victory Over Error* (Glasgow, 1725), xix.
[27] George Christie, "Scripture Exposition in Scotland in the Seventeenth Century", *RSCHS* 1(1926), 97.
[28] Christie, "Scripture Exposition in Scotland", 98-111; Walker, *The Theology and Theologians of Scotland*, 16-17.

	1 and 2 Peter	1658	
Alexander Nisbet	Ecclesiastes	(1660 ready) delayed until 1694	
James Durham	Revelation	1658	
	Song of Songs	1668	
	Job	1759	

We find George Hutchison acknowledging his debt to David Dickson in his introduction to his exposition of *The Twelve Minor Prophets:*

> Being some years ago seriously invited with divers others, by the Reverend Author of that Exposition on Matthew, to concur with him in prosecuting that purpose which he had begun, and hath since made further progress into, upon the booke of Psalms; I did then essay some of these Prophets, being at that time recommended unto me, and of late at his desire.... I have looked upon them over again, and adventured to present these to public view, if so be it may invite others who have more ability and leisure, to mind and help forward such a work upon the whole Bible.[29]

It was a masterful plan and, as we note with Alexander Nisbet's second contribution to the scheme with Ecclesiastes, though it was ready for press in 1660, it was suppressed due to the Restoration. Eventually when it was published, the preface acknowledged the fact that it was part of a great endeavour "that had happily begun, but [was] sadly interrupted work and design, of these burning and Shining Lights of this Church, Mr. Dickson, Mr. Hutcheson, Mr. Fergusson, etc...."[30]

Dickson acknowledged the existence of commentaries, but most were too large, too expensive and too detailed. Dickson's own contributions to this Scottish Covenanter Expositor's Series were based mainly upon his lectures to his theology students at Glasgow and Edinburgh, with the exception of his work on Hebrews.[31]

The name of Principal William Guild of King's College was not attached to this Covenanter Expository Series, even though he was a prolific writer and much of his work was expository. Henry Sefton described Guild as a "reluctant Covenanter", and it appears his writings have been eclipsed by other

---

[29] Christie, "Scripture Exposition in Scotland", 103, quoting from George Hutchison, *A Brief Exposition of the Prophets of Obadiah, etc...* (London, 1653).

[30] Christie, "Scripture Exposition in Scotland", 109, quoting from Alexander Nisbet, *An Exposition With Practical Observations Upon the Book of Ecclesiastes* (Edinburgh, 1694).

[31] Reid, *Divinity Professors in the University of Glasgow*, 48-50.

Covenanter expositors.³² Many of his works were in print prior to his becoming principal at King's and several more came following his dismissal. This should not allow them to be ignored. His works show evidence of devotion to Christ; for instance, his volume *The only Way to Salvation, or the Life and Soul of True Religion* (1608).³³ Biblical commentary was a predominant feature of his writings; for example, *Moses Unveiled; or those figures pointing out to Christ Jesus*,³⁴ which went through at least ten printings from 1618 to 1893, and also his commentaries on 2 Samuel, the Song of Songs, and Revelation. Since these last two received much attention in this period, one must take note of Guild in an attempt to perceive the views of professors of divinity in the 1640s.³⁵ Guild's other works were polemical treatises against Roman Catholicism, specifically on transubstantiation, the Anti-Christ or the "man of sin", and purgatory.³⁶ Two years after Guild's death, John Owen had Guild's commentary on 2 Samuel (which Guild had planned to dedicate to John Owen) published at Oxford in 1659.³⁷

Dickson, while at Glasgow University, gave lectures (dictates) upon each of the chapters of the then new Westminster Confession of Faith. He continued to do this at Edinburgh University for the first two years and then, when Robert Leighton arrived in 1653, Dickson concentrated more fully on biblical exposition. His son, Alexander Dickson, joined the Edinburgh Divinity Hall in 1656 as professor of Hebrew.³⁸

Dickson's theological lectures (dictates) on the Westminster Confession of Faith were written in Latin. *Prealectiones in Confessionem Fidei* is his collection of class notes from these lectures, but these were not published until 1684, when they were translated into English as *Truth's Victory Over Error* and subsequently republished in 1725, 1752, 1764 and 1787. This provided the first

---

[32] *DSCHT*, 380; *DNB*, 23:323-324.

[33] William Guild, *The Only Way to Salvation, or the Life and Soul of True Religion* (London, 1608).

[34] William Guild, *Moses Unveiled: or those figures pointing out Christ Jesus whereunto is added the Harmony of All the Prophets* (London, 1620).

[35] William Guild, *The Sealed Book Opened, being an explication of the Revelations* (Aberdeen, 1656); *Love's Entercours between the Lamb and his Bride, or A Clear Explication...of the Song of Solomon* (London, 1658); *The Throne of David, an Exposition of II Samuel* (Oxford, 1659).

[36] William Guild, *Anti-christ in his true Colours, or the Pope of Rome proven to bee that Man of Sinne,...* (Aberdeen, 1655); *The Noveltie of Poperie discovered and chieflie proved by Romanists out of themselves* (Aberdeen, 1656); *Three Rare Monuments of Antiquita, or Bertram, a Frenchman, Aelfricus, an Englishman, and Maurus, a Scotsman: all stronglie convincing that grosse error of transubstantiation* (Aberdeen, 1624).

[37] *DNB*, 23:324.

[38] Reid, *Divinity Professors in the University of Glasgow*, 61 - 62.

full commentary on the *Westminster Confession*. The full title in English, along with a "purpose statement" on the title page, are worth quoting in full here:

Truth's Victory over Error or, An Abridgement of the Chief Controversies in Religion, which since the Apostles Days to this Time, have been, and are in Agitation, between those of the Orthodox Faith, and all Adversaries whatsoever; a List of whose Names are set down after the Epistle to the Reader. Wherein, by going through all the Chapters of the Confession of Faith, one by one, and propunding out of them, by Way of Question, all the controverted Assertions; and Answering by Yes, or No, there is a clear Confirmation of the Truth; and an evident Confutation of what Tenets and Opinions are maintain'd by the Adversaries.

A TREATISE

Most useful for all Persons, who desire to be instructed in the true Protestant Religion, who would shun in these Last Days, and perillous Times, the Infection of Errors and Heresies, and all dangerous Tenets and Opinions, contrary to the Word of God.[39]

It is worthy of note that it served as a teaching system in this period at both Glasgow and Edinburgh Universities.[40] This is significant as most of the ministers "in the West, South, and East Parts of Scotland, from the year 1640 to the happy Revolution, were under his Inspection and from this very Book we may perceive his Care to educate them in the Form of sound Words, and to ground them solidly in the excellent Standards of Doctrine agreed to by this Church".[41] Clearly these dictates constitute one of the chief Scottish theological textbooks for divinity students in Period III. The work itself takes the chapters of the Confession of Faith in consecutive order, Dickson first posing a question and then providing an answer. The answers either cite Scripture or quote it, and "confute" false doctrines concerning the particular chapter under study. Taking chapter one as an example of how Dickson dictated upon the Confession, we find he formed fifteen questions and provided answers for each, making for nineteen pages of "commentary". (It is not a commentary in the same style as Robert Shaw's.) In listing all the errors dealt with in these fifteen questions the following list is found:

---

[39] David Dickson, *Truth's Victory over Error...*, original 1684 Latin (Glasgow, 1725), title page. The editor of this 1725 edition refers to the contents as Dickson's "Dictates" because he "had dictated to his scholars, in Latine upon the Confession of Faith", iii. The 1725 edition has a total of 340 pages.

[40] Torrance, *Scottish Theology*, 112, 123; *DSCHT*, 243.

[41] R– W–, preface to Dickson, *Truth's Victory Over Error*, xxi. Reading beyond R. W.'s high praise and generous historical dating, the point he makes still remains valid. Dickson as a federal theologian of great influence can also be found in *The Sum of Saving Knowledge...* (a work attributed in part to his authorship). See C. G. McCrie, *The Confessions of the Church of Scotland* (Edinburgh, 1907), 70-73.

Socinians	1
Papists	11
Libertines	1
Quakers	8
Enthusiasts	2
Arminians	2
Anabaptists	1[42]

It is not surprising that the errors of the Papists head the list. Perhaps more interesting is the addressing of Quakerism; however, in Aberdeen it was making an impact. The work overall reveals a teaching method which was catechetical, dogmatic and biblical but without extensive exegesis, as Dickson only rarely referred to the Greek text of the New Testament.[43] Baillie did not produce a commentary on the Confession like Dickson's, but he came close in *Catechesis Elenctica Errorum*, which was intended as a supplement to the Confession and two Catechisms.[44]

The other work that arose from Dickson's ministerial experience is *Therapeutica Sacra*. Again, it was delivered to his students and written for the "use of young students in Theology". First issued in Latin in 1656, then in English in 1664, it was a work which combined doctrinal elements with practical divinity or case divinity.[45] Its English subtitle reads, *The Method of Healing the Diseases of the Conscience Concerning Regeneration*, a work worthy of a comparative study with some of the English Puritan writers. This shows Dickson's pastoral heart, which no doubt clearly came across to his

---

[42] Dickson, *Truth's Victory Over Error*, 1-19. If one is in doubt about any of these terms, a glossary of terms with definitions is given in the book.

[43] Dickson, *Truth's Victory Over Error*, 51.

[44] Reid, *Divinity Professors in the University of Glasgow*, 101.

[45] David Dickson, *Therapeutica Sacra: Shewing Briefly the Method of Healing the Diseases of the Conscience Concerning Regeneration* (Edinburgh, 1664), i, 3. The work focuses on a general discussion on the conscience and deals much with matters of doubt and assurance. See also: MacLeod, *Scottish Theology*, 84-85; Walker, *Scottish Theologoy and Theologians*, 15-16; Riddell, *Divinity*, 5-6. Riddell wrote "*Therapeutica Sacra*, one of the few Scottish contributions to the literature of the cure of souls, was derived partly from his own spiritual experiences in the Covenanting period, but still more from the revivalist movement in his Irvine ministry known as the 'Stewarton sickness'." Riddell is helpful on Dickson, but the thesis that he was "one of the few" certainly could be challenged. There are others, albeit not as many as England produced. See Guthrie of Fenwick, Rutherford, Scougal, Leighton, John Brown of Haddington and George Gillespie. Each of these contributed in various ways to "soul literature" in the seventeenth century in Scotland. Even the poet Zachary Boyd contributed one prose work of Calvinistic devotion – *The Last Battell of the Soule in Death*. See: D. W. Atkinson, "Zachary Boyd as Minister of the Barony Parish", *RSCHS* 24 (1990-1992), 22; Adam Philip, *The Devotional Literature of Scotland* (Dunfermline, n.d.).

students. This, too, was the focus of the co-authored *The Sum of the Saving Religion*, based upon Dickson's sermons at Inverary.[46]

In summary, we see Dickson, the professor, as one who was clearly a doctor of the Church. He obviously desired to ensure that men were well equipped for the ministry of the Word and its application. Like Baillie and Rutherford, he expounded Reformed orthodoxy in the classroom to ensure that the next generation of preachers knew and confessed truth and were kept on the narrow road against error. When Dickson and Rutherford's writings are taken together as a whole, one finds strong Reformed orthodoxy and an experimental Calvinism of the highest order.

The next in our quintet of stars in the colleges during the Covenanter Period is Patrick Gillespie, the younger brother of George who was famous for his involvement in the Westminster Assembly and his writings on church government. Patrick Gillespie was appointed principal of Glasgow College in 1653 in conjunction with his duties within East Parish.[47] He remained principal until 1660, when he was in London for a year. In 1661 he was imprisoned in Stirling and Edinburgh on charges of treason. He escaped execution but did not return to the ministry and spent the following years writing *The Ark of the Testament*, first published in 1661 and then 1677. When this work was reprinted in 1677, John Owen wrote the preface stating: "I do freely declare my judgement, that for order, method, perspicuity in treating, and solidity of argument, the ensuing discourse exceedeth whatsoever single treatise I have seen written with the same design." Walker added, "Teaching the same doctrine as Rutherford and Dickson, Gillespie unfolds it with a richness and fulness peculiar to himself. There is little doubt his books were a quarry from which succeeding writers on the Covenants drew materials, even though in some points they diverged from Gillespie's views!"[48]

Patrick Gillespie stands as heir of the rich, Scottish federal theology of Rollock of the former century and of Rutherford and George Gillespie of the seventeenth century, and he draws us to the continent where Cocceius and Witsius were in the forefront.[49] Some believe that Patrick Gillespie was also the author of *A Treatise of the Covenant of Redemption Between God and Christ, as the Foundation of the Covenant of Grace*.[50]

Thus, Patrick Gillespie's time as principal at Glasgow College was one in which a biblical exposition of federal theology would have been evident. Yet it

---

[46] MacLeod, *Scottish Theology*, 85.
[47] *FES*, 3:462.
[48] Walker, *Theology and Theologians of Scotland*, 20.
[49] T. M. Lindsay, "The Covenant Theology", *British and Foreign Evangelical Review* 28 (1879), 521-538. Lindsay helps provide a good context for relating Scottish Covenantal theology with the continent.
[50] Woolsey, "Unity and Continuity in Covenantal Thought", 2:323. Compare with the article on Patrick Gillespie in *DSCHT*, 360.

seems that his involvement as a lecturer was very "part-time". He did not teach the languages, as this was Baillie's role. He took more of a leading role as expounder (he was highly regarded as a pulpiteer at East Parish) and combined this with an aggressive building campaign at the college. During Gillespie's time there were tensions between him and Baillie. Baillie openly wrote about these in his *Journal*, but acknowledged Gillespie's gifts as a preacher. It was a difficult time as tensions mounted between the two Covenanting parties, the Resolutioners and the Protestors; Baillie being a Resolutioner and Gillespie a Protestor.

When the Restoration came, Baillie was made principal, but died in 1662 a broken-hearted man, for he saw that episcopacy was being forced upon the church by the King, whom as a Resolutioner he had supported.[51] It is grievous to find that the Glasgow divinity professors were men estranged from one another. When Baillie became principal, John Young, for whom Baillie had obvious dislike, was appointed first divinity professor.[52]

The last of our quintet is John Row of Aberdeen, principal at King's College from 1652-1661. He followed Principal William Guild, who had been principal of King's from 1640-1651. Guild had been dismissed as principal in 1651 by Oliver Cromwell's military commissioners due to his royalist sympathies. Row's chief contributions were the supplement he provided for his father's *The History of the Kirk of Scotland, 1558-1639* [53] and his assistance in the final version of the 1650 *Scottish Psalter,* of which more will be said later.

It is helpful to sketch briefly some of Row's early life in order to learn about the training of ministers in this period. Row's grandfather was a reformer with Knox, an able Hebraist and involved in the composition of the *FBD*. Row's father, it is said, mastered Hebrew at age seven, studied at Edinburgh, and spent his life as a minister in Carnock from 1592 until 1646. It was into such a pedigree that John was born in 1598. He graduated from St. Andrews in 1617, M.A., and then became master of the grammar school at Kirkcaldy in 1619. It is not known whether or not he attended the theology class at St. Mary's in 1618. He transferred to become headmaster of the grammar school at Perth in 1632, where he remained until 1641. While at Perth he gave instruction in Latin, Greek and Hebrew and composed a Hebrew grammar in 1637, which was well received by the faculty at St. Andrews.[54] In 1641 he was ordained as

---

[51] Reid, *Divinity Professors in the University of Glasgow*, 118-119.

[52] Reid, *Divinity Professors in the University of Glasgow*, 127-130.

[53] John Row, *The History of the Kirk of Scotland*, original *MS* 1650, (reprinted by Wodrow Society, Edinburgh, 1842). Row added the history of 1637-1639 to his father's work.

[54] David Laing, "Life and Writings of John Row, Principal of King's College, Aberdeen", in John Row, *History of the Kirk of Scotland*, xl - xliii. Samuel Rutherford added a word of commendation to it in 1644 when it was published in Glasgow as two volumes in one – the original grammar plus a Hebrew Dictionary. The two volume work was viewed as the first of its kind to be printed in Scotland.

minister of St. Nicholas Church (Third Charge), Aberdeen. Evidence cannot be found that he took the theological classes in Aberdeen or St. Mary's. He may have done so, but often a schoolmaster was taken on trials and became a minister. Obviously with Row's academic abilities in the languages, he had a good start. By the next year, 1642, Row was also lecturing in Hebrew at Marischal College in addition to his ministry at St. Nicholas Church. In 1646 the General Assembly passed an act wherein Row's *Hebrew Grammar* was recommended to all ministers. The Synod of Fife went one step further and asked that every minister within that Synod be provided with a copy of Row's *Grammar and Dictionary*.[55] It certainly appears that John Row was the leading scholar and Covenanter at Aberdeen. He kept in contact with Baillie and Dickson, to whom he sent an *MS* treatise, *Praxis Praeceptorum Hebrae Grammaticae*, with additional material.[56]

It was under Row's principalship at King's, 1652-1661, while he was still minister at St. Nicholas Church, that new buildings were erected at the college. He was ejected in 1661 and returned to being a schoolmaster, this time in New Aberdeen. Row had adhered to the strict Protestor Party in the 1650s, and like some others became Independent for a time. He returned shortly afterwards to the Presbyterian fold, perhaps due to Rutherford and Wariston's visit to check the rising schism in Aberdeen. John Menzies, the divinity professor at Marischal, had joined with Row in this brief-lived Independency movement, but he also returned to Presbyterianism and later embraced Episcopalianism.[57]

Row's interest while principal at King's is chiefly seen in the Cromwell Tower, which remains today and was built at Row's instigation. He also busied himself in revising the regulations for King's and ensuring that the students (or mere boys, as Henderson calls them) received proper religious education. His second abiding interest was the Scripture, specifically Hebrew or the text of Scripture. In 1657 he produced for the Lord Protector, *Ane Overture and humble adwyse hou the leatter translatione of the Byble imprinted first in the yeir 1612 may be much bettered, with a supplicatione to the Protector*.[58] Here was a principal and primarius of theology who was deeply interested in Scripture and the text of Scripture. No doubt this was communicated to the arts and theology students in Aberdeen.

---

[55] Laing, "Life and Writings of John Row", xiv-xvi.

[56] Laing, "Life and Writings of John Row", 1. Row's *Hebrew Grammar and Vocabulary*, printed in Glasgow in 1644, was the first book ever printed in Scotland using Hebrew type. Prior to this all Hebrew letters were done by hand. See: James Maclehose, *The Glasgow University Press 1638-1931* (Glasgow, 1931), 28-29.

[57] Henderson, *Religious Life in Seventeenth Century Scotland*, 107-108; *DSCHT*, 132, 559-560.

[58] Henderson, *Religious Life in Seventeenth Century Scotland*, 271, 109-110. Strict Puritans and Covenanters were far from satisfied with the Authorized Version of 1611.

Row's last contribution for our purposes here was his answering the call of the General Assembly of 1647 to be part of a four man committee to revise the "Paraphrase of the Psalms" sent from England. Row was given forty Psalms to paraphrase (Psalms 90-130). The Assembly Act also assigned Zachary Boyd the task of translating the "other Scriptural songs in meter".[59] It would appear that Row may have had his own metrical version of the Psalter, as many others did at that time in Scotland. In 1650 the committee's work was done, and the new *Scottish Psalter* of 1650 was printed. Unconsciously perhaps, the contributions of Row lived on for several generations.[60] The other members of the Assembly committee included: John Adamson, principal of Edinburgh College; Thomas Crawford, professor of mathematics and regent in philosophy at Edinburgh College; and John Nevay of London Parish Church.[61] Such work gives evidence that these professors were committed to church life and matters of liturgy.

Row was a linguist, a teacher, an historian, a churchman, a minister, a religious instructor and to a certain extent a liturgist of the church. The students at Marischal and King's, both arts and theological, would have had a most interesting man from whom to learn.

There is one other name that must receive brief mention, that of Robert Leighton. He was the principal at the Town College in Edinburgh for ten years during this Covenanter Period. Leighton, like David Dickson, made a firm contribution to expository works with his commentary on 1 Peter, which John MacLeod described as "admirable".[62] Leighton was born into a solid Covenanter family, his father being a minister at Leiden, where he was dismissed for his Puritan views of worship. Alexander Leighton, Robert's father, was severely punished under Charles I, and his most famous written work was an attack on episcopacy.[63] Robert, the son, signed the National Covenant, yet he ran into some controversy in the Presbytery of Dalkeith because he did not preach on the covenant enough (meaning the national covenant). However, he told his fellow presbyters, "If all you preach up the

---

[59] *Acts of the General Assembly of the Church of Scotland 1638 to 1842*, ed. Thomas Pitcairn (Church Law Society, Edinburgh, 1843), 159. It is of interest that the Assembly act refers to this as the revision of a "paraphrase". The "paraphrase" in question here is, Frances Rous' metrical version of the Psalms.

[60] J. Stewart Wilson, "The Story of the Scottish Metrical Version of the Psalm", *British and Foreign Evangelical Review* 28 (1879), 61-64.

[61] Millar Patrick, *Four Centuries of Scottish Psalmody* (London, 1949), 97. *FES*, 3:119-120. J. W. MacMeeken, *History of the Scottish Metrical Psalms with an Account of the Paraphrases and Hymns* (Glasgow, 1872), 43.

[62] MacLeod, *Scottish Theology*, 86. Robert Leighton, *A Practical Commentary on the First Epistle of Peter*, original 1693-1694 (London, 1870).

[63] *DSCHT*, 477-478.

times, you may surely allow one poor brother to preach up Christ Jesus and eternity."[64]

In 1653, when he became principal and professor of theology in Edinburgh, there was no doubt as to his abilities. His intimate command of Latin, Greek and Hebrew were well known, as was his grasp of Scripture. Instruction at Edinburgh College had declined by the end of Period II in that the principal did virtually no lecturing in theology. Under Leighton this changed. He returned the principalship to include the active post of professor of theology.[65] Students thronged to hear his divinity lectures, which were delivered in Latin and combined exacting scholarly work with practical and devotional life.

Again, as at Glasgow, there were at times tensions between the Edinburgh professors of divinity. Evidently David Dickson was not always in agreement with Leighton. Torrance stated that one such tension between these two men was over Leighton's promotion of Thomas à Kempis' *Imitation of Christ*.[66]

Leighton continued in the college to emphasize instruction in the catechism, using the Heidelberg Catechism and perhaps Principal John Adamson's Latin metrical version of Calvin's Geneva Catechism. Since Leighton had studied at Edinburgh College using Adamson's Latin catechism, it is possible that he continued to use it alongside the Heidelberg.[67] Leighton was not the only one to use the Heidelberg Catechism in teaching during this time. The standard work at King's College for all students doing arts during the Covenanting Period was also *Catecheseas Palatinae*.[68]

While we are discussing Edinburgh College, mention needs to be made that in Period III a new professorship was established. This was the professorship of Hebrew and Semitic Languages, founded in 1642. The first person to hold the office was Julius Conradus Otto, a former Jew from Vienna, of whom very little is known. Otto remained in this position until 1656 and then either resigned or died. The Town Council replaced him with Alexander Dickson, the son of David Dickson.[69]

---

[64] Torrance, *Scottish Theology*, 150.
[65] E. A. Knox, *Robert Leighton, Archbishop of Glasgow* (London, 1930), 155. Knox is quoting here at length from Gilbert Burnet's autobiography, a sympathetic contemporary of Leighton.
[66] Torrance, *Scottish Theology*, 158. Also, C.G. McCrie, *Confessions of the Church of Scotland*, 73-75.
[67] D. Butler, *The Life and Letters of Robert Leighton* (London, 1903), 50. Torrance, *Scottish Theology*, 167.
[68] Rait, *The University of Aberdeen*, 156.
[69] Andrew Dalzel, *History of the University of Edinburgh*, vol. 2 (Edinburgh,1862), 175; Grant, *The Story of the University of Edinburgh*, vol. 1 (London, 1884), 214-215.

General Assemblies

We now turn from the "Galaxy of Divines" to the role and contribution of the General Assemblies during the Covenanter Period. In reading through the Acts of the General Assembly of the Church of Scotland from 1638 to 1649, we learn other matters which are of relevance to theological education and training. Beginning in 1638 by an act of the Glasgow Assembly, all ministers and masters of universities, colleges and schools were required to subscribe to the Confession and Covenant.[70] This Confession of Faith was the 1580 Confession plus The National Covenant.[71] This basic matter of subscription for those who taught in the universities established the theological position being taught. In the next year, 1639, the General Assembly spelled out more clearly their understanding of subscription by adopting a formula for subscription. The 1639 act also stipulated that "all scholars at the passing of their degrees" were required to subscribe to the Confession of Faith by this formula:

> The article of this Covenant, which was at the first subscription referred to the determination of the General Assembly, being determined, and thereby the Five Articles of Perth, the government of the Kirk by Bishops, the civill places and power of Kirkmen, upon the reasons and grounds contained in the acts of the General Assembly, declared to be unlawfull within this Kirk, we subscribe according to the determination foresaid.[72]

In terms of formula it is rather convoluted, yet it certainly makes the point concerning what the church stood for as well as to what the church opposed. Further acts followed in 1640, strengthening the meaning of this subscription. No one was allowed to speak against the Confession or Covenant and if a minister did so, he was removed from office. Such an act certainly affected the theological curriculum and the manner of instruction. Likewise, if any who was aspiring to teach or preach one day refused to subscribe, then he was refused residence in a burgh, university or college.[73] Thus, the professors of theology were under the Confession, as were also potential students in the college.

Other issues dealt with were somewhat more in the realm of finances and fabric. One act allowed Dr. Robert Howie of St. Mary's College to receive financial assistance in his old age.[74] Another called for the King and Parliament to offer financial assistance to the universities and colleges and "especially in divinities" for a competent number of professors and bursars and for the fabric of the college and libraries.[75]

---

[70] *AGACS*, 31.
[71] *The Confession of Faith etc.* (Glasgow, 1958 and reprinted since), 347-354.
[72] *AGACS*, 42.
[73] *AGACS*, 45.
[74] *AGACS*, 46, Sess. 5, July 30, 1641.
[75] *AGACS*, 46-47, Sess. 9, August 3, 1641.

In 1641 the General Assembly also recommended to the Parliament that there be an annual meeting of commissioners from each university and college "to consult and determine upon the common affairs". It was encouraged that, for the promotion of piety and learning, a good correspondence be held between the colleges. This was something that Andrew Melville would certainly have applauded in an earlier time.[76] A brief point was also made concerning the standards sought in those who would teach in the colleges:

> That special care be had that the places of the professors, especially of professors of divinity, in every university and college, be filled with the ablest men, and best affected to the Reformation and order of this Kirk.[77]

It was the 1641 Assembly at Edinburgh which also established an important act wherein each presbytery was to provide support for a bursar of divinity. Each presbytery that consisted in a minimum of twelve ministers was to maintain one bursar of divinity. If a presbytery was smaller, then they were to join hands with another presbytery for this purpose. This was to be undertaken without delay by the presbyteries, if such was not already being done.[78] This scheme for the financial provision of bursars for divinity was a common one, not only in Scotland but in other places and at other times. Samuel Miller, at the founding of Princeton Seminary in America in 1812, made a similar plea in his inaugural sermon.[79]

The early General Assemblies of the Covenanting Period returned to the standards of the 1580s and 1590s concerning the trials of students for the ministry. This 1596 act stated that in a trial both learning and ability to preach as well as conscience and feeling were to be inquired after. It was to be acknowledged in these trials that some candidates were more suitable for certain locations, such as "landword" parishes as opposed to burghs.[80]

The General Assembly desired that the best ministers became professors of divinity, yet the one problem with this was that it depleted the number of ministers labouring full-time in the pastorate. In 1642 the General Assembly passed an act as a partial solution to this problem. It was decided to recruit professors of divinity from the continent to avoid robbing the parishes of their ministers at this critical time.[81] The Assembly also decided in 1643 that professors of divinity could be chosen as commissioners to the General

---

[76] *AGACS*, 46-47.
[77] *AGACS*, 47.
[78] *AGACS*, 48.
[79] Samuel Miller, *An Able and Faithful Ministry*, ed. Kevin Reed, original 1812 (Dallas, 1984), 18-19. "The church is bound to provide funds for the partial or entire support of those who need this kind of aid, while they are preparing for the work of the ministry..."
[80] *AGACS*, 23.
[81] *AGACS*, 62.

Assembly since they were ministers.[82] Such thinking shows that generally the Scottish Church saw the office of "doctor" as a specialized task within the office of minister and not as a separate office.

Returning to the need for bursary money from the presbyteries, the General Assembly desired to settle more ministers in the Highlands who knew the "Irish" tongue. Thus, presbyteries were to give preference for allotting bursary aid to divinity students who knew Irish.[83] It would appear that the actual practice of supporting a bursar student never did occur in many of the presbyteries in the 1640s. Repeated admonitions from the General Assembly were issued to the presbyteries to put the bursar support system into practice.[84]

The General Assembly acts for the Covenanting Period tell us that the Church asserted its control over the teaching of the professors of divinity. If a professor was coming to the General Assembly, he was to bring with him "one perfect and well written copie of his dictates"; and if he were not going, then he could send them with a commissioner.[85] The dictates constituted their compendium of the system of theology they taught and were distinct from their Bible expositions.

One curious overture which the General Assembly did adopt in 1646 stated: "That for the better breeding of young men to the ministrie, who are not able to furnish themselves or charges to attend in the universities, that the Presbyteries where they reside appoint some to direct their studies."[86] Perhaps this provided for a measure of flexibility to allow for exceptions to the accustomed rule of attending university for arts and then proceeding onto divinity. Mechie comments on the adoption of this overture as making for "a pretty large loophole"![87]

The Westminster Standards

A further contribution of the Scottish General Assembly during the Covenanting Period may be seen in their approval of what has collectively been referred to as the *Westminster Standards*. Two of these documents are relevant to the study of Scottish theological education and training: The Form of Presbyterial Church-Government and The Directory for the Publick Worship of

---

[82] *AGACS*, 74.

[83] *AGACS*, 82-83.

[84] *AGACS*, 110. See the General Assembly ordinance of 1644 and also on page 119 the adopted overtures of the 1645 General Assembly, which clearly state the support of bursars included the amount, the dates for payment and that it was the responsibility of the moderator of every presbytery to collect the funds. Bursars were not to receive assistance for more than four years. Also, page 163 for the 1647 overture on bursars' support by the presbyteries.

[85] AGACS, 142.

[86] *AGACS*, 142.

[87] Mechie, "Education for the Ministry in Scotland", 1:123.

God. Both of these documents were agreed upon by the Assembly of Divines at Westminster and by the Scottish General Assembly. The Directory was agreed upon by the General Assembly on February 3, 1645, and The Form of Church Government on February 10, 1645.[88] We quote from two passages that clearly formulated the ideals of the Westminster Assembly for the education of ministers. The Directory under the "preaching of the Word" states:

> It is presupposed (according to the rules for ordination), that the minister of Christ is in some good measure gifted for so weighty a service, by his skill in the original languages, and in such arts and sciences as are handmaid unto divinity; by his knowledge of the whole body of theology, but most of all in the holy scriptures, having his senses and heart exercised in them above the common sort of believers; and by the illumination of God's Spirit, and other gifts of edification, and an humble heart, resolving to admit and receive any truth not yet attained, whenever God shall make it known unto him...[89]

We also quote from The Form of Church Government before making comment. Prior to ordination the candidate was required to bring a testimonial of his subscription to the Covenant and a listing of the degrees he had taken at a university along with the amount of time he spent there. The minimum age for ordination was set at twenty-four years. Testimonials were also to be furnished of the man's "life and conversation". After this preamble there were nine "Rules for Examination" stated. Rules two through seven we quote now:

> 2) He shall be examined touching his skill in original tongues, and his trial to be made by reading the Hebrew and Greek Testaments, and rendering some portion of some into Latin; and if he be defective in them, enquiry shall be made more strictly after his other learning, and whether he hath skill in logick and philosophy.
> 3) What authors in divinity he hath read, and is best acquainted with; and trial shall be made in his knowledge of the grounds of religion, and of his ability to defend the orthodox doctrine contained in them against all unsound and erroneous opinions, especially these of the present age; of his skill in the sense and meaning of such places of scripture as shall be proposed unto him, in cases of conscience, and in the chronology of the scripture, and the ecclesiastical history.
> 4) If he hath not before preached in publick with approbation of such as are able to judge, he shall, at a competent time assigned him, expound before the presbytery such a place of scripture as shall be given him.
> 5) He shall also, within a competent time, frame a discourse in Latin, upon such a common-place or controversy in divinity as shall be assigned to him, and exhibit to the presbytery such theses as express the sum thereof, and maintain a dispute upon them.

---

[88] *The Confession of Faith, etc...*, 371-372, 396. See also *The Westminster Directory*, ed. and notes by Thomas Leishman (Church Service Society Edinburgh, 1901).
[89] The Directory, in *The Confession of Faith*, 379.

6) He shall preach before the people, the presbytery, or some of the ministers of the word appointed by them, being present.
7) The proportion of his gifts in relation to the place unto which he is called be considered.[90]

All these are viewed as the ordinary rules and course for ordination, but the Form of Church Government did state that it acknowledged extraordinary ways, especially in the late 1640s, as presbyteries may not have been working up to their full strength and there was a crying need for ministers. The Form made provision for a body of ministers in London to examine and ordain ministers "keeping as near to the ordinary rules fore-mentioned as possibly they may".[91]

This caveat at the end was more of a temporary measure, but it did show a spirit of flexibility in the interpretation of the ordinary rules at the time. Subsequent periods exercised these extraordinary ways in varying degrees, which will be discussed in Periods V and VI. The examination was never to lose sight of heart religion and a right piety. This is clearly evidenced in the passage in The Directory and also in what we refer to as a preamble to the ordinary rules in the Form of Church Government.

We see next that a study of the arts and sciences was to be as a handmaid to divinity. This was nothing new; rather it was consistent with the vision and ideals of Calvin in the Academy, and others, such as Melville, in Scotland. Obvious ability in Latin, Greek and Hebrew was the standard, and it was the presbytery's task to examine the student in all three languages. A certificate from a college stating attendance in such classes was insufficient. Knowledge of the sound Reformed divines would be scrutinized for the purpose of seeing if a student could defend the truth. A public disputation in Latin on a theological common-place would assure the presbytery of the student's oral skills, knowledge and orthodoxy. Examinations also occurred in scriptural interpretation, casuistry and biblical history. Preaching was also a part of the examination, although the rules allowed for either a full presbytery meeting or "some of the ministers" to be present. Rule number seven allowed for certain exceptions to some of the above, dependent upon the particular charge in view. The degrees referred to here would have been limited in Scotland to the M.A.. The B.D. or D.D. degrees were never given in Scotland during this period at the five colleges where divinity was taught.[92]

The language requirements of "The Form of Church Government" adopted by the General Assembly on February 10, 1645, really follow on from what the

---

[90] The Form of Church Government, in *The Confession of Faith*, 412-413.
[91] The Form of Church Government, in *The Confession of Faith*, 415-416.
[92] *Officers and Graduates of University and King's College*, 98, 109. *A Catalogue of the Graduates;...University of Edinburgh*, 239, 254. See also *Munimenta Alme Universitatis Glasguensis*, 3:304, where we learn that the first recorded D.D. at Glasgow was to Daniel Williams, the English Dissenter.

General Assembly had passed a few days earlier on February 7th. These were the adoption of "Overtures for advancement of Learning, and good Order on Grammar Schools and Colleges". Again we find a constant theme that the standards of the grammar schools affected what could be achieved in the universities and subsequently in the divinity halls. These adopted overtures required that all grammar schoolmasters be well skilled in the Latin tongue and that they be examined by the presbytery on this requirement. The grammar schools were to concentrate upon Latin, and no one was to study Greek in any college until he had mastered Latin.[93] The teaching of Latin in the grammar school was generally accomplished by using Andrew Duncan's *Latin Grammar* and his Latin catechism of 1595, the *Rudimenta Pietatis*.[94] Thus, one can see the close link between grammar school, college and divinity hall, not only in terms of language preparation but also in doctrine.

College and Student

Before we conclude our examination of the Covenanter Period, some further remarks need to be made in order to round out our views of aspects of theological education during this period. The 1640s was in many ways another period of reform in the colleges. This change occurred under a General Assembly commission established to visit and reform the colleges. Ronald Cant has suggested that this commission of the General Assembly virtually controlled St. Andrews from 1642 to 1649. Our focus primarily concerns St. Mary's, the College of Divinity. All professorships there were under the direct appointment of the General Assembly. There were four professors – the principal and three others. College life had a strong religious atmosphere with the principal leading the evening prayers, the grace at meals and catechism on Wednesdays. On Sundays the morning began with an exposition on "controversies of religion" before morning worship. St. Mary's College attended the Town Kirk where the principal and divinity professors took their turn at preaching.[95] Evidently the St. Mary's divinity students had daily contact with their principal, Samuel Rutherford. In the two arts colleges at St. Andrews, the commission allowed the regents to marry.[96] Such medieval policies were slow in changing in the universities from 1560 onward. The perception was that the college was a residential community as much as possible. The commitment

---

[93] *AGACS*, 117.
[94] D. F. Wright, "Andrew Duncan", in *DSCHT*, 261-262. *The School of Faith*, trans. and ed. Thomas Torrance (London, 1959), 277-288.
[95] Cant, *The University of St. Andrews* (3d ed.), 78-84. It appears that the commissioners of the General Assembly also had the power to appoint David Dickson to become the professor of divinity in Glasgow. See *Munimenta Alme Universitatis Glasguensis*, 3: 381.
[96] Cant, *The University of St. Andrews* (3d ed.), 82.

for faculty dwellings to be within the college precinct therefore remained in some colleges until the early twentieth century.

Since theology students at the college did not graduate during the Covenanting Period as we know it today, it is difficult to calculate accurately the number of students who studied. For example, at Glasgow College between 1638 and 1661, we only have theology student lists for 1644, 1645-1646, 1654-1655, and 1659.[97] It was not until the year 1692 that class registration lists for theology students were kept with consistency at Glasgow College.[98] The full recording of the bursars of theology is also incomplete for this time, and for most years non-existent. It was in the Episcopal Period, 1662-1688, that accurate records began to be kept of the theology students who were receiving bursaries.[99] Therefore it is difficult from the records at Glasgow University to assess to what extent the Acts of the General Assembly (urging the presbyteries to provide for theological bursars) were put into effect. From the continual admonitions of the General Assemblies, it would appear that the presbyteries during the Covenanting Period provided little by way of bursary assistance to theology students.

The General Assembly guarded the appointment of professors of divinity very carefully during this period. For example, when the Edinburgh Town Council chose Alexander Colvill of St. Andrews to become the new professor of divinity in 1648, the General Assembly refused his translation. Yet in the appointment of Julius Otto as the first professor of Hebrew at Edinburgh, the Town Council alone made the appointment.[100] Furthermore, the General Assembly desired an annual meeting of the commissioners from Glasgow, Aberdeen, St. Andrews and Edinburgh for the purpose of common consultation. Reference has already been made to such meetings, but this shows the General Assembly oversight.[101] When a replacement was finally found for the professorship of divinity at Edinburgh, the Town Council proposed him along with the ministers of Edinburgh Presbytery, but it was the commission of the General Assembly that agreed upon David Dickson's appointment.[102]

Although the presbyteries did not always provide bursaries as the General Assembly desired, we do find other individuals providing them as well as also the Town Council in the case of Edinburgh. The Edinburgh Town Council of 1658 made an extensive list of nine rules or regulations for bursars along with an oath. These rules and the oath were not only for arts but also for divinity

---

[97] *Munimenta Alme Universitatis Glasguensis*, 3:237-238.
[98] *Munimenta Alme Universitatis Glasguensis*, 3: 241 (from 1692-1727).
[99] *Munimenta Alme Universitatis* Glasguensis, 3: 262.
[100] Andrew Dalzel, *History of the University of Edinburgh*, vol. 2 (Edinburgh, 1862), 121, 145-146.
[101] Dalzel, *History of the University of Edinburgh*, 2:149.
[102] Dalzel, *History of the University of Edinburgh*, 2:156.

students. We quote part of the oath, which clearly shows the extent of Reformed piety:

> I, A.A., now admitted a student in the College of Edinburgh, and to the benefit of a yearly allowance out of the revenues thereof, do solemnly and sincerely promise, as in the sight of God, that I will, through the assistance of his grace, endeavour in my whole conversation to behave myself suitably, not only to the present station... but, which is much more, to the high name and calling of a Christian, walking in the fear of God, neither giving evil example to others nor taking it from them...[103]

Summary

This Covenanting Period often received the nickname of being the "golden-age of Scottish Presbyterianism". There is little doubt that it was a period of intense activity in which the professors of divinity were involved in writing textbooks, biblical expositions, divinity works (both thematic and controversial), chronologies (the handmaid to covenant theology), and casuistry studies. In this sense it truly was "a golden-age".

For the first half of the time, it was a period of General Assembly assertion of power in the universities, especially in the area of divinity studies. The Assemblies often had ideals which the presbyteries were slow to put into effect. The General Assembly was certainly willing to assert its control over who taught and what was taught. This is surely in contrast to our day where inspection of a divinity professor's lecture notes is hardly common-place.

We also notice that the curriculum and methods were confessional and catechetical. Mastery of the Reformed creeds was universal. John Leith, writing at the end of the twentieth century, stated that "the first task of the seminary is to teach the church's faith; more particularly, a Presbyterian Seminary is to teach the faith of the Presbyterian Church".[104] He went on to write of the seminary as distinct in that its role must be inclusive of being a catechetical school of the Church's faith.[105] The evidence for the Covenanting Period is conclusively in harmony with Leith as to the nature of theological education in the Scottish colleges at this time.

The arts course was absolutely integral to the overall training and education of a minister. Here critical language studies were undertaken, catechisms were studied and a systematic religious devotional life was followed. Skills in speaking were also learned in the arts course. While the actual divinity hall was quite small in terms of staff, two to three members only, it must be borne in

---

[103] Dalzel, *History of the University of Edinburgh*, 2:180.
[104] John Leith, *Crisis in the Church: The Plight of Theological Education* (Louisville, 1997), 40.
[105] Leith, *Crisis in the Church*, 43-46.

mind that the arts course was an integral part of the preparation for ministry.[106] The divinity class was far less structured than what we know today. Final examinations or graduation did not occur. The final tests were clearly in the hands of the presbytery, covering languages, preaching, chronology, casuistry, church history, controversies and common-places. The premise was that an actively involved presbytery was essential to the training of ministers. Accordingly, presbyteries met frequently, in many instances weekly, except for certain times of the year.

There were two other aspects of note in this period. We find this a period where on occasion the divinity professors' relationships with one another could be quite strained. Unity in the halls was frequently not more than superficial. In addition, governance and support in "the Golden Age" could be a complex matter involving Church, Town Council and individuals.

---

[106] Leith, *Crisis in the Church*, 43, 49. Leith has some interesting comments in this regard.

CHAPTER 5

Period IV: 1662-1689, Episcopal Restoration

Introduction

We turn now to the Episcopal Restoration Period of 1662-1689. While it has been characterized as a period of educational decline in the training of those who became ministers, the actual evidence paints quite a varied picture which does not support this characterization. Covenanters claimed that many of the northern farmers who went south in Scotland to become curates lost their cowherds! Burnet, the Episcopalian, stated that many "were the worst preachers I ever heard; they were ignorant to a reproach..."[1] and, "Further what sorry and insignificant tryals are these of the Presbytery? Shall the Bishops sit down upon the dregs of the presbyterians and rise no higher with their reforme? Shall a few jejune discourses which the weakest capacity pick out of books be sufficient qualification for a minister?"[2] Yet, as Mechie has pointed out, in 1662 and shortly thereafter, of eighty-one men ordained, seventy-nine were graduates of a Scottish university.[3] So the picture seems far from clear concerning the educational abilities of the ministers in this period.

Six[4] sample parish lists of ministers and those obtaining the M.A. degree have been examined and found to be quite similar in most respects from Period III to Period IV. Granted these are only samplings, yet samples from quite diverse regions. So we can certainly see a different picture emerging. The

---

[1] Mechie, "Education for the Ministry in Scotland", 1:117.
[2] Mechie, "Education for the Ministry in Scotland", 1:117, where Mechie is quoting from Burnet in *Miscellany of Scottish History Society*, 2:351.
[3] Mechie, "Education for the Ministry in Scotland", 1:117.
[4] These six sample parish lists were in Greenock, Wester-Ross, Leith, Dunlop and Orkney. A careful reading of the "List of Clergy in the Dioceses of Argyll and the Isles from the Restoration to the Revolution" (1661-1689) found in *Records of the Dioceses of Argyll and the Isles 1560-1860*, ed. J. B. Craven (Kirkwall, 1907), 147-153, tells much the same story. Here we find that the majority of the ministers in the Dioceses of Argyll and the Isles were graduates of either Glasgow, Edinburgh or Aberdeen, with M.A.'s. It definitely appears that Glasgow furnished by far the largest number of graduates. A few ministers are listed without M.A.'s, yet this is not fully conclusive as not all who studied "took" the degree. We also note two references to ministers translating material into Gaelic (the Irish tongue).

educational standards for ministers were not significantly different than they were in the previous period. Thus, since this was the case, we need not rehearse the typical M.A. course of the mid-seventeenth century. It offered a solid background to handle the later divinity lectures and in many ways was the "first chamber" of the Theological Seminary.

Exercise/Presbytery and Diocesan Synod

In Period IV we possess ample records of exercise or presbytery and Diocesan Synod rulings, enactments and practices concerning students for the ministry. By briefly citing some examples, we will clearly understand the standards expected in this period.

The exercises continued to take interest in bursary support for divinity students. One of the first enactments of the Exercise of Alford in October, 1662, was that:

> Payment be made to the bursars of Divinitie according to use and wont , viz: the one half at the winter synod, and the other half in the spring, and because they cannot be payt at this present Synod, that they be payt betwixt and the eleven day of November, under the pane of censure; as also it is enacted that the severall bursars shall come into Aberdeen immediately the foresaid eleven day of November, and attend the professione of Divinitie, exhibit and present to the brethren of the severall Exercises the professa dicta, and if the foresaid bursars shall not attend the professione of Divinitie at the time above expresse, then, and in that case, their places to be declared vacant.[5]

The intent of the act was clear. Failure to provide for divinity bursars would provoke censure upon brethren of the exercise. Also, bursars who failed to attend the divinity classes and show the dictations would no longer be deemed bursars.[6]

The Exercise of Alford affords us several examples of divinity students being assigned Scripture passages upon which to give "additions". Mr. John Mair delivered one on Romans 5:19 with approval,[7] Mr. Wm. Garrioch on Genesis 3:15, and Mr. Robert Cheyne on Matthew 5:48.[8] The other aspects of

---

[5] *Records of the Meeting of the Exercise of Alford 1662-1668*, ed. Thomas Ball (New Spalding Club, Aberdeen, 1897), 4.

[6] When the Synod of Aberdeen convened to examine the work of the exercises/presbyteries, it included careful rules for checking on presbyteries collecting for bursars. See *Records of the Exercise of Alford* wherein the Synod of Aberdeen 1678 action is recorded, page 299. We find in the *Records* that sometimes bursars were asked who had not paid their "dues" for the bursary. In one instance the student could say all churches did except two. There follows no note of censure in the *Records*, 173.

[7] *Records of the Exercise of Alford*, 9.

[8] *Records of the Exercise of Alford*, 273 in 1677; 352 in 1684.

the trial appear to have been equally serious. Repeated reference was made to taking examinations in Hebrew and Greek. Often the Greek was open to any passage of the New Testament, whereas the Hebrew appears to have been a Psalm, announced in advance.[9] It would appear that a committee of two would first meet with a student to determine if they were ready for public trials and, if so, would then bring in a recommendation to proceed. Then public trials would follow.[10] The exercise had a standard which was similar to what we have seen before, that "no young man be admitted to tryals before Exercises, until they have studied divinity some years they be graduatt, unless extraordinar pregnancie in learning be seen in theme, which is first to be reported to the Bishope".[11]

Usually the presbytery met in Alford, although periodically in King's College, Aberdeen. Since there was often a student sermon or part of a trial, obviously divinity students were in attendance. The meetings usually had to include a "commone heads of controversie" by one of the ministers, or an exercise on an assigned Scripture text. These frequent meetings functioned as a pastors' training school to the ministers in attendance and no doubt as important training for the students as well. We read frequently that a minister gave a sermon on ministerial duties and some of the other discourses were on the sacraments, justification, pelagianism and ecclesiology. These were either by ministers or students. There is a record of Professor Henry Scougal bringing such a discourse.[12]

Sometimes the records tell of the giver of a discourse or exercise receiving definite censure from the brethren present, as in 1667 when Mr. James Ross was "exhorted to studie more clearness in his doctrin"[13], and one student's theses on the Trinity was not satisfactorily handled in the ensuing question period.[14] Another, Mr. John Irving, in conducting an exercise met with censure as he lacked "exact method of exercise and addition, and was gravely admonished".[15] The Alford Presbytery also evidently had clear language expectations, as one student failed to satisfy the presbytery in his knowledge of Hebrew, and he was told to study more.[16]

---

[9] *Records of the Exercise of Alford*, 185, 294, 280, 193, etc.
[10] *Records of the Exercise of Alford*, 294.
[11] *Records of the Exercise of Alford*, 58.
[12] *Records of the Exercise of Alford*, 25, 7, 15, 196, 231. These discourses were in Latin, and we list some of them: *De efficacia gratiae, De formali ratione justificationis, De visibilitate Ecclesiae, De Iconolatria, De presentia Christi in Eucharistia, De principie formali mediationis in Christo mediatore, De paedo-baptismo, De Eucharistia sub utraque, De Trinitate, De Satisfactione Christi.*
[13] *Records of the Exercise of Alford*, 100.
[14] *Records of the Exercise of Alford*, 179.
[15] *Records of the Exercise of Alford*, 157.
[16] *Records of the Exercise of Alford*, 280, 403.

In casting a brief glance at some of the registers of the Diocesan Synod of Dunblane, ever since associated with Bishop Robert Leighton, we find some reference to theology students. Leighton presented a paper to Synod in 1667 including "Training for the Ministry" which stated:

> Something hath lykwyse bene said concerneing the training upe of such young men amongst us as intende the ministry, not onely as to their straine of preaching, but moving of their myndes to more inwarde thoughts, and the study of a devout lyfe, and more acquainteance with the exercises of mortificacioun and purgeing of their owne heartes by these divine truethes which they are to preach to others for the same purpose; for how shall they teach what they have not learnit?[17]

One is not surprised by such an emphasis being recommended and accepted by the Diocesan Synod of Dunblane. It combines learning with a strong emphasis on experimental religion.

The common feature of the Dunblane Register with that of the Alford Exercise and the Aberdeen Synod is the number of times matters arose for the support of divinity bursars. One student appeared before the 1667 synod explaining that several of the ministers in the various presbyteries had given him no bursary assistance to continue his studies at St. Mary's College.[18] Likewise a bursar was not to assign his bursary to another and was required to submit a testimony to the synod (likely annually) as to his studies in divinity.[19] Regulations were also set as to the manner of conducting the trials of students in the synod's presbyteries. The bishop did not have to be present; he simply needed to know the trials were to occur. The trials were clearly in the hands of the presbytery, but ordination was in the possession of the bishop. The induction was in the hands of the presbytery.[20]

We find one exhortation in 1682 that presbyteries be more diligent in conducting trials of students:

> does appoint and ordaine that a more strict and impartial accompt be taken of intrants through all the several stages and periods of their trials; and whereas part of them usuallie called questionairie trialls have been generallie more slightlie and perfunctoriouslie performed, and therefore enjoine a whole entire diet to be set

---

[17] *Register of the Diocesan Synod of Dunblane 1662-1688*, ed. John Wilson (Edinburgh, 1927), 52-53. It must be acknowledged that Leighton's writings continued to be admired by Presbyterians in later generations for their warm gospel emphasis and piety, which lies behind this quotation. See also the anonymous review, "Evangelical Beauties, selected from the *Works of Archbishop Leighton* with a Short Account of his Life", by John Brown, Whitburn, in *Edinburgh Theological Magazine* 2 (1827):264, where the reviewer applauds Leighton but confesses confusion over Leighton's "strange" Episcopal alignment.

[18] *Register... Synod of Dunblane*, 55-56.

[19] *Register... Synod of Dunblane*, 66. See also 77, 114, 124, 173, 181, 193, 198, 202.

[20] *Register... Synod of Dunblane*, 64-70

apart for a thorough examination of them in the grounds of the Christian religion, and other enquiries which have a more direct aspect upon and immediate tendencie to the superstructing Christian practise, and that they may be observit and keepit as a standing rule in tyme coming.[21]

Gilbert Burnet

The first of the Episcopalian divinity professors appointed to Glasgow after the Restoration was Gilbert Burnet, who was later to become the Bishop of Salisbury and is still widely known for his *History of His Own Times*.[22] Burnet spent his five years at Glasgow as virtually the sole instructor in divinity, where he was professor. We record here how Burnet himself described his programme of teaching, to which Mechie comments, "No wonder Burnet reports that everyone approved of his scheme, but thought it ought to be the work of two or three men!"[23]

> My chief business was to form the students of Divinity right, and I laid down a plan for it which made all my friends uneasy... Yet I let no part of it fall all the time I stayed there...On Monday I made all the students in course explain a part of the body of Divinity in Latin with a thesis, and answer all the arguments. On Tuesday I had a prelection in Latin, in which I designed to go through a body of Divinity in ten or twelve years. On Wednesday I went through a critical commentary on St. Matthew's gospel which I delivered in English... On Thursday I expounded a Psalm in Hebrew, comparing it with the 70, the vulgar, and our version. And by turns the next Thursday I explained the Constitution and the ritual, and made the Apostolical canons my text, bringing every particular I opened to them to one of the canons. On Fridays I made the students in course preach a short sermon upon a text that I gave them and... shewed them what was defective or amiss in the sermon, and the text ought to have been opened and applied. Besides all this, I called them all together in the evening everyday to prayers. I read a parcel of Scripture, and after I had explained it I made a short sermon for a quarter of an hour upon it. I then asked them what difficulties they met with in their studies and answered such questions as they put to me. Thus I applied myself for eight months in the year to answer the ends of a professor with the dilegence of a schoolmaster. This obliged me to much hard study. I rose early

---

[21] *Register... Synod of Dunblane*, 188. It is perhaps difficult to define just exactly how long an "entire diet" would have been, but at a minimum it would have been a few hours.

[22] Burnet's *History of His Own Time* has again been printed for a new generation. See G. Burnet, *History of His Own Time*, abridged by Thomas Stackhouse (London,1986).

[23] Mechie, *"Education and the Ministry in Scotland"*, 1:121. Mechie is actually reading from Burnet on this point.

and studied close from four to ten, six hours, but was forced to throw up the rest of the day.[24]

Mention is made of instruction by way of Latin and the teaching of Hebrew exegesis, yet nothing is mentioned of Greek. We can assume that this was covered within commentary on "St. Matthew's gospel". Student work on the common places of theology and on their own sermons seems standard to what we have noted before. Also Burnet's involvement in their daily lives, forming a college community for divinity, is nothing new. We learn from an English, Non-Conformist student at Glasgow College while Burnet was there that college life was very similar to the preceding period. This student recorded that the day began with the bell at five o'clock. The Lord's Day was "strictly observed, all the scholars called to the several classes, where, after religious exercises, all attend the Primar and Regents to church, forenoon and afternoon.... Then in the evening called again to classes, and then to come under examination concerning the sermons heard, and give account of what was appointed the foregoing Sabbath in some theological treatises, viz., Wollebius or Ursin's Catechism...."[25] This is comment by an arts student, yet it shows the tenor of what constituted the life of a university student at Glasgow during this period of Episcopal restoration. Life was lived in a religious environment. Sunday had student exercises with a regent or professor presiding before the two church services. Finally, the day ended with "recall", whereby the day's sermons were reviewed as was the catechism. The study of the Heidelberg was obviously one of the catechetical mainstays in Glasgow at this time. We also know that Burnet was busy most Sundays preaching.

It would certainly appear that at Glasgow during the Episcopalian period, none of Burnet's successors, either David Liddell, Alexander Rose or James Wemyss, rivaled 1's energy and abilities. The number of candidates studying divinity at Glasgow during this period evidently fell in number. Burnet sees this as due to the fact that the west coast had strong Presbyterian sympathies.[26]

The actual number of theology students while Burnet was professor is difficult to determine. If we read the bursar list, it would suggest from seven to nine students per year. However, this figure may be slightly low as perhaps there were other divinity students who did not need bursaries or obtained their bursary from other means.[27] The total figure was certainly under fifteen students each year, and this was probably the maximum for Glasgow during the Episcopal period. There is nothing to suggest that the numbers for any of the other colleges were much different; perhaps some were even smaller.

---

[24] *A Supplement to Burnet's History of My Own Time, derived from His Original Memoirs, etc.* ed. H. C. Foxcroft (Oxford,1902), 477-478.
[25] T. E. S. Clarke and H. C. Foxcroft, *A Life of Gilbert Burnet* (Cambridge, 1907) 81.
[26] Riddell, "Divinity", 8.
[27] *Munimenta Alme Universitatis Glasguensis,* 3:262-277.

"School of Theology"

There remains one question concerning Burnet and his successors for the professorship of divinity – what school of theology did they teach? It was clearly Protestant and with evident articulation against Popery.[28] But how close was it to the school of theology in the preceding period? We know someone like Burnet had read and travelled extensively in the lands of the Protestants on the continent.[29] He was very well acquainted with the field of Reformed theology in the Covenanting period. Burnet's theology, as we have said, was clearly anti-Roman. He also fell into conflict with his own party, the Episcopalians, at various times throughout his life before, during, and even after his time in Glasgow. In 1668 he took a hard knock against Episcopal abuses of absentee bishops, worldliness and little pastoral care in his *Memorial of Diverse Grievances*. His alliance with Robert Leighton was not popular with all in the Episcopal party, nor were his rigorous demands and standards at Glasgow College. His own *History* does display which party he belonged to and remains an invaluable work. Thus, what begins to emerge is a picture of someone who had moderate sympathies and, as is often the case, had enemies on both sides – in this instance both Covenanters and Episcopalians.[30]

Reference has been made to the use at Glasgow during Burnet's time of the Heidelberg Catechism and Ursinus' treatises on it and the dogmatics of Wollebius. Wollebius was a German Reformed theologian whose *Compendium* was very popular in Britain among the Westminster Divines. He was infralapsarian.[31] Yet the employment of such texts in a college does not necessarily constitute strict conformity to the school of Calvinism formulated at Dort or Westminster. The characterization given today of Gilbert Burnet is that he was a "Latitudinarian" of the seventeenth century and, even more pointedly, "a decided Arminian" and "a non-high" churchman, as evidenced in Burnet's *Exposition of the Thirty-Nine Articles*.[32] He clearly did not view the application of federal theology in the same ways as the opposing Covenanters. On another matter, distinctions have been found comparing Burnet with David Dickson on casuistry, and the conclusion is that Burnet certainly did not develop as in-

---

[28] Robert Wodrow, *The History of the Sufferings of the Church of Scotland from the Restoration to the Revolution*, vol. 4, original 1721-1722, ed. R. Burns (Glasgow, 1828) 411.

[29] Gilbert Burnet, *History of His Own Times*, vol. 2 (London,1838), 437-438.

[30] *DSCHT,*112. Also, in Wodrow, *History of the Sufferings of the Church of Scotland*, see preliminary remarks of Burns, 1:xi and 4:535.

[31] Muller, *Post-Reformation Reformed Dogmatics*, 1:46; *ERF,* 398.

[32] *ODCC*, 254-255 and 956 on Burnet and Latitudinarianism; MacLeod, *Scottish Theology*, 111, 134; Torrance, *Scottish Theology*, 160-161; Reid, *Divinity Professors*, 150, 158, 168.

depth answers as Dickson or the Puritans.[33] It appears, in conclusion, that in some respects all of the above interpretations are correct, and various schools of theology were brought together under Burnet.

Perhaps H. M. B. Reid summarized it best: "In truth he was a curious though not unparalleled mixture of all sorts of Churchmen."[34] Ultimately, it will be admitted by all that such professors do have an effect upon their students and therefore upon the life of the church, just as Baillie or Dickson did in the previous period.

Academically, there does not appear to be any difference between Periods III and IV in terms of languages, controversies, common-places, chronology or exegesis. It appears that confessional instruction was conducted, yet obviously it was latitudinarian in approach. The best of the professors attempted to combine piety with learning.

The overall student numbers were not large, nor was the divinity hall staff. In tabulating the staff in divinity at the five halls/colleges, they read as two or three.[35] However, it appears that in many instances the principal took a very limited role during this period, and thus in some halls we find one professor solely in charge of the theology education. Again, this does not show the entire picture because the presbyteries/exercises were responsible for extensive annual reviews and conducted the trials. As we have intimated before, the rules may not have always paralleled the practices.

Perhaps the most enduring piece of writing to come from this period by any of the Scottish professors of divinity was Henry Scougal's *The Life of God in the Soul of Man*, published first in 1677 while he was professor at King's and one year before his death. Scougal is generally accorded the position of an evangelical or, as MacLeod writes, a "mystical Erastian".[36]

Scougal's immediate successor at King's for a brief two year period was John Menzies, followed by the long professorship of James Garden, who served both in the Episcopal Period and the Revolutionary Settlement Period.

It would appear that Garden went even further than Scougal as a mystical theologian, imbibing the writings of Antoinette Bourignon of the Netherlands. This begins to raise several questions as to the nature of theological confessionalism at King's, particularly with Garden, but also Scougal. James Garden was deprived of his professorship in 1697 for his refusal to subscribe to the Westminster Confession. This perhaps points us to an indication that his theology lectures, like his *Comparative Theology*, were mystical.[37] G. D.

---

[33] Reid, *Divinity Professors*, 162-163, where Reid recounts Burnet's casuistry, which on one point makes polygamy lawful in some cases under the Gospel.
[34] Reid, *Divinity Professors*, 168.
[35] See Appendix A.
[36] G. D. Henderson, *The Burning Bush* (Edinburgh, 1957), 101; MacLeod, *Scottish Theology*, 65. Also, C. G. McCrie, *Confessions of the Church of Scotland*, 79-82.
[37] *DSCHT*, 351. Also, C. G. McCrie, *Confessions of the Church of Scotland*, 95-96.

Henderson, in a brief study of *Comparative Theology*, describes it in terms of the famous desideratum: "In essentials unity, in non-essentials liberty, in all charity", and in Henderson's words that:

> When true piety and charity are greatly decayed, when unimportant views are violently propagated and harmless ideas fiercely attacked, when this or that ceremony is the centre of acrimonious dispute, while meantime vice and error flourish without interruption, it is very necessary that some attempt be made to recall men to a better sense of proportion and to insist that repentance, charity and humility are more urgent than orthodoxy, and that sin is in fact more serious than incorrect observance.[38]

Thus, it clearly emerges that a certain strain of pietism which was of a mystical nature was characteristic of the teaching of theology at King's College during the Episcopal Period. Therefore, it is not shocking at all to learn that Scougal, even when he was a regent in arts, took the spiritual well-being of his students very seriously and enquired after them both collectively and privately.

Henderson brings this charge against the general tendency of the Scottish divinity halls: "One of the weaknesses of Scottish Divinity Halls is said to be a tendency to allow [the] intellectual to crush out spiritual training." He then adds in this context:

> There was nothing of this fault when Scougall taught theology at King's College. He made it his great design to fit his students for what he believed to be a most weighty and responsible function, which would not be so much the handling of controversies and debates about religion as the guiding of men's souls to eternity. Scougall, indeed, acted not simply as a lecturer but as a spiritual director.[39]

However, in the field of dogmatics, Henderson asserts that Scougall and his circle expressed themselves inconsistently and "confusedly" for "they were interested in religion" and for them theological controversies were as irrelevant as were disputes over Episcopacy or Presbytery.[40] With this we now end our brief look into the "School of Theology" in this Episcopal Period and turn to discuss the academic degrees.

---

[38] Henderson, *Burning Bush*, 113. What follows is a summary of the contents of Garden's *Comparative Theology*, 114-116.

[39] Henderson, *Burning Bush*, 102.

[40] Henderson, *Burning Bush*, 101. The only other leading divinity professors were John Menzies at Marischal and briefly at King's, who is characterized as a vacillator, yet known for attacking Popery and Quakerism, and Alexander Monro at St. Mary's and Edinburgh, known for strong views against Presbyterianism. See *DSCHT*, 559, 603.

Degrees

As we have seen before under Episcopal influence in Period II, the higher degree of Doctor of Divinity was awarded for the presentation of a thesis on a common-place of theology. Thus, it is not surprising to learn that in this period of Episcopal Restoration the conferring of the D.D. degree returned in some of the colleges. None were given at Glasgow, at least according to the records,[41] nor at Edinburgh College.[42] Both King's College and St. Andrews awarded the D.D. degree for theses presented during the Episcopal Period.[43] Since there was no such thing as the B.D. degree in this period, this can be passed over quickly.

Summary

To a certain extent we have already included a summary of Scottish theological education in the Episcopal Period in the subsection "School of Theology". The theology taught in the five divinity halls was preceded by a preparatory course (usually resulting in the M.A. degree). It was thoroughly Protestant, yet contained a spectrum of theological positions. It lacked the precision of the federal theology of the earlier period, yet often used theological works of the Reformed writers. At least one hall was mystical and had extremes in this area, which included Bourigionism.

It would appear that, as in preceding periods, the struggle in raising bursary support remained a problem and presbyteries needed chastisement for their neglect.

Divinity hall staffing remained small, and this was not a time in which the staff produced theological texts or expository works of note; in fact, very few works have come from this period.

The presbyteries continued to stress the study of Greek and Hebrew. One can only speculate as to whether or not this was universal, yet some students were rejected or admonished for deficiency in this area. The presbytery or exercise exerted its influence over student sermons, discourses and additions, all of which continued to make the presbytery meetings integral to the theological training of ministers, not limiting theological education to the confines of the divinity halls of the universities.

---

[41] *Munimenta Alme Universitatis Glasguensis*, 3:34-41.

[42] *Catalogue of Edinburgh University Graduates*, 239.

[43] Cant, *University of St. Andrews*, 75; *DSCHT*, 351. Henry Scougal and James Garden both received D.D.'s.

Chapter 6

Period V: 1690-1825, Revolution Settlement

Introduction

Period V covers the long time span from 1690 to1825, and though it shows many continuities in the Kirk's attitude towards theological education, this period also contains many complexities. The period begins with the restoration of Presbyterianism in Scotland and, for our purposes, ends with university reform and restructuring about to occur. We will examine the General Assembly directives on theological education, certain memoir material, the university changes in this period, and the leading Scottish educationalists. Key books and texts will be discussed as well as extended discussion on George Campbell. This will lead us to the matter of the Scottish Enlightenment, and an attempt will be made to see its connection to theological education and the church parties, Moderate and Popular.

The General Assembly: 1690-1825

One of the best ways to formulate a systematic history of Scottish theological education and training in the Church of Scotland in Period V, which begins with the Revolution Settlement, is to mine the Acts of the General Assembly during the years 1690 to 1825. They provide us with the official intentions of the Church throughout this period and, as we will note, the continual struggle to implement General Assembly standing laws within the presbyteries and synods. In the 1690s the General Assembly retraced much of the same ground of the 1640s and 1650s, so that as the eighteenth century passed, the system was very much in place and in many ways became routine. The period ended with the anticipation of a time of change.

Subscription

One of the first acts of the General Assembly of October, 1690, was to bring about a return to the subscription of the Confession of Faith, not only for the ministers but also the probationers and entrants for the ministry: "All probationers licensed to preach, all entrants into the ministry, and all other ministers and elders... be obliged to subscribe their approbation of the Confession of Faith, approven by former General Assemblies of this Church..."[1] The year 1690 was also a time when the visitation of the Scottish universities occurred, in essence to do "housekeeping". The first to go as a result of this was James Fall, principal of Glasgow University, for refusing to acknowledge Presbyterianism.[2]

Twenty-one years later the General Assembly passed an act concerning probationers and their licensure questions. This act included more specific language and formulation. The second question to a probationer began: "Do you sincerely own and believe the whole doctrine of the Confession of Faith... and do you own the whole doctrine therein contained as the confession of your faith?"[3] The fourth vow strengthened this by calling not only for an "owning" but also a "defending". The questions have to be read in their entirety in order to capture the intentions of the General Assembly of 1711.[4] The matter of subscription as defined by the Assembly set a standard for those men entering the ministry in the fifth period. This closely related to the three General Assembly rulings in this period involving three professors and their conformity to the Confession's doctrine.

There was an attempt during Period V to abolish the subscription to the Confession of Faith. This was chiefly the work of MacGill and Dalrymple of Ayr and it failed.[5] In actuality, Socinianism was tolerated in many quarters, although a stringent subscription formula was in place.

The Exercise and Addition and the Rise of "Societies"

As in the former Covenanting Period, the presbyterial exercise and addition was observed in the presbyteries. There is no need to retrace former ground, but we summarize these exercises and additions as also including the divinity students and being an integral part of their theological education and pastoral training. The act included the use of "privy censures" at the conclusion of the exercise, as had formerly been practiced. Such acts show the continuity with

---

[1] *AGACS*, 225. See the article by J. Ligon Duncan for a fuller discussion on subscription. J. Ligon Duncan, III, "Owning the Confession: Subscription in the Scottish Presbyterian Tradition", in *The Practice of Confessional Subscription*, ed. D. W. Hall (Lanham, Maryland, 1995), 77-91.

[2] *FES*, 7:396. Also, Tristram Clarke, "The Williamite Episcopalians and the Glorious Revolution in Scotland", *RSCHS* 24 (1992), 43-44.

[3] *AGACS*, May 22, 1711, 454.

[4] *AGACS*, 454. The fourth question reads: "Do you promise, that, through the grace of God, you will firmly and constantly adhere to, and in your station to the utmost of your power assert, maintain, and defend the said doctrine, worship, and discipline, and the government of this church...?"

[5] Thomas McCrie, Jr., *The Story of the Scottish Church*, original 1874 (Glasgow, 1988), 507.

the practice of the church in the past and the ongoing involvement of the presbytery in more than a functionary, business mode.[6]

The 1705 General Assembly listed seven rules for the observance of presbyterial exercises. These rules included assigning the exercise texts by the presbytery. Rule three concerned probationers. Rules six and seven concerned the exercise of a "Common Head", usually but not necessarily in Latin. When involving Scripture, the exercise was to proceed systematically, verse by verse, from meeting to meeting.[7] However, we find that although Period V began with the ideal of the exercise, by the end of this period it was no longer practiced, and presbytery meetings had become much more administrative.[8]

Though we are looking specifically at the official Assembly acts, it must be acknowledged here that Period V was clearly a transitional time for the older exercise. It is noteworthy that during the second half of the eighteenth and the beginning of the nineteenth century two things emerged – theology student societies and clerical societies. The functions of these societies in many respects resembled those intended for the traditional presbyterial exercise meeting. For example, the theology students at St. Mary's formed a theological society in 1760. It would appear that during session the society met weekly and had one or more discourses by students, followed by discussion or debate.[9] We discover the same in Aberdeen, where George Campbell, later to become professor of divinity, formed the Theological Club in January, 1742. Alexander Gerard also became a member. The society had fourteen rules for the members. Its stated purpose was for the improvement of her members and the pursuit of sacred literature and "pleasures of conversation".[10] McElroy makes a striking point:

> Campbell's theological education was not confined to the classroom. Student societies had become important parts of a young Scot's education, providing venues for public speaking, not to mention conversation and debate.[11]

Perhaps in a limited way the demise of the presbytery exercise made some contribution to the development of theology student and clerical societies.

---

[6] *AGACS*, April 16, 1694, 243.
[7] *AGACS*, April 15, 1705, 366.
[8] *DSCHT*, 311-312.
[9] H. R. Sefton, "St. Mary's College, St. Andrews, in the Eighteenth Century", *RSCHS* 24 (1990-1992), 170-171. J. H. Baxter, "The Theological Society 1760-1960", *St. Mary's College Bulletin* 3 (1961), 11-18. Similar will be noted for Edinburgh theology students when we come to Thomas Somerville in this chapter.
[10] Jeffrey M. Suderman, "Orthodoxy and Enlightenment: George Campbell (1719-1796) And the Aberdeen Enlightenment" (unpublished Ph.D. thesis, University of Western Ontario, London, 1995), 22-23.
[11] D. D. McElroy, *Scotland's Age of Improvement: A Survey of Eighteenth Century Literary Clubs and Societies* (Washington, D.C., 1969), 104.

However, it could also be argued that these were results of the Scottish Enlightenment. These are just two of a complex ring of origins of these societies. The eighteenth century saw the founding of an incredible number of clubs and societies. Daiches offered this prefatory remark concerning these clubs and societies: "The literati of the Enlightenment believed profoundly in human contact, by means both of personal engagement and of published discourse."[12] Social conversation was also an Enlightenment ideal, and we know these clubs and societies for theology students were in harmony with such Enlightenment stirrings.

The divinity student societies were not limited to the confines of the divinity halls in the universities, as societies for students, both divinity and otherwise, existed in various locations in the eighteenth century. In a prefatory remark to "The Gaelic Students' Society" (Glasgow), this comment was made: "Divinity students supplemented more collegiate instruction by meeting with their fellows and discussing questions that puzzled them but were neglected by their stated and more academic teachers."[13] The composition of the students who formed this society were members of the Church of Scotland, the Relief Church and the Associate Church. The compiler, [William J. Couper], in an effort to identify the ordination source for the members of the Society, concluded the majority for the years 1786-1831 were "dissenters". The students were from Glasgow or vicinity and from Ireland. The most noteworthy Seceder student who belonged to the Society was Andrew Marshall, later of Kirkintilloch, who was involved in the Atonement controversy. Some eventually joined the Free Church at the Disruption in 1843. One went to Quebec and taught classics. Another taught at a Dissenting Academy in York, then in Chatham. Still another became an eminent mathematician.[14] Since the Associate Seceders' Hall was in Selkirk for most of the time period 1796-1831 (it was in Selkirk under Lawson from 1787-1820), it can be assumed that this Gaelic Chapel Students' Society made for further ongoing fellowship, interaction and sharpening of the students outside the short hall sessions for students around Glasgow. Later, in 1820, when the United Secession Hall moved to Glasgow, we note that this society continued to meet through to 1831. Since it was not limited to Seceders, there was a mixing of students, a dynamic which one may not have expected.

The minute book for 1796 to 1831 lists twenty rules for the society which were adopted in 1796. A summary of these rules included the following:

---

[12] David Daiches, "The Scottish Enlightenment", in *The Scottish Enlightenment 1730-1790 A Hotbed of Genius*, eds. David Daiches, Peter Jones and Jean Jones, original 1986 (Saltire Society, Edinburgh, 1996), 34.

[13] Anon, "Two Glasgow Society Minute Books", bk. 1 [1796-1831], in "The Gaelic Chapel Students' Society", *RSCHS* 5 (1935), 175. I believe the editor of these minute books was William J. Couper. The article was simply signed W. J. C.

[14] "The Gaelic Chapel Students' Society", 176-177.

prescribed weekly meetings; penalties for lateness or absenteeism; all meetings opened by a "Theological Discourse from one of the members, and that the members shall succeed each other in rotation according to their seniority of standing in the Society". Following each "oration", members gave their opinion, and this was concluded by the president. Debates could also be conducted (if time allowed) on a "controverted point in divinity" and each be given two minutes to speak. Rules for the taking of minutes were clearly stated. The society was to be limited to a maximum of twelve students at any one time, and these were to be students of theology who had finished a regular course of philosophy in a university. New members were voted upon by the society and first had to be intimated to the society at the previous meeting. Very clear procedures for misconduct of members were to be followed. In order to ensure good order in the society:

> No old law shall be repealed, nor new one enacted, unless it shall have occupied the attention of the Society upon a part of three several meetings successively; on the first of these any motion for that purpose shall be made; on the second it shall be repeated and considered, and on the third, after what further deliberation may be necessary, it shall be finally decided;

Secret ballots were used for membership and the annual dues were collected in January.[15] If nothing else, the students were certainly learning order, something which would prepare them for the courts of the church!

That the society took the admission of new members very seriously is evidenced from the number of individuals who were denied admittance. The society's name came originally from the fact that it met in the Gaelic church on Duke Street. However, other subsequent locations were obtained. Topics covered included issues that have an Enlightenment flavour about them; for example, "Can miracles be proven from human testimony?", "Is the Preparation of Christianity a proof of its truth?" and "Whether the Egyptian Magi had the power of the working of miracles?" Such questions occupied the second half of the meeting after the orator's paper or essay. Other questions included ecclesiastical matters of current debate; such as, "Whether the right of electing their own pastors belong to the people?"[16] Given the backgrounds of the students, it is logical to perceive that the Church of Scotland students were evangelical and probably had much sympathy with the Dissenting Presbyterians on this point.

Such a divinity student society as this suggests that student societies must not be ignored in examining theological education and training amongst Scottish Presbyterians, 1790-1840. It is significant to note that this society extended beyond one Presbyterian body. The topics heard or debated were very

---

[15] "The Gaelic Chapel Students' Society", 177-179.

[16] "The Gaelic Chapel Students' Society", 180-181.

much reflective of the time. However, not all divinity students joined such a group or were admitted. Only about thirty names are listed for this society between 1796 to 1831, so it was small given the overall student numbers for divinity. Also, since it was limited to twelve members, it appears as elitist and secretive (a word used in their rules). It offered an alternative to the hall societies, which would have been held during sessions of the hall and also limited by denomination. This society stood in a most unique position.

Clergy also founded their own societies. The most notable of this period was the one founded chiefly under the efforts of the Rev. Stevenson MacGill in 1800 in Glasgow, where he was then minister of the Tron Church. This society, the Clerical Literary Society, met monthly to hear essays read and to discuss such "literature of the clerical profession, or that species of learning to which a clergyman should chiefly direct his views and attention".[17] Since MacGill's essays were published in *Considerations Addressed to A Young Clergyman* (Glasgow, 1809), we can examine their contents and see that they were essays in practical theology, including some themes which formerly would have been suited to exercise meetings. The rise of such clubs and societies in the eighteenth century must be noted as we examine theological education and training and the Assembly acts.[18] Professor Hunter, in his introductory theological lectures (delivered twenty-two times), commended attendance at the societies from his own experience.[19] Thus, professors were recommending to students to join such clubs, and they were also popular with the professors. In the minds of some, notably Alexander Carlyle, the literary clubs in part compensated for the few exercises demanded of students, as "one discourse in a session was by no means sufficient to produce a habit of composition".[20] A. M. Clark's summary on this craze of "clubbability" was:

> Association and Improvement became the watchwords of the Scottish Enlightenment of the eighteenth century...Practically every star of the Scottish Enlightenment, every man of any eminence in the professions, and every man whose rank and position as a great landowner gave him authority and influence was also a member of one or more of [these] fellowships.[21]

When we come to chapter fifteen of this thesis we will note Thomas McCulloch's involvement with such societies and clubs.

---

[17] Robert Burns, *Memoir of the Rev. Stevenson MacGill* (Edinburgh, 1842), 59-60.
[18] See the helpful article on "Clubs and Societies, Eighteenth Century", in *DSCHT*, 191-192, and D. D. McElroy, "The Literary Clubs and Societies of Eighteenth Century Scotland" (unpublished Ph.D. thesis, Edinburgh University, 1952).
[19] David F. Wright, "Andrew Hunter of Barjarg (1744-1809): Evangelical Divine in an Age of Improvement", *RSCHS* 26 (1996), 150.
[20] Wright, "Andrew Hunter of Barjarg", 150.
[21] A. M. Clark quoted in Wright, "Andrew Hunter of Barjarg", 155.

Bursars

A constant theme throughout the Acts of General Assembly in this fifth period concerned raising bursary assistance for divinity students. The first mention was in the General Assembly of 1694 with the recommendation to the presbyteries to "be careful to keep and maintain bursars of theology", conforming in this regard to the "ancient practice" and Acts of the General Assemblies.[22] In reality, it would seem that for several years presbyteries and synods were generally quite negligent in carrying out the directives of the General Assembly on this matter. It would certainly appear that many bursars did not receive their assistance very punctually from the presbyteries.[23] However, it does appear that bursary aid was more forthcoming as the eighteenth century progressed.

Bursary aid can be found being given to three categories of students: Lowland students whose language was English constituted the first category, Gaelic speaking students made up the second category (they were referred to as the Irish Language students), and the foreign bursary aid students composed the third.

In the eighteenth century the Highlands were the focus for church planting, establishing schools, securing preachers and settling ministers. This became expressed as well in the Church's pronouncements concerning theological education. Students who knew the "Irish tongue" were singled out for particular bursary assistance, and it would appear that students destined for the Highlands could have a shorter divinity course.

The General Assembly created quite exacting formulas for the Lowland presbyteries, as well as others, as to how they were to support Irish language bursars.[24] In 1717 the General Assembly had to safeguard the abuse of these "Highland Bursaries", as they were occasionally called. Some students received these bursaries, but upon completion of their studies it became evident that they were actually incapable of preaching in Gaelic. The solution was to have a committee examine the students of the Irish language bursaries before they were given the bursaries in order to prevent abuse.[25]

The third category of bursary support was for foreign students studying in Scotland. The only references in the fifth period to foreign students was in regard to the awarding of bursaries to Lithuanian students in 1722, 1736, and 1740. Each of these lasted for four years. The Lithuanian students came to Edinburgh from the Protestant Synod of Lithuania, and to receive aid they were

---

[22] *AGACS*, April 16, 1694, 243.

[23] *AGACS*, April 13, 1706, 395. See also the problem of many commissioners failing to come to the Assembly. This may explain part of the reason for General Assembly recommendations to be conveyed into effect at the presbytery level, 434 (Act for Better Attendance at General Assembly) and 439, 500.

[24] *AGACS*, March 4, 1701, 304 and March 27, 1704, 329. See also, 418.

[25] *AGACS*, May 13, 1717, 517.

required to show testimonials from their church affirming that they were candidates for the ministry.[26]

By 1737 the General Assembly observed that the number of candidates for the ministry was increasing, and the former rules and quotas for supporting bursars were relaxed, thereby giving more control to the individual presbyteries.[27] Then in 1756, seeing that there was a scarcity of Gaelic preachers, the former acts were restored along with a formula to provide bursaries for students of the Irish language.[28] The General Assembly's provision of bursaries showed its concern for financing the training of ministerial students.

Libraries in the Highlands

A review of the establishment of presbytery libraries in the Highlands in the early eighteenth century needs to be included in our understanding of theological education in Period V. One reason these libraries were established is that few ministers were able to afford books in the early eighteenth century and therefore needed to be able to borrow commentaries, etc. However, these libraries served another important purpose. Divinity students had large blocks of time between sessions in the divinity hall and were often employed as schoolmasters or family tutors. During these times their studies were under presbytery oversight. Therefore, a student would often continue his reading (for example, in chronology) and then present a paper or exercise to the brethren of his presbytery.[29]

In 1704 the Society for Propagating Christian Knowledge in England gave thirty-one libraries to the General Assembly of the Church of Scotland. The Assembly divided these by giving one to the Dumbarton Presbytery, two to Dunblane, three to Ross, one to Sutherland, two to Caithness, one to Orkney, one to Zetland (Shetland), four to Moray, and four to Dunkeld. Twelve were given to the Synod of Argyle to distribute as they deemed appropriate, but with particular attention to Lewis.[30] These presbytery libraries each had about seventy volumes of books and represented continental and English authors.[31] Besides these presbyterial libraries, there were also fifty-eight parochial libraries distributed as follows:

---

[26] *AGACS*, May 17, 1722, 546; May 22, 1736, 660; May 19, 1740, 660.

[27] *AGACS*, May 24, 1737, 645.

[28] *AGACS*, May 31, 1756, 727.

[29] David Lachman, *The Marrow Controversy* (Edinburgh, 1988), 78-80; Donald MacLean, "Highland Libraries in the Eighteenth Century", *Transactions of the Gaelic Society of Inverness* 31 (1922-1924), 92-94.

[30] *AGACS*, March 29, 1704, 332.

[31] Lachman, *Marrow Controversy*, 80.

Shetland (2)
Orkney (3)
Caithness (2)
Sutherland (2)
Ross (4)
Inverness (3)
Aberlour (2)
Abernethy (1)
Alford (1)
Kincardine (2)
Synods of Angus and Mearns (3)
Dunkeld (4)
Auchterarder (2)
Dunblane (2)
Dumbarton (2)
Synod of Argyle (23)

These libraries were to be "fixed at such places as the representative Synods and Presbyteries shall find most convenient".[32]

One of these presbytery libraries which was kept intact was the Dumbarton Presbytery Library, now housed in Special Collections at the University of Glasgow Library. A survey of the contents of the Dumbarton Presbytery Library provides an amazing record of theological study around 1705 in the Church of Scotland presbyteries.[33]

We discover that several volumes are English Puritan authors such as Flavel, Burgess, Manton, Shepard, Reynolds, Baxter, Gouge and Jenkyn. These tend to be in the category of practical divinity, although some are commentaries on individual books of Scripture; for example, Jude, Colossians or specific portions of Scripture. It is interesting to note several copies of Robert Leighton's *Praelectiones Theologicae* and volume two of his 1 Peter commentary. Some of Calvin's commentaries in Latin are included, as are some other continental commentaries. In addition, we find Willet's 1611 *Hexapla of Romans*, which contains a massive quarry of information; commentary by Church Fathers (Origin, Ambrose, Chrysostom, Augustine); Greek philosophers; Reformers (Bucer, Beza, Calvin); and Church history volumes by Eusebius, Crakanthorpe, and Acominatus. We also find theological works on the Creed and the Lord's Supper; writings by Erasmus, Zanchi (eight volumes) and François DuJon; and lectures on the catechism and the covenant of grace, as well as Acts of the Synod of Dort. One copy of John Duns Scotus' *Commentary on the Sentences of Peter Lombard* is in this collection, as is a parallel version of the Rheims and Bishops' *New Testaments*, all of which made the Dumbarton Presbytery Library a rich mine of resources. It should be noted also that Gilbert Burnet's *Four Discourses Delivered to the Clergy of the Diocese of Sarum* was included in the library, so one cannot say everything reflected strict Puritan theology.[34]

---

[32] *AGACS*, April 10, 1705, 338.

[33] *A Guide to the Major Collections in the Department of Special Collections*, 3d ed. (Glasgow University Library, 1995), No.15.

[34] The reader should note that the author has made a complete list of the contents of the Dumbarton Presbytery Library, which may be found in J. C. Whytock, "Appendix B – A Catalogue of the Dumbarton Presbytery Library, 1705", in "The History and

One work which provided teaching on pastoral ministry was Samuel Annesley's collection of exercise sermons which had been delivered by ministers gathering at Cripplegate for a morning exercise. The ministers were many of the leading Puritans – Poole, Watson, Gouge, Manton, Doolittel, etc. – and dealt with "cases of conscience" such as backsliding, vows, advice to merchants who travel, assurance, alms and visiting the sick.[35]

Suffice it to say that the Dumbarton Presbytery Library contained in its approximately seventy volumes (which would have amounted to more than seventy individual books, as some were several volumes and others were bound together) quite an amazing divinity library for this time. It certainly shows that considerable effort was made that resources might be available in order that Scottish ministers could study and students of divinity could continue their studies under presbytery supervision. The closest way of describing the usage of these libraries is to view them more as study centres outside of the university system.

Assembly Standing Laws for Licensure of Students

Several times between 1690 and 1825 the General Assembly formulated a complete act of Regulations or Standards for the Licensing of Probationers. It is to these acts that we turn to find the official standards expected of a student from his entrance through to his ordination. The first of these complete acts for students came in 1696. It began with a preamble extolling the virtues of a qualified ministry and the inherent dangers when such was not the case:

> The General Assembly, taking into their consideration the danger that ariseth to the church and to the souls of people, and the contempt that may be brought on the ministry, by licensing or ordaining young men, without sufficient proof of their piety, gravity, prudence, sobriety, orthodoxy, and learning, do, therefore, appoint, that strict inquiry be made into all these qualifications of such as are offered to Presbyteries... and that such be rejected who have not sufficient testimonials from universities of their good behaviour and proficiency; (and that the usual school-degrees be inquired after, though not made a necessary qualification) or, at least, should not be found to have retrieved their lodt time at schools by after diligence...[36]

Development of Scottish Theological Education and Training, Kirk and Secession (c.1560-c.1850) (unpublished Ph.D. Thesis, University of Wales, Lampeter, 2001), 481-486. See also the forthcoming article by W. M. Jacob, "Libraries for the parish: individual donors and charitable societies", in *The Cambridge History of Libraries in Britain and Ireland*. Vol. 3. [forthcoming].

[35] Samuel Annesley, *The Morning-Exercise at Cripple-gate or, Several Cases of conscience practically resolved by sundry ministers...*(London, 1677).

[36] *AGACS*, Jan. 4, 1696, 253-254.

The Master of Arts degree was perceived as the ideal preparation for divinity students, but it was not a necessity. This allowance held true throughout all of Period V, with the result that often ministers were ordained in the Church of Scotland without possessing a degree in arts. Since B.D. degrees were not conferred, the full test lay with the presbytery.[37] However, we find that the General Assembly upon occasion issued acts exhorting the presbyteries to make proper enquiries into the educational attainments of students whom they were about to license. The synods were expected to make "strict inquiry how the Presbyteries within their bounds have observed this...".[38] The exhortation of 1704, urging more thoroughness by the presbyteries, warned of not allowing the examinations to become "perfunctorious" and instructed that presbyteries were to appoint certain fellow presbyters to examine the students in the heads of divinity, church government, and the reason of their faith and the "settlement in these matters... and that this be not done hastily....".[39]

The 1696 act also required that no student could be licensed unless he gave proof of understanding Greek and Hebrew. The study of Chaldee and Syriac was only recommended, not required, and ended with this proviso, "so far as they can".[40] When we turn to memoirs and ministerial autobiographical sketches, we find that the possession of Hebrew was sometimes lacking, not to mention any attempts at Chaldee and Syriac.

The other major acts in Period V were adopted in 1782 and 1813, setting forth the educational standards. Several times during the eighteenth and early nineteenth century, overtures were sent down to the presbyteries, but these continued to be either amended or simply never adopted.

The early 1820s were years of revising the General Assembly Standing Laws of the Church on the course of study for students. This was subsequently adopted in 1826. Both the 1782 and 1813 Standing Laws insisted upon a presbytery trial of a student's knowledge of Greek and Hebrew.[41] Also, for this entire period the student still had to be examined for proficiency in Latin prior to his trials. At his public trial he was required to deliver in Latin a "controverted head in Divinity".[42]

In both the 1782 and 1813 Acts, the student did not have to possess the M.A. degree, but a certificate stating the nature of his studies in a course of philosophy (arts) was sufficient for a presbytery. The 1782 Act stated actual attendance at the divinity hall was to be for four years, if the student gave "close attendance", or if this was not possible, for six years, along with the

---

[37] A. L. Brown and Michael Moss, *The University of Glasgow: 1451-1996* (Edinburgh, 1996), 17-18.
[38] *AGACS*, March 27, 1704, 328; *AGACS*, May 25, 1736, 641-642.
[39] *AGACS*, March 27, 1704, 328.
[40] *AGACS*, Jan. 4, 1696, 254.
[41] *AGACS*, May 30, 1782, 813; *AGACS*, May 31, 1813, 937.
[42] *AGACS*, May 30, 1782, 813. *AGACS*, May 31, 1813, 936-937.

delivery of the usual number of discourses. Likewise, the 1813 Act maintained six sessions, but went on to qualify this by saying that if a student did three sessions at "regular attendance", then he could be considered complete in four sessions. If a student only attended two sessions in regular attendance, "his course shall be considered complete in five sessions".

The 1813 Act gave further details than that of 1782 Act by stating what students were to deliver in the divinity hall during the several sessions:

1.) an exegesis in Latin on a Divinity Controversy
2.) a homily in English
3.) a lecture on some large portion of Scripture
4.) a popular sermon
5.) "together with such other exercises as the professors shall think proper to prescribe"[43]

Concerning age requirements, the 1782 Act, which became the Standing Law of the Church, stipulated that for a student to undergo presbytery trials for licensure, he had to be twenty-one years of age.[44] As we shall see, this stipulation was on occasion over-ruled by the presbyteries. The 1813 Act also stipulated that the candidate had to be twenty-one years old before taking his trials.

In order for the trial to proceed, several procedures were to be followed. A certificate had to be presented to the presbytery from the professor or professors of divinity under whom the candidate had studied stating that he had prosecuted his studies, delivered the necessary discourses, and that "his conduct, as far as it consists with the knowledge of the said Professor or Professors, been in every respect suitable to his views in life".[45] This latter point in the 1782 Act was worded to read "his testimonials shall certify his proficiency in his studies and in his moral character".[46] Since divinity diplomas were not issued, the professors' certificates served as a testimonial of the studies attended and as verification that the discourses had been delivered and that knowledge and morality were held together.

It is interesting to note that the 1813 Act stated that the presbytery was to first examine a student "strictly and privately in Greek, Latin, philosophy and theology", yet nothing was stated concerning Hebrew in this pre-trial examination.[47] This private examination was to be held before the public trials and, if positive, due notice was given to every presbytery within the bounds of the provincial synod. Thus we learn that the synod had a function in the trials of

---

[43] *AGACS*, May 31, 1813, 935.
[44] *AGACS*, May 30, 1782, 812.
[45] *AGACS*, May 31, 1813, 935.
[46] *AGACS*, May 30, 1782, 812.
[47] *AGACS*, May 31, 1813, 936.

a student for the ministry. The synod meeting provided an opportunity for other presbyteries to make objections against a student having public trials. Hence, it rested with the synod to grant authorization to the presbytery to proceed with the public trials of its students.[48] The most noteworthy acts were 1742, 1782 and 1813, and all three held to this principle of synod ratification before a presbytery proceeded to the public trials of a student.[49]

Once authorization had been given to a presbytery to proceed with the public trials of a student, the 1813 Act stipulated which trials were to be conducted:

> 1st, Catechetic trials on Divinity, Chronology, and Church History; 2nd, A trial on the Hebrew and Greek languages; 3rd, An exegesis in Latin, on some controverted head in Divinity; 4th, A Homily in English; 5th, An exercise and addition; 6th, A lecture on some large portion of Scripture; 7th, A popular sermon; it being understood, that if the Presbytery see cause they may examine the student upon the subject of these several discourses.[50]

One final item of the official acts of the General Assembly during Period V concerns the work of evangelism in the Highlands. We have noted the efforts to provide presbytery and parochial libraries, but there were other measures undertaken for the Highlands which affected the divinity students. The most obvious of these was the sending of probationers into the North. All eighteen probationers sent in 1700 were "to be sent on the same terms and conditions, and with the same encouragements, that the twenty probationers were sent by the last Assembly".[51] This "sending" can be interpreted as travelling north to preach there for three or four months commencing March 1st. It would appear that this was one of the few incidents of extended student ministry, other than what may have occurred amongst presbyteries in the Lowlands, where students were used for pulpit supply. The only other form of placement ministry was by more private arrangement or by presbytery consent, and that was when the divinity students served as schoolmasters and/or clerks of session.

Memoirs and Autobiographical Sketches

We now turn our attention from the role of the General Assembly in this period to records of the training of some of the leaders of the time. The leading evangelical divine of the Church of Scotland in Period V was certainly Thomas Boston, some of whose writings continue to be popularly reprinted 250 years

---

[48] *AGACS*, May 31, 1813, 936.
[49] *AGACS*, (1742), 666; (1782), 813; (1813), 936.
[50] *AGACS*, May 31, 1813, 937.
[51] *AGACS*, Feb. 19, 1700, 299. See also 286 concerning the twenty sent in 1799 to the North, including to Orkney.

after his death.[52] (Ebenezer and Ralph Erskine have purposely been omitted here; sketches of them will be given in Part Two of this thesis.)

Thomas Boston matriculated at the University of Edinburgh in January of 1692 at the age of sixteen. He was passed into the second year class after being examined in Greek. His graduation occurred in July, 1694, making for a three year M.A. course.[53] In the autumn of 1694 he began the private study of divinity by reading Pareus' compiled commentary of Ursinus' notes on the Heidelberg Catechism, *Explicationum catecheticarum* (1594).

Boston's higher education illustrates much of what was common in Period V. His arts course at Edinburgh was under Herbert Kennedy, a regent. Edinburgh, like Glasgow, did not abandon regenting until the beginning of the eighteenth century, and therefore Boston studied arts under the old regenting system. He only attended one divinity session[54], and this was for three months in 1695, during which time the divinity professor was George Campbell and the professor of Hebrew was Alexander Rule. Campbell used Leonard van Ryssen's *Compendium Theologiae*[55] and Andrew Essenius' *Compendium Theologiae Dogmatieum* as the theology texts, both orthodox Dutch Calvinistic authors.

Following this time, Boston's studies were directed by the Presbytery of Stirling, then by the United Presbyteries of Duns and Chirnside. Boston became a private tutor and a family chaplain; while serving as the latter he led family worship, catechized the servants and encouraged prayer. He wrote that while he tutored at Kenneth Clackmannan, "I gave myself to my study, [and] kept correspondence with the neighbouring ministers."

In 1697 at the age of twenty-one Boston was licensed, having sustained his trials by doing the following: two Scripture discourses upon assigned texts for the presbytery (some presbyteries made written critiques); additional assigned texts for English homilies; a Latin common-place, with addition; a Latin chronology discourse; an exercise and addition on Psalm 18:25-29; language

---

[52] See Thomas Boston, *The Art of Man-Fishing* (Fearn, Ross-shire, 1998); *Human Nature in its Fourfold State* (Edinburgh, 1720); *Memoirs of Thomas Boston*, new edition, ed. George Morrison, 1899 (Edinburgh, 1988); *The Complete Works of Thomas Boston*, ed. Samuel McMillan, 12 vols., original 1853 (Wheaton, Illinois, 1980).

[53] Philip Graham Ryken, *Thomas Boston as Preacher of the Fourfold State*, Rutherford Studies in Historical Theology (Carlisle/Edinburgh, 1999), 2, provides some biographical data on Boston, but also more fully analyses his preaching and gives excellent bibliographies.

[54] Thomas Boston, *A General Account of My Life*, ed. George Low (London, 1907), xix, 21.

[55] Also spelled Riissen. He had studied at Utrecht, and though he received his doctorate from Utrecht, he remained a pastor. The text which Campbell used was based upon Francis Turretin's *Instititio theologiae elencticae*. It was Ryssen's most famous work and was also entitled *Summa theologiae*. See Richard A. Muller, *Post-Reformation Reformed Dogmatics Volume I Prolegomena to Theology* (Grand Rapids, 1987), 49.

exams; and "catecheticks". His theology studies lasted three years up to his licensure on June 15th, 1697, after which he spent the next two years as a probationer before being settled at Simprin.[56]

It would appear that Boston did not know Hebrew, or virtually none, at his licensure. It was at Simprin that he made progress in Hebrew, and in 1718, thirteen years after his licensure trials, he came to possess a Hebrew Bible.[57]

Such a case study of Boston illustrates the impact Assembly Acts at the early stages of Period V. Actual attendance in Hebrew classes was inconsistent, and how much teaching and examination of Hebrew took place was certainly subject to variety. We conclude that presbytery retained the right to oversee theological education and training as it saw fit within Assembly rulings.

A contemporary of Boston's at the beginning of Period V, also well known and who continues to be read, was Thomas Halyburton. He lived for a time in Rotterdam and was schooled there, where he learned Latin in Erasmus' school.[58] Upon returning to Scotland, he continued at school before going to St. Andrews University, where he graduated M.A. in 1696. It is asserted that Halyburton greatly excelled in his studies there, rising above his fellow students. After the M.A. he became a chaplain for a noble family, and it was during this time that he became embroiled in a dispute with a friend about Deism. The result was that he read widely on this subject and came to write against the Deists. While working for this family he was able to attend the divinity lectures at St. Mary's College; the result was that he "read divinity only two years". This means that he only attended two sessions in the divinity hall of St. Mary's College. The Presbytery of Kirkcaldy desired him to undergo his licensure trials despite his having only taken two formal sessions of divinity. Halyburton himself wrote that he was approached sometime in April or May, 1698, by the presbytery and believed he was not ready for trials:

> I had not read extensively, wanted the languages, and had been diverted from study by the foregoing exercise [Deist controversy], which had filled my thoughts for nearly a year and a half; and it was not then two years since I came from the college. In a word, I answered, 'I am a child, and cannot speak'.[59]

The presbytery assigned John 1:12 for his first discourse, but Halyburton was reluctant to take it up. Further solicitations were exchanged and, following a homily in the college (Job 28:28 on Feb. 28, 1699), he then consented to the trials and thus began them on April 20, 1699. He commenced with a discourse on a "common head", then a sermon on Psalm 119:9, then "the exercise and

---

[56] Boston, *A General Account of My Life*, 25-26, 27-35, 87.
[57] Boston, *A General Account of My Life*, xxxix.
[58] *The Works of the Rev. Thomas Halyburton*, ed. Robert Burns (Glasgow, 1837), 677-678. See also *Memoirs of the Rev. Thomas Halyburton*, ed. Joel R. Beeke, (Grand Rapids, 1996). This latest edition attests to the abiding interest in Halyburton.
[59] *The Works of the Rev. Thomas Halyburton*, 758.

addition, which I delivered before the synod", followed by another presbytery "popular sermon" on Romans 8:36. One more popular sermon was preached on Psalm 73:24. Halyburton wrote he "...was licensed after I had gone through the usual trials". The date was June 22, 1699. His ordination trial followed, and Halyburton recorded this experience with good detail:

> Upon accepting the call to Ceres, the first discourse was upon the common head 'De Comminicatione Idiomatum', on February 13, at Cupar, and my exercise and addition, on Galations iii,9, March 19; and April 16, I delivered my popular sermon on Revelation i,6, and underwent the other parts of my private trials; and last, on May 1, 1700, was ordained at Ceres.[60]

When the public discourses at Halyburton's licensure and ordination are added up, they total nine public discourses, plus "the usual trials" and "private trials". We notice that one year he did not attend the divinity lectures, although he returned to the college to deliver a discourse. This appears to have been a common occurrence in the eighteenth century, as we will see in a quotation from Professor Campbell.

Turning to the middle of the eighteenth century, a sample case study can be found with Thomas Somerville. Somerville attended the University of Edinburgh from 1756 to 1759, entering at the age of fifteen. He studied arts in what appears to be the "full course of philosophy" – Latin, Greek, logic, mathematics, moral philosophy and natural philosophy. Some of the lectures were still conducted in Latin for these courses in Edinburgh during the 1750s. Not all arts students started with Latin, but he estimated that over half of the first year students began with Greek and logic, the result being that "some of them were extremely deficient in classical learning".[61]

Somerville attended the arts course at Edinburgh for three sessions and in the last year of arts was enrolled as a student of divinity "by special favour".[62] Mechie concludes that this arrangement gave Somerville one of his required sessions in divinity which normally was to occur after the completion of the arts course.

Somerville finished his record of this phase of his life with a personal glimpse into the divinity hall at Edinburgh and student attendance. Concerning Hebrew, taught by Professor Robertson, he tells us that "when I was a student of Divinity Hebrew was a little cultivated, or altogether omitted, by the greater number of the theological students".[63] And Church history during Somerville's student days did not fair much better:

---

[60] *The Works of the Rev. Thomas Halyburton*, 760.
[61] Thomas Somerville, *My Own Life and Times 1741-1814* (Edinburgh, 1861), 11-12.
[62] Mechie, "Education for the Ministry in Scotland Since the Reformation", 1:125. There is no record that Somerville took the M.A. degree at Edinburgh. See, *Catalogue of the Edinburgh Graduates*, 330.
[63] Somerville, *My Own Life and Times*, 18.

Dr. Cuming, Regius Professor of Divinity, as required by the terms of his appointment, delivered a lecture once a week, during four months of the session, on Church History. Attendance at this class not being an indispensable qualification for probationary trials, few of the divinity students attended. The lectures were composed in Latin; but after the first, the professor began every prelection by recapitulating the preceding one in English. This practice seemed to imply a concession to the opinion I have stated with regard to the preference due to the use of the vernacular language in academical teaching.[64]

Professor Cuming was also the minister of the Collegiate Church and it would appear his time spent with students was not of a significant nature. Since the principal, though a professor of divinity, was not lecturing, it fell upon the one professor of divinity, Robert Hamilton, to conduct the majority of lecturing in the Edinburgh Divinity Hall and to interact with the divinity students.

Professor Hamilton, who held this post for thirty-three years, (1754-1787), delivered theological lectures on Benedict Pictet's *Theologia Christiana* [65] as often as four times on week days during sessions, plus a weekly lecture on Biblical criticism. Somerville believed that it took Hamilton five or six sessions to go through Pictet's *Theologia Christiana*. He lectured on Pictet in English, though the text used was the Latin. On Saturdays Professor Hamilton heard the students deliver their exercises, ending with his remarks and critiques of each discourse.[66] Hamilton was clearly the centre of the Edinburgh Divinity Hall during Somerville's student days there and for several years afterwards. Professor Hamilton's assistant from 1779 to 1787 was Professor Andrew Hunter, whom Somerville did not have as a professor. However, in comparing Somerville's description of Hamilton's work as a professor with that of Hunter, there are very few differences. Both professors used Pictet's *Theologia Christiana* as their textbook, and Hunter delivered up to three lectures each week "on the system" and conducted student examinations on Thursdays, thus making for a maximum of four times per week on systematics (although sometimes examinations were held twice a week), plus a critical exegetical lecture on Mondays or "fortnightly".[67] Hunter's pattern was virtually the same as that of Hamilton, which means this was the accepted pattern at Edinburgh in the divinity hall from 1754 to 1809. In fact, we can go back a generation before both men to Professor Gowdie, who also used Pictet. Therefore, we can chart

---

[64] Somerville, *My Own Life and Times*, 18-19.

[65] Benedict Pictet, known for his high orthodox Calvinist theology, was a pastor in Geneva, professor of theology at the Geneva Academy and a hymn writer. His texts were highly popular in Scotland. See Muller, *Post-Reformation Reformed Dogmatics*, 1:48, and *ERF*, 278.

[66] Somerville, *My Own Life and Times*, 17-18.

[67] Wright, "Andrew Hunter of Barjarg", 144. This information comes from A. Bower, *The History of the University of Edinburgh*, vol. 3 (Edinburgh, 1830), 207.

from 1733 to 1809 at Edinburgh a virtual succession and unity of teaching.[68] Gowdie was a Moderate who had caste the deciding vote removing the Secession brethren in 1734. Hunter was an Evangelical, or at least "an evangelical moderate", yet the teaching method varied little in the eighty years.[69] Though there were chairs in Church history and Hebrew, their impact was minimal. James Robertson, the professor of Hebrew, also served as the university librarian, not just for divinity but for the whole university.[70]

It appears from Somerville's personal account that his formal studies were supplemented in divinity by way of private reading, of which he wrote:

> In the course of my reading, I do not think that any of the books that treat of the evidences of natural and revealed religion were omitted. Of all such works, however, I consider myself to have profited most by Butler's *Analogy*...[71]

Two other things must be mentioned as preparing Somerville for Christian ministry during his time at the divinity hall. The first is his involvement in the Theological Society, which he attended from 1759 to 1764 (Somerville was not ordained until 1766). Writing of the society he says, "[it] was not only a school of mental improvement, but a nursery of brotherly love and kind affections...." He went on to describe the lasting ministerial friendships which arose out of this Theological Society, and he attributed activities in this society as providing improvement in reading, composition and correct expression. However, the one negative was the time spent in the tavern after the society meetings which should have been more temperate.[72] The documentation of the influence of such a society upon a divinity student is somewhat difficult to access, yet it must not be ignored.

Another influence on Somerville's theological studies in Edinburgh concerned his acquaintance with the leading preachers of the city, whom, it appears, he made a point of going to hear preach. Somerville's book reads at this point like a "who's who" of the Edinburgh pulpits of his divinity days, including mention of his visit to hear George Whitefield. It appears that Somerville listened intently to each preacher in order to study his communication skills, and he was not always in agreement with the more evangelical preachers.[73] Again, it is difficult to access the influence of such

---

[68] Alexander Carlyle, *The Autobiography of Dr. Alexander Carlyle of Inveresk 1722-1805*, ed. J. H. Burton (London/Edinburgh, 1910), 63. Carlyle described Gowie as "dull and Dutch". See Wright, "Andrew Hunter of Barjarg", 149. Wright's article has "Professor Goldie", but it should be Gowdie.
[69] *DNB*, 373; *FES*, 7:.382.
[70] See Appendix A.
[71] Somerville, *My Own Life and Times*, 36-37.
[72] Somerville, *My Own Life and Times*, 39-40, 42-45.
[73] Somerville, *My Own Life and Times*, 37, 57-74.

listening, but many have mentioned that the proper teaching of homiletics requires the hearing of good preaching.[74]

In the eighteenth century we see that divinity hall assignments consisted mainly in presenting student discourses. There can be many positive points made about this method, as writers on theological education in the twentieth century have noted.[75] However, it does appear that something which was designed for good became abused in Period V. Principal George Campbell had worked at both King's and Marischal and had reservations and major criticisms of these discourses and of student attendance at lectures:

> That their attendance was only to give, not to receive instruction, and that it would be just as beneficial to them if they had sent their discourses by post, and gotten somebody to read it in the Hall.[76]

One last brief sketch of a student's trials for licensure will now be noted before we turn to our next point. In an article by Jane B. Fagg on Adam Fergusson's ministry from 1700 to 1754, we see several significant details about student trials. Adam Fergusson was the father of the Adam Fergusson who became professor of moral philosophy at the University of Edinburgh in 1759. Fergusson senior studied at St. Leonard's College, St. Andrews and graduated with the M. A. degree in 1693 at the age of twenty-one. Following this he taught school and then became a tutor in Dumfriesshire. In 1700 he underwent his trials in hopes of filling a Gaelic-speaking parish. In June of 1700 he was assigned a homily on Matthew 28 and an exegesis on the Pope as Anti-Christ. Passing both of these in July of 1700, he was assigned his presbytery examinations in Hebrew and Greek and other assignments that same month. He was quickly licensed "temporarily" because "the Presbytery believed it was imperative to send a Gaelic-speaker to Crathie and Braemar". The presbytery sent him to preach for two Sundays at these churches, and then he continued with the following trials: an addition on John 3:16, a sermon, a thesis on the "cult of images" and a popular sermon on John 2:1. Having satisfied the Presbytery of Kincardine O'Neil, he was ordained at Crathie on September 25, 1700.[77] Overall, it appears that the presbytery took the student trials seriously with Fergusson. The anti-Roman Catholic emphasis is obvious and reflects the situation which the Presbytery of Kincardine O'Neil was facing locally; that is, parishioners were being converted to Catholicism under Father Forsyth. *FES,* on the Presbytery of Kincardine O'Neil, states that Fergusson

---

[74] See, Martyn Lloyd-Jones, *Sermon on the Mount*, vol. 1 (Grand Rapids, 1959), vii - viii.
[75] Leith, *Crisis in the Church*, 108.
[76] Archibald Bruce, *Collected Works*, 7:243. Here Bruce is quoting from Campbell's *Lectures on Ecclesiastical History* but does not cite the volume or edition used.
[77] Jane B. Fagg, "'Complaints and Clamours': the ministry of Adam Fergusson, 1700-1754", *RSCHS* 25 (1995), 290-293; *FES*, 6:92; *FES*, 4:188.

was called to Crathie *Jure devoluto*. There is a very strong possibility that Fergusson did not complete the normal number of sessions in a divinity hall, if any. Hew Scott, in *FES*, credited Adam Fergusson with having been the original mover against Ebenezer Erskine after his famous synod sermon. Jane Fagg believes that Fergusson actually had a smaller role in that event than Scott assigned.[78]

University Changes in Period V

The most radical change for the M.A. students in the Scottish universities in Period V was the abandonment of the regenting system. This did not happen at once, but was fully effected in all the universities by 1800. Edinburgh was the first to abolish regenting in 1708. The credit for this must not be interpreted as a return to a Melvillian ideal, but rather was the result of Principal William Carstares and reflected his experience with the new Dutch universities. Carstares remodelled the Edinburgh College along the lines of the Dutch system of faculties and prepared the way for the University of Edinburgh to become a leader in the Enlightenment. While a student at Utrecht, Carstares studied divinity under Witsius and Hebrew under Leusden. He advocated that Glasgow College obtain professors of theology and philosophy from Holland "for good men are to be found there". Typical of this period at Edinburgh, students boarded with Carstares.[79]

Given in terms of Adam Smith's thought, the abandonment of the old regenting system exhibited the principle of the division of labour.[80] The result was that instead of four part-time professors (regents) of Greek, there was only one. Horn tells us that a consequence of this reorganization, along with the restructuring of the fields of philosophical study, was that students began to choose which classes they would attend, with the result that many in the first year of philosophy did not attend the Latin or Greek classes. This in part explains the rise in the number of students that Edinburgh attracted during the early eighteenth century, both from home and abroad.[81]

Several new chairs were established throughout the eighteenth century. These chairs were mainly in science, but since a separate science faculty was not created in the eighteenth century, they were linked with the existing faculties of arts or medicine. This helps to explain why the third year classes in natural philosophy were in arts, yet chairs in astronomy or agriculture were included under natural philosophy. The creation of new faculties out of arts did

---

[78] Fagg, "Adam Fergusson,1700-1754", 307; *FES*, 4:188.
[79] *DNB*, 5:9, 189-190; A. Ian Dunlop, *William Carstares and the Kirk by Law Established* (Edinburgh, 1967).
[80] Horn, *A Short History of the University of Edinburgh*, 40.
[81] Horn, *A Short History of the University of Edinburgh*, 41.

not arise until the nineteenth century and really belongs to our Period VI and beyond.[82]

After the abandonment of the regenting system at Edinburgh, there appears to have been some confusion as to exactly what was meant by graduating M.A. Since only arts and medicine gave degrees to students at the end of a course of instruction, it should have been easy to determine what this would mean. However, in both faculties graduation was the exception – so much so in arts that the faculty was never sure what the requirements were for an M.A. degree.[83] It was only in 1814 that a regular order of study was formally adopted for those who wanted to graduate M.A.

Therefore, the eighteenth century was a time of transition with new chairs and new courses. Obtaining a degree was not always the chief concern. One instance is known of a student attending classes for three years, leaving the University of Edinburgh, and diligently publishing. Since this showed "sufficient proofs of his learning", he was awarded the M.A. without any degree examination. The year was 1734. In the early nineteenth century some former students were being awarded honourary M.A.'s.[84] This is in the background to the 1820s, when the Royal Commission began its enquiry into university reform, and we see that change was imminent regarding academic regulations.

The arts course in the eighteenth century continued to reflect the influence of the Church. The moral philosophy professor was to give one weekly prelection on "the truth of the Christian religion", and this professor was to show the students anything contrary to the Scriptures or the Confession of Faith in any of the books used in class. A divinity student who held to heretical opinions could be removed from the university. If he repented, the student could return to study in any faculty except divinity.[85]

Several changes had occurred in the rules of conduct at Edinburgh University by the middle of the eighteenth century. Students were no longer required to speak to each other in Latin, corporal punishment was removed and classes were to start at eight o'clock rather than at seven o'clock. The use of Latin in lecturing was clearly diminishing, and after the mid-eighteenth century few arts professors retained it for lectures. The use of Latin was retained the longest in the Faculty of Medicine, until 1834, with a few medical theses still

---

[82] Horn, *A Short History of the University of Edinburgh*, 43.

[83] Horn, *A Short History of the University of Edinburgh*, 43.

[84] Horn, *A Short History of the University of Edinburgh*, 44.

[85] Horn, *A Short History of the University of Edinburgh*, 46; John Ross, *The Present State of the Edinburgh Divinity Hall* (Edinburgh, 1813), 34, 38, 41. Ross graduated M.A. from the University of Edinburgh and then entered the Edinburgh Divinity Hall but was expelled in 1812. He wrote this small book afterwards, and in it he is highly critical of student attendance, student discourses, etc., in the Edinburgh hall.

written in Latin.[86] An interesting question to pose here would be, "Why the change to lecturing in English?" We know that language was a theme in Scotland after the Union in 1707. Educated Scots would avoid "Scotticisms" in written prose, yet at the same time there was a defensiveness about the Scots language.[87] It would appear that the rise of "North Britain" sympathy was not related to the switch to English in the lecture halls in the Scottish universities. The answer to the question concerning the reason for the change does not appear to be directly related to the Enlightenment, nor the Union. At best these reasons would be indirect.

Divinity students did not pay class fees to attend lectures. This is important to note, even though it does not reveal a change in university policy. This explains in part why the divinity professors often sought additional employment as parish ministers or preachers. The salaries of divinity professors were meagre. Another source of income was to board students, which it appears virtually all professors did.[88]

Moving on to other Scottish universities, we see that many similar changes and developments occurred throughout the eighteenth century. Glasgow University in the opening years of the eighteenth century established several new chairs: Greek, humanity, oriental languages, medicine, law, ecclesiastical history, anatomy and botany. By 1727 the remaining regents were given their choice of chairs in logic and rhetoric, moral philosophy and natural philosophy. In the words of Brown and Moss: "The age of the professors had begun – literally so because they were almost the only teachers until the late nineteenth century."[89]

Likewise at Glasgow teaching changed from lectures in Latin to lectures in English. Adam Smith, the professor of logic in 1750 and then the professor of moral philosophy in 1751, lectured in English. Professor George Jardine, professor of logic in Glasgow from 1774 to 1827, wrote, "Nothing, certainly, can more retard the progress of science, and particularly of elegant literature, than the practice of teaching in a foreign language."[90]

Also, during the eighteenth century when teaching such things as astronomy (which had been taught in Glasgow since 1451), there was a change to teaching along the Newtonian lines; apparatus was important, as was experiment, for many subjects. Hence an observatory was built for the university in 1757. Throughout the eighteenth century and into the nineteenth, the other branches of science were adapting to these teaching methods in "experimental philosophy".

---

[86] Horn, *A Short History of the University of Edinburgh*, 47.
[87] Daiches, "Scottish Enlightenment", 16-17.
[88] Horn, *A Short History of the University of Edinburgh*, 60-61.
[89] Brown and Moss, *The University of Glasgow: 1451-1996*, 18-19.
[90] George Jardine, *Outlines of Philosophical Education*, 2d ed. (Glasgow, 1825), 21.

From 1774 the B.A. degree was awarded at Glasgow University to those who elected for it after passing examinations in Latin, Greek, logic and moral philosophy, a course of study embracing three years. If they stayed on longer to be examined in mathematics and natural philosophy, then they could take the M.A. degree. Thus, we see that some Church of Scotland ministers possessed a Glasgow B.A. before entering the divinity hall, rather than an M.A. degree.[91]

St. Andrews University was the next to move from the regenting system to having professors as we know them today. The break was clearly made in 1747, the year the two colleges of St. Salvator and St. Leonard were united. The masters of both colleges became professors at the union, whereby each was responsible for the teaching of a specialized branch of knowledge. Moves toward a "professorial system" had partially begun at St. Salvator's in 1724, when a "fixed" professor of natural philosophy was created and at St. Leonard's in 1727.[92] Both colleges were clearly moving towards "fixed" professorships before the 1747 union, and this was the standard afterwards.

Marischal College followed by completely abandoning the regenting system in 1753. The original charter of Marischal College had actually encouraged a "fixed professorial model", yet this had not won the day, nor had the efforts in 1733/1734 to abandon regenting. The Senate finally abandoned the regenting method because "of the thing itself" and of "the almost universal practice of other universities".[93] The first reason was likely for efficiency and better teaching of a subject, although the Senate did not spell this out. Also in 1753 curriculum changes were made and logic was moved from year one to year four, a change also made at King's College, but not at the other Scottish colleges. Professor Gerard was mainly responsible for this radical curriculum change.[94] Gerard argued that the reform took the university curriculum from basically a scholastic curriculum to a philosophic curriculum – "not of human phantasies and conceits, but of the reality of nature and truth of things. The only basis of Philosophy is now acknowledged to be an accurate and extensive history of nature, exhibiting an exact view of the various phenomena for which Philosophy is to account, and on which it is to found its reasoning."[95] Suderman offered his opinion that the reason Marischal College abandoned regenting in 1753 was rooted more in keeping with the adopting of an enlightened approach to education which was also Baconian.[96] This theory may have some merit.

---

[91] Brown and Moss, *The University of Glasgow: 1451-1996*, 28.
[92] Cant, *The University of St. Andrews: A Short History*, 3d ed. (St. Andrews, 1992), 108-109.
[93] Rait, *The Universities of Aberdeen*, 299-300.
[94] See A. Gerard, "A Plan of Education in the Marischal College and University of Aberdeen, with the Reasons of it" (Aberdeen, 1755).
[95] Rait, *The Universities of Aberdeen*, 301-302, quoting from Gerard, "A Plan of Education ...".
[96] Suderman, "Orthodoxy and Enlightenment: George Campbell", 32.

However, as stated above, the original charter envisioned something other than regenting (Marischal was founded in 1593 – see chapter three, Period II), and Andrew Melville had wanted to see specialized regenting almost two hundred years before the Scottish Enlightenment. Thus, Suderman's reasoning for the Enlightenment as the impetus for the change to specialized teaching has certain difficulties.

Likewise, we learn that at Marischal College the methods of learning science changed to a new curriculum which emphasized mathematical proficiency and the natural sciences.[97] An observatory was built in 1780, a symbol of the new change.[98] Should we, however, interpret this as Baconian or Newtonian?

Finally, King's College was the last of all the Scottish colleges to abandon the regenting system and did not do so until 1799. King's College Senate defended the regenting system, stating:

> Every Professor of Philosophy in this University is also a Tutor to those who study under him, has the whole Direction of their studies, the Training of their Minds, and the oversight of their Manners; and it seems to be generally agreed that it must be detrimental to a student to change his Tutor every session...[99]

Again, Suderman argued that King's resistance to abandoning regenting went beyond the quotation from the Senate. Regenting implied that knowledge remained constant and was thus best communicated by a single teacher. The Senate's reason does not seem to strongly articulate such as clear educational philosophy. Suderman went on to state that for Marischal to change from regenting was to adopt a philosophy of education "that reflected more enlightened pedagogical notions...".[100]

Yet, as has been stated above, King's did change the ordering of its curriculum, displacing logic to year four, but it remained opposed to a reform of regenting. It would appear that this was mainly due to Thomas Reid's influence as regent at King's from 1751 to 1764, before he went to Glasgow to be the professor of moral philosophy. Also, King's continued the College Table throughout Period V, when both Glasgow and Edinburgh had basically been forced to abandon it due to the increase of student enrolment. It would appear that the smaller colleges, like King's, Marischal and St. Andrews, retained these customs for their students longer than the larger two universities.[101]

---

[97] Suderman, "Orthodoxy and Enlightenment: George Campbell", 34.
[98] Rait, *The Universities of Aberdeen*, 304.
[99] Rait, *The Universities of Aberdeen*, 201, quoting from the Senate Rules of King's College, 1753.
[100] Suderman, "Orthodoxy and Enlightenment: George Campbell", 35.
[101] Rait, *The Universities of Aberdeen*, 203-206; Brown and Moss, *The University of Glasgow: 1451-1996*, 16.

In summary, the main changes which occurred at all the Scottish universities in Period V were: the move to use English in lecturing; the establishment of the professorial system; and the reform of the curriculum, in varying degrees, from medieval scholasticism to Newtonian science. The other matter which is perhaps somewhat harder to define is that during the eighteenth century the leading minds of the day encouraged the rise of Scottish Enlightenment thought in the universities. This was the apex of the "Scottish School" of Thomas Reid and Dugald Stewart. In certain respects it was a reaction against the skepticism of David Hume. It gave rise to a popular school of philosophy and certainly made an impact on arts and divinity students.[102] This was also the period of Adam Smith, author of *Wealth of Nations* and professor of moral philosophy.

How can the Scottish Enlightenment be summarized for our purposes as it relates to theological education? First, it can be said that in terms of much of its theological presuppositions, it was rational yet undogmatic. As Drummond and Bullock wrote of Francis Hutcheson (which could characterize much of the movement), "He was a humanist whose understanding of man's nature was dominated by the idea of benevolence rather than that of the fall."[103] Thus, the traditional Calvinism of man's depravity was "watered down", as was revelation, and in its place reason, nature and morality were exalted. The divinity halls within the Scottish universities do not exhibit such theological tenants when the writings of the professors are examined, but the old evangelical applications are noticeably absent. Attacks on extreme rationalists and sceptics were made. George Campbell of Marischal College, in his *A Dissertation on Miracles,* was perhaps the Church of Scotland's professor of divinity who challenged Hume the most directly. Hume had included in *Inquiry Concerning Human Understanding* a chapter on miracles in which he argued that there is no miracle which has been sufficiently attested.[104] We will treat Campbell separately momentarily.

One of the influential Scottish university professors of divinity during the Scottish Enlightenment was Principal William Wishart (Jr.) of the University of Edinburgh. John R. McIntosh wrote that Principal Wishart had "significant influences on the theology of later eighteenth century Scottish ministers as a result of his University teaching".[105] He was charged with heresy by the Presbytery of Edinburgh, but he was acquitted by the General Assembly in 1738. Supposedly, he introduced God as the "Universal Governor" to the

---

[102] See *The Glasgow Enlightenment*, eds. Hook and Sher, (East Linton, 1995).

[103] Andrew L. Drummond and James Bullock, *The Scottish Church 1688-1843: The Age of Moderates* (Edinburgh, 1973), 86.

[104] McGrath, *Christian Theology,* 360; Drummond and Bullock, *Scottish Church,* 95-100.

[105] John R. McIntosh, "Wishart, William", in *DSCHT*, 879.

Popular party.[106] It is but a short step between what Wishart was saying and the basic tenets of Scottish common-sense philosophy with its fundamental stress on intuitive beliefs of these matters being common sense. Thus it was not of the nature of Hume's scepticism. Thomas Reid, the professor of moral philosophy at Glasgow from 1764 until his death in 1796, is viewed as the great architect of common sense philosophy. He was never a divinity professor, nevertheless his influence in the Church of Scotland as a leading Moderate and educator cannot be ignored.[107] He was their chief critic of David Hume and, as John McIntosh has shown, the Enlightenment thought of Thomas Reid influenced more than the Moderate party. It also extended to the Evangelical party within the Church of Scotland. Reid's common sense realism was also highly influential on Princeton, being mediated there through the Scottish Evangelical, John Witherspoon.[108]

Despite the differences which are clearly seen between Moderate and Evangelical, we must recognize the matter of "shared attitudes", as Voges called it, between the two groups. These shared attitudes can be found in matters relating to the Scottish Enlightenment, in particular common sense philosophy, societies and clubs, and education. Voges specifically noted four points of common ground between Moderates and Evangelicals: "1. apologetics or, in the term used at the time, the 'evidences' for Christianity; 2. exegesis; 3. dogmatic theology as such; 4. views on politics and the relationship of church and state."[109] Voges brought out the fact that every Scottish student came under "the influence of the Common Sense school through his attendance at moral philosophy lectures. This could well be one of the reasons why after the turn of the century party differences became less and less important. Old style Moderatism was on the decline, whereas Evangelism took on certain features of the old Moderate school."[110]

Though the arts course was undergoing these changes, the divinity halls in the universities did not undergo such radical changes. The Church of Scotland continued to use the Scottish universities for their students during the rise of the

---

[106] John R. McIntosh, *Church and Theology in Enlightenment Scotland: The Popular Party, 1740-1800* (East Linton, East Lothian, 1998), 39.

[107] Frederick Copleston, *A History of Philosophy: Volume V Hobbes to Hume*, The Bellarmine Series 16 (London, 1964), 364-375. Reid saw in Hume the "*reductio ad absurdum* of scepticism".

[108] *ERF*, 316-317, 396. Also, Boyd S. Schlenther, "Scottish Influences, Especially Religious, in Colonial America", *RSCHS* 19 (1977), 144-145. Schlenther wrote that "Witherspoon's main philosophical concern was to show that the ideas of Enlightenment thought could be made fully compatible with his orthodox Calvinism."

[109] Friedhelm Voges, "Moderate and Evangelical Thinking in the later Eighteenth Century: Differences and Shared Attitudes", *RSCHS* 22 (1985), 147.

[110] Voges, "Moderate and Evangelical Thinking", 147-148. Voges in a footnote wrote: "In Cook [George Cook] and Moncrieff, both party leaders agree that there is now little difference between both sides", 147, n.15.

Leading Scottish Educationalists

One of the leading writers and thinkers on higher education during Period V was George Jardine, professor of logic and rhetoric at Glasgow. His *Outlines of Philosophical Education* appeared in two editions near the end of his teaching career, and he included comment on three departments: theology, law and medicine. A comment in the biography of Ralph Wardlaw, one of Jardine's students, speaks most accurately about Jardine's position: "His name does not stand among those who have enlarged the bounds or added to the resources of philosophy; but, as a master of the science and practice of education, he occupies a place of the highest distinction."[111]

We learn much about the arts course at Glasgow during Jardine's time and how it could benefit candidates for the ministry. It also reflects an age very different from the modern secular university. Jardine set a rigorous routine for the undergraduate student who belonged to the Church of Scotland and attended his logic class. On Monday he called for an abstract from such students who had attended the college chapel on Sunday. This abstract had to be from memory and without the aid of notes. A prize was given at the end of the session for the essay that was the best account of the sermon delivered. The minister who preached the sermon served as the judge. Jardine's philosophy behind this exercise was to develop the power of attention, reasoning and style.[112] Another practical exercise Jardine assigned to all logic students in order to develop their abilities in analysis and classification was for them to take a chapter from Proverbs from which they were to arrange the verses into topical headings.[113] (Much of Proverbs can be viewed as but a collection of various sayings or proverbs, and Jardine was having the students create order and forcing the student to develop mental organizational skills). Such pursuits were included in the undergraduate curriculum before studying divinity at Glasgow.

It is most helpful to read Jardine in order to gain insight into the philosophy of a Scottish Master's course during the second half of Period V. He drew a clear distinction between the universities in Scotland and those in England:

---

[111] William L. Alexander, *Memoirs of the Life and Writings of Ralph Wardlaw* (Edinburgh, 1856), 15-16. Wardlaw was in Jardine's logic class 1794-1795.
[112] Jardine, *Outlines of Philosophical Education*, 288-289.
[113] Jardine, *Outlines of Philosophical Education*, 303-305.

> In all our [British] colleges, a considerable part of the under-graduate course is devoted to the study of Greek and Latin but in those of Scotland, the attention is not exclusively confined to the learned languages, as in the Universities of the south. We do not, in this part of the kingdom, attach to classical learning that high and almost exclusive degree of importance which is ascribed to it elsewhere; thinking it of greater consequence to the students, to receive instructions in the elements of science, both mental and physical, than to acquire even the most accurate knowledge of the ancient tongues; of which all that is valuable may, it is thought, be obtained without so great a sacrifice of time and labour.[114]

> The business of the undergraduate course ought to comprehend, besides the learned languages, the elements of philosophy in all its branches, – of the science of mind, logic, ethics, geometry, and physics…. A teacher must not expect to carry his pupils, in the course of a few months, to the higher parts of those sciences, which it may, notwithstanding, be proper to put them in the way of studying for themselves. All that he can accomplish, in so short a period, is to open up the path which they are afterwards to pursue…[115]

Jardine also maintained that logic should be properly taught in the first years of the arts course, not waiting until the third or fourth years. This was in marked contrast to King's College, or Marischal College under Gerard's influence. Jardine was very certain on this point: "the anatomy of the mind must be studied before the mental powers can be thoroughly known or successfully exercised".[116]

Bearing these introductory points in mind, we turn to see what Jardine had to say about the professional department of theology. He was quite critical about the teaching of theology in the Scottish universities during his time as a professor. Jardine believed insufficient time was given to its teaching, poor attendance by students occurred, poor methods of teaching were practised and there was a need for stricter and more definite regulations. Expanding on the theme of attendance (the four year requirement, often extended to six due to two sessions being irregular), Jardine suggested these sessions needed stricter guidelines. Jardine believed that divinity students should not be allowed to have irregular attendance during the first two years, because this ought to be the time when the professor of theology gave careful instruction on theological method and the selection of theological books in his lectures on theology. A solid foundation in these first two regulars would then allow for more direction in private studies. Since divinity students often served as tutors in families or schoolmasters during their studies, they needed to be carefully prepared for reading theology. They did not have a lot of time, and thus proper guidance at

---

[114] Jardine, *Outlines of Philosophical Education*, 418.
[115] Jardine, *Outlines of Philosophical Education*, 421.
[116] Jardine, *Outlines of Philosophical Education*, 424.

the beginning could create a closer study while they were occupied as tutors and headmasters.[117]

Jardine was also very critical of the fact that no examinations occurred in the divinity halls, which must have meant no written examinations. The student discourses were unsatisfactory, and Jardine even suspected that some of these discourses were not of the student's own composition.[118]

On the matter of attendance, he stated that in many of the halls attendance at the lectures was entirely optional and many of the students were too young.[119] He also criticised the divinity professors for not taking enough time to teach properly since they only took one hour per day, during which time they had to hear student discourses, leaving little time remaining for lecturing. Jardine mentioned that one divinity professor in an unnamed college took twenty years to complete his course of lectures![120] Since there were no regulations, the bare minimum had been adopted by some of the students and the professors.

With his critique ended, Jardine then presented a positive model as to how a divinity hall should be organized and conducted in the Scottish universities. He turned to his colleague at Glasgow University, Dr. Stevenson MacGill, professor of divinity (from 1814 to 1840), who had restored and renewed the teaching of theology at Glasgow: "I shall do an essential service to the public in publishing the detail of his method of teaching, with which he has favoured me. His example, I hope, will be followed by other professors of divinity in Scotland."[121] Then followed an extensive quotation from the pen of Professor MacGill about his method, after which Jardine made comment (ten pages, both MacGill and Jardine).

Professor MacGill's plan was to divide the students into two classes: the Junior Class, which was all the first year divinity students, and the Senior Class or Division which included the second, third and fourth year students. The Junior Class can be summarized in six parts:

1.) The divinity professor gave a series of lectures on the proofs for natural and revealed religion; necessity of revelation; various proofs etc...; evidences for Mosaic and Christian dispensations; books of the Canons; nature of inspiration; advice on the manner of studying the Scriptures;
2.) Essays were assigned to be written during the session on the subjects of the lectures. The essays were handed in to the professor, who after a few days returned them;
3.) The students then read their essays in the class and observations were made particularly by the professor. The topics of the essays were

---

[117] Jardine, *Outlines of Philosophical Education*, 471-472.
[118] Jardine, *Outlines of Philosophical Education*, 472.
[119] Jardine, *Outlines of Philosophical Education*, 472.
[120] Jardine, *Outlines of Philosophical Education*, 473.
[121] Jardine, *Outlines of Philosophical Education*, 475.

assigned on the basis of their importance and by consideration of the errors students could encounter;

4.) Oral examinations of the lectures were conducted frequently and were often in the form of the students recapitulating the topics of the preceding lecture;

5.) During the last month of the first session, each student was required to deliver a sermon before the professor and fellow students on a prearranged subject. Remarks were made in public on each sermon; and,

6.) After delivering this sermon, the student met in private with the professor who "[gave] him such instruction and admonitions as circumstances may require."[122]

The Senior Division attended a course of lectures during their three sessions which when taken together formed one complete system. MacGill summarized this course of lectures for the three years as commencing with lectures on the duties of a student of theology, including the dangers, temptations, difficulties and causes to be expected. Next were lectures on the Bible, dealing with all matters which would aid in the critical study of the Scriptures. Following closely onto this were matters of biblical theology, taught by going through the scriptural dispensations. Also included were the principal "controversies". In summary, these three years of lectures "consist[ed] of a selection of all the principal subjects which [were] usually comprehended under the name of a system of divinity".[123]

MacGill subdivided the Senior Divisions into its three natural parts. He met Fridays with the second year students for the reading of essays, examinations on the lectures, and occasional instructions as needed. The third year students, in addition to attending the lectures stated above, met separately with the professor fortnightly. This fortnightly meeting was mainly for translating a chapter from the New Testament and to discuss customs, places and allusions in the chapter. Sometimes an Old Testament chapter was considered.

The fourth year students, in addition to attending the lectures, were preparing for their presbytery trials. Thus, they were expected to prepare for these and deliver the last of the discourses in the hall. They were also to open each of the classes with public prayer. Occasional oral examinations occurred on the common *loci* of theology during this fourth year.[124]

During the long summer recess between sessions, Professor MacGill assigned essays to be written and prizes were given according to their merit.

---

[122] Jardine, *Outlines of Philosophical Education*, 476-477. Much of this was later reprinted in Robert Burns' biography of MacGill, *Memoir of the Rev. Stevenson MacGill* (Edinburgh, 1842), 70-74.

[123] Jardine, *Outlines of Philosophical Education*, 477-478.

[124] Jardine, *Outlines of Philosophical Education*, 478-480.

Other essays were encouraged and likewise rewarded. Divinity students could read books in the divinity library and were charged a small fee that helped to purchase more books.[125]

Jardine then concluded his comments upon MacGill's method and manner of teaching in the Glasgow divinity hall by writing: "The method of teaching which has been so fully described, and which occupies at an average three hours each day, has, for some years, [MacGill started in 1814], been tried in this university, and found productive of the happiest effects. It has infused a spirit of activity, as well as of attention to the lectures, – an attention formally unknown here, or in any other Divinity Halls in Scotland...."[126]

Jardine went on to make a brief comparison of the Scottish divinity halls in the universities to the teaching of divinity for ministers at Oxford and Cambridge at the beginning of the nineteenth century.[127] The teaching of divinity for ordinands was acknowledged to be very inadequate at this time in England and a period of vast expansion of divinity halls was about to occur there, which is beyond our concern at this point.[128]

We have already noted Stevenson MacGill's name in Jardine's *Outlines of Philosophical Education*. He was a man of clear methods and opinions on the subject of theological education towards the close of Period V. MacGill spanned both Period V and Period VI and in many ways is the theological educator who led into the next period.

Some of the details surrounding MacGill's appointment in 1814 bear attention now. He was the successor to Professor Robert Findlay, who died in 1814 at the age of 93 years. Some questions have been raised about Findlay's effectiveness as a divinity professor in these latter years (he held the professorship from 1782 to 1814).[129] He held to certain practices in his professorship, such as never taking student fees, and maintained that theology should be taught without student payment. During this time both Church history and Hebrew chairs collected student fees. He also opposed pluralities of a theology professor, whereby a professor held a parish alongside his teaching responsibilities. This is noteworthy as Stevenson MacGill likewise believed this.[130]

---

[125] Jardine, *Outlines of Philosophical Education*, 480.
[126] Jardine, *Outlines of Philosophical Education*, 480.
[127] Jardine, *Outlines of Philosophical Education*, 485-489.
[128] The best treatment recently done on the rise of divinity halls in England in the nineteenth century is: Trevor Park, "Theological Education and Ministerial Training for the Ordained Ministry of the Church of England, 1800-1850" (unpublished Ph.D. thesis, Open University, 1990).
[129] Reid, *The Divinity Professors in the University of Glasgow*, 301. The study of divinity at Glasgow under MacGill represented a transition from the Moderate sterility to a time of renewal. Under Findlay attendance at classes had fallen, newspapers were openly read in class and there was virtually no discipline.
[130] Reid, *The Divinity Professors in the University of Glasgow*, 270-273.

MacGill was appointed to the Chair of Divinity in 1814 through the efforts of Professor George Jardine, who wrote, "I thought you better qualified than any others who were, or were likely to become candidates...."[131] The two other individuals who pressed for MacGill's appointment were Sir Henry Moncrieff Wellwood and Dr. Andrew Thomson, two prominent members of the Evangelical Party. Sir Henry Moncrieff Wellwood was chiefly engaged in this, and, in Burns' words, "at this time he was in the zenith of his influence and fame".[132] MacGill and Sir Henry were friends for years, going back to MacGill's days as tutor to the Henry Erskine family, and MacGill often consulted Sir Henry on public matters. Sir Henry wrote a long, well articulated letter to MacGill upon his nomination to the professorship at Glasgow. This letter was in accord with MacGill's thoughts and bears extensive quoting:

Tullibole, 22 Sept. 1814

My Dear Sir,

You are fully aware how much I must have been gratified by your election, every way so honourable to you, and, in my apprehension, so important to the best interests of religion in this country. The University have done honour to themselves, by their firmness and their unanimity; and to do then justice, even the politicians there, have for once preferred the interests of the college to their private views.

I can say little which can be useful to you in arranging your plan of teaching. The great object certainly is, to give the young men such a general view of the whole subject within a reasonable compass, as shall be sufficient to direct their studies, so as to render them most efficient and complete. My observations must be very general.

1. I think the business of the professor is rather to give the students an exact view of the opinions and arguments of other men, than to lay down dogmatically his own opinions; on each head of divinity to represent the substance of the opinions of Arians, Socinians, Arminians, Calvinists, etc., with the rise and progress of the controversies on the subject; mentioning at last, the doctrine asserted in the Confessions of different churches, and concluding with that laid down in the Articles of England and the Confession of Scotland.

2. I think that instead of a detailed or minuted discussion of any one subject, his real business is to give merely the outline of each head of divinity, and of each controversy; and to direct the students to the best selection of books on the subject, on different sides of the question, with such a view of each of them as can be given in a short compass.

3. I think the chief object of the Divinity Chair is to teach Christianity, and to prepare others for teaching it. It has therefore always appeared to me a deviation from the chief business of the professor, to spend a great proportion even of one session on the doctrine of Natural Religion, which should really belong to another class. Certainly there ought to be given an outline of that subject, chiefly with a

---

[131] Burns, *Memoirs of Stevenson MacGill*, 64.

[132] Burns, *Memoirs of Stevenson MacGill*, 65; *DSCHT*, 860, 819-820.

view to show, 1st. What the real foundations of Natural Religion are; and, 2nd. How inefficient Natural Religion has ever been, where there has been no positive revelation. Even on these points the field is so wide, that it would require both a clear apprehension of the subject, and a steady adherence to an original plan, to abridge it as it ought to be.

4. I think all minor points, and even minor controversies, are beneath the notice of a professor of divinity. He should, if possible, confine himself to the important subjects, and to the chief writers. He will of course be obliged sometimes to allude to even things of less consequence; but he at least should not spend his time on them, or treat them so as to give them a consequence in the eyes of the student which does not belong to them.

5. I think the arrangement of divinity lectures can have but three divisions, - the evidences, the doctrines, and the practical applications of Christianity; and that under these may be comprehended all the learning, and every controversy on the subject.

6. I think that though the professor should give no opinions in his lectures, he is bound to give such remarks on discourses as will show that he abides by the doctrines of the church, without severity or partiality of any kind – with no bigotry, and not catching at straws on purpose to find fault; but yet pointing out, in mild and inoffensive language, where the student might have expressed themselves more correctly.

7. I think much might be done by regular examinations on the lectures, and by prescribing essays on the history or substance of particular controversies. This of course would require a separate hour, which I presume might be easily found. For this first session, perhaps, before your lectures can be digested, you might examine every second day, even on the lecturing hour. It would be useful to the students to do so, and a relief at present to yourself; though you take afterwards a separate hour.

Above all, have confidence in the effects of industry; and never despair, though you find yourself behind occasionally, nor attempt to do more than your health will admit of.

When are you to be admitted? Have you prepared your introductory discourse? Let me hear how your preparation goes on.

Ever your, my dear Sir,
    Most sincerely and affectionally,
        H. Moncrieff Wellwood[133]

Burns provided an insightful commentary about Sir Henry's line "giving no opinions". By this he meant that a Scots professor of divinity was not at liberty to do what many of the German professors did, to throw out their own opinions and show contempt towards the standards they had pledged to maintain. However, a Scots professor was "bound to teach the theology of his church".[134] Though fresh illustration could be used, the professor was to "lay a restraint on

---

[133] Burns, *Memoirs of Stevenson MacGill*, 66-69.
[134] Burns, *Memoirs of Stevenson MacGill*, 69.

fancy, and check the exuberance of airy speculation".[135] Sir Henry's point that "the chief object of the Divinity Chair [was] to teach Christianity, and prepare others for teaching it" is a point which accords well with John Leith writing today critiquing modern Presbyterian seminaries in America.[136]

Of MacGill's method, it appears that he excelled as a critic on the discourses of the students. "In this department he stood pre-eminent." He had a wonderful ability here to be accurate and impartial, and he could listen to five or six discourses at a time, yet could give careful assessments on each one. It was MacGill's private meetings with students which increased his fame amongst them. It would appear that he had these private meetings over breakfast. Reading through student testimonials of these meetings, we find that MacGill was a professor who was able to provide keen analysis of discourses, compassion and evangelical fervour.[137] MacGill's influence in the rising Evangelical party in the Church of Scotland in the early nineteenth century has not received adequate acknowledgement.

Before leaving Professor MacGill, mention should be made of the occasional Saturday lectures which he gave to divinity students. They were mainly on biblical criticism and on composition or public speaking.[138] Another pursuit of MacGill, together with William MacGavin, was the erection of the John Knox monument in the Glasgow Necropolis in 1824. In fact, MacGill's portrait, housed at the University of Glasgow, has this Knox monument as the background.[139] He was also very involved in the S.S.P.C.R. (Scottish Society for Propagating the Christian Religion), the Clerical Literary Society,[140] and missions to Jews and Indians, not to mention his philanthropic endeavours locally in Glasgow. MacGill's influence was quite far ranging, and he certainly stands out as one of Glasgow's more influential divinity professors.

Pluralities

We have already noticed Professor Findlay's opposition to professors of divinity holding a parish. It was with Professor Stevenson MacGill that this issue was asserted most strongly at the end of Period V. Principal Brown of Marischal College shared Professor MacGill's opinion in this regard, although

---

[135] Burns, *Memoirs of Stevenson MacGill*, 69.
[136] Leith, *Crisis in the Church*, 40-43.
[137] Burns, *Memoirs of Stevenson MacGill*, 102-109.
[138] Stevenson MacGill, *Lectures on Rhetoric and Criticism* (Edinburgh, 1838). This is the substance of his Saturday divinity lectures.
[139] Burns, *Memoirs of Stevenson MacGill*, 292-294. "Near the base of the monument of John Knox, stands a cenotaph to William MacGavin, esq. Author of 'the Protestant', and that was the individual who, of all others, lent Dr. MacGill the most effective aid in the accomplishment of the undertaking."
[140] Anon. "Two Glasgow Society Minute Books", bk. 2, in "The Clerical Literary Society", *RSCHS* 5 (1935), 181-184.

MacGill went farther on this than Brown. It was not until 1817 that the General Assembly came to prohibit holding a professorship along with a country parish, but it remained acceptable if the parish was in the town.[141] This was a compromise act of General Assembly and was proposed by Principal George Hill. Hill, along with other Moderates, maintained "that the union of parish livings with university chairs was legal and that such pluralities strengthened ties between learning and religion".[142] On the one side, the issue does raise the nature of the connection between the university, particularly its divinity hall, and the church; yet in these debates it was more an issue of the likelihood of a Moderate elite dominating both church and university.[143] Not all Moderates held to such a perspective on pluralities. George Cook, Hill's nephew, "vigorously opposed pluralities and non-residence as detrimental to the Church and a violation of Reformation principles".[144] It is interesting to note that this followed shortly after Professor Alexander Murray's death in 1813. He had been professor of Hebrew at Edinburgh and the parish minister in Urr in Kirkcudbrightshire.[145] MacGill saw it as a fixed principle "that the pastoral office was sufficient of itself for one man, and that unions of offices always had a very pernicious effect on both sides".[146] Thus MacGill, along with others, kept overtures against pluralities before the Assembly throughout the early years of the nineteenth century. Brown and MacGill worked as "strategists" in this regard, supported and encouraged by Professor George Jardine.[147]

Likewise, MacGill opposed the presentation of Principal Duncan MacFarlane of Glasgow University to St. Mungo's Parish in 1823, which was upheld by the General Assembly in 1824. He went on to memorialize the Senate of Glasgow University. In his memorial he listed four reasons for his opposition to pluralities. The second reason is the most important. Here MacGill argued that to hold both offices was not for the best interests of religion and learning nor of the university. Both positions were very demanding, especially in a large parish.[148] Further, since the principal was primarius professor of theology, how would he have adequate time to lecture and spend time with students amidst a parish of 9,000 souls?[149]

---

[141] Reid, *The Divinity Professors in the University of Glasgow*, 302-303.
[142] Donald P. McCallum, "George Hill, D.D.: Moderate or Evangelical Erastian?" (unpublished M.A. thesis, University of Western Ontario, 1989), 107-108. Also, Drummond and Bulloch, *Scottish Church 1688-1843*, 154-156.
[143] See Stewart J. Brown, *Thomas Chalmers and the Godly Commonwealth in Scotland* (Oxford, 1982), 86.
[144] McCallum, "George Hill", 109.
[145] See Appendix A on the professors.
[146] Burns, *Memoirs of Stevenson MacGill*, 169.
[147] Burns, *Memoirs of Stevenson MacGill*, 172-176.
[148] Burns, *Memoirs of Stevenson MacGill*, 180.
[149] Burns, *Memoirs of Stevenson MacGill*, 216,219.

In 1823 and 1824 Thomas Chalmers and Stevenson MacGill were closely aligned in speaking out against pluralities, as evidenced by Chalmers 1823 speech to the Glasgow and Ayr Synod, prefaced by MacGill.[150] In Period VI, MacGill's views on the plurality issue became that of the Royal Commission.

On the Matter of Books

The reorganization of theological teaching at Glasgow after the Revolution Settlement was clearly in the hands of James Wodrow. He was "informally" professor from September, 1687, to February, 1692, and formally appointed on February 22, 1692, holding the position until 1722.[151] Wodrow provided a very exhaustive list of the theology books he was using with the students.

1.) The primary texts were:
   Marcus Friedrich Wendelin, *Minus Systema Theologiae* (1656)
   Paraeus, *Explicationum Catecheticarum* (1594)
   John Calvin, *Institutio* (1559)

2.) The next texts used were:
   Francis Turretin, *Institutio theologiae elencticae* (1679-1685)
   Antonius Waleus, [likely – *Loci communes* – (1643)]
   Samuel Maresius, *Collegium theoligicum*...(1645)
   plus works by Essenius, Altingius, Maccovius, the *Theses leidenses*, Polant Syntagma, etc.

3.) Then for private reading, students were directed to:
   Daniel Chamier of Montauban and Gisbert Voetius for the controversies on Papacy and Arminianism. Other works were by Bellarmine, Socinus, Arminius and Limborch.[152]

Wodrow made use of the above works, particularly those in category one, as he dealt with Wendelin on Friday's and then proceeded to hear the students report on their private reading. He used a five-day a week teaching schedule, except on presbytery weeks. Wodrow lectured in Latin but made abundant use of English in disputations. He wanted each student to master one systematic theology text before reading others. Wodrow came to see less success with

---

[150] Burns, *Memoirs of Stevenson MacGill*, 227. See also *Edinburgh Christian Instructor*, years 1824, 1825 and 1826, for articles on the plurality question of the time.

[151] Reid, *Divinity Professors in the University of Glasgow*, 184-186. The *University of Glasgow: History and Constitution 1977-1978*, xxii, is not very clear on this point but the next is: Robert Wodrow, *Life of James Wodrow* (Edinburgh, 1828), 81,86.

[152] Reid, *Divinity Professors in the University of Glasgow*, 187; Muller, *Post-Reformation Reformed Dogmatics*, 1:43-49.

lecturing and came to rely more heavily on offering "compends", or brief summaries, following which the discussion was focussed on the textbooks.

An interesting development at Glasgow under Wodrow was the dividing of the students into small societies for prayer and "practical cases". These small societies met weekly and made a record of their answers. Then once a month a joint meeting was held when all the answers were read and, when approved, inserted into a book. This book was deposited into the Glasgow Divinity Library as *Cases Answered by the Societies of the Students under Mr. James Wodrow together with A Comparative, Relative, and Synonimous Index*. The cases were on alms, fasting, calling to the ministry, etc., all combining piety and Scripture. From these societies Wodrow then selected eight or ten students whom he met with in his dwelling to discuss "abstruse and knotty subjects of divinity".[153]

Lastly, James Wodrow published a short work on homiletics, which is of value for studying the training of ministers at Glasgow during Wodrow's time. It is entitled *A Compend of the Treatise Methodus Homiletics, Being A Short Directory to Students of Theology for Making of and Criticising Upon Homilies, As Also for the Making of Popular Sermons, As They are Called Thereto*.[154]

An overview of the main theology textbooks used post-Wodrow in the Scottish universities reveals that there were two works which appear to have been predominate. These were Johannes Marck's *Compendium theologiae christianae* (1686) and Benedict Pictet's *Theologia Christiana* (1696). Further comment on their use will be made momentarily.

Professor John Simson, who was subsequently tried for heresy, used Marck, although his opponents accused him of not using Marck's terms in the way the author meant them to be used.[155] The use of a work viewed as orthodox and Calvinistic does not guarantee orthodoxy in the classroom, a point which Sir Henry Moncrieff Wellwood made.

William Leechman, the longstanding professor of divinity at Glasgow from 1743-1761, then principal from 1761-1785, used Pictet's shorter systematics as his textbook and in latter years changed to Ostervald.[156] As we have already noted, Somerville likewise was taught using Pictet while a student at Edinburgh

---

[153] Reid, *Divinity Professors in the University of Glasgow*, 188-189.

[154] See the appendix of R. Wodrow, *Life of James Wodrow*, 208-245, for the printed text. This is only part of a much larger work by J. Wodrow, *Methodus Studii Theologici – a Directory or Guide to Students in their Study of Theology, MS* in the Special Collections of the University of Glasgow.

[155] Lachman, *Marrow Controversy,* 187, referring to John McLaren.

[156] Reid, *Divinity Professors in the University of Glasgow,* 205, 255; Mechie, "Education for the Ministry in Scotland", 3:16. Drummond's comment that "at Glasgow Professor Leechman was popular with students because he avoided quoting Dutch divines" is a problematic statement since it must be asked, how different was Marck from Pictet? See Drummond, *The Kirk and the Continent*, 141.

Divinity Hall in the 1760s under Professor Hamilton. In the preceding generation (Boston's era), Professor George Campbell had used the two Dutch *Compendiums* by van Ryssen and Essenius. In the era after Somerville's student days at Edinburgh, Professor Andrew Hunter (1779-1809) was lecturing still from Pictet's *Theologia Christiana*.[157] Thus, throughout Period V the focus of the theological texts in the divinity halls was clearly with continental authors of the orthodox Calvinistic school. (For an excellent summary of Professor Hunter's lectures in theology, see David Wright's article "Andrew Hunter at Barjarg (1744-1809): Evangelical Divine in an Age of Improvement". Hunter's complete set of 118 lectures is available in manuscript form and would make for a worthwhile comparison to the Secession works by Brown of Haddington and to John Dick, not to mention the Kirk theologian George Hill.[158]) Hunter also continued the custom of giving an introductory lecture, which he delivered twenty-two times. The 118 lectures were based upon Pictet's *Theologia Christiana,* not Pictet's shorter *Medulla Theologiae.* Wright noted that he cited few other authors.[159]

Hunter published very little, and what he did publish was not a direct result of his work as a divinity professor. Wright summarized Hunter's writings as devotional in nature. Perhaps the most important work was his 1797 sermon preached to the Edinburgh Missionary Society – *Christ Drawing All Men Unto Him* – a work which enthusiastically supported worldwide missions.[160] The other material which concerns us more here is the manuscript lectures Hunter delivered on Romans, James and Ephesians. It would appear that he never delivered critical lectures on any other Scripture books except these three. These were delivered several times during his post as professor.[161]

A further note on William Leechman is in order at this point. Though he used Pictet for several years before switching to Ostervald, Leechman's commitment to Calvinistic orthodoxy must be questioned for several reasons. First, Ostervald has been viewed as a moderating Calvinist more in keeping with the transitional theology of Alphonse Turretin.[162] Second, though Leechman escaped the charge of heresy, there remain some question marks here. Third, and perhaps most to the point, was Leechman's relationship with John Taylor (1694-1761), the professor of divinity at the English Dissenting

---

[157] *DNB*, 28:284.

[158] Andrew Hunter, "Theological Lectures", *MS*, Edinburgh University Library, Dc. 3.22-7. See David F. Wright, "Andrew Hunter of Barjarg (1744-1809): Evangelical Divine in an Age of Improvement", *RSCHS* 26 (1996), 145. Wright also refers to a set of student dictates of Hunter's lectures for the year 1794-1795, 147.

[159] Wright, "Andrew Hunter of Barjarg", 146.

[160] Andrew Hunter, *Christ Drawing All Men unto Him* (Edinburgh, 1797).

[161] Wright, "Andrew Hunter of Barjarg", 144-145. These critical lectures also may be found in the Edinburgh University Library, Dc.3.30-32.

[162] Briggs, *History of the Study of Theology,* 2:164. Briggs at this point is correct; however, on the next page, 165, he is incorrect concerning Pictet.

Academy at Warrington. It was under Leechman's instigation that Glasgow University awarded the D.D. degree to Taylor in 1756. In 1759 Leechman travelled to Warrington to holiday with Taylor and, as has been written of these two men, they were two kindred souls".[163] Taylor was the author of *The Scripture-Doctrine of Original Sin*, a work which was widely read in the eighteenth century. It passed through four editions between 1738 and 1767, with one printing in Glasgow. This work reveals Taylor's theological drift into Arianism and Unitarianism.[164] He charged the Westminster Assembly of Divines with inheriting the doctrine of original sin from the Roman Catholic Church.[165] Several took up their pens against Taylor at this time, with the fullest work against Taylor being Jonathan Edwards' 1757 work, *The Great Christian Doctrine of Original Sin Defended; Evidences of its Truth Produced and Arguments to the Contrary Answered.*[166] It is no wonder that we find Taylor was immensely popular amongst many in Ireland (the non-subscribing Presbyterians) and the growing Unitarian movement in New England.

This raises many questions about William Leechman's theological classes. Were they very much the same as John Simson, and did he continue to teach as the Covenanters in Period III? The answers appear to be obvious. He was clearly a Moderate and is rightly ranked by Alexander Carlyle as such.[167] However, a curious fact is that Seceder students also attended his divinity lectures. It did not conflict with their own session in their hall and, if they were at the University of Glasgow for their final courses, it can be seen how they could attend. However, it is difficult to conceive of them as being Antiburghers. They were probably Burghers.[168]

The early part of Period V was a time when treatises were being written to defend the Presbyterian way, as opposed to the preceding Episcopal time. Gilbert Rule, who replaced Alexander Monro (who had been deposed as principal of Edinburgh University and an active promoter of Episcopacy), as the principal and primarius of divinity of Edinburgh, wrote *The Good Old Way Defended* (Edinburgh, 1697) and to expound the faith, *A Plain and Easy Explication of the...Shorter Catechism* (Edinburgh, 1697).[169] Rule's chief work to vindicate Presbyterianism was issued at the request of the General Assembly; *A Vindication of the Church of Scotland, being an answer to a Paper entitled,*

---

[163] McLachlan, *English Education Under the Test Acts...*, 31.

[164] *DNB*, 55:439-440. Taylor's views were described as "old deism in a new dress".

[165] John Taylor, *The Scripture-Doctrine of Original Sin* (London, 1746), 127-128.

[166] Edwards' works remain in print and the full text of this polemical work can be found in the following: Jonathan Edwards, "The Great Christian Doctrine of Original Sin Defended", in *The Works of Jonathan Edwards*, vol. 1, ed. Edward Hickman (Edinburgh, 1974), 143-233. An older edition is: Jonathan Edwards, *The Great Christian Doctrine of Original Sin...* (Glasgow, 1819), 15-16.

[167] Sher, *Church and University in the Scottish Enlightenment*, 161-162.

[168] Mechie, "Education for the Ministry in Scotland", 3:16.

[169] *DNB*, 49:393-394.

Some questions concerning Episcopal and Presbyterial Government in Scotland' (Edinburgh, 1691), and again that year, *Second Vindication of the Church of Scotland.* From his other works on this subject, it can be concluded that between 1690 and 1700 there was a raging controversy on church polity and that Gilbert Rule was one of those divinity writers at the centre of the controversy. No doubt this whole matter attracted the attention of the divinity students within each of the divinity halls.[170]

The beginning of the eighteenth century saw the Marrow controversy. The clearest writer in the divinity halls against this controversy was James Hadow. He wrote, *The Antinomianism of the Marrow of Modern Divinity Detected* (Edinburgh, 1722). Other theological works were against Simson and the Episcopalians.[171] The professors of divinity in Period V continued to write, and no doubt communicate to their students, on the religious controversies. These were on matters of church government, the nature of grace, the person of Christ and the rising scepticism.

If one wants to mine the writings of the principals and professors of divinity and examine their writings in Period V, there is no shortage of materials and the range is quite impressive. William Wishart (Sr.), principal of Edinburgh, produced a two volume *Theologia or Discourses of God* (Edinburgh, 1716), which has been compared to Charnock's *magnum opus* on this subject, if not relying upon it.[172]

Minor works on historical themes were produced, several of which were lectures in print form, but certainly not all. George Campbell's work *Lectures on Ecclesiastical History* (London, 1800) falls into the first category but William Robertson's *Histories of Scotland, America,* or *India* do not.

Several theological works which were popular for some time also came out of this period. Thomas Blackwell's three volumes, *Ratio Sacra* (Edinburgh, 1710), *Schema Sacrum* (Edinburgh, 1710), and *Methodus Evangelica* (London, 1712), were popular in Scotland and America for one hundred years and dealt with theological errors, a positive statement of divinity and homiletics. Principal George Hill's *Lectures in Divinity* (Edinburgh, 1821 – first edition as *Theological Institutes*, Edinburgh, 1803) was popular after this period; this is evidenced by Chalmers using it at New College, Dabney in the southern states of America, and McCulloch in Nova Scotia.[173] A. C. Cheyne has recently written concerning George Hill that he was "possibly the most distinguished theological teacher of the unreformed Establishment". Cheyne then goes on to

---

[170] Thomas Maxwell, "The Scotch Presbyterian Eloquence – A Post-Revolution Pamphlet", *RSCHS* 8 (1944), 225-253. This is a most helpful article to gain insights to the debates of 1690-1700.

[171] *DSCHT*, 384.

[172] *DSCHT*, 878.

[173] *DSCHT*, 408; Sefton, "St. Mary's College, St. Andrews, in the Eighteenth Century", 178; Thomas McCulloch, *Calvinism, the Doctrine of the Scriptures* (Glasgow, 1846).

discuss Hill's understanding of the different degrees of biblical inspiration. Hill had no difficulty in stating that there were various degrees. On this point Hill resembles Philip Doddridge, the English Dissenter.[174] (Hill will receive further comment separately in this chapter.) Typically one would expect to find eighteenth century theology professors publishing works in natural religion within the Scottish context. There was certainly an abundance of such material coming forth.[175]

It does not seem to have been a period when the professors were producing biblical commentaries. There are virtually none to be found. Several works on rhetoric or homiletics were produced and several on the pastoral office or piety.[176] It comes as no surprise that rhetoric was a popular pursuit, much more than biblical exegesis. The form of a sermon was most important. This can be said of both Moderates and Evangelicals in the eighteenth century. The emphasis was different in each, but often the form or stress on structure in a sermon (not a "lecture") was remarkably similar. Reference here could be made to the sermons by Hugh Blair of the High Church, Edinburgh, and professor of rhetoric in Edinburgh University. His preaching style reflected his *Lectures on Rhetoric*, and his sermons were "long considered models of style and taste".[177] Likewise, the Moderate preacher Alexander Carlyle (1722-1805) was not noted for biblical exegesis in the pulpit or gospel piety, but David Hume, it is said, once rebuked his preaching for that of one of "Cicero's Academics".[178] Thus, it is little wonder that within the Kirk halls we do not find large amounts of gospel-styled published sermons or lectures. This was not the emphasis from these Kirk professors of divinity as a whole in the eighteenth century, and their published writings reflect this.

---

[174] Cheyne, *Studies in Scottish Church History*, 125-127. Compare George Hill, *Lectures in Divinity*, original 1821 (Philadelphia, 1844), 154, with John Dick, *An Essay on the Inspiration of the Holy Scripture*, original 1800 (Edinburgh, 1840), x-xi, 236.

[175] See William Hamilton, *The Truth and Excellency of the Christian Religion* Edinburgh, 1732); William L. Brown, *Essays on the Existence of a Supreme Creator* (Aberdeen, 1816); Alexander Gerard, *Dissertations on Subjects Relating to the Genius and Evidences of Christianity* (Edinburgh, 1766); Thomas Halyburton, *Natural Religion Insufficient* (Edinburgh, 1714).

[176] George Campbell, *Philosophy of Rhetoric* (London, 1776); Alexander Gerard, *The Influence of the Pastoral Office* (Aberdeen, 1760); William Leechman, *The Temper, Character, and Duty of a Minister* (Glasgow, 1755); Stevenson MacGill, *Considerations Addressed to a Young Minister* (Glasgow, 1809).

[177] Edwin C. Dargan, *A History of Preaching*, vol. 2, original 1905 (Grand Rapids, 1970), 341.

[178] Dargan, *History of Preaching*, 2:339.

Principal George Campbell: Lectures, Books, Student Training and The Scottish Enlightenment

Perhaps within the Church of Scotland divinity halls in the eighteenth century the most prolific author was Professor George Campbell of Marischal College, Aberdeen (b.1717-d.1796).[179] By way of comparison for an approximately parallel time period, the most prolific of the Secession professors would have been John Brown of Haddington. Archibald Bruce, also a Secession professor, would have overlapped with most of Campbell's time as professor, but not to the same extent as Brown. Campbell's works were collected together and published as *The Works of George Campbell* in 1840, consisting of six volumes.[180] Several of the writings were actually published posthumously. Since there is no table of contents to these volumes, a brief contents list will provide a place to begin an assessment:

Vol. I	Dissertation on Miracles (134 pp.); Sermons; Addresses on the Alarms raised concerning toleration of Catholics.
Vol. II	Philosophy of Rhetoric (426 pp.)
Vol. III	Dissertation on the Gospels I (558 pp.)
Vol. IV	Dissertation on the Gospels II (562 pp.)
Vol. V	Ecclesiastical History (458 pp.) – 28 lectures
Vol. VI	Introductory Discourses to Systematic Theology – 4 lectures
	Of Systematic Theology – 6 lectures
	On Pulpit Eloquence – 12 lectures
	On Pastoral Character – 9 lectures

Several items from Campbell's *Works* had their origins as lectures to the students of divinity at Marischal; namely, those on ecclesiastical history, introductory discourses to systematic theology, systematic theology, pulpit eloquence and pastoral character.[181] Jeffrey Suderman's extensive research on George Campbell's lectures and writings is most helpful here and supports the above summary of what constituted Campbell's lectures to divinity students from within his *Works*.[182] It does not appear that the remainder of his *Works*

---

[179] See *DNB*, 8:357-358; J. Valentine, *An Aberdeen Principal of Last Century* (Aberdeen, 1856).

[180] George Campbell, *The Works of George Campbell*, 6 vols. (London, 1840).

[181] Campbell, *Works*, vols. 5 and 6.

[182] Jeffrey M. Suderman, "Orthodoxy and Enlightenment: George Campbell (1719-1796) And the Aberdeen Enlightenment" (unpublished Ph.D. thesis, University of Western Ontario, London, 1995), 404-408, 100-101. Suderman has examined student notebooks for the period 1786-1787 and then has found the student notes within Campbell's *Works*. Suderman here also includes the lectures of Alexander Gerard and concludes that most of these are to be found in Alexander Gerard's, *Pastoral Care*, ed. Gilbert Gerard (London/Aberdeen, 1799).

were directly given as lectures to the divinity students. Much of *Dissertation on Miracles* originated as sermons delivered in Aberdeen. Thus they were formally outside the college.

It is no doubt in part this work that brought Campbell to fame at this time as the opponent of David Hume.[183] In the eighteenth century, Christian apologetics centred around "two basic theistic proofs: the argument from miracle and prophecy, and the argument from design". Hume was attacking these touchstones, in particular the first, in his essay *Of Miracles*. Campbell's response was to become the chief Christian response in Scotland to Hume's philosophy of skepticism. Campbell's work here stresses "evidences", a word which will be encountered in both Moderate and Evangelical writing within the Kirk. It has affinities with several other titles: George Gerard's *Dissertations on Subjects relating to the Genius and Evidences of Christianity*, Sir Henry Moncrieff Wellwood's *Discourses on the Evidences of the Jewish and Christian Revelations,* and the two Gerard's (Alexander and Gilbert and edited by George) *A Compendious View of the Evidences of Natural and Revealed Religion.*[184] Even a Seceder such as John Brown of Haddington used language which reflected the enlightened world of the Scottish theologians in the title of his systematics, *A Compendious View of Natural and Revealed Religion.* Brown, of course, was careful to state the limits of reason; nonetheless, he too reflected the age and intellectual environment of Scotland in the eighteenth century. Hence Voges' conclusion is perceptive: "Perhaps it is now clearer that what Moderates and Evangelicals had in common outweighed the impact of their differences."[185] It would appear that both parties were united against the skepticism of a Hume but could work well with Common Sense Realism. I believe the difference between the two centres around piety, or personal religion, as stressed by the Evangelical party; and as the eighteenth century progressed, even this became blurred. Thus, it becomes difficult to use the labels of Moderate and Evangelical consistently in the eighteenth and in the first three decades of the nineteenth century.

We turn now to Campbell's *Philosophy of Rhetoric*, which would more properly be used within the arts curriculum. We find many scholars today saying that this was Campbell's greatest contribution and that he was the

---

[183] See Drummond and Bulloch, *The Scottish Church 1688-1843*, 99-100; McIntosh, *Church and Theology in Enlightenment Scotland*, 18. In Colin Brown's estimation, David Hume has been discussed more than any other British philosopher. Brown goes on to write about Hume that once he "...opened Pandora's box of skepticism in the interests of attacking religion and rival philosophies, Hume found that he could not close it. In the end, he had to fall back on 'nature' and make a virtue out of the necessities of his skepticism." Colin Brown, *Christianity and Western Thought: A History of Philosophers, Ideas and Movements*, vol. 1 (Leicester, 1990), 243.

[184] Voges, "Moderate and Evangelical Thinking", 148-149.

[185] Voges, "Moderate and Evangelical Thinking", 156.

leading eighteenth century philosopher of rhetoric.[186] Campbell does state that it is a subject which had employed his inquiry since 1750 and was read in part to a "private literary society".[187] Likewise, his *Dissertation on the Gospels* (over one thousand pages) does not appear to have originated in the divinity hall in the first instance. It began while Campbell was in a country parish, where he collected criticisms on the text of the New Testament while translating.[188] The work certainly displays a man acquainted with Greek, Latin, German, French, the Church Fathers and textual criticism. One can only conclude that some of this must have been conveyed to divinity students. He produced his own English translation of the four Gospels, including textual notes.

The remainder of Campbell's collected works constitute fifty-nine lectures which he gave within the divinity hall.[189] These serve as the largest collection of lectures of any divinity professor within the divinity halls of the Scottish universities in the mid to late eighteenth century. The subject matter compares closely with that of John Brown of Haddington, but the content generally is of a different kind. Unlike Brown, Campbell's lectures on ecclesiastical history do not direct the student through the vast corpus of ecclesiastical writers.[190] Brown stated that he had chiefly consulted Mosheim and then proceeded to direct the student or reader to the works in the various fields – a bibliography of eight pages.[191] Campbell's goal was "to lay a wide foundation, on which a goodly edifice may in time be erected, though I should make but little or no progress in raising the walls".[192] The two ecclesiastical history sets are also fundamentally different in that Campbell began his lectures with sacred history as a study in the history of the Old Testament. He commended students to read the Old Testament and indirectly suggested that they read Josephus in Greek and Prideaux's, *The Connexion of the Old Testament History with that of the New*. It is interesting that Campbell originally stated he was not going to be

---

[186] Wilbur Samuel Howell, *Eighteenth-Century British Logic and Rhetoric* (Princeton, 1971), 602.
[187] Campbell, *Works*, 2:iii-vi.
[188] Campbell, *Works*, 3:1.
[189] Campbell, *Works*, 5:i. Since the main body of these lectures was on ecclesiastical history, I quote from the prefatory "advertisement" to these: "The following discourses on Church History are a considerable part of a course of Theological Lectures delivered in Marischal College. The author had transcribed and revised them, and was every year making considerable alterations and additions to the Work. For more than the last twenty years of his life, his Lectures to the Students of Divinity occupied the greater part of his time, and those now offered to the Public were distinguished as the most curious and entertaining branch of the whole."
[190] Compare Campbell, *Works*, 5:6, with John Brown, *A General History of the Christian Church*, vol.1 (Edinburgh, 1771), v-xiii.
[191] Brown, *A General History of the Christian Church*, 1:v-viii.
[192] Campbell, *Works*, 5:7.

recommending works and then shortly thereafter was continually referring to books. In fact, we find such recommendations in each lecture![193] Since lecture one was on sacred history and the Old Testament was commended for reading, one would think this would be where the history would continue in lecture two. Instead, he turned to the question of the history of the sacred canon and then spent several lectures on church government in the early Church (ten lectures of about two hundred pages). His conclusion was that there is not one form of church government by divine right:

> The notion, that it was the intention of the apostles that the particular mould which they gave the church should be held inviolable; or that it was their doctrine, that the continuance of the same mould is essential to the being of the church, appears to me not indeed problematical, but utterly incredible.[194]

Finally, in lecture fourteen he began to examine the doctrinal controversies of the early Church. In lecture fifteen he returned again to church government, this time on the Roman hierarchy, and continued this for several more lectures. He wrote in lecture eighteen:

> In my preceding lecture on the rise and progress of the papacy, I have been more particular, and treated things more in detail, than I had first intended. But on so complex a subject, to which so great a variety of different, and even dissimilar circumstances contributed, it is not so easy to consult at once brevity and perspicuity...[195]

Several more lectures dealt with the papacy and empire through to the medieval period. In lecture twenty-eight Luther received a few pages and the Reformed about three pages to conclude the *Ecclesiastical History*.[196]

In summary, if these church history lectures were "a considerable part of a course" for church history at Marischal College, one concludes that the students were subjected to Campbell's own "hobby-horses", and they quite possibly would have never managed to complete a survey of church history. They certainly would have heard his interpretation on the history of church government. Campbell's history is an utter contrast to Brown's, which is very much a survey of historical theology written as a chronology. This is no doubt reflective of the fact that students were required to give a chronological discourse on a period in church history at their trials. Campbell's history would have made it more difficult for the student to prepare for his trials and would have demanded much additional study by the student. Suderman is definitely

---

[193] Campbell, *Works*, 5:10, 13, 17, 19, 20, 47, 51, etc.
[194] Campbell, *Works*, 5:141.
[195] Campbell, *Works*, 5:300.
[196] Campbell, *Works*, 5:433-446.

correct that Campbell was latitudinarian on church government and essentially these

> are less a narrative history of the church than a series of topical arguments designed to illustrate certain historical tendencies in the development of the church, particularly the growth and domination of the hierarchical form of ecclesiastical government.[197]

Concerning Campbell's other divinity lectures available to us, we know they were first delivered in 1772 and 1773, and subsequently he "read them to the students, as they had been at first composed".[198] They reveal a professor who urged his students to stay away from religious controversies, contending that they were of an abstract and exhausting nature. Also, Campbell delivered all of his lectures to the divinity students in English, not Latin.[199] In his "Introductory Discourses" to theology, he laid out the four fields for the students: biblical criticism, sacred history, systematics or polemic divinity and practical theology. He then reviewed all their presbytery requirements for the student trials for licensure:

1.) Explain and analyze a selection from the Hebrew Psalter, given to the student at a previous meeting
2.) Explain a passage in the Greek New Testament
3.) Give an exercise on one or two assigned verses. This selection will be a different passage where interpreters differ.
4.) A Latin lecture as a chronological discourse of the memorable events ecclesiastically, as assigned by presbytery (if no discourse is required, an examination in English on a period will be done).
5.) An English homily with doctrinal addition (assigned).
6.) In Latin, an exegesis of a doctrinal controversy. He is to be prepared to defend this thesis *ex tempore*. (Campbell adds that this rarely ever occurred anymore, and that these *viva voce* disputations had been abandoned in the halls and presbyteries.)
7.) An English popular lecture and popular sermon (to try the candidates abilities and fitness for the pulpit).[200]

Campbell was doing his duty in laying before the divinity students a reminder of the presbytery's expectations. He admitted that four winters of classes was very brief and that divinity st1udents were continually coming and going, thus acknowledging the erratic attendance patterns.[201] Suderman

---

[197] Suderman, "Orthodoxy and Enlightenment: George Campbell", 92-93.
[198] Campbell, *Works*, 6:3.
[199] Campbell, *Works*, 6:4, 9, 12.
[200] Campbell, *Works*, 6:22-24.
[201] Campbell, *Works*, 6:22.

provided some light on the poor attendance of divinity students. Statistically, King's and Marischal had, on average, a total of sixty to eighty divinity students, but only one third attended lectures regularly.[202] Therefore, Campbell did not propose to take them through "controversial theology" as a branch, but only to give introductory lectures here. The students could read the compendiums on this at leisure.[203] Likewise, on the matter of church history he commented, "I am not of opinion, that attending what are commonly called historical lectures, that is, an abridgement of history distributed into lectures, whether the subject be sacred or civil, is the best way of acquiring a sufficiency of knowledge in this branch."[204] As we have already seen from his ecclesiastical lectures, they were very limited in scope. Again, Campbell concluded that such lectures were to advise the student as to how to proceed to acquire knowledge.[205] For biblical criticism he wanted to steer students away from commentaries and to encourage them to focus chiefly upon New Testament criticism.[206] We assume then that the first half of his *Dissertation on the Gospels* may have worked their way into lectures.

Lastly, on the subject of practical divinity, Campbell wrote that he chiefly gave lectures on pulpit eloquence, "propriety of conduct in private life" and "propriety" in the role as minister.[207] There is a noted contrast between Campbell and John Brown on the theme of pulpit eloquence. The chief contrast is that Campbell surveyed it from a technical perspective, whereas Brown focused upon the spiritual or evangelical. When Campbell offered advice to his students on the various forms of address, he did not turn to a casuistry of preaching, that is the converted, the doubters, etc.. Rather his focus was purely technical. Under the lecture on pronunciation, he dealt with straining the voice, rapidity of utterance, theatrical and too violent manners of speech, monotony, sing-song, etc.. He offered the practical advice that students should attend to the conversations of the best speakers and keep company with them. He further stated that young preachers should never commence their sermons too high, they should not raise their voice as they proceeded, and they should begin very

---

[202] Suderman, "Orthodoxy and Enlightenment: George Campbell".

[203] Campbell, *Works*, 6:24-25, and pages 39-122 of his "Of Systematic Theology" lectures (six in number), which, as he said in his introduction to the study of theology, were all introductory and really in no fashion a compendium for a systematic theology text. This is in direct contrast to Brown's compendium or *System*. Campbell is essentially "anti-systems" in theology and in Suderman's estimation reflects the enlightened attitude of being cautious towards Covenant theology. See also Suderman, "Orthodoxy and Enlightenment: George Campbell", 97.

[204] Campbell, *Works*, 6:25.
[205] Campbell, *Works*, 6:26.
[206] Campbell, *Works*, 6:26.
[207] Campbell, *Works*, 6:27.

deliberately and slowly, never rapidly, yet not be uniform throughout the sermon.[208]

The remaining nine lectures on the minister's exemplary character extol virtue, morality and steadiness as the goals. Campbell did not turn to historical figures (as John Brown did), nor did he become highly personal or soul searching. He set Christ before the students as their example, but he did not do it with the evangelical strains of others.[209] He advised the students to be disciplined, wisely scheduling their day and avoiding sloth.[210]

From the survey of Campbell's vast collection of lectures read to the divinity students at Marischal College, we have an invaluable record of what was being taught there in the late 1760s through to 1796. It was Alexander Carlyle who described Campbell as one of "the leading writers in their fields in the English speaking world".[211] The conclusion is that it was of a very different piety than his contemporary at Haddington. Also, in terms of actual lecture material, it was of a very different order. Moderatism and Evangelicalism were different in the classroom. Furthermore, George Campbell, Alexander Gerard (his fellow professor at King's), and his good friend James Beattie all belong to this group of the "literati" of the Scottish Enlightenment in some sense of the term. It is easy to see how Campbell reacted against Hume when Campbell issued his *Dissertation on Miracles*, yet that in itself presents us with a problem. Many regard Hume as typical of the Scottish Enlightenment.[212] Thus, with a more generalist definition, we could say that Campbell's lectures reflected polished lectures of a stimulating intellectual order, "enlightened", yet not reflective of those of a former century, nor of the Dissenting Presbyterian divinity halls of his time. Campbell is likewise representative of Moderatism on Catholic relief, evidenced in his *Address to the People of Scotland*, published in 1779. This contrasts with John Brown of Haddington's anti-Catholic emancipation position as seen in his *The Absurdity and Perfidy of all Authoritative Toleration of Gross Heresy, Blasphemy, Idolatry, and Popery in Britain*.[213] Campbell's views were shared with his Kirk colleague, Principal Robertson of Edinburgh University. Brown's views were shared by his Antiburgher compatriot, Professor Bruce. Such comparisons only highlight the fact that although methods may not have been very different, philosophies were.

---

[208] Campbell, *Works*, 6:156-165.
[209] Campbell, *Works*, 6:265, 294, 301, 313, 358-359.
[210] Campbell, *Works*, 6:369-370.
[211] *DSCHT*, 128, Also Richard B. Sher, *Church and University in the Scottish Enlightenment: The Moderate Literati of Edinburgh* (Edinburgh, 1985), 161-162.
[212] Sher, *Church and University in the Scottish Enlightenment*, 6-8.
[213] John Brown, *The Absurdity and Perfidy of all Authoritative Toleration of Gross Heresy, Blasphemy, Idolatry, and Popery in Britain* (Glasgow, 1780); George Campbell, *Address to the People of Scotland* (Aberdeen, 1779); Sher, *Church and University in the Scottish Enlightenment*, 288-289.

George Hill (1750-1819)

As has already been noted, George Hill commanded a dominant position in the Moderate Party of the Church of Scotland. He must also receive proper attention as a theological educator. Hill took his full arts course at the United College, St. Andrews, graduating M.A. in 1765 at the age of fifteen. He proceeded immediately to the study of divinity at St. Mary's College, St. Andrews. Like most divinity students, Hill also tutored during the years of divinity, tutoring for the family of Pryse Campbell. This tutoring took him to London in 1767 and in the winters of 1768 and 1769 to Edinburgh, where he also completed divinity with Principal Robertson.[214] In 1772 Hill became the professor of Greek at the United College, St. Andrews and held this position until 1788, when he became professor of divinity at St. Mary's College. While professor of Greek, he also held concurrently the Second Charge from May, 1780. He held the Second Charge until 1808, when he was inducted to the First College. In 1791 he was made principal of St. Mary's College. Hill's ecclesiastical positions in church and university illustrate his commitment to pluralities. In addition to those positions mentioned above, he was also made Dean of the Thistle Chapel in 1787 and Dean of the Chapel Royal in 1799.[215]

Sefton comments that George Hill "was more than an ecclesiastical careerist". He was obviously a most diligent worker, starting each day at four in the morning. He is credited with having helped raise the standard of both Greek and the teaching of theology at St. Andrews.[216] Hill has also been given credit for producing the "most influential Scottish compendium" of systematic theology.[217] MacLeod affirmed that the Reformed Church in Scotland had produced many expert theologians, yet "few of them produced compendia of theology". This dearth of such works perhaps resulted from the conviction of many Scottish theologians that "they could not improve on the work of the seventeenth-century continental Reformed dogmatics".[218]

Hill's *Lectures on Divinity* were the lectures (prelections) he gave to the students of divinity at St. Mary's during their four sessions.[219] They are arranged into six books (by comparison, John Brown's *Compendious View*... is

---

[214] McCallum, "George Hill", 4-5; *DSCHT*, 407- 408.
[215] McCallum, "George Hill", 6, 7, 13; *DSCHT*, 408.
[216] *DSCHT*, 408; McCallum, "George Hill", 6; Alexander Hill, ed., preface to *Lectures in Divinity*, by George Hill, original, 1821 (Philadelphia, 1844), iii, where Alexander Hill mentions his father's continual revising of his lectures, and page iv, where he quotes from his father's inaugural address upon becoming professor of divinity.
[217] *DSCHT*, 810. This is Donald MacLeod's article on "systematic theology".
[218] *DSCHT*, 810.
[219] George Hill, *Lectures in Divinity*, ed. Alexander Hill [revised from the original edition of 1803 which was entitled *Theological Institutes* and was re-issued posthumously in 1821 as *Lectures in Divinity*. This volume went through various printings in both Britain and America in the nineteenth century] (Philadelphia, 1844), iii-iv.

arranged into seven books).[220] As MacLeod has noted, the lectures gave a large amount of space to Christian evidences (that is, all of book 1, 150 pages), before proceeding in the other books to a general view of the Scripture system, the Trinity, the nature and extent of redemption, the application of redemption, and ecclesiology.[221] Evidence can quickly be found in examining these lectures that Hill was well read in the Church Fathers and included many references to such (these were often printed in Greek in the text). This is reflective of his sixteen years of teaching Greek.[222] Although Thomas Chalmers relied heavily upon Hill's *Lectures on Divinity,* he believed that it lacked a *sal evangelicun*. It lacks an obvious Christian piety that can be found in John Brown's *Compendious View*. Hill does not give the reader "reflections", or strong sections on heart application.[223] Hill used scripture, but not with reference after reference like John Brown. Yet, as Donald McCallum has pointed out, Hill "formulated a Calvinist theology which increased the common ground between the Moderate and Evangelical factions in the Church of Scotland…".[224] Hill also included the names of the writers he was making reference to, often as a polemical dogmatic text. These are almost never footnoted. Mosheim's name appears several times, and this same work was used by Brown as the basis for his church history/historical theology text. Hence, it can be concluded that Hill's *Lectures on Divinity* covered systematic theology in a different way from what Brown did in the Secession.[225]

Concerning covenant theology as treated by Hill, it is covered in book 5 in one chapter, but not as extensively as by Brown. Hill held to a two covenant theology, the covenant of works and the covenant of grace; yet interestingly he did not mention one continental Reformed author. This is a stark contrast to the

---

[220] John Brown, *A Compendious View of Natural and Revealed Religion* (London, 1817), xix-xxii.

[221] *DSCHT*, 810; Hill, *Lectures in Divinity*, ix-xvi.

[222] Hill, *Lectures in Divinity*, 3:231-389. John Brown arranges one chapter of sixteen pages on the Trinity in book 2. Then one would turn to book 4 in Brown, chapter 1 on Christ, to find more related material, which Hill treats under the Trinity. The conclusion – Hill is much more extensive on the Trinity. Brown, *Compendious View of Natural and Revealed Religion*, 130-146, 256-279.

[223] *DSCHT*, 810; Hill, *Lectures in Divinity*.

[224] McCallum, "George Hill", 3. Hill was definitely not a Moderate in the way that John MacLeod characterized the Moderates as Arminian, Pelagian or Socinian. MacLeod viewed Hill as "definitely and ably Calvinistic", yet on "church policy" a Moderate. Compare MacLeod, *Scottish Theology*, 203 with 208.

[225] Hill, *Lectures in Divinity*, 388-389. It is unusual in a systematic theology text to see a chapter entitled, "History of Calvinism", such as Hill does, bk. 4, ch. 11, 587-600. Such a chapter cannot be found in either Brown or Dick in their systematic texts. It is more along the lines of what would be expected in William Cunningham's *Historical Theology*.

way he referred to authors when writing on the Trinity.[226] Either Hill dealt with this elsewhere, or it was a matter he did not treat extensively in his divinity lectures. Generally Hill's systematic theology would be classified more as a dogmatic theology text and unlike Daniel Dewar's (Aberdeen) work in systematics. John MacLeod wrote of Dewar's work that it "was inclined to be more Biblical than dogmatic".[227]

One area in Hill's writings which has attracted attention concerns his position on the inspiration of Scripture. Hill, like some others, distinguished among three levels of inspiration of Scripture. Donald MacLeod stated that Hill and Dick both shared this approach to inspiration, yet it must "not be confused with the idea of partial inspiration".[228] It was Hill who made reference to Dick's *Inspiration of Scripture*, which had been first published in 1800 and then went through more editions prior to Hill's *Lectures*.[229]

Within the Church of Scotland at the close of the eighteenth and beginning of the nineteenth century, it is accurate to conclude that in certain aspects George Hill, as a professor of divinity, did not neatly reflect the label of a Moderate, but at the same time neither did he fit the label Evangelical. Thomas Chalmers summed it up well when he wrote concerning Hill's divinity lectures that "there will not often be a substantial, but often at least a complexional difference between us".[230] George Hill's systematics stands alone in the divinity halls of the Scottish universities at this time as a published work and provides an invaluable tool to uncover the nature of the divinity lectures at St. Mary's College between 1788 and 1819. It was Calvinistic; polemical against Arminianism, Deism, Pelagianism and Socinianism; strongly Trinitarian; and gave a strong emphasis upon a rational faith. It did not exude a warm piety in print form, yet this does not necessarily mean that Hill did not attempt to inculcate such in pulpit and classroom. Donald McCullum has provided sufficient evidence which counterbalances any who would say Hill was only a cold Moderate Calvinist.[231] However, certainly neither was he an "enthusiast" or romantic. Hill's *Lectures upon Portions of the Old Testament: Intended to Illustrate Jewish History and Scripture Characters* were lectures given to his congregation and not in the divinity hall.[232] It is highly probable that several of

---

[226] Hill, *Lectures in Divinity*, 640-655.
[227] MacLeod, *Scottish Theology*, 267; Daniel Dewar, *Elements of Systematic Theology*, 3 vols., (Glasgow, 1867).
[228] *DSCHT*, 811. See Hill, *Lectures in Divinity*, bk. 2, ch. 1, 154-171.
[229] Hill, *Lectures in Divinity*, 171; *DSCHT*, 242. One of the Scottish critics of Hill and Dick in the nineteenth century was: James Bannerman, *Inspiration: The Infallible Truth and Divine Authority of Holy Scriptures* (Edinburgh, 1865), 140-141, 249. See also A. C. Cheyne, *Studies in Scottish Church History* (Edinburgh, 1999), 125-127.
[230] Chalmers quoted in McCallum, "George Hill", 119. See also Thomas Chalmers, *Posthumous Works*, ed. William Hanna, vol. 9 (Edinburgh, 1849), 125-126.
[231] McCullum, "George Hill", 116-119.
[232] George Hill, *Lectures upon Portions of the Old Testament* (Edinburgh, 1812).

the divinity students heard them preached, but this is difficult to evaluate. Several of the discourses are on Bible characters – Abraham, Balaam, Joshua, Samuel, Saul and David. The application at the conclusion of each discourse is unlike that of Lawson. It tends in the direction of moral exhortation.[233] Christ's name is mentioned, but the evangelical tradition of the Seceders is absent and, as such, tempers McCullum's statements in this regard. Perhaps in conclusion, the best we can say is that Hill was a member of the Moderate Party, a Calvinist, but not an Evangelical.

Summary

Period V in the history of Scottish Theological education in the Scottish universities began with a reassertion in the halls of "the old way" theologically. This was more-or-less universal, yet Garden was tolerated for several years before he was removed. The Assembly Directives, on the whole, were consistent throughout Period V in terms of the arts curriculum and the divinity course, with its strong emphasis on student discourses in hall and presbytery. It must be acknowledged that though the presbytery continued hearing the many student discourses, the atmosphere of the presbytery meetings had greatly changed by the mid-eighteenth century.

While this period saw immense changes within the universities in the arts course and also in the professional school of medicine, the divinity halls appear to have been virtually unaffected except in the increased use of English and an increase in certain chairs. However the transition was beginning, as seen in Stevenson MacGill. The divinity halls were about to undergo radical changes that had not been paralleled for virtually two hundred years.

Though there was an emphasis on mastering orthodox systematic tomes, it was not a time known for producing lasting biblical commentaries. The one exception was James MacKnight's exegetical studies from 1756 to 1795, yet MacKnight never did gain a professorship of divinity, nor is he still read today, as is Bengel.[234] The other two exegetes were George Campbell and Gilbert Gerard. All three of these were Moderates, and although Friedhelm Voges considered them as basically at one with Kirk Evangelicals in exegesis, he has ignored matters of piety in his generalization.[235]

Outside the Church of Scotland at the close of Period V, George Lawson was busy producing such expository or exegetical works. Again this marked a

---

[233] Hill, *Lectures upon Portions of the Old Testament*, 323-324, 403-404.

[234] James MacKnight, *A New and Literal Translation from the Original Greek, of all the Apostolical Epistles, with a Commentary and Notes Philological, Critical, Explanatory and Practical*, 4 vols. (Edinburgh, 1795).

[235] Voges, "Moderate and Evangelical Thinking", 150.

transition.[236] A comparison of the divinity professors of Period III with Period V and their writings makes this point.

A close study of some of the teaching models in Period V merits our attention. Oral examination and a heavy emphasis on discourse are far removed from our modern era, yet when one reads the methods of Wodrow or MacGill, one cannot help but be impressed. We see that men were being trained who could communicate Christian truth. Appropriate models and methods for such must not be ignored. An examination of Wodrow's society classes certainly shows that the divinity hall of his day was not divorced from Christian life and church life. Yet at the same time these very models present another question – can one professor do an adequate job and combine this teaching with a parish or with weekly preaching in a church? As student numbers continued to increase throughout Period V, so did the number of discourses for each professor to critique.

Though extra professors were being added during Period V to teach Hebrew and Church history, it must be said that since student fees had to be paid for these subjects, students often opted out, even though the fee was small. Closer examination of patronage of the chairs and regulations were clearly needed in Period V.

The chief systematic textbooks were continental Reformed works, with Marck and Pictet predominating for most of Period V. However, an orthodox Calvinistic text was not to be taken as a guarantee that the professor was in sympathy with the text. Note for example Professor Simson. Also we have seen that many did respond to the challenges of Enlightenment thinking.

This period has also highlighted the issue of resources beyond the university libraries. The unique place these libraries have held in Scottish Theological studies for students and ordained clergy has not been fully appreciated.

---

[236] *DSCHT*, 525, 474.

CHAPTER 7

Period VI: 1826-1860, Universities' Commission

Introduction

Period VI can be characterized as a time of university reform, regulation and standardization such as had not been seen in Scotland since the Melvillian period. The Commission on Universities in Scotland was appointed by the House of Commons and produced weighty documents as to their investigations and recommendations. In Period VI there were two such Commissions, the first being 1826-1830 and the second 1858-1862. The 1826-1830 Commission *Report* was printed as a whole in 1831. The 1858-1862 Commission *Report* was printed as a whole in 1863. Our primary concern is with their reports concerning the teaching of divinity in the Scottish universities, but we will note also some of their remarks on arts, as this does form a critical basis for the learned ministry in the Scottish Kirk.

In an article on Thomas Chalmers and the University of Glasgow, Gareth Davies and Lionel Ritchie have highlighted problems and tensions within the Scottish universities from the 1820s onwards. They wrote, "The university [Glasgow] itself was aware of the problem of professorial delinquency, but could see no way of tackling it without a wholesale reform of the whole system."[1] In short, the Universities' Commission must be viewed as an effort to bring about much needed change. One example will make the point. Professor William Ritchie was the professor of divinity at Edinburgh from 1809. However by 1827 he was almost eighty and physically unable to lecture. The Town Council in December, 1826 offered Ritchie "full salary and emoluments for life in return for his resignation in favour of a conjoint-professor to carry out the full duties of the office".[2] Instead, Ritchie had Principal Baird read his [i.e. Ritchie's] lectures. By October, 1827 Professor Ritchie realized this arrangement had to end and accepted the earlier offer of the Town Council. The

---

[1] Gareth Davies and Lionel A. Ritchie, "Dr. Chalmers and the University of Glasgow", *RSCHS* 20 (1980), 213.

[2] Iain F. MacIver, "'I did not seek....but was sought after': The Election of Thomas Chalmers to the Chair of Divinity at Edinburgh University, October 1827", *RSCHS* 20 (1980), 224.

students had wanted his retirement for years. Ritchie was to have Thomas Chalmers as the conjoint-professor.

Royal Commission into the State of the Universities of Scotland, 1826-1830

As we have already noted, this commission lasted four years and completed its report in October, 1830. The report was ordered to be printed by the House of Commons October 7, 1831.[3] The printed 1831 *Report* consists of six parts. Part one is a general report on the constitutions of the colleges; the faculties of arts, theology, law and medicine; and some miscellaneous matters. Parts two through six are reports on the five universities: Edinburgh, Glasgow, King's, Marischal and St. Andrews. The Commission worked within the general principle that things could remain as they were in the respective colleges "unless it appeared on satisfactory evidence that an abuse or defect existed...".[4] One example of a recommendation of the 1831 *Report* was that King's and Marischal become one university with one principal.[5]

The Royal Commission reviewed the arts course and acknowledged that a large number of Scottish students exempted themselves from some of the first and second year classes and instead elected to take classes in moral or natural philosophy, the third and fourth year classes. The Commission recognized that they could not stop this because the students would simply go elsewhere for instruction. The Commission therefore recommended that "the Curriculum of Arts should be imperative only on those who may be candidates for degrees, or who may require certificates of a regular university education".[6] The uniform arts course was to be as follows:

> 1st Year: First Latin and Greek classes from Oct. to May 1st – two hours per day, five days per week.
> 2nd Year: Second Latin and Greek classes from Oct. to May 1st – two hours per day, five days per week. First mathematics class – one hour per day, five days a week.
> 3rd Year: Second mathematics class – one hour per day, five days per week. Elementary logic and rhetoric – two hours per day, five days per week (with one hour for lecture and one hour for examination, exercise and composition.
> 4th Year: Natural philosophy class – two hours per day, five days per week. Moral philosophy class – two hours per day, five days per week. (Both to

---

[3] *Report Made to His Majesty by a Royal Commission of Inquiry into the State of the Universities of Scotland* (House of Commons, London, 1831), i. (Hereafter *Royal Commission...1831*).
[4] *Royal Commission...1831*, 8.
[5] *Royal Commission...1831*, 22.
[6] *Royal Commission...1831*, 25.

have one hour for lecture and one hour for examination, exercise, themes, etc).[7]

The Royal Commission concluded that logic and rhetoric could not be studied until year three because in general the Scottish students were very young and had not mastered Greek and Latin. In addition, improvements needed to be made in the Parish Schools or Grammar Schools in Scotland.[8] Another standard established by the Acts of Parliament of 1690 and 1707 which the Commission found lagging was one which stated that all professors, principals, regents and masters must subscribe to the Westminster Confession of Faith. The Commission found that this was not being uniformly followed in the colleges and recommended "that in future it should be regularly enforced".[9] Examinations, it appears, were not universally carried out, and often in many classes there were no examinations. The Commission recommended that examinations should be conducted at a separate hour from the lecture hour. They noted the one exception was the University of Glasgow, which for a long time had been examining students in the philosophy classes, theology, law and medicine. They also noted that the universities of Aberdeen had recently begun to conduct philosophy examinations. Therefore, St. Andrews and Edinburgh evidently were the culprits in view.[10] Completing this triad of "E's", after examinations were "exercises" and "essays", both of which the Commissioners recommended be conducted. The abuse of students presenting someone else's exercise or essay was no warrant for the colleges not to conduct exercises and assign essays.[11]

The commissioners highly valued the use of prizes "as the reward of eminence, or of distinguished propriety of conduct on the part of students".[12] These prizes, plus a better regulation of class certificates concerning attendance, behaviour and examinations, went a long way towards encouraging students in the Scottish universities to prosecute their studies seriously.[13] Also flowing out of this was a recommendation for a universal revival of the Bachelor of Arts degree prior to the Master of Arts degree. With both degrees the Commission outlined the examination procedures to be followed.[14] It had been found that in many instances there were no longer examinations occurring to award degree; rather, the student paid his fees and received the degrees. Many never proceeded to pay such fees, thus never obtained a degree.

---

[7] *Royal Commission...1831*, 25.
[8] *Royal Commission...1831*, 27.
[9] *Royal Commission...1831*, 33.
[10] *Royal Commission...1831*, 35.
[11] *Royal Commission...1831*, 35-36.
[12] *Royal Commission...1831*, 36.
[13] *Royal Commission...1831*, 36-39.
[14] *Royal Commission...1831*, 39-44.

When we come to the 1831 Report regarding theology, we find a wealth of information concerning the teaching of divinity in the five Scottish universities between 1826-1830. The Report begins by outlining the length of sessions in divinity in the universities: King's and Marischal, both three month sessions; Aberdeen, four month sessions; Edinburgh, "although nominally longer, it is not so"; and Glasgow, six month sessions. The Commission recommended that all the divinity halls should be uniform, with a session lasting six months.[15]

The Report openly acknowledged that improvements for theological education could be proposed by the Commission, but unless the church judicatories accorded, little would be improved. It stated that some students only enrolled their names with their professor of divinity and delivered their discourses but never attended lectures. Such students could take their trials for licensure just as students who attended lectures. However, this was beginning to change, albeit rather slowly. Also, the study of Hebrew remained a matter "no less remarkable" in the eyes of the Commission. Since Hebrew was to be part of the presbytery trials, it is strange that very few students for the ministry attended Hebrew classes in the universities. The Commission was pleased to learn that the General Assembly was transmitting an act to the presbyteries for their approval which would require all students to attend one session in Hebrew in a university prior to licensure.[16]

The 1831 Report recommended that within each of the four universities (King's and Marischal to become one) there would be four professors in theology. In broad terms the outline of their duties and courses would be:

1.) Professor of Divinity or Systematic Theology:
First Class – Evidence of Natural and Revealed Religion: comprehending the genuineness, authority and inspiration of Scripture and its sufficiency as a rule of faith. To meet one hour each day for five days of the week, three days for lecture and two for examination.
Second Class – Theology, strictly so called: embracing the great doctrine of revelation and the ground upon which they rest, view of systematic theology, and the qualifications and duties of the pastoral office. Three lectures each week, with two hours for examinations upon lectures or upon standard theological works appointed to be read by the students. That the professor of divinity complete the course of this second class in two sessions.

2.) Professor of Oriental Languages:
First Class – Elements of Hebrew and translation of the historical books of the Old Testament. One hour for five days of the week.

---

[15] *Royal Commission...1831*, 45.
[16] *Royal Commission...1831*, 46.

> Second Class – Political and prophetical books of the Old Testament, Chaldee and Syriac, and occasional lectures on Hebrew antiquities. One hour for five days of the week.
>
> 3.) Professor of Ecclesiastical History:
> First Class – Historical view of the Old Testament dispensation, introduction of Christianity, and Apostolic Age and historical and critical account of the Apostolic Fathers. To meet five hours a week, four for lecturing and one for examination.
> Second Class – History of the dissemination and establishment of Christianity, of the opinions which have been entertained as to its doctrines and morality, and of the various forms under which it has been administered. The polity, laws and government of the Church of Scotland. Five hours a week, four for lecturing and one for exercises and examination. The whole course to be concluded in two years.
>
> 4.) Professor of Biblical Criticism:
> One Class – This class to meet five hours a week, three for lecturing and two for examinations and exercises. The critical discourse, denominated exercises and addition delivered by the students according to the requisition of the Church to be heard by this professor.[17]

At this time none of the divinity halls in the universities had a professor of biblical criticism and generally each only had a professor of divinity and a professor of Hebrew. Since by this time the principal did virtually no lecturing, his title as primarius for divinity was honourary. Students at King's and Marischal attended lectures in both colleges. By 1830 Glasgow, Edinburgh and St. Andrews each had a professor in Church history, so they had three staff members each. The Commission discovered that there was a wide variance in how many lectures were given by any professor each week. Some lectured daily, some on three days and some only two hours a week. Often the student discourses occurred during the lecture hours, which considerably reduced the amount of time given to lectures.[18] Hence the proposed arrangement by the Royal Commission added considerable lecture time. The result meant that a divinity student was in class two hours per day, excluding discourse time.

In addition, the Commission recommended that student attendance become compulsory and in order to encourage such, they proposed to institute the degree of Bachelor of Divinity. To obtain this degree, a student was required to regularly attend and be examined in theology, biblical criticism, ecclesiastical history and in Hebrew, provided he possessed a Bachelor of Arts degree. Also, such candidates had to subscribe to the "Confession of Faith and the Formula of

---

[17] *Royal Commission...1831*, 47-48.
[18] *Royal Commission...1831*, 47.

the Church of Scotland".[19] Connected with this was the fact that after the adoption of these recommendations, the Doctor of Divinity degree could only be given to those who had studied divinity regularly at a university and obtained the B.D. and the M.A.. No one who entered a university after this came into effect could secure a D.D. if they lacked these two degrees. Also, in future the D.D. was only to be awarded to those who had received their education in one of the universities of Scotland.[20]

Finally, the Report recommended that fees would be charged in all the divinity classes. The times were now different from before, when it was difficult to procure a sufficient number of young men for the ministry. Also, if some type of fee was not charged, the education would not be highly valued. The fee structure that was proposed was very moderate to avoid becoming a burden for any.[21]

The Royal Commission brought in one other recommendation that concerned the teaching of theology in Scotland. This was the recommendation to establish the Dumfries University in Dumfries. This proposed Dumfries University was to have a regular arts course and a regular course of theology. It was envisaged that "in the first instance" no classes in law or medicine would be given. They recommended that there be a professor of systematic theology, a professor of Church history and a professor of oriental languages, all teaching divinity for the B.D. degree, plus the principal. The principal was to be a clergyman of the Established Church and was to give lectures on biblical criticism rather than making this a separate professorship.[22] The chief patron of this proposed Dumfries University was Mrs. John Crichton of Friar's Carse, Dumfries, but the Commissioners recognized that not all of the capital promised could be secured immediately. The total funds amounted to eighty-five thousand pounds, but some of this was in annuities and could not be secured until the death of two individuals, who at the time of the *Report* were aged 45 and 54.[23] Had this recommendation been carried into effect in its entirety, the Dumfries University would have followed the proposed course in arts and divinity which we have outlined above, together with all the regulations on examinations, etc. It would, in essence, have become a model university of the 1831 Royal Commission.

The general portion of the *Report* ended with a qualifying paragraph above the signatures of all the Commissioners stating that on certain recommendations they were not all united. The differences of opinion which concern us are as follows: first, there was a diversity of thought about the principal and professors holding a plurality of offices; second, not all agreed to

---

[19] *Royal Commission...1831*, 50-51.
[20] *Royal Commission...1831*, 51-52.
[21] *Royal Commission...1831*, 52-53.
[22] *Royal Commission...1831*, 85-86.
[23] *Royal Commission...1831*, 86-87.

the proposed arts curriculum; and third, not all agreed upon the uniting of King's and Marischal. Interestingly, there is no dissent recorded over the regulations and requirements for the theological curriculum.[24]

The Commission Report recommended allowing a plurality of offices for the divinity halls' or universities' principals and professors. The reason recorded for allowing this was to ensure the connection between the Church and the universities of Scotland and "because the nature of the studies in which a Professor of Theology must engage, and the Lectures he has to deliver, so far from interfering with the due performance of the duties of a parochial minister, are such as will enable him to exhibit in the pulpit a practical example of the utility of those doctrines and instructions which it is his province to inculcate in his class".[25] The opposing significant reason given was that "the duties about to be imposed on the Professor of Theology and the Principals of the Universities, by the recommendations contained in the *Report to His Majesty*, are such as to preclude a faithful and efficient discharge of them, in conjunction with those attached to the Ministry of a Parish Church, in the city or the suburbs, where the University is situated...".[26] This dissent was signed by seven of the Commissioners, one half of the total Commission, and clearly reflects one of the intense debates within the Commission itself and also in the Church of Scotland of the 1820s and 1830s.

It must be stated here that there was chiefly one man behind the recommendations of the Universities' Commission, Professor Stevenson MacGill. This applies to both the 1826 Commission and also the less important Commission of 1836. In reviewing a letter of John Wilson, one of the 1836 Commissioners, Robert Burns concludes:

> It is a matter of record, that to no man in any one of the Universities were the Commissioners of 1826 and 1836, more amply indebted in all matters of information and of reform than to Professor Macgill; and it must have been extremely gratifying to him to find that, in most instances, his suggestions were adopted by them.[27]

In a *MS* which Stevenson MacGill made of his answers to the Commissioners, we learn that he recommended that the divinity students be divided into two classes, junior and senior, along the lines he used (see Period V on MacGill for details). He further recommended that the principal, as primarius professor of divinity, should take charge of the students in the fourth

---

[24] *Royal Commission...1831*, 89.

[25] *Royal Commission...1831*, 90.

[26] *Royal Commission...1831*, 89-90.

[27] Burns, *Memoir of Stevenson MacGill*, 345. See also pages 75-94 for a printed copy from the *MS* answers which Stevenson MacGill gave to the Commissioners in 1827. Some of this material was incorporated into their final printed *Report* issued in 1831, but not all.

session and hear their discourses and give whatever lectures may be needed.[28] MacGill also wanted all professors of Hebrew and Church history to be clergymen, not laymen. He saw this as important for maintaining a marriage between religion and learning. Also on that same theme, he desired to see proper attendance by professors and students "on divine worship on the Sabbath".[29] In this matter MacGill felt the universities were departing from their "original constitution" to provide "religious instruction of our students". Thus, chapel services were to be shared once a month by the principal and the professor of divinity. A list of certain clergymen who would come and preach before the university at chapel was to be established.[30]

Some of the other points raised in this *MS* show MacGill's desire to have divinity students well grounded in the arts curriculum before taking up divinity. In fact, MacGill had worked upon overtures to the General Assembly to this effect, that a student must appear before a presbytery to be examined "upon his classical attainments, and his knowledge of philosophy". In this regard he applauded others: "so do the respectable dissenters in the same way among ourselves in Scotland".[31] Since he did not define "dissenters", it could be Seceders or Covenanters. When pressed by the Commissioners, he stated it as possible for the Church to insist upon the student first graduating M.A. before proceeding to the divinity hall.[32] He also concurred with the need for a professor of biblical criticism, and he saw an advantage for divinity bursaries.[33] He did not elaborate at length on either of these two points.

In Burn's biography of MacGill, following the quotation from the *MS* are six pages of discussion on the needs in the divinity halls in the Scottish universities. It becomes difficult to separate Burns from MacGill at this juncture, with the result that the reader is left to speculate whose views are being expressed. To summarize the six pages, MacGill (via Burns) first dealt with the need for a fifth professorship on pastoral care to go beyond the "occasional lectures" of the past. Second, he argued that the teaching of Church history must include the constitution and practice of the Church of Scotland and the general principles of Christian establishment. Third, he advocated the "Formation of Ministerial Character and Habits". That is, occasional lectures on experimental religion and cases of conscience must be given in addition to private interviews between a student and a professor, much like Charles Simeon's private interviews with students. Fourth, he wanted "Enlargement of the Church", meaning that students of divinity need to be encouraged to meet

---

[28] Burns, *Memoir of Stevenson MacGill*, 75.
[29] Burns, *Memoir of Stevenson MacGill*, 76.
[30] Burns, *Memoir of Stevenson MacGill*, 78-79. "I conceive it is due to religion that there should be an excellent example of preaching set before the students."
[31] Burns, *Memoir of Stevenson MacGill*, 84-85.
[32] Burns, *Memoir of Stevenson MacGill*, 85.
[33] Burns, *Memoir of Stevenson MacGill*, 85, 93.

monthly for prayer and to hear reports on "religious intelligence regarding the progress of the gospel". Here students could learn about the churches on the continent, the British Colonies, the mission in India or other heathen lands, and in general learn of "the great missionary enterprises of the Protestant Churches at large."[34]

Some of the other appended dissents in the *Report* go on to cite the need for the principal to be a clergyman of the Church and those in the chairs of the faculty of theology to be clergymen, called "Placed Ministers", thus clearly under the discipline and control of the Church. It appears that once again this was all within the framework of not wanting to sever the connection between the Church and the universities.[35]

Several signed dissents with reasons were also given in the *Report*, which had placed logic and rhetoric in year three. Again, much in the spirit of Professor Jardine, it was argued that this gave too much emphasis to the classics and the development of the mind needed to occur early in the curriculum.[36]

The General Assembly Acts

Thus, we have seen that the recommendations of the Royal Commission of 1826-1830 contained many significant reforms. The logical question is, "How did the Church of Scotland and the universities respond?" The answer can be best summarized as "slowly". In 1832, after a long process, the Church of Scotland succeeded in making attendance at Church history and Hebrew in the divinity halls the standing law of the Church. These standing laws of 1832 required that a student submit a certificate to his presbytery of "having regularly attended the class of Church History during two of the sessions which he claims to be considered as sessions of regular attendance at the Divinity Hall, if such a class exist in the University or Universities at which he has prosecuted his theological studies".[37] The certificate was to be submitted prior to a student's trials. Likewise, every divinity student was required to "attend the Hebrew class in one or other of the Universities during two of the sessions which he claims as sessions of regular attendance at the Divinity Hall".[38]

In 1835 several overtures were transmitted within the Church dealing with presbyteries and their examination of students. These examinations were to be conducted yearly, and a certificate was to be issued to the student from his professor of divinity. Another overture added a new examination "upon their [the students'] knowledge of the Christian religion as it is exhibited in the

---

[34] Burns, *Memoir of Stevenson MacGill*, 96-100.
[35] *Royal Commission...1831*, 90.
[36] *Royal Commission...1831*, 91.
[37] Mechie, "Education for the Ministry", 2:167.
[38] Mechie, "Education for the Ministry", 2:167.

catechetical standards of the Church". The third overture of 1835 concerned the place of learning Hebrew and asserted that the way of promoting it was "that a Critical Hebrew exercise on some portion of the original text of the Old Testament be appointed to be prepared and delivered by every Theological Student in the course of his attendance at the Divinity Hall, in addition to those exercises that are already prescribed by the Church".[39] These 1835 overtures each subsequently became standing laws of the Church in 1836 and 1837.[40]

The other way the Church responded in the 1830s was that in 1839 the General Assembly passed an act concerning the establishment and endowment of a professorship of biblical criticism in each of the universities of Scotland. With the exception of Edinburgh University, it was to be over twenty years before this would become a reality in all of the Scottish universities. Edinburgh was the first to appoint such a professor in 1847, followed by Aberdeen in 1860, Glasgow in 1861 and St. Andrews in 1862.[41]

Concerning the introduction of the B.D. degree, this was not implemented for several decades. Much debate ensued concerning this in the latter half of the 1850s due to varying requirements in each of the universities as to who was entitled to the B.D. degree. In 1855 a delegation of professors from the different universities proposed the introduction of the B.D. degree in Scotland. Glasgow University Senate refused to implement these proposed regulations on the basis that the universities were national institutions and that a degree should not be limited to members of the Church of Scotland only.[42] Aberdeen concurred with Glasgow on this point; but St. Andrews and Edinburgh held that, in order for the B.D. to be given by a university, a student had to study theology one year in the university from which he proposed to graduate. This would mean that the Scottish universities maintained the exclusive right to grant the B.D. degree, thus continuing to exclude the Free Church and United Presbyterian Halls. In 1862 Glasgow University presented a proposal before the Royal Commission to secure an ordinance that any M.A. graduate who attended

---

[39] Mechie, "Education for the Ministry", 2:168; *AGACS*, June 1, 1835, 1052.

[40] *AGACS*, May 29, 1837, 1073; *AGACS*, May 29, 1837, 1073-1074; *AGACS*, May 30, 1836, 1059-1060.

[41] Mechie, "Education for the Ministry", 2:168; *DSCHT*, 279.

[42] *Scottish Universities Commission: General Report of the Commissioners under the Universities (Scotland) Act, 1858 with an Appendix* (Edinburgh, 1863), 370. In 1856 the *Senatus Academicus* of Glasgow University stated: "that, by the creation of the degree of B.D. in the manner proposed, the Universities, would place themselves in the position of having instituted public academical honours, which can be enjoyed by no student of Theology, not belonging to the Church of Scotland, and that in present circumstances, it is not desirable to erect a distinction which must be invidious, and might be prejudicial to large numbers of young men received, educated, and admitted to all honours in the curriculum in Arts, but, who, through effect of differences of opinion widely prevailing and with which, as representing a National University, the Senate is not concerned, attend other Theological Halls." 370.

one of the university divinity halls or another in Scotland could present themselves for the degree. This proposal went on to define these other halls as, "such other Theological Halls or Colleges presided over by one or more graduates of Divinity of this or some other Scottish University, as shall have been specifically recognized for this purpose by the University Court, with consent of the Chancellor of the University, was to be sufficient".[43] The Commission concluded it was not desirable for them to regulate by ordinance the conditions by which degrees in divinity were conferred. The result was that the Scottish universities each began to confer the B.D. degrees in the ensuing years to any candidate, whether a member of the Church of Scotland or not. By 1876 all the Scottish universities were conferring the B.D. degree.[44]

Following the Disruption, the General Assembly passed interim regulations concerning the trial and licensing of students. By the 1850s the emergency had passed and regulations were clarified once again stating the will of the Church for students. In 1856 a standing law was made by the Assembly in which "the course of attendance at the Divinity Hall shall be completed in four sessions, provided that the student's attendance during three of these sessions shall have been regular; but students giving only two sessions of regular attendance shall be required to give an additional attendance of three partial sessions to complete their course".[45] Ten years later in 1866, the General Assembly made it a standing law that the divinity course attendance ordinarily be three regular sessions, "henceforth all candidates for the ministry be required to attend at the Divinity Hall either three full and regular sessions, without the fourth partial session, or two full and regular sessions and three partial sessions".[46]

By 1842 the General Assembly had agreed to transmit an Overture on Pluralities of Office to the presbyteries. It read as follows:

> The General Assembly, being desirous to promote the interests of religion and literature, direct all the Presbyteries of the Church to employ all means competent to them in order to prevent the same person from holding at the same time a Principality or Professorship in any University and a parochial or pastoral charge, and that this direction may be uniformly carried into effect, the General Assembly do, with the consent of a majority of the Presbyteries of the Church, enact and ordain, that if a Principal or Professor in any University be hereafter presented to a parochial or pastoral charge, he shall, on his admission thereto, forthwith resign his Principality or Professorship and that if any Minister of a Parish, or any Pastor of a Congregation, be hereafter presented or elected to any Principality or Professorship in any University, he shall, at the first ordinary meeting of

---

[43] *Report of the Commissioners...1858*, 370.
[44] Mechie, "Education for the Ministry", 2:169.
[45] Mechie, "Education for the Ministry", 2:171.
[46] Mechie, "Education for the Ministry", 2:172. It was not until 1918 that the Church of Scotland made it the standing law of the Church that a student must attend three full sessions of twenty weeks each, and partial sessions were abolished.

Presbytery which shall take place after his induction into the Principality or Professorship, resign into the hands of the Presbytery his Parochial or Pastoral Charge; and in the event of this injunction not being complied with by the persons holding such offices, the General Assembly, with the like consent of the Presbyteries of this Church, ordain the Presbytery of the bounds to serve him, in his character of Minister, with a libel for the break of this statue, and to proceed therein according to the rules of the Church.[47]

The following year, 1843, General Assembly made no mention of what became of this matter. No doubt the matter of that year's Disruption was in the forefront, and matters such as this were not a high priority. Yet we do find three days after the "Act of Separation", this General Assembly received the results of the majority of presbyteries approving an Overture concerning "Attendance on the Latin Class", which the General Assembly passed into the standing law of the Church. This act stated "that no student shall be admitted into any of the Divinity Halls, unless he shall produce to the Professor or Professors of Divinity, and to the Presbytery within whose bounds he resides, a certificate of having attended the Latin Class in some University for at least one session, and made satisfactory proficiency as a Latin scholar".[48] This standing law came at a most unusual time since virtually all the classes in the Scottish universities were by then conducted in English.

In the 1845 General Assembly of the Church of Scotland, much discussion occurred about students in the light of Interim Acts of 1843, which allowed presbyteries to take students on trials for license who had never received the authorization of the synod. The reason for this was that of expediency to quickly fill the vacant charges. The other interim matter was that a student could be taken on trial who had delivered all his discourses in the theological hall and had attended three regular sessions. The presbyteries were not to lower this standard. The only allowance was for a student who had completed two sessions of regular attendance and two sessions of occasional attendance. He could then be admitted to trials.[49] Also in 1845 the General Assembly gave a "Declaration as to the course of Literary and Philosophical Study to be attended by Students of Divinity". This Declaration was intended to make clear for all the standards of the Church. Again, it did not demand the M.A. degree but declared that the student would produce certificates of attendance for all classes which made up the M.A. course; namely Greek, Latin, logic, mathematics, moral philosophy and natural philosophy. The Declaration also stated in what order these classes had to be studied; first, Greek and Latin in session one; then logic, moral and natural philosophy. It was to be understood that the divinity

---

[47] *AGACS*, May 30, 1842, 1145.
[48] *The Principal Acts of the General Assembly of the Church of Scotland, 1843* (Edinburgh, 1843), 27 May, 1843, 30.
[49] *The Principal Acts of the General Assembly of the Church of Scotland, 1845* (Edinburgh, 1845), 29 May, 1845, 17-18.

professors were "to make allowance for such deviations from the order of the course as may have arisen from misinformation".[50]

A further Declaration was issued by the General Assembly of 1846 on another matter, the language of which we have already seen before in the 1830 Royal Commission *Report*. This 1846 Declaration reads that the General Assembly "feel themselves called on to declare, in the strongest manner, that the Church of Scotland regards the connection between the Universities and the Church as of the utmost importance to the best interests of the country".[51]

In 1849 the General Assembly issued an act consolidating the various acts of former Assemblies respecting the study of divinity and the licensing of probationers. Thus, this 1849 Act of Consolidation assembles in one location the ideals for the training of ministers and their education in Period VI. We do not find anything new added, but the fourteen sections of this Act of Consolidation make for easy reference.[52] This Consolidation document does not single out the requirement of Latin specifically, but assumes it at two points. First, it assumes that the student took Latin in university and had a certificate to that effect. Second, it also assumes that the student had sustained the presbytery examinations in such and that he completed an exegesis discourse in Latin in the divinity hall and in presbytery on some controverted head in divinity – one of the last vestiges of the old Latin disputations of the medieval university in the study of theology.[53] Immediately following this Consolidation Act was the usual act making the full standards of the General Assembly subject to the unique interim situation. These interim measures were ratified each year until 1850, as we have already noted.[54]

Later throughout the 1850s on an annual basis overtures were sent down to the presbyteries of further consolidation and amendment to the Acts of Assembly regarding students of divinity and the licensing of students and probationers. Each year a committee issued a report on this abstract and finally, in the General Assembly of 1863, an "Act of Declaratory of and Consolidating the Acts of Assembly presently in force, in regard to the Study of Divinity, – to the Licensing of Students, – and to Probationers" was enacted. This Act Declaratory was considerably longer than that of the 1849 Act of Consolidation owing to the incorporation of two previous acts: an 1851 act requiring a student to be six months in residence prior to examination for becoming enrolled as a

---

[50] *The Principal Acts of the General Assembly of the Church of Scotland, 1845* (Edinburgh, 1845), 2 June, 1845, 31-32.
[51] *The Principal Acts of the General Assembly of the Church of Scotland, 1846* (Edinburgh, 1846), 28 May, 1846, 17.
[52] *The Principal Acts of the General Assembly of the Church of Scotland, 1849* (Edinburgh, 1849), 4 June, 1849, 34-39.
[53] *Principal Acts, 1849,* 34-35, 38.
[54] *The Principal Acts of the General Assembly of the Church of Scotland, 1850* (Edinburgh, 1850), 30 May, 1850, 20.

student of presbytery, and the 1856 Act of the Rules for Conducting Presbytery Examinations of Students.[55] One other addition took little space but is significant; that is the 1855 act prohibiting students from preaching in public before being regularly licensed.[56] Thus, Period VI ended with the General Assembly issuing a well formulated document on the ideals for students of the ministry. Regularized attendance at the divinity halls, along with the completion of the discourses, had become very much the norm. The 1865 Act Declaratory and Consolidating Acts lists these hall discourses as:

1.) an exegesis in Latin on a controverted head in divinity,
2.) a homily in English,
3.) a critical exercise on some portion of the original text of the Old Testament,
4.) an exercise and addition on some portion of the original text of the New Testament,
5.) a lecture on some large portion of Scripture;
6.) a popular sermon, and
7.) any other exercise the professor sees proper.

Likewise, the 1863 Act lists the trials before presbytery:

1.) catechetical trials on divinity, chronology, and Church history,
2.) a trial in Hebrew and Greek,
3.) an exercise in Latin on a controverted head in divinity,
4.) a homily in English,
5.) an exercise and addition,
6.) a lecture on some large portion of Scripture,
7.) a popular sermon, and
8.) if presbytery sees cause, an examination of any of the student discourses listed above.[57]

Today we are surprised that students of divinity would not be allowed to supply pulpits until they were licensed. Yet we should bear these critical factors in view: first, the young age of a first year divinity student; second, the whole nature of a probationary period after licensure which could last for a year or, as was often the case, several years, thus allowing for preaching experience; and third, the general seriousness of the ministry of the Word being in the hands of men properly qualified to handle it. There was certainly no regard for lay preaching, whether it be Methodist or of the Haldane variety of Period V.

---

[55] *The Principal Acts of the General Assembly, Church of Scotland, 1863* (Edinburgh, 1863), 29 May, 1863, 33-34.
[56] *Principal Acts, 1863*, 35.
[57] *Principal Acts, 1863*, 37-38.

However, the insistence by acts of Assembly that students should not preach raises the question of pastoral theology and training. The extended probationary enterprise was an informal way of handling it while also supplying schools and families with teachers and tutors.[58] However, the latter half of Period VI was the beginning of the end of this arrangement. By the end of the nineteenth-century, schooling in Scotland had undergone many radical changes.

Since the ancient practice of the Geneva Academy of Calvin's day of placing students in vacant charges was not followed, it is valid to wonder how pastoral training was going to be undertaken in the Scottish divinity halls and presbyteries. The void was acknowledged by the General Assembly in a small manner in 1842. That year the General Assembly declared it to be expedient that a pastoral superintendent be appointed at each of the Scottish universities. A committee was appointed to bring in full recommendations on this to the next Assembly. It appears that this matter was "swallowed whole" in the crisis of the Disruption, and nothing was done about it. In fact, there were no concrete developments in this regard until 1870 to 1872, when "Lecturers" were appointed for each of the divinity halls and mandated to give a short series of lectures in pastoral theology. At first two lecturers were appointed, with one to give twelve lectures each at Glasgow and Aberdeen and the other at Edinburgh and St. Andrews.[59] These lecturers fell outside of the category of professor and were parish ministers.

Royal Commission and the Five Universities' Divinity Halls, 1826-1830

In reading through what constitutes the appendices to the *General Report*, we find each of the five colleges were thoroughly described. It is very valuable to review some of the salient points on each of the five universities. These supplemented the *Report* itself in providing very clear information on the state of the divinity halls within the universities and clarified the situation that prompted the Commission to make its detailed recommendations.

Both Glasgow and Edinburgh divinity halls were averaging around two hundred students each in 1825-1830. However, it must be borne in mind that this was inclusive of regular and irregular students. For example, students at the Edinburgh Divinity Hall for the 1825-1826 session included 131 regular and 92 irregular. King's College for the 1826-1827 session actually listed more irregular students than regular – 81 irregular, 69 regular.[60] St. Mary's College appears to have been the exception, the Commissioners finding that the professors there were very strict about attendance and refused to issue certificates to any who were not regular or did not remain until the end. It should also be remembered that the definition of a divinity session at St.

---

[58] Mechie, "Education for the Ministry", 1:132, 133.
[59] Mechie, "Education for the Ministry", 1:174-175.
[60] *Royal Commission... 1831*, 161, 322.

Mary's College was from December 1 to the beginning of April, a time of four months.[61]

The Commissioners also help us to understand more about Thomas Chalmers' work as a professor of divinity at Edinburgh. Chalmers was appointed in 1828 following Professor William Ritchie. Chalmers immediately went to work increasing the number of lectures given (Ritchie only gave a total of forty per session). His goal was to go through a complete series of lectures on divinity in three or four sessions. He began with Butler's *Analogy* and Paley's *Evidences*, then proceeded to his own lectures on natural theology and Christian evidences, which were subsequently published. Chalmers told the Commission that in Session One he heard 160 student discourses (which would not have been unusual).[62] Clearly Chalmers was moving away from the practice of his predecessor, who was the minister of the High Kirk and the professor of divinity and hence not free to devote as much time to class work.

Another change at Edinburgh by 1830 was the increase in attendance in the class of ecclesiastical history. In 1799 there were only thirty students taking the Church history class, but in 1825-1826 there were 126. The Church history continued to be taught in two parts; first, the chronology of the Old and New Testaments and then ecclesiastical history. The mode of instruction in the class was by lectures and student discourses, with examinations on the lectures (oral) but none on the textbooks.[63]

Turning to the Commissioners specific report on Glasgow University and its divinity hall, we find that the Commission recognized Professor Stevenson MacGill's goal and organization in teaching the divinity class. They recorded MacGill's distaste for irregular attendance: "that partial attendance ought not to be permitted, at least to the extent which is at present allowed by the church".[64] They also noted MacGill's desire to see a second divinity professor at Glasgow besides himself. The principal, though technically primarius of divinity, was virtually uninvolved in the divinity hall, though he was the minister of the cathedral. The professor of Church history taught both in the divinity hall and in the faculty of arts, where he was also the professor for civil history. Likewise, the subject matter at Glasgow for Church history was the same as that at Edinburgh.[65]

The Commission found that the Glasgow Hebrew classes in the late 1820s averaged thirty-five to fifty students in year one and about fifteen students in year two. The Commissioners wrote that the professor also taught classes in

---

[61] *Royal Commission... 1831*, 400.
[62] *Royal Commission... 1831*, 153-154.
[63] *Royal Commission... 1831*, 154.
[64] *Royal Commission... 1831*, 251-252.
[65] *Royal Commission... 1831*, 252.

French, Persian and Arabic, but they did not state if this was in arts or divinity.[66]

The Commissioner's Report on King's College Divinity Hall is not very encouraging. Again, the principal, though primarius of divinity, did not teach. The professor of divinity neither conducted examinations of students in public or private; and though students of divinity attended the lectures of both the professors of divinity at King's and Marischal, the two professors did not work in concert. Therefore students may have received lectures on the same subject from each. The King's professor of divinity lectured for one and a half hours per week and on Saturdays heard student discourses.[67] The Commission also reported that for many years there was no Hebrew class taught at King's, but during this time it was meeting for one hour a day during session, from December 22 to the first of April. About eight to ten students attended this Hebrew class; and if there was a second class, about two or three students attended.[68] Finally, the Commission simply stated that the library at King's showed that divinity students borrowed on average thirty books per session.[69] The Commissioners did not state if the King's students used other libraries such as presbytery, parochial or Marischal library. In the 1826-1827 session, only fourteen students borrowed any books from the Marischal library, totaling sixty-nine books.[70] However, this could mean that students simply went to read and never borrowed.

Likewise, at Marischal College the Commissioners found that the teaching of Hebrew was at a poor standard. In the 1826-1827 session, nineteen students took Hebrew but often did not show up to any class. The Commissioners concluded:

> The students might perhaps be able to consult lexicons for themselves for a little while after they leave College, but have attained so little familiarity with the process, that it is for the most part soon forgotten.[71]

On a positive note, in 1825 both King's and Marischal introduced a series of special lectures on themes in the field of pastoral theology. In both instances these lectures came about from estates which provided endowment. At Marischal these started in 1825 from the trustees of the will of John Gordon and at King's from the bequest of Alexander Murray of Philadelphia. The Murray Lectures were delivered on Sunday mornings and many were published, as required by one of the provisions of the bequest.[72] It would appear

---

[66] *Royal Commission... 1831*, 253.
[67] *Royal Commission... 1831*, 321-322.
[68] *Royal Commission... 1831*, 322.
[69] *Royal Commission... 1831*, 332.
[70] *Royal Commission... 1831*, 362.
[71] *Royal Commission... 1831*, 355.
[72] *Royal Commission... 1831*, 348, 315.

that there was only one Gordon Lecture on "Practical Religion" each year, whereas the Murray Lectureships formed a series each Sunday over the winter months.

In the *Report* St. Mary's College came the closest to what the Commissioners envisaged as the ideal for a divinity hall, having four professors. The Commissioners found that at St. Mary's the principal was primarius professor of divinity, the only principal in Scotland actually still teaching in 1826. The St. Mary's principal taught on Monday, Wednesday and Friday in the four month session, and on Saturdays he heard student discourses. His chief focus was to teach systematic theology. He was using Paley's *Evidences* and George Hill's *Lectures in Divinity*. The principal at this time was Robert Heldane, who delivered his lectures in a two year cycle.[73] The second professor of divinity (John Mitchell) taught on Tuesdays and Thursdays. The Commissioners noted that he concentrated on matters of biblical criticism and examined in Greek. The third chair was Church history, also taught two days a week, Tuesday and Thursday. The Church history course had three parts – Old Testament chronology, historical theology disputes, and New Testament and ecclesiastical history. However, the Commissioners discovered that the Church history classes had not yet managed to get beyond A.D. 1400. The attendance of students in the Church history class was the same as for the primarius and second divinity professor's classes, as the standard at St. Mary's required all regular students to attend all classes. The Hebrew professor taught on Mondays, Wednesdays and Fridays and encouraged his students to keep up their Hebrew studies over the summer. In the third session this professor also taught some Syriac and Chaldee.[74] The student numbers in the first and senior sessions were all high, indicative of a very different atmosphere from King's or Marischal. Also, two features of student life at St. Mary's were particularly mentioned by the Commissioners. First, St. Andrews appeared to be the strictest of all the universities concerning student attendance at church. The United Colleges' students went to St. Leonard's Church, whereas the St. Mary's Colleges' students went to the Town Church. The second unique feature was the Prayer Hall at St. Mary's College, where at 9:00 A.M. each day the divinity students took turns in leading in prayers, reading Scripture and singing Psalms. The Commissioners applauded this, yet noted that at some point the professors had stopped coming, and they thought the professors should once again rotate in attending to the Prayer Hall.[75]

The 1831 printed *Report* in its entirety provides one of the finest summaries of the nature of theological training in the five existing Scottish universities of the late 1820s. Likewise, the many comments and recommendations which

---

[73] *Royal Commission... 1831*, 405.
[74] *Royal Commission... 1831*, 406-407.
[75] *Royal Commission... 1831*, 410-411.

were given in this *Report* can be traced throughout the remainder of Period VI to discover how Church and university responded.

The Chair of Biblical Criticism and Robert Lee

One of the prominent recommendations of the 1826-1830 Royal Commission was the establishment of a Chair of Biblical Criticism in each of the Scottish universities. In a formal sense only one university, the University of Edinburgh, had complied with this. They appointed Robert Lee to this chair in 1847. However, the Commissioners of 1858-1862 did find that St. Mary's College was functioning as if one professor of divinity was also the professor of biblical criticism.[76]

Robert Lee held this professorship for twenty-one years in conjunction with being the parish minister of Old Greyfriars and Dean of Chapel Royal. Professor Lee's contributions in the direction of innovations in the Church of Scotland's worship services are generally more recognized today than those as a professor of biblical criticism. Lee is remembered for introducing standing in worship for singing, printed prayers and the use of the harmonium.[77] However, it is necessary to briefly review Lee's contributions as Chair of Biblical Criticism as he was the first to formally hold this position in the Scottish universities.

Lee's contemporaries did not see him as a Tischendorf or a Delitzsch, but rather as a "gatherer" and a "disseminator" of what others wrote. "[H]e stood mid-way between the scientific and the popular spheres, knowing how to take from the one, and how to transfer to the other."[78] Evidently he was a great admirer of the works of Principal Campbell of Aberdeen and read extensively from what was coming from Germany, Holland, America and France in the field of biblical criticism.[79] One of his former students, Robert Wallace, described Lee's classes as full of variety. One year was chiefly Old Testament and one year chiefly New Testament. Within these yearly divisions, Lee broke up the material into weekly sub-divisions:

> one day was given to archaeology from a text-book; another to lecturing and examination; another to familiar Scriptural exposition; another to criticism of exercises by students.... The subjects of textual criticism and hermeneutics were treated very much in the way of exhibiting general principles by the discussion of

---

[76] *Report of the Commission... 1858*, 522.
[77] *DSCHT*, 476; R. H. Story, *Life and Remains of Robert Lee*, vols. 1 and 2 (London, 1870), 1:114-126; 2:186-211; Douglas Murray, "Disruption to Union", in *Studies in the History of Worship in Scotland*, second edition, eds. D. Forrester and D. Murray (Edinburgh, 1996), 91-92, 99.
[78] Story, *Life and Remains of Robert Lee*, 2:201-202.
[79] Story, *Life and Remains of Robert Lee*, 2:253-254. While in Germany and Switzerland, Lee visited several churches and commented on their worship services.

opposite specimens and illustrations... while the whole handling of the topics treated of was pervaded with such a spirit of devotion to truth, and jealousy for its proper assertion, as to make it not merely a contribution to intellectual enlightenment, but a valuable moral discipline.[80]

Lee's chief writing was *Prayers for Public Worship*, in the field of liturgy, for which he is mainly remembered today. Yet he was involved in one work in the field of biblical studies, a *Reference Bible*, which he completed in 1853 and was published in 1854. It was attacked by one Free Church reviewer as propagating heretical teachings such as Socinianism and the doctrine of universal redemption. In 1854 he was invited to become the principal of St. Mary's College but declined the invitation.[81] The *Reference Bible* was chiefly Lee's production except for Proverbs to Malachi, which was written by his friend Thomas Barclay, subsequently the principal of Glasgow University.[82]

Lee's contribution to theological education at the time included his vocal support for the instituting of the B.D. degree. The 1826-1830 Commissioners had recommended the instituting of the B.D. degree, and it was instituted at Edinburgh University very briefly from 1836-1843 and conferred upon those who were in regular attendance in the Edinburgh Divinity Hall and subscribed to the Confession of Faith and Formula of the Church of Scotland. After 1843 it fell into disuse until the 1858-1862 Commission again recommended its use. It was re-instated in Edinburgh in 1864 under these terms: all students had to possess the M.A. degree, and if a member of the Church of Scotland, they must have studied one regular session in the Edinburgh Divinity Hall. If not members of the Church of Scotland, they must have attended one session in the Edinburgh University Divinity Hall and taken two classes. All students had to be examined for the degree.

Needless to say, this resulted in much controversy, chiefly it appears with the Free Church of Scotland, whose spokesman was Dr. Robert Candlish. The leading opponent for the Edinburgh University was Lee, who argued that in 1836 both Thomas Chalmers and David Welsh recommended that the B.D. of 1836 be awarded only to Church of Scotland students who had prosecuted all their theological studies in the University of Edinburgh.[83] The exchange between Lee and Candlish appears to have been heated, and Lee's final two concluding points in a lecture on the topic stated that:

> [1] our degree of B.D. is in no sense and to no extent a certificate of the faith or the religious opinions of the holder, but simply of his having made a certain proficiency in theological studies. So that any student is entitled to take a degree who has complied with the academical conditions, if he can satisfy the examiners

---

[80] Story, *Life and Remains of Robert Lee*, 2:210.
[81] Story, *Life and Remains of Robert Lee*, 1:223-224, 227.
[82] Story, *Life and Remains of Robert Lee*, 1:319.
[83] Story, *Life and Remains of Robert Lee*, 2:194-195.

that he possesses the requisite amount of knowledge – in short, by granting him this degree we only certify what he knows, not what he believes; this important point we leave to be inquired into by the Church to which he belongs, and in which he seeks to be a minister...

[2] Nor can I allow to pass without remark the assertion that our 'Theological Faculty is simply the Divinity Hall of the Established Church.' It is the Divinity Hall of the country – of the Kingdom of Scotland...[84]

Professors and Their Writings

We have already mentioned the literary output of Robert Lee on liturgy together with his *Reference Bible*. The nineteenth century Scottish divinity professors did produce some lasting works in the field of history, which have been passed on as a more enduring contribution than anything else they produced. The three leading historical writers of Period VI were James Seaton Reid, John Lee and Alexander F. Mitchell. Reid's contributions were two-fold. He edited Mosheim's *Institutes of Ecclesiastical History*, which was widely used as a textbook. Mosheim's work was popular for well over a century both in Seceder and Church of Scotland divinity halls. John Brown of Haddington's *Church History* is basically a compendium from Mosheim. Reid's other major work was his three volume *History of the Presbyterian Church in Ireland*, reprinted recently in 1998, 150 years after the first issues of 1834-1853.[85]

John Lee, one of the leading Establishment ministers of the Church of Scotland before and after the Disruption, contributed two major historical works, *Lectures on the History of the Church of Scotland* and *The University of Edinburgh, 1583-1839,* both of which were published posthumously. The third divine known for his historical writings was Alexander F. Mitchell, who during Period VI was professor of Hebrew in St. Mary's College and did not move to the Chair of Divinity and Ecclesiastical History until 1868. His writings on the Westminster Assembly and Confession did not actually begin to appear until 1866 and thus technically take us into the next period, yet we must at least make mention of him here.[86]

Since Stevenson MacGill spans both Period V and VI, we will not repeat here his literary efforts which in Period VI were edited and reprinted. The leading theological writers in the Scottish universities in Period VI were Thomas Chalmers and Daniel Dewar. Chalmers left the Church of Scotland in 1843 and hence his professorship of divinity at Edinburgh University, but much of his writing material was printed by then. In fact, his *Collected Works* were printed between 1835 and 1842 and ran to twenty-five volumes. After his death

---

[84] Story, *Life and Remains of Robert Lee,* 2:200.
[85] *DSCHT,* 701; James S. Reid, *History of the Presbyterian Church in Ireland,* 3 vols., ed. W. D. Killen, original 1853 (Stoke-on-Trent, 1998).
[86] *DSCHT,* 475, 594.

ten volumes of posthumous works were published. None of the other professors of divinity in Scotland could compare with Chalmers in pure magnitude of material published. Much of these writings were for his classes, whether it be lectures on Butler or on systematic theology.[87] Daniel Dewar certainly was not such a prolific writer of theology as Chalmers, yet he likely ranks second in terms of volumes written at this time. Dewar wrote two volumes on *Elements of Moral Philosophy and Christian Ethics* and three volumes published posthumously, *Elements of Systematic Theology,* plus *The Nature and Obligations of Pastoral and Family Religion.* John MacLeod has treated Dewar as one of the competent Calvinistic theologians within the state church and "a prominent Evangelical. His Systematic Theology inclined to be more Biblical than dogmatic".[88]

The last three writers who were also in the divinity halls in Period VI were James Kidd, Duncan Mearns and William Laurence Brown. The latter, Brown, died in 1830, so he was also a professor spanning Periods V and VI. Brown's most influential writing was *A Comparative View of Christianity, and of the Other Forms of Religion* (1826). This work was highly acclaimed as orthodox and was used by Secession theologians and Church of Scotland divines.[89] Both Kidd and Mearns made contributions to biblical studies and pastoral theology amongst other things. Kidd wrote *A Catechism, for Assisting the Young Preparing to Approach the Lord's Table for the First Time*, and Mearns wrote two volumes of *Lectures on Scripture Evidence.* Referring to MacLeod again, we see that in passing he notes that Mearns critiqued Chalmers early work on *The Evidences* "for its exclusively objective character" and for not giving proper place to the character of special revelation.[90]

Summary

Only by examining the *Report* of the Universities' Commission, 1826-1830, can a proper understanding be found of the theological education of ministers within the Church of Scotland in this period. This then must be viewed alongside how the General Assembly responded. As we have seen, this was not always quickly, but by the end of Period VI the recommendations of the Royal Commission were principally in place. The study of divinity in the university

---

[87] *DNB,* 9:454; *DSCHT,* 160.
[88] MacLeod, *Scottish Theology,* 267.
[89] See the review in *Edinburgh Theological Magazine,* 2 (1827), 35.
[90] MacLeod, *Scottish Theology,* 197. Chalmers' work was influenced by Scottish Common Sense Realism and properly belongs to the evidentialist school of apologetics in contrast to Abraham Kuyper's *A Priori* theological methodolgy, which was presuppositionalist. These modern classifications, however, do have certain problems which one finds alluded to in Donald MacLeod's article on "Systematic Theology" in *DSCHT,* 810: "It is also very difficult to distinguish between the 'Common Sense' of the philosopher and the theistic presuppositionalism of Calvin and St Paul...."

divinity halls was taking on a new look as the nineteenth century emerged, and by 1860 the foundations for the study of theology for the ministry were being laid for the future and would be built upon in subsequent periods. There had certainly been major changes from preceding periods. In fact, we find it is not that many steps from 1860 to the course of such education in our age.

As may appear obvious to some readers, this period of Universities' Commissions will highlight the relationship of Church and State in training for the ministry. The call for change/reform was not always driven by the Church.

PART TWO

Theological Education and Training in the Secession

CHAPTER 8

Introduction: Origins of the Secession and First Efforts for a Divinity Hall

Introduction

We come now to Part Two of this book, which will concentrate upon the work of the Secession Church (1733) and its branches in the area of theological education and training through to 1847. In this first chapter of Part Two, brief mention is made concerning the origin of the Secession which eventually led to the need to train their own ministers. Consequently their patterns for theological education and training were established. Thus, this opening chapter will serve as an introduction to the first efforts for a divinity hall in the Secession Church up to 1747. Subsequent chapters will trace the developments up to 1847.

Origins

Thomas McCrie in his *The Story of the Scottish Church*, a volume of his popular lectures, provided the wisest and best way of stating the origin of the Secession of 1733. He asserted that there must be a proper distinguishing between the "occasion" and the "cause"; that is, the immediate "occasion" is one thing, but the underlying "cause" is much wider. McCrie wrote:

> The real origin of this movement [the Secession], if we may judge even from recent measures, has been misunderstood. It has been generally ascribed to direct opposition to the Act of Queen Anne restoring patronage.[1]

However, the immediate "occasion" of the Secession "was the action of the church rather than that of the state".[2] The action of the Church was an overture before the Church of Scotland's General Assembly of 1731 whereby the Church undermined its own Acts of 1690. It proposed to give absolute rights to

---
[1] Thomas McCrie, Jr., *The Story of the Scottish Church*, original 1875 (Glasgow, 1988), 465.
[2] McCrie, *Story of the Scottish Church*, 465.

elders and heritors.[3] These heritors had to be Protestants, but this could include Protestants who were of the "Prelatist" party. Despite much protest from several presbyteries and a petition of protest signed by seventeen hundred people, the General Assembly of 1732 enacted the controversial legislation.[4]

The leading individual who spoke out in opposition following this Assembly ruling was the Rev. Ebenezer Erskine. In October, 1732, as Moderator of the Synod of Perth and Stirling, he delivered a sermon from the text Psalm 118:22. In the sermon Erskine referred to the passing of the 1732 act on patronage by the General Assembly as a direct attack on the crown rights of Jesus Christ:

> I am firmly persuaded that, if a remedy is not provided, that act will very soon terminate in the overthrow of the Church of Scotland, and of a faithful ministry therein; in regard that the power of electing ministers is thereby principally lodged in the hands of a set of men that are generally disaffected by the power of godliness, and to the doctrine, discipline, worship, and government of this Church.[5]

Erskine was immediately placed under censure by the Synod, and he subsequently appealed to the Assembly. The General Assembly of May 15, 1733, concurred with the censure of the Synod of Perth and Stirling and "appointed him to be rebuked and admonished by the Moderator at their own bar".[6] This led to the protest of Ebenezer Erskine, Alexander Moncrieff, William Wilson and James Fisher. Later that same year (November), the Commission of the General Assembly voted to censure the four men by declaring them now suspended from the ministry. This action thereby brought the four men together on December 5, 1733, at Gairney Bridge, Kinross to constitute the Associate Presbytery.[7]

The General Assembly of 1734 made an effort to restore the four seceding brethren, and this can be attributed to sympathizers within the Kirk, men like John Willison.[8] Perhaps it was a case of "too little, too late", yet even William Wilson (one of the four), who contemplated a possible return to the Kirk, concluded that the defections within the Kirk were too numerous.[9]

The writings by the "Four Brethren" throughout the 1730s were clear apologetic works stating the reasons for the Secession.[10] They were formally

---

[3] *AGACS*, 614.
[4] *AGACS*, 620-612; McCrie, *Story of the Scottish Church*, 465.
[5] McCrie, *Story of the Scottish Church*, 466; Ebenezer Erskine, *The Stone Rejected by the Builders, Exalted as the Headstone of the Corner* (Edinburgh, 1732).
[6] *AGACS*, 624.
[7] McCrie, *Story of the Scottish Church*, 467.
[8] *DSCHT*, 874.
[9] McKerrow, *History of the Secession Church*, 88-89; *AGACS*, 629.
[10] There are many sources to read for primary documentation for the Secession as formulated by the Seceders themselves. Mention is made here of some of these: *Acts*

Introduction: Origins of the Secession and First Efforts for a Divinity Hall 171

deposed in 1740. The reasons they provide for their Secession went beyond the Assembly Act of 1732 and patronage. These include failure to formally repeal the censures against Ebenezer Erskine and his sermon at the Synod of Perth and Stirling. In addition, the Assembly was still not acting upon the injustice whereby local congregations had ministers "thrust" upon them. Rescinding the 1732 Act would have necessitated reforms to be executively carried forth. Doctrinal errors were continuing to be tolerated. This was evidenced in the admitting of men into the ministry who were not fit candidates, morally and doctrinally, as well as allowing the heresies of Professor Simson of Glasgow and Professor Archibald Campbell of St. Andrews.[11] There is a large body of literature available which discusses the reasons for the Secession and outlines how it came about. A full study needs to include a discussion on the Marrow and the doctrines of grace, as this was also integral to the origins of the Secession.[12]

---

and Proceedings of the Associate Presbytery, Met at Edinburgh, May 1739 Containing their Declinature... (Edinburgh, 1739); *Acts of the Associate Presbytery: Act concerning the Doctrine of Graces... Act for Renewing the National Covenant of Scotland, and the Solemn League and Covenant...* (Edinburgh 1744); William Wilson, *Defence of Reformation Principles* (Edinburgh, 1739); A. Gib, *The Present Truth: A Display of the Secession Testimony*, 2 vols. (Edinburgh, 1744); "Minutes of the Associate Presbytery, 1733-1740", National Archives of Scotland, Edinburgh *MS* CH3/27/1. See the 1734 "Testimony", 7-88. The full title reads: "A Testimony to the Doctrines, Worship, Government and Discipline of the Church of Scotland: or Reasons by Mr. Ebenezer Erskine, Minister at Stirling, Mr. William Wilson, Minister at Perth, Mr. Alexander Moncrieff, Minister at Abernethy, and Mr. James Fisher, Minister at Kinclaven, for their Protestation entered before the Commission of the General Assembly, November 1733, upon the intention of a Sentence of the said Commissions, loosing their Relations to their respective Parishes..."

A pamphlet warfare issued at the time of the Secession and lasted for several years afterwards. These help provide insight into the nature of the Secession and its causes. See: Alexander Ferguson, *A Display of the Act and Testimony published by Mr. Ebenezer Erskine and his Associates who separated from the Church of Scotland in the year 1734, and were deposed by the General Assembly in the year 1740...* (Glasgow, 1761) – a work which charges the Seceders with schism, 3-47; David McLerie, *The Clergy-man Corrected by the Weaver; in a letter from David McLerie, Weaver in Paisley, to the Rev. Mr. Alexander Ferguson, Minister of the Gospel at Kilwinning* (Glasgow, 1761) – a defense of the Secession, ii-47.

[11] McKerrow, *History of the Secession Church*, 89-90. See: "Minutes of the Associate Presbytery – Testimony..." [*MS* 1734], 56-60 concerning Simson, and 60-61 concerning Campbell.

[12] William MacKelvie, *Annals and Statistics of the United Presbyterian Church* (Edinburgh, 1873), 4-8. MacKelvie in an interesting fashion treats the rise of the "praying societies" as an "anterior cause" to the Secession (pp. 1-4). This may have some merit; however, for the purposes of this book, I will treat the praying societies as connected to the Secession's theological educational endeavours.

First Efforts: William Wilson, "the face of an ox" (Perth)[13]

Very soon after the Secession of 1733, "the Four Brethren", as they were often referred to, began to receive applications from societies and groups of families to supply them with a preacher. These individual societies would meet weekly, and then several societies would meet together once a month as "The Association". Delegates from these Associations would convene once a year at "The Correspondence". According to MacKelvie, these meetings at the various levels served "as the remote origin of many Secession congregations" and

> in several places "The Correspondence", in its collective capacity, tendered a written adherence to the Presbytery formed by "The Four Brethren", and at once became a congregation in connection with the Presbytery.[14]

The requests were not limited to Scotland. In 1736 the presbytery received an application from a group of families in Lisburn, Ireland, requesting a minister. McKerrow summarized the response: "But at that time the request could not be complied with, as the Presbytery had no preachers to send."[15] It is within the context of this pressing need for ministers and with a clear commitment to having an educated ministry, that the Secession at the presbytery meeting of November 4, 1736, proposed that one of the Four be appointed to teach and train men for the ministry.[16] The Revs. Ebenezer Erskine and Alexander Moncrieff were appointed as a committee to "prepare an overture, which should regulate the Presbytery's procedure in this important matter".[17] The next day they submitted their overture:

> Considering the lamentable and desolate condition of many parishes in Scotland, by reason of the violent intrusions that have been made upon them, and likewise considering the frequent and repeated applications to this Presbytery, from several quarters of the land, for sending forth labourers into the Lord's vineyard, that so they might have the benefit of the gospel, and the ordinances thereof, therefore the

---

[13] P. Landreth, *The United Presbyterian Divinity Hall, in its Changes and Enlargements for 140 Years* (Edinburgh, 1876), 37. Wilson was referred to as "the ox" of the Four Fathers of the Secession to symbolize the patience with which he bore the yoke of toil for the Secession. See Andrew Ferrier, *Memoirs of the Rev. William Wilson* (Glasgow, 1830), 357. The allusion comes from Ezekiel – Moncrieff is "the lion", Ebenezer Erskine "the face of a man", and Fisher "the eagle".

[14] MacKelvie, *Annals and Statistics of the UP Church*, 2. For an example see, East Church, in Haddington, 216, in MacKelvie which reads: "A number of praying societies in East Lothian acceded to the Associate Presbytery in March, 1737. They were united in a General Association, and designated 'The Correspondence of East Lothian'. They were publicly recognized as a congregation in connection with the Presbytery in October of that year...."

[15] McKerrow, *History of the Secession*, 177, 100.

[16] Landreth, *The UPD Hall*, 34.

[17] McKerrow, *History of the Secession*, 101.

Introduction: Origins of the Secession and First Efforts for a Divinity Hall

committee are of opinion that this Presbytery should make some step towards the relief of the Lord's oppressed heritage, especially considering the loud call in Providence thereto, by nominating and appointing one of their number to take the inspection of the youth that should offer themselves to be trained up for the holy ministry, and also that every one of the brethren should carefully look out for faithful men, to whom the ministry should be committed.[18]

The Rev. Wilson was unanimously appointed the first professor, and at the next meeting of presbytery he announced that he would begin the first session in March to May, 1737. The presbyters were to correspond with the various societies to make this announcement and to advise everyone that students who were properly recommended would be received.[19] All of the lectures were to be conducted in Latin.[20]

William Wilson (1690-1744) was born in Glasgow and graduated M.A. from the University of Glasgow in 1707. His father had fled to Holland to seek refuge during the "killing times". He was named William in honour of William, Prince of Orange.[21] It is believed he matriculated at Glasgow in 1704 following his personal covenant to God in August of that year. The following summer Wilson wrote in his diary of the blessings he experienced in going to the various communions throughout his area, especially where the ministers were evangelical.[22] He took his divinity studies at the divinity hall within Glasgow University. The two professors of divinity at this time were Principal John Stirling and Professor John Simson.

Ferrier tells us of the personal covenants which Wilson undertook during his study of divinity, for example:

30th October, 1708 [and subscribed to 1st November, 1708]
  I, William Wilson, do declare that my coming and now entering on the study of Theology, is (or, at least, the desire of my soul is that it should be) for God's glory, and the good of souls;... therefore, I do beg that he may be pleased to give me capacity, memory, and other qualifications, for this end; and make good his promises of assisting me by his grace... And I do promise, in his strength, to spend my time better than hitherto, and not to trifle the same away, but to lay it out for God, in my day and generation, improving it for his glory. And, I do bless him who hath, in any manner, determined my mind to the great study of Theology, and

---

[18] McKerrow, *History of the Secession*, 101-102; "Minutes of the Associate Presbytery" (5 Nov.1736).
[19] "Minutes of the Associate Presbytery, 1733-1740", *MS*, Oct.20,1736, 249.
[20] McKerrow, *History of the Secession*, 102.
[21] *DNB*, 62:145-146; John Eadie, *Life and Times of the Rev. William Wilson in Fathers of the United Presbyterian Church* (Edinburgh, 1849), 97; Ferrier, *Memoirs of William Wilson*, 29-30.
[22] Ferrier, *Memoirs of William Wilson*, 35. Evidently this diary of his early years has been lost.

bless him have opportunity for the same, and plead that he may be forthcoming with his Spirit, that I may apply my mind to my mind to my studies.

I do devote myself, with all my heart, to serve God in the gospel of his Son, in my day and generation; and I desire to guard against seeking myself in this most solemn work, and pray for pardon through the blood of Christ, for all my past sins, and to be kept from wavering in my studies; and, in hope of God's gracious assistance in promoting my end, and giving all that is necessary for the study....[23]

Such a covenant is reflective of a student who was strongly influenced by Scottish Covenant theology and piety and who became one of the Marrowmen. We have no reason to doubt the sincerity of the covenant, as the whole tenor of his life was of this order. Possibly this 1708 covenant was at the commencement of his divinity course.

Wilson provided a schedule of his day while studying divinity at Glasgow. Although he had completed the philosophical course in 1707, he continued to study in certain philosophical subjects. The schedule was as follows:

> Rise at 6 in the morning: in summer at 5.
>   Time divided
> From rising till 9 – prayer and Scripture reading
> From 9 to 11 – Natural Philosophy & Biblical Criticism
> From 11 to 12 – Latin
> From 12 to 2 – Hebrew and Greek
> From 2 to 5 or 6 – Systematic Theology
> From 6 to 7 – History
> From 7 to 9 – Common-place Book
> The rest in prayer.
> Prayer also at 10, at 2, and at 6. At lying down and rising up: read three chapters of the Bible every day: read through the Hebrew Scriptures, three chapters a day.
>
> Glasgow, 2nd June, 1710.[24]

It appears that he interrupted his studies in divinity at Glasgow in 1711, as he then spent time in Angus with friends from July, 1711, to April, 1712. Then he did one more session in Glasgow in divinity (or a part session) in 1712, hoping to be taken on trial for licensure by Glasgow Presbytery. However, Glasgow Presbytery, under the influence of Professor Simson, did not take him on trial because of his evangelicalism. The Presbytery of Dunfermline invited him to undergo his trials there.[25] This presbytery had several noted evangelicals in its membership. In April, 1713, he delivered his first discourse to the Dunfermline Presbytery. It was approved and he was assigned his second

---

[23] Ferrier, *Memoirs of William Wilson*, 43-44.

[24] Ferrier, *Memoirs of William Wilson*, 52.

[25] Ferrier, *Memoirs of William Wilson*, 62-63; Eadie, *Life of William Wilson*, 105.

Introduction: Origins of the Secession and First Efforts for a Divinity Hall   175

discourse on the question: "What kind of covenant was it that God made with Adam in a state of innocence?" Wilson recorded most of the other discourses which were also assigned to him: Hebrews 3:14, 15, Ephesians 3:16 and Genesis 6:6. Then on September 23, 1713, he delivered a "popular sermon" and "was carried through the rest of my trials". He was approved for licensure and exhorted by the Rev. Ralph Erskine. It would appear that Wilson gave at least six discourses to the presbytery plus other oral examinations prior to his licensure. These questions were probably on church government, the Confession and perhaps Church history.[26] Wilson's licensure trials are reviewed here as they highlight the presbytery's work in the examination process.

The next three years were spent as a probationer before he was settled and ordained at Perth in 1716. The parish of Dalry in Ayrshire had wanted Wilson, but evidently the influence of Professor Simson on the Presbytery of Irvine prevented his settlement there.[27]

His involvement in the Marrow and with the founding of the Secession has been noted, so we turn to Wilson, the professor of divinity for the Associate Presbytery. Since he wrote very little, it is difficult to reconstruct his lectures in the divinity hall, unlike the noted John Brown of Haddington. Wilson did not write any works on biblical exegesis or extensive doctrinal treatises. Rather his writings were polemical and apologetical for the support of the Secession; for example,[28] *A Defence of the Reformation – Principles of the Church of Scotland...* (Edinburgh, 1739; expanded Glasgow, 1739), a work which defended the Secession against attacks by a Church of Scotland minister, the Rev. John Currie. Wilson's chief literary place was to clearly set forth the rationale for the Secession.

The other main work is a collection of his sermons which were published posthumously in 1748. Several of these sermons had been published singly prior to his death. This posthumous collection contains seven sermons, over half of which were given at communion seasons.[29] (If one reads the list of

---

[26] Ferrier, *Memoirs of William Wilson*, 82-91.
[27] Eadie, *Life of William Wilson*, 113.
[28] *FES*, 4:237; Ferrier, *Memoirs of William Wilson*, 364.
[29] William Wilson, *Sermons by the Reverend and Learned Mr. William Wilson, late Minister of the Gospel at Perth* (Edinburgh, 1748). The table of contents reads as follows: [I have inserted the texts]
    I. The Church's Extremity Christ's Opportunity. (Mic.4:10)
    II. The Lamb's Retinue attending him whithersoever he goeth. (Rev.14:4)
    III. The Father's Promise to the Son, a clear Bow in the Church's darkest Cloud. (Ps.89:29)
    IV. The Watchman's Duty and Desire. (Ps. 90:17)
    V. Steadfastness in the Faith recommended. (1 Cor.16:13)
    VI. The Blessedness lost in the first Adam, to be found in Christ the second Adam. (Ps.72:17)
    The communion season messages are within I, II, and V.

sermons published by the Erskines, one would notice the same percentage).[30] Though the table of contents lists six sermons, there are really seven in total. However, several sermons are compilations from two or three sermons "run together". This accounts for their considerable length. One sermon is prefaced by a very long apologetic for the Secession.[31]

From this brief sketch of Wilson's life with a focus on his own education, we can conclude that he was a most earnest and zealous student. His sympathies were clearly that of a Marrow divine and with Scottish covenant theology. He was a man of great discipline and aptly earned the title "the ox". Thus, it is no surprise that he was appointed the first professor of divinity.

Wilson selected Marck's *Medulla* as his chief textbook for systematic theology. Evidently Wilson's copy was bound with blank sheets of paper interleaved to allow him to make comments of his own. This was not unlike what Brown had done to his *System of Divinity*. Wilson's copy of the *Medulla* made its way into the possession of Professor Archibald Bruce.[32] His two chief biographers, Ferrier and Eadie, provided few other details about his professorship. We know the number of students was more than that of the four divinity halls in the universities, with the exception of Edinburgh. This was stated in a letter from Ralph Erskine to George Whitefield, April 10, 1741: "Our Professor of Divinity has more candidates for the ministry under his charge than most of the public colleges except Edinburgh."[33]

The first session of 1737 at the hall in Perth had six students. Since one student, John Hunter, had previously studied in the Church of Scotland and one of its halls, he only did one session under Wilson. Thus, John Hunter was the first to be licensed and subsequently ordained in the Secession churches. This

---

[30] Pieter van Harten, *De Prediking van Ebenezer en Ralph Erskine* (Gravenhage, Netherlands, 1986), 283.

[31] Wilson, "Steadfastness in the Faith... to which is prefixed a Short Account of the Occasion of publishing this, together with some reasons for his condemned conduct; directed by the Author to the People of his Pastoral Charge", in *Sermons*, iii - xxvii.

[32] Ferrier, *Memoirs of William Wilson*, 315. I have endeavoured to locate Wilson's interleaved *Medulla* but with no success. If it went to Bruce's personal library rather than to the General Associate Divinity Hall Library, it would be difficult to trace its current location. Adam Gib, the noted Antiburgher, was one of Wilson's students. See David M. Forrester, "Adam Gib, The Anti-Burgher", *RSCHS* 7 (1944), 143-144. Here Forrester discusses Gib's keen Hebrew abilities and views on the "points" as inspired by God. This reflects Thomas Boston's *Tractatus Stigmologicus Hebraco-Biblicus*. Since Hebrew was studied in university before entering the hall, Gib would have done this at Edinburgh University, and it does raise the question concerning Wilson's position on Hebrew exegesis and the points. I have yet to find any mention how this was handled in the Associate Synod divinity hall or after the Breach in either of the Secession halls.

[33] Eadie, *Life of William Wilson*, 170.

Introduction: Origins of the Secession and First Efforts for a Divinity Hall 177

first licentiate of the Secession died four months after his ordination.[34] However, George Brown's manuscript work on the "Annals of the Divinity Hall of the Secession Church..." lists John Hunter as beginning in the divinity hall in 1736. Yet, MacKelvie says the first session of the hall did not start until 1737.[35] One explanation is that Brown was out by one year on John Hunter. However, if we check his dates for the other five students in the hall session of 1737, we find that Brown recorded 1737 for all except Adam Gib, whom he also noted as starting in 1736.[36] Thus, the other possible explanation is that Hunter and Gib may have been private divinity students with William Wilson in 1736, prior to the formal opening of the hall in 1737. The Associate Presbytery Minutes are silent on this point, yet are quick to show that Wilson was the logical choice as their first professor for divinity. The matter may not be overly critical, but it raises the line of awareness between the formal and informal education and training that existed in Scotland.

Of the other students in the 1737 session, four were settled into charges in Scotland and one went to America.[37] Wilson's intake of the first session students for the duration of his professorship averaged six, thus he would likely have had around twenty to twenty-three students in total by 1740/41, when Ralph Erskine made the comment about the hall's student enrolment to George Whitefield.[38]

Though Wilson set the hall to meet at Perth for March, April and May, this should not be taken to mean it would have lasted a full three months. Likely up to two and a half months at most would have been the standard length of a

---

[34] Landreth, *The UPD Hall*, 46-48; MacKelvie, *Annals and Statistics of the UP Church*, 383; George Brown, "Annals of the Divinity Hall of the Secession Church of Scotland...", New College Library, Edinburgh, *MS* UPC3, 110-111. Brown writes about John Hunter: "The first licensed and ordained by Associate Presbytery. Zealous and popular. Preached sometimes 30 sermons in 15 days. Left a widow and family." Note this Brown *MS* goes to the year 1847.

[35] George Brown, "Annals of the Divinity Hall of the Secession Church of Scotland", 110; MacKelvie, *Annals and Statistics of the UP Church*, 652.

[36] George Brown, "Annals of the Divinity Hall of the Secession Church of Scotland", 86, 2, 50, 110, 224 and unpaginated list at beginning for "Students of Divinity, the Rev. William Wilson, Perth, Professor, 1736, John Hunter and Adam Gib". In Brown's other *MS* entitled "Alphabetical List of the Students of Divinity of the United Secession Church, from the Rise of the Secession, till the year 1840...", New College Library, Edinburgh, *MS* USC 5-11, unpaginated, Brown listed Gib as starting in 1736 and Hunter as 1737. The others all correspond with MacKelvie as 1737.

[37] Landreth, *The UPD Hall*, 46-48, 62; MacKelvie, *Annals and Statistics of the UP Church*, 652.

[38] MacKelvie, *Annals and Statistics of the UP Church*, 653; Landreth, *The UPD Hall*, 62. This is assuming that all students came and remained. That is why I suggest a maximum of twenty to twenty-three.

session.[39] In terms of method of instruction, Wilson examined the students orally and combined this with lectures. Landreth, without solid support given in his *The United Presbyterian Divinity Hall*, says that Wilson was influenced by the seventeenth century Burnet of Glasgow University in structuring the order of the hall.[40] (See Part One of this thesis, chapter 5, the section on Gilbert Burnet, for details on this method.)

No details survive as to the housing arrangements for the students in each session. We assume they stayed with various families in the congregation in Perth, as was often the custom in the other halls. For example, in Haddington Professor Brown would often go around the town early in the morning to the private dwellings where students boarded to enquire that the students were up and studying.[41]

Gleanings from the Associate Presbytery Minutes

By reading the Associate Presbytery Minutes alongside Professor Wilson's labours in the divinity hall 1737 to 1741, we gain a better perspective on theological education and training. One of the first men to be licensed and then ordained by the Associate Presbytery was Mr. John Hunter. We now follow some of the requirements he performed for the presbytery.

On May 17, 1738, Hunter delivered a popular sermon and lecture before the presbytery, both of which were approved. Then at the very next presbytery meeting, June 7, 1738, he undertook the remainder of his licensure trials:

1.) presented a thesis
2.) explained an assigned portion of the Hebrew Bible
3.) explained a portion of the Greek New Testament
   "Ad apetivirain libri"
4.) extempore questions, and
5.) chronological questions on the first half century.[42]

All of this was approved and he was licensed. Then he formally commenced ministry for the presbytery. On July 18, 1738, he was given his preaching assignments for July, August and September in Kinross, Morbattle, Stitchell, East Lothian, Linton, Cambusmethen, Fenwick, Balfour and Larbert.[43] Many of these were not beyond society status, somewhat like what today would be referred to as core groups for church planting.

---

[39] Landreth, *The UPD Hall*, 64. Based upon the fact that in 1740 the last Sunday the hall was in session was May 17th, I conclude then it was not a full three month session.
[40] Landreth, *The UPD Hall*, 35-57.
[41] Landreth, *The UPD Hall*, 60; MacKenzie, *John Brown of Haddington* (1964), 143.
[42] "Minutes of the Associate Presbytery, 1733-1740" (May 17, 1738), June 7, 1738, 320.
[43] "Minutes of the Associate Presbytery, 1733-1740", 326.

Introduction: Origins of the Secession and First Efforts for a Divinity Hall 179

It was only after licensure that the students were sent out on such a circuit. These assignments met a need of the presbytery by supplying new works, gave the student valuable experience (like an internship or a student field assignment) and allowed vacant congregations to meet candidates whom they might consider calling in the future. Thus, the post-licensure probationary period was very important to the students' training. The pattern which had started with Hunter of having a student be a probationer on average for about two years was carried through for several decades.

As we continue to follow Mr. Hunter's name in the minutes, we find that he was given more assignments at the December 14, 1738, presbytery meeting for December (1738), January and February (1739) to preach in Falkirk, Kilmacolm, Kilmaurs, Mearns, Straven, Stitchell, Morebattle, Jarrow, Stow, East Lothian and Linton.[44] As one would expect, a vacant church or society would then ask Mr. Hunter to become their minister by petitioning presbytery, and Morebattle did such on October 10, 1738. Presbytery moved slowly but finally approved the call on March 16, 1739. At this meeting they also assigned Hunter more preaching engagements for March, April and May at Balfrom, Easthouses, Dreghorn, "societies in and about Edinburgh", and Yarrow.[45]

Thus, we come to Hunter's ordination trials on May 29, 1739, which were not unlike his licensure trials: an exegesis and addition on Ephesians 1:3 and an exegesis on *An datur pecatium vemiale*. In addition he was given assignments for the next month's meeting: a lecture on 1 John 2:10-18, a popular sermon on 1 John 2:12, Psalm 3 explained from the Hebrew, an explanation of any passage presbytery would choose from the Greek New Testament, a chronology of the first half of the second century, a defense of his thesis, and extemporary questions. Presbytery approved his May 29, 1739, assignments and took up the lecture, popular sermon and remaining assignments on June 19, 1739.[46] Even though he was fully approved for ordination, he was given another preaching assignment for July and August, this time to Neilston, Kilmaurs, Galston, Wallacetown, Sanquhar and Annandale.[47]

Finally we read of John Hunter's ordination on October 17, 1739,[48] one year after the church's request and about one and a half years after his licensure. In those eighteen months he covered many miles in lowland Scotland and had about twelve presbytery assignments to complete. Divinity training was not restricted to the hall! It also tells us something about the spread of the Secession Church by 1738 and the role of the students. By 1742 we notice in the minutes that due to the large number of requests for pulpit supply a

---

[44] "Minutes of the Associate Presbytery, 1733-1740", 342.
[45] "Minutes of the Associate Presbytery, 1733-1740", 333, 351, 354.
[46] "Minutes of the Associate Presbytery, 1733-1740", 408-409, 412.
[47] "Minutes of the Associate Presbytery, 1733-1740", 415.
[48] "Minutes of the Associate Presbytery, 1733-1740", 433.

committee was erected, called appropriately the Committee for Supply. Students had a large role to play in the Secession fulfilling pulpit requests.[49]

By selecting Hunter and chronicling his time with presbytery from licensure to ordination, we are given one individual to focus upon. However, we could select the others who followed after Hunter, and we would see much of the same pattern of probationers being assigned two and three month preaching assignments amongst the churches or groups.[50] Also, it is curious to observe the way the chronology assignments were handed out – literally chronologically: Mr. Gib – assigned second half, second century; Mr. Smyton – assigned first half, third century; and Mr. Hutton – assigned second half, third century.[51] Perhaps it does not appear novel or interesting, but this was not likely a "notion" which concerned them.

Presbytery took the education of the students seriously, and one of the earliest things done was to send out the Revs. Wilson and Fisher to have each church take a collection for the students. The report for March 14, 1739, mentions that many were liberal in their givings towards this collection.[52] The collection was undertaken annually in all the churches. In the May 18, 1739, minutes of presbytery, there is a complete record of the forty-three groups who gave to the offering for the students; then follows the names of eight students who were given money from the collection.[53]

One of the Associate Presbytery's first clerks was William Hutton, a student of divinity.[54] This no doubt could be viewed today as ministerial training but was a pragmatic necessity for the presbytery at this time.

Finally, there is a curious use of words for student discourses. Sometimes the students delivered popular sermons, other times "homilies".[55] It would appear that these terms were virtually synonymous and may have depended more upon the scribe than anything else. The presbytery minutes never define exactly the nature of the various assignments. The terms employed within the Associate Presbytery divinity hall and presbytery meeting were not dissimilar from the terms used in the Church of Scotland's divinity halls or presbyteries.

As we proceed from 1734, we notice one detail which was addressed several times prior to formally beginning a student's trial for licensure. This concerned enquiring into the students "experience in religion", or "Principles of Religion

---

[49] "Minutes of the Associate Presbytery, 1741-1747", National Archives of Scotland, Edinburgh, *MS* CH3/28/1, 610 (July 13, 1742).

[50] "Minutes of the Associate Presbytery, 1733-1740", See, March 5; May 15; and July 23, 1740, and the various preaching assignments for five students, 452, 459, 477.

[51] "Minutes of the Associate Presbytery, 1733-1740", on November 6, 1739, 436-437 and for October 23, 1740, 494, where it makes it to the second half of the fifth century.

[52] "Minutes of the Associate Presbytery, 1733-1740", 344.

[53] "Minutes of the Associate Presbytery, 1733-1740", 407-408. Also, more disbursements to students, 420, and another collection and disbursement, 490.

[54] "Minutes of the Associate Presbytery, 1733-1740" (July 18, 1738), 326.

[55] "Minutes of the Associate Presbytery, 1733-1740", 408-409, 426.

and their own experience of the Power of it, were put to them". The presbytery would make this enquiry prior to the trial and then send the student out and discuss if they should proceed with the trials.[56] The Seceders saw a marriage between theology (their Marrow theology) and piety. This was reflected even in the preliminaries leading up to trials for licensure as well as in many of the texts assigned by the presbytery to the students for their popular sermons. The texts, such as Acts 16:31 or Ephesians 1:13b, clearly highlight the fullness of the gospel of grace.[57] For the Associate Presbytery and the "Four Brethren", there was a strong conviction that ministers were to preach the gospel. Such trials as this would not only have kept a student focused, but they would also have allowed the presbytery to assess the student's clarity on the gospel as well as their personal experience of it.

The Associate Presbytery divided into three presbyteries in 1745 and formed the Associate Synod. One of the first recommendations of the synod to each presbytery was to have presbytery exercises, "unless when they have young men passing trials before them".[58] From the number of student discourses of various kinds which were to be heard, it is very doubtful how many presbyterial exercises did occur. They did happen upon occasion, but the stress appears to have been upon hearing the students' discourses. With the establishment of the synod came the practice of first securing synod's approval for a student to be taken under their trials for licensure by the presbytery.[59] We have encountered this previously with the Church of Scotland synods, so the Seceders were not innovators on this point. It was also the synod that would assign students to preach in Ireland as probationers.[60]

Alexander Moncrieff, "the face of a lion" (Abernethy)

Alexander Moncrieff (1695 - 1761) was appointed the divinity professor upon the death of William Wilson, and hence the divinity hall moved from Perth to Abernethy.[61] Since there was no library at this time, the move simply meant a change of venue for instruction with a new professor. Moncrieff was heir to a Covenanter heritage, had graduated with the M.A. degree from St. Andrews in 1714, and had proceeded to study divinity under Professor James Hadow of St.

---

[56] "Minutes of the Associate Presbytery, 1741-1747", 525, 582.
[57] "Minutes of the Associate Presbytery, 1741-1747", 529, 532. The conviction on gospel and grace was a paramount matter. See further their "Act of the Associate Presbytery Concerning the Doctrine of Free Grace", 651-721, Oct. 21, 1742, in the above "Minute" volume.
[58] "Minutes of the Associate Presbytery, 1741-1747" (May 16, 1745), 891.
[59] "Minutes of the Associate Presbytery, 1741-1747" (April 10,1746), 939.
[60] "Minutes of the Associate Presbytery, 1741-1747", 939.
[61] "Minutes of the Associate Presbytery, 1741 1747", 582. The date was February 10, 1742. The presbytery also agreed that during the hall's session, the Rev. Moncrieff's pulpit would be supplied.

Mary's College, St. Andrews for three sessions. Moncrieff spoke highly of Professor Hadow's abilities.[62] Hadow was an opponent of the teaching of Professor Simson of Glasgow, a matter he had in common with Moncrieff. However, Hadow and Moncrieff saw very differently on the Marrow controversy.[63]

Hadow had studied divinity in Utrecht before taking a church, and Moncrieff also ventured to Holland, but to Leiden, to study theology. Moncrieff went to Holland in 1716 to study under the illustrious Reformed divines Wesselius and Marck. Marck wrote very favourably of Moncrieff and classified him as one of his elite students. David Young, Moncrieff's biographer, believed he recovered one of Moncrieff's printed theses from Leiden, "On the Future Subjection of the Son to the Father" on 1 Cor.15:28.[64] In common with William Wilson, Moncrieff early in his life had a keen awareness of his sin and need of the blood of Christ. He, too, recorded in diary format his attendance at various communion seasons and the spiritual effects of these times. Also, he engaged in personal covenants with God.[65]

During his year at Leiden, Moncrieff wrote a defense of the truth which Professor Simson at Glasgow was denying. Young believes that Marck and Wesselius were helpful in this defense.[66]

Moncrieff returned to Scotland and passed his licensure trials in 1718 within the Presbytery of Perth. In 1720 he was ordained and settled at Abernethy. The story of his involvement in the founding of the Secession is well known, so we pass on to his work as professor of divinity.

Like under Wilson before him, the divinity hall under Moncrieff met for three months starting in March, 1742. The first class session that year had six students, and from 1742 to 1747 (the six years he was professor for the hall of the Associate Presbytery), the first year class averaged eight students, thus making an average total enrolment each year of around thirty, somewhat larger than in Wilson's time.[67] As with Wilson, the systematics textbook was Marck's *Medulla*, and Moncrieff would give comments upon it, not lectures, along with the oral examinations. Landreth writes that Moncrieff changed to holding these examinations in English, whereas Wilson had done the examinations in Latin. (Recall that the students still had to read the *Medulla* in Latin).[68]

---

[62] David Young and John Brown (Broughton Place/Edinburgh), *Memorials of Alexander Moncrieff and James Fisher* (Edinburgh, 1849), xvii - xxiii. Also, "Memoir of the Rev. Alexander Moncrieff of Culfargie, Minister of the Gospel at Abernethy", *The Christian Magazine* (1804), 89-96, 133-140.

[63] *DSCHT*, 384.

[64] Young and Brown, *Memorials of Moncrieff and Fisher,* xviii; *DSCHT*, 384.

[65] Young and Brown, *Memorials of Moncrieff and Fisher*, xxix-xxx.

[66] Young and Brown, *Memorials of Moncrieff and Fisher*, xxxiii-xxxiv.

[67] MacKelvie, *Annals and Statistics of the UP Church*, 652-653.

[68] Landreth, *The UPD Hall*, 76, 78-79.

Following the pattern established by Wilson, Moncrieff took "special and increasing care of the discourses and the critical and exegetical exercises that were delivered or read annually by each student".[69] Evidently this work was most important to Moncrieff, who desired to form men who preached in the evangelical way. Much time was given to these students' exercises, many of which were delivered from memory. Following a student discourse, the students were asked to give their criticisms, both positive and negative. Then Professor Moncrieff would make his comments upon the discourse.[70] This practice was not unique to Moncrieff but would have been common in virtually all Scottish divinity halls, Kirk or Secession, in the eighteenth century.

Since we possess no written lectures by Alexander Moncrieff, we are unable to examine what practical divinity or ecclesiastical history he may have taught in the hall at Abernethy. His published remains are chiefly sermons, two brief treatises and then polemical matters related to the Burgess Oath and George Whitefield's visit to Scotland.[71] The sermons were clearly in the Marrow tradition and were full of the free offer of the gospel. Such titles as "The Glory of Emmanuel" and "Christ's call to the rising generation" are evidence of this tradition.[72] Thus, we know what focus Moncrieff would have given to any lectures on homiletics. "An Enquiry into the Principle Rule, and End of Moral Actions" was written to challenge Professor Archibald Campbell, professor of ecclesiastical history at St. Andrews, concerning his defective views on virtue.[73]

The final comment to be made about the divinity hall under Alexander Moncrieff was the spirit of godliness or piety which pervaded Moncrieff's labours. There is a ring of Protestant hagiography in the stories which come from Moncrieff's life and tutoring, yet taking this into consideration, we are left with a clear understanding that piety was not to be divorced from theological knowledge.[74]

---

[69] Landreth, *The UPD Hall*, 79.

[70] Landreth, *The UPD Hall*, 80-82.

[71] Alexander Moncrieff, *Practical Works* 2 vols. (Edinburgh, 1779).

[72] Moncrieff, *Practical Works,* 1:39-87. "The Glory of Emmanuel", which ends as follows: "We conclude this discourse, inviting you in the name of our Lord Jesus Christ, who have never to this day, seen the King in his beauty, to 'go forth and behold King Solomon.... Our Lord Jesus saith, 'Behold me, behold me.... 'The Spirit and the Bride say, Come,...." (p. 87).

[73] Alexander Moncrieff, "An Inquiry into the Principle, Rule, and End of Moral Actions", in *Memorials of Moncrieff and Fisher*, 63-116.

[74] Landreth, *The UPD Hall*, 76-77; McKerrow, *History of the Secession*, 831; "Memoir of the Rev. Alexander Moncrieff", *Christian Magazine*, 140.

Development of a Philosophical Class/College

Under Alexander Moncrieff's urging, a philosophical class was begun at Abernethy in 1742. The purpose of this class was to afford students an opportunity to study the various branches of philosophy without being exposed to the errors within the Scottish universities.[75] It would appear that the languages of Greek and Latin as "enlargements of their attainments" were stressed in these philosophical classes.[76]

The first tutor for this philosophical class was Mr. Robert Archibald, a student of divinity. He had been in the first class with Professor Wilson in 1740. (Since the divinity professor or a minister did not serve as the instructor for the philosophical class, the post was filled by a divinity student or another teacher.) Archibald only taught the class one year and was subsequently ordained and called to Haddington in 1744.[77] The philosophical class was originally intended to meet for two years in eight week sessions and then was later changed to meet for three years. Students were not required to attend it; however, they were to be routinely examined in philosophy to see if they were imbibing errors. The teacher for these classes was to receive six pounds per annum, plus he was to collect a student fee of either five or ten shillings quarterly depending upon the student's ability to pay.[78]

Archibald's successor was Mr. David Wilson, who taught the philosophical class for four or five years, evidently resigning at the time of the Breach.[79] Wilson joined the Associate Church after being a divinity student with the Church of Scotland and was ordained by the Antiburghers in 1748 to Kirkcaldy. The class was under the supervision of the presbytery and of the professor of divinity, namely Alexander Moncrieff.[80] However, it would appear that there was then, and continues to be still, some uncertainty as to just exactly how the Associate Presbytery as a whole viewed this philosophical class at Abernethy. John Brown's *MS* "Memoirs of the Secession" (which needs to be read separately from his printed work, *A Historical Account of the Rise and Progress of the Secession*, because the latter is only an abridgement of this *MS* and misses much of what is contained in the *MS*) contains one paragraph on the philosophical class at Abernethy. Brown's comments are rather curt, yet nevertheless do give us further insight upon this subject:

> In the end of this year [1741] not the Associate Pby for divers members of [it(?)] were mightily against it on sundry accounts but Mr. Moncrieff sets up a kind of College for Philosophy at Abernethy which as a learned professor thro' that

---

[75] McKerrow, *History of the Secession*, 176.
[76] McKerrow, *History of the Secession*, 333.
[77] McKerrow, *Annals and Statistics of the UP Church*, 652, 216.
[78] McKerrow, *History of the Secession*, 176; Landreth, *The UPD Hall*, 83-84.
[79] McKerrow, *History of the Secession*, 176.
[80] Landreth, *The UPD Hall*, 84; Mackelvie, *Annals and Statistics of the UP Church*, 443.

science without acquaintance of several of the branches of that science some so judged it tended not a little to train up ministers in a shiff and new disposition it being a common notion that want of acquaintance with the rest of mankind render person's bigots and self-conceited. In the beginning of 1742 Mr.Moncrieff is chosen in the Room of Mr. Wilson to inspect and teach the Students of Divinity...[81]

Though brief, and with little detail, it appears that Brown had some personal insight into the controversy concerning Moncrieff's push for this "College for Philosophy". This in part may explain why after the Breach of 1747 the Associate Synod never established a class or college of philosophy. Yet as we will see, the Associate Synod was active in correcting any philosophical defects in her divinity students (see chapter 10 of this book). Perhaps they perceived they did not possess the resources for such a large undertaking and that it could distract them from their chief ministries.

In a biographical study on the poet Michael Bruce, we also gain some further insights into the philosophical class. Bruce applied to study at the Antiburgher's philosophical class at Alloa sometime in 1765 or 1766. However, since the Antiburghers required all students for admission to be members or regular hearers within their body, he was refused admittance since he did not regularly attend an Antiburgher church. Instead Bruce went to Edinburgh University. The above incident illustrates the entrance requirements for this class. It also affirms again that the reason for the philosophical class was to counter the Scottish Enlightenment thinking in the Scottish universities, such as that of Professor Adam Ferguson at Edinburgh University and Professor Hutcheson at Glasgow University.[82] The Scottish Enlightenment did have a direct effect upon the attempts of the Secession in educating her ministers by causing them to establish a "College of Philosophy". The above mentioned professors were not in the faculties of divinity and illustrate why many Seceders had their reasons to be skeptical of the orthodoxy of the professors in the Scottish universities. Hutcheson was professor of moral philosophy at Glasgow University from 1729-1746, several years before Michael Bruce attended university. However, it was professors like Hutcheson who caused the Seceders to react as they did. Also, Hutcheson's influence extended to the students of divinity, as William Leechman acknowledged: "He was especially solicitous to be serviceable to students of Divinity, endeavouring... to give them just notions of the main design of preaching."[83] Hutcheson was an innovator in education and gave "extramural classes in Religion and Theology" with free seminars to the public, using Hugo Grotius'

---

[81] John Brown, "Memoirs of the Secession" *MS*, New College Library, Edinburgh, BRO 70, 258.
[82] James MacKenzie, *Life of Michael Bruce of Loch Leven* (Edinburgh, 1908), 46-49.
[83] William Leechman's preface to Hutcheson's *System of Moral Philosophy,* quoted in Hazlett, "Ebbs and Flows of Theology in Glasgow", 17.

work, *On the Truth of the Christian Religion*, a work which was non-dogmatic and represented "a scaled down Christianity".[84] Thus, it is not difficult to see why Secessionist evangelicals would be highly skeptical of the professors in the Scottish universities, and they were not alone. John Witherspoon was also disturbed, although he represented a certain approach to the Scottish Enlightenment in that of Scottish Common Sense Philosophy, distinct from Hutcheson.

Summary

The very origins of the Secession churches resulted in the need for them to develop their own divinity hall. Their halls in this early period had a solo professor acting as a "theological regent" for the divinity curriculum. This "theological regenting" was somewhat more concentrated than in the case of the divinity halls in the Scottish universities, where often there was more than one professor. Though the university divinity halls may also have had longer sessions, there really is a question whether or not actual attendance, or the actual amount of class-room time, would have been much greater than in the Secession. The size of the Secession hall may be surprising to some in that there was quite a large number of students going up to the hall each year. Patterns for theological examination or pedagogy do not appear to be radically different, whether Kirk or Seceder. In both cases presbytery and synod were heavily involved. One unique feature was the Secession's creation of a philosophical class or "college". This symbolically highlighted the theological tensions between Kirk and Seceder.

---

[84] Hazlett, "Ebbs and Flows of Theology in Glasgow", 19.

CHAPTER 9

The 1747 Breach and Two Halls

Introduction

The purpose of this chapter is to trace the development of theological education and training after the 1747 Breach in the Secession churches. A brief defining of the Breach and the two parties will begin the chapter. Then the chapter will treat each hall chronologically. Since more professors served the Associate halls, the study of this hall in this chapter will end in 1767 and be recommenced in chapter 10. In contrast, the General Associate hall had more continuity (or what some might interpret as a family dynasty with a father and son in succession), so we will take this study through to 1785. Brown has been given a separate chapter for various reasons: the vast corpus of written material he authored in comparison to any others in either of the Secession divinity halls from 1747 to c.1785; the absence of current research; and Brown's influence both inside and outside of the Secession on several different fronts.

The Associate Hall: 1746-1767

Ebenezer Erskine, "the face of a man" (Stirling)

The Burgess Oath was taken by citizens in Edinburgh, Glasgow and Perth from 1744 onward in which the taker endorsed "the religion professed in the realm". The Seceders quickly fell into two parties, with those who condemned the oath receiving the popular name of Antiburgher. Sherman Isbell wrote that, "The issue was important to the Associate Synod because, within a burgh, none but the burgesses were permitted to engage in commerce, belong to a trade guild, or enjoy the privilege of voting. Moreover, much of the synod's strength lay in the three cities affected."[1] The oath read as follows:

> Here I protest before God, and your Lordships, that I profess, and allow with my heart, the true religion presently professed within this realm, and authorized by the

---

[1] *DSCHT*, 109.

laws thereof: I shall abide thereat, and defend the same to my life's end; renouncing the Roman religion called papistry.[2]

This oath was variously interpreted by the two parties within the Secession. The chief Antiburgher faction was led by Alexander Moncrieff and Adam Gib and the Burgher faction by the Erskines, James Fisher, and Archibald Hall. There is a tremendous corpus of pamphlet literature on this subject, which does not need to be analyzed here.[3] Suffice it to say that the Antiburghers viewed the oath as not simply a renouncing of Roman Catholicism, but as an adoption of current practices in the Church of Scotland. Others believed that by taking the oath they were approbating "the Protestant Reformed faith itself" (without its corruptions) and that the intent of the oath was to exclude Roman Catholics from becoming burgesses. Therefore, the latter group pleaded that the taking of the oath was not worthy of church censure or excommunication, but the Antiburghers insisted that there could not be "ministerial nor Christian communion with those who should take it." When the synod was divided in April, 1747, at what is called "The Breach", nineteen ministers formed the Antiburgher or General Associate Synod and fourteen ministers the Burgher or Associate Synod. That emotions were high is evidenced by the fact that Ralph Erskine was censured by his own son John Erskine.[4] The Burgess Oath remained in effect in Scotland until 1819, when it was abolished.[5]

Ebenezer Erskine and James Fisher, two of the original "Four Fathers" of the Secession, adopted the position of allowing the Burgess Oath to be viewed as a matter of forbearance. The Breach centred around this question: "Whether the decision anent the Religious clause in some Burgess Oaths, shall be made a Term of Ministerial and Christian Communion or not?"[6] It was the Burghers who adopted the answer of forbearance, and thus with two parties the newly formed synod divided.

The Associate Synod, having only been formed in June, 1747, met again in September, 1747 at Dunfermline, to address the matter of what to do for the students who belonged to the Burgher party.[7] The synod desired Ebenezer Erskine to become the professor of divinity, but he believed he was too old (he

---

[2] McKerrow, *The History of the Secession Church*, 210.
[3] Some of this literature includes: Adam Gib, *The Present Truth: A Display of the Secession Testimony*, 2 vols. (Edinburgh,1774); Archibald Hall, *Impartial Survey of the Religious Clause in some Burgess-Oaths* (Edinburgh, 1771); Ralph Erskine, *Fancy no Faith: or, A Seasonable Admonition...* (Glasgow, 1747).
[4] *DSCHT*, 302.
[5] *DSCHT*, 109-110; Robert Lathan, *History of the Associate Reformed Synod of the South*, original 1882 (Charlotte, NC, 1982), 136. Lathan provides a very readable review of the Burgess controversy.
[6] "Minutes of the Proceedings of the Associate Synod, 1747-1766", in National Archives of Scotland, Edinburgh, *MS* CH3/28/2, 976.
[7] Landreth, *The UPD Hall*, 151-152; *DSCHT*, 298-300.

was 67). Synod then requested James Fisher, but he deferred, being unwilling. Finally Ebenezer Erskine accepted the position, agreeing to serve for a time but advising the synod that James Fisher should begin to prepare to take the post.

Ebenezer Erskine served only one year as professor of divinity,[8] although some writers state he served two years. MacKelvie's student statistics are highly reliable, so if Erskine served for a second session, which I do not believe he did, it must have been a very small student body, likely under ten.[9] (There is a discrepancy between MacKelvie and Landreth on how long Erskine taught at the divinity hall. MacKelvie records only one session whereas Landreth, two.)[10]

Erskine resigned the professorship in 1749, and in September of that year James Fisher of Glasgow was appointed the professor of divinity.[11] Since Erskine needed help in the pastorate, to which his nephew was ordained as his colleague in June of 1752, it would appear that Erskine's labours were too much, so he probably only conducted the hall at Stirling for one session (that of 1748).[12]

It is helpful to briefly review Ebenezer Erskine's own education. Erskine was a full M.A. graduate of the University of Edinburgh, commencing his studies, it is believed, in November, 1693, at age 14 and graduating June, 1697. The university was under the principalship of Gilbert Rule at that time and had five regents.[13] We know that Hebrew was taught from 1694 to 1701 by Alexander, Principal Rule's son. Students going into divinity were to take this language in their senior year, which would mean Ebenezer Erskine would have studied Hebrew. Divinity normally lasted five sessions, and Professor George Campbell would have taught Erskine. Campbell was the founder of the Divinity Library at Edinburgh University, which at the time of his death consisted of 996 volumes.[14] During his theological studies Erskine served as chaplain and tutor to the Earl of Rothe's household, a position he may have held until his licensure.[15]

---

[8] "Minutes of the Proceedings of the Associate Synod, 1747-1766", 979, 1033; Landreth, *The UPD Hall*, 152-154; Donald Fraser, *The Life and Diary of Ebenezer Erskine* (Edinburgh, 1831), 451-452.

[9] To occupy the theological chair for two years is different from serving two sessions in the divinity hall. Brown in Fisher's *Memorials* uses "occupied" the chair for two years. John Brown (of Broughton Place), *Memorials of the Rev. James Fisher* in *Fathers of the United Presbyterian Church* (Edinburgh, 1849).

[10] MacKelvie, *Annals and Statistics of the UP Church*, 664; Landreth, *The UPD Hall*, 156.

[11] Landreth, *The UPD Hall*, 157.

[12] Fraser, *Life and Diary of Ebenezer Erskine*, 452, is not conclusive either on this point.

[13] Fraser, *Life and Diary of Ebenezer Erskine*, 64-65.

[14] Fraser, *Life and Diary of Ebenezer Erskine*, 65.

[15] Fraser, *Life and Diary of Ebenezer Erskine*, 65-67

The 1748 session for the Associate Synod divinity studies began at Ebenezer Erskine's residence at Stirling in early February, 1748. It was smaller than the year before, as three of the fourth year students were away preaching because of the pressing need of the hour.[16] However, there were four new first session students: John Brown (afterwards of Haddington); Daniel Cock (afterwards of Londonderry, Nova Scotia); William McEwen (afterwards of Dundee); and Hugh McGill (afterwards of Ireland).[17] All four students in this first session class adhered with the Burgher party and were eventually all ordained as Burgher ministers. Cock later became the first settled minister of the Associate Church in Nova Scotia, McGill the second Associate minister in Ireland and John Brown the noted professor of divinity.[18] Thus, from Erskine's first session class came several leaders of the Associate Church.

Erskine did not give formal lectures to the students but used Francis Turretin's *Institutio Theologiae Elencticae* (in Latin) as his system, adding comment and conducting student examinations. There is no evidence that Erskine changed to English for the observations or student examinations on Turretin. The strength of his professorship was with the examinations, which were no doubt formulated from years of catechizing.[19] The student discourses were delivered along with student and professor critiques.

Ebenezer Erskine is chiefly remembered as a preacher of the Marrow, and therefore it is reasonable to conclude that this would have been the focus in the comments on the discourses – not to preach "legally", but rather to freely offer the gospel and emphasize grace. Pieter van Harten aptly contrasts the Enlightenment preaching of the Moderates as "characterized by an inner alienation from received dogmas. The change of opinion mainly showed in the more strongly moralistic character of preaching."[20] Erskine's preaching was not of this new Enlightenment order; rather it was "strongly Christocentric and of an evangelical and invitatory nature".[21] In Erskine's most famed student, John Brown of Haddington, we read of this same emphasis. No doubt as Erskine was in the pulpit, so he was with his students.

---

[16] Landreth, *The UPD Hall*, 154.

[17] MacKelvie, *Annals and Statistics of the UP Church*, 664, 559; Small, *History of the Congregations of the UP Church*, vols. 1 and 2.

[18] McKerrow, *History of the Secession*, 542; Small, *History of the Congregations of the UP Church*, vols. 1 and 2.

[19] MacKenzie, *John Brown of Haddington* (1964), 76-77; Landreth, *The UPD Hall*, 156. Fraser makes the comment that Brown of Haddington said about Erskine that he "gave them not only instruction lectures but many serious and affecting advices." Fraser, *Life and Diary of Ebenezer Erskine*, 452.

[20] van Harten, *De Prediking van Ebenezer en Ralph Erskine*, 282.

[21] van Harten, *De Prediking van Ebenezer en Ralph Erskine*, 287. Further on Erskine's preaching see, *DSCHT*, 300, and Joel Beeke, "Ebenezer and Ralph Erskine: Dissenters with a Cause" (1), *Banner of Sovereign Grace Truth* (November,1999), 231.

A brief divergence to Erskine's understanding of the Marrow is helpful. Basically, the Marrowmen upheld the "evangelical view that faith in Jesus Christ is the very essence of the Gospel and that every sinner is warranted to lay hold of Christ freely offered therein. The opposing view was that a sinner must prepare himself by repentance and the forsaking of sin before he is entitled to trust in the Saviour."[22] Thus, the Moderate view attached conditions to the covenant of grace, thereby making the gospel a legal presentation and not offered from the perspective of the free promises of the Saviour in the covenant.[23] These two contrasting theologies were not simply confined to the pulpits but were also found in the divinity halls of Kirk and Secession in the eighteenth century (Erskine representing the Marrow in the Secession Hall). For the Moderates there was *eloquentia* but little *sapientia*.

Unfortunately we possess nothing by Ebenezer Erskine in the way of printed works which would shed light on his divinity hall lectures. His writings are chiefly sermons, in addition to which there are a few materials related specifically to the rise of the Secession.[24] In a consideration of his published sermons, the context or occasion for them needs to be carefully reviewed. The sermons we possess generally would be classified as evangelical, no doubt having been preached during communion seasons. Few selections of ordinary Sabbath sermons remain.

Edwin Dargon provided a most precise description of both Ebenezer and Ralph Erskine's sermons in his *A History of Preaching*:

---

[22] MacKenzie, *John Brown of Haddington* (1964), 69.

[23] John Brown (of Whitburn), "The Life of Ralph Erskine", in *The Sermons and other Practical Works of Ralph Erskine*, vol. 7, original 1764-65 (London, 1865), viii-ix.

[24] For the fullest collection of his sermons, see Ebenezer Erskine, *The Whole Works of Ebenezer Erskine Consisting of Sermons and Discourses*, ed. James Fisher, original 1761 (Edinburgh, 1871). Volume 1 contains eighteen sermons, volume 2 contains twenty-four sermons, and volume 3 contains twenty sermons. Sometimes "one" sermon will run into two or three sermons, as it would be a communion sermon, thus the number of sermons according to the index is actually much lower than in actual fact.

Other works more directly related to the rise of the Secession include: Ebenezer Erskine, W. Wilson, A. Moncrieff, and J. Fisher, *Reasons by Ebenezer Erskine, William Wilson, Alexander Moncrieff, and James Fisher, why they have not aceded to the judicatories of the Established Church* (Edinburgh, 1735); Ebenezer Erskine, *The Stone Rejected by the Builders, exalted as the Head-Stone of the Corner* (Edinburgh, 1732); Ebenezer Erskine, *The True State of the Question* (Edinburgh, 1747).

Landreth maintains that Ebenezer Erskine did the first part of what is traditionally referred to as James Fisher's *The Assembly's Shorter Catechism Explained*, which would have been influential on the method of orally examining divinity students on Turretin. The point is somewhat difficult to press towards much of a conclusion. See, Landreth, *The UPD Hall*, 156; James Fisher, *The Assembly's Shorter Catechism Explained* (Glasgow, 1753), with various editions afterwards. Ebenezer Erskine did the shortest section of this volume, and the larger was done by Ralph Erskine and James Fisher.

Their published sermons are of the extreme analytical type, with elaborate introduction, formal statement of heads, divisions, doctrines, points, etc. They abound in Scripture quotations, but are sparing in use of illustration. Definition, distinction, argument, and appeal are the main things; but there is a spiritual glow through all the bony structure and wearisome refinement of analysis. There is a warmth of conviction and pastoral concern in the quaint modes of expression that still make appeal, even to the reader whose taste is offended by the faults mentioned...[25]

Dargon's description shows the contrast between the Erskine sermons and the Scottish pulpit lectures.[26] Likewise, his comments concerning the structure of an Erskine sermon could be applied to sermons by Moderate preachers as well Evangelicals. The difference between the two – Evangelical and Moderate – centres on a moral religion versus a gospel proclaimed with conviction and in confidence in the doctrines of grace.

As we have noted in the education and training of ministers for the Kirk, there was also the expectation of the Associate Presbytery that students attend the exercise and addition. In the early years of the Secession, the custom continued whereby the ministers of the presbytery took turns in giving critical exercises. We learn about Ebenezer Erskine taking his turn at these. Donald Fraser brought this to our attention from one of Erskine's shorthand "Notebooks", where he found the title "Exercises and Addition" on Jude 1 (then follows): "The Associate Presbytery of Glasgow having appointed a Presbyterial exercise upon the Epistle of Jude, – I, as the oldest, had the first verse appointed me, – to be delivered at their next meeting, April 1750, in Stirling."[27] Again, it is difficult to make any real assessment relative to how these presbyterial exercises and additions were part of the training for students. The best way to view it is not to look at contemporary models of presbytery meetings. It is most likely that the exercises were being laid before the students as models of what they also were expected to do before presbytery in the course of their licensure trials. Thus, the presbytery exercise and addition must be viewed as part of the educational and training process.

Since Erskine's term as professor of divinity was so brief and no literature can be found on his work in the hall, he does not rank as one of the seminal leaders in theological education for the Associate Church. His significance is primarily threefold: in being a founder of the Secession; in being a preacher who influenced many in his day and whose sermons still continue to be reprinted, especially amongst the Dutch; and in his involvement concerning the Marrow controversy. As an educator these influences extended to his students

---

[25] Edwin C. Dargon, *A History of Preaching*, vol. 2, original 1905 (Grand Rapids, 1970), 338.

[26] See Appendix D in Whytock, "History and Development of Scottish Theological Education and Training", 493-498.

[27] Fraser, *Life and Diary of Ebenezer Erskine*, 451.

and took them in a different direction from the Enlightenment thinkers. John LaShell sums it up best: "In an age when Enlightenment-influenced 'Moderatism' threatened the vibrancy of faith in the Church of Scotland, the secession of the Erskines helped preserve evangelical life both in their own synod and in the national church."[28]

James Fisher, "the face of an eagle" (Glasgow)

As Ebenezer Erskine himself intimated, James Fisher (1697-1775) prepared to become the Associate Synod's professor of divinity, and thus was officially assigned this duty September 5, 1749, a post he held until 1764.[29] Fisher was the youngest of the "Four Fathers" of the Secession and exhibited a keen commitment to the Marrow and to the principles of the Secession. He studied at the University of Glasgow beginning in 1712, where he took Greek under Professor Alexander Dunlop, the author of the Greek grammar used in the Scottish universities for a considerable time. Fisher also studied at St. Andrews in the 1715-1716 session before going to the divinity hall at the University of Edinburgh for six sessions, studying under Professor William Hamilton.[30] Hamilton appears to have been "more moderate" than his father, a staunch Covenanter, yet it is difficult to classify him as a full Moderate. Sefton summarizes him well: "His material contribution to emergent Moderatism remains an open question."[31]

James Fisher's probationary period ended in 1725, when he was ordained to Kinclaven in the Presbytery of Kinclaven. Brown reviewed some of Fisher's ordination trials as follows: give a lecture on Psalm 121 and a popular sermon on Psalm 121:2; prepare a thesis on *"de deitate Filii"*; explain Psalm 19 from the Hebrew; read from the Greek New Testament *ad aperturam libri*; answer catechetics and chronological questions from the second half of the tenth century.[32] He was also to be called upon to show his sermon notebooks to the presbytery. These would have contained the sermons preached during his probationary period and were generally done in a shorthand. Evidently it was a very normal custom for the presbytery to examine these notebooks in order to determine that the student was preaching doctrine catechetically and that he was careful in preparing for the pulpit.[33]

---

[28] *BDEB*, 1:362.

[29] "Minutes of the Proceedings of the Associate Synod, 1747-1766", 1047.

[30] John Brown (of Broughton Place), *Memorials of the Rev. James Fisher* in *Fathers of the United Presbyterian Church* (Edinburgh, 1849), 9-13.

[31] *SDCHT*, 431.

[32] Brown, *Memorials of James Fisher*, 16.

[33] Brown, *Memorials of James Fisher*, 17. I have yet to locate any of Fisher's short hand sermon books, but they would have been similar to that of William Fraser's notebook at

In summarizing Fisher's fifteen years as professor in the Associate divinity hall, Brown says that Fisher did not vary the patterns which had already been established. However, it does appear that under Fisher the length of each session was reduced from three to two months. The emphasis continued to be upon a system of theology and assigned student exercises and discourses.[34] During Fisher's professorship the hall met in Glasgow, as Fisher went there from Kinclaven in 1741. We lack records telling what system he used, likely either Turretin or Marck. We also lack any of his lectures in divinity, Church history or practical divinity. Since Fisher's publications were either sermons or about matters related to the Secession (with the exception of his work on the Shorter Catechism), we are hard pressed to learn much about the hall from anything he published.[35] Undoubtedly it was this work on the Shorter Catechism that has kept his name most alive. Ebenezer Erskine did the section from question viii (8) to question xxviii (28) on Christ the King, Ralph Erskine did lxxvi to xcv (76 to 95), and James Fisher the remainder. It received an affectionate name, "The Baw-bee Bible", in Scotland.[36]

We have Fisher's register for the divinity hall meeting at Glasgow from 1750-1763. This allows us to learn much about the student numbers, their assignments and the schedule as well as a way of verifying MacKelvie's student lists.[37] First, we observe that MacKelvie's list of first session students matches the names in Fisher's register except for one year. Fisher has all of the students in the various sessions listed as a whole, whereas MacKelvie's list is neatly ordered. This helps us to confirm that MacKelvie's data is generally reliable. However, according to MacKelvie's statistics,[38] the number of first session students varied during Fisher's professorship from a low (in 1761) of one student to a high (in 1757) of twelve. On the other hand, according to

---

New College Library, Edinburgh. See William Fraser, "Sermons, Written A.D. 1816, 1817, and 1818", *MS*, which contains 28 sermons in shorthand. FRA 5.

[34] Brown, *Memorials of Rev. James Fisher*, 67-68.

[35] Landreth, *The UPD Hall*, 159-160. Some of his publications were: James Fisher, *A Review of the Preface to a Narrative of the Extraordinary Work at Kilsyth and other Congregations in the Neighbourhood, written by the Rev. Mr. James Robe, Minister of Kilsyth...* (Glasgow, 1742), 68; *A Review of a Pamphlet entitled 'A Serious Enquiry into the Burgess Oaths of Edinburgh, Perth, and Glasgow;' wherein the most material arguments against the Burgess Oath are impartially weighed and examined* (Glasgow, 1747), 120; *Christ the Sole and Wonderful Doer in the Work of Man's Redemption; an action sermon...to which is subjoined The Door of the Heart summoned to open to the King of Glory; an action sermon...* (Glasgow, 1755), 32, 36.

[36] Brown, *Memorials of Rev. James Fisher*, 66. The accurate statement of who did what was taken from the shorthand *MS* of the work which Donald Fraser possessed in 1831, when he did the *Life and Diary of Ebenezer Erskine*, 494.

[37] "Fisher's Register of the Divinity Hall, 1750-1763" is printed as Appendix 3 in Brown, *Memorials of Rev. James Fisher*, 96-116.

[38] MacKelvie, *Annals and Statistics of the UP Church*, 665.

Fisher's class register, 1762, not 1761, was the year with the fewest students.[39] This variance probably highlights the common problem of inconsistent attendance in the Scottish divinity halls, where their names at times appear only two or at the most three times in the class register.

Taking examples from the class register of the late 1750s and early 1760s and tracing Fisher's comments on these examples reveals the problem of irregular attendance. John Beaty, who had been in the first session of the divinity hall in 1758, failed to deliver his exercise from Exodus that year or the next and had the words "Did not deliver it" attached to his name. On April 7, 1760, another John, John Bennet, was assigned a popular lecture on Ezekiel 24:23-26, yet did not return until the 1762 session and delivered it on April 5, 1762 – two years after his professor had assigned it. When he did arrive, it was week five! Is one reading too much to perceive some frustration on the part of the professor of divinity? What causes a professor to put into his register: "Five weeks after I was begun to teach came up Mr. John Bennet, detained (as he said) by his aunt's indisposition from coming up sooner"?[40] The conclusion appears obvious: student attendance could be erratic – and frustrating.

From reading the class registers by Fisher, we conclude that, with all sessions together, he would never have had more than twenty students at any spring meeting of the divinity hall.[41] This assumes that Fisher was accurate in his records, and it also assumes some students did not leave after their discourse, thus affecting the total number for the duration of the hall in that season.

Reading the class register, one finds that there were several students who came across from Ireland to study. Usually Fisher would write "Irel." next to their names, but this was not completely consistent. The Irish students do not appear to have attended any more than two or three sessions in the hall. Fisher's final entry in his class register concerns these Irish students and specific assignments given to them:

> January 11th, 1764. – As the Irish students, who came over here, had not access to attend their own Presbytery in Ireland; according to recommendation of last Synod, in case I was not to teach, as I am resolved to do this year, I prescribed them the following Discourses.
> To –
>
> | | |
> |---|---|
> | Samuel Kennedy, | Exercise and addition on Jude ver.20. |
> | | Lecture on Rev.1 verses 4, 5, and 6. |
> | John Rogers, | Exercise and addition on Jude ver.21. |
> | Joseph Little, | Exercise and addition on Jude ver.17.[42] |

---

[39] "Fisher's Register of the Divinity Hall, 1750-1763", 112-113.
[40] "Fisher's Register of the Divinity Hall, 1750-1763", 112, 114.
[41] "Fisher's Register of the Divinity Hall, 1750-1763", 96-116.
[42] "Fisher's Register of the Divinity Hall, 1750-1763", 116.

Are we to infer from this that the Irish students could complete more of their assigned discourses before a presbytery rather than in the hall? From their less frequent attendance at the hall, this would appear as the logical answer. In effect, Fisher was giving their assignments and having others do the grading, a method that today would resemble distance learning.

We see a wide range of terms used when we come to the actual list of assigned discourses prescribed for the student. Some of the assignments were exegetical, others used the words homily, lecture, or exercise and addition, and sometimes popular sermon, thesis, disputations, or discourses. No doubt some of these words served as synonyms for each other, but not all of them. In some cases it is very obvious what was implied. For example, in 1734 twelve theses were assigned, to begin February 23rd and conclude on March 25th. We have a list of these, including the thesis title in Latin, the student's name in Latin, the date for delivery of the thesis, the respondent and the name(s) of the opponents. Only once are two delivered on any single day. Here is a portion of the list:

> Thesis 1 ma. Mars et Satisfactio Christi, ex Dei Consilio et Christi Voluntate, non omnium et singulorum Loco, facta est, sed Electorum tantum. – Joan. Beveridge, Respondens; Gul. Coventry et Dav. Smith, Opponentes,... Feb.23
>
> Thesis 3tia. Revelatio necessaria est Naturaliter et per se Nota. – Gul. Atnot, Resp.; Joan. Beveridge, Opponens,... Mar.11
>
> Thesis 8va. Imago Dei ad quam Homo ab Initio conditus fuit, non in solo Dominio consistebat, sed justitia Originalis fuit potior et praecipua ejus Pars. – Joan. Beveridge, Resp.; Gul. Arnot, Opponens,... Mar.19 [43]

If we take these three arbitrary dates, February 23, March 11 and March 19, and look across the class register for 1754 to the column marked "Discourses Prescribed to the students", we are able to reconstruct further what took place in the hall on those three dates. On February 23rd, in addition to hearing thesis number one, a discourse by John Anderson of a popular sermon on John 17:17 was heard and then student and professor critiques followed. On March 11th two students were assigned the following:

> David Smith, Exercise and add. on I Tim.4:10, and
> William Archer, Exeg. An Revelatio necessaria sit ad Satutem?
> Exeg. An circa futura contingentia et libera, Deo competat Praescientia jecturalis tantum? [44]

Obviously March 11, 1754, was a very full day in the divinity hall. We can hardly imagine Professor Fisher had much time for long lectures in Church history or practical divinity that day.

---

[43] "Fisher's Register of the Divinity Hall, 1750-1763", 103.
[44] "Fisher's Register of the Divinity Hall, 1750-1763", 102-103.

For the last date, March 19th, there were no other student discourses to be delivered.[45] Thus, we can only speculate what else Professor Fisher may have done either in systematics, Church history or practical divinity. Since these were more under the professor's domain, he did not record these within his class register.

In reviewing Fisher's class registers, we come to the conclusion that two central ingredients of the divinity hall curriculum were preaching and the proper interpretation of Scripture. MacKenzie summarizes Fisher's classes well in relating John Brown of Haddington's experience in the one session he attended in 1750:

> A prominent feature of the class work was the delivery of discourses, and the reading of critical and exegetical exercises. Training in exact interpretation of the Word, and effective preaching of it, was the dominant aim. Pulpit-work was never lost sight of. A considerable proportion of the time, in consequence, was spent in hearing and criticizing students' sermons...[46]

Fisher found the workload of a pastorate, church extension or itinerant ministry, and the divinity hall much to bear. In 1751 he complained to the synod, asking to be relieved of the professorship and that someone else be nominated.[47] He did not stand alone in making such a request, as we find John Brown of Haddington (Associate Hall) and Archibald Bruce (General Associate Hall) both made similar requests. Although synod in April, 1752, did agree to discuss the matter, they delayed action until October, 1752. Somehow Fisher was encouraged to continue on for another session in the hall, and this extended into many more.[48]

However, in October, 1763, Fisher firmly requested the synod to replace him in the professorship due to his age and health. He was asked again to take one more session, if possible, or else "each Presbytery take the care and inspection of the students in their own bounds... directing them in their studies..."[49] When we again compare this synod action to Fisher's hall register for 1764, we find this entry only:

> January 11th, 1764.– As the Irish students, who came over here, had not access to attend their own Presbytery in Ireland; according to the recommendation of last

---

[45] "Fisher's Register of the Divinity Hall, 1750-1763", 102-103.
[46] MacKenzie, *John Brown of Haddington* (1964), 78.
[47] "Minutes of the Proceedings of the Associate Synod, 1747-1766", 1110.
[48] "Minutes of the Proceedings of the Associate Synod, 1747-1766", 1124, 1142.
[49] "Minutes of the Proceedings of the Associate Synod, 1747-1766", 1436-1437. Also, "Letter No.9 To Mr. John Gray, from the Rev. James Fisher, Dec.26,1764", appendix 4 in Brown, *Memorials of James Fisher*, 124, where Fisher describes his health problems as swelling in his legs.

Synod, in case I was not to teach, as I am not resolved to do this year, I prescribed to them the following Discourses. To –

Samuel Kennedy,	Exercise and addition on Jude 20
	Lecture on Rev.1:4-6
John Rogers,	Exercise and addition on Jude21
Joseph Little,	Exercise and addition on Jude 17 [50]

Though Fisher gave the assignments for the Irish students, the presbyteries were in fact the "divinity hall" for 1764, and this was later replicated in the Secession churches, as we shall see. If one reads MacKelvie's list of students only, it would appear that no divinity education occurred in 1764; yet, as we have seen, this was simply not the case.[51]

Fisher continued in his pastorate after resigning from the hall, eventually receiving a colleague to assist him in 1771, three years before his death in 1774.[52]

As professor of divinity, James Fisher was very much aware of the time and sacrifice required to be involved in theological education in addition to a pastorate. This was not unique to Fisher.

John Swanston (Kinross)

Upon the resignation of James Fisher, the Rev. John Swanston of Kinross (1720-1767) was appointed to the professorship for the Associate synod on May 18, 1764.[53] However he died in 1767 at age forty-six, having only served three sessions in the divinity hall. Swanston had studied arts at Edinburgh University and theology at the Secession divinity hall at Perth under Professor William Wilson.[54] Since he published nothing during his lifetime, we are only left with a collection of sermons published posthumously in 1773.[55] As one would expect of someone close to the Erskines and of one who remained with them at the Breach, in his preaching (as described by a fellow presbyter), he:

> shewed himself in earnest to win souls to Christ; by applying the law to the conscience of the sinner, for convincing him of his guilt and pollution; and by

---

[50] "Fisher's Register of the Divinity Hall, 1750-1763", 116.
[51] MacKelvie, *Annals and Statistics of the UP Church*, 665.
[52] McKerrow, *History of the Secession*, 834-835.
[53] "Minutes of the Proceedings of the Associate Synod,1747-1766", 1452.
[54] *DSCHT*, 807-808; McKerrow, *History of the Secession Church*, 850-852.
[55] John Swanston, *Sermons on Several Important Subjects* (Glasgow, 1773). McKerrow said of these sermons: "These sermons have been very much esteemed by those who set a value on the marrow of the gospel." McKerrow, *History of the Secession of the Church*, 852.

holding forth the Redeemer in glory of his grace, as the only means of recovery...[56]

The collection of sermons is simply full of Christ, with such titles as "God in Christ, a God of Kindness", "The Riches of Grace Displayed", "Christ, the Sun of Righteousness, arising with Healing in His Wings", and "A Sight of Christ, the Christian's Joy".[57]

Swanston, like Professor Wilson, continued to use Marck's *Medulla* as the systematic text, but he evidently added "his own prelections upon the leading doctrines of the Dutch system...from his studies of the old English theology."[58] We assume this is a reference to the English Puritans.

On average there were eight first session students during Swanston's three sessions.[59] Therefore we assume that the hall had thirty to thirty-five students each year. Perhaps one of Swanston's most noted students was Michael Bruce, who was never ordained as he, too, died in 1767, just three weeks after his professor. Michael Bruce's fame rests with his poetry, some of which was included in the *Scottish Paraphrases* (1781 edition). His most famous poem was "The Ode to the Cuckoo"; however, strong evidence suggests that John Logan pirated several of Bruce's poems in Logan's published volume of *Poems*, 1781. Bruce stands as one of the important figures in the history of Scottish psalmody and hymnology. He is included in Julian's monumental *Dictionary of Hymnology*, Julian taking the position that Logan's work was inferior to that of Bruce and that Bruce was really responsible for several works which Logan attempted to pass off as his own. Bruce evidently composed his hymns and paraphrases for a singing school he conducted at Kinnesswood while a divinity student.[60]

From biographies on Bruce we learn some details about the Associate hall at Kinross. For example, the students were boarded amongst families in the congregation. Evidently these were the well-to-do families, and they took no remuneration for the board of the students. Michael Bruce boarded with the household of George Henderson, a fellow student with Bruce at the University of Edinburgh. When the hall was not in session, Bruce taught school at Forest Mill, between Kinross and Alloa.[61] Some of this gives us insight into certain of the more social and practical aspects of how the students of the divinity hall

---

[56] John Smith, preface to *Sermons on Several Important Subjects by John Swanson*, vii-viii.
[57] Swanston, *Sermons on Several Important Subjects*, xi-xii.
[58] Landreth, *The UPD Hall*, 164.
[59] MacKelvie, *Annals and Statistics of the UP Church*, 665.
[60] John Julian, ed., *A Dictionary of Hymnology*, rev. ed. (London, 1907), 187-189, 834, 1033, 1651; Michael Bruce, *Works of Michael Bruce*, ed. A. B. Grosart (Edinburgh, 1865); *DNB*, 8:111-113.
[61] James MacKenzie, *Life of Michael Bruce: Poet of Loch Leven* (Edinburgh, 1908), 60-62.

lived. Another class-mate of Michael Bruce was George Lawson. He eventually became a professor of divinity for the Seceders.[62]

Discontinuation of the Philosophical Class

After the Breach of 1747, there is no mention within the Associate Synod of the continuation of the philosophical class in addition to a divinity hall. There is ample evidence which confirms that those who continued to constitute the Associate Synod, like the Erskine brothers, James Fisher and Swanston's successor, John Brown of Haddington, were not in sympathy with the leading lights of the Scottish Enlightenment. (We will see how Brown was very direct with students who imbibed such Scottish Enlightenment thought.) So why is there no mention of abandoning the class if their sympathies were with it? One may deduce some tentative reasons for its abandonment. One such reason we have already hinted at from the Brown *MS* "Memoirs of the Secession";[63] namely, that there was an opposing undercurrent within the Associate Synod before the Breach at least as early as 1742, when Alexander Moncrieff urged that a philosophical class be established. The Associate presbytery minutes from 1742 to 1746 certainly do not indicate a divided court on this issue, but perhaps this was due to some forbearing comment, allowing Moncrieff to pursue the project.[64] Or was the reason they now abandoned the philosophical class more to do with pragmatism, as the synod after the Breach simply could not engage in any extra activity in light of the pressing needs of reorganizing divided churches, re-establishing the hall and coming to grips with the highly emotional state which had divided families? One has only to recall the tension in the Erskines' extended family caused by the Breach to keep in view the intensity of the situation in 1747.[65] Thus, with perhaps some in the synod not as committed to having their own philosophical class, together with the situation of 1747 and the resulting limited man-power, the project was abandoned, never to be resurrected in the Associate Burgher branch of the Secession.

However, in saying this, we do not mean that the Associate synod lost interest in what their students were being taught in the Scottish universities. Rather, the responsibility was more clearly upon the local presbyteries to guide their students and enquire about their philosophical studies. Much of what was being taught in the universities was not a matter for debate; for example, Greek, Latin, Hebrew, and logic or rhetoric. It was the moral and natural philosophy classes which were more to be enquired about.

---

[62] John G. Barnet, *Life and Complete Works of Michael Bruce* (London, 1926), 46.
[63] John Brown, "Memoirs of the Secession", *MSS,* New College Library, Edinburgh, BRO 70, 258.
[64] "Minutes of the Associate Presbytery,1741-1747", 582, 743, 939, 953.
[65] *DSCHT*, 302.

The General Associate Hall: 1748-1785

Alexander Moncrieff (Abernethy)

After the Breach of 1747, Alexander Moncrieff continued as professor for the General Associate Synod from 1748 to his death in 1761. Since the hall under Alexander Moncrieff has already been analyzed, his teaching methods and curricula will not be repeated here. There is no evidence that would lead us to conclude that he made any major changes to his established pattern. In reviewing the statistics for first year students between 1748 and 1761 under Professor Alexander Moncrieff, we are able to conclude that this divinity hall was larger than the Associate hall for the same time period under Professor Erskine and then Fisher.[66] Yet, in this connection it needs to be said that Landreth claims that under Alexander Moncrieff there was a marked increase in attention given to the student discourses. This shift started under Professor Wilson and continued to be strengthened under Moncrieff. Again Landreth, without citing references, wrote, "Mr. Moncrieff was more solicitous still that the occupations of each session should directly tend to make the students more persuasive preachers and faithful ministers."[67]

Under Alexander Moncrieff, as in the Associate hall at this time, many of the students who trained were either Irish or went to minister in Ireland, and several went as well to the Thirteen Colonies or to Nova Scotia. One of Alexander Moncrieff's students who was later to distinguish himself in America was the Rev. John Mason, who went to New York in 1761. Mason had also taught the philosophy class in connection with the Antiburghers in Scotland.[68]

William Moncrieff (Alloa)

Upon the death of Alexander Moncrieff in 1761, the General Associate Synod appointed the Rev. William Moncrieff, Alexander's son, to become their professor of divinity after Adam Gib refused the position. William Moncrieff has the distinction of being the Antiburgher's longest serving professor (twenty-four years) and Professor Archibald Bruce comes second (nineteen years). Thus, the hall moved from Abernethy to Alloa in 1762.[69]

John McKerrow was able to obtain a personal account of the divinity hall at Alloa under William Moncrieff from Alexander Pringle, a student in his first

---

[66] MacKelvie, *Annals and Statistics of the UP Church*, 654-655.
[67] Landreth, *The UPD Hall*, 79.
[68] MacKelvie, *Annals and Statistics of the UP Church*, 654-655; *DSCHT*, 552.
[69] MacKelvie, *Annals and Statistics of the UP Church*, 655-661.

session in 1772. Pringle was later ordained to North Church, Perth. His account provides us with several interesting details about the hall at Alloa.[70]

Pringle was one of the students who did not attend the philosophy class conducted by the Antiburghers. He noted that the class had about twenty students, but thirty students were applying to the divinity hall in 1772. Those who did not attend the class mostly went to Edinburgh or Glasgow Universities (Pringle went to Edinburgh). All thirty students met with the synod's committee for admitting students into the divinity hall, which could meet for up to two days. The students were examined in logic, metaphysics, and moral philosophy, but we read in the account of Pringle:

> So far as I recollect we were not examined on the languages. Then after the public examination, each student was called in alone, and examined on personal religion and his views concerning theological studies. The Professor of course was always in the committee.[71]

Pringle affirms for us that the course was for five sessions, thus five years, "but when the church demanded preachers, some were licensed after four years' attendance."[72] This seems to have been a common theme in the divinity halls in Scotland; namely, pragmatically shortening the course for pressing needs, whether it be for Gaelic preachers in the Highlands and Islands or for Ireland – a point of similarity between the Church of Scotland and the Secession.

William Moncrieff's systematic theology class was again on Marck's *Medulla*, but the students were advised to consult Turretin, we assume to purchase and read outside of the classroom as a supplement to Moncrieff's lectures on the *Medulla*. Although we do not learn from Pringle an exact weekly schedule at the hall, he affirmed clearly that the hall was to last nine weeks and "none were allowed to depart unless they attended six weeks. The Professor kept a statement of the time which each attended."[73] Pringle states that the professor gave four lectures per week "unless there was a great press of discourses". One senses that some students were pressed to return to their teaching posts in schools and therefore tried to schedule their discourses together so that they could leave early. Once or twice a week students were assigned "theological difficulties", likely theological theses for presentation and subsequent critique by opponents. On Saturdays they heard a lecture on a chapter from the Westminster Confession of Faith, and "two students were employed in prayer". Pringle also made a general statement that each student was called by name to make "remarks" on the discourse delivered. He must be referring here to the student exegetical discourses or homilies. Then in

---

[70] McKerrow, *History of the Secession Church*, 780, where he quotes from the Rev. Alexander Pringle's private correspondence to him about the divinity hall.
[71] McKerrow, *History of the Secession Church*, 780.
[72] McKerrow, *History of the Secession Church*, 780.
[73] McKerrow, *History of the Secession Church*, 780.

summary he writes: "The exercises prescribed were just such as we now prescribe to young men on trials for license."[74]

In order to deal with the attendance problem, the General Associate Synod, towards the end of Professor William Moncrieff's time, tightened the attendance requirements. Students being taken on for trials for licensure were given preference if they had been regular in their attendance at the divinity hall. "The Professor should not give a recommendation to any, with a view to their being licensed, unless they had not only attended the full number of sessions, but given a certain amount of attendance at each session."[75] Also, all ministers who had students connected with their congregations were "to become acquainted with them, to assist them in their studies, and to be ready to report to the synod concerning their diligence and general deportment".[76] Likewise, students were to cultivate a positive relationship with the ministers of the churches to which they belonged, and they were to be diligent in prosecuting their studies, not only in the sessions at the hall but also during the "vacations".[77] All of this tells us that the hall was very important in theological education, but the presbyters also played a major role in the process.

During Professor William Moncrieff's professorship, the length of each session went from three months to nine weeks, and nothing less than six weeks attendance was sustained as satisfactory.[78] Presbytery and synod also exercised a firm hand on the placement or settlement of students who had completed their trials for licensure. For example, young men would be appointed to go to Ireland or North America, and if they refused, their license was removed.[79]

It was during William Moncrieff's professorship that the first General Associate divinity library began. This library commenced in 1776 at Alloa and upon Moncrieff's death was transferred to Whitburn under Professor Archibald Bruce's care.[80] There appears to have been a vision for a library for several years, yet the actual agreement for the library only came about on the 18th of October, 1776. William Moncrieff served as the president of the divinity hall library, and several appointed managers, both ministers and students, aided the library. The library welcomed donations and subscriptions and also adopted rules for the reading of the books. Unfortunately these rules are not to be found in the published history of Moncrieff Church Alloa.[81]

---

[74] McKerrow, *History of the Secession Church*, 780.
[75] McKerrow, *History of the Secession Church*, 781. Landreth views this in terms of "bribes and threats" to secure better attendance in the hall by the synod. See: Landreth, *The UPD Hall*, 108-109.
[76] McKerrow, *History of the Secession Church*, 781.
[77] McKerrow, *History of the Secession Church*, 781.
[78] Landreth, *The UPD Hall*, 107.
[79] Landreth, *The UPD Hall*, 109.
[80] *Annals of Moncrieff United Free Church, Alloa. 1747-1904* (Alloa, 1904), 17-18.
[81] *Annals of Moncrieff United Free Church, Alloa*, 65-67.

Continuation of the Philosophical Class

The analysis and history of the Antiburgher philosophy class appears as virgin territory. The teachers were usually senior divinity students. The list of teachers included:

R. Archibald	Abernethy	1742
David Wilson	Abernethy	1743-1746
John Heugh	Abernethy	1749-1751
John Mason[82]	Abernethy	1756-1760
Alexander Pirie	Abernethy	1760-1762
James Bishop	Alloa	1762-1772
Isaac Ketchen	Alloa	1772-(?)
John Smart	Alloa, Kirkcaldy, Edinburgh	1778-1788
William Graham[83]		

An interesting story about one of the philosophy teachers is worthy of rehearsing here. Mr. Alexander Pirie had taught the philosophy class for two sessions (1760-1762) and then resigned. He passed his trials for licensure but managed to claim ill-health and thus was not appointed to the Colonies. Pirie was eventually censured, first by the Antiburghers and then latterly by the Burghers. It appears the matter revolved around Pirie's teaching the students "Affectations"; that is, more emphasis on style than on truth, Gospel, and conscience. The Antiburghers also disciplined one of their students, Laurence Wotherspoon, for imbibing this teaching. The source of the problem was traced to Pirie, who had been his philosophy teacher.[84] Here we certainly gain an insight into how the Antiburghers perceived the purpose of these classes and their goals; namely, as reactionary classes to those offered within the public universities.

That the Antiburgher Synod took seriously a watchful eye over her students, whether in philosophy or divinity, cannot be denied. McKerrow provides a

---

[82] Jacob Van Vechten, *Memoirs of John M. Mason, D.D., S.T.P. with Portions of His Correspondence* (New York, 1856), 8. Although this volume is about John Mitchell Mason, the first chapter is entitled "Biographical Sketch of His Father" (John Mason) and thus is most helpful for our purposes here.

[83] Landreth, *The UPD Hall*, 98. I have tried to ascertain the location where the philosophical teachers actually taught and to verify Landreth's list. See: Small, *History of the Congregations of the UP Church*, 2:567, 671; "Minutes of the Associate Presbytery, 1741-1747", 743, 954.

[84] McKerrow, *History of the Secession Church*, 288-293; Small, *History of the Congregations of the UP Church*, 2:586-588. Pirie was an Antiburgher and with the Relief before becoming Independent or Glassite. A brief entry on Pirie can also be found in Julian's *Dictionary of Hymnology*, 896, where we learn of Pirie's interest in hymnology and contributions in this field.

sample, synod minute extract of the report of that year's examination of students. The extract states that students were examined "concerning their knowledge in philosophy, their soundness in the faith, their acquaintance with experimental religion, and their motives for prosecuting their studies".[85] Then those who were admitted to study divinity were listed, followed by those conditionally admitted to study divinity, subject to their "joining in the bond for renewing our covenants". Finally, the names of two students (John Graham and Andrew Arnot) who were not admitted to study divinity are given. They were refused for "not having given evidence of their proficiency in the study of philosophy".[86] One additional student (William Buchanan) was not admitted to the hall because he did not give satisfactory reason for leaving his current employment to commence studies in divinity.[87] Later the "renewing the covenants" was omitted for incoming students, this being reserved for the licensure of students. In MacKelvie's "List of Students" we find that none of the three men – Graham, Arnot or Buchanan – can be found as ever entering the divinity hall.[88] The General Associate Synod committee for examining students to enter the hall maintained a strong hand upon the process.

At each synod there was generally a committee of examiners appointed whose task it was to examine the students attending both the synod's philosophical class and the public universities. Since the minutes do not record a list of students in the philosophical class, it is difficult to assess the actual number of these students as opposed to those in the public universities. One has the impression that some years the philosophical class had the larger number of students coming for committee examination. However, as time passed the numbers decreased, and more students were opting for the universities. We learn that in 1773 and again in 1781 this was certainly the situation.[89] For several years synod voted to continue the class and approved moving it from place to place so that it was not always in the same location as the divinity hall. When John Smart was the teacher, the philosophical class was in Kirkcaldy and then in Edinburgh (1784).[90] Smart appears to have taught the class for several

---

[85] McKerrow, *History of the Secession Church*, 294.

[86] McKerrow, *History of the Secession Church*, 294.

[87] McKerrow, *History of the Secession Church*, 294; "Acts and Proceedings of the General Associate Synod, 1767-1781", National Archives of Scotland, Edinburgh, *MS* CH3/144/1, 14 (Sept.3,1767). I found that McKerrow's *History* was based substantially upon the minutes of the two main branches of the Secession and that he generally was accurate. The one disappointment was that McKerrow did not always give the year and the minute from which he obtained his information, nor did he always supply names. I found these student names in the "Acts and Proceedings".

[88] MacKelvie, *Annals and Statistics of the UP Church*, 656.

[89] "Acts and Proceedings of the General Associate Synod, 1767-1781", 115-116; "Acts and Proceedings of the General Associate Synod,1781-1794", National Archives of Scotland, Edinburgh, *MS* CH3/144/2, 8.

[90] "Acts and Proceedings of the General Associate Synod, 1781-1794", 74.

years, starting in 1778 in Alloa, then 1779 in Kirkcaldy and finally in 1784 in Edinburgh, before he was settled as minister at Stirling in 1788.[91] Since there is no record of the synod approving teachers for the philosophy class in the 1790s, we must conclude the class ceased to exist, probably due to lack of support from students.

It is not only today that committees are forced to react rather than first give direction. In 1775 the examining committee of the synod had to make a decision about three students who had not attended one of the public universities in Scotland nor the synod's philosophical class but had studied privately. The minutes actually record nothing about these students being deficient; rather the issue was the question of accepting students who had undertaken philosophical studies privately. Evidently the three were accepted, but the next year, 1776, the synod adopted regulations which stated that no student was to study philosophy from "non-regular" means. Clearly the synod was reacting to the situation of the previous year.

One of the best descriptions to be found on the nature of the philosophical class was written by the Rev. John Young, an Antiburgher minister who was at Harick from 1767 to 1806.[92] Young had been a student in the philosophical class at Abernethy taught by John Mason and gave this description of the class:

> In the year 1756, the Synod appointed Mr. Mason their Professor of Philosophy at Abernethy. In that office he continued four years; consequently he taught two classes, to the last of which I belonged. The first year he taught us Logic, a system of which he himself had compiled. He then gave us prelections on De Vries' Ontology and Pneumatology. The second year he gave us a sketch of Mathematics, with Moral and Natural Philosophy. His Compendium Logiciae, I believe is the best extant. He always delivered his prelections in Latin, which language he spake with a fluency and propriety which I never knew equalled. We always met twice a day. He began with examining us on his last prelection, and then delivered another, generally of an hour's length; so that he lectured two hours every day, unless when some of the students had an exegesis or something of that kind to deliver. We also met once a week for prayer and religious conversation, in which he excelled.[93]

Young's description omits comment on further instruction in Latin and the teaching of Greek and Hebrew. Since Mason continued his lectures in Latin, perhaps this infers the competence of the students in this field. Whether the philosophical class included Greek and Hebrew cannot be conclusively determined by Young's comment. However, the testimony is very clear as to Mason's abilities in the classics and in Hebrew, as he gave private instruction

---

[91] Small, *History of the Congregations of the UP Church*, 2:668; "Acts and Proceedings of the General Associate Synod, 1767-1781", 202 (1778), 219 (1779), and 274 (1784).
[92] Small, *History of the Congregations of the UP Church*, 2:456.
[93] Van Vechten, *Memoirs of John M. Mason*, 8-9.

to his son in America prior to sending him to Columbia College and Edinburgh University.[94] Thus Mason functioned as regent for the entire college curriculum for the Antiburgher philosophical class.

Summary

The infant Secession Church's Breach of 1747 resulted in two divinity halls, and this chapter has traced their early development. The one obvious point of difference between the two synods was that the latter continued to operate a philosophical class or college. This chapter lacks in-depth analysis of the lectures in each hall, something subsequent chapters dealing with later periods will be able to develop more fully because of published sources. There were no radical alterations discovered in this study as to methods, curriculum and student numbers or attendance. Synod involvement, primarily through its examination committees, played an active role, as did the presbyteries. The establishment of a theological library in 1776 in the General Associate hall was a significant development and a matter which received increasing attention in the decades which followed.

---

[94] Frank Dixon McCloy, "John Mitchell Mason, Pioneer in American Theological Education", *Journal of Presbyterian History* 44 (1966), 141-142. McCloy is incorrect when he writes that John Mason taught in the Antiburgher theological school of Abernethy; rather it was the Philosophical Class. Mason, in writing his son (in what came to be published under the title *Hints to Theological Students*), was very strong on the Bible languages plus Arabic, Syriac and Chaldaic and the continuous reading of the Greek and Latin classics, "with specified emphasis on Plato, and also, of French literature." (145) This can be cross referenced in VanVechten, *Memoirs of John M. Mason*, 34.

CHAPTER 10

The Associate Divinity Hall With John Brown of Haddington (1767-1787)

Introduction
The history of theological education and training in the Seceder Church generally has one notable contrast with the divinity halls of the Kirk in that the Seceders had only a single professor versus two or more in each of the Kirk halls. Thus such a history becomes a study of these individual Seceder professors and their contributions to theological education and training. One of the most noteworthy in the Associate Synod was John Brown of Haddington, who held the position of sole professor of divinity for twenty years, 1767-1787. Having outlined the reasons in the last chapter for a focused study on Brown, we now turn to that study.

A Biographical Sketch
Brown was born in 1722 at Carpow, near Abernethy, and received little formal schooling. He possessed a keen desire for learning and disciplined himself to learn Latin, Greek and Hebrew. The Seceders expected all candidates for the ministry to attend one of the Scottish universities to study arts. Brown never did; rather, he was admitted to the divinity hall without the normal course of studies. Since presbytery examinations in philosophy and Latin were conducted for all students applying to enter the divinity hall, it was quickly seen that John Brown had a better grasp of these subjects than students who had studied at one of the Scottish universities. In order that the student did not have to actually possess the M.A. degree, the presbytery allowed for "testing out". Such was the case with Brown, although later this "testing out" allowance was annulled. Brown's theological studies commenced under Ebenezer Erskine and then transferred to James Fisher due to Ebenezer Erskine's death. Robert MacKenzie wrote:

> A university career was demanded of all entrants to the ministry, but Brown had made such progress by his self-education in classes and general literature, that in his case a university curriculum was dispensed with. He was now twenty-six years

of age, and he had mastered more than most after a university training, Latin, Greek and Hebrew, and was even knocking at the gates of Arabic and Persian. What theological works were available he had devoured....[1]

Some wanted to block Brown from becoming a candidate for the ministry on the assertion that he must have obtained his learning from Satan. Ralph Erskine came to John Brown's defense declaring, "I think the lad has a sweet savour of Christ about him."[2] It should also be borne in view that Brown was a schoolmaster prior to his commencing at the divinity hall, a common practice for many students for the ministry.

Brown probably spent two sessions under Professor Ebenezer Erskine at the Associate divinity hall at Stirling, 1747 and 1748. These sessions lasted a little over two months in order to allow students to keep their teaching posts. The chief systematic text Erskine used was Francis Turretin's *Institutio Theologie Elencticae*. Erskine read from this and made comments, and then each student was orally examined. The students also gave formal discourses, after which the professor made remarks. It would appear that Erskine did not present formal lectures.[3]

The professorship was transferred to the Rev. James Fisher in 1749, and therefore situated in Glasgow. MacKenzie wrote that Fisher's professorship was characterized by the delivery of student discourses, chiefly exegetical, and effective preaching. Students shared with the professor in the criticism of these student discourses.[4]

Such was Brown's education and training. This led to his licensure in November, 1750, and his ordination on July 4, 1751, in Haddington at the Associate Church.[5]

---

[1] Robert MacKenzie, *John Brown of Haddington*, original 1918 (London, 1964), 76. The 1964 edition was abridged, so upon occasion the 1918 edition will also be used. This can be supplemented with: McKerrow, *History of the Secession Church*, 854-859; Small, *History of the Congregations of the UP Church*, 1:516-518; *DSCHT*, 99-100; *DNB*, 7: 12-14. I acknowledge the mention by Philip Ryken in *Thomas Boston as Preacher*, 8-9, of the rediscovery of *MSS* at the Dept. of Special Collections, Kings College University of Aberdeen Library, entitled: "Sermons and related writings of Thomas Boston, James Fisher, John Brown and other members of the United Free Church in Scotland 1699-1851", specifically John Brown of Haddington (1722-87; MS.3245/9). See also, D. S. Cairns, "From Union to Union: 1900-1929", in *The Church College in Aberdeen* (Aberdeen, 1936), 19. The U. P. Brown-Lindsay Library became the property of Christ's College, Aberdeen.
[2] MacKenzie, *John Brown of Haddington* (1964), 76.
[3] McKerrow, *History of the Secession Church*, 786; A. R. MacEwen, *The Erskines*, Famous Scots Series (Edinburgh, 1900), 138.
[4] MacKenzie, *John Brown of Haddington* (1964), 78-79.
[5] MacKenzie, *John Brown of Haddington* (1964), 79, 83.

One aspect of Brown's life which needs to be highlighted in this brief sketch is that of his correspondence, and specifically that with Selina, the Countess of Huntingdon, while he was professor. This has also been generally ignored by scholars, including Schlenther and Welch in their recent biographies of the Countess.[6] However, Brown's correspondence with the Countess is worthy of note as it reveals his wider influence in theological education and training and a link to the Countess's college at Trevecca in Wales.[7] The influence of the Scottish Free Church in Wales in the nineteenth century relative to theological education and other matters is commonly recognized, but Brown's influence in Wales in the previous century has received virtually no attention.[8] It was perhaps not of the same magnitude, yet it did exist. The parameters of this book only allow this relationship and influence to be recognized here.

Professor Brown

In 1767 the Associate Church lost its only professor of divinity with the death of the Rev. John Swanston. Brown was chosen as his successor on August 27, 1767, and for twenty years he remained the Associate Church's sole professor.[9] MacKenzie summarized the role as follows: "The arrangement at this period was for one Professor to undertake the work for two months in the year under a curriculum extending at first over four and later over five years; and for presbyteries to superintend the students' further studies in theology during the other ten months."[10]

Brown commenced his duties as professor in August, 1768, but not until after he attempted to withdraw from the position. In May, 1768, Brown appealed to the Associate Synod to release him from carrying out the professorship as he felt overwhelmed by what would be expected of him. The synod responded by taking another vote on the position on May 3rd with three names on the "leet", Brown being one of them. The result of the vote was that

---

[6] Boyd Stanley Schlenther, *Queen of the Methodists: The Countess of Huntingdon and the Eighteenth-Century Crisis of Faith and Society* (Durham, 1997), 201; Edwin Welch, *Spiritual Pilgrim: A Reassessment of the life of the Countess of Huntingdon* (Cardiff, 1995), 226.

[7] It is with the nineteenth-century biography on the Countess that such a theme can be found. See [Aaron Seymour], *The Life and Times of Selina Countess of Huntingdon*, vol. 2, original 1839-1844 (Stoke-on-Trent, 2000), 479-483; MacKenzie, *John Brown of Haddington* (1964), 158-164; Geoffrey F. Nuttall, *The Significance of Trevecca College 1768 -91* (London, 1969), 8, 23.

[8] *DSCHT*, 849-850. The influence of John Brown of Haddington's grandson, John Brown of Broughton Place, upon Lewis Edwards, the founder of the college at Bala, would also be an interesting matter for pursuit concerning Brown of Broughton Place.

[9] "Minutes of the Proceedings of the Associate Synod, 1766-1787", National Archives of Scotland, Edinburgh *MS* CH3/28/3, 1562.

[10] MacKenzie, *John Brown of Haddington* (1964), 131.

the synod unanimously called him to the professorship.[11] Thus, his speech to persuade the synod to release him from the professorship failed. He duly submitted to the will of the synod and thereafter held the professorship from 1767 to 1787. Hence the students of divinity made their first trip to Haddington in August, 1768, and met there each year from 1767 to 1787 for the months of August and September. The hall was conducted in the Associate Church directly behind the manse. On average Brown had about thirty students per session.

Classes were held at ten o'clock in the morning and went until noon or one o'clock. Brown had been taught Turretin but was himself a master of several systematic works, including Marck, Pictet and Owen. He produced his own systematic text, and hand written copies were produced for the students to use and copy from until it was eventually printed (first edition, 1782). This ten o'clock meeting was chiefly spent in learning the "system" section by section. The classes were begun and concluded with prayer "by the Professor and the students in the order of the roll."[12] Brown's systematic textbook had citations of Scripture liberally provided, and he would ask the students to quote the Scriptures to him to show scriptural proof for the system. Brown, like his former professor (Erskine), did not lecture on any of the divisions of divinity. Rather, he provided occasional lectures (which were really readings from his manuscripts) on some historical matter or delivered a paper on pastoral duty.

There was a second formal meeting time on four afternoons each week – Monday, Tuesday, Thursday and Friday – at which time the class met to hear students' sermons and lectures (discourses). The students were called upon in a pre-arranged order to make comment. Peddie wrote that "the Professor protected the preacher against unjust or unduly severe censures".[13] These afternoon discourses were open to the public and followed a particular pattern. First year students were assigned a text on the opening day of the hall, and each delivered a discourse before the close of that session. The second year students had to deliver a lecture from an Old Testament text which included an exercise with addition (exegesis and exposition). The third, fourth and fifth year students were given three discourses each to give during the session – a lecture on a passage of Scripture, a thesis lecture on one chapter of the Confession, and a popular sermon.[14]

On Wednesday afternoons the students met by themselves without the professor for debate and discussion. Saturday was a meeting with the professor

---

[11] "Minutes of the Proceedings of the Associate Synod, 1766-1787", 1581.

[12] McKerrow, *History of the Secession Church*, 788. McKerrow is quoting from a narrative of the Rev. James Peddie, a student of Brown's from 1777-81.

[13] McKerrow, *History of the Secession Church*, 788; MacKenzie, *John Brown of Haddington* (1964), 136.

[14] MacKenzie, *John Brown of Haddington* (1964), 136-137; McKerrow, *History of the Secession Church*, 788.

for prayer. One or two evenings were usually devoted to dealing with Church history. The session always ended with a stirring address from the professor about commencing the ministerial life, and this generally stressed an aspect of experimental Christianity. The most impressive of these was issued as "Address to Students of Divinity" and has appeared in various editions.[15] Evidently these final addresses and partings at the close of a session of the hall were solemn and moved many to tears.

One of the best sources for learning about the methods Professor Brown employed in instructing the divinity students comes from the *Memoir of the Rev. Alexander Waugh*.[16] This biography establishes a most helpful portrait of the path of education for an Associate divinity student. Waugh (b.1754-d.1827) was a student of Professor Brown in the first session of 1774. He was later ordained to the Associate Church, Newtown, in Roxburghshire, and from there he went to Wells Street (Associate) Church, London. He served a noted ministry there and was also involved in the London Missionary Society. Waugh was one of the leaders in the Secession to enlarge the content of praise within that denomination; that is, to formally move the Associate synod to include more than Psalms in its praise.[17]

Waugh was a student for four sessions at the University of Edinburgh, commencing there in 1770. He took Latin, Greek, logic, natural philosophy and moral philosophy. While at the divinity hall at Edinburgh, he returned to take Hebrew at Edinburgh University under Professor James Robertson. In addition to four sessions at Edinburgh University, he took one session at Marischal College, Aberdeen, under Professors Beattie and Campbell and took his M.A. degree from there. (Beattie was professor of moral philosophy and Campbell was principal and professor of divinity. Waugh may also have attended Professor Gerard's divinity lectures at King's College, Aberdeen.)[18] Later in 1815 he was awarded the D.D. from Marischal.[19] We find in the record of Waugh's life what was commonplace for the time; namely, students entering

---

[15] MacKenzie, *John Brown of Haddington* (1964), 139-141; John Brown, *A Compendious View of Natural and Revealed Religion* (London, 1817), iii-xviii. The *Address* was printed on both sides of the Atlantic in various editions. One of the last in America was the 1864 edition of it by the American Tract and Book Society under the title: *The Gospel Ministry: An Address to Ministers and Students of Theology* by John Brown of Haddington (Cincinnati, 1864).

[16] In part this may have come via the Rev. John Brown (Whitburn) and the Rev. Ebenezer Brown, who furnished it to Hay and Belfrage. However, it also seems to be interspersed with Waugh's own thoughts. Since there are no footnotes, it is difficult to reconstruct its origins completely.

[17] James Hay and Henry Belfrage, *Memoir of the Rev. Alexander Waugh*, 3d ed. (Edinburgh, 1839), 100-101; MacKelvie, *Annals and Statistics of the UP Church*, 520, 497; Small, *History of the Congregations of the UP Church From 1733-1900*, 2:464.

[18] Hay and Belfrage, *Memoir of Alexander Waugh*, 46-47; *DNB*, 60:76-77.

[19] Hay and Belfrage, *Memoir of Alexander Waugh*, 30, 102.

the divinity hall had not necessarily graduated or completed their arts course for the M.A. In fact, Waugh did not actually graduate with his M.A. until 1778, which would have been his fifth session in the divinity hall.[20] We also notice Waugh did his Hebrew at Edinburgh University.

Prior to commencing his studies in the divinity hall, he was examined "by the Presbytery regarding his proficiency in Philosophy and the learned language...".[21] Waugh began his divinity studies in August, 1774, under Professor Brown.

The students were required to transcribe Brown's *System of Divinity, Cases of Conscience* and *Letters on the Behaviour of Ministers and on Gospel Preaching*.[22] This parallels what was stated above about Brown's method in general. Brown was not in the habit of delivering lectures; rather he would have the students do transcriptions of his works. "Previous to the printing of the first of these works, [ie. the System, the Histories, etc.] each student was, in the course of his attendance at the Divinity Hall, required to write out a copy of it."[23] Then followed Brown's mode of instruction by oral examination, whereby the students would repeat from memory the *loci* of doctrine, together with the Scripture reference(s) in Brown's writings, supporting the various positions. This allowed Brown to supplement material into the examinations as he proceeded. He would highlight deficiencies in the students' understanding of what was read as well as correct weak oral formulations.[24] These oral examinations took place each forenoon during the weekdays for the two-month session each year. Since the students were required to commit to memory passages from *Cases of Conscience* together with the Scripture references, we would assume oral examinations/lectures occurred at some time during the week also.[25]

In the *Memoir of Alexander Waugh*, the comments which Brown added to his works are referred to as "observations". Waugh's biographers then stated that in the evenings Brown read for an hour from Church history. Although the authors were not specific, it was most likely his Church history – *A General History of the Christian Church*. There does seem to be some confusion between various books as to whether or not the students had previously copied out this Church history lecture or if Brown read and made "observations" rather than conducting a full one-hour examination session on the subject. Since Brown's *General History of the Christian Church* was published in 1771, it can

---

[20] *DNB*,60:77.
[21] Hay and Belfrage, *Memoir of Alexander Waugh*, 34.
[22] Hay and Belfrage, *Memoir of Alexander Waugh*, 35.
[23] *Memoir and Select Remains of John Brown of Haddington*, ed. William Brown (1856), 57.
[24] *Memoir and Select Remains of John Brown of Haddington*, 57-58.
[25] Hay and Belfrage, *Memoir of Alexander Waugh*, 35.

be assumed that Brown was not having the students transcribe it, but rather he reviewed it with occasional lecture and observation.

Further reading in Waugh's memoirs provides brief comment on three other features of the divinity hall at Haddington: the debating society, the prayer meeting and the student discourses. On Wednesday afternoons the students held their debating society on orthodox and heterodox doctrines. Then on Saturday afternoon a prayer-meeting was held.[26] Concerning student discourses, in the first session the students were assigned a "homily"; in the second session, "a critical discourse on a passage of the Greek Testament, with a lecture"; and in the third, fourth and fifth sessions each student was expected to deliver a lecture and a popular sermon. This sermon was to be preached in public. Following each of these discourses the students gave their criticisms, after which Professor Brown would give his remarks.[27]

Waugh has furnished us some personal insight into these discourses and the times of criticism which followed. While Waugh was in his second year, a friend in his first year delivered a homily on Romans 8:2. Evidently the criticism did not go very well for the student, as Professor Brown detected an attachment in the man to the system of moral philosophy as taught by Professor Ferguson of Edinburgh. We learn that the student subsequently came to accept his divinity professor's rebuke and corrected his views. It seems this also happened the year before with Waugh himself at the conclusion of his homily. Professor Brown had said to Waugh, "I hope I shall never hear such a discourse again in this place". Evidently by year two Waugh was in agreement with his professor and ever after spoke of Professor Brown with "veneration and gratitude".[28]

It seems that Waugh lost all confidence in Professor Ferguson after Brown's admonitions. Thus, we can observe Brown's method of guiding his students into what he viewed as the proper role of the philosophy course – never to exalt itself above Scripture. It was to be "subsidiary to the great object which constituted its chief value, by enabling him to illustrate, in a more forcible manner, those all important truths which the Scriptures alone reveal, and the knowledge of which is necessary to make men wise unto eternal life".[29]

It seems that Professor Beattie's moral philosophy lectures at Marischal College also were influential in Waugh changing his thoughts on human nature. Therefore the credit cannot all go to Brown. Beattie, like Brown, stressed piety and virtue as the chief principles for man's pursuits. Both Beattie and Campbell were noted in the 1770s for writing against David Hume.[30] It would appear that

---

[26] Hay and Belfrage, *Memoir of Alexander Waugh*, 35-36.
[27] Hay and Belfrage, *Memoir of Alexander Waugh*, 35.
[28] Hay and Belfrage, *Memoir of Alexander Waugh*, 40-41.
[29] Hay and Belfrage, *Memoir of Alexander Waugh*, 42.
[30] George Campbell, *Dissertation on Miracles* (Edinburgh, 1762); James Beattie, *Essay on Truth* (Edinburgh, 1770), various editions.

Campbell, Beattie and Brown were really not all that far apart in some of their views, even though Campbell was a Moderate within the Church of Scotland.

Waugh's contact with Marischal College helps us to see some parallels there with Brown's methods of instructions. Campbell was an able scholar of the biblical languages and offered some advice to his students: study the text in the original languages, study the ancient customs, but do not turn to the commentaries until need be. The stress was upon reading the Scripture and seeking wisdom and truth with fervent prayer: "But put no confidence in commentators: consult them sparingly: never use them till the last, and then use them only as dictionaries."[31] This last point will similarly be noted concerning Brown under the sub-heading "Brown and Scripture".

Brown and the Marriage of Theology and Piety

One theme which was prominent in the pattern of theological education and training by John Brown of Haddington was the marriage of theology and piety, especially evident in his systematic theology text, which was described by his grandson as his "most elaborate work".[32] *A Compendious View of Natural and Revealed Religion In Seven Books* was first published in 1782 for the aid of the theology students.[33] No doubt it was a great relief for the students to have it in published form and saved them endless hours of copying it out by hand. The contents of the seven books (sections/divisions) may be summarized as follows:

Book I: The Law of Nature, Its Insufficiency, Scripture
Book II: Of God
Book III: The Covenants of Works and Grace
Book IV: Of Christ
Book V: Effectual Calling, Justification, Adoption, Sanctification, Holy Spirit Comforts, Glorification
Book VI: Law, Gospel and Ordinances

---

[31] Hay and Belfrage, *Memoir of Alexander Waugh*, 43-44; George Campbell, *Lectures on Ecclesiastical History* (London, 1800).

[32] John Brown (Broughton Place, Edinburgh), ed., preface to *Address to Students of Divinity...* (Edinburgh, 1859), 17. I will only insert the location after the name "John Brown" when it is not John Brown of Haddington. Thus, if no location is attached, the reader will assume it is John Brown of Haddington.

[33] John Brown, *A Compendious View of Natural and Revealed Religion. In Seven Books.* (Glasgow, 1782). Two subsequent editions were the Edinburgh edition of 1796 and the London edition of 1817. New College, Edinburgh, has an interleaved copy of the 1782 *Compendious View...* with Brown's *MS* notes on the interleaves plus notes on "Textual Difficulties" and "Textual Difficulties Solved", which may have been class examples and were his notes. (New College *MSS*, BRO59). This 1782 interleaved copy also has the *MS* notes which Brown's grandson added into it in preparation for the reprinting of *Address to Students of Divinity* which he worked on in 1858 and was published in 1859.

Book VII: The Church: Her Constitution, Members, Offices and Government.[34]

Before addressing the theme of the marriage of theology and piety in this volume, we need to ask a basic theological question to place the work within a context; namely, how does one theologically classify the *Compendious View*? Brown's grandson, John Brown of Broughton Place, Edinburgh, answered this question accurately in the 1859 preface to the "Address":

> This work, which, being a body of Federal Theology, is, in a great degree, a compilation from the writings of Witsius, Boston, etc., who modified the most ingenious scheme of Cocceius, and suited it more accurately and completely to be an exhibition of Scriptural truth, formed the substance of the instructions read by the author in the Divinity Hall, Haddington.[35]

A cursory examination of the table of contents reveals that Brown not only had access to, but also a profound familiarity with, these authors. It is clearly reflective of a high, orthodox Reformed theology and is structured around federal theology. Brown's name for his systematics at first appears as reflecting the impact of the Enlightenment, since he used "natural and revealed religion". However, John Owen, a century before Brown, entitled book one of his *Biblical Theology*, "Natural Theology". Owen, like Brown, was saying basically what is found in the first chapter of the Westminster Confession of Faith. So one must be careful in interpreting Brown's title, as Brown was a student of Owen and yet lived in eighteenth century Scotland.[36] His polemical, doctrinal work, *A Brief Dissertation on Christ's Righteousness...*, is very clear in setting before the reader Brown's library sources and references. Chief of these were John Owen, Francis Turretin, Thomas Boston, William Flavel, Anthony Burgess, David Clarkson and William Bradshaw. Brown contended that he was representative of these authors' theology concerning the thesis he was arguing on the imputation of Christ's righteousness. Brown then concluded by writing that if his readers were still not convinced, they should read the following exhaustive list of authors to see the unity of his thought with general Reformed

---

[34] Brown, *Compendious View of Natural and Revealed Religion* (1817).

[35] Brown (Broughton Place), ed., preface to *Address*, 18.

[36] See, John Owen, *Biblical Theology*, trans. S. P. Westcott, original 1661 (Morgan, Pennsylvania, 1996), Book One, 1-144. See Westcott's notes on Owen's use of the term "natural theology". Westcott uses the American terminology that describes Owen as broadly "presuppositionalist" rather than the way the Princeton theologians used "natural theology" as a middle ground for believers and non-believers.

thought: Brown of Wamphray, Rutherford, Durham, Calvin, etc. (listing thirty-nine names in total in the first edition and fifty in the second edition).[37]

Returning again to another reference by Brown of Broughton Place, Edinburgh, he stated that Brown of Haddington used five chief writers to form his own compilation called *A Compendious View of Natural and Revealed Religion*, namely: Calvin, Turretin, Mastricht, Marck and Witsius.[38] This is quite similar to what he said in the 1859 preface to the "Address", except that Boston's name was absent. Brown's sons wrote in the 1793 *Memoir* of their father that he chiefly used Turretin, Pictet, Mastrict, Owen, Boston, Erskine and Hewey.[39] The reason we must refer to other conjectures of Brown's sources for his systematic text is that there does not appear to be one direct quotation from any of the divines listed above. Brown was forming his own compilation and purposely did not want to interject a host of names into the chief textbook for the students.[40] In summary, Brown relied heavily upon the federal theologians; the references above confirm the authors he was summarizing.[41]

In addition, although Brown's approach was biblical rather than strictly scholastic, when one reads, for instance, his chapter on "The Insufficiency of the Law, and especially of the light of Nature, to conduct Men to true and lasting felicity" (book 1, chapter 2), there is not one biblical reference! Thus, to categorize Brown's writing as in the style of Cocceius, as more of a history of biblical revelation, misses the full content of what Brown wrote. MacKenzie saw this chapter as an attack on David Hume, the Deists and Rationalists.[42] To label Brown's work as a federal tome is not to exclude also the scholastic and

---

[37] John Brown, *A Brief Dissertation on Christ's Righteousness* (Edinburgh, 1759), 7, 16-21. In the second edition of *A Brief Dissertation*, published in *The Posthumous Works of John Brown of Haddington* (Perth, 1797), on page 289 the additions may be found.

[38] Brown (Broughton Place), ed., preface to *Address*, 29.

[39] "Memoir", in *Posthumous Works of John Brown of Haddington*, 26.

[40] This was not the approach adopted by certain other divines both before and after John Brown. For example, Robert L. Dabney, *Syllabus and Notes of the Course of Systematic and Polemic Theology*, 2d ed., 1878 (Edinburgh, 1985), 183, 193, who gave extensive reference to authors and extensive reference to Scripture; and Francis Turretin, *Institutes of Elenctic Theology*, trans. G.M. Giger, ed. J. T. Dennison, 3 vols. (Phillipsburg, N.J. 1992-199), who very much adopted the scholastic approach.

[41] For helpful discussions along with primary sources on covenant theology in Bullinger, Calvin, Ursinus, Wollebius, Ames and Cocceius, see, William S. Johnson and John H. Leith, eds., "Classical Beginnings,1519-1799", in *Reformed Reader: A Sourcebook in Christian Theology*, vol. 1 (Louisville, 1993), 115-131. The subtitle on Cocceius is very good – "Johannes Cocceius: Covenant as the Foundation of a Systematic Theology". For an excellent discussion on the difference between the two Reformed Covenant schools of Cocceius and Voetius, see Francis Nigel Lee, *The Covenantal Sabbath* (Lord's Day Observance Society, London, 1969), 262. Lee summarizes this very well.

[42] MacKenzie, *John Brown of Haddington* (1918), 209.

pietistic.[43] After all, Brown wrote of Turretin, Mastricht and Marck that their systematic works were "extremely judicious",[44] so one needs to be careful in stating what Brown actually did in his systematics text.

It appears Brown was following an approach similar to Benedict Pictet in his *Christian Theology*. Pictet set forth in a briefer compendium, free of the controversies, the truth simply and plainly. The fuller system could be found in Turretin. The English translator of Pictet made the following remarks:

> [It] claims attention as a body of Christian divinity, more concise and perspicuous, and therefore more acceptable to general readers.... [T]he author [Pictet] has, by the omission of formal controversies, and, as far as possible, of the scholastic terms in which such controversies were generally conducted, rendered it a suitable work for Christian readers in general, as well as for professed students of Christian theology.[45]

Brown, like Pictet, simplified a "compendium" of federal theology into one volume. Brown also set out to issue a work which was "an exhibition of Scriptural truth", so much so that Robert MacKenzie found 1,792 scripture references in Brown's chapter on the "Covenant of Grace" (book 3, chapter 2), really an astounding number! In this respect MacKenzie saw clear likenesses to the work of Cocceius.[46] The system was rooted in the Bible. Thus, we find scores of Scripture references yet virtually no direct quotations from writers outside of the Scripture. Again, quoting his sons in the *Memoir*:

> But above all, he studied the Scripture of Truth. His acquaintance with the Bible was singular. Seldom was a text quoted but he could repeat it, explain its meaning, and point out its connection with the context.[47]

(The one exception concerns establishing the canon of Scripture. Here Brown referred to the Church Fathers and Councils.)[48] It would thus appear that his two volume ecclesiastical history entitled *A General History of the Christian Church... and the Disputes, Heresies, and Sects... to which is subjoined a List of Errors* was set forth as an "historical theology". Today we would expect to see some of it incorporated into a systematic theology textbook.[49]

---

[43] I conclude that the categories Berkof erects in the history of dogmatics do not always make for the neat inserting of Brown's name into these categories. See Louis Berkof, *Introductory Volume to Systematic Theology*, rev. ed. (Grand Rapids, 1932), 76-83.

[44] John Brown, *A General History of the Christian Church*, vol. 2 (Edinburgh, 1771), 248.

[45] Benedict Pictet, *Christian Theology*, trans. F. Reyroux (London, 1834), viii, iii-iv.

[46] MacKenzie, *John Brown of Haddington* (1918), 210-211.

[47] "Memoirs", in *Posthumous Works of John Brown of Haddington*, 26.

[48] Brown, *Compendious View of Natural and Revealed Religion* (1817), 62-63, 69.

[49] John Brown, *A General History of the Christian Church...*, 2 vols. (Edinburgh, 1771). See bibliography for a more complete title to show support for the point being presented.

Each edition of Brown's *Compendious View* or *A System of Divinity*, as it was sometimes called, included an extensive introductory "Address". This "Address" was also variously reprinted as a separate work and was still being given to all students of the United Presbyterian Divinity Hall in 1850.[50] It combines a clear statement that the study of doctrine must be held together with piety or experimental religion. Brown's grandson wrote that as a "treatment" it was to:

> guard against a style of theological instruction, the introduction and prevalence of which in the Church of Scotland the dying Halyburton so strongly deprecates, and which is the plague that threatens to overwhelm our time as well as his – 'a rational'... 'sort of religion – ordinances without power, doctrine without influence...'[51]

Brown did not want to see a division come between the academic study of theology and the "experimental acquaintance with the great facts of revealed truth in their influence on the conscience and the heart".[52] We read further that Brown:

> earnestly warned them against a merely philosophical way of studying divinity, and strenuously insisted, that, without heart religion, they could not be profitable students of theology. His address to them, in his system, plainly shows that he regarded this as a matter of the first importance.[53]

There are very obvious parallels between Brown's marriage of theology and piety as expressed in his "Address" and throughout his systematics text and that of John Owen as seen in his "Evangelical Theology", book six, chapters eight and nine in *Biblical Theology*. Owen dealt with the subject in sections entitled "Digression on the Mingling of Philosophy with Theology" and "On the Study of Theology".[54] Here Owen set forth a definition and context for theology and stated that the "sole frame of mind by which such heavenly knowledge may be grasped and so lead to salvation" and "the true principles for the study of theology and, in a word, how a man [may] become a gospel student". Further, Owen wrote: "Let a man appoint himself this goal, experiencing communion with the Holy Spirit and steadily rejecting all reliance on his own strength and

---

[50] Brown (Edinburgh), ed., preface to *Address*, 19-20.
[51] Brown (Edinburgh), ed., preface to *Address*, 19-20. The reference to Halyburton will be found in: *Memoirs of the Rev. Thomas Halyburton. With an introductory essay by the Rev. D. Young* (Glasgow, 1824), 325.
[52] Brown of Edinburgh, ed., preface to *Address*, 21.
[53] "Memoir", in *Posthumous Works of John Brown of Haddington*, 36.
[54] Owen, *Biblical Theology*, 668-703.

nature...."[55] Owen was one of Brown's favourite Puritan authors, and on this point of the marriage of theology and piety they have many parallels.

The very ordering of the chapters and books of Brown's *System of Divinity* reflects this marriage of truth and piety. All seven books in his system have sections with the heading "Reflect". Generally these are found at the end of each book, except in book six, *Law, Gospel and Ordinances*, where there are four sectional Reflect(s). Occasionally other books received an extra Reflect.[56] These Reflects are laden with personal questions stressing devotion, pilgrimage, self-examination, worship, faith, religious experience and the Gospel call – matters today more commonly referred to as "spirituality".[57] Some examples from these Reflects include:

> Ponder now, my soul! Are these oracles of God, these testimonies and testaments of Jesus Christ, my heritage...
>
> But, O my soul, in what form am I to die, - to rise again, - and to live forever? Shall I certainly die *in the Lord?* (Italics by John Brown)[58]

Brown not only used such Reflects in his *System of Divinity*, but we find this same basic layout in his *Self-Interpreting Bible*. Here the Explanatory Notes at the bottom of the page provide a brief, verse-by-verse commentary. These are followed by a set of notes for each chapter and verse set under "Reflections Upon Chap. I" (or whatever chapter it was). Thus, the division is commentary first (explanatory notes), followed by "Evangelical Reflections", as the title page describes them.[59] In comparing these Reflections in the *Self-Interpreting Bible* to the Reflections in Brown's *System of Divinity*, the immediate difference of note is grammatical. The divinity text uses mainly the interrogative, whereas in the biblical text the Reflections are either exclamatory or assertive. However, the intent in each remains the same, to stress man's need for the Saviour, Jesus Christ, and to come to worship God. For example, on Matthew chapter three we read in the Reflections:

---

[55] Owen, *Biblical Theology*, 685, 694. Owen's concluding exhortation to students is on keeping up a regular communion with the saints: "Living interaction with saints and believers is essential to the student. It will sharpen, by exercise and practice, those spiritual gifts on which true gospel wisdom is founded, and that wisdom itself will be strengthened and increased by the holy practice."

[56] I have used here the 1817 edition to look at these "Reflect" sections. Brown, *Compendious View of Natural and Revealed Religion*, 97, 191, 225, 335, 397, 449, 496, 500, 517, 546, 575-576.

[57] See article on "Piety" in *ERF*, 278-279.

[58] Brown, *Compendious View of Natural and Revealed Religion*, 97, 449.

[59] John Brown, *Self-Interpreting Bible*, 2 vols. (London, 1791). This edition has no page numbers, therefore citations will refer to volume number, followed by the Bible book and chapter. For example, 2, Proverbs, chs. 1 and 2 and Romans, chs. 1and 2.

multitudes often seem fond of hearing the gospel, while few really believe it: and most men are ready to rest in external professions or privileges, without any experience of the power of religion. Indispensable is the necessity of true repentance, marked by an holy life, under the influence of the Holy Ghost: and happy forever are they who are once partakers of this grace![60]

Thus, this chapter's Reflections are similar to those in the *System of Divinity*; however, generally the explanatory notes are considerably shorter here.[61]

Brown's goal of the marriage of theology and piety and his structure in his systematic text are not dissimilar to the late twentieth century systematic text by Wayne Grudem (aside from theological positions). Grudem's work, like Brown's, contains a prefatory address, although somewhat shorter than Brown's. Grudem raised and also answered the questions "Why Should Christians Study Theology?" and "How Should Christians Study Systematic Theology?" Interestingly, Grudem included "Questions for Personal Application", "Scripture Memory Passage", and a "Hymn" at the conclusion of every chapter. Much of this is quite comparable in spirit to Brown's work.[62]

The prefatory "Address" in Brown's systematics stands at a most important juncture, not just for laying before the reader the approach they are to take in studying theology, but also because Brown ended every session of the divinity hall with such an address. These were always of the same order – to speak of personal religion and to make earnest and solemn appeal on the matters studied. In the Rev. Alexander Waugh's *Memoirs*, we find two excerpts recorded from such closing addresses. (Waugh, having been a student of Brown, issued two letters to his own son when this son was studying theology, exhorting him to: "Read over and over good old Mr. Brown's Address to Students... and apply to your own soul the deep and impressive sentiments which you will find

---

[60] *Self-Interpreting Bible*, 2, Matt., ch. 4.

[61] See, *Self-Interpreting Bible*, 2, Eph., ch. 6, for an example of this. Also, the explanatory notes were in a much smaller type-set from the Reflections. For some reason, however, in the book of Acts there are no explanatory notes but only reflections. In the other books where there are explanatory notes, each verse will receive some commentary, although not always as a single verse, but often two or three verses taken together.

[62] Wayne Grudem, *Systematic Theology: An Introduction to Biblical Doctrine* (Leicester and Grand Rapids, 1994), 23, 26-30, 32-38, 41-43, 51-53, etc. I am not identifying exact style in Brown and Grudem. Grudem certainly combines more dogmatic controversies, but in Scripture, theology and piety they are remarkably similar. There is much less of a similarity in these aspects if one does a comparison with Robert L. Reymond, *A New Systematic Theology of the Christian Faith* (Nashville, 1998).

there.")[63] Evidently a student of Brown's made full notes of these addresses and they were inserted into Waugh's *Memoirs*:

> Thinking this morning of your departure, two passages of Scripture came to my mind, and you will do well to take them into your serious consideration. "Have I not chosen you twelve, and one of you is a devil?" One may be called to special service, may fill a public station in the church, may be a preacher... and yet be a devil... a traitor at heart, and act the part of an open traitor at last, may betray the Master he professed to serve... Jesus knows all things; he searches the heart... To commend a Saviour one has no love for; to preach a Gospel one does not believe..., to enforce a saving acquaintance with religion, and to be an entire stranger to it one's self, how sad....
>
> The other passage comes more closely home, and is still more alarming. "And five of them were wise, and five were foolish." Is it only one-half of the number here present that are wise, that are truly serious, prudent, and thoughtful,... Surely they who propose to undertake an office, the design of which is to win souls, had need to be convinced, about their own souls.
>
> The most profound silence reigned while from these passages he addressed the students: all were dissolved in tears. The language, the tone, the general manner, every circumstance, was calculated to make a deep impression.[64]

Clearly from the foregoing, the structure and composition of Brown's major theological tome reveal him as concerned with orthodoxy and the transmission of it as truth. However, that is far from the entirety of the matter. Brown's goal was to wed theology and piety both in the textbooks and in the sessions of the annual divinity hall at Haddington.[65] Although the study of doctrine wedded to piety in Scottish theological education has not received a great deal of attention, it is certainly deserving of renewed study. Andrew Hoffecker, in writing about Princeton and Archibald Alexander, Charles Hodge and Benjamin Warfield in *Piety and the Princeton Theologians*, offered a good paradigm which could have equally characterized John Brown of Haddington. He stated that:

> Within the Princeton theology the subject of religious experience was as integral a part of any discussion of strictly doctrinal issues...because they constantly related experience to doctrine, they composed a theology of religious experience that is as

---

[63] Hay and Belfrage, *Memoir of the Rev. Alexander Waugh*. Also, "The closest attention to the state of your own heart, and to the progress of religious principle and feeling there, is indispensably necessary." 325, 331.

[64] Hay and Belfrage, *Memoir of Waugh*, 36-38.

[65] The pattern which emerges here is that of the fusion of religious sympathy between professor and student. Several standard works provide analysis of this at the level of application or analysis. See William Adams Brown, "Ministerial Education In America: Summary and Interpretation", in *The Education of American Ministers*, vol. 1 (New York, 1934), 155. The author centres upon chapel services in the "seminary". Brown's "Addresses" went beyond a chapel service to establishing a method and an ethos in the hall.

important for understanding the Princeton theology as any other of their writings on theological topics.

Unfortunately, scholars of American theology and church history have neglected the Princeton piety...[66]

Hoffecker went on to write that these Princetonians charted a *via media* so that the cognitive powers together with that of the subjective were both stressed.[67] Brown was certainly in harmony with Hoffecker's paradigm.

Brown and Practical Divinity

Casuistry

The literary output of Brown was quite phenomenal, amounting to over thirty publications, several of these going through numerous editions.[68] It is commonly acknowledged that some of these, and in particular his *Self-Interpreting Bible*, were household possessions and therefore part of the ordinary religious life of many.[69] Yet, as in the case of his systematic tome, much of what he wrote was aimed at the instruction, edification and training of Secession divinity students. In this regard we turn to an area where his output was prodigious – practical divinity. As we will see, this discipline encompasses many distinct topics which we will endeavour to categorize as we proceed.

In the 1797 *Posthumous Works*, drawn together chiefly by his ministerial sons, the Revs. John Brown of Whitburn and Ebenezer Brown of Inverkeithing, we read: "In his system of divinity and cases of conscience, the public have a view of the particular topics which he used to explain at large to his pupils."[70]

We possess a complete *MS* transcription of Brown's *Cases of Conscience* by one of his students, William Taylor, who is listed as having attended the divinity hall in Haddington in 1778. Whether he transcribed it at that session or in 1781, the date on the *MS*, it is difficult to access. William Taylor was ordained January 3, 1786, as the first minister of Renton, Associate Church (Burgher) Dumbartonshire.[71] The reference here to "cases of conscience" is obviously to the second half of his 1783 work, *Practical Piety Exemplified, in the Lives of Thirteen Eminent Christians... And Illustrated in Casuistical Hints*

---

[66] Andrew Hoffecker, *Piety and the Princeton Theologians* (Phillipsburg, New Jersey, 1981), 5.
[67] Hoffecker, *Piety and the Princeton Theologians*, vi-vii.
[68] *DSCHT*, 99.
[69] *DNB*, 7:13.
[70] "Memoir", in *Posthumous Works of John Brown of Haddington*, 8.
[71] MacKelvie, *Annals and Statistics of the UPC*, 575, 667.

or *Cases of Conscience*.[72] The section *Casuistical Hints* is almost two hundred pages in length and is divided into five chapters:

    I. Satan's Temptations
    II. Indwelling Sin
    III. Spiritual Experiences
    IV. Christian Conversation
    V. Scandalous Offences[73]

Brown wrote in the preface to *Casuistical Hints* that it was "originally formed for my own use: and may now be considered as an appended illustration of the *Lives*: or, as an Appendix to my *System* on the head of SANCTIFI-CATION...".[74] Thus Brown was simply reworking material formerly used in the divinity hall and offering it as a published body of practical divinity. It bears a close comparative study to that of David Dickson's *Theurpeatica Sacra* of an earlier period in Scottish theological education. Brown, in typical Puritan fashion, was taking his students and readers into conviction of sin and to crying out in their consciences for Christ's grace and enablement by the Spirit. His chapter on Satan's temptations to various "sorts and ranks" of peoples (young persons, old persons, the afflicted, the rich and great, learned, magistrates, lawyers, ministers, the unlearned, those under convictions, the unconverted, the converted, those under "divine desertion", and those who have "remarkable fellowship with God") gave a careful analysis of Satan's methods and was followed by appropriate applications.[75] As practical divinity for candidates for the ministry, the application was clear – they would minister to a variety of people, and as physicians of the soul they had to be wise and well trained. No doubt, in dealing with Satan's temptations to ministers, Brown exhibited an utmost solemnity, as was the case with such addresses.

In chapter two, "Indwelling Sin", he again began by setting forth a theological framework and then proceeded to deal with twenty-two "spiritual plagues" from indwelling sin, all matters ministers would encounter in their pastorate; such as lukewarmness, carnality, superstitious inclinations and legality.[76] Following an analysis of these twenty-two aspects of indwelling sin, an extensive application was given on the mortification of sin with a strong

---

[72] John Brown, *Practical Piety Exemplified, in the Lives of Thirteen Eminent Christians ... And Illustrated in Casuistical Hints of Cases of Conscience...* (Glasgow, 1783).
[73] Brown, *Practical Piety... Casuistical Hints*, 171. [This work can be found in *MSS* form in the New College Library, Edinburgh, *MSS*, BRO 44. It was transcribed by William Falkirk in 1781 and is 348 pages of hand-written text.]
[74] Brown, *Practical Piety...Casuistical Hints*, iii.
[75] Brown, *Practical Piety...Casuistical Hints*, 179-183.
[76] Brown, *Practical Piety...Casuistical Hints*, 207-225.

development on the ministry of the Holy Spirit.[77] Also an extensive listing of scriptures to be used when dealing with the various "plagues of sin" was provided. Brown dealt with thirty indwelling sins and generally furnished one, two or more scripture texts to be applied.[78] Again the work is reflective of a Puritan tradition in practical divinity and no doubt students were to make these lists as class-notes.[79] Chapter three, "Spiritual Experiences", began with a discussion on the dangers of those who delight in experience without being rooted in scriptural knowledge. Likewise, the problems of those who are serious in self-examination yet lack assurance or have problems with doubt was addressed. Again there was a very strong stress on the work of the Holy Spirit.[80] Many of the themes in this chapter were "common-growth" matters in Puritanism.[81]

Brown went on to deal with six matters of the spiritual life of a believer in chapter four: the Christian walk, fellowship with God (which is sub-divided several ways), spiritual mindedness, keeping the heart, keeping the conscience, and affliction and death. Point five, "conscience", began with a definition of conscience as "that power of our soul, not which makes laws for our conduct, – but which declares the law of God, and witnesseth and judgeth what actions are agreeable to it, and what not, and approves or condemns accordingly".[82] The definition was followed by the various states of one's conscience – deluded or erroneous, silent, truly good, sincere and well informed.[83] Matters of the heart and conscience surfaced often in the writings of Brown and appear to have been directed towards his students.

The last chapter in *Casuistical Hints*, "Scandalous Offences", would have been of very practical importance for men training for the ministry as they could incur offence from members of a church or vice-versa. Also they would be called upon to settle disputes, act in church trials, provide wisdom and give

---

[77] Brown, *Practical Piety...Casuistical Hints*, 225-243.

[78] Brown, *Practical Piety...Casuistical Hints*, 240-242.

[79] In the late twentieth century there was the rise of the "nouthetic school of Christian counseling". Though it is not Puritan, it has certain methodical parallels. It is not our purpose here to divert into a full comparative study of the Puritans, John Brown of Haddington and nouthetic counseling.

[80] Brown, *Practical Piety...Casuistical Hints*, 243-278.

[81] See John Flavel, "A Familiar Conference Between a Minister and a Doubting Christian Concerning the Sacrament of The Lord's Supper", in *The Works of John Flavel*, original 1820 (London, 1968), 460; John Owen, *The Works of John Owen*, ed. William Goold, original 1850-1853 (London, 1965-1967), vols. 3, 4, 6 and 7.

[82] Brown, *Practical Piety...Casuistical Hints*, 311.

[83] Brown, *Practical Piety...Casuistical Hints*, 312-317; William Brown, ed., *Memoir and Select Remains of John Brown of Haddington* (Edinburgh,1856), 72, where several comments are made about Brown's preaching as close and addressing the conscience. His sermons were not cold but awakened the conscience. Also see Brown, *Posthumous Works*, 30.

advice to members on fellowship matters. Here there were direct applications to elders and ministers:

> When offensive practices abound, church-rulers ought to shew themselves eminent patterns of sobriety, meekness, holiness and humility: – they ought to be deeply affected with that giving or taking of offence, which they perceive in others, and by prayer, reproof, advice and intreaty, labour to prevent offences, or root them out before they spread; and ought to cultivate the most intimate union and ardent affection among themselves. – Ministers ought to avoid the mentioning of any thing which tends toward doubtful disputations, and to endeavour leading their hearers to the most important and practical points of religion...[84]

Brown was obviously grieved to observe the hurt and offence caused by the division within the branches of the Secession and strove to lay before his students the marks of God's people to strive together for peace. His passions ran high in writing this chapter. In speaking about "private offences" and how to handle these, he wrote that one should:

> carefully conceal the offence from others who are not necessarily concerned to knowing it, that he may not involve himself in backbiting and reviling, – in which one may sometimes hurt his neighbour and the church more, by reporting a truth which ought to be concealed... *Oh! Would professed Christians ponder this!* [85] (italics-Brown)

This section also presented a theology and commentary on church discipline: "public scandals, the honour of Jesus Christ..., the general edification of souls, and the recovery of the offender are to be carefully kept in view...."[86] Brown devoted several pages to "scandals and errors", offering a theological framework on heresy and the ensuing duty of church judicatories to practice church discipline.[87] His final concentration in this last chapter concerned the harm done by scandalous offences:[88]

> they are contrary to that love, reconciliation, study of peace, unity of affection, and intimacy of fellowship among Christians, so much recommended in scripture... they proceed from the most shameful causes, produce the most sinful and ruinous effects, and are very hard to be cured.[89]

---

[84] Brown, *Practical Piety...Casuistical Hints*, 323.
[85] Brown, *Practical Piety...Casuistical Hints*, 324.
[86] Brown, *Practical Piety...Casuistical Hints*, 324-325. Brown continues his discussion here on church discipline and church judicatories.
[87] Brown, *Practical Piety...Casuistical Hints*, 330-338.
[88] Brown, *Practical Piety...Casuistical Hints*, 338-352.
[89] Brown, *Practical Piety...Casuistical Hints*, 338.

Brown wrote pastorally, singling out the various reasons for division – divisions about non-fundamental doctrinal points, divisions on the manner of worship, divisions over alleged personal faults, divisions concerning the authority of a church court, divisions over practices established by church courts, divisions over admitting someone to the ministry, etc., – including advice with each.[90] All this reads as a practical manual to resolve division in local churches. One wonders if his years as clerk of synod and close involvement in church life could not supply behind the scenes examples to each division. He then closed with a warm plea to overcome division and depicted the problem as a "want of that heart-melting fellowship with Christ, which powerfully inclines to a tender love to his church and people...".[91] There are obvious parallels to Richard Baxter's *A Christian Directory,* volume one, particularly part three, "Christian Ecclesiastics", and also chapter eight and some of the "Ecclesiastical Cases of Conscience".[92]

There is no clear evidence that the first half of *Practical Piety...And Casuistical Hints*, the lives of thirteen Christians, was ever delivered before the students of the divinity hall.[93] This is not to say that it was not; however, it appears to have been written more for readers by way of illustration of the practical divinity set forth in part two of the book.

Another of Brown's published works on practical divinity is his translation into English of portions of Charles Drelincourt's (the elder) *Charitable Visits*.[94] This is a work which, broadly speaking, can be placed in the category of casuistry. The work contains sixty-one sections dealing with a variety of spiritual issues.[95] Brown did not leave us a hint anywhere within it that he used this as part of a pastoral course with the students in the divinity hall. His sons stated that he translated it "chiefly for his own amusement and information".[96] It gives us more insight into Brown's reading and study of casuistry, all

---

[90] Brown, *Practical Piety...Casuistical Hints*, 347-351.
[91] Brown, *Practical Piety...Casuistical Hints*, 352.
[92] Richard Baxter, *The Practical Works of Richard Baxter: A Christian Directory*, vol. 1 (Morgan, PA, 2000), 595.
[93] Brown, *Practical Piety...Casuistical Hints*, 1-120. These potted sketches are mainly of Scots. The one on James Mitchel is highly fascinating as he tells about sitting under David Dickson's ministry in Irvine and receiving personal admonitions from him (142-149). Common themes in these sketches are the blessings connected to the communion seasons, struggles with sin, the glories of Christ and approaching death. The story of Alexander Archibald includes mention of the blessing he had in joining a society for prayer, joining the Four Seceeding ministers and hearing Ebenezer Erskine preach to great profit (76-91).
[94] Charles Drelincourt (the elder), *Les visites charitables, on les consolations chretiennes, pour toutes sortes de personnes afligées* (Genève, 1666).
[95] Charles Drelincourt, "Extracts from Drelincourt's Charitable Visits", trans. John Brown (Haddington), in *Posthumous Works*, 200-240.
[96] "Extracts from Drelincourt's Charitable Visits", *Posthumous Works*, 200.

forming background for instruction in the hall. Topics surveyed included: doubting one's salvation because one does not feel the grace of God, overwhelmed by sin and fear of God's judgment, doubting one's salvation because of great afflictions, of one imprisoned for professing gospel truth, for one in "a long languishing disease", for a young man dying, of one healed of the plague, of a woman whose child died without baptism, for orphans, for those grieving for truth and piety in the world, of a dying minister and of one whose faithful minister has died.[97]

That Drelincourt was being studied by others in Scotland on the matter of casuistry is evidenced by a selection of Drelincourt's *Consolations* published in Glasgow in 1790. However, these selections are not the same as John Brown's. The editor or translator is unnamed, and they are included in a collection with consolations by Bradbury, Harvey and Halyburton.[98]

Homiletics, Catechising and Sacraments

We turn now from casuistry to homiletics. There are several published letters on homiletics by John Brown of Haddington which were "originally composed for the use of his students".[99] These do not furnish us with a complete set of notes of what Brown taught for homiletics, but they are more than we possess for many other halls. These letters have little to say concerning sermon structure and delivery. However, in "On the Composition of Pulpit Discourses" there are more hints in that direction. The letters focus upon the goal or aim of preaching, as Brown himself states in the opening sentences of "Letter 1. On Preaching the Gospel": "Let me here touch the principal point. A preacher's elocution may be charming, his action perfectly regular, his language elegant, his method exact, and his manner scarce chargeable with error, and yet he may not truly preach the gospel of Christ."[100] Brown then contrasted true gospel preaching with much of the current preaching of his day, and we infer this to refer to Moderate preaching. He wanted his students to preach about sinful human nature and the glories of the Saviour Jesus Christ. For Brown, cursed were all who would preach anything else. He appealed to apostolic preaching as the example to follow. Further, he wrote about true preaching:

---

[97] "Extracts from Drelincourt's Charitable Visits", *Posthumous Works*, 200-240
[98] Charles Drelincourt, "The Resurrection a Comfort against the Fears of Death" and "Consolation of Felicity after the Glorious Resurrection" (Consolation Nos.10 and 11 of Drelincourt's Consolation), in *The Christian's Consolations in Times of Trouble and at Death*, no trans., no ed. (Glasgow, 1790), 177-212; 212-286. Charles Drelincourt, *Les consolations de l'aime fidele contre les frayeurs de la mort* (Amsterdam, 1699).
[99] Brown, "Two Letters", in *Posthumous Works*, 160; John Brown, "On the Composition of Pulpit Discourses", in *Christian Repository* (1817), 661-671.
[100] Brown, *Posthumous Works*, "Letter 1. On Preaching the Gospel", 160.

Nothing is more common, easy, or agreeable to corrupt nature, than to preach a multitude of the precious truths of God in a broken and disjointed manner, without ever preaching the gospel of Christ. If a preacher descant upon the perfections of God, but do not represent him, as in Christ, well appeared... there is no gospel, no glad-tidings without this...

He [the preacher] acts but the part of a heathen who acquaints me with the multitude, the pollution, the absurdity of my vices and indwelling lusts, and with the charms, the profits, the pleasures, the honours, the duty of virtue, or my obligation to it, and calls me off from the one to the other, without setting before me Jesus Christ, as sent by God to save me from sin, and to sanctify them with his blood, – Jesus Christ... through which, imputed to us, we become dead to, and delivered from the broken covenant of works... that being married to Christ, and created anew in him,... we, in his strength, may bring forth fruit unto God....[101]

Brown then went further by telling his students that those who would preach about Christ's imputed righteousness "but neglects[ed] to point him forth as a Saviour from the power and pollution of sin..." also were defective preachers.[102] The goal and purpose of training the students in homiletics was that they would preach in the tradition of the Marrowmen, of Boston, and of the Erskines. Philip Ryken's study on the preaching of Thomas Boston would provide a noble point of comparison to Brown's homiletic discourse. Ryken sees in Boston's sermons a preacher who "discriminates between the regenerate and the unregenerate in the application of his doctrine...Of all the possible distinctions that might be drawn between one hearer and another, it was the distinction between belief and unbelief which most concerned Thomas Boston."[103] Similarly, it was evangelical preaching that was John Brown's goal.

In a further set of letters which were also read to his students, we find a brief setting forth of seven "Rules" to follow when preaching. These are in summary:

1.) Keep in view that it is the gospel you are preaching, and it is God ordained.
2.) Found the sermon on the Scripture as your text and proof.
3.) "Insist chiefly on the greater points of revelation concerning Jesus Christ, faith in him, and repentance toward God through him." [the number 3 was missing but I have inserted it to keep the intent]
4.) Make application that it may awaken, and "captivate their affections to Christ".
5.) Let your language be adapted to that of the hearers, and let it be scriptural. Do not be philosophical.

---

[101] Brown, *Posthumous Works*, "Letter 1. On Preaching the Gospel", 162-163.
[102] Brown, *Posthumous Works*, "Letter 1. On Preaching the Gospel", 165-168.
[103] Philip Graham Ryken, *Thomas Boston as Preacher of the Fourfold State*, Rutherford studies in Historical Theology, eds. David F. Wright and Donald MacLeod (Carlisle and Edinburgh, 1999), 41-42.

6.) Avoid anything which will detract, for example, speaking too quickly, or indistinctly, poor pronunciation, awkward gestures, wandering from the subject, useless questions, expressions which would promote laughter. Also do not adhere too scrupulously to your notes. "Avoid all descriptions of an offender from personal circumstances...."

7.) Never draw attention and focus upon your own honours. You are to promote the glory of Christ.[104]

Rule number six is the longest of these, yet it needs to be kept in view that Brown would have "enlarge[d] upon"[105] each point as he read them to the students. Though we are fortunate in being able to see some general rules he laid down in homiletics, these are "bare-bones" and would have certainly been more extensively delivered to the students. It will be noticed that these rules do deal with certain points on delivery and gesture, yet the focus comes out once again that gospel preaching was the goal and nothing else.

Interestingly, Brown attached an exhortation on catechising to this homiletic lecture. In fact, he linked it with preaching: "Catechising, and the private visitation of families and the sick, are but subordinate forms of preaching, of which catechising explains, and visitation, rightly performed, closely applies, the truths of God and men."[106] Again he set forth rules, but this time they appeared unnumbered and took up less than two pages. Thus, we may presume that they too were enlarged upon in the classroom. Brown assumed that the minister would perform catechism work within the congregation twice a year. His rules included using an approved catechism or a passage of Scripture, with clear stress that the Scripture must also be brought forth in the catechising. He also believed that catechising should be done in groups, classified according to age and ability to encourage each in his group. His admonition: be gentle as Jesus was gentle with the children – "You cannot deal too much with young ones in a kind and prudent catechising of them." In addition, he advocated that at the end of a catechism session a suitable "warm" address could be formed and addressed to "the consciences of the catechised and others".[107]

Elsewhere we learn that John Brown had a high regard for ministry to children. This was certainly expressed above in the homiletic lecture, but in addition we can draw together four other points as they related to children's instruction. First, his "Children's Catechism" or "A Short Catechism for Young

---

[104] John Brown, *Letters on The Exemplary Behaviour of Ministers: Originally Composed for the Use of His Students*, ed. John Brown (of Whitburn), part 3, "Directions with Respect to Preaching the Gospel, and Administering the Sacraments" (Edinburgh,1827), "Letter 1", 29-33.

[105] Brown, *Letters*, ed. John Brown (of Whitburn) iii.

[106] Brown, *Letters*, part 3, "Letter 1", 33.

[107] Brown, *Letters*, part 3, "Letter 1", 33-35.

Children" was to be "taught children before they can read"[108] and was offered to them that they might know the way of salvation. Second, he desired to have children in attendance during the Lord's Supper.[109] Third, often in his preaching he addressed the children in the congregation, and on occasion he delivered a series of sermons for the youth.[110] Fourth, on Saturday evenings he regularly gathered for half an hour with children who would come to the manse, when he would "converse" with them and pray.[111]

Further lectures or letters on homiletics return us to casuistry, but this time the casuistry of preaching. Brown contended to his students that simply preaching truth was not sufficient – "You must rightly divide and address them to the consciences of your hearers, as unconverted or converted, as strong or weak, as legally or evangelically wounded in spirit, or as fallen into scandal or error."[112] Brown then arranged the hearers of sermons into various casuistical categories and offered applications as to how the students should preach to each group. The categories were: the unconverted sinners, the converted, those "strong in faith and knowledge", those "weak in the faith", those with wounded spirits (various sub-divisions within this category), those who are "lapsed" (backsliders).[113]

Though Brown has given us this casuistry on preaching, it was not that distinct from his *Cases of Conscience*. Thus there is little need to repeat those things here. What we find is a strong evangelical or gospel emphasis, a reliance upon the influence of the Holy Spirit and an assertion that the preachers' task is to labour and exhort people to fellowship with God the Father. There is a sense of great gravity which flows throughout these letters, combined with an exhortation to the preacher to be meek and gentle, yet bold. Brown asserted that the preacher must practice wisdom, "never proposing things in their hearing which they are not able to bear".[114] The final category of dealing with the lapsed in preaching appears to be applied definitely at two levels, public preaching and private counsel.[115]

Brown's "On the Composition of Pulpit Discourses" provided some very clear directives on sermon organization, introduction and delivery. For example, he commended the preacher to commit the sermon to memory after it was written; introduce the sermon with "serious, warm, and evangelical prayer"; speak calmly in the introduction, then rise with the sermon's advance;

---

[108] John Brown, *Two Short Catechisms Mutually Connected*, original 1764 (Edinburgh, 1818), 5-20 for "Children's Catechism".
[109] *DSCHT*, 99.
[110] Brown, *Posthumous Works*, "Memoir", 32.
[111] Brown, *Posthumous Works*, "Memoir", 33.
[112] Brown, *Letters*, part 3, "Letter 2", 35.
[113] Brown, *Letters*, part 3, "Letter 2", "Letter 3" and "Letter 4", 35-49.
[114] Brown, *Letters*, part 3, "Letter 2", 38.
[115] Brown, *Letters*, part 3, "Letter 4", 47-49.

and above all, for the preacher's life to be a living testimony.[116] Brown explained that these elements grew from a preacher who had an "abundant grace and experimental fellowship with God" whereby "the better he will understand his subject, the more deeply he will be affected with it, and with the spiritual state, or condition of his hearers…".[117]

Attached to Brown's letters/lectures on homiletics we find one letter which was devoted solely to the practical administration of the sacraments of baptism and the Lord's Supper.[118] Today in many seminaries this would be taken up in a worship course intended for candidates for the ministry. Nonetheless, he gave four rules on the administration of the sacraments, but again they were so brief that we must conclude that he enlarged upon them in class with the students. The four rules were: to administer the sacraments as prescribed by Christ, not to administer the sacraments privately but rather publicly, to administer them to "visible believers" – the scandalous were not to be admitted, and to possess reverence and "lively affection" in all discourses at such times as "ought to correspond with these things".[119] Rule four could be interpreted either to mean that the discourses or sermons at the time of the sacrament should be fittingly chosen or that these sermons should be serious. I adopt the first opinion.

This particular series of letters/lectures, chiefly on homiletics, concluded with eight exhortations, all of which discussed the high calling and importance of the ministry plus the character of a minister and the account ministers must render for their labours. His eighth exhortation was an encouragement not to become discouraged, and here he mentioned the labours of Moses, Isaiah, Jeremiah, Ezekiel and of Jesus Christ:

> Your ministrations may be secretly useful, though you perceive it not. Though they should not be blessed for the conversation of sinners, they may be useful for the building up of believers in holiness and comfort… Your diligence, faithfulness, and order, may provoke or excite others, whose ministrations will be more remarkably useful… May the Lord make these scriptural hints very profitable to your soul![120]

The conclusion we reach is that these lectures were very pastoral in nature. Brown was desirous to guard the students from as many pitfalls as he could. He wanted his students to leave the divinity hall as ministers of the gospel, not philosophers.

---

[116] Brown, "On the Composition of Pulpit Discourses", 663-670.
[117] Brown, "On the Composition of Pulpit Discourses", 661.
[118] Brown, *Letters*, part 3, "Letter 5", 49-53.
[119] Brown, *Letters*, part 3, "Letter 5", 49-50.
[120] Brown, *Letters*, part 3, "Letter 5", 50-53.

Polity

Normally in the theological curriculum of a Presbyterian seminary, there is a place given to church polity or church government. Brown dealt with much of this in his systematic work, book seven. However, as we have seen before, he often took a section and "expanded" upon it, as he did with book five under "Sanctification", by giving lectures in casuistry. Some of these would fit properly under sanctification, but the latter "cases" (such as on scandals and church discipline) would more properly be studied under polity. Thus, there is some overlapping and ambiguity when we attempt to place Brown's curriculum into our modern curricular categories. Chapter five, "Scandalous Offences", listed under casuistry, could in its entirety be included under polity studies today.[121] It was first given as a lecture in the divinity hall at Haddington, so we know polity issues were taught there.

However, a more formal polity work which Brown authored was *Letters on the Constitution, Government, and Discipline, of the Christian Church.*[122] This was first printed in 1767, the year he began his professorial labours, and again in 1799. Brown provided us with no preface or direct clue within the work to indicate whether these became or already were lectures in the divinity hall. Since Brown did not always give formal lectures, we could surmise that this book was made available to the students, and that subsequently they may have been orally examined upon it. The work contained nineteen letters, with the first addressed to Amelius, who is rarely mentioned again.[123] We print out below the nineteen "chapters":

1. Of the Nature and Foundation of Divine Right
2. Of the Divine Warrant for Church Government
3. Of Christ's Headship over the Visible Church
4. Of the Qualifications of Church-members
5. Of Private Christians Privileges and Power
6. Of Magistrates Power in the Church
7. Of Diocesan Bishops Office and Power
8. Of the Subject of Church-power, etc.
9. Of the Qualifications of Church Officers
10. Of the Election of Ministers
11. Of the Ordination and Duty of Ministers
12. Of Ruling Elders and Deacons

---

[121] John Brown, *Practical Piety...Casuistical Hints*, "Chapter Five – Scandalous Offences", 171.

[122] John Brown, *Letters on the Constitution, Government, and Discipline, of the Christian Church*, original 1767 (Edinburgh, 1799).

[123] Brown, *Letters on the Constitution...Church*, 4, 5, 23-24, 30, 104. The students may have even transcribed the book or a select lecture from it for themselves. See also MacKenzie, *John Brown of Haddington* (1964), 151.

13. Of the Nature of Church-power
14. Of the Warrant for Congregational Sessions
15. Of the Warrant for Classical Presbyteries
16. Of the Warrant for Synods
17. Of the Calling, etc. of Church Courts
18. Of Scandals and Discipline
19. Of Church-Fellowship and Separation[124]

Again like most of Brown's writings, it abounded with Scripture references. Chapters four, ten and eleven had obvious pastoral implications for students. The whole tenor of the book was to clearly defend Presbyterianism as the only biblical form of church government, a matter which the Secession no doubt wanted to be upheld in their hall. Brown wrote in chapter eleven:

> Knowledge of languages, knowledge of the history and sciences of this world, are useful handmaids to assist us in the study of divine things. To preach from the oracles of God, without capacity to persue the originals, especially if verrant in romances and plays, I abhor; I detest. This aptness to teach, however, consists not chiefly in any of these; but in a capacity to conceive spiritual things, and with some distinctness express their conceptions to the edification of others...[125]

In this work Brown set forth at length the duties of the minister beginning with his duty to acquaint himself with the spiritual state of the flock and then to feed them truth "according to their diversified state and condition", never reading the sermon from the pulpit. He was to catechise, visit from house to house "to awaken their conscience; promote the conversion of sinners...", faithfully administer the sacraments, tenderly care for the poor, visit the sick, govern the church, admonish and rebuke and absolve the penitent; habitually pray. "Finally, he is constantly to walk before his flock, a distinguished pattern of sobriety, righteousness, holiness, humility, heavenliness, temperance, charity, brotherly kindness, and every good word and work. Without this his ministrations appear but a solemn farce of deceit."[126] Then Brown concluded these duties with two practical questions: could ministers accept civil office and could ministers read their sermons, to both of which he gave an impassioned NO! [127]

In addition to this discussion by Brown on ministerial labours, we find similar material in two tracts found in the 1789 *Select Remains* – "Reflections of a Candidate for the Ministerial Office" and "Reflections of one entered into

---

[124] Brown, *Letters on the Constitution...Church*, i.
[125] Brown, *Letters on the Constitution...Church*, 58.
[126] Brown, *Letters on the Constitution...Church*, 74-76.
[127] Brown, *Letters on the Constitution...Church*, 75-76.

the Pastoral Office".[128] There is no conclusive evidence that Brown used these directly in the hall. Rather, the first of these tracts was probably sent out to potential candidates wrestling with the call to ministry and the latter to his students who were newly settled into their first charge, as was his custom. In reading MacKenzie's extractions from Brown's correspondence to students, it can be concluded that these two tracts would have also been sent forth to students or potential students. Seceder divinity students received correspondence from their professor throughout the year or following their licensure, which tells us that the formation of the students was not limited to the divinity hall. Thus Brown's correspondence to his students became part of their ministerial training and formation and some of his tracts such as those named above must not be ignored in establishing the overall picture of theological education and training by the Associates.[129]

From a pastoral perspective, "Of Qualifications of Church Members" would certainly have generated interest amongst candidates for the ministry. Brown argued that members are not admitted on the basis of a "change" or "regeneration". Rather, it was on the basis of "probable appearance; not infallible evidence of men's faith and repentance". Examiners were to look for "visible conversation, correspondent to regeneration".[130] Next he raised the question of whether profession of assent to histories, etc., should be necessary. His answer – no. Rather the candidate should confess to the "leading truths".[131] Brown then proceeded very carefully to set forth much pastoral advice for the examination of someone to see if they knew the "leading truths".

Unto Exemplification

Amongst the writings of John Brown we find several works dealing with biography. These are of varied nature, some of ministers and theologians and some of ordinary Christians who left journals, etc. His son, the Rev. William Brown, stated that his *Christian, Student, and Pastor, Exemplified in the lives of Nine Ministers* was "prepared with a special view to the improvement of his students", like his systematics and his church histories, general and British.[132] There is one word in the full title of this work which serves as a key to how Brown would use these, and this is the word "exemplified". The biographies were of James Fraser, James Hogg, Thomas Halyburton, Owen Stockton,

---

[128] John Brown, "Reflections of a Candidate for the Ministerial Office" and "Reflections of One Entered into the Pastoral Office" (Tracts 5 and 6), in *Select Remains of John Brown*, eds. John and Ebenezer Brown (London,1789), 113-125, 126-141.
[129] MacKenzie, *John Brown of Haddington* (1964), 147-154.
[130] Brown, *Letters on the Constitution...Church*,18-20.
[131] Brown, *Letters on the Constitution...Church*, 20.
[132] William Brown, ed., *Memoir and Select Remains of Rev. John Brown, Haddington* (Edinburgh,1856), 57.

Matthew Henry, Philip Doddridge, Thomas Shepherd, Cotton Mather and Jonathan Edwards – three from Scotland, three from England and three from America.[133] They cannot be properly called biographical sketches as little by way of fact is given about the individuals. Brown set out to abridge the memoirs of each and to promote in the reader devotion and practice, thus using the memoirs for exemplification. Addressing "my pupils, or others", Brown urged them to have deep foundations in their religion, no formalities, but an "experimental knowledge of Jesus Christ".[134] Hebrews 6:12 was the text Brown used in addressing his "Reader" – "Be not slothful, but followers of them...."[135]

The Scottish ministers Fraser, Hogg and Halyburton receive the largest space in the book, with approximately eighty pages devoted to each.[136] We will sample Fraser's "Life" as Brown extracted it to gain insights into what Brown was giving his students. The first chapter begins with Fraser discussing his "convictions, conversion, and particular backslidings and recoveries". Fraser recorded what works he was reading beside Scripture, and how these were blessing his soul – Shepherd and Ferrier's works, the *Practice and Piety* and the Westminster Confession of Faith.[137] His reflections are highly experimental and very much reflect Puritan piety:

> My backslidings were many and dreadful; I neglected, or but slightly performed, the duties of God's worship, in public or private. I idled away my time, neither glorifying God, edifying others, or profiting myself... From this decay, I learned, (1) Saints are very apt to fall from that measure of grace, or comfort, which they receive at their conversion, Rev. ii:4, 5. (2) Saints never fall totally from grace, I John iii:9. Song v.2....[He lists 15 things he learned during his backslidings!][138]

Fraser described some of the critical facts about his life, such as in 1663 when he stopped hearing the Episcopalian clergy and joined with "the poor people of God" (the Covenanters). Reference was made to his ordination by

---

[133] John Brown, *The Christian, the Student, and Pastor, Exemplified in the lives of Nine Ministers* (Edinburgh, 1781), i-iv. Brown evidently wanted to include Thomas Boston in this list. For Brown's other such studies see "Pleasant and Practical Hints, Chiefly from Samuel Rutherford", collected by John Brown in *Posthumous Works*, 109-153. Much of this appears to be for Rutherford's people in Anwoth and for afflicted believers in Ireland. Thus, it is aimed at pastoral edifications and strengthening. It very much extols the "sweetness of Jesus": "Oh that I could employ all the tongues in Britain and Ireland in helping me to sing new songs to my well-beloved!... How fearful the guilt of rejecting the offers of Christ in the gospel!" (127).

[134] Brown, *Christian, Student and Pastor*, iii.

[135] Brown, *Christian, Student, and Pastor*, iv.

[136] Brown, *Christian, Student, and Pastor*. See Fraser, 1-76; Hogg, 77-150; Halyburton, 151-230; Stockton, 231-253; Henry, 254-269; Doddridge, 270-283; Shepherd, 284-286; Mather, 286-289; and Edwards, 290-295.

[137] Brown, *Christian, Student, and Pastor*, 9.

[138] Brown, *Christian, Student, and Pastor*, 14, 16-17.

Presbyterian ministers, his preaching and his various confinements.[139] Sprinkled into the loose narrative were certain opinions, such as his very negative view of Richard Baxter "whom I looked upon as a stated enemy to the grace of the gospel".[140] This is intriguing in that on the atonement Baxter and Fraser do not appear all that far apart, and their writings both possess the same introspective piety and analysis. It is possible his concern was the same that Hogg had – the issue of Baxter legalizing the gospel.[141] Other sidelights of wisdom and advice were also given, such as what Fraser advised concerning choosing a marriage partner:

> ...(3) The great end of Christians, in their marriage, ought to be the getting of a help meet, for the furtherance of their spiritual and eternal welfare. (4) They ought, therefore, to take the most earnest heed, that the person they marry be prudent, pious, and virtuous. It is dreadful to take a lump of God's wrath into our bosom....[ten points in total here on marriage][142]

The final pages devoted to Fraser were his "Observations", of which there were thirty-six, chiefly centring around earthly trials and the Christian. Brown then concluded the "life" by stating Fraser's last words: "I am full of the consolations of Christ...."[143]

The three main "lives" all commenced the first chapters with a discussion on conversion and temptations or backslidings. Also, Fraser and Halyburton both gave wisdom on marriage, and Halyburton also briefly touched upon devoting children to God and family education.[144]

In pursuing other "lives" in this book, we quickly see how Brown could have used these ministerial sketches to advantage in the divinity hall as "exemplifications". For example, in the section on Matthew Henry, Brown included the extensive six questions of self-examination Henry used at the time of his ordination.[145] Likewise, Brown included extensive descriptions of Henry's daily schedule and routine, along with such hints as to take note that Henry memorized his sermons, rose between four and five and had monthly communion.[146]

---

[139] Brown, *Christian, Student, and Pastor*, 35, 67, 72-73.
[140] Brown, *Christian, Student, and Pastor*, 66.
[141] Brown, *Christian, Student, and Pastor*, 100.
[142] Brown, *Christian, Student, and Pastor*, 71-72.
[143] Brown, *Christian, Student, and Pastor*, 73-76. The three chapters on Fraser were:
Chapter One: Of his convictions, conversion, and particular backslidings and recoveries;
Chapter Two: Of more general concerns of his spiritual estate and condition;
Chapter Three: Of his entrance on the ministry; marriage; imprisonments; and death.
[144] Brown, *Christian, Student, and Pastor*, 213-214, 151, 77.
[145] Brown, *Christian, Student, and Pastor*, 257-260.
[146] Brown, *Christian, Student, and Pastor*, 260-265.

Brown did not restrict himself to biography in order to lay before the students of the divinity hall examples of the Christian life and of being students and pastors. Sometimes his lectures were direct, not using an example from Church history. We have several of these direct lectures on "exemplification". Again, they are printed in the form of letters to the divinity students. Thus they parallel in style the letters on homiletics he gave in the hall which we have already examined.

In one of these letters, "Letter II: On the Exemplary Behaviour of Ministers", Brown began by laying out various doctrines upon which ministers must have a firm intellectual grasp; for example, the differences between and harmony of justification and sanctification. However, he emphasized that one must go beyond an intellectual grasp for "a deep experience of these truths is necessary to make one clearly apprehend them. None can rightly understand the power of mens (sic) indwelling corruption, unless he have savingly felt his own...."[147] In this letter Brown again united knowledge with the heart, then proceeded to lay before the students examples of how to properly set out the gospel before people. He explained that "exemplary behaviour" begins with the preacher rightly being "acquainted" with the gospel.

The other letters on exemplary behaviour take us on from this point into matters of advice and daily conduct. These are grouped under two main headings: "Cautious with respect to personal conduct" (which contains two letters) and "Directions with Respect to the exercise of every saving grace, Christian temper and practice" (which contains three letters).[148] A variety of subject matter is covered in these letters, beginning with the exhortation never to take up the ministry without both the inward and the outward call.[149] Here are some examples of the advice Brown offered his students:

> Shun intimate friendship with obstinate atheists and scorners.
> Never speak lightly of religious discourses.
> Be most careful about becoming dependent upon financial loans from folks.
> Be cautious about accepting loans or gifts if it might lead to your being held dependent or in a state of bondage to such individuals.
> Do not be anxious about money, etc.
> Do not begrudge giving money to the poor.
> Do not have an ambitious spirit in the church.
> Do not envy the success and prosperity of others.

---

[147] "Two Letters on Gospel Preaching and on The Exemplary Behaviour of Ministers, originally composed for the Use of his students", in *Posthumous Works of John Brown*, "Letter 2", 168-169.

[148] John Brown, *Letters on the Exemplary Behaviour of Ministers Originally Composed for the Use of His Students*, ed. John Brown of Whitburn (Edinburgh, 1827), 5-28.

[149] Brown, *Letters on the Exemplary Behaviour of Ministers*, 5-6.

Do not be obstinate in matters which are really indifferent or doubtful.
Do not have a contentious spirit.
Do not indulge anger for matters which are the defects of men.
Be temperate in both eating and drinking.
Do not become drunk.
Do not turn to riotous living after ordinations and the Lord's Supper.
Desist all "unbecoming familiarities" with women.[150]

Brown urged the students to avoid all the vices and lusts summarized above and then proceeded to lay before them the Christian virtues or graces they were to pursue. He began with an extended exhortation for them to pursue holiness and devotion towards God in public and secret worship. Each was to keep his own soul "burning with love and zeal".[151]

The students were to choose pious servants for their household and, in particular, they were to choose a wife who was pious, affable and a true help. Brown explained that in the family you are responsible for love, harmony, order and the exercise of authority along with

> affectionate delight in your wife, sympathy with her in trouble, and patient bearing of her infirmities. The children whom God may give you, should be brought up in the nurture and admonition of the Lord, without either sinful indulgence, or cruelty in your dealings with them, and in due time appointed to some proper business, answerable to their inclinations, abilities, and station in life.[152]

Brown proceeded to the minister's dealings outside of the home, namely, his report amongst all men. He was never to be condescending to those of low estate. He was to be humble with others, to love all men, to help the poor, to forgive injuries, to show hospitality to strangers, to be moderate towards all and to seize opportunities to bring spiritual good into conversations with all people, thus being like Jesus in His conversations.[153] He concluded these virtues with the charge to become godly examples, explaining that otherwise they would hurt the preaching of the gospel and the Church. Brown asserted that bad examples would be told of far and near, and they would introduce much error and corruption into the Church.[154]

Finally, in Brown's last letter on exemplary behaviour, he laid before the students the need for them to remain good "learners". When ministers, the students must give themselves to reading, meditation and prayer. Brown assumed that the minister would be reading widely in natural history,

---

[150] Brown, *Letters on the Exemplary Behaviour of Ministers*, 7-15.
[151] Brown, *Letters on the Exemplary Behaviour of Ministers*, 16-17.
[152] Brown, *Letters on the Exemplary Behaviour of Ministers*, 19.
[153] Brown, *Letters on the Exemplary Behaviour of Ministers*, 20-22.
[154] Brown, *Letters on the Exemplary Behaviour of Ministers*, 23-24.

biography, histories of nations and churches, and doctrine, but in so doing must ask God's blessings so that he would not read it like an atheist. However, he emphasized that the minister's chief reading should ever be the Scriptures in the original languages. Brown gave some practical advice also on how to read divinity when he stated that one should always seek to discern in what age and for what reason the author wrote the book.[155]

In conclusion, Brown's writings on exemplification were to set historical examples before the students and directly challenge them through exhortation to become an example (1 Thess. 1:4-7, etc). His lectures and writings to his students to this end do not seem to have a parallel in the divinity halls of the Kirk of the same time period. And, though Brown wrote positively about Halyburton, there is no evidence Halyburton gave such lectures in the early eighteenth century. Brown was not completely unique in this area, as Samuel Miller of Princeton in a later generation wrote *Letters on Clerical Manners and Habits, Addressed to a Student in the Theological Seminary at Princeton, N.J.* (1827).[156] Yet Brown does appear to stand alone in this regard in Scotland in the late eighteenth century.

Brown and History

In the mid-eighteenth century Scotland saw a whole host of histories being produced. Coming from the Kirk divinity professors, we have already noted William Robertson's *History of Scotland*, one of three histories he wrote. The enlightened writers David Hume and Adam Ferguson likewise produced their histories (Hume: *History of the Stuarts*, 1754, and *History of England*, 1762, and Ferguson: *History of the Roman Republic*, 1782). Robert Watson, divinity professor and also principal of St. Andrews, wrote *History of Philip II of Spain* in 1777.[157] However, one notices that the theme of these histories is more that of civil rather than ecclesiastical history, even though two of these authors were divinity professors for the Church of Scotland. Brown was not satisfied with this approach, nor, one suspects, would Brown be overly impressed by Ferguson's writing. Brown believed that the history of the Church of Christ was being neglected and that there was an abundant "usefulness" in studying Church history – it instructs in "favours" received and in sins committed.[158]

---

[155] Brown, *Letters on the Exemplary Behaviour of Ministers*, 24-28.

[156] Samuel Miller, *Letters on Clerical Manners and Habits, Addressed to a Student in the Theological Seminary at Princeton, N.J.* (New York, 1827).

[157] MacKenzie, *John Brown of Haddington* (1918), 166-167.

[158] John Brown, *A Compendious History of the British Churches in England, Scotland, Ireland and America. An Account of the most material Transactions since the introduction of Christianity to the Present Time. With an Introductory Sketch of the History of the Waldenses*, 2 vols. (Glasgow, 1784), iii.

Thus we can see how Brown would have used his evening Church history lectures to counteract this neglect and edify his students.

Brown's general Church history appeared in print in 1771 and his *British Churches* in 1784. In essence they were the print form of what the students would have transcribed and heard "observations" upon at the divinity hall. For his general Church history, Brown acknowledged his debt of gratitude to Johann von Mosheim, professor of theology first at Helmstedt, then at Gottingen. Mosheim's *Institutiones historiae ecclesiasticae* appeared first in 1726 but went through various revisions. It was said of Mosheim that, "His historical work was marked by a hitherto unprecedented objectivity and penetration and he may be considered the first of modern ecclesiastical historians."[159] Brown's general Church history may have relied upon Mosheim, yet he demonstrates an acquaintance with a vast array of writers – numbering over 240 in the two volumes. His method was to read both sides of the controversies in Church history and then to formulate his historical statement on the matter. Brown's structure for his *General History* basically follows Mosheim's structure in his *Institutes of Ecclesiastical History*, dividing the history by centuries.[160] Within each century Brown subdivided the century into four categories: external events, state of learning, practice of religion, and contentions and heresies. These subdivisions come close to Mosheim's, although not identical. In the sixteenth century Brown took a different structure from Mosheim.[161] Mention has already been made of the appendices. These make the work fall more into historical theology than the more modern teaching of Church history.[162]

Brown's other major historical work, the *History of the British Churches*, opened with a chapter on the Waldensians, then in nine chapters he dealt with England, beginning at approximately A.D. 300, then one chapter on the Church in Ireland and one chapter on the Protestant churches in America. This concluded volume one. Volume two contained seven chapters on the history of the Church in Scotland in the ancient period, but with marked emphasis on the Reformation and Second Reformation. Subsequent editions attached Brown's "An Historical Account of the Rise and Progress of the Secession" to volume two, although it was absent from the 1784 edition.[163] This appended historical

---

[159] *ODCD*, 119; John Brown, *General History of the Christian Church*, 1:i.

[160] *ODCD*, 119.

[161] John Brown, *General History of the Christian Church*, 1:v; 2:28; Johann Lorenz von Mosheim, *Institutes of Ecclesiastical History, Ancient and Modern*, trans. James Murdock, revised by James Seaton Reid, 6th ed. (London, 1868)

[162] MacKenzie, *John Brown of Haddington* (1918), 169; Brown, *General History of the Christian Church*, 2:341.

[163] Brown, *A Compendious History of the British Churches* (Glasgow, 1782), 1:v-viii, 2: iii-iv; John Brown, *A Compendious History of the British Churches...*, 2d ed. (Edinburgh,1820), 1:v-viii; 2:iv-v; appendix to vol. 2, 1-96.

account of the Secession also had an appendix attached to it as "A Brief Explanation of the Terms used in the preceding Pages".[164] Here thirty-one terms were defined, similar to what Alister McGrath has recently included at the back of his historical theology.[165]

Brown's other historical writings were on the history of the Secession and, of note here, *A Brief Chronology of Redemption*, which was simply issued as a tract. Brown had hoped to give a fuller treatment to this subject yet never had opportunity. He was glad that Jonathan Edwards had attempted such in *A History of the Work of Redemption*, but believed it to be too meagre. This tract by Brown is interesting to read. Whether or not he had the students memorize the chronology from it cannot be stated with conviction. There does seem to be a hint at the end of the tract that he was offering practical advice as to how to read histories of churches and nations, perhaps with his students in view.[166] The tract follows Ussher's chronology of the world, and the final three chronological sections reveal Brown's historic post-millennialism.[167] It would certainly make for an interesting comparative study to Edwards as well as other Puritans.[168] Brown, like many others, approached the writing of history with a much larger scope towards Church history than we would use today. We would put many of Brown's historical writings within the biblical department of a seminary curriculum. Further comment will be made upon this in the sub-section "Brown and Scripture".

Brown and Baxter

It would appear obvious to many that there was a similarity in ministry and writing between Richard Baxter and John Brown of Haddington. There are striking parallels on casuistry, catechising and the call for conversion. Brown commended both Joseph Alleine's *Alarm to the Unconverted* and Richard Baxter's *Call to the Unconverted* in his "Dying Advices to his Younger Children". Yet he added this caveat: "…but beware of some legal directions in the last two [Alleine and Baxter]".[169] This qualified commendation is set within Brown's exhortation on their being concerned for their eternal salvation. As a Marrow follower, Brown was concerned over Baxter not having the same grasp

---

[164] Brown, appendix to *A Compendious History of the British Churches*, vol. 2 (1820 edition), 93-95.
[165] McGrath, *Historical Theology* (rev. ed.), 564-577.
[166] John Brown, "A Brief Chronology of Redemption, Representing all the Noted Events of Time and Eternity as Promoting it, and the Glory of the Divine Perfections in and Through it", in *Posthumous Works*, 58-92.
[167] Brown, "A Brief Chronology of Redemption", 87-92.
[168] Jonathan Edwards, *The Works of Jonathan Edwards*, ed. Edward Hickman (Edinburgh, 1974 from the 1834 edition), 532-619.
[169] John Brown, "Dying Advices to his Younger Children", in *Select Remains of John Brown*, eds. John Brown and Ebenezer Brown (London, 1789), 252.

of the nature of grace (thus leaning to legalistic tendencies) and also that of Amyraldianism. Brown's younger son in the ministry, William, wrote of his father: "Probably few men have come nearer than Mr. Brown to Richard Baxter's style of preaching, as described by him in these memorable lines, 'I preach'd as never sure to preach again; and as a dying man to dying men.'"[170] William then goes on to quote one of Brown's former students (unnamed) who had once said to Professor Brown: "Mr. Brown, you are often speaking against Richard Baxter, but I see no man so like Richard Baxter as yourself."[171] This particular reference exemplifies the parallel between Baxter and Brown in their similar, earnest appeals to the hearts and consciences of the unconverted.

Brown and Scripture

It appears that Brown's approach in relation to scriptural instruction within the divinity hall did not centre around intense instruction in Greek and Hebrew. All students would have taken Greek in their arts course, and several in their fourth year in arts would have taken Hebrew. However, Brown did produce an unpublished, simplified Hebrew grammar and vocabulary for the use of some students.[172] This was possibly the only Hebrew some would have received if they had not done it in their arts. This was not radically different from the Church of Scotland students within the university divinity halls, many of whom would have not studied Hebrew. In the Scripture discourses and exegetical exercises which the students delivered, Brown would have been able to make his "observations" and thus teach exegesis in some form.[173] It seems Brown assigned passages to be done in the Hebrew before the students arrived at the hall, and then they were called upon in turn to read and give an explanation.[174]

We notice that Brown did not write any commentaries, though he certainly was teaching biblical exegesis in the divinity hall as noted above. John MacLeod in *Scottish Theology* casually asserted that John Brown of Haddington was responsible for bringing out an edition of John Brown of Wamphray's commentary on Romans.[175] In an examination of this particular commentary, there is no mention of Brown of Haddington being the editor or preparer.[176] MacKenzie is silent on this, as are all of Brown's sons in *Select Remains* or *Posthumous Works*. The title page only reads, "Carefully printed

---

[170] John Brown, *Memoir and Select Remains of John Brown of Haddington*, ed. William Brown (Edinburgh, 1856), 72-73.
[171] John Brown, *Memoir and Select Remains*, 73.
[172] MacKenzie, *John Brown*, (1918), 133.
[173] MacKenzie, *John Brown*, (1918), 132.
[174] MacKenzie, *John Brown*, (1918), 140.
[175] MacLeod, *Scottish Theology*, 85.
[176] John Brown (of Wamphray), *An Exposition of the Epistle of Paul to the Romans with Large Practical Observations; delivered in Several Lectures* (Edinburgh, 1766).

from the Author's own Manuscript" and is unsigned. The preface of six pages follows, also unsigned.[177] Obvious clues are not there to help us.

In the preface we are informed that the introduction also had to be written, but nothing else had to be added. There are various hints in the preface and the introduction to lead one to conclude that it may have been executed by Brown of Haddington: a good acquaintance with Samuel Rutherford and the Covenanters in general;[178] a clear reference to the Covenanter expository series by Durham, Dickson, Ferguson, Hutcheson and Nisbet and that this is but in the same class;[179] reference to Henry's commentary and how this will aid where Henry ended his commentary;[180] obvious Secession theology concerning evangelical preaching, free grace and lifting high the honours of Christ in contrast to the legal preaching of the Moderates;[181] and finally, the constant references to Christ's righteousness and the sinners justification.[182] In 1759 Brown had issued his pamphlet *A Brief Dissertation on Christ's Righteousness...*, and the first name he mentioned in his concluding list of Reformed authors who were in unity with his thoughts was Brown of Wamphray. This was not due to alphabetical listing as he did not employ such.[183] Did Brown of Haddington have Brown of Wamphray's manuscript or access to it prior to 1766 while he was writing the *Dissertation*? (Brown of Wamphray's work on justification [1696] is viewed by James Walker as one of Scotland's best Reformed expositions on the subject.[184]) Lastly, at the end of the printed text of the commentary is "A List of the Encouragers of this Work". In this list there are fifty-six ministers included (Brown being one), and of these over ninety per cent belong to one of the Secession branches.[185] Thus, there is a very high probability, reading through this list of names and with internal evidence, that John MacLeod's brief statement is on solid ground. This tells us that Brown was continuing in the Puritan tradition of exposition. As he was a professor the year following the publication of this commentary, we are confident to assert that the "old paths" were taught to the students:

---

[177] Brown (Wamphray), preface to *Exposition on Romans*, i, iii-viii.

[178] Brown (Wamphray), preface to *Exposition on Romans*, iv-v. See Brown's own "Pleasant and Practical Hints from Samuel Rutherford", in *Posthumous Works*, 109.

[179] Brown (Wamphray), preface to *Exposition on Romans*, vi.

[180] Brown (Wamphray), preface to *Exposition on Romans*, vi. Also Brown's life of "Matthew Henry", in *Christian, Student, and Pastor*, 254.

[181] Brown (Wamphray), preface to *Exposition on Romans*, vii-viii. This theme was amply explored in Brown's lectures to aid students in homiletics.

[182] Brown (Wamphray), preface and introduction to *Exposition on Romans*, vii-2.

[183] Brown, *Brief Dissertation on Christ's Righteousness* (1759).

[184] Walker, *The Theology and Theologians of Scotland 1560-1750*, 24.

[185] For verification I examined Small, *History of the Congregations of the UP Church*, vols. 1 and 2.

> Ever since the decline of our national reformation, a set of pulpit men have arisen, who set themselves in direct opposition to the gospel and doctrine of Christ: instead of knowing nothing but Jesus Christ, and him crucified, they appear determined to know and teach some other thing of their own framing and invention; rarely do they mention the name of Christ in their pulpit harangues, as if they were ashamed of this glorious name; or when they mention him, it is only under the notion of a heavenly teacher and pattern of imitation, robbing him of the glory of his Deity and Godhead, and the merit of his obedience and righteousness; and thereby do they frame a gospel of their fancy...
>
> Morality in its finest dress, and true godliness in its greatest simplicity, do widely differ both as to their spring and tendency; the one is bred in; and formated by a carnal proud heart, the other flowing from a new covenant state of union to, and interest in Christ; the one tending to exalt self, whilst the other ascribes all to God, and the sovereignty of his grace...
>
> It may be justly lamented, that few know the meaning of true religion in its power and efficacy upon the heart....[186]

This brings us to briefly consider how Brown conceived of teaching his students to exegete and exposit upon the text. Brown explained his method in *The Christian, the Student, and Pastor* in the course of dealing with the memoir of James Hogg. Recall that these memoirs of nine ministers were used first in the classroom with his divinity students. In dealing with Hogg, Brown easily stepped into a lecture "observation" on the science of biblical hermeneutics. Hogg gave six rules to follow in "searching the scripture". Brown then added a footnote to these rules:

> From experience, I am persuaded, that this method of searching into the meaning of God's word, is by far the most delightful, edifying, and instructive; and that commentaries ought to be used chiefly as helps, to assist us in comparing parallel passages of Scripture.[187]

The six rules emphasize such things as the absolute necessity of the illumination of the Spirit and that if a matter is taught we must hold to it. Also, we must never impose our meaning upon the text but rather must dig further and draw together parallel passages whereby we will derive the true explanation.[188] Brown's vision for interpretation, like that of Hogg, was very much akin to what Hugh Oliphant Old wrote about Matthew Henry:

> The biblical interpretations of Matthew Henry are an expression of that age. Far from expressing a partisan backlash, this interpretation of Scripture sought a

---

[186] Brown of Wamphray, preface to *Exposition on Romans*, vii-viii.
[187] John Brown, "James Hogg", in *The Christian, the Student, and Pastor*, 135.
[188] John Brown, "James Hogg", in *The Christian, the Student, and Pastor*, 134-135.

practical meaning, easily applicable to the Christian life as an informal worship expressing a simple and sincere inward devotion.[189]

This quotation certainly applies to Brown's *Self-Interpreting Bible* and his *Bible Dictionary*, for he interpreted Scripture with a strong desire to edify and to be edified. Thus Brown's scriptural studies were pastoral, aimed at strengthening the Christian and the Christian family. They cannot be compared as in the same vein as his contemporary at Marischal College, Principal and Professor George Campbell and his *Dissertation on the Gospels*, which was a critical work. Brown's hall and the vision for a pastoral ministry remained the focus. None of this detracts from Brown's analytical and linguistic abilities and his understanding of biblical imagery. Old's comments on Henry read almost like a mirror of Brown: he was quite capable of grammatical-historical exegesis; he did not allegorize but understood the types, intimations and foreshadows of the Old Testament to the New; he sought the *sensus spiritualis*; and the critical issues were not paramount, rather God's Word was to direct us to eternity.[190] We noticed in Brown's *MS* at New College his interleaves on "Textual Difficulties" and "Textual Difficulties Solved", showing that he was prepared to struggle and think, but with a purpose in view – preaching – and that very much falls within the Puritan tradition.

Three other noteworthy publications from Brown in the field of biblical theology were: *Sacred Typology* (1767), *An Evangelical and Practical View of Old Testament Types* (1781) and *The Harmony of Scripture Prophecies and History of their Fulfilment* (1784).[191] The first and third of these went through various editions. No doubt today several biblical scholars would view these works as pressing typology too far.[192] The popular nineteenth century text in this same field, Patrick Fairbairn's *Typology of Scripture* (published 1845-1847), omits any reference to John Brown's writings in his first chapter on the "Historical and critical survey of the past and present state of theological opinion on the subjects".[193] It appears these biblical theological writings did not have a lasting influence on into the nineteenth century, particularly by the time of Fairbairn. In the second half of the nineteenth century in conservative Presbyterian circles, Hengstenberg's and Patrick Fairbairn's writings were more influential than Brown's on the Old Testament, typology and messianic prophecy. Brown's lacked substantial scholarly interaction and concentrated upon organization, brief explanation and the citing of Scripture references.

---

[189] Donald K. McKim, ed., *Historical Handbook of Major Biblical Interpreters* (Downers Grove, Illinois / Leicester, England, 1998), 196.

[190] *Historical Handbook of Major Biblical Interpreters*, 197-198.

[191] MacKenzie, *John Brown of Haddington*, 312-313.

[192] I have consulted the 1812 American edition of John Brown, *A Brief View of the Figures and Explication of the Metaphors Contained in Scripture* (Middlebury, Vermont, 1812).

[193] Patrick Fairbairn, *Typology of Scripture,* orig. 1845-47 (Grand Rapids,1989), 1-46.

Works additional to the three mentioned above need to be consulted to gain a true perspective on how Brown handled typology and prophecy. These include both his *Self-Interpreting Bible* and the *Dictionary*. However, the other work which must not be omitted is *The Psalms of David, in Metre with Notes, Exhibiting the Connection, Explaining the Sense, and for Directing and Animating the Devotion*. This work went through several editions, the last in 1991. Brown's preface gives some information as to how he approached the Psalms beyond merely the prophetic. He also stated that what "is *historical*, as it relates to David and the Jewish church, is often *typical*, and so *prophetic*, as it relates to Jesus Christ and the Gospel church, or heavenly state".[194] In reading through the "notes" that prefix each metrical psalm, one finds they are both Christocentric and devotional in emphasis. The note on Psalm 149 is most interesting:

> While I sing, let mine eyes be fixed on Jesus Christ, going forth in his chariots of salvation, subduing his enemies to himself, by the Gospel-rod of his strength, in the Apostolic and Millennial periods, Rev.20:2; and in the chariots of vengeance, destroying his incorrigible opposers, by the iron rod of his wrath, and treading them under the feet of his saints.[195]

Brown's *Self-Interpreting Bible*, *Bible Dictionary*, *Concordance* and *Psalms of David in Metre with Notes* remained popular long after his death in 1787. The *Self-Interpreting Bible* went through at least twenty-six editions, the last in 1909, and the *Dictionary* went through eight editions (plus at least five pirated editions), the last in 1868.[196] The *Dictionary* usually included Brown's *Concordance*, although often the *Concordance* was printed as a separate volume.[197] MacKenzie wrote that Brown's *Dictionary of the Bible* was the first undertaking by a Scot and only the second in Britain; the first was written by Thomas Wilson of Canterbury (1563-1622). Brown's *Dictionary* made full use of the best of the then published dictionaries: Matthias Illyricus, Thomas Wilson, Honore Simon and Augustine Calmet. Calmet's had been abridged and translated into English, yet according to MacKenzie it was defective on the oriental languages, the classics, history, divinity and the natural sciences. Brown's *Dictionary* pursued these subjects, thus producing in its age a work for students and lay people to use in their homes unlike any before it.[198] This final

---

[194] John Brown, *The Psalms of David in Metre with Notes, Exhibiting the Connection, Explaining the Sense, and for Directing and Animating the Devotion* (Dallas, Texas, 1991), xx-xxi.

[195] Brown, *Psalms of David*, 460.

[196] MacKenzie, *John Brown of Haddington*, 312-313.

[197] Brown's *Concordance* was last printed in America as a separate volume in 1871. John Brown, *A Concordance to the Holy Scriptures* (New York, 1871).

[198] MacKenzie, *John Brown of Haddington*; John Brown, *Dictionary of the Holy Bible*, ed. John Brown Patterson (London and Edinburgh, 1845), i.

comment emphasizes the readership for whom Brown's two greatest biblical works were produced. As a professor in the divinity hall, the church was always close by, and Brown was not a professor in an "ivory tower" setting. Thus, even the title, *Self-Interpreting Bible*, had this same goal: to aid the reader to understand the Bible and to help them by cross-referencing the Scripture text in question.[199] It is not a scholarly study Bible, but rather the notes and reflections are devotional in orientation and give a simple and plain comment upon the text. Questions such as the identity of the "virgin" in Isaiah 7:14 did not concern Brown, nor did word studies on "covenant" or "testament" in 1 Corinthians 11:25.[200]

Brown's Old Testament Cocceian approach can be found also in his *Dictionary*. For example, in the entry under Boaz, Brown pressed the typological window:

> Was Boaz a figure of our Blessed Redeemer, who though great and wealthy, thought on us sinners of the Gentiles, and after manifold tokens of kindness, espoused us to himself, as his church and people?[201]

Such a question posed to the reader was clearly reflective of Cocceius' approach to the Old Testament in one branch of the federal theologians. It is also reflective of Brown's Christ-centred preaching. The story of David Hume hearing John Brown of Haddington preach illustrates this: "That man preaches as if Jesus Christ stood at his elbow."[202] Fairbairn, in his critique of the Cocceian School, stated that by the eighteenth century a coldness was gripping Protestant orthodoxy; however, in contrast the Cocceians "...kept the work and kingdom of Christ ever prominently in view, as the grand scope and end of all God's dispensations".[203] Likewise in Brown's writings or lectures, evangelical teaching was the centre; he never succumbed to the rationalistic spirit of his age.

Brown was not alone in the Secession in this regard. William McEwen, his fellow class-mate in the divinity hall at Stirling under Ebenezer Erskine and then at Glasgow under James Fisher, authored *Grace and Truth; or the Glory and Fulness of the Redeemer Displayed, in an Attempt to Explain the Types, Figures, and Allegories of the Old Testament* (1762). McEwen's work follows the Cocceian School, Vitringa and others and was highly popular in Scotland in the eighteenth century.[204]

---

[199] "Biblical Exegesis", in *DSCHT*, 310.
[200] *Self-Interpreting Bible*, 2, Isaiah, ch. 7 and 1 Corinthians, ch. 11.
[201] Brown, *Dictionary of the Bible*, 114.
[202] MacLeod, *Scottish Theology*, 96.
[203] Fairbairn, *Typology of Scripture*, 15.
[204] Fairbairn, *Typology of Scripture*, 17; *DSCHT*, 512-513; MacKelvie, *Annals and Statistics of the UP Church*, 664; MacKenzie, *John Brown of Haddington*, 98-99; MacLeod, *Scottish Theology*, 181.

The area in Brown's *Dictionary* which would draw the most attention today would be on eschatology. Brown's approach to Revelation would be that of a continuous interpretation or what could be classified as historicist post-millennialism – what most theologians today would call historic post-millennialism.[205] Brown, like many others, expected the downfall of "AntiChrist and Mahometanism" in A.D.1866 and then the occurrence of the millennium in 1941 (or possibly A.D. 2085 or 2091).[206] Likewise, in Brown's 1784 *Harmony of Scripture Prophecies, and History of Their Fulfilment*, he used A.D.1866 as the date for the "complete and final ruin of Popery" or "150 years after". In his *Self-Interpreting Bible* on Revelation he wrote this most interesting introduction:

> This book contains the visions which the apostle John received in the desert isle of Patmos, to which the Emperor Domitian had banished him about A. D. 96. (1) After a preface and introductory vision of Christ, it contains seven doctrinal epistles to the seven churches of Proconsular Asia, which also contain warnings and directions to the church in every age; i-iii. (2) After an introductory vision of an enthroned God and Redeemer, it represents the state of the church, and of the world as connected with it, from the ascension of Christ till the end of time, under the emblems of seven seals of a book opened, the seventh of which introduces seven trumpets, and the seventh of which trumpets introduces seven vials for the destruction of Antichrist, after which the glorious thousand years, the last judgment, and eternal state, take place; chap. iv-xxii. The series of the predictions is carried on in chap. vi, viii, ix, xi, xx: and the other chapters are explanatory digressions. The first six seals represent the state of the church and Roman empire from A. D. 33 to 323. The first six trumpets represent their state from A. D. 338 to 1866, or 2016. The seventh trumpet extends from thence to the end of the world; in the beginning of which period the seven vials will be poured upon Antichrist.[207]

The explanatory notes in Revelation clearly show Brown's historicist interpretation. For example, in Revelation 6:4 his comments are that the red horse and its rider were the emperors Nero, Domitian, Trojan and Adrian between A.D. 66 and 138. Brown went on to apply similar interpretation

---

[205] According to Strong's terminology, Brown would hold to a "continuous" interpretation of the book of Revelation. Others may call this "historicist", and some "historic". See A. H. Strong, *Systematic Theology* (Burlington, Ontario, 1907), 1009-1010.

[206] Brown, *Dictionary of the Bible*, 47-48, under the article on "AntiChrist"; also, "A Chronology of Facts Relative to the History or Predictions of Scripture", 802; Strong, *Systematic Theology*, 1009-1010. It appears that John Brown was close to the eschatological interpretation of that of Campegius Vitringa (1659-1722). See also, John Brown, *Harmony of Scripture Prophecies, and History of Their Fulfilment* (Glasgow, 1784), 409-411.

[207] *Self-Interpreting Bible*, 2, in introduction to Revelation.

throughout this chapter[208] and in the chapters following. Brown's interpretation of Revelation 12:7-8 is that it "may" describe the Reformation and verses 12-15 may denote, amongst other things, the missionaries of the Papacy after the Reformation who attempted to persecute and destroy Protestantism.[209] That Brown's eschatological views continued to be popular in Scotland after his death can be confirmed in a curious 1835 reprinting of Brown's *Psalms*, with the new title *The Family and Church Psalm Book, with Notes and Illustrations, designed to explain the sense, and to aid in the exercise of Christian Devotion by John Brown. – With an Appendix, Containing the whole of the Author's Commentary on the Book of Revelation....* The commentary on Revelation is simply taken from the *Self-Interpreting Bible* and reset as a commentary with the text of the Authorized Translation. The title page states that the *Psalm Book* was printed for the editor, but never identifies the editor. The curious point here is that in the 1830s Brown's historicist post-millennialism was still popular with some.[210] A worthy study would be to see if there was an interaction with the eschatology of Edward Irving or the Bonars and Brown's position in early to mid-nineteenth century Scotland. Without exhaustive analysis, I believe there is a relationship between *The Geneva Bible* (1602 edition) and Brown's "commentary" on Revelation.[211] The 1602 edition of the *Geneva Bible* contains marginal notes by Franciscus Junius on the book of Revelation and had replaced the original notes by Theodore Beza. Thereby the 1602 edition represented the form of the Bible which was popular with Puritans in the first half of the seventeenth century, and Junius' notes "display a robust millenarian impulse together with unrestrained polemics with Roman Catholic positions".[212] Modern post-millennialism was not founded by Daniel Whitby (1638-1735) but followed from many of the Reformers and early seventeenth century Puritan divines as well as from later Puritans such as Jonathan Edwards. John Brown must be studied within this framework and should not be shallowly confused with the late twentieth century version of post-millennialism of the reconstructionist circle.[213]

---

[208] *Self-Interpreting Bible*, 2, Revelation, ch. 6.

[209] *Self-Interpreting Bible*, 2, Revelation, ch. 12.

[210] John Brown, *The Family and Church Psalm Book, with Notes and Illustrations, designed to explain the sense, and to aid in the exercise of Christian Devotion by John Brown. – With an Appendix, Containing the whole of the Author's Commentary on the Book of Revelation...*, editor not identified (Edinburgh, 1835).

[211] *The Geneva Bible (The Annotated New Testament 1602 Edition)*, ed. Gerald T. Sheppard (New York, 1989), 125-135. (Pagination is only on the right side not on the left.) See the chart which prefaces the book of Revelation which is entitled "The Order of Time whereunto the Contents of this booke are to be referred", 125-left.

[212] Gerald T. Sheppard, "The Geneva Bible and English Commentary 1600-1645", in *The Geneva Bible (The Annotated New Testament 1602 Edition)*, 1-2.

[213] Stanley J. Grenz, *The Millennial Maze* (Downers Grove, Illinois, 1992), 67-69.

Concerning Brown's explanatory note on the millennium or the thousand years, he wrote that he could not determine if it denoted "precisely a thousand of our years, or only many years".[214] This last point does remind the reader of Brown's somewhat cautious interpretations on eschatology. It cannot be known with certainty how he communicated such topics to the students within the divinity hall. However, he was widely read in this field and wrote on the matter in several of his works, so it must have been a topic for discussion upon occasion.

Brown's approach to Scripture was clearly in the tradition of Cocceius, Witsius and Vitringa in terms of a covenantal biblical theology. Beginning with Cocceius, these theologians attempted to search the Scriptures in order to establish an exegetical basis for Reformed dogma. Cocceius viewed much of Reformed systematics as proof-texting without substantial biblical support. Brown's approach in terms of typology also appears to be close to that of these three Dutch authors.[215] More work is certainly needed in placing Brown's biblical interpretations in eschatology, but a cursory investigation points in the direction of Vitringa as a possible forerunner of Brown, along with John Brown of Wamphray or Thomas Boston in Brown's continuation of postmillennialism.[216]

Cocceius remained a covenantal theologian, but many saw fundamental problems in his approach to the Old Testament which resulted in over allegorization, etc.[217] Brown definitely sought to approach Reformed theology from the perspective of a biblical theology which was covenantal.[218] However, the depth of his biblical theology did not establish him as a renowned Scottish biblical exegete. He "piled up scripture texts" rather than setting forth detailed exegesis. In contrast to his grandson, John Brown of Broughton Place, Edinburgh, he did not write exegetically. If one were to speculate, it would appear that Brown further set the Secession advancing on its course from dogmatic theology to biblical exegesis. The relation of systematics and exegesis needs to be explored more than it has been in Brown and also in general in Scottish Church history and theology. The same would be said of Brown's eschatological views.

---

[214] *Self-Interpreting Bible*, 2, Revelation, ch. 20.
[215] Fairbairn, *Typology of Scripture*, 11.
[216] *DSCHT*, 563. This article on "Millennialism" shows the Secession tradition of postmillennialism but makes no direct reference to John Brown of Haddington nor of Vitringa.
[217] Bartel Elshout, *The Pastoral and Practical Theology of Wilhelmus à Brakel* (Grand Rapids, 1997), 49-51.
[218] Drummond and Bulloch, *Scottish Church 1688-1843*, 111.

The Associate Divinity Library (1770)

During Professor Brown's time, the Associate Synod responded to a petition from the students in their hall to begin a library. It was begun in 1770, and the books were kept in Professor Brown's house at Haddington.[219] The library was then moved to wherever the professor lived, thus transferring from Haddington to Selkirk with Professor Lawson. The library catalogues for the Associate divinity hall library were kept at the University of Glasgow but unfortunately were discarded in 1997 due to severe water damage.[220] These records would have provided a valuable source of information as to theological study in the Associate divinity hall.

The Theological Society: Kinross, Haddington, Selkirk

The students of the Associate (Burgher) divinity hall had started a Theological Society in 1765 in Kinross under Professor Swanston. The first act of the Society was to elect a president and establish rules for the Society. Eight rules were established which in summary are:

1.) meet weekly on Saturday at 10:00 a.m.,
2.) the president would be chosen at the close of each meeting for the next,
3.) the president opens the meeting with prayer,
4.) the president appoints a committee to prepare questions for consideration of the Society,
5.) that the speaker address the president,
6.) that the president have full powers for ensuring "decorum",
7.) "that no member divulge anything said or done under pain of extrusion", and
8.) no one could join the Society but students under Professor Swanston, and they must also submit to all these rules.[221]

The rules do not seem that unusual today, with the exception of rule number seven. The exact import of this is difficult to ascertain. Given the nature of some of the matters to be considered, it may be that they were wanting to guard themselves from having heretical aspersions attached to their names. Following the rules is a list of the members of the Society through to 1792, at which time they ran out of space. We read at another place that the Society agreed to purchase another book in which to record their rules and minutes. Thus, we do not have the full record of the Society's proceedings, except in part to 1788 and

---

[219] Landreth, *The UPD Hall*, 171.
[220] Personal conversation between the writer of this book and library staff at the University of Glasgow, Reference Library Division, spring, 1998.
[221] "Rules to be observed in the Theological Society instituted February 16th at Kinross, 1765", New College Library, Edinburgh *MS* ASS-B unpaginated.

the list of members to 1792. In reading the membership list, we find that generally all the first session students joined the Society, so most Burgher students were members of the Society during part or all of their time in the hall. The men who succeeded John Brown as professor in the hall, George Lawson and John Dick, were both named on the role of members for the Society. We can conclude that in terms of membership the Society basically encompassed all the students of the divinity hall for the period 1765-1792.[222]

The records indicate that the Society was very consistent in holding meetings in each session of the divinity hall. In reviewing the records from 1765 to 1788, I conclude that on average the Society had eight meetings per session. This corresponds fairly closely with the average length of each hall session, which was two months during this time period. Sometimes there would have been an additional meeting on the first Friday and on a week day during the last week of the hall's session.

In 1768, when John Brown of Haddington became professor, the Society changed its meetings from Saturday to Wednesday. These were not for discussion purposes but for prayer or "for prayer and practical conversations". This latter phrase reveals the purpose and significance or the role of such a society for theological students. It certainly was beyond the formal theological questions and debates. This was a fraternity of students who would not see each other very often except for during this annual two month session. Since they were not all of the same presbytery, even the opportunity of meeting one another at ecclesiastical meetings would have been limited. Matters of "practical conversations" no doubt opened a wider window within the student life of the Burgher divinity hall. By rotating presidents the way the Society did, it allowed the students opportunity to practice their moderatorial skills, something they would have simply observed at presbyterial exercises. Lawson and Dick both took their turn as president.

The formal portion of the Society meeting was to discuss a question which had been assigned in advance by the president to a committee of three plus the next president. This question was considered at the following meeting, and another would be assigned before they adjourned. Assigned questions included:

1.) Whither ought a seventh-day sabbath to be observed under the New Testament? Which of the seven must Christians observe?
2.) Whither is a Presbytery or Independency most agreeable to Scripture?
3.) Whither Christ gave full satisfaction to Divine justice?
4.) Whither is there such a thing as original sin?
5.) Whither is the Glory of God or the enjoyment of him to be man's chief and ultimate end?

---

[222] "Rules to be observed in the Theological Society instituted...at Kinross". See their membership lists and compare these with MacKelvie, "Annals and Statistics of the UP Church", 665-692, and George Brown, "Annals of the Divinity Hall".

6.) Whether Foreseen Faith and good works be the cause of election.
7.) Whether God intended Christ's death a satisfaction for all men.
8.) Whether Presbyterian Church Government be the only Government agreeable to the Word of God?
9.) Whither all sins past, present and to come are pardoned in justification?
10.) Whither repentance be necessary to the obtaining the pardon of sin in justification?
11.) Whither our public covenants national and Solemn League are binding upon posterity?
12.) Whether the light of nature in our present state is sufficient to conduct men to happiness.
13.) Whether the internal evidence of the Scriptures afford sufficient Marks of their divine authenticity?
14.) Whether perfection in holiness be attainable in this life?
15.) Whither human oratory be necessary for a preaching of the Gospel?
16.) Whither infant baptism be of Divine institution?
17.) Whither the books commonly called the Apocrypha be divinely inspired?
18.) Whither civil establishments of Religion be agreeable to the Word of God?
19.) Whether is faith or repentance first in order?
20.) Whither the immortality of the soul can be proven from reason?
21.) Whether the soul is immortal?
22.) If it was right to allow a toleration of every different religion?
23.) Was there a real Covenant made between God and Man in Paradise?
24.) Are the Covenants of grace and redemption two distinct Covenants?
25.) Is the conversion of a sinner possible without the almighty influence of God's Spirit?
26.) Did God enter into any real covenant with Adam as the representative of all his posterity?
27.) Is Popery Anti Christ?
28.) Whether the Prophets and Apostles knew themselves to be divinely inspired or not?
29.) Is an exact acquaintance with the Bible in Greek and Hebrew necessary to Preachers?
30.) Have women a right to vote in the election of Ministers?[223]

The Society amended its rules four times between 1765 and 1788. Some of the amendments were minor; such as one in 1778 that stated the president must be chosen from the fourth and fifth year students and at the end of a dispute the president must summarize the principle arguments presented on both sides of a question. Also, a time limit of eight minutes maximum was given to each

---

[223] "Rules to be observed in the Theological Society instituted...at Kinross".

speaker on a dispute. In 1783 another rule was added that prevented irregular attendance by some members. If a member was to be absent, he had to obtain permission to be excused from the president. The member was to appeal to the Society if the president was unreasonable.

In 1786 a more radical change took place in the Society whereby for the first time reference was made to the Theological Society as the "Debating Society". From this time on each member was to give an "Essay", either read or delivered from the pulpit, and after the essay members were to "make observations upon the sentiment, composition and delivery". The Society also allowed probationers and ministers, but these could not vote. Following the observations on the essays, time for disputes was to be given. Though we find the word "Essay" introduced here for the first time in 1786, the meetings after this date never used the word again. Rather, the same pattern occured as before; namely, with questions such as "Can the saints totally or finally fall away?" or "Did Christ die for all men?" being presented.

In 1788 the Society again restructured the selection of the president. The position would now alternate between an "Irish Gentleman" of the second or third session and a "Scotsman" of the fourth or fifth. An addendum was made that if anyone acted improperly, the president had the power to impose fines "in proportion to the offence". Perhaps this reflected a move to raise money in the Society for building up the library in the divinity hall. In 1788 the Society imposed an annual fee on all members, more for the Scots than the Irish, and formed a committee to consider books to purchase.[224]

Summary

Professor John Brown of Haddington did not deviate from the early efforts of Erskine, Fisher and Swanston in the Associate divinity hall. In fact he very much continued in this model. One of the most striking features of Brown's professorship clearly was his marriage of theology and piety. This was evidenced in his *Compendious View of Natural and Revealed Religion*, but it was not exclusive to this work. The entire ethos of the hall was this same marriage of theology and piety.

This study has attempted to take seriously the wider corpus of Brown's writings and to establish a record of what the divinity students were taught in hermeneutics, polity, casuistry, homiletics and Church history. Clearly these "subjects" were secondary to dogmatics. Brown functioned like the others as a theological regent for the curriculum, yet presbytery also had its role.

In the final analysis, it clearly emerges that what Brown was actively doing has been eclipsed in Scottish church history studies. Serious theological education outside of the Scottish universities and their divinity halls was

---

[224] "Rules to be observed in the Theological Society instituted...at Kinross".

energetic, reaching a significant number of students and making a contribution to Scottish ecclesiastical life.

During Brown's professorship the divinity library began, a feature symbolic towards permanence for the hall. Also, the Theological Students Society remained very active after its inception two years prior to Brown's professorship. The minutes attest to its importance for the students' intellectual and social development at Haddington. While it does not appear that during Brown's time this Theological Society took on a position of significance equal to the prayer concerts and mission societies at Princeton Seminary in the 1820s,[225] this Society in the Associate hall was to take on expanded roles in subsequent generations. Therefore this foundational period of the society remains of great relevance and importance.

---

[225] David Calhoun, *Princeton Seminary* (Edinburgh, 1994) 1:137-159.

CHAPTER 11

The Associate Divinity Hall with George Lawson (1787-1820)

Introduction

With the death of Professor Brown of Haddington, the Associate Synod elected the Rev. George Lawson of Selkirk to the vacancy. He was succeeded by the Rev. John Dick of Glasgow. The primary focus of this chapter is to chronicle the history of the Associate divinity hall in the Lawson era. During this time the Associate Synod kept to a solo professorship. The study will close in 1820, the eve of the union of the majority of Burghers and Antiburghers and the reorganization of a new single divinity hall.

Biographical Sketch

George Lawson was born into an Associate family in 1747 near West Linton, Peebleshire.[1] He was tutored by John Johnstone, who was a schoolmaster in West Linton before becoming a Seceder minister at Ecclefachan.[2] Following this, Lawson studied at the University of Edinburgh, where he took his Hebrew under James Robertson. His closest student friends while at the University of Edinburgh included fellow Seceders Michael Bruce, George Henderson, David Greig and Andrew Swanston.[3] He attended the Associate divinity hall for one session, that of 1766, under Professor Swanston at Kinross, whose chief text was that by Marck. At Kinross his fellow students again included Bruce, Henderson, Swanston and Greig. MacFarlane's biography of Lawson provides a good vignette into the happy fellowship these divinity students enjoyed

---

[1] J. MacFarlane, *The Life and Times of Dr. Lawson*, original 1862 (Edinburgh,1880), 14-15.
[2] Small, *History of the Congregation of the UP Church*, 1:44; MacFarlane, *Life and Times of Dr. Lawson*, 27-28. Evidently George Lawson was highly attached to his teacher at West Linton and "wept for days" when Johnstone left.
[3] MacFarlane, *Life and Times of Dr. Lawson*, 30-37.

during their session at Kinross. Lawson lived with David Greig at his home, Bruce lived with Henderson and Swanston lived in the manse.[4]

With Professor Swanston's death, the hall was transferred to Haddington, where Lawson continued his theological studies, probably for three sessions as he was licensed in 1769 by Edinburgh Presbytery.[5] While a student at Edinburgh University and at the divinity hall, Lawson did not usually spend the intervening months between sessions teaching school; rather, he returned home to his parents' farm near West Linton. However, one winter he tutored a family in Dalwich and for a shorter period a family in Romano.[6] Thus, at the age of twenty-one years (1769), Lawson was licensed to preach and for the next two years laboured as a probationer. MacFarlane's work gives us some interesting details on the life of a Seceder probationer. For instance, Lawson's first sermon as a licentiate was delivered *memoriter*, a practice which he continued for all sermons and lectures over the next fifty years. Also, some probationers were given a pony if funds were available; otherwise they would travel by foot. However, Lawson's father gave him a pony, which one family (of the vacant charge) fed while another family housed the student. Such an arrangement lasted from Friday to Friday. This long period of being a probationer allowed the churches both to meet prospective ministers and to receive preaching.[7]

There was nothing extraordinary in these biographical details concerning Lawson's education or training to become a Secession minister. Rather they establish a fairly typical portrait of a Seceder student probationer, which in many ways could be reviewed as an institution in its own right.[8] George Lawson served as a probationer from the time of his licensure in 1769 until his ordination in April, 1771, to the Burgher Church in Selkirk. This was his sole charge until his death in February, 1820.[9] In 1787 he was made Professor Brown's successor, a position he held through to the time of his death.[10]

---

[4] MacFarlane, *Life and Times of Dr. Lawson*, 30-40.

[5] MacFarlane, *Life and Times of Dr. Lawson*, 41-44. See pages 43-44 for two incidents of Lawson and Professor Brown at the hall. Also, *DSCHT*, 474.

[6] MacFarlane, *Life and Times of Dr. Lawson*, 45-46.

[7] MacFarlane, *Life and Times of Dr. Lawson*, 48-54.

[8] James Brown, *The Life of a Scottish Probationer: Being a Memoir of Thomas Davidson with poems and extracts from his letters* (Glasgow, 1908), 82. Although Brown's book on Davidson includes helpful descriptions of Davidson's life as a student of theology in the UP Divinity Hall, 1859 to 1867, and his work as a probationer afterwards, it is still very much the pattern of that of Lawson's day. Thus, it is helpful reading to see where and how UP's of the 1850s and 1860s educated and trained prospective ministers. In the 1860s the UP probationer still received one week's lodging when going from pulpit to pulpit.

[9] Small, *History of the Congregations of the UP Church*,2:441-442; MacFarlane, *Life and Times of Dr. Lawson*, 54.

[10] "Minutes of the Proceedings of the Associate Synod, 1766-1787" (May 2, 1787), 2043.

Lawson was the first Secession professor to receive a D.D.; this was bestowed upon him in 1806 from Marischal College, Aberdeen.[11]

Synod Actions in the Lawson Era

At the May 2, 1787, Associate Synod meeting, where the replacement for Professor Brown was discussed, the synod asked all presbyteries to discuss before the next meeting of synod

> whether it may not be expedient that the Teacher of the Students in Divinity have no congregational charge, that he reside in Edinburgh and have a subsistence afforded him by the Body at large and that the Presbyteries endeavour to form a scheme for raising subsistence.[12]

When the synod met again four months later and heard the reports of the presbyteries, the overwhelming sentiment was that they were not in "readiness" for such a scheme. Thus the idea died, and synod agreed to keep Lawson on as professor while still having him serve the congregation in Selkirk. Obviously the hall therefore remained at Selkirk.[13] This synod discussion highlights that there were certain problems with the arrangement of a short annual session, the work-load upon the professor being the chief issue. This pattern also demanded that the presbyteries be rigorous in their student assignments between hall sessions.

During Lawson's professorship the synod began to make a more concerted effort to improve the divinity hall library. Their first action was to have the library moved from Haddington to Selkirk in 1887.[14] The library had grown under Professor Brown, but very slowly. Only a few individuals had given money to it, and the custom that each student upon his ordination would give a book to the library did not advance its size very rapidly.[15] In 1792 the synod instituted an annual library fee of a few shillings to be charged to each divinity student to help purchase books.[16] Then in 1812 a memorial came before the synod reminding the body that they had done very little since 1772 in advancing the cause of the library.[17] Synod's major action on the 1812 memorial was to state that the library was clearly the property of the synod and

---

[11] *DSCHT*, 474.
[12] "Minutes of the Proceedings of the Associate Synod, 1766-1787" (May 2, 1787), 2043.
[13] "Minutes of the Proceedings of the Associate Synod, 1787-1820", *MS*, CH3/28/4, National Archives of Edinburgh, Sept. 5, 1787, 2056.
[14] "Minutes of the Proceedings of the Associate Synod, 1787-1820", 2056.
[15] "Minutes of the Proceedings of the Associate Synod, 1787-1820", 2449.
[16] "Minutes of the Proceedings of the Associate Synod, 1787-1820", 2449.
[17] "Minutes of the Proceedings of the Associate Synod, 1787-1820", 2449.

not that of the professor and that there should be proper library trustees.[18] Obviously the synod gave virtually no support to the divinity hall library during most of Lawson's time as professor and did not view it as a high priority.

What was a much higher priority for the synod was the assigning of probationers to the various presbyteries in Scotland, England and Ireland. This was a longstanding tradition and went on uninterrupted during the Lawson era. The assignments went from October to May and from June to September and were given out respectively at the spring or summer meetings of synod.[19] These probationers continued the custom of traveling throughout the synod rather than remaining as an assistant in one charge.[20]

The synod was also proactive in collecting funds from all the congregations to support the work of the students and to offer assistance. Delinquent congregations on occasion were listed by name in the synod minutes, evidence that the task of collecting funds was taken seriously within the synod.[21] It is difficult to reckon the full impact of such a disciplinary measure, but it certainly affirms a level of commitment to collect funds for students.

The Divinity Hall at Selkirk

The pattern of theological education under Professor Lawson and the hall at Selkirk was not radically altered from that of Brown at Haddington. As before, the whole course was covered over five sessions of two months each (August and September). On the Sabbaths while the hall was in session at Selkirk, "deputies" of the synod supplied the pulpit for Professor Lawson, although it appears that upon occasion Professor Lawson would have had to supply the pulpit if there was a problem with one of these probationers or deputies.[22] The normal daily schedule at the hall was to divide the day into two meetings, each lasting approximately one and a half hours. On select evenings the senior students would deliver "popular sermons", and these evening meetings were open to members of the Associate Church in Selkirk.[23]

While a session lasted nine weeks, these weekly public meetings went for six weeks; thus one may assume that these public meetings were not held during the first couple of weeks. Three students led the meeting. One "gave out" a psalm or hymn to be sung followed by a prayer; then the other two students delivered

---

[18] "Minutes of the Proceedings of the Associate Synod, 1787-1820", 2449.
[19] "Minutes of the Proceedings of the Associate Synod, 1787-1820", 247, 2411.
[20] *DSCHT*, 679. This article on "Probationer" does not view the practice of probationers in the Secession churches but only within the Church of Scotland and this only in more recent times.
[21] "Minutes of the Proceedings of the Associate Synod, 1787-1820", 247, 2411.
[22] MacFarlane, *Life and Times of Dr. Lawson*, 274, 279.
[23] Landreth, *The UPD Hall*, 182-184.

short prepared and practical discourses or addresses. Often the whole, and always a part, of the exercises at these meetings, was connected with the great and most interesting subject of evangelizing the world, by the dissemination of the divine word among all nations, in their vernacular languages, and by the labours of Christian missionaries.[24]

Professor Lawson concluded these public meetings with prayer. Evidently the attendance was very good and no doubt continued to make for a good relationship between the hall and the church. Since the meetings were to create a "missionary spirit", they also were reflective of Lawson's personal involvement and commitment to the rise of the missionary societies in the second half of the eighteenth and beginning of the nineteenth century. Lawson preached for the Edinburgh Missionary Society and supported their work as well as that of the London Missionary Society.[25] These public meetings also had a second purpose; to help the students develop "ease and readiness" in addressing the public.[26]

Other patterns in the hall at Selkirk were consistent with what had occurred at Haddington; for example, each meeting in the hall was opened and closed by the students taking turns in prayer. The students gave their remarks on their fellow students' discourses, but the professor supervised these criticisms and had the last word. Student assignments for the next year were given at the close of each session of the hall. Generally first session students only delivered a homily while the other session students were assigned two or three discourses, and these were either critical lectures or popular sermons.[27] All student discourses were delivered from memory and never read (an infraction which Lawson would not tolerate).[28]

It appears that a major focus of Professor Lawson was in what would be termed the department of biblical exegesis. This is not to imply that this was absent under Professor Brown, for in terms of ability he was equally able and also stressed scripture memorization in his systematics work. However, the fact that Lawson has not left us his published theological lectures, but rather his

---

[24] McKerrow, *History of the Secession Church*, 791. McKerrow has extracted from *The Christian Repository* magazine a three page account of the daily schedule of the hall at Selkirk. It is a valuable source of information and much more detailed than Landreth. It is also mentioned in the biography of Ralph Wardlaw. See W. L. Alexander, *Memoirs of the Life and Writings of Ralph Wardlaw* (Edinburgh, 1865), 28. Also MacFarlane, *Life and Times of Dr. Lawson*, 279-283, where the author is identified as Andrew Lothian. Lothian had been a first session student of Lawson at Selkirk in 1788. MacKelvie, *Annals and Statistics of the UP Church*, 668.
[25] MacFarlane, *Life and Times of Dr. Lawson*, 140, 467.
[26] McKerrow, *History of the Secession Church*, 791.
[27] McKerrow, *History of the Secession Church*, 790-791.
[28] MacFarlane, *Life and Times of Dr. Lawson*, 289.

work on the Scriptures, coupled with the following summary from the *Christian Repository*, makes a clear impression of Lawson's focus and strength.

> The Dr. was accustomed also, every session, to make his pupils read with him, and critically analyze a part of the Holy Scriptures in the original Hebrew and Greek. Pertinent questions were proposed by him, on such occasions, leading, at once, to the formation of the sound critic, and the edifying practical exposition of the divine word. The continued study of the original languages of the Holy Scriptures, and of their criticism, and of the practical use of the sacred volume, were thus strongly recommended. A laudable ambition to excel in these important exercises was excited and kept alive, and, in many cases, led to very valuable results.[29]

We can conclude that the level of Greek and Hebrew done prior to coming to the hall had prepared the student for such an oral exegesis class. It is fair to deduce that these classes were a significant part of the Selkirk hall curriculum.

The compiler of the account of the hall at Selkirk in the *Christian Repository* made his own calculations on the number of hours in class for each session and arrived at 144 hours per session over the nine weeks. He then compared this with the divinity halls in the Scottish universities and arrived at 120 hours per session over an average of twenty-four weeks. His conclusion was that though the Secession hall only lasted nine weeks, more time was given to actual instruction and examination than in the Scottish universities.[30] The calculations appear reasonable and accurate.

Lawson generally departed from his predecessor's custom of ending each session with an "exhortation" or as Lawson called them a "valedictory" address. Instead he read a few passages of Scripture, gave some brief practical counsel and sang a hymn. Sometimes Lawson read from John Brown's closing exhortations and began to weep and upon occasion so would the students.[31]

Statistically, during Professor Lawson's time in the hall the highest number of first year students was in 1795 when there were twenty-two. However, by 1801 it reached its lowest number, that of four first session students. Thus, it is not surprising that in 1806 the synod issued an address by the Rev. James Peddie concerning the scarcity of probationers and also appealed that a more liberal remuneration be made for ministers' stipends.[32] In student notes of William Fraser (one of Lawson's students), Fraser provided a breakdown of the number of students for the meeting of the hall at Selkirk in 1798:

---

[29] McKerrow, *History of the Secession Church*, 789-790.
[30] McKerrow, *History of the Secession Church*, 791.
[31] MacFarlane, *Life and Times of Dr. Lawson*, 351.
[32] Landreth, *The UPD Hall*, 184-185. The number of first session students in 1819 had gone up to nineteen, showing a marked improvement from 1801. See MacKelvie, *Annals and Statistics of the UP Church*, 674.

1st Session Students   12
2nd Session Students   11
3rd Session Students   8
4th Session Students   12[33]

Noticeably absent are any statistics for fifth session students, which is a confirmation of a common student pattern – to attend only four sessions of the hall. Since MacKelvie's *Annals and Statistics of the United Presbyterian Church* only lists first session students, it is difficult to ascertain a total number attending the hall each year and also whether or not the fifth session was well represented. Fraser's note book is therefore valuable in providing a clear statistic that forty-four students attended the Selkirk hall in 1798. Given the number of student discourses then to be heard by the professor during the session, in addition to oral examinations and lectures, it certainly confirms the fact that it was an immense burden to be placed on one person. George Lawson was sole professor of divinity in the Associate Synod for thirty-three years, a remarkable feat.

Another statistic which can be found on record for the total numbers in each year is for the divinity hall of 1811. This was the first year that the Associate Synod minutes gave a complete list of Dr. Lawson's students. It was as follows:

1st Session Students   16
2nd Session Students   11
3rd Session Students   3
4th Session Students   4
5th Session Students   2[34]

In this case there were two fifth session students, yet if one counts back in MacKelvie's *Annals and Statistics of the United Presbyterian Church*, this fifth session class had six students when it was a first session class in 1807.[35] What happened to the other four students that they did not proceed to the fifth session? In all likelihood they did not attend a fifth session, as it was not generally a hard pressed point. Some went to the fifth session and some did not.

The students continued to engage one another at Selkirk through their own society meetings and actions. These meetings were to deliver, hear and criticize essays on important subjects and to conduct correspondence. One example of such a letter of correspondence was sent to the Antiburgher students in their hall, which was meeting concurrently in Whitburn under Professor Bruce. The

---

[33] William Fraser, "Book K – Sermons by William Fraser together with Statistics of Students in the Burgher Divinity Hall, Selkirk 1798", *MS*, New College Library, Edinburgh FRA 5.
[34] "Minutes of the Proceedings of the Associate Synod 1787-1820", 2440.
[35] MacKelvie, *Annals and Statistics of the UP Church*, 72.

purpose of their letter was to "express our good wishes for their general welfare and the success of their studies...".[36] This letter was dated 1798, twenty-two years before the union of the Burghers and Antiburghers, and shows the sentiment of at least many of the students in the late 1790s concerning the Breach. Such society meetings and gatherings are worthy of note as they formed a vital part of the ethos of divinity studies. Wardlaw's homely comments about the "juggling of cups" and "popular discourses immediately after tea" remind the reader that the meeting of students over the nine weeks was for more than theological knowledge.[37]

The Professor and His Writings

Several of Professor Lawson's published works are not directly related to his work in the divinity hall at Selkirk but were either sermons or discourses on polemical topics within the church courts. Such works include his two volumes of sermons: *Sermons on Various Relative Duties* (1809) and *Sermons, on the Death of Faithful Ministers, On Wars and Revolutions, To the Aged* (1810).[38] These two volumes contain practical sermons related to a variety of subjects on living the Christian life. For example, the first volume contains practical sermons on "The Duty of Parents to Their Children", "The Reciprocal Duty of Husband and Wife" and "The Duty of Hearers of the Gospel to Help Their Ministers".[39] The second volume contains several sermons from Jeremiah on the theme "On Wars and Revolutions" and sermons addressed to the aged.[40] These two volumes did not have a direct bearing on the hall.

Lawson was recognized by many of his contemporaries and by several of his students as possessing vast scholarship. He was given the nickname the "Christian Socrates" and was well regarded by John Lee and Ralph Wardlaw, two of his students who left the Secession churches. His knowledge of the classical authors and the Church Fathers was attested to by many, as was his use of the scriptural languages and French.[41] Several of his students gave testimony of his favourite authors and his exacting knowledge of their writings. These included the works of Chrysostom (in Greek), Owen, Massillon and Saurin (in French), Jonathan Edwards, Campbell on the Gospels, Traill, Boston,

---

[36] Alexander, *Memoirs of the Life and Writings of Ralph Wardlaw*, 31. This was stated in a letter by Ralph Wardlaw, a student in the hall at Selkirk, August 27, 1798, back to his father in Glasgow.

[37] Alexander, *Memoirs of the Life and Writings of Ralph Wardlaw*, 32.

[38] George Lawson, *Sermons on Various Relative Duties* (Edinburgh, 1809); and *Sermons, on the Death of Faithful Ministers, On Wars and Revolutions, To the Aged* (Hawick, 1810).

[39] Lawson, *Sermons and Various Relative Duties*, iii-iv and 1, 154, 270.

[40] Lawson, *Sermons, on the Death of Faithful Ministers*, iii-iv, 31, 53, 83, etc.

[41] MacFarlane, *Life and Times of Dr. Lawson*, 205, 283-284, 288.

Brown of Haddington, Plutarch's *Lives* and Homer.[42] MacFarlane stated that Lawson's personal library consisted of two thousand volumes and then proceeded to give a sample listing from the library of one hundred authors and their works. Amongst the Reformed writers are several that were common to his predecessor: Boston, Calvin, Cartwright, Flavel, Grotius, Goodwin, Marck, Manton, Owen, Pictet, Turretin, Ursinus, Vitringa and Witsius.[43] Also included in MacFarlane's select list were lexicons, grammars, writings from the Church Fathers, classical writers, church histories, hermeneutical texts and commentaries. These were in addition to the students' library, which was also housed in Selkirk, thus giving him access to an unusually vast corpus of material in an isolated town. He also freely allowed the divinity students ready access to his personal library and permission to borrow from it. This also included some of the manuscript volumes which he possessed, some of which were borrowed and copied by the students. MacFarlane cited one example of such, in that John Brown (later of Broughton Place), when one of Lawson's students, was in the habit of borrowing some of Lawson's manuscript volumes from Lawson's library.[44] It appears to have been common for students upon occasion to transcribe manuscript works in whole or in part.

Lawson's interest was in the works mentioned above, and he never developed an interest in novel reading. Though Sir Walter Scott lived not far from Lawson, this form of book did not overly interest him. Although he saw merit in some of the Waverly Novels, he stopped reading them after *Old Morality* was published because "the character and conduct of the Scottish Covenanters are so impiously caricatured".[45] Lawson accepted Thomas McCrie's critique in this regard, and although Lawson and McCrie differed on the matter of the civil magistrate in the Confession of Faith, they shared a similar position here.

The chief focus of Lawson's written contributions were clearly within the biblical department, and likewise it was here that he made his chief contributions to his students. Laying aside hagiographic praise in any of the biographical sketches of Lawson, it does appear without question that he had an unusual memory (not only of the English Bible but also of the Hebrew and Greek texts), as he would often lecture or examine upon the Hebrew or Greek texts without a copy in front of him. This was also the case with the sermons of Ralph Erskine and the epistles of Paul in Greek, all of which he could repeat

---

[42] MacFarlane, *Life and Times of Dr. Lawson*, 210-212.
[43] MacFarlane, *Life and Times of Dr. Lawson*, 216-217.
[44] MacFarlane, *Life and Times of Dr. Lawson*, 219-220.
[45] MacFarlane, *Life and Times of Dr. Lawson*, 230. Also Henry Belfrage, "A Short Account of Dr. Lawson and His Writings", in *Discourses on the History of David* (Berwick, 1833), xxix.

from memory.[46] Thus his published Bible works were really an extension of his class lectures. Before he died three works were published in this connection: *Discourses on the Book of Esther* (1804), *Lectures on the Book of Ruth, with a few Discourses on the Sovereignty and Efficacy of Grace* (1805), and *Lectures on the History of David*, two volumes (1807). These were followed after his death by the *Exposition of the Book of Proverbs* in 1821 (two volumes) and *Discourses on the History of David* in 1833.[47] He also left a total of eighty volumes of his own manuscript material which were never published. These were lectures and expositions on doctrinal topics or Bible books, such as on justification, sanctification, Chronicles, Psalms, Isaiah, Luke, John, Romans, Galatians, etc. Evidently some of these manuscript volumes were also borrowed or loaned to students, and where they may be today is not altogether certain.[48] Whether or not Lawson planned to create a full devotional commentary on the Bible is difficult to determine.

In more closely examining Lawson's *Exposition of the Book of Proverbs* (to select it for analysis amongst his published expositional works), certain features emerge. It is not a critical work on the text of Scripture; rather it is full of instruction for Christians and is "pious and sensible, full of sound doctrine and salutary admonition and instruction". Thomas Horne, writing further on Lawson's work on Proverbs as well as on Joseph and Ruth, claimed that:

> There is rarely anything of a critical nature to be found in them, which indeed was not the writer's object; but they everywhere discover a minute acquaintance with the Bible and the human heart, and reflect a deep concern to profit the reader. The style is plain and the illustrations very brief.[49]

For the first nine chapters of the book of Proverbs, Lawson made a brief one to two paragraph introduction for each, followed by a verse by verse exposition. With the remainder of Proverbs, he gave a verse by verse exposition without chapter introductions and without an attempt to group them or categorize them by theme. There were absolutely no other commentaries mentioned, and only about ten times did he refer to textual matters or to the

---

[46] MacFarlane, *Life and Times of Dr. Lawson*, 234-235. MacFarlane brought forth a host of examples all of which bore testimony to Lawson's unusual abilities to quote the Bible in the original languages and to give comment. (For example, Dr. Simpson of Sanquhar, Dr. Kidston of Glasgow, Dr. Johnston of Limekilus, etc.)

[47] MacFarlane, *Life and Times of Dr. Lawson*, 255.

[48] MacFarlane, *Life and Times of Dr. Lawson*, 255.

[49] Cyril J. Barber, in his foreword to the 1984 reprint of George Lawson's *Proverbs*, is quoting from Thomas Hartwell Horne's *Introduction to the Critical Study and Knowledge of the Holy Scriptures*, but Barber fails to identify which edition and the page number he is referring to in Horne. See Cyril J. Barber, foreword to George Lawson, *Proverbs*, original 1821(Grand Rapids, 1984), vii.

Septuagint text.[50] The chief references were to other scriptural texts, and these were referenced at the bottom of the page as footnotes. The next major category of references was to the Greek philosophers or culture and on occasion also to Roman antiquities.[51] This was not surprising due to Lawson's knowledge of the classics. Upon occasion Lawson made very obvious anti-Roman Catholic applications reflective of his theological perspective.[52] Other references beyond the classics were limited to single references and included Dodderidge, Augustine and Latimer but were merely illustrative and not of a deep theological nature.[53] Lawson's chief aim was to explain the text and bring forth applications that would be illustrative of Christian morality based upon the moral law. Thus his expositions viewed the law as showing man's sin and as being a guide for righteous living for the Christian. Lawson aimed at bringing a Christ-centred perspective to the book and probing the heart of the reader, often by asking questions by way of application, not unlike the preacher in a sermon.[54]

For covenantal theologians Proverbs 22:6 and its interpretation reveal two things: first, how the book of Proverbs is approached hermeneutically – that is, as principle and precept or as promise; and second, the stress of the writers' covenantal position. Lawson treated Proverbs 22:6 as principle and not presumptively, thus telling the reader a great deal.[55] He did have a hermeneutic fixed in expositing Proverbs, and he also as a Calvinist had an experimental piety that was not presumptive.

Lawson evidently used the book of Proverbs regularly in the hall to draw forth illustrations on "duties". On occasion this can be discovered in Lawson's commentary, where he wrote that this proverb may be applied this way to the minister and in this manner to the congregation.[56] Whether or not he did an extensive lecture series on Proverbs at the hall cannot be proven from the published book. Perhaps the book originated from the manuscript of his congregational lectures more than directly from hall lectures, other than as occasional exhortations on "duties". Likewise, Lawson's books on Joseph,

---

[50] George Lawson, *Proverbs*, original 1821 (Grand Rapids, 1984), 176, 363, 366, 2-163. All references below are to the 1984 reprint edition.

[51] Lawson, *Proverbs*, 4, 223, 245, 289, 302, 328, 376, 383, 386, 425, 444, 510, 632, 729, 868 and 888 for Greek references. Pages 564, 708, 791, 820, 826, 856 for Roman references.

[52] Lawson, *Proverbs*, 394, 447.

[53] Lawson, *Proverbs*, 511, 867.

[54] Lawson, *Proverbs*, 168. "Salvation is by grace through faith, and this faith works by love, producing universal obedience to the law of our Creator and Redeemer. This law is summarily comprehended in the ten commandments, and published with more particularity in this divinely inspired body of Christian morality." From the introduction to the second portion of Proverbs at chapter ten.

[55] Lawson, *Proverbs*, 585-588.

[56] MacFarlane, *Life and Writings of Dr. Lawson*, 299; Lawson, *Proverbs*, 379.

David and Ruth were no doubt incorporated in some way into the hall's curriculum; however, it cannot be asserted with certainty that they were hall lectures. Belfrage testified that in his Bible lectures Lawson provided well researched Bible background material on the history of the Holy Land, and no doubt such would have included information on Joseph, Ruth and David.[57]

Lawson's other main biblical work, which went through different editions and printings, is now entitled *The Life of Joseph*.[58] Although its original title was *Lectures on the History of Joseph*, this title should not necessarily be interpreted to mean that in its original form it appeared in lecture format in the divinity hall at Selkirk. Rather, Lawson was using the word "lecture" here in the old Scottish tradition of a continuous Bible exposition given, in Lawson's case, at the "forenoon" of the Sabbath.[59] In all likelihood these lectures on Joseph were from these Sabbath lectures and not from hall discourses (lectures). Lawson prefaced this published volume on Joseph by giving an exhortation to parents: "May not this book assist parents in speaking of it to their little ones, in a manner fitted to insinuate into their minds some of the most important lessons of religion."[60] This confirms that these lectures were aimed at the breadth of an assembled congregation, not the hall. The series of lectures on Joseph covers Genesis 37:1-48:22 and chapter 50, and in addition the book contains a series of seven sermons in the appendix entitled "Lectures on the Blessings Pronounced by Jacob on His Twelve Children", covering Genesis 49:1-33. The purpose of the volume was certainly not to show forth critical Hebrew exegesis, although Lawson clearly interacted with the Hebrew text, but was a devotional, verse-by-verse exposition for a congregation. If anything, the expositions on Proverbs come closer to the hall than his lectures on Joseph. Thus, Lawson's published Bible expositions only provide a limited insight into the divinity hall.

His other noteworthy literary composition was his 1797 *Considerations on the Overture lying before the Associate Synod, respecting some alterations in the Formula concerning the power of the Civil Magistrate in matters of Religion, and the Obligation of our Covenants, National and Solemn League, on Posterity*. Again, this work does not directly bear upon lectures in the divinity hall. Rather it reveals Lawson's theological position, which no doubt was influential upon the scores of students who trained under him in the hall. Lawson advocated "toleration and progress" on these two theological issues

---

[57] Belfrage, "A Short Account of George Lawson", xvi.

[58] George Lawson, *The Life of Joseph*, original 1807 (Edinburgh, 1988).

[59] MacFarlane, *Life and Times of Dr. Lawson*, 134.

[60] Lawson, *Life of Joseph*, xv. Lawson's Bible lectures would not be dissimilar to the Bible notes recently published on Genesis done by William Still, the noted evangelical Scottish expositor of the twentieth century. William Still, *Theological Studies in Genesis and Romans, Collected Writings of William Still*, eds. David C. Searle and Sinclair B. Ferguson, vol. 3 (Edinburgh/Fearn, 2000).

raised in this eighty-three page book. That is, forbear with one another as to the Westminster Confession of Faith's teaching that the magistrate may assume ecclesiastical power in the Church to call and dismiss church courts and as to whether the Covenants are binding on posterity. Both of these points were assumed in the Formula for those to be licensed and to be ordained. Since the issue created such a stir in the Burgher Synod, it is logical to assume that the events of the 1790s came into the daily discussions of students with their professor at the hall.[61]

Likewise, on other matters Lawson had definite opinions which in some manner would have influenced the students. He was very interested in missions, as evidenced by his close relationship with Dr. Alexander Waugh. Upon one occasion he gave the hall over to a visiting minister from America, the Rev. John Mason, Jr., who gave a guest lecture to the students and set forth the need for ministers in America. Such activities in a hall, accompanied by the blessing of the hall's sole professor, established an ethos which is significant in understanding the history of theological education.[62] Also Lawson, in the tradition of Brown of Haddington, supported more frequent communion, that is, more than once a year in a congregation and, like many at the turn of the century in the Burgher fold, sang the Scottish Paraphrases and Hymns. All of these subjects were no doubt at issue in some way in the Burgher division into New Lights and Auld/Old Lights in 1799 and must have been topics at least informally in the hall.[63]

Despite Lawson's name being associated with certain "innovations" within the Burgher Synod, there remains this curious fact concerning Lawson and Walter Scott's *Tales of My Landlord*. Having read Thomas McCrie's extensive review on this novel, Lawson refused to read the book. He likewise adopted the position that the Covenanters were dishonoured by Scott.[64] Although McCrie was an Auld Light and Lawson a New Light, it does raise some questions as to how to evaluate Lawson. Did he really have a romantic understanding of the Covenanters, or could he separate respect for them from their understanding of a covenanted magistrate in Scotland? Such questions have not really been

---

[61] More on this controversy can be found in: William Willis, *A Smooth Stone from the Brook. or, an Humble Attempt to Prevent Backsliding from the Principles of the Covenanted Church of Scotland, in Some Letters to the Rev. George Lawson* (Glasgow, 1799); McKerrow, *History of the Secession Church*, 587-591; William Taylor, *An EffectualRemedy to the Disputes Presently Existing in the Associate Synod, Respecting the Formula: in a Series of Letters to the Rev. Mr. Lawson* (Glasgow, 1799).

[62] MacFarlane, *Life and Times of Dr. Lawson*, 317-319.

[63] MacFarlane, *Life and Times of Dr. Lawson*, 381; *DSCHT*, 474; MacLeod, *Scottish Theology*, 237-238. MacLeod describes Lawson as "a hot advocate for change". It is questionable as to whether or not MacLeod has given a proper description of all the issues on this matter.

[64] Belfrage, "A Short Account of George Lawson", xxix.; MacFarlane, *Life and Times of Dr. Lawson*, 230.

addressed by church historians today. Was there a fundamental tension amongst the Seceders as to how they approached the covenants in Scottish civil and religious life and the failed efforts to have union discussions between Seceders and Covenanters in the eighteenth century? Did the Secession tradition have a completely homogeneous position from 1733 to 1800 on these matters? A possible interpretation could be made that eventually the issue did arise within the Secession, and John MacLeod's interpretation here could be in need of re-examination.

George Lawson had the distinction of being the first Seceder professor of divinity to receive the D.D. degree. He was awarded this from Marischal College in 1806.[65] Several of Lawson's friends in the Associate Synod had pursued this honour because of his contributions to learning in Scotland, chiefly his publications. (At the time of the granting of the D.D. degree, Lawson had only published his expository works on Ruth and Esther.) Lawson sent Marischal College complimentary copies of his *Lectures on Joseph*, which was published in 1807, for the honour he had received. Evidently some were of the opinion that Marischal had "dishonoured itself" by granting the degree to a "Dissenter".[66]

Summary

It seems appropriate enough to entitle this period "the Lawson era" if only for the fact that he single-handedly conducted the hall for almost thirty-three years. Yet the title can be given for other reasons also: Lawson was the last of the main body of Secession Burghers to conduct the hall, and he represents the last of the solo professors. In 1787 the Synod had questioned having only one professor and by the mid-1820s (shortly after Lawson's death) had changed this. In part, increased student numbers made it more difficult, but the other factor was that as the nineteenth century emerged, specialization became more established. No doubt as the four-fold encyclopaedia of theology emerged as systematic, biblical, ecclesiastical and practical, the fact became obvious that a solo professor could not cover everything.

Lawson's ethos and pedagogical approach in the conducting of the hall was virtually identical to that of his predecessor, Professor John Brown of Haddington. In fact, Brown's "exhortations" and systematic text were standard fare for these thirty-three years. The traditional features of federal theology were the foundation, together with a marked evangelical piety. It is clear that Lawson could stand strong intellectually in the field of classical literature, the writings of the Church Fathers and the scholastic Reformed divines from the continent. He was willing to have more forbearance in the judicatories of the Church than the previous generation, but he was not a Voluntarist nor an

---

[65] MacFarlane, *Life and Times of Dr. Lawson*, 243-245.
[66] MacFarlane, *Life and Times of Dr. Lawson*, 249.

Amyraldian on the Atonement. In John Brown (of Broughton Place) there was a worthy successor and an emerging exegete, and Lawson must be viewed as part of this progression. The steps from 1787 to 1820 were significant theologically, yet not radical. These were stages in exegetical theology and a part of the history of Scottish exegesis. Lawson was not a father of the exegetical movement but a link in the chain of Secession exegetes. It would also be fair to say that with both John Brown of Haddington and George Lawson of Selkirk, the Burgher Seceders had two men who were "large" individuals. A. C. Cheyne's quote from John Baillie on educators could be appropriately applied to Brown or Lawson: "The greatest chapters in the history of education are those that tell of individual magnetic personalities, of men whose power lay as much in the inherent transmissive quality of their own consecration as in any counsels they gave."[67] The Socratic Lawson aptly conducted the hall with such a magnetism during his thirty-three years, and MacFarlane's Victorian styled biography of him rightly conveys that impression.

---

[67] Alec Cheyne quoting from John Baillie's "The Fundamental Task of the Theological Seminary", *Reformed Church Review*, no. 3, (July, 1922), 281. This is in Cheyne's article "John Caird (1820-1898) Preacher, Professor, Principal", in *Traditions of Theology in Glasgow 1450-1900. A Miscellany*, ed. W. I. P. Hazlett, 57.

CHAPTER 12

The General Associate Hall (1786-1820)

Introduction

The most noteworthy theological professor of the General Associate Hall was Archibald Bruce, who served the hall from 1786 to 1804, then in the Constitutional Hall 1806-1816. He was a voluminous author, thus helping to make it somewhat easier for posterity to gain an understanding of classroom materials used.[1] A study of Archibald Bruce as a pattern of Scottish theological education is also an important link to British North America as he was Thomas McCulloch's professor, more of which will be discussed in Part Three. Upon Bruce's removal to form the Constitutional Hall, the General Associate Synod appointed George Paxton as sole professor to their hall. Paxton also became the first Seceder professor to hold this position without a pastoral charge. However, this must not be misinterpreted. Stewart Mechie is accurate in accessing that change: "This seems, however, to have been rather a concession to Dr. Paxton's health than a decision on principle."[2]

The Archibald Bruce Era

Biographical Sketch

Bruce was born in 1746 at Broomhall, a farm near Denny, Stirlingshire, and was raised in the Antiburgher (General Associate) Church in Dennyloanhead. In a 1954 doctoral thesis on Bruce, Robert Hall stated that Bruce went to

---

[1] In the New College Library, Edinburgh, the *Collected Works of Archibald Bruce* ran to nine bound volumes; however, it needs to be noted that not everything Bruce wrote is in *Collected Works*. For example, he wrote several articles in *The Christian Magazine*, such as "The Marrow", "Gospel Ministry", "Ignatius" and "Weather in the Holy Land". It appears that the *Collected Works of Archibald Bruce* is a unique set found only in New College Library, Edinburgh. Since this was the set I consulted, all reference to *Collected Works of Archibald Bruce* (1774-1817) will be to the set at New College.

[2] Stewart Mechie, "Education for the Ministry in Scotland since the Reformation" III, *RSCHS* 15 (1966), 2.

Glasgow University at age fourteen or fifteen, or 1760-61.[3] Checking the matriculation lists, class lists and prize lists for Glasgow University in the early 1760s, no concrete evidence of such can be found. This is not very conclusive as the matriculation lists for this period are not always reliable. (The university at this time was under Principal Leechman and a full arts course took five sessions and covered moral philosophy, natural philosophy, Latin, Greek, logic, and mathematics).[4] McKerrow tells us that Bruce studied the languages and philosophy at Glasgow University after a classical education "at a country school".[5] His theological studies were under Professor William Moncrieff, Alloa, and the superintendence of the presbytery. Since Bruce was ordained in 1768 at age twenty-two and the normal period of study was five sessions under the theological professor, he possibly started around 1763/4. Some students studied arts and philosophy concurrently, and Bruce may have been one of them. A full description of Professor William Moncrieff's teaching has already been given; thus we will omit this in our brief biographic sketch of Bruce.

Bruce remained pastor in Whitburn for forty-eight years and never married. In his early years at Whitburn, he taught himself French for the purpose of reading French Protestant theology.[6] He was known as a man of liberality, returning the synod's professor's stipend of fifty pounds for the purchase of books for the students' library and to improve their accommodations.[7]

The chief controversy of his life centred around the General Synod's adopting a *New Narrative Testimony* in 1804 whereby "the Synod altered its teaching and denied that civil magistrates are obliged to exercise their authority in behalf of the new religion".[8] This eventually brought him to form the Constitutional Presbytery along with such a leader as Thomas McCrie.

An interesting side of Archibald Bruce is found in his poetry. Though not directly related to his work as a theological professor, it presents the aspect of a gentle-natured individual, in contrast to his satirical work, *The Catechism Modernized and adapted to the Meridian Patronage.*[9] Some of the poems are light-hearted, and as he admitted, were not to stir up passionate love. Yet one is entitled "Elegiac Verses on the Death of Mrs. E. W. Spouse of the Rev. J. B." (the Rev. John Brown of Whitburn, the Burgher minister), another "Reflections

---

[3] Robert G. Hall, "Archibald Bruce at Whitburn (1746-1816) with a special reference to his view of church and state" (unpublished Ph.D. thesis, New College, Edinburgh, 1954), 1-8.
[4] *The Matriculation Albums of the University of Glasgow 1728-1858*, ed. and compiler W. Innes Addison (Glasgow, 1913); *DNB*, 7:89.
[5] John McKerrow, *History of the Secession Church* (Glasgow, 1841), 896.
[6] R. R. Hobart, "Archibald Bruce of Whitburn", *Original Secession Magazine* (4th series), I (1903), 486. It is interesting to note that Bruce's student, Thomas McCulloch, in the first years of his pastorate conducted an extensive study of constitutional law.
[7] Hall, "Archibald Bruce", 24.
[8] *DSCHT*, 103.
[9] *CWAB*, vol. 9, *The Catechism Modernized...*, 1-50.

on the death of a fellow student".[10] Though Bruce could be rigid and dogmatic, there certainly was another side to him. His last epitaph in the section on "epitaphs" was occasioned by the death of a Rev. J. B. (In all likelihood, the Rev. John Brown of Haddington):

> The world he left in evil times;
> But saints remove to peaceful climes,
> Where Jesus' friends shall one day meet,
> And free of fault, each other greet.
> No more his human voice can teach,
> But from the dust his ashes preach;
> They tell how soon our days will fly;
> That we may learn to live and die.
> Ye who approach to gaze, or mourn,
> Be warn'd; and wiser hence return.[11]

Bruce's Vision as Theological Professor

Our chief focus will be to examine Archibald Bruce's advocacy of reform in theological training. His writings will also be examined, and in conclusion we will note the students he trained who went to British North America.

Bruce was Professor William Moncrieff's successor and was appointed by the General Synod on September 7, 1786. It must be noted that Bruce was aware of the immense pressure which Professor Moncrieff laboured under, as were others.[12] In 1790 Professor Bruce complained to the General Synod of the difficulties and work load involved in conducting the hall, and in 1791 he resigned as professor. The synod deferred the matter and received a petition from the students in the synod imploring the synod not to accept Professor Bruce's resignation. In an effort to show some support to Bruce, the General Synod admonished the lower courts to remind all students to be "regular" in attendance at the hall and also promised to provide pulpit supply for Bruce's pulpit during the hall session.[13] There was high regard by the students for their professor, but there were also problems in the arrangements of the hall.

In *Annals of Moncrieff Church Alloa 1747 to 1904* we find this statement: "There is direct evidence of overwork and threatened breakdown of Mr.

---

[10] *CWAB*, vol. 9, *Poems Serious and Amuzing by a Rural Divine*, 1-172. There appears to be some parallel between Ralph Erskine's "Gospel Sonnets" and some selections Bruce himself wrote or adapted, for example, "A morning hymn to Christ, from Buchanan".

[11] *CWAB*, vol. 9, *Poems Serious and Amuzing by a Rural Divine*, 1-172.

[12] *CWAB*, 8:246; "Acts and Proceedings of the General Associate Synod, 1781-1794", *MS*, National Archives of Scotland, Edinburgh, CH3/144/2, 121, 123.

[13] "Acts and Proceedings of the General Associate Synod, 1781-1794", 211, 218.

Moncrieff under the strain of class and congregation."[14] This is an issue that cannot be ignored in the pattern of theological education and training adopted by the Secession churches whereby one man carried such an immense workload.

Bruce accepted the professorship with reluctance, yielding to the authority of the church court. Taking up his new task, he found many problems, thus dispelling all notions of a perfect theological training programme. He was well aware that Whitburn did not possess adequate student accommodations during the sessions.[15] It was a highly practical matter. Where would the students stay during each session? It was impossible for the professor to accommodate them all, contrary to a notion that appears to linger in some circles that it was a glorious time in theological education in which the students would journey to their professor's manse and live with him during their studies.[16] The General Synod had promised pulpit supply for the professor during the weeks of the annual session of the hall because the professor was so busy and overworked. In reality such pulpit relief never did materialize.[17]

Two other major defects in the pattern of theological education which Bruce inherited concerned student attendance and student discourses. Bruce encountered a real problem with inconsistency in attendance at the lectures "commonly owing to their being engaged in teaching either public schools or private families".[18] This was not only a Secession problem or circumstance; it has been noted as well as a common occurrence in the Kirk halls within the universities. Students needed to earn a living. It appears that being a school teacher or a family tutor were the most common forms of employment for students of theology. This meant that students would often miss most of the hall's annual session, which at the time Bruce became professor was in the spring. Seemingly some arrived for the beginning of the annual session but had left before the end. However, closely related to the issue of poor attendance was the purpose for which the students often were there, namely, to deliver their discourses. Having delivered their student discourses, they would opt out of lectures and return to their jobs. Thus Bruce at times felt himself to be more of an "auditor" of student discourses than an instructor. Typically he would listen to up to fifty student discourses per session, and these were up to one hour in duration. Bruce wrote about the students who gave their discourses and left:

> It seemed as if some had considered this as their chief business and design in attending a hall; which being over, and having seen and mutually interchanged

---

[14] *Annals of Moncrieff United Free Church, Alloa. 1847-1904* (Alloa, 1904), 18.
[15] *CWAB*, 8: 242; "Acts and Proceedings of the General Associate Synod, 1795-1820", *MS*, National Archives of Scotland, Edinburgh, CH3/144/3, 165.
[16] Personal correspondence with the author from the Rev. Thomas Aiken, May 18, 1999.
[17] *CWAB*, 8:242.
[18] *CWAB*, 8:243.

compliments and news with their comrades, they would hasten away, with the name of having studied divinity so many years.[19]

These complaints were not unique to Archibald Bruce. Principal George Campbell, Aberdeen, (known as a Moderate in the Kirk) similarly said of the divinity students of King's and Marischal that they came only for a few days and:

> that their attendance was only to give, not to receive instruction, and that it would be just as beneficial to them if they had sent their discourses by post, and gotten somebody to read it in the hall.[20]

Thus George Campbell, a contemporary of Bruce, gave a very similar evaluation of the problems in the divinity halls of the day, and Bruce in his *Collected Works* acknowledged Campbell's truthful evaluation.[21]

A final criticism which Bruce had about the state of theological education within the General Synod was that incoming students needed better training in philosophy than they were then receiving at the Scottish universities. Bruce saw their arts course as suspect because he felt many teaching the philosophical course in these universities were "Semi-Arminians".[22] This is reminiscent of the General Associate's efforts earlier to have a separate philosophical class. Yet in reality resources were never adequate to cover the long term teaching of a separate philosophical class.

Under Professor Bruce the annual session for the hall changed from March to September and lasted for eight weeks. Bruce taught a total of 190 students during his nineteen year professorship with the General Synod, with an average of ten new students entering the hall each year. Of these 190 students, nine went to British North America.[23]

We find in Bruce a man with an immense vision for theological education and training within the Secession. Many of his ideas were implemented in generations to come by Seceders of a different theological perspective. His vision was for an entire academy to be created by the General Synod and staffed by several professors teaching arts, languages and theology. It would be a virtual university.[24] We can ask if he had a model other than the Scottish universities. Perhaps he looked to the continent, in particular Geneva, or to one of the Dutch universities. It is difficult to give an adequate answer to this

---

[19] *CWAB*, 8:243.
[20] George Campbell, *Lectures on Ecclesiastical History* (London, 1800), 77.
[21] *CWAB*, 8:243
[22] *CWAB*, 8:244.
[23] Hall, "Archibald Bruce", 39; David Brown, *Life of the Late John Duncan* (Edinburgh,1872), 28. "Rabbi" Duncan had been a student of Bruce's.
[24] Hall, "Archibald Bruce", 40, referring to Bruce, *Review*, 246; also *CWAB*, 8:246.

question, as there does not appear to be any direct reference in Bruce's writings as to possible models.

Although the General Synod did not adopt Bruce's proposal, they did add certain regulations gleaned from his work. The first of these was that young men had to undergo an examination as to their proficiency in Latin by the presbytery within the bounds of which they resided before beginning university. It was a common problem that the first year university students coming from the "higher" schools had very poor knowledge of Latin. Also, once the student was in university, he was required to have an annual examination by his presbytery or a presbytery committee. In conducting this examination, the presbyters were "to have their eye particularly on those dangerous opinions which are taught in our universities".[25] Once a student was then ready to study at the divinity hall, the presbytery would carry forth another examination covering their ability in Greek and Latin, their understanding of the various branches of philosophy – specifically mathematics, logic, moral philosophy, and natural philosophy, if they had studied these – and their "personal religion". Therefore, the presbytery served as an examining board and conducted an entrance requirement examination before a student could be admitted into the divinity hall. Furthermore, the presbytery was free to recommend additional books to be read during the students' university course. The General Synod did not state which texts were to be used but left this to the discretion of the local presbyteries.[26] The General Synod thus conceded to Bruce's vision only in a very small way.

The General Synod also stipulated that the annual session in the divinity hall was to last eight weeks, of which a student had to attend five weeks for it to count towards the four or five year requirement for the theological course. However, it appears that synods or assemblies in the eighteenth century were always quick to add a rider to their standards. Such was the case with the five week minimum attendance requirement, because if a student could provide a satisfactory reason for his absence, the presbytery could override the five week minimum. Evidence suggests that the presbyteries were not overly rigid on this nor on the requirement of five sessions at the hall if the student was preparing for missions or if there was a scarcity of preachers. In addition to attending the annual sessions with Professor Bruce, each divinity student was expected to deliver at least one discourse each year before the presbytery. In addition the presbytery would examine the student on assigned books.[27] This was not unlike requirements made for Church of Scotland candidates in this time period. These presbytery discourses were in the form of a lecture/exegesis on an assigned biblical text together with reading from the biblical languages. The book assignment took the form of a discourse, usually on a textbook for ecclesiastical

---

[25] McKerrow, *History of the Secession Church*, 782.
[26] McKerrow, *History of the Secession Church*, 782-783.
[27] McKerrow, *History of the Secession Church*, 41.

history, whereby the material was basically summarized. Alternately, the discourse could be a "discussion" of a particular theological point from Francis Turretin's *Institute*.[28]

Turning to Professor Bruce's conduct of the theological hall, we are given a minister's verbatim account of his student days with Bruce in a one page report in McKerrow. The student was Peter Taylor, and we now refer to it extensively.

The first to fifth year students each had a particular assignment to do during each session:

First Year	an exegesis in Latin and a lecture on a portion of the Westminster Confession of Faith.
Second Year	a homily.
Third Year	an exercise with additions on some portion of the Greek New Testament.
Fourth Year	a lecture.
Fifth Year	a popular sermon.

These assignments were in addition to oral examination on some point of theological controversy and textual difficulties.[29]

Taylor went on to say that, "In the business of the Hall, order was not strictly adhered to, and cannot be well-stated." He then made an effort to summarize a typical week in the divinity hall under Professor Bruce. Generally they met each day at twelve noon:

Monday – a miscellaneous lecture by Professor Bruce.
Tuesday – student discourses.
Wednesday – a lecture by Professor Bruce from Marck's *Medulla*.
Thursday – oral examination on Wednesday's theological lecture.
Friday – student discourses.
Saturday – a Confessional (*WCF*) lecture by Professor Bruce and a
   'conference' on some practical subject by Professor Bruce.[30]

The students would also meet amongst themselves and host a Theological Debating Society.[31] This suggests that there did develop a certain comradery amongst the students, and no doubt such societies and friendships were beneficial and important to their education and training. Since they were not

---

[28] Hall, "Archibald Bruce", 41.
[29] McKerrow, *History of the Secession Church*, 783, quoting from the Rev. Peter Taylor.
[30] McKerrow, *History of the Secession Church*, 783, quoting from the Rev. Peter Taylor.
[31] McKerrow, *History of the Secession Church*, 783. The role of student theological societies must not be ignored when consideration is given to the training of students for the ministry. In a later period we know of the incredible influence of student societies for missions upon theology students.

with each other as students on an ongoing basis throughout the year, these annual sessions at the divinity hall were very important. Taylor then added a comment that though the session was to last eight weeks, attendance was not enforced.[32] Since there are no records of student attendance, it is difficult to arrive at an average, but likely four to five weeks would be reasonable.

Taylor then offered a concluding paragraph whereby he evaluated the divinity hall at Whitburn. High praise is given to Professor Bruce for his qualifications, piety, and examinations and critical comments. Taylor states that his judgments were all sound "except the magistrates power". Bruce was a strong leader in the Old Light/New Light Controversy, and Taylor went into what became the United Secession Church, whereas Bruce joined the Constitutional Presbytery, upholding an unmodified Confession on the magistrate. In a passing comment Taylor suggests the system of theological education as practiced in the 1830s to around 1840 was superior to that of the hall at Whitburn. It is noteworthy why he thinks it was better. It was because the presbyteries were doing a superior job by having more student compositions and discourses delivered. Thus he noted "a decided improvement".[33]

Bruce's approach to theological studies continued to use the standard three elements in terms of teaching method: lecture, student discourse and oral examination. There was no real departure here from his predecessors, nor in his focus upon Marck or Turretin as the chief theology texts. As Bruce himself wrote about Marck's *Medulla*, it "has been put into the hand of every student of Divinity in the Secession, as a textbook on which lectures have been delivered by all that have filled that chair".[34] Marck was also used in the Scottish universities, in Holland and England at John Condor's Homerton Academy.[35]

Bruce's Writings

Turning now to Bruce's writings, we are immediately drawn to the two volumes of *Introductory and Occasional Lectures, for Forming the Minds of Young Men, Intending the Holy Ministry*.[36] These volumes constitute the occasional lectures he delivered to the students at the annual sessions of the divinity hall. They were distinct from the systematic lectures, and probably only one or two were delivered at each annual session. Bruce viewed them as

---

[32] McKerrow, *History of the Secession Church*, 783.
[33] McKerrow, *History of the Secession Church*, 783.
[34] *CWAB*, 3:205.
[35] *CWAB*, 3:205.
[36] Archibald Bruce, *Introductory and Occasional Lectures, for Forming the Minds of Young Men, Intending the Holy Ministry* (Edinburgh, original 1797 and reprint 1817) 1:212 and 2:321. Vol. 1 went through two printings, whereas vol. 2 was printed posthumously in 1817. These are bound together in the *CWAB* in New College Library as vol. 7.

more a practical theology with this stated purpose: "Their chief design is to form a Theological taste, to recommend a proper disposition of mind to those engaged in sacred studies, due attention to religion, and good conduct."[37] He tells us that it was the students who requested that he print them. Bruce admits that he freely borrowed from other writings and writers. Some of these can be clearly discerned, whereas others lie buried in the text. The Church Fathers and the Councils of the Early Church are referenced and show Bruce's profound knowledge of the Ancient Church. References to the Reformers, Calvin and Andrew Melville are made plus many references to Puritan Divines, Owen, Baxter, etc., as well as the later English Dissenters, Watts and Doddridge.

The nature of several of these "occasional lectures" parallels a tradition which was followed by many in the seventeenth and eighteenth centuries, namely, to deliver lectures to the students to stress piety combined with knowledge, or set the context for undertaking theological studies. Parallels can be found with Herman Witsius' classical work, *On the Character of a True Theologian*, which he delivered upon his election as professor of divinity at the University of Franeker and to the pastoral charge of the church in Franeker.[38] The aim of this work was for theological students to marry the intellect with spirituality. Several of Bruce's "occasional lectures" parallel the oft-printed "Address to Divinity Students" by Bruce's counter-part in the Associate Synod's divinity hall, John Brown of Haddington.[39]

One quotation from Bruce gives the flavour of several of these lectures:

> However the most of human learning may sometimes prove hurtful, yet this is not the one, or the main thing, needful for the teachers of religion. There is a treasure more to be desired, and 'oil in the house of the righteous.' Though a weak illiterate ministry may greatly injure the interests of the church, yet a graceless one, though polite and learned, is more to be dreaded, and has done much more hurt...[40]

Below we give a brief listing of the contents of the two volumes to learn the content of the students' instruction:

---

[37] *CWAB*, vol. 7, *Occasional Lectures*, 1:iii.
[38] Herman Witsius, *Sacred Dissertations on the Apostles' Creed*, trans. Donald Fraser, original Latin 1681, original English 1823 (Escondido, California, 1993), "Memoir", xvii-xviii; and *On the Character of a True Theologian*, ed. J. Ligon Duncan (Greenville, SC, 1994), 7-8.
[39] John Brown, "Address to Divinity Students", in *A Compendious View of Natural and Revealed Religion,* several editions (London, 1817).
[40] *CWAB*, vol. 7, *Occasional Lectures,* 1:193-194.

Volume 1

Introductory Address to the Students at the Opening of the Divinity Hall, in the First Session at Whitburn, 1787.
1. The Excellency of Knowledge in General
2. The Vanity of Human Knowledge, and Defects of Learning
3. The Excellence of Theology
4. The Disposition of Mind, and Qualities Requisite for Theological Studies
5. ["V" is missing in the text]
6. Of Solitude and Retirement
7. Of Social Intercourse and Conversation
8. The Importance of Moral Character and Conduct
9. Necessity of Personal Religion
10. Improvement of Prayer Distribution of Time

Volume 2

Author's Preface
Address to the Students at the Beginning of a Session
1. The Importance of Early Instruction, with Remarks on Rousseau's System of Education
2. Cont'd – Advantages of Early Piety
3. Of the Seminaries, and Teachers of Sacred Learning, among the Ancient Jews
4. A View of Theological Education, and the State of Ecclesiastical Literature in the early ages of Christianity[41]
5. On the subserviency and utility of Academical Literature and Philosophy to the study of Theology
6. Con't – Philosophy consistent with and subservient to Divinity – the perversion of it dangerous
7. Con't – Logic, Metaphysics, Natural Philosophy, Astronomy
8. Of Ancient and Modern Scepticism and Cartesian Doubt
9. On the Right of Private Judgment, and due Freedom of Inquiry
10. Con't – Objections Answered – Abuses pointed out
11. Con't – Abuses Pointed Out

Volume one clearly appears to emphasize aspects of piety, whereas volume two focuses more on the mind or the intellect. Bruce was obviously aware of Enlightenment thinking and was concerned with training the theology students

---

[41] Bruce did continue his historical account through the Middle Ages and the Reformation, but it was not included in this 1817 volume. *CWAB*, vol. 7, *Occasional*, 2:128.

in orthodox Calvinistic theology. The lectures in volume two clearly reveal the intellectual rigour of Bruce's abilities as professor of theology.

Turning to the long list of Bruce's other writings, his *magnum opus* was no doubt *Free Thoughts on the Toleration of Popery*, running to almost five hundred pages, for which he adopted the pen name of Calvinus Minor.[42] This work exhibits a keen knowledge of the history of Roman Catholic dogma and is paralleled in the largest theological work written by his student Thomas McCulloch, *Popery Condemned,* in two volumes.[43] Bruce must be viewed in the context of being but one Scottish minister writing on the issue of Roman Catholic dogmas and emancipation. The Rev. William Porteous, a leading Church of Scotland minister, wrote a similar work, *The Doctrine of Toleration & Applied to the Present Times* (1778).[44] Bruce also wrote *Annus Secularis*, or *History of Religious Festivals*, which again was a polemic against Roman Catholic liturgical practices.[45]

Bruce had a keen interest in the Huguenots and produced a biography on Alexander Morus as well as translating several of Morus' sermons into English. A reviewer suggested that Bruce was highly capable of producing a history of the Protestant church in France.[46] This, taken with what he wrote (listed above) on historical theology and liturgy plus other short historical articles, reveals Bruce's knowledge to instruct the students in church history. He also edited *Memoirs of J. Hog* (1798), which combines Marrow theology, piety and biography/church history.[47] Clearly the General Associate students had someone well versed in ecclesiastical history. Bruce defended his choice of Alexander Morus with a variety of reasons: to acquaint English readers with this individual, to set forth the controversies of his life, to exhibit his discourses and because his father was from Scotland. Morus was born of a Scottish father in 1616 at Castres, Languedoc, France, where his father was the principal of the Reformed Academy and also a pastor of the Reformed Church.[48]

The writing by Bruce of a biography on Alexander Morus and the translation of his sermons does raise an interesting theological issue for

---

[42] Hobart, "Archibald Bruce", 487: *CWAB*, vol. 2, *Free Thoughts on the Toleration of Popery* (Whitburn, 1780). The second edition was printed in 1810.

[43] Thomas McCulloch, *Popery Condemned,* 2 vols. (Edinburgh, 1808 and 1810).

[44] William Porteous, *The Doctrine of Toleration & Applied to Present Times: in a sermon, preached in the Wynd Church of Glasgow, 10th December, 1778. Being a Public Feast, appointed by the Provisional Synod of Glasgow and Ayr* (Glasgow, 1778); John R. McIntosh, *Church and Theology in Enlightenment Scotland: The Popular Party, 1740 - 1800* (East Linton, 1998), 235, 242.

[45] *CWAB*, vol. 1, *Annus Secularis*.

[46] John Brown (Broughton Place), "Review of Archibald Bruce's 'A Critical Account of the Life, Character, and Discourses of Mr. Alexander Morus'", *Edinburgh Christian Instructor* 8 (March, 1814), 195.

[47] *DSCH*, 103.

[48] *CWAB*, vol.6, *Life of Alexander Morus*, 2-20.

students of Bruce today. Morus, it appears, may have been sympathetic to the Amyraldian teaching about hypothetical redemption coming from Saumur; that is, "that Christ has purchased redemption for each and every human being provided they themselves do not reject this salvation".[49] Dennison wrote that Morus "implied" this Salmurian theology. From Bruce's esteem of Francis Turretin and Benedict Pictet, it is unreasonable to detect within Bruce's theology any Amyraldian teaching. However, it is somewhat perplexing why he devoted such extensive writing and translation of Morus. John MacLeod in *Scottish Theology* makes no reference to Bruce and Amyraldianism via Morus. Perhaps the best assessment is that Bruce appreciated the stress on the free offer of the Gospel in the sermons and writings of Morus, something emphasized by many of the Amyraldians.[50] Furthermore, Dennison may have over-stated the case: Morus was twice examined for heretical notions, once prior to his ordination for suspected Amyraldianism and second, for teaching that Adam's sin was not imputed to his posterity. Both times Morus was found to be orthodox. He held to infralapsarianism and not supralapsarianism, and perhaps this led to suspicion.[51] Furthermore, Francis Turretin studied under Morus, and there appears to have been high respect between them, as there also was with Pictet, who saw in Morus a man of eloquence.[52]

A whole host of Bruce's writings concern polemics on church and state, patronage and satires on Moderatism. These do not chiefly concern us here. However, what is of more direct bearing for us is the fact that Bruce translated Benedict Pictet's *True and False Religion Examined and the Protestant Reformation Vindicated* (1797). The motive for Bruce in translating this work was to help students. He saw the study of Pictet's theology and that of Turretin as "sufficient to give candidates for the ministry a competent idea of the principal heads of divinity...".[53] The work aids the student to see the chief articles of religion stated and defended, to examine world religions, to state Reformation principles and to aim that Roman Catholics would "profess the truth as in Jesus". Bruce adds several footnotes commenting upon Pictet's text and also includes a biographical sketch of the life of Pictet. Bruce's clear objective was to provide a teaching aid for the students in the field of systematic and historical theology. Since presbyteries required students to give

---

[49] James T. Dennison, "The Life and Career of Francis Turretin", in Francis Turretin, *Institutes of Elenctic Theology* (Phillipsburg, NJ, 1977), 3:643.

[50] MacLeod, *Scottish Theology*, 114, 160, 236, 238.

[51] John Brown (Broughton Place) Place, "Review of Bruce's '...Alexander Morus'" ,183.

[52] *CWAB*, vol.6, *Life of Alexander Morus*, 25.

[53] Benedict Pictet, *True and False Religion Examined and the Protestant Reformation Vindicated* (Whitburn, 1797), bound as vol. 4 in *CWAB*. See v and viii. Pictet was Francis Turretin's nephew and the opponent to J. A. Turretin. Pictet is viewed as the last of the old orthodox Calvinists in Geneva. See James I. Good, *History of the Swiss Reformed Church Since the Reformation* (Philadelphia, 1913), 176.

discourses on certain controversies or points of doctrine, Bruce was working towards this goal. As a theologian Bruce was continuing to write and teach in the high orthodox vein of what has often been referred to as "Reformed scholasticism". Muller's definition of "scholasticism" can be well illustrated in the work of Archibald Bruce, that is:

> A highly technical and logical approach to theological system, according to which each theological topic or *locus* was divided into its component parts, the parts analyzed and then defined in careful propositional form. In addition, this highly technical approach sought to achieve precise definition by debate with adversaries and by use of the Christian tradition as a whole in arguing its doctrines. The form of theological *system* was adapted to a didactical and polemical model that could move from biblical definition to traditional development of doctrine, to debate with doctrinal adversaries past and present, to theological resolution of the problem. This method is rightly called scholastic both in view of its roots in medieval scholasticism and in view of its intention to provide an adequate technical theology for schools, seminaries and universities. The goal of this method, the dogmatic or doctrinal intention of this theology was to provide the church with "right teaching," literally, "orthodoxy."[54]

As we have seen with many of the Church of Scotland divinity professors in the eighteenth century, few solid exegetical works were produced. This is also the case with Professor Bruce. A few short articles such as "Weather in the Holy Land" can be found, but nothing substantive, unlike his Associate counterpart John Brown of Haddington, who wrote extensively in the biblical department. (See chapter 10.) There are some hints in Bruce's twice published *An Historical Account of the Most Remarkable Earthquakes and Volcanic Eruptions,* but this was hardly a work to be classified as in the biblical department!

The writings of Bruce bring us to the conclusion that he possessed vast knowledge of the classics, patristics and Reformers. He also possessed a well stocked library of sermons and theological writings by French divines. David Scott wrote that Bruce "was , moreover, familiar with the whole vast field of Papal theology and history – no man of his time nearly so much so".[55] His students wrote very highly of him and through the Student Theological Society urged him to publish his lectures. He also clearly influenced Thomas McCrie and can be attributed with launching him into his historical studies and

---

[54] R. A. Muller, *Dictionary of Latin and Greek Theological Terms* (Grand Rapids, 1985), 8. For an analysis of this definition, see Martin I. Klauber, "Continuity and Discontinuity in Post-Reformation Reformed Theology: An Evaluation of the Muller Thesis", *Journal of the Evangelical Theological Society* 33, No. 4 (1990), 467-475.

[55] David Scott, *Annals and Statistics of the Original Secession Church* (Edinburgh, 1886).

biographies. Some have suggested as well that he had influence upon Thomas Dick, the philosopher. "Rabbi" Duncan once wrote to Thomas McCrie saying:

> "O man do you mind about Whitburn and Professor Bruce? He was a wonderful old man that" – doubtless transporting himself to the days when the venerable Professor sat before us in his full bottomed wig and silver buckles, lecturing... in the muffled tones of the Dead March in Saul, but uttering a depth of wisdom worthy of being listened to by a whole conclave of bishops.[56]

George Paxton

Biographical Sketch and the Hall

George Paxton (1762-1837), born at Dalgowry, East Lothian, went to Edinburgh when about eighteen years old. He did not take the M.A. degree, as was often the custom at this time – "which was then very seldom done".[57] He did four sessions at Edinburgh, not taking Latin but only Greek in addition to the philosophy classes. Belonging to the Antiburghers, he then proceeded to their divinity hall at Alloa under Professor William Moncrieff and was a member of the first session, 1784.[58] Since Professor Moncrieff died in 1786, it is uncertain if Paxton only did three sessions in the divinity hall, each under Moncrieff, or if he attended a fourth session under Professor Archibald Bruce in 1787, when Bruce became Moncrieff's replacement. Since John Mitchell wrote Paxton's brief memoir, it is interesting that he only states Paxton as attending the hall at Alloa. Mitchell was in Professor Bruce's first class (1787), and therefore he would know this information about Paxton.[59] The conclusion appears to be that Paxton only attended three sessions of the divinity hall prior to his licensure in March of 1788, thus also missing the hall that year since it met later. He spent a year and a half as a probationer and very quickly became popular for his pulpit oratorical skills. Mitchell comments upon his pulpit abilities at some length. He had three calls – to Greenlaw, Craigend and the united charge of Kilmaurs and Stewarton. The General Associate Synod determined that he would go to Kilmaurs and Stewarton and was ordained there in August of 1789. It was while there that he took very sick and in 1795(?) resigned Stewarton but remained as the minister of Kilmaurs. Stewarton Church remained without a minister until Thomas McCulloch was ordained there in June, 1799. Mention is made here of this fact as Thomas McCulloch,

---

[56] Brown, *Life of John Duncan*, 39 - 40.
[57] John Mitchell, "Biographical Memoir" [of George Paxton], in George Paxton, *Illustrations of Scripture: From the Geography, Natural History, and Manners and Customs of the East*, 3d ed., ed. Robert Jamieson (Edinburgh, 1842), 26; *DNB*, 44:102.
[58] MacKelvie, *Annals and Statistics of the UP Church*, 658.
[59] MacKelvie, *Annals and Statistics of the UP Church*, 658.

George Paxton and John Mitchell formed a triangle as close friends and encouragers.[60]

In 1807 the General Synod appointed Paxton as the new professor of divinity in their hall due to Archibald Bruce's withdrawal into the Constitutional Presbytery (Auld Light Antiburghers). The synod reviewed the arrangements in its hall, and it was decided to have a second professor for biblical literature as soon as possible. In addition, to promote an improvement of education, the professor of divinity was to be "loosed from his charge", given a suitable salary and was to move to Edinburgh for the conducting of the hall. The professor would also teach Hebrew during the year to students there and "superintend the university education" of those General Associate students in the university with a view to becoming ministers. The Antiburghers, unlike the Burghers, had taken a different approach to their students in the arts course. Often they had conducted their own "philosophy college", but now their method was modified by having their divinity professor in Edinburgh act as a superintendent for the arts students. Mitchell comments with perhaps a flourish of hagiography that Professor Paxton gave himself over thoroughly to these new synod arrangements and carried them out with diligence and devotion and had the fondest of attachments of his students.[61]

Paxton served as the sole professor of divinity in the General Associate divinity hall from 1807 to 1820, with the second professorship never materializing. In December, 1820, he joined in with those Antiburghers who protested the terms of union with the Associate (Burgher) Synod and thus left and became this minority's professor of divinity.[62] He served the Protestors until 1827, when they united with the Auld Light Constitutionalists to form the

---

[60] MacKelvie, *Annals and Statistics of the UP Church*, 411. Concerning Paxton's resigning from Stewarton, there are two dates in MacKelvie (pages 403 and 411) either 1795 or 1797. Mitchell remained a close friend of Paxton's after the 1820 union and valued his friendship. This was likewise true with Thomas McCulloch and George Paxton. McCulloch sent the Nova Scotia students to Paxton's church when they went to Edinburgh in 1824. See William McCulloch, *Life of Thomas McCulloch, D.D. Pictou*, eds. Isabella and Jean McCulloch (Truro, N.S., 1920), 80-82.

[61] J. Mitchell, "Biographical Memoir (Paxton)", 30-31.

[62] MacKelvie, *Annals and Statistics of the UP Church*, 403; "United Associate Synod Minutes, Sept. 8, 1820-Sept.17, 1834", *MS* (Microfilm) United Church of Canada Archives, Victoria University, Toronto (1821), 34. Paxton resigned on December 5, 1820, from the Presbytery of Edinburgh (United Associate Synod) and the Synod accepted his resignation at its 1821 meeting. It would appear that Paxton took some time before he actually withdrew himself. The 1820 United Associate Synod Minutes only record his name as dissenting/protesting to the terms of union (14). An 1821 Synod appointed a committee to "return him the Synod's best thanks for his past services" (34). Thus it appears that Paxton taught the Antiburgher hall session of 1820. Mitchell confirms that Paxton took "a few months" before severing ties with the United Associate Synod. See Mitchell, "Biographical Memoir (Paxton)", 31.

Original Secession Church, for which again he was professor until his death in 1837.[63] The University of St. Andrews awarded him the D.D. in 1834.[64]

From 1807 to 1820 Paxton continued the Antiburgher custom in the General Associate Synod divinity hall of using Marck's *Medulla* as the chief systematic theology textbook. There is no evidence which lends us to believe that after 1820 he stopped using Marck when he left with the Protestors and eventually joined the Original Secession. Like his predecessor, Archibald Bruce, Paxton gave lectures upon Marck each "forenoon", covering the entire work over the five sessions of the hall.[65] The student discourses under Paxton were held at the afternoon meeting, always followed by critical response by the students and last by Professor Paxton. The afternoon session included the professor's examination of the students on his systematic theology lectures. Monday and Saturday allowed for different lessons, with exegetical lectures on different passages usually on Monday followed by readings in the Greek New Testament. Matters related to practical religion were covered on Saturday mornings, when also the students met for essay reading and "conversation", likely as a society. The only substantial change from Bruce in the General Synod divinity hall under Paxton was Paxton's introduction of the exercise of having students produce "skeletons" from assigned texts.[66] Previous to Paxton this term has not been found. Thomas McCulloch also used the term. It appears to mean very simply that the student analyzed the Scripture text and developed a sermon outline with the main points and sub-divisions.

Following the union of 1820, Paxton conducted the Protestors divinity hall for a period at his house at 12 Archibald Place, Edinburgh.[67] Since the minority party of Protestors also had no library, the students availed themselves of Paxton's library. Upon his death in 1837, the library was given to the Original Secession divinity hall. Two years later another Original Seceder minister died, and his library was also given to the Original Secession hall.[68]

Writings

Paxton's chief work was his *Illustrations of Scripture*, which shows his keen interest and knowledge of Scripture and its backgrounds. The contents of this four volume set "consists of the materials of those lectures which were prepared for his students, and delivered from time to time as a portion of the

---

[63] Mitchell, "Biographical Memoir (Paxton)", 31-32. See Appendix B, Section C.
[64] MacKelvie, *Annals and Statistics of the UP Church*, 403.
[65] David Scott, *Annals and Statistics of the Original Secession Church* (Edinburgh, 1886), 606.
[66] Scott, *Annals and Statistics of the Original Secession Church*, 606.
[67] Scott, *Annals and Statistics of the Original Secession Church*, 606.
[68] Scott, *Annals and Statistics of the Original Secession Church*, 551 and 549. The other minister was the Rev. Richard Black (died, 1839).

theological course".[69] These volumes went through various printings and are like an encyclopedia of knowledge relating to the geography of Palestine and the countries bordering the Holy Land; the natural history of the Bible lands, particularly on botany and zoology; and the manners and customs in Bible Lands. This last category took two volumes in the 1842 edition, and likely not all of this material on manners and customs was given in the divinity halls of the General Synod, Protestors or United Original Seceders.[70] *Illustrations of Scripture* represents what emerged in Scotland as a fruit of the Scottish Enlightenment – a flourish of studies in all aspects of knowledge, a proper collecting of the material, and its organization. It thus comes as part of a movement, yet Paxton's foremost goal was to aid the student of Scripture. As he wrote on what he included in the volumes, he admitted that the work did not embrace every "place, or plant, or custom", rather "it embraced those only that are connected with the exposition of some important passage, or that contribute to the general elucidation of the scripture".[71] The tone is evangelical; for example, he draws a parallel between the price of slaves, the average price being thirty pieces of silver according to Maimonides, and Christ – "And this, it will be recollected was the price at which the traitor sold the Redeemer of our souls; it was a part of the deep humiliation to which he submitted...."[72] This evangelical tone is fairly consistent throughout the volumes.

The volume on natural history shows that Paxton studied extensively in this field and consulted a vast range of authorities. He gives the common name first, then followed by the Latin name, and with some of the herbs and shrubs also the class name and the order. For example "aloes": "*Excoecaria Agallocha.* Class, *Dioecia.* Order, *Triandria*" and "The Mouse": *Jerboa*".[73] Many of these articles are of a similar order to those in some of the Edinburgh societies of the period. It is easy to see how entries in "Manners and Customs" would have been used in the hall or by the students; for example, dipping hands in a dish, dancing, privacy of the harem, giving of names, adoption, anointing with oil, musical instruments, kissing the ground, etc.[74]

Overall, Paxton's *Illustrations of Scripture* combines "solid learning and fervent piety".[75] It continues in the tradition of Secession professors before Paxton, particularly Brown, even though he was a Burgher; but it also to a degree parallels some of Bruce's writings as an Antiburgher professor.

---

[69] Mitchell, "Biographical Memoir (Paxton)", 35.

[70] George Paxton, "Author's Preface to the First Edition", in *Illustrations of Scripture*, original 1819 (Edinburgh, 1842), 18, where Paxton stated that he commenced lectures to the theological students on these subjects but stopped and then simply prepared the rest of his "prelections" for the press, as this would be as helpful to the students.

[71] Paxton, "Author's Preface to the First Edition", in *Illustrations of Scripture*, 19.

[72] Paxton, *Illustrations of Scripture*, 4:458.

[73] Paxton, *Illustrations of Scripture*, 2:9, 396.

[74] Paxton, *Illustrations of Scripture*, 3:6-8; 4:5-8.

[75] "Advertisement", in *Illustrations of Scripture*, 3:5.

Most of Paxton's other writings did not originate as lectures in the divinity hall at Edinburgh but chiefly represented his role in the Secession polemics of the period concerning the establishment principle and the civil magistrate.[76] His volume of published poetry likewise was not related to his work in the divinity hall.[77] If anything, this shows his diverse interests and talents, much like Bruce or McCulloch. The last two small published works which may have been used in the divinity hall concerned the office of the deacon, possibly used in a polity series, and his writing against the Apocrypha and its inclusion in the Scripture. This latter may have been circulated, or have been discussed in the divinity hall of the Original Secession when he was their professor.[78] Paxton shared this position with many, and no doubt it was at least a topic in student society discourses or debates.

Summary

The General Associate divinity hall continued the tradition of solo divinity professors from 1786 to1820; however, with certain changes or modifications. Professor Bruce's ideal plan for a virtual Secession (Antiburgher) university was too ambitious for the Scottish Seceders. Hence they continued, in part, to use the Scottish universities for arts and conducted their own divinity hall. Pedagogically Bruce continued the methods established before this time which were lecture, oral examination, criticism and student discourse. A strong commitment to federal theology was maintained by both Bruce and Paxton, as was the commitment to theology and piety in the hall. Alastair Heron suggested that Bruce was more dogmatic than the first generation of Seceders on the Auld Light/New Light matter. He argued that Adam Gib, notorious for his "intolerance", found in Bruce someone "intolerant". Heron seems to have missed the fact that Bruce was highly regarded by his students, and there is evidence that this was the case even after he became a Constitutionalist in 1806. Bruce's writing output was voluminous, and an effort was made to access this particularly in relation to its use in the divinity hall.

Though Paxton remained the General Associate solo professor of divinity from 1806 to 1820, there were significant changes. First, the position was not

---

[76] George Paxton, *An Inquiry into the Obligation of Religious Covenants upon Posterity* (Edinburgh, 1801); and *Letters to Rev. W. Taylor on Healing Divisions in the Church* (Edinburgh, 1802).

[77] George Paxton, *The Villager and Other Poems* (Edinburgh, 1813).

[78] George Paxton, *The Sin and Danger of Circulating the Apocrypha in connection with the Holy Scriptures* (Edinburgh, 1828); Scott, *Annals and Statistics of the Original Session Church*, 550, mentions George Paxton's *The Office and Duty of Deacons*, yet I have been unable to secure a copy to examine. It possibly could provide some insight into Paxton's teaching of polity. Unfortunately Scott did not tell us the year Paxton's work on deacons was published, thus not providing a clue as to when Paxton may have prepared this material.

held as a plurality in connection with a church, and even though this was not on principle, it did represent a change. Further, Paxton took up assisting students in Edinburgh throughout the year and thus not limiting his involvement to the hall session. Paxton made no noticeable theological contributions in dogmatics; rather, his chief contribution was with literature on Bible backgrounds. Whether this should be read as a step away from dogmatic theology to more focus on exegetical theology cannot be conclusively stated. If anything, much like with George Lawson, it was a step, albeit, a small one.

CHAPTER 13

The United Secession Divinity Hall (1821-1847)

Introduction

This chapter will examine the history and development of theological education and training in the United Secession Synod, 1821 to 1847. This was the majority portion of Burghers and Antiburghers, who were united in 1820, and were of the New Light Party. The divinity hall of the United Secession Synod had a relatively short existence. However, there were very clear and marked developments in the hall. These are seen in the change from a solo professor of divinity to two professors and then to four. With the increase in the number of professors, there also arose a degree of specialization in these chairs. This was also a time of theological transition, particularly towards the close of this time period. The chief focus will be first upon the Secession professors and their contributions; next upon Synod directives, pedagogical customs and presbytery involvement.

John Dick: Solo Professor

Biographical Sketch

John Dick was born in 1764 in Aberdeen, where his father, the Rev. Alexander Dick, was the minister of an Associate church. His father was known for his evangelical preaching and evidently stood alone in this category in Aberdeen during the period of his pastorate there, 1758 to 1793.[1] John Dick attended King's College, Aberdeen, beginning when he was twelve years old, having won a bursary competition. Since the philosophy course was still done in the regenting system, he was probably taken through his course under Professor Dunbar. In addition he had Greek from Professor Leslie and Latin from Professor Ogilvie.[2] He received his M.A. degree from King's on the 30th

---

[1] *ERF*, 102; *DNB*, 15:14-15; Andrew C. Dick, "Memoir of the Rev. John Dick, D.D.", in John Dick, *Lectures on Theology* (Edinburgh, 1834),1:ix-x. Alexander Dick was described as having a religion which was "warm, but not enthusiastical" (p. x).

[2] By comparing the two "Memoirs", we arrive at this conclusion concerning Dick's course at King's College. See J. F., "Memoir of the Rev. John Dick, D.D.", in John

of March, 1781, yet had entered the Associate divinity hall for the first session in 1780 under Professor Brown at Haddington.[3] This was not out of the ordinary, as often students attended one or two sessions in divinity while still working on the arts course at a Scottish university. Thus Dick was sixteen years old during his first divinity session, and he completed all five sessions in the divinity hall, something not always accomplished.

It appears that John Dick did not serve as a schoolmaster between sessions in the divinity hall but rather went and lived with relatives in Kinross-shire, where he spent much time with the Secession minister, the Rev. Grieg of Lochgelly. He also spent one summer in Banff-shire with the Church of Scotland minister, Mr. Dunbar, a relative, whom Dick was surprised to discover actually knew Hebrew, a rarity in that presbytery.[4] These months spent in relatives' homes allowed Dick to learn from other ministers and also afforded him time to develop two passions he had, the reading of classical writers and the use of the English language with purity and accomplishment. In the latter Dick had been greatly influenced by Dr. Beattie of Aberdeen. Thus, Dick endeavoured to rid "Scotticisms" from his speech and written work.[5]

After being licensed in 1785 at the age of twenty-one, Dick spent only one year as a probationer, receiving several calls before being settled with the Slateford Associate congregation in 1786. It was shortly after his ministry at Slateford that he issued his first printed sermon, *The Conduct and Doom of False Teachers*, which was an attack on William McGill of Ayr and his Socinian views.[6] His next published sermon was on a controversy within the Associate Church over the Westminster Confession of Faith and the civil magistrate. This published sermon stressed the positive need and use of confessions of faith but encouraged forbearance on what Dick considered a more minor article of the Confession, namely, on the civil magistrate.[7] The issue of the civil magistrate was resolved in the Associate Synod in 1799 by the enactment of a new Preamble to the Formula, which stated that the church did not require assent to compulsory religious matters being imposed by the civil magistrate. Dick sided with the majority portion of the Synod, while the minority became affectionately termed the Auld Light Burgher Synod.[8]

In 1801 he left Slateford and became the minister of Greyfriars (Shuttle Street) Associate congregation in Glasgow, remaining there until his death in

---

Dick, *Lectures on Theology* American Edition, (1841), 1:viii; and Andrew C. Dick, "Memoir of the Rev. John Dick", 1:x.

[3] Andrew C. Dick, "Memoir of the Rev. John Dick", xi-xii.

[4] Andrew C. Dick, "Memoir of the Rev. John Dick", xiii.

[5] Andrew C. Dick, "Memoir of the Rev. John Dick", xiii-xiv.

[6] *DSCHT*, 242; John Dick, *The Conduct and Doom of False Teachers* (Edinburgh, 1788).

[7] John Dick, *Confessions of Faith shown to be Necessary, and the Duty of Churches with Respect to them Explained* (Edinburgh, 1796).

[8] *DNB*, 15:15.

1833. Princeton College awarded him the D.D. degree in 1815, in part for his *Essay on the Inspiration of the Scriptures*. He was also an advocate for foreign missions and preached for the Edinburgh Missionary Society.[9]

In the spring of 1820, he was appointed professor of divinity for the Associate divinity hall (Burgher) following the death of Professor Lawson. Later that year, after the union of the Burghers and Antiburghers resulted in the formation of the United Secession Church, he was appointed this body's professor of divinity. Thus the newly united hall was to be conducted in Glasgow. What follows is a brief description of the United divinity hall while Dick was professor of divinity.[10]

The United Divinity Hall

The hall met twice each day except on Saturdays and Wednesdays, on which days it met only once. On Wednesday's during the afternoon the students met for their society meeting, where the custom was to hear a student's essay and then to offer criticism. The students also met again on Friday evenings to promote "brotherly affection" or to develop a missionary spirit. It would appear that these Friday evening meetings were a continuation of the Wednesday society meetings but were more centred on matters of piety, fellowship and mission.[11] The society meetings during the hall session were important for developing student friendships since many would only see one another annually except for those in the same presbytery. These society meetings always included praise and prayer as well.

Professor Dick had the tradition of inviting students to the manse twice during each session of the hall. The students would be divided into "separate parties", and they would go to the manse for the purpose of cultivating fellowship with one another and in particular to allow the professor to become acquainted with the students. Dick's goal in meeting the students in his home twice each session was to learn about the history of each student and other particularities. He was known for continuing to follow his students after they left the hall in much the same manner as John Brown of Haddington had done.[12] It was an effort to foster warmth and pastoral interest in the hall. Since

---

[9] *DSCHT*, 242; Andrew C. Dick, "Memoir of the Rev. John Dick", xxiv; John Dick, *A Sermon on the Qualifications and the Call of Missionaries* (Edinburgh, 1801).

[10] This description has said little about Dick's personal life. Mention should be made of the intense grief he bore while a minister in Glasgow. He lost a daughter at age ten, a son at age four, and another son at age twenty-three, who had just completed a medical course. Andrew C. Dick, "Memoir of the Rev. John Dick", xxxii.

[11] J. F., "Memoir of the Rev. John Dick", xvi-xvi.

[12] J. F., "Memoir of the Rev. John Dick", xvi-xvii.

there were upwards of eighty or ninety students attending the hall, the group size was probably up to ten for these manse meetings.[13]

The morning sessions in the hall were spent listening to two student discourses with student response and criticism after each. The last to offer criticism was Professor Dick. It appears that during Dick's professorship the student criticism declined at these morning meetings, and it increasingly became only the professor who offered criticism. The reason for this seems to be that the students found opportunity at their Wednesday society meetings to do such criticisms.[14] Dick took great interest and time in the oral criticisms that he offered, which perhaps in part led to a decline by the students as formal respondents to the student discourses.

The afternoon meetings were given over to hearing Professor Dick lecture, and at least once a week he conducted oral examinations on his lectures. Although Dick chiefly concentrated on theological lecturing, as his published lectures reflect, his understanding of systematic theology was to combine theology with scriptural study. Thus, both were covered to some extent in his lectures.[15] In addition, occasionally Dick offered an analysis from a portion of the Scripture in the original languages in a morning session rather than hearing the normal student discourse.[16] However, for his entire thirteen years in the United Secession divinity hall, Dick retained the title Professor of Divinity, which was his chief concentration in the lectures. After six years as sole professor, the synod appointed a second professor in September of 1825. It would appear that, with the enlargement of the hall after the two halls became one, there was less time in each session and too much work for one professor. This new professorship within the department of biblical literature augmented considerably the range of instruction in the hall.[17] After Professor John Mitchell was appointed professor of biblical criticism, Dick only had the third, fourth and fifth session students, thus decreasing the class size.

The *United Associate Minutes* of 1821 reveal that Secession students from Ireland desired to study in the the new united hall in Scotland. The synod had no objections to welcoming the Irish students "if properly attested"; but by studying in Scotland, they would still have to return to Ireland for their licensure. Also, the Scottish synod left it to the discretion of the Irish synod as to whether or not that body would consider the Scottish hall "as equivalent to their studying at their own Hall, it belonged not to us to determine".[18] John

---

[13] MacKelvie, *Annals and Statistics of the UP Church*, 674-677.

[14] J. F., "Memoir of the Rev. John Dick", xvi.

[15] J. F., "Memoir of the Rev. John Dick", xvi.

[16] Andrew C. Dick, "Memoir of the Rev. John Dick", xxxi.

[17] Andrew C. Dick, "Memoir of the Rev. John Dick", xxvii.

[18] "United Associate Synod Minutes" (May, 1821), 40. The exchange between Ireland and Scotland amongst the Seceders was ongoing. In September, 1821, delegates from Scotland reported back to the Scottish Church about their recent visit to the Irish Synod

Dick had managed the hall in 1820 during the time of transitions. The 1821 synod asked him to continue to manage the hall and agreed to pay him one hundred pounds for his work as professor. This synod also appointed a committee to investigate adding a second professor and report back to the 1822 Synod.[19] The United Synod's 1821 Regulations for the Divinity Hall were the following:

1.) The hall session be nine weeks (with authority for the professor to extend it to ten weeks if necessary).
2.) The session to begin the second Wednesday of August.
3.) The student is to attend the whole session of nine weeks unless "he can satisfy the Professor with sufficient reasons for abridging the term; and that even in this case, the minimum of attendance must be six weeks".
4.) A student is to do five sessions; and "if any student has not during any of these years attended full six weeks, he shall attend another year".
5.) "That no one shall be admitted to the study of Divinity, who is not in full communion with the United Body, and who has not attended in one of the Universities and been examined and certified by a Presbytery; and that if he has not studied Natural Philosophy, he shall attend said class, and be examined by the Presbytery before his second year's study of Divinity."[20]
6.) "That the Synod take care to supply the Professor's pulpit during the Session and at the Synod's expense."[21]

The United Associate Synod continued the practice of "distributing probationers" at their synod meetings. The minutes listed the names of students licensed by the presbyteries since the last meeting of synod. These men were referred to as the "Preachers".[22] At the September 1821 synod, seven "Preachers" were listed.[23] The synod had a committee which was charged with

---

of Seceders, where they sat as corresponding members. In their report they laid before the Scottish Synod the "Rules for the Education of Candidates for the holy ministry". See "United Associate Synod Minutes" (Sept., 1821), 51.

[19] "United Associate Synod Minutes" (May, 1821), 40-41.

[20] This rule was altered in 1822 to read that a student who had not attended the natural philosophy class prior to entering the hall could attend such a class concurrently while in the hall provided it was finished before being taken of their trials. See United Associate Minutes" (May, 1822), 60.

[21] "United Associate Minutes" (May, 1821), 42-43.

[22] Since this was a bi-annual occurrence, I will cite only one example: "United Associate Synod Minutes" (April, 1825), 134.

[23] "United Associate Minutes" (Sept., 1821), 46. The first full list with the probationers' names and where they would preach for June, July, August, September and October appeared in the May, 1822 Minutes. "United Associate Synod Minutes" (May, 1822), 68. At the September, 1822, Synod meeting, another table can be found showing where

drawing up the rota for the distribution of the probationers.[24] Synod also continued to give active direction to the presbytery concerning the students under their "inspection". Before a presbytery could take a student under trials for licensure, the synod first had to grant permission. The students were to complete their session and "be duly attested by the Professor of Divinity".[25] Most years when the Committee on Theological Education delivered their report to the synod, it simply stated that the report was read and received. Since the report was not included in the minutes, it is difficult to determine what was the nature of the report.[26] However, we do know that the synod continued to give directives to the various presbyteries to fill the professor's pulpit during the annual session of the divinity hall.[27]

Also, at each synod the committee was appointed "to converse with the students" present at that meeting of synod. We again lack a full report as to the nature of these "conversations", but it would have included, as a minimum, the hearing of reports on the progress of each student and a challenge to those who were irregular in attendance. In essence, this committee functioned as a "quality control" agency for the students. Knowing the stress on piety in the Secession, it can be assumed that matters of piety were also in the "conversation".[28]

Student Petition

In September, 1822, the students of divinity petitioned the United Associate Synod concerning the need for more books. The synod appointed a committee to recommend means to promote the "improvement of the Library".[29] The committee reported back to the synod in May, 1823, with a full report and recommendations. The synod "deliberated", but in the end gave approval for the committee to prosecute their report. Unfortunately, once again we lack the report in the minutes of synod, so we are left to wonder what action synod took.[30] However, in 1824 the synod purchased the Robertsonian Library in

---

each probationer was assigned for November, 1822, through to May, 1823. Occasionally there was a month that a probationer would have off. "United Associate Synod Minutes" (Sept., 1822), 82.

[24] This was also done bi-annually. I cite two examples: "United Associate Synod Minutes" (May, 1823), 92; "United Associate Synod Minutes" (September, 1823), 97.

[25] "United Associate Synod Minutes" (Sept., 1821), 54.

[26] "United Associate Synod Minutes" (May, 1823), 88.

[27] "United Associate Synod Minutes" (May, 1823), 91. This also continued when the synod added a second professor in 1825. We read that Professor Dick's and Professor Mitchell's pulpits were filled. See "United Associate Synod Minutes" (April, 1826), 167.

[28] Once again I have only selected one example: "United Associate Synod Minutes" (April, 1825), 136.

[29] "United Associate Synod Minutes" (Sept., 1822), 80.

[30] "United Associate Synod Minutes" (May, 1823), 92.

Glasgow for the use of divinity students, which was one definite action the synod authorized this committee to perform.[31] The Robertsonian Library could also be used by Secession ministers; and it is assumed they had free access, whereas the students were charged an annual fee. In order to pay for the Robertsonian Library, the synod directed that collections would be received in all the churches and that the funds would be collected by each presbytery treasurer and then remitted to the synod treasurer.[32] Needless to say, some congregations did not respond to the call for collections in 1825, and so in 1826 the synod urged those congregations to take collections before September, 1826.[33] Evidently this did not work all that effectively either, so in 1827 the synod requested that each presbytery appoint a treasurer for the library collections, and this individual was to be diligent in promoting this cause to all the churches.[34] The synod did take the student petition of 1822 seriously, and as the 1820s moved forward, concrete improvements could be seen regarding the synod's attempt to provide an adequate library for its students.

Professor Dick and His Printed Divinity Lectures

When we come to review the systematic theology lecture material which Professor John Dick gave during his thirteen year professorship, we are not left to wonder about its content. As with Brown, we possess the complete syllabus for Dick's systematic theology. His lectures in systematics were first published in 1834, the year following his death, being prepared for the press by his son Andrew Coventry Dick. The son wrote in the preface to the first edition that:

> The Lectures of which it is composed, were read by him to the students attending the Divinity Hall of the United Secession Church...
> They were not prepared by him for the press, nor is it known that he had any intention that they should ever be published.
> They are printed from his MSS nearly *verbatim*...[35]

The son then continued in the original preface with valuable information concerning Dick's conduct in class:

---

[31] "United Associate Synod Minutes" (May, 1824), 117. The report only stated that the library fee for students was to remain the same in 1824 and made no mention of fees for ministers.

[32] "United Associate Synod Minutes" (September, 1825), 159. Synod also directed the Library Committee which had negotiated the purchase of the Robertsonian Library to circulate "Regulations" for the use of the library. One of the negotiators for the library was Andrew Lothian. See Ian D. L. Clark, "The Reverend Andrew Lothian 1763-1831 United Secession Minister", *RSCHS* 20 (1980), 146.

[33] "United Associate Synod Minutes" (April, 1826), 168.

[34] "United Associate Synod Minutes" (May, 1827), 189.

[35] John Dick, *Lectures on Theology*, ed. Andrew C. Dick (Edinburgh, 1834), 1:v.

> A wish was expressed by some, that the questions which the Author put to his Students in his examinations upon the Lectures, should be added to each. But it has been found impossible to furnish either those questions, or a complete list of the books which, at the conclusion of each subject, he was accustomed to recommend for perusal, giving at the same time, characteristic notices of their merits and defects.[36]

Thus, it appears that Dick read each lecture as found in the printed textbook, then followed up with an oral examination of the students plus a "post-lecture" on sources with commentary. The latter point explains the near absence of reference to Reformed compendiums of systematic theology, as this was all done extemporaneously by the professor. Presumably what happened was that Dick delivered the formal lecture, then proceeded to go through the commentary on source works for that particular lecture. He probably brought the books on the particular doctrine to class from his personal library or from the small hall library, of which he was chief custodian and which was housed with him in the manse or church. Notice that Dick provided both positive and negative commentary on the authors' books. This would chiefly have been to assess their orthodoxy and clarity on the subject. The class was then dismissed; and at the beginning of the next day's class, oral examination would occur on the previous day's lecture. As this was the accustomed pattern in most of the halls, Dick followed this pedagogical method.

The oral examination would have been much like conducting a catechism class upon the lecture and material. It demanded recall of the dogmatic point plus reference and oral recital of the appropriate biblical texts. Oral examination was still an entrenched practice in pastoral visitation, presbytery meetings and in the divinity hall exercises. Though Dick's published lectures contained much of what went on in the classroom, these qualifiers were significant. Secondly, another qualifier must be made. Dick's published lectures did not contain the introductory addresses with which each session of the hall would begin. These introductory addresses were a long-standing tradition in the Secession halls and were always given. They were a reminder to the students of the "why's and how's" of the study of divinity. They were full of Christian piety as the proper "prolegomena" to the study of theology. Fortunately a portion of one of Dick's introductory addresses has been preserved in the preface, which we now quote:

> You come to this place to hear such an explanation of the doctrine of religion as will furnish you with materials of reflection, and the means of assistance in your private inquiries. Of one thing it may be proper to admonish you, that you ought not to expect to be entertained with things which can be properly called new. To

---

[36] Andrew Dick, preface to John Dick, *Lectures on Theology* (1834 edition),1:vi. The American edition of 1841 omits these facts. See John Dick, *Lectures on Theology* (Philadelphia, 1841), 1:3-4.

some of you, indeed, many things may be new in this sense, that you have not heard them before; but in general, the subject to which your attention is directed, are truths as old as the Bible, which have been topics of discussion from chairs and pulpits from the first age of our religion. It cannot be supposed that, in a field which has been so often and so carefully surveyed, there is anything left to be gathered by the persons who shall walk over it again. Our purpose is gained, if we are able to communicate to the rising race the knowledge which was imparted to ourselves by our predecessors; we have not the presumption to hope that we shall make any material addition to it; and the utmost at which we could reasonably aim is, to suggest some small matter which had been overlooked, to propose a new argument, or a better statement of an old argument, or, it may be, to throw some light upon a portion of Scripture not yet fully understood. In human sciences, discoveries may be made by superior penetration and more patient inquiry; and their advanced state in the present age, is proof of the success of the moderns in the investigation of the secrets of nature. Discoveries might have been made also in religion while Revelation was in progress, and its light was increasing, like that of the morning; but as seventeen centuries have elapsed since it was completed, and during this long interval it has engaged the attention of the wise, the learned, and the pious, there is every probability that we have been anticipated in all our views.[37]

Though this is only a portion from one of Dick's introductory lectures, it nevertheless is instructive for several reasons. The study of systematic theology has a practical end in view, namely, to assist ministers in their studies in the future (this no doubt being sermon preparation). Dick's choice of language is interesting – "to admonish you". The professor was clearly to be the master in the hall. Next, these lectures were not for entertainment or to promote novel ideas; rather they were to represent a great chain in the study of truth. The proper study of divinity was to promote the communication of these truths to the next generation. The premise here is that truth does not change and the canon of Scripture is complete and sufficient, and this is what wise and pious men ought to study. Though Dick does not state it categorically, he was really affirming confessional, creedal Christianity as the path of study. This was not to be a school of doubt and questioning.

In lecture one, which defined theology and gave introductory material on natural theology and supernatural theology, Dick interestingly included such topics as "Qualifications of a Student of Theology: Piety, a competent Share of natural Talents and Learning, and a Love of Truth". He termed these subjects "the sequel of this lecture". It clearly emphasizes the same theme that was common-place in the Burgher hall under Brown and Lawson, the marriage of theology and piety. Dick warned against "cold speculation" and urged that the conscience be deeply impressed with the authority of God "and the heart" affected. He added that as the student acquired knowledge, "it should be his

---

[37] Dick, *Lectures on Theology* (1834 edition), 1:vi-vii.

first care to convert it by faith and prayer to his own use, that he may be nourished with heavenly food which he is preparing for the household of God. If we are destitute of piety, we cannot enjoy the divine blessing on our studies...."[38] Then Dick balanced what he wrote by stating:

> But piety, although indispensably necessary, is not the only qualification. The study of theology demands, if not the power of genius, yet certainly a competent portion of intellectual ability, a mind capable of attention and patient investigation, of distinguishing and combining, and of communicating the result of its inquiries by accurate arrangement, and perspicuous exposition...[39]

Dick then gave comment upon the value of the university course being properly executed before studying divinity.

> Learning, then, is necessary to the study of theology; and without its aid, our knowledge must be very incomplete. Can he be called a divine, whose accomplishments are little superior, if they be superior, to those of many pious mechanics; or can he expound the Scriptures, who is unable to consult them in the original languages, and is unacquainted with the histories, and laws, and manners, and opinions, to which they so often refer? In this view, it may be justly said, *philosophia theologiae ancillatur*, – philosophy is the handmaid, although not the mistress, of theology.[40]

His last point in this "sequel" was that students must be lovers of the truth for their aim must be "to ascertain the mind of God in the Scriptures, by reading and reflecting upon them".[41] The trail from Brown's "reflections" is not too difficult to follow through to Dick. Although in most of his lectures Dick did not have separate "reflects", he did on occasion sprinkle questions throughout the lectures to draw forth personal application by the student or use assertive sentences of exhortation.[42] These, however, were less pronounced than in Brown.

The text consists of one-hundred and five lectures.[43] If Dick kept to a five year cycle, then he presented twenty-six lectures in systematic theology per session, with a session being up to two months in length, but probably shorter for the most part. This would mean Dick gave four theology lectures per week, these being in the afternoon and exclusive of the oral examination, but inclusive of the source commentary. After 1825, when Professor Mitchell was added as

---

[38] Dick, *Lectures on Theology* (American edition, 1841), 1:12 (Lecture One).
[39] Dick, *Lectures on Theology* (American edition, 1841), 1:12-13.
[40] Dick, *Lectures on Theology* (American edition, 1841), 1:13.
[41] Dick, *Lectures on Theology* (American edition, 1841), 1:14.
[42] Dick, *Lectures on Theology* (American edition, 1841), 1:25, 56.
[43] Dick, *Lectures on Theology*, (1841 edition), 1:v-vi; 2:iii-iv. Technically there are 105 lectures plus an appendix, which was a lecture which the editor/son omitted to include under Lecture Number 58.

professor of biblical criticism, Dick had to condense his lectures into three sessions.[44] The printed lectures begin much like Brown of Haddington's with the topics of reason and revelation and then proceeding in a fairly orderly arrangement to that of the Westminster Confession of Faith. Lectures sixteen through twenty-seven basically follow the Fourth Question from the Shorter Catechism, "What is God?". Following the lecture on "The Final State of the Righteous", there are several lectures on "The External Means of Grace" and "The Government of the Church", and finally "The Law of God". The only noticeable deviation from the arrangement of the Confession was that the text concludes with the lecture on the Law. Dick explained this was in part because of the "practical" nature of the Law.[45] As would be expected, Dick gave several lectures on the covenant of works and covenant of grace and represented a strict adherence to federal theology and to a federal soteriology of *ordo salutis*. In a recent American doctoral thesis by William Evans, brief reference is made to "John Dick: The Federal Textbook Tradition". Evans acknowledges Dick's influence upon Charles Hodge and also the fact that Dick's D. D. came from Princeton College in 1815, but Evans likewise states that John W. Nevin of Mercersburg used Dick's published systematics lectures. Briefly, Evans sees much continuity between Turretin, Dick and Hodge on the matter of federal theology.[46]

Like Brown, Dick's systematics were taught in English. The Burgher halls were doing their theological lectures in English from at least the 1770s. Dick used Latin terms in his text without translation, but this was generally limited to theological terms.[47] The nature of both Brown's and Dick's systematic theology lectures can be adequately summarized by borrowing a description from Hermann Venema's *Institutes of Theology*, where he addressed what should be the component elements of "a theological system":

> It should be *didactic*, or explain and prove from Scripture or from reason the truths which it teaches – it should be *polemic* or *critical*, i.e., the truths explained and proved should be vindicated from the objections and difficulties of adversaries, and a fair view given of the various opinions of those who differ. It

---

[44] "Memoir of the Rev. John Dick, D.D.", in *Lectures on Theology* (American edition, 1841), 1:xv-xvi. This memoir is signed J.F.

[45] Dick, *Lectures on Theology*, (American edition, 1841), 2:513.

[46] William Evans, "Imputation and Impartation: The Problem of Union with Christ in Nineteenth-Century American Reformed Theology" (unpublished Ph.D. thesis, Vanderbilt University, Nashville, Tennessee, 1996), 323-326; Dick, *Lectures on Theology*, (American edition, 1841), 1:455.

[47] Dick, *Lectures on Theology*, (American edition, 1841), 1:433.

should moreover be *practical*, or exhibit the moral use and tendency of the truths which have been thus, in a didactic and polemical form, set forth and discussed.[48]

The latter element could also be termed "piety", but on the whole Venema's description helps us to categorize several of the Scottish theological works in the Secession tradition and beyond it. Brown and Dick fit within Venema's description. Others, such as Dickson's *Truth's Victory Over Error*, fit also somewhat into this, except that he employed the catechetical style. George Hill's *Lectures in Divinity* also approached Venema's description, however, towards the third part tended toward morality rather than piety. These were all in contrast to the Rev. Alexander Rankin's *Institutes of Theology; or, A Concise System of Divinity* (1822), which appeared to combine the didactic element of Scripture in chapter four, "Of the History of Revelation, or, of the Canon of Scripture" (which took over one hundred pages), with almost a biblical chronology or biblical theology. Though Rankin's work was published in 1822, it does not appear to have gained wide acceptance, perhaps in part due to its different organization as a systematic theological work.[49]

Dick's two other written works, which by their titles would appear to have borne directly upon his work as a professor, were written prior to his becoming the United Secession's professor of divinity. His *Lectures on the Acts of the Apostles* was published first between 1805 and 1808, and his *Essay on the Inspiration of the Holy Scriptures of the Old and New Testaments* was first published in 1800.[50] Dick's lectures on Acts were delivered at intervals of every two months and appear to have been a special series of lectures he offered at his church in Glasgow as Sabbath evening lectures. They did not constitute a complete exposition of the entire book, so were not comparable to Lawson's Sabbath lectures on Joseph. Rather, each is a Scripture exposition on a large passage of a chapter from Acts with full explanation given, including background material. Each concludes with orderly reflections, generally of three to four points and two to three pages in length.[51]

It was no doubt in part due to the popularity of Dick's *Lectures on Acts* that his name came forward to stand as the new professor in 1820. It was in keeping with the Scottish custom of expository lectures in distinction from sermons. Dick's American biographer, J. F. (see footnote 2), stated that ordinarily Dick

---

[48] Hermann Venema, *Institutes of Theology*, trans. Alexander W. Brown (Edinburgh, 1850), 8.

[49] On Rankin of Ramshorn Parish (St. David's), Glasgow, see *FES*, 3:434 and *DNB*, 47:289. Rankin was Moderator of the Church of Scotland General Assembly, 1811, and received a Glasgow D. D. in 1801. There is no entry article for him in *DSCHT*.

[50] *DSCHT*, 242.

[51] John Dick, original preface to the first editions of *Lectures on the Acts of the Apostles*, (Glasgow, 1848 edition), vii-viii. The twenty-nine lectures on Acts took five years for Dick to complete. See p. 451; also John Dick, *Lectures on Acts*, 286-288; Andrew C. Dick, "Memoir of the Rev. John Dick", xxv-xxvi.

gave an expository lecture at the morning Sabbath service and a sermon at the afternoon service. Thus, the Acts lectures constituted a special Sabbath evening monthly lecture series.[52] Dick's published volume of sermons is precisely that – sermons. Each sermon is based upon a short, scriptural text, read somewhat topically. For example, titles include "On the Divinity of the Messiah", "On the Easy Yoke of Christ", "On Humility" and "On the Purification of the Young". These sermons are arranged with an introduction, often setting forth context and theme, before taking up the main points which are quite doctrinal, and then ending with applications. The sermons refer to other Scripture and are Christ-centred, in keeping with the Secession evangelical tradition.[53]

Concerning Dick's *Essay on the Inspiration of the Holy Scriptures*, although it was published before he became professor of divinity, portions of it can be found in his *Lectures on Theology*.[54] Dick held to the plenary inspiration of the Scriptures while seeing this as not negating "degrees of inspiration", for "sometimes a larger and sometimes a smaller degree was necessary to the composition of the books, according to the previous state of the minds of the writers, and the matter of their writings".[55] This approach does not imply a "doctrine of partial inspiration", something he rejected; rather he was attempting to classify various genre of Scripture rationally.

The Appointment of a Second Professor (1825-1833)

It was not only in the Kirk halls within the Scottish universities that serious evaluations were being made. Evaluation was also occurring within the United Secession Synod and her United divinity hall. The critical years for change here were 1825, when a second professor was added to the hall, and 1833, when a synod committee was appointed to study the conducting of the United hall. It is the appointment of a second professor for the United divinity hall to which we now turn.

John Dick remained the professor of divinity in the United hall through to 1833, but in 1825 he was joined by John Mitchell, who became professor of biblical literature.[56] Actual discussion concerning the appointment of a second professor had been ongoing in committees, presbyteries and in the synod since 1823. McKerrow summarized the arguments for the change as two-fold: "for the sake of the students, and also for the sake of cementing more firmly the union". Since Professor Dick came from the Burgher portion, there was obviously an element of the Antiburghers who wanted to see someone from

---

[52] J.F., "Memoir of the Rev. John Dick", x.
[53] John Dick, *Sermons* (Glasgow, 1816), v-viii, 1-33, 226-253, 175-199, and 307-331.
[54] John Dick, *Lectures on Theology*, (Edinburgh, 1834), 1:187.
[55] Andrew C. Dick, "Memoir of the Rev. John Dick", xxii.
[56] McKerrow, *History of the Secession Church*, 678-679; "United Associate Synod Minutes" (April, 1825), 135.

their ranks also a professor. It is difficult to fully assess then the motives and reasons for the change, but it was for more than simply the best interests of the students in the minds of some of the members of synod. McKerrow stated that some in the synod saw no need to add a second professor and believed that the studies of the students would be better served by having only one.[57]

In April, 1825, the synod did decide to appoint a second professor "for promoting the improvement of the system of theological tuition" and set forth that this second professor

> give a course of lectures on the history, evidence, and interpretation of the sacred books; to direct the reading of the students; and to examine them on these subjects; to read to them portions of the scriptures in the original critically; and to require from them explicatory and critical exercises.[58]

Dr. John Mitchell was appointed the second Professor in the United divinity hall in September, 1825.[59] His interest, the purpose for which he was appointed, appears to be very parallel with that of his close friend, George Paxton, whose publications were virtually in the exact areas in which Mitchell was being asked to serve as professor. He protested becoming the second professor due to his age (fifty-seven years), but the will of the United synod carried. Mitchell had been ordained August, 1793, to Anderston (Antiburgher) Church, Glasgow, which was Wellington Street Church after 1828. In 1842 he informed the United synod that he was unable to take the junior class of the hall, and arrangements were made for ministers to take his classes. This fell upon the shoulders of the Rev. John Eadie, who was later appointed to be professor of biblical literature.[60]

From 1825 to 1833 the United divinity hall was divided into two divisions, junior and senior. Students were to attend five sessions in the hall with each session lasting eight weeks, but "every student was required to be present at least six weeks of the session, otherwise it did not count as one of the prescribed sessions".[61] The junior division was for students in their first two sessions, and they attended the classes of Dr. Mitchell, professor of biblical literature, while the senior three sessions were spent with Dr. Dick, the professor of divinity (systematic theology). The hall had approximately one hundred students in total with Professor Dick, 1820-1825; and with the two professors, from 1825 to 1833, it would have been the same. Thus Professor Mitchell taught about fifty students in total in the junior classes; and, owing to attrition, Professor Dick probably had about fifty students in the senior

---

[57] McKerrow, *History of the Secession Church*, 678-679.
[58] McKerrow, *History of the Secession Church*, 679; "United Associate Synod Minutes" (April, 1825), 137.
[59] "United Associate Synod Minutes" (September, 1825), 157.
[60] Small, *History of the Congregations of the UP Church*, 2:44-45.
[61] McKerrow, *History of the Secession Church*, 679.

classes.[62] Both professors did not preach in their pulpits during the eight weeks the hall was in session, and each received one hundred pounds per annum from the synod for their work in the hall.[63] With the size of the student body in the United divinity hall, it appears obvious that the synod had no choice in having a second professor. It would have taken a most remarkable individual to process the number of student discourses in such a student body single-handedly!

Professor Mitchell did not publish any of his Bible lectures or any other discourses which he may have delivered in the hall. Two of his published works, a *Sermon on the Death of Dr. John Dick* (1833) and his *An Essay on the best means of civilizing the subjects of the British Empire in India, and of diffusing the light of Christian religion throughout the eastern world* (1805), were not composed for the divinity hall. The latter is his chief published work and won him one hundred pounds in an essay competition sponsored by Claudius Buchanan, an Anglican evangelical chaplain of the East India Company. It was no doubt as a result of the publishing of this essay that he received the D.D. degree from Princeton College, New Jersey, in 1807.[64] Mitchell's other published work, which has been already referred to, was his memoir of George Paxton. In the absence of evidence to the contrary and knowing Mitchell's high regard for Paxton, it can be concluded that Paxton's *Illustrations of the Holy Scriptures* were a valuable resource for Mitchell's work in the divinity hall. It is very difficult to assess Professor Mitchell's impact in the United Secession divinity hall from 1825 to 1842 without knowing for certain how he conducted his lectures and examinations. It would appear that the hall met in Glasgow in the two church buildings of the professors from 1825 to 1833. From 1835 to 1842 it met mainly in Edinburgh, which would mean Professor Mitchell would have had to travel there. However, MacKelvie records that for one of these years, 1836, the junior classes met in Glasgow with Professor Mitchell.[65]

Professor Mitchell's title was "Professor of Biblical Literature", not "Professor of Exegetical Theology"; and the two titles reflect two very different classes. Professor Mitchell's lectures were on biblical history, evidences, hermeneutics, geography and chronology. He also gave some lectures on the history of the Christian Church. During session the class met for at least two hours daily starting at ten in the morning. The classes opened with prayer taken in turn by the students except on Monday, when Professor Mitchell led in prayer. The first hour of the class was spent in reading a passage either in the Hebrew or Greek Scripture. Particular focus on Hebrew was directed towards

---

[62] MacKelvie, *Annals and Statistics of the UP Church*, 674-681.
[63] Landreth, *The United Presbyterian Divinity Hall*, 222.
[64] *DSCHT*, 594, 105; *DEB*, 2:777. The entry article here dates Mitchell's D.D. from Princeton as 1814, whereas the *DSCHT* dates it as 1807. Mitchell received also the D.D. degree from the University of Glasgow in 1837.
[65] MacKelvie, *Annals and Statistics of the UP Church*, 682-685.

the Psalms. The reading included analyzing the passage. A break occurred at the end of the reading class before Professor Mitchell delivered a lecture "according to the order of the course". An oral examination of this lecture occurred after every third lecture, which probably meant once or twice a week. It was also at the second class that the students gave the discourses based upon their assignment at the conclusion of the hall the year before. It is uncertain whether Professor Mitchell required the first session divinity students to give a discourse. These discourses were criticized by the professor and one or two students. If time permitted near the conclusion of the session, supplementary lectures were given on style, composition of discourses and the study of the biblical languages. Professor Mitchell then closed the hall with a brief recapitulation of what had been covered in that session and gave advice and direction as to how the students could "improve" and use their time during the hall's recess.[66] Essentially the heart of what Mitchell lectured upon was parallel to the contents of Paxton's *Illustrations*.

In the *Edinburgh Theological Magazine* of 1828, we discover an interesting article signed simply by "A Member of the United Synod". The editors did not identify the writer and entitled the article "Theological Discourses of the Students in the Secession Church". It describes the impact in the synod of moving to having a second professor in the divinity hall. The writer was not opposed to having a second professor; rather, he was opposed to a trend that quickly arose in the United Associate Presbytery of Stirling, namely, the reduction by two of the number of required student discourses, thus removing a homily and a lecture in the student's first two years. The writer of the article saw a problem developing, a defect in the education of Secession students:

> in not accustoming them early enough, and often enough, to theological writing – to the composition of sermons – in short, to the *preaching* of the gospel. This, one would suppose, should be the grand end of his education – the tendency of all his studies – not merely to inform his own mind, but to enable him to communicate his ideas clearly and forcibly to others, without which talent as a preacher he would be useless. Now, Sir, how is this talent to be acquired? Is it merely by listening to the preaching of others?... We must try the thing ourselves, and try it often ere we can do it well...
>
> Now, Sir, if the art of preaching (for there is an art in *it* as in every thing) is to be acquired in the same way, namely, by *practice*, would not any man be surprised to learn, that all the practice a student was required to have had, previous to his being taken on trials for license, was confined to *seven* sermons? I except the critical exercises, for they are not preaching... He may be perfectly well acquainted with theology, and utterly unable to *explain* it. It is his education for *this* that I consider so defective. It is to be the business of his life to *speak to the people* on these subjects; and will such limited practice qualify him for *that*?

---

[66] McKerrow, *History of the Secession Church*, 797-798.

But this is not the whole of the evil. The people must be addressed in a style different from that in which students write college essays and critical exercises; and to prescribe the latter immediately after they quit college, is to confirm them in a style too dry and uninteresting for the pulpit, and which the people neither relish nor understand. Delaying, then, their writing theological discourses till the third year of their studies, not merely leaves them little time to cultivate that species of composition, but may also unfit them for it, by their style being previously formed on a wrong model for pulpit eloquence.[67]

This anonymous writer then went on to state that he knew one of the presbyteries voted to require the students to do four "theological discourses" during their first two years of studies and that another presbytery was considering such action. In view of how this writer used the term "theological discourses", here it really means a homily, popular sermon or expository lecture in contrast to the "critical exercises", which were more in the style of essays on Bible customs, geography, manners, etc. The article does not directly mention Professor John Mitchell, but one does wonder if this was a criticism of his style, which was known as "cultivated" and "classical" and was distinct amongst Secession preachers.[68] This is only speculative and cannot be determined conclusively.

The article not only raises the question of the work of the second professor but also the issue of the practical training and development of the students for their life-work. Since students of divinity did not preach in churches until they were licensed and thus probationers, they gained no experience in teaching the Scriptures in a congregation while students in the divinity hall for four or five years. That this was the case throughout the entire period of study in the Secession halls from 1734 to 1847 is quickly verified. However, three facts must be acknowledged: first the students in the divinity halls were relatively young, late teens to early twenties; second, after licensure there were generally one to three years of probationary preaching (as now they were "preachers"), whereby they did their field work or internship for the church; and third, while they were divinity students their usual source of income was derived by teaching in a school or as a tutor for a family, where it would be their task to give instruction in Scriptural knowledge, catechism and psalm singing. Thus, while they were students, a form of public training was going on, albeit not in the formal sense as perceived in the twenty-first century.

The Hebrew instruction which Professor Mitchell gave in the United divinity hall would not have been the alphabet and basic grammar. Students were to have received this in their college classes and in the presbytery examinations for entrance to the divinity hall in addition to Latin, Greek and

---

[67] Anon, "Theological Discourses of the Students in the Secession Church", *Edinburgh Theological Magazine* 3 (1828), 205-206.
[68] *DSCHT*, 594.

philosophical subjects. Once a presbytery was satisfied, then the students were admitted to the hall.[69]

The actual amount of Hebrew reading required in the divinity hall and the quality of such was a point of criticism in a review in an issue of the 1831 *Edinburgh Theological Magazine*. The review was on Adam Thomson's *A Comparative View of the English and Scottish Dissenters*, where the reviewer freely admitted that Hebrew studies in the United Secession hall were inferior to those done in English Dissenting academies and that presbyteries are generally too "easy" with Hebrew translation work. Usually the presbytery assigned a short Psalm six months in advance and then required the student to translate it. However, the reviewer did acknowledge that things were improving because Hebrew was being read in the hall as an exercise in the junior classes. Yet he went on to argue that the current practice of an annual session of six weeks (does this mean students usually opted for the minimum?) was not enough and that it should be changed to a six month session, thereby making the hall "a standing hall" and allowing the presbyteries liberty to increase the number of student discourses required.[70]

Varying opinions within the United Secession Church in the 1820s and 1830s were also expressed on the question of students paying fees to the professors of the hall. The *Edinburgh Theological Magazine*, as we have seen, was a source for Seceders to give vent to their views on theological education. In another letter to the editor of this magazine in 1830, a reader identified as "X.Y.Z." wrote concerning an overture that was to have been raised at one of the synods of 1829 or 1830. He stated that he was not the originator of the lost overture and could not speak as to what happened about it.[71] In arguing that the divinity students should be paying fees to the professors, he first gave proof that the students could afford such. In 1829 the divinity students gave two hundred pounds "to a foreign seminary", and they pledged to do this again in 1830. This foreign seminary was the Pictou Academy and Divinity Hall with Professor Thomas McCulloch. He further argued that the students had completed their literary classes, thereby qualifying them to teach and thus have "more money at command". Next, since the teaching session was so short – only six weeks – and it had only one professor, it would not cost that much for board and fees for the professor. If the students could afford board for six months and fees for two or three professors at the university in their arts course, then surely could not such a short course in the Secession divinity hall include

---

[69] For an example of this see the United Associate Presbytery of Stirling and Falkirk and its August 5, 1828, meeting which is described under, "Ecclesiastical Intelligence", *Edinburgh Theological Magazine* 3 (1828), 500-501.

[70] Anon, "Review of Adam Thomson's, *A Comparative View of the English and Scottish Dissenters*," *Edinburgh Theological Magazine* 6 (1831), 323-324.

[71] Anon, "Is it Expedient to Require Students of Divinity in the Secession to Pay Fees to Their Professors?", *Edinburgh Theological Magazine* 5 (1830), 505-506.

fees? Also, many began their studies at the hall (on average, he calculated, twenty-five new students annually), yet less than half of that first session class made it through to licensure in the Secession Church. Some entered "other societies", yet it was the Secession who paid for their theological education.[72]

The writer's conclusion was that the students of divinity should pay fees; and if there was a truly talented student with no finances available, then his presbytery should pay the fees, providing he refund the money to the presbytery after taking office.[73] The writer drew attention to the fact that two Scottish universities were collecting fees in their divinity halls, which was sanctioned by the General Assembly of the Church of Scotland, as were the English Dissenters in their academies.[74] Thus, it appeared logical to "X.Y.Z." that student fees should be paid. Since this matter was a mute point in the Synod *Minutes*, we conclude that this writer represented a minority opinion within the United Secession Synod.

The Appointment of a Third and Fourth Professor (1834-1847)

Professor John Dick died in January of 1833. For the session of 1833, the students were put directly under a committee appointed by their respective presbyteries who directed their studies during that year.[75] Also, from April to September, 1833, a synod committee studied the "scheme of theological tuition" in the hall, and in September recommended to the United Session Synod that four professors rather than two be in charge of the hall. In April, 1834, synod accepted the recommendation and proceeded to appoint four professors. Since this move took so long, it does raise the question if there was opposition to this in the synod. The minutes do not appear to reflect this, but rather the question raised from the minutes centred around the exact division of labour among the four professors.[76] Dr. John Mitchell remained the professor of biblical literature and the new appointments were: the Rev. John Brown of Broughton Place, Edinburgh, to be the professor of exegetical theology;[77] the Rev. Alexander Duncan to be the professor of systematic theology; and the Rev. Robert Balmer, the professor of pastoral theology and Church history.[78] The synod committee further recommended that the junior students (first and

---

[72] Anon, "Is it Expedient...?", 506-507.
[73] Anon, "Is it Expedient...?", 507-508.
[74] Anon, "Is it Expedient...?", 508.
[75] McKelvie, *Annals and Statistics of the UP Church*, 682; "United Associate Synod Minutes" (April, 1834), 398; McKerrow, *History of the Secession Church*, 689-690.
[76] "United Associate Synod Minutes" (April, 1834), 400-401.
[77] The minutes refer to this professor as "Professor of Exegetical Theology, or Exposition of the Holy Scriptures". See "United Associate Synod Minutes" (April, 1834), 401.
[78] McKelvie, *Annals and Statistics of the UP Church*, 682; "United Associate Synod Minutes" (April, 1834), 398.

second sessions) attend the classes in biblical literature and exegetical theology and that the senior students (third, fourth and fifth sessions) attend the classes in systematic theology, pastoral theology and Church history. The sessions were to last for two months, with the students remaining for the entirety of each session. Alexander Duncan and Robert Balmer made a private arrangement to change what they taught in their classes, which was endorsed by the synod, so that Balmer became the professor of systematic theology and Duncan the professor of practical theology and Church history.[79] Balmer requested the change because his eyes would not allow him to write full lecture notes, and he thought he could conduct the systematics class mainly by examination and student discourse.[80]

Since Professor Mitchell's class in biblical literature has already been dealt with, we will proceed to make comments upon the work of Brown, Balmer and Duncan. It should be noted that synod continued to supply the pulpits of all four professors during the annual hall session.[81]

John Brown: Exegetical Theology

John Brown of Broughton Place (1784-1858) was the grandson of John Brown of Haddington and the son of John Brown of Whitburn. He studied at the University of Glasgow and with Professor Lawson at Selkirk because he belonged to the Burgher Seceders. His first charge was in Biggar (1806-1822), then Rose Street, Edinburgh (1822-1829), and, the one with which he was most associated, Broughton Place Church (Edinburgh) from 1829 to the time of his death in 1858. He is remembered for three controversies with which he was involved: the Apocrypha Controversy (the 1820s), the Voluntary Controversy (1835-1843), and the Atonement Controversy (1840-1845).[82] Chiefly what concerns us here are his labours as professor of exegetical theology or "Exposition of the Holy Scriptures" from 1834 to 1847 in the United divinity hall. He continued as professor in the United Presbyterian divinity hall after 1847 until 1858. Thus, in total he was a professor for twenty-four years, thirteen in the United Secession hall and eleven in the United Presbyterian hall. While professor he continued to hold his pastoral charge, as did the three other professors. Each professor received fifty pounds per annum to cover his expenses while working in the hall. Since generally the hall alternated between Glasgow and Edinburgh, the professors sometimes lived away from home. For

---

[79] McKelvie, *Annals and Statistics of the UP Church*, 682; "United Associate Synod Minutes" (April, 1834), 402.
[80] "United Associate Synod Minutes" (May, 1834), 407.
[81] "United Associate Synod Minutes" (April, 1835), 439.
[82] *DSCHT*, 100-101; Wayne Livingston McCoy, "John Brown of Edinburgh (1784-1858), Churchman and Theologian" (unpublished Ph.D. thesis, New College, University of Edinburgh, 1956), 286-269.

someone like Professor Balmer, this was always the situation, as his pastoral charge was at Berwick-upon-Tweed in England.[83] Both Brown and Balmer tried to resign from their respective professorships in 1835, the year following their appointments, but synod urged them each to "discharge the duties to which they have been elected".[84] Both men complied with the wishes of the synod.

According to the reorganized plan of synod for the United Secession hall, the students in the junior class of 1834 were to have select Scripture books critically expounded to them. This became the focus of Professor Brown's classes. Brown gave John McKerrow a description of the class he was conducting for McKerrow's *History of the Secession*. In the Old Testament Scriptures, Professor Brown gave lectures on the history of creation, the fall of man, select Messianic Psalms (numbers 2, 16, 18 and 110), and the Messianic prophecies in Isaiah (chapters 11, 52, 53, etc.). In the New Testament he gave "minute critical exposition" of Christ's discourses in the four Gospels and lectures on Romans, Galatians and Hebrews. He desired to provide more lectures from Acts and the New Testament prophecies and on the Messianic predictions in the Old Testament but could not take these up as there was insufficient time with only two sessions allotted to such.[85] Professor Brown took between two and three hours each weekday that the hall was in session and divided this time equally between lecturing and student discourses. Student exercises were exegetical and were always followed by his critical comments, and each student prepared and delivered one each session in his junior years. These were still delivered *memoriter* and were to be "pieces of strict exegesis; a clear exposition of the words, phrases, and sentiments of the passage with a statement of the reasons on which the exposition is founded".[86]

In reviewing McKerrow's written account received from Professor Brown, a quick comparison to the published works of Professor Brown reveals a virtually identical listing. Wayne McCoy's doctoral thesis of 1956 furnishes the best bibliography of the published works of Brown. McCoy divided Brown's works into four categories: books, pamphlets, articles and essays, and works edited by Brown. The bibliography is eight pages in length and accords with what McCoy says about Brown as being very "industrious".[87] Under Brown's published works on the Old Testament can be found *The Sufferings and Glories*

---

[83] McKerrow, *History of the Secession Church*, 691; Stewart Mechie, "Education for the Ministry in Scotland since the Reformation III", *RSCHS* 15 (1966), 3; "United Associate Synod Minutes" (April, 1836), 486, for an example of where the classes would meet.

[84] "United Associate Synod Minutes" (April, 1835), 444.

[85] McKerrow, *History of the Secession Church*, 798.

[86] McKerrow, *History of the Secession Church*, 799.

[87] McCoy, "John Brown of Edinburgh", 295-302. I will not list here or in the bibliography all the printed works of John Brown of Broughton Place but rather refer the reader to the bibliography in McCoy's thesis.

of the Messiah: An Exposition of Psalm XVIII, and Isaiah LII:13-LIII:12.[88] There are no published lectures from Brown on Genesis. All of the lectures he gave on the New Testament were later published:

> Discourses and Sayings of Our Lord Jesus Christ:Illustrated in a Series of Expositions (1850)
> An Exposition of the Epistle of the Apostle Paul to the Hebrews (1862)
> An Exposition of the Epistle of Paul the Apostle to the Galatians (1853)
> Analytical Exposition of the Epistle of Paul the Apostle to the Romans (1857)[89]

The *Discourses and Sayings of Our Lord Jesus Christ* has been selected for brief comment to gain further insight into Professor Brown's contributions to the United Secession divinity hall. These expositions must be viewed as often having originated in the pulpit of Broughton Place Church and then re-worked for the students by adding "philological discussions of the Hebrew and Greek texts, the detailed opinions of authorities on all controverted questions of interpretation, and the nomenclature of Biblical Exegesis". Thus, these lectures were utilized in the pulpit and in the divinity hall.[90] Hence the world of the church was not far away in these lectures, something for which Brown did not apologize, because merely critical discussions in a divinity hall without what has been called piety in this book turns the study of Scripture into an intellectual pursuit.[91] The lectures in the hall had a quality of godliness, humility and solemnity about them, for the Scripture was revered; and a love for Christ came through in all that was studied.[92] The overall thrust of these volumes is clearly evangelical and Christ-centred. While not devoid of piety, they also contain "*scholia*, on particular words and phrases", continuous comment and "illustrated analysis". Brown states that "in all the Discourses, Exposition will be found to be the staple; whatever is doctrinal, experimental, or practical, being presented as the result of the application of the principles of strict exposition to the passage under consideration".[93]

---

[88] John Brown (of Broughton Place), *The Sufferings and Glories of the Messiah: an Exposition of Psalm XVIII, and Isaiah LII:13-LIII:12* (Edinburgh, 1853).

[89] John Brown (of Broughton Place), *Discourses and Sayings of Our Lord Jesus Christ: Illustrated in a Series of Expositions*, 3 vols. (Edinburgh,1850); *An Exposition of the Epistle of the Apostle Paul to the Hebrews*, ed. David Smith, 2 vols. (Edinburgh, 1862); *An Exposition of the Epistle of Paul the Apostle to the Galatians* (Edinburgh, 1853); and *Analytical Exposition of the Epistle of Paul the Apostle to the Romans* (Edinburgh, 1857).

[90] McCoy, "John Brown of Edinburgh", 223-224.

[91] McCoy, "John Brown of Edinburgh", 224.

[92] McCoy, "John Brown of Edinburgh", 249.

[93] John Brown (of Broughton Place), preface to *Discourses and Sayings of Our Lord Jesus Christ*, original 1850, second edition 1852 enlarged (Edinburgh, 1990), v, ix.

In his preface Brown stated which works he had found most helpful in doing the exposition, but the definitive list of works consulted can be found in the third index, "Authors Quoted or Referred To". This list contains reference to almost three hundred different authors and can be viewed as a working bibliography. Of these three hundred authors, several are referred to numerous times throughout the volumes. Those which were referred to most often by Brown were: Augustine, Bengel, Beza, Brewster, Calvin, Campbell, Chrysostom, Erasmus, Fuller, Grotius, M. Henry, Josephus, Kuinoel, G. Lawson, Lightfoot, Luther, Neander, Olshausen, J. Brown Patterson, Quesnel, Scott, Pye Smith, Tholuck, Trench and Wetstein.[94] And of these in this list of "those most often referred to", the top three were Bengel, Olshausen and Tholuck, with Bengel and Tholuck leading the number. Brown was in many ways a Scottish counterpart to these German pietists/scholars, although he never held a university appointment.

Brown's approach in his lectures was not to give lectures on the principles of hermeneutics but rather to apply such principles in class by expositing large portions of Scripture. McCoy stated that Brown's two questions were: "What was this oracle in sense to those who first received it?" and "What is it still to us?" Further, his plan of exegesis was "'to make the Bible the basis and test of the system' of theology and not 'to make the system the principal and, in effect, sole means of the interpretation of the Bible'".[95]

Commenting upon Brown's exegetical work, McCoy stated that Brown largely limited it "to philological, grammatical, or linguistic criticism..." and, "To Lower, Higher and Historical Criticism, he contributed little or nothing." He read the German writers' works which were written in Latin or made available in English translation, as he did not read German. This led McCoy to his conclusion that by the time Brown's exegetical lectures were actually published, they were "already outdated".[96] By this McCoy meant that Brown wrote and published prior to the time when the German Higher Critical writings were introduced to Scotland, and McCoy argued that Brown must be read within his time period. McCoy attributed Brown a special place in what he called "the general forward movement in exegetical theology in Scotland" in that Brown helped originate this movement.[97] William Taylor, in *The Scottish Pulpit From the Reformation to the Present Day*, said much the same concerning Brown's influence upon exegesis in Scotland:

> ...the name of John Brown marks the beginning of an era not only in his own denomination, but in Scotland generally. He was in that country very much what

---

[94] Brown, Index 3: Authors Quoted or Referred To, in *Discourses and Sayings of Our Lord*, 3:505-507.
[95] McCoy, "John Brown of Edinburgh", 264.
[96] McCoy, "John Brown of Edinburgh", 264.
[97] McCoy, "John Brown of Edinburgh", 264.

Moses Stuart was in New England, the regenerator, if not the father, of exact Scriptural exegesis, and for that he deserves to be held in lasting honor.[98]

McCoy's words concerning Brown's place in Scottish exegesis in the nineteenth century are accurate. Brown certainly did inaugurate a new era in exegesis, which continued to develop and came "to supersede his work".[99] Brown certainly represented a movement to interpret the Bible historically and represented in Scotland the early steps in the nineteenth century towards the historical-critical method of biblical interpretation. Glenn Miller wrote that it was Friedrich Schleiermacher who was "the first notable Reformed thinker to struggle with the new approach...".[100] It is not unusual to read that Brown viewed Schleiermacher with very positive accolades and mentioned him in the introduction to his *Discourses of Our Lord*.[101]

In examining the *Discourses and Sayings of our Lord*, there are a total of twenty-five expositions. However, the twenty-fifth exposition has twenty-two "parts", each of which on average is fifteen pages in length, thus making them separate expositions or lectures in themselves. Also, just because he numbered them Exposition I, Exposition II, etc. does not mean that these expositions each constituted one lecture in the divinity hall. Several of these would likely have been three or four lectures.[102] These published lectures interpreted Scripture by

---

[98] McCoy, "John Brown of Edinburgh", 258. McCoy is quoting from William M. Taylor, *The Scottish Pulpit from the Reformation to the Present Day* (London, 1887), 227.

[99] McCoy, "John Brown of Edinburgh", 259.

[100] Glenn Miller, "Theological Education", in *ERF*, 365.

[101] Brown, introduction to *Discourses and Sayings of Our Lord Jesus Christ*, 1:vi. Brown saw Schleiermacher as opposing the German rationalists and emphasising a personal Saviour – "the soul of revealed religion".

[102] For example, Brown, *Discourses and Sayings of our Lord Jesus Christ*, vol. 1, "Exposition I", goes from pages 1 to 52, yet is subdivided into:
Introduction (1-11)
  I. Of the Messiah (12-15)
    1. The Son of God
    2. The Son of Man
    3. Sent by the Father
  II. Of the Design of the Messiah's Mission (15-18)
    1. Negatively - not to condemn the world
    2. Positively - to save the world
       (i) That the world may not perish
       (ii) That the world may have eternal life
  III. Of the Means by Which the Design of the Messiah's Mission was to be Accomplished.... Figuratively.... Literally (18-22)
  IV. Of the Manner of Obtaining the Blessings Procured by the Messiah:
  Figuratively... Literally... (22-27)

Scripture, thus making reference to other Scripture passages and either citing these passages in the text or as footnotes. The footnotes often refer to authors consulted and quite often include a quotation from them in Latin, English, French, Greek or Hebrew. They are quite extensive and are usually comments directly upon the Greek text, explaining its meaning, its difficulties and how it was treated by the Church Fathers, Reformers, etc. They further show that Brown had a vast acquaintance with the authors in his massive library.[103]

In reading the titles of Brown's expositions, it becomes clear that in his opinion several of these were particularly valuable for students training for the ministry; for example, Exposition XII, "The Church and Its Office-Bearers – True and False" (John 10:1-9), and Exposition VI, "The Christian Ministry; And the Character and Destiny of Its Occupants – Worthy and Unworthy" (Luke 12:35-37, 41-47).[104] Brown's audience of the junior classes of the divinity hall were the recipients of such teaching, which was more than exegesis. It was exhortation, encouragement and a call to self-examination. The strains of his grandfather, John Brown of Haddington, can be detected in the spirit of these expositions. We know that he continued to use his grandfather's "Address to Students of Divinity" in the United Secession and in the United Presbyterian divinity halls and had it reprinted.[105] The hall existed for the formation of men for the ministry who were spiritually right with God and whose characters reflected maturity for office. The study of divinity was not a mere academic or intellectual pursuit. Nonetheless, he attempted to be as precise as possible in his lectures. For example, on that twelfth exposition, "The Church and Its Office-Bearers – True and False", he opened up the lecture with a discussion on the distinction of seeing John 10 as an "allegorical discourse" rather than a parable, with reference to Olshausen's views on this distinction. This type of discussion has a fairly modern ring about it, as is evidenced by similar discussions in Craig L. Blomberg's *Interpreting the Parables*, where a parable's relation to an allegory is discussed.[106]

V. Of the Primary Source of this Economy of Salvation, the Love of God to the World (28-36)
   1. The love of God, the origin of the plan of salvation
   2. The love of God to the world...
VI. Of the Guilt and Danger of those who do not Avail themselves to this Economy of Salvation (37-47)
Notes A, B, C, D, E (47-52)

[103] These statements are based upon a summary analysis of "Exposition I", outlined in footnote 102 above.

[104] Brown, *Discourses and Sayings of our Lord Jesus Christ*, "Exposition XII", 2:90-106; *Discourses and Sayings of our Lord Jesus Christ*, "Exposition VI", 1:387-410.

[105] John Brown (of Broughton Place), *Hints to the students of Divinity: An Address at the opening of the Annual Session of the Theological Seminary of the United Secession Church* (Edinburgh, 1841).

[106] Craig L. Blomberg, *Interpreting the Parables* (Downers Grove, Illinois, 1990), 29.

In reviewing Brown's exegetical lectures in the hall, we find that they really were just that – exegetical expositions. They do not classify either in the older Coccejan or Voetian field or in the more modern field of what may be viewed as biblical theology. This can quickly be seen in the three-hundred authors Brown quoted or referred to, where some of the older covenantal theologians receive only a few references in comparison to those who were more exegetical, like Bengel or Tholuck. The older writers like Witsius, Voetius, Vitringa and Coccejus are not prominent.[107]

It is also interesting to notice that Amyraut only receives two references, yet Brown was supposedly moving in the same theological circle as Amyraut on the atonement of Christ. Ian Hamilton in *The Erosion of Calvinist Orthodoxy* covers the background and development of thinking on the extent of Christ's atonement very well. He deals with Professor John Brown and Professor Robert Balmer at length. That both these professors had moved to adopt an Amyraldian position is a fair conclusion. Since Balmer died before the matter was settled with him (he died in 1844) and Brown's name was cleared by the United Secession Synod from heresy, the matter may have appeared to have ended in 1845. Yet Hamilton rightly shows that Brown and Balmer represented a doctrinal shift within the Secession. Clearly by 1847 this shift was apparent, and the two professors in the hall were at the centre of this development.[108] In 1830 the United Associate Synod had passed an act condemning the doctrine of universal atonement. This was no longer the case by the mid-1840s. Hamilton quotes Balmer in 1842 as stating:

> Twelve years ago, the supreme court of the United Secession passed an act condemning the doctrine of a universal atonement, and forbidding the phrase. But how great the change effected in the last two years... and although the expression (universal atonement) is not yet stamped by the seal of judicial approbation, the chief lets to the use of it are taken out of the way; and already it is sanctioned by such authority as will speedily ensure its all but universal adoption.[109]

Hamilton argues his case well that with both Balmer and Brown (and John McLeod Campbell), the motivation for the change fundamentally came from a pastoral concern "to render the universal offer meaningful... Particular atonement was thought to be an inadequate and even an impossible, basis on which to rest the universal gospel offer."[110] By 1847 Brown's views were

---

[107] Brown, *Discourses and Sayings of our Lord*, "III - Authors Quoted or Referred To", 3:505-507. It is also interesting that in Index 1 – "Principle Matters" discussed in these *Discourses*, the word "covenant" does not appear, even though this was a seven page index of "Principle Matters" discussed, 497-503.

[108] Hamilton, *Erosion of Calvinistic Orthodoxy*, 41-44, 49-51, 57-59, 62-67; also, C. G. McCrie, *Confessions of the Church of Scotland*, 138-145.

[109] Hamilton, *Erosion of Calvinistic Orthodoxy*, 66.

[110] Hamilton, *Erosion of Calvinistic Orthodoxy*, 71.

clearly being tolerated and in some fashion accepted in the synod. Thus it can also be assumed these views were being conveyed to the students in the late 1830s and throughout the 1840s.

Before leaving Brown, mention should be made that upon his death (1858) his former students raised one thousand one hundred pounds to purchase his library, which was described as a "magnificent library". It was then transferred to the divinity hall library of the United Presbyterian Church in Glasgow and in 1900, by the terms of union, was transferred to the Library of Christ's College, Aberdeen.[111]

Brown's library catalogue of 1847 gives us some valuable information, revealing the fact that he was an avid book collector and had tremendous resources to work with for his lectures. The catalogue shows that Brown had fourteen volumes of Amyraut's works, all editions printed between 1631 and 1676, and this included Amyraut's *Defensio doctrinae Calvini de reprobatione* (Salmur, 1641). The library also had thirty-seven volumes of Richard Baxter's works, including a first edition of *Reformed Pastor* (1656). There are dozens of Greek New Testaments in a whole variety of versions and a vast collection of John Owen's writings and several volumes particularly of Morus, Mosheim and Pictet, not to mention Zanchi, Turretin, Ursinus, Venema, Leighton and Rollock. The students generally had access to their professor's library, and there is no evidence to suggest that Professor Brown ended this custom.

After 1820 the divinity libraries of the Burgher and the Antiburgher synods became the sole possession of the United Secession Synod, and hence were joined together as one divinity hall library by 1841, if not before. McKerrow wrote his *History* (second edition) in 1841 and stated that:

> in consequence of arrangements lately made (and now carried into effect) for uniting three libraries into one, the students attending the Divinity Hall of the Secession will henceforward enjoy the benefit of an extensive and valuable library, containing in it a well-assorted collection of books -- ancient and modern -- on all the branches of theology, and also of general literature.[112]

The three libraries were the Burgher Hall Library, the Antiburgher Hall Library and a library called the Robertsonian Library, Glasgow, which the United Synod had purchased for eight hundred pounds. It was the combining of these

---

[111] McCoy, "John Brown of Edinburgh", 274. See Ryken, *Thomas Boston as Preacher of the Fourfold State*, 6-9, for comments on this library, which also includes *MSS* of John Brown (1784-1858) now in the Historic Collections, Special Libraries and Archives, Kings College, Aberdeen, *MS* 3245/11. See also, "Catalogue of the Library of the Rev. John Brown, D.D. March, 1847" [to which is added], "Index of Pamphlets" [indexed into two sections – Nos.1-150; Nos.151-267], *MS* in Historic Collections, Special Libraries and Archives, Kings College, Aberdeen. *MS*, but no identification number.

[112] McKerrow, *History of the Secession Church*, 807.

three libraries into one in the early 1840s which constituted the United Secession Divinity Library. Unfortunately, the only catalogue lists known to exist were recently destroyed, so at present it is difficult to make a full assessment of this United Secession Hall Library of the early 1840s.[113] One conclusion that can be made is that, since the hall alternated between Glasgow and Edinburgh for several years (at least from 1834 to 1843), a library in each city was available until the hall centralized in Edinburgh.[114] The junior classes were permanently situated in Edinburgh upon Professor Mitchell's retirement from office, while the senior classes from 1835 were in Edinburgh. Thus, by the early 1840s two sites for a library were no longer needed in the United Secession Synod.

Robert Balmer: Systematic Theology

The other two professors who were appointed to the United divinity hall in April, 1834, were Robert Balmer and Alexander Duncan. Balmer (1787-1844) served ten years as professor of systematic theology (1834-1844). Like Brown, he was from the Burgher Associate Synod prior to the 1820 union of New Light Seceders and had studied at the University of Edinburgh and at the Burgher hall at Selkirk (first session, 1805) under Professor Lawson.[115] Throughout his ministry he remained at the Associate Church (then the United Associate Church) of Berwick-upon-Tweed from 1812 to 1844. He received the D.D. degree from Glasgow University in 1840. His published works included a controversial preface to the re-publication of Edward Polhill's *Essay on the Extent of the Death of Christ* and posthumously *Academical Lectures and*

---

[113] The catalogues of these three libraries are listed as being in the library of the University of Glasgow but were all badly water damaged and destroyed in the mid-1990s.

    a) *Robertsonian Theological Library: Laws and Catalogue of the Robertsonian Theological Library, Glasgow, instituted in 1814* (Glasgow, 1815) [Call Number: CP1O, 1812-6, TA 0653]

    b) *Library Catalogue of Books Belonging to the Students' Library at Selkirk, Sept., 1817* [Associate Synod Hall] (Edinburgh, 1817) with *MS* additions. [TA 0653]; *Catalogue of books in the Students' Library, Selkirk* [Associate Divinity Hall] (c.1800) with *MS* additions. [TA 0653]

    c) *A Catalogue of Books in the Theological Library Presently in Edinburgh, for the use of students in Divinity and other subscribers, under the inspection of the General Associate Synod* (Edinburgh, 1812) [General Associate Synod Hall] [Call Number: CP1O, 1812-6, TA 0653]; *A Catalogue of the Books Belonging to the Theological Library, established at Alloa, 1777, now in Nicolson St., Edinburgh* (Edinburgh, 1825). [TA 0653]

[114] McCoy, "John Brown of Edinburgh", 217.

[115] *DSCHT*, 54-55; MacKelvie, *Annals and Statistics of the UP Church*, 671.

Pulpit Discourses.[116] Balmer's fame is chiefly connected today with the Atonement Controversy within the United Secession Church (1840-1844). The chief opponent of Balmer and Professor Brown was their fellow United Secession minister Andrew Marshall, Kirkintilloch, who accused Balmer and Brown of being promoters of Amyraldian and Arminian theology.[117]

The best written account of Professor Balmer's systematic theology classes for the senior division of the hall is again found in McKerrow's *History*, where he provides a very detailed account. This account was based in part upon a personal report from Balmer himself to McKerrow.[118] The conduct of the class was virtually identical with that of all the other professors in that it consisted of two meetings each weekday and only one on Saturday. In total these two meetings constituted two to three hours of class time. The first meeting consisted of one student discourse followed by two or three students giving responsive criticisms. The professor would then make concluding observations. At this first meeting Professor Balmer read a lecture of systematic theology. Like Professor Mitchell, Balmer conducted student examinations, usually twice a week. All meetings opened and closed with prayer by the students on a rotational basis. The first and last meeting of each week the professor led in prayer. The Saturday meeting was more devotional in nature and was led either by Professor Balmer or by a student.[119] On Wednesdays Balmer often delivered a "miscellaneous lecture" on a topic or question "not falling naturally under any of the divisions of the foregoing plan".[120] The "plan" was given to each student as they began their senior classes and was a series of lectures as follows:

PART I.

Evidences of Revelation. Preliminary inquiry into the principles of natural religion assumed as the basis of these evidences. Evidences external – internal – miscellaneous. Objections. Inspiration. Other supplementary topics.

PART II.

Doctrines of Revelation, which are either of a miscellaneous character, or which may be regarded as preparatory to the scheme of redemption. The nature and attributes of God. The Trinity. Divinity of Christ. Creation. Providence. Fall of man and its consequences.

---

[116] Edward Polhill, *Essay on the Extent of the Death of Christ* (Berwick, 1842). Polhill was an Amyraldian, and this essay was taken from his 1673 work, *The Divine Will*. See also Robert Balmer, *Academical Lectures and Pulpit Discourses* (Edinburgh, 1845), 2 vols.; MacLeod, *Scottish History*, 249.

[117] *DSCHT*, 55; A.C. Cheyne, *Studies in Scottish Church History* (Edinburgh, 1999), 24; MacLeod, *Scottish History*, 243.

[118] McKerrow, *History of the Secession Church*, 799-806.

[119] McKerrow, *History of the Secession Church*, 799.

[120] McKerrow, *History of the Secession Church*, 801, where McKerrow is quoting from Balmer.

PART III.
Work of the Redeemer. His sacrifice. Other operations necessary to carry the designs of his sacrifice into effect.

PART IV.
Blessings of Redemption. Introductory topics. Work of the Spirit. Faith, &c. 1. Justification. 2. Sanctification. 3. Other blessings conferred in the present life,– at death, – and at the resurrection. Appendix on the final state of those who reject these blessings.

PART V.
Christian Morals. 1. Doctrinal and speculative questions relating to the grounds of moral obligation, the rule of duty, &c. 2. Practical duties. Our duty to God: to our fellow men: to ourselves.[121]

Balmer wrote that he attempted to cover all of these topics in the three sessions, but some were handled only "in a very meagre and perfunctory manner". However, he relied heavily upon examinations for extending knowledge of divinity. For these examinations he used the textbook of his predecessor, John Dick. The students were required to read Dick's *Lectures on Theology* and then were examined upon this textbook (perhaps Balmer did this because of his poor eyesight). Balmer stated that upon occasion he would use additional books such as Jonathan Edward's *Sermon on Justification* "as the groundwork of examination on that doctrine".[122] During the examinations Balmer also told the students about the best books on the particular *loci* or topic under discussion and pointed "out at considerable length their principle excellences and blemishes".[123]

Student numbers in the senior classes for the United Secession divinity hall averaged between seventy and ninety. This meant the professors in the senior classes would hear fifty to sixty student discourses per session. Balmer's discourses consisted of "popular sermons", whereas Professor Duncan's consisted of either lectures or expository discourses. There is no mention in Balmer's personal account that he gave confessional lectures or that the students each presented a confessional discourse. It would appear that this must have been dropped from the student assignments within the hall after its 1834 reorganization. However, the ongoing use of Dick's *Lectures on Theology* did make for a continuity in the teaching of the United Associate divinity hall. It also ensured that one systematic textbook was mastered by the students. Questions may nevertheless be raised as to how Professor Balmer dealt with

---

[121] McKerrow, *History of the Secession Church*, 800.
[122] McKerrow, *History of the Secession Church*, 801.
[123] McKerrow, *History of the Secession Church*, 801.

matters related to the atonement when conducting the examination on Dick, what books he cited as the best on the subject and how he evaluated these for their "excellence and blemishes".

Finally in connection with Professor Balmer, we are informed that he occasionally analysed a chapter either from the Hebrew or the Greek New Testament with the senior class. Also upon occasion he gave a lecture "on the character and duties of the Christian minister".[124] It is presumed that the latter were given at the conclusion of the hall's session, which would have followed the tradition of the conduct of the Secession hall. The former tells us that the professorial titles still allowed for digression into other disciplines or fields. This needs to be borne in view when seeing the switch from a solo professor in the hall to two and then to four.

Alexander Duncan: Pastoral Theology and Ecclesiastical History

The fourth professor appointed by the United Secession Synod in April, 1834, was the Rev. Alexander Duncan (1776-1844). He was the minister at Mid-Calder (Antiburgher) Church, then United Associate, from 1800 until the time of his death.[125] Duncan had attended the Antiburgher divinity hall at Whitburn under Professor Bruce (first session, 1794).[126] Once again, the conducting of Professor Duncan's class was arranged much like that of the other professors. On average there were two class meetings each weekday and the students opened and closed the classes in prayer, except at the beginning and end of the week, when Professor Duncan led in prayer. The morning meeting was a lecture on pastoral theology, with the exception of Monday morning, when there were readings from the Hebrew or Greek Scriptures which related to pastoral duties. Again, at first instance this would not necessarily be implied in reading the title "Professor of Pastoral Theology". The afternoon class was for examinations based upon the professor's morning lectures and the giving of student discourses, all in addition to ecclesiastical history. Thus, it can be concluded that ecclesiastical history received very little attention in the United Secession divinity hall even though there were now four professors.[127] McKerrow then followed with exactly what Duncan covered in Church history:

1.) the professor gave no lectures in a regular fashion;
2.) he selected important subjects in sacred and uninspired history upon which to give lectures;

---

[124] McKerrow, *History of the Secession Church*, 801.
[125] Small, *History of the Congregations of the UP Church*, 1:595-596. Alexander Duncan had six sons, all of whom became United Secession ministers. See *BDEB*, 2:332.
[126] MacKelvie, *Annals and Statistics of the UP Church*, 659.
[127] McKerrow, *History of the Secession Church*, 803.

3.) these were "intermingled with critiques on certain celebrated works in present or past times" (no authors are cited) prepared by the fifth session students, done as essays written during the recess time between sessions in the hall;

4.) the professor gave lectures at the commencement of each session on the following topics: "the utility of church history, – the beauties, the peculiar character, and the use of sacred history, – the importance of the gospels, – the design of the book of Acts, – the heresies of the primitive age, – and the different modes of arrangement adopted".[128]

Duncan's method was perhaps not radically different from the method used in the Kirk or Secession halls prior to Duncan's day. The most orderly treatment of Church history was by John Brown of Haddington based upon Mosheim, but whether he ever fully took the students through it is questionable. Generally Church history was still "sacred and uninspired" and select themes, such as the Church Fathers, heresies, and Acts, were all favourites. Church history was often viewed as something to be studied between sessions and to be dealt with by the presbyteries within the student chronology assignments.

We turn now to Professor Duncan's work in pastoral theology with the senior classes in the hall. This work was divided very concisely into three separate divisions:

1.) "The first division relates to the method of ascertaining the mind of the Spirit, or discovering the truth to be presented and urged by the minister of the gospel in discharging his office." In essence these lectures were on the nature of revelation, the restoration of fallen man, the Saviour, the divine economy among the persons of the Godhead, the covenant between the Father and the Son, etc., the Noahic Covenant, the Sinaitic Covenant, the terms *Berith* and *Diatheke*, the Promise, the Law, the Gospel, etc.[129]

The topics of these lectures consisted of many things which may be termed prolegomena of systematic theology. We also find covenant theology, which one might have thought would be in either systematic theology or biblical theology. Again, the professional title does not necessarily match the actual division of the lectures undertaken.

2.) "The second division gives views of the mode of ministerially exhibiting the mind of the Spirit, or proclaiming and inculcating the truth." This included lectures on exposition (its history, warrants and different forms), the structure and delivery of sermons, kinds of

---

[128] McKerrow, *History of the Secession Church*, 803.

[129] McKerrow, *History of the Secession Church*, 802.

sermons (sentimental, didactic, catechetical, etc.), and the universal call of the Gospel and "its consistency with particular election".[130]

This division dealt with two things – homiletics and the theology of preaching. These lectures introduced the topic of homiletics but clearly dealt with issues which should be viewed as a theology of preaching, for example, the free offer. It is interesting that Professor Michael Willis, the Auld Light professor, then the Free Church professor, also explored matters that were beyond homiletics and really belonged to the theology of preaching (see chapter fourteen).[131]

3.) "The third division embraces other ordinances founded on the system of revealed truth, intended to be also its organs, and subservient to the full accomplishment of its ends." This included lectures on the Sabbath, prayer, liturgy, psalmody, sacraments, polity or church order, rights of church members, ordination, discipline, catechizing, visitation of families, visitation of the sick, casuistry, etc.[132]

This division basically covers matters on worship, church government, pastoral ministry and counsel and is what one would expect of a professor of pastoral theology in a Scottish hall of the Secession tradition in the 1830s and 1840s. Professor Duncan of Mid-Calder published on the Lord's Supper and the subject of its more frequent occurrence. He also published some theological essays on providence, the being of God, the origin of moral evil, plus some sermons. It is doubtful if any of these were for the divinity hall.[133]

Both Professors Mitchell and Duncan were unable to conduct their classes in the United Secession hall in 1842. The result was that synod appointed a committee of four ministers to take charge of Professor Mitchell's classes and also a committee of four to take charge of Professor Duncan's classes. Professors Brown and Balmer continued to conduct their classes as normal for the year 1842. The committee members for Professor Mitchell's classes for 1842 were Dr. Andrew Marshall (Kirkintilloch), Dr. Hugh Heugh (Stirling), the Rev. John Eadie (Glasgow) and a Rev. Robson. The Rev. John Eadie actually "discharged the duties" for the committee, and thus it was not surprising that on May 5, 1843, the synod appointed him as the new professor of biblical literature, officially replacing John Mitchell. The last year for the junior classes to be held in Glasgow was 1842, after which time the junior and senior classes

---

[130] McKerrow, *History of the Secession Church*, 802.
[131] I am not clear as to where Professor Duncan was on the Atonement Controversy within the United Secession Church, yet these lectures would be most informative if they were available.
[132] McKerrow, *History of the Secession Church*, 802-803.
[133] McKerrow, *History of the Secession Church*, 929.

were held in Edinburgh in the final years of the United Secession hall. The synod committee members to oversee Professor Duncan's classes for 1842 were Dr. James Harper (Leith), Dr. Smart, the Rev. James Robertson (Edinburgh) and the Rev. David Duncan (Howgate). The classes in pastoral theology and Church history for the 1842 session were conducted by David Duncan, who "read his father's lectures".[134] In 1843 the synod did not appoint David Duncan to become Professor Duncan's replacement but instead appointed Dr. James Harper of Leith as the new professor of pastoral theology.

In 1843 the United divinity hall again had four official professors: Brown, Balmer, Harper and Eadie. This was the last year in which the United Secession hall had four professors, as Professor Balmer died July 1, 1844, before the 1844 hall session began that August. In 1844, 1845 and 1846 Brown, Harper and Eadie shared the hall classes in Edinburgh, and in 1846 Dr. Harper's title was changed to that of Professor of Systematic Theology rather than Professor of Pastoral Theology and Ecclesiastical History.[135]

Since Professors Harper and Eadie served so briefly with the United Secession hall and most of their major contributions to church life were in the United Presbyterian Church, we have omitted extensive comment here on them.[136]

Summary

In summary, the United Secession, as an enlarged church body, was forced to add to its number of professors in the divinity hall from 1820 to 1847. The process of adding demonstrates the change that the Seceders were making in theological education, namely, specialized professors. Yet as we have seen in the analysis of what the professors actually covered, there were not always the clear divisions that might be expected. The hall averaged one hundred students per session for its whole duration. The professors retained their pastoral charges while being professors for the two month annual hall. Clearly what did emerge, particularly through Professor John Brown, was a new day in exegetical lecture and examination in the Secession hall. The United hall maintained a unity of piety and learning and was closely identified with the Church.

John Dick's *Lectures on Theology* provided a certain continuity throughout the hall's existence. Dick's contributions need to be recognized more than they have been. It is not without coincidence that he received the D.D. degree from Princeton in 1815 after three editions of his *Essay on the Inspiration of the Holy Scriptures* had been released. Princeton's continued writing and teaching

---

[134] MacKelvie, *Annals and Statistics of the UP Church*, 686.
[135] MacKelvie, *Annals and Statistics of the UP Church*, 686-687; *DSCHT*, 282.
[136] See the helpful articles on Eadie and Harper with bibliographical references in *DSCHT*, 270, 393.

on the inspiration of Scripture cannot ignore Dick.[137] Likewise, his systematic theology textbook was extremely influential among Secessionist Presbyterians in the Lower Provinces of British North America; Princeton Seminary, New Jersey; Southern Presbyterians; and very much so amongst the Associate Reformed Seminaries in the United States. This contribution was the influence of a commitment to the federal theology of Westminster. This was Dick's contribution. The Seceders contribution to Princeton's theology was not that of Scottish Common Sense philosophy, as this can be traced through other Scottish writers who were not Seceders but Kirk men or Free Church men. Dick did make a considerable theological contribution in the Secession tradition and beyond.

It must be plainly stated that throughout this period, 1820 to 1846, the hall was only one component of the students' studies. It was a most vital component, and probably the greatest, but the work of the local presbyteries must not be ignored. After all, it was by the presbytery that the student was examined in Latin, Greek, Hebrew, logic, moral philosophy and natural philosophy as verification of his competence to enter the hall.[138] It is apparent that virtually all Seceder students continued to attend the Scottish universities for their literary and philosophical studies. We do read of one instance in the synod minutes of Edinburgh Presbytery granting a student approval for taking his natural philosophy studies through the Royal College of Surgeons. Interestingly, this came to the floor of synod for its judgment. The synod declined to make an immediate ruling, and I was unable to find if they ever did.[139] Between hall sessions the students of divinity delivered at least one discourse annually before their respective presbyteries. In addition, they alternated between an annual examination of a *loci* of theology and bi-annual examinations in Church history, theology and heretical controversies. For example, they might be examined on Deism in year one, Arminianism in year two, Socinianism in year three, and in "practical and experimental religion" in year four (this was the order followed in the United Associate Presbytery of Stirling and Falkirk).

Following his studies in the hall, the student was taken on his trials for licensure to become a probationer. For these trials there would be a series of discourses: a homily, a lecture, an exercise with addition, a thesis or controversy, and a popular sermon. Further examination included a selected Hebrew passage, a Greek text and a portion of Church history. Following this, if successful, he was ready to preach, was licensed, and took up preaching as determined by the Synod's rota and superintendence.[140] Thus, the divinity hall,

---

[137] David Calhoun, *Princeton Seminary*, 2 vols. (Edinburgh, 1994-1996). Dick's name does not appear in either volume.
[138] McKerrow, *History of the Secession Church*, 691-692.
[139] "United Associate Synod Minutes" (April, 1835), 450.
[140] McKerrow, *History of the Secession Church*, 804-805.

the annual superintendence and assignments by the local presbytery, the trials for licensure, and the preaching under the superintendence of the Synod's committee for preachers all need to be seen as a complete system that operated within the United Secession Church for the education and training of students for the ministry from 1820 to 1847.

CHAPTER 14

The Auld Light Divinity Halls

Introduction

Most church historians concur that the divisions within the Scottish Secession from 1799 to the mid-nineteenth century can be rather confusing to follow. In a simplified fashion they are included here as a separate chapter of study to note their contributions to theological education in Scotland amongst the Dissenting Presbyterians. The focus will not be so much to analyze these Auld Light groups, but rather to identify those who were chiefly involved in conducting their divinity halls. Chapter 14 should be read with appendix B, sections B, C, and D as the guide.[1]

The Auld Light Burghers

Introduction

In the late 1780s and 1790s, much attention was given to France by Scottish Presbyterian ministers. Naturally this related to the discussion of the role of the civil government and the church. Specifically in the 1790s the question arose – did the Westminster Confession of Faith espouse Erastianism (many within the two branches of the Secession were beginning to question if a change was needed)? It was the Burghers who first had a division on this issue in 1799, with the majority party adopting a position of forbearance on the matter of the magistrate within the Confession. This majority party were popularly also referred to as New Lights and the minority party, Auld Lights (Old Lights).[2] It

---

[1] There is very little by way of journal material on the Auld Lights. See A. MacWhirter's "The Last Anti-Burghers A Footnote to Secession History", *RSCHS* 8 (1944), 256-259, which includes an overview on the various branches of Auld Lights.

[2] We will adopt the spelling of "Auld Lights" for the majority of references rather than "Auld Lichts". J. M. Barrie in his novels uses "Auld Lichts", the language of the Scots tongue. See J. M. Barrie, *The Little Minister*, original 1891 (Cleveland, 1933). Spelling for the various Secession parties is not consistent. For example, some may use "Antiburgher" while others use "Anti-Burgher". Also, some texts will use "Remanent Auld Burghers" and others "Remnant Auld Light Burghers". Every effort has been made

is incorrect to apply the term "Voluntaryism" to the New Lights at this stage. This thinking would develop more fully by 1847.[3]

The Burgher Synod of 1799 adopted a Preamble to its Formula of Questions for preachers and ministers that "disowned all compulsory measures in religion; and, whilst acknowledging the obligation of the Covenants, giving everyone the fullest liberty to put his own construction upon the nature of such obligation".[4] This Preamble resulted in the withdrawal of the minority party of Auld Light Burghers, which constituted themselves a separate body from the "apostate judicatories" on October 2, 1799.[5] This body was not large in size, as can be seen by the fact that in 1805, when they formed a synod, they numbered only fifteen ministers.

The majority of these Burgher Auld Lights joined the Church of Scotland in 1839; and the Remnant Burghers of this union existed from 1839 to 1842, when they joined with the Original Seceders (Auld Light Antiburghers) to form the United Original Secession Church in 1842. McKerrow gave a highly critical opinion concerning the Auld Light Burghers joining the Church of Scotland. His opinion called into question why they would join a church with Socinian, Pelagian and Arminian heresies tolerated; where patronage still existed; and which virtually practiced no ecclesiastical discipline.[6] Obviously the majority of Auld Light Burghers, or Original Burghers, interpreted the situation within the Church of Scotland very differently.

One of the chief leaders for union amongst the Original Burghers was the Rev. Michael Willis, the professor of divinity for them from 1835 to 1839. In 1839, when the union occurred, the Original Burghers had forty-one ministers on the role of its Scottish Synod, twenty-nine of whom joined the Church of Scotland. The others continued as a Remnant Synod for three years. In Ireland the Original Burghers had five ministers and these dispersed in various ways.[7]

---

to be consistent in this book with the adoption of "Antiburgher" and "Remnant" in spelling. See Alastair Heron, *Kirk by Divine Right* (Edinburgh, 1985), 68-87.

[3] Scott, *Annals and Statistics of the Original Secession Church*, 88. Stewart Gill states that Voluntaryism did not become a major issue in the Secession Churches until 1828 and this in the United Secession Church. Even then the issue was not fully developed, but by 1847 it was. See Stewart D. Gill, *The Reverend William Proudfoot and the United Secession Mission in Canada* (Lewiston, New York, 1991), 196.

[4] Scott, *Annals and Statistics of the Original Secession Church*, 41. See McKerrow, *History of the Secession Church*, 579-597, for a full account of the controversy.

[5] Scott, *Annals and Statistics of the Original Secession Church*, 42. Three ministers formed this new judicatory in 1799.

[6] McKerrow, *History of the Secession Church*, 615-617.

[7] Scott, *Annals and Statistics of the Original Secession Church*, 75-76. The spelling for "Remnant" Synod is not consistent. See footnote 2 above.

The Original Burgher Synod Divinity Hall (1799)

From 1800 to 1839 the Auld Light Burghers had four professors in their divinity hall, each serving in succession. The Rev. William Willis was elected professor of divinity in June, 1800, and he was followed by the Rev. George Hill in 1803. Scott writes in *Annals and Statistics of the Original Secession Church* that:

> no record of the way in which either Mr. Willis or his successor, Mr. Hill, conducted their classes, has been handed down, there can be little doubt that though the Old Light Hall might be smaller than its New Light contemporary (sic), the students that issued from it would be equally well furnished for the work of the ministry.[8]

Thus the information on these halls is very difficult to pull together and all which follows is very general.

The Original Burghers did not provide a salary for their professor of divinity until 1812, and this was not really a salary but viewed as a help for purchasing books. Since Professor Hill lived in Cumbernauld, it was believed this money would aid him in buying books and thus help the students. The synod agreed to pay twenty-five pounds annually to be collected by Mr. Stewart of Pollokshaws by "a scale of rates from the different congregations". It would appear that little of this money was ever collected.[9]

William Willis, first of Greenock, then of Stirling, only conducted the Auld Light Burgher hall for three sessions, 1800, 1801 and 1802, since he resigned in 1803 and was succeeded in that session by George Hill. The 1800 session had five students, three of whom had previously studied with Professor Lawson at Selkirk; in 1801 four students; and in 1802, five or six students in total.

It is believed that the chief systematic theology textbook used by Professors William Willis, George Hill and William Taylor was John Brown of Haddington's *A Compendious View of Natural and Revealed Religion*. There is a strong likelihood that Michael Willis also used Brown's systematic work as the chief textbook, but evidence has not yet been found verifying this.

Professor William Taylor's son gave Scott a brief description of the hall, which is virtually all that is known of the hall of the Auld Light Burghers. It ordinarily sat for eight weeks each autumn, and students were to attend four sessions. Oral examinations continued to be made upon Brown's systematic theology text, and occasional lectures were given by the professor. Student discourses continued to be held as before, one including a "confessional lecture" in which "some portion of the Confession was the subject, and in which it was expected of the lecturer not to give a treatise of his own, but to show how the passages of Scripture adduced support for the proposition the

---

[8] Scott, *Annals and Statistics of the Original Secession Church*, 43.
[9] Scott, *Annals and Statistics of the Original Secession Church*, 49.

compilers had laid down".[10] The study of the subordinate standard of the church thus received focused attention in the hall, as was often the case within the various Secession halls and in certain halls in the Scottish universities.

On Saturdays the Greek New Testament was read and on Monday afternoons the Hebrew Psalter and "observations" were made upon the text. The students were to have studied Hebrew in their arts course in the Scottish universities prior to coming to the divinity hall. Again, it is difficult to verify if this was always the case. On Monday mornings the students delivered their popular sermons without a manuscript before the professor, fellow students and other "general hearers" who were available to attend (presumably members of the professor's congregation). This last point is not unusual, as Brown did the same at Haddington.[11]

The students also had their own Theological and Debating Society, which by this time was common in all the divinity halls. Scott tells us via Taylor that instructions were given in how to prepare sermons and to do pastoral work, and "there was a deep religious feeling, as was becoming a school of the Prophets". Thus we see here the continuing emphasis on the marriage of theology and piety and the office of the minister as the reason the hall existed.[12] Scott made reference also to the motto of the hall at this time as being "*Multum in parvo*". Since hall sessions were so short, the motto certainly was appropriate.[13]

The Auld Light Burghers look back to the period of Professor Brown of Haddington as their "golden era", and not that of George Lawson. Since Brown's systematic theology text was in print, it was easy for them to attempt to perpetuate Brown's approach. Also, the first three Auld Light Burgher professors – William Willis, George Hill and William Taylor – had attended the divinity hall at Haddington under Brown, thus cementing their common vision for the hall; and the fourth professor, Michael Willis, trained under Hill and Taylor, both "Brown men".[14]

The Church of Scotland Act, concerning reunion with the Seceders, included two articles on the terms of union which concerned students and theological education as undertaken by the Auld Light Burghers:

> 6. The licentiates or probationers of the Associate Synod [Auld Light Burghers] shall be received and treated as other probationers within the bounds of the presbytery, on their making application to the presbytery to that effect, and on their subscribing the Westminster Confession of Faith, and Formula of the Church of Scotland, and shall be held equally capable with them of receiving a

---

[10] Scott, *Annals and Statistics of the Original Secession Church*, 604-605.
[11] Scott, *Annals and Statistics of the Original Secession Church*, 604.
[12] Scott, *Annals and Statistics of the Original Secession Church*, 604-605.
[13] Whether it is translated "much in little" or more fully "a great deal in a small time", the point is well taken.
[14] Scott, *Annals and Statistics of the Original Secession Church*, 472, 473, 474, 493.

presentation, or of being elected and called to a vacant congregation within the bounds of this Church.

7. The students of divinity of the Associate Synod at the time of the passing of this Act shall, on producing certificates of their having finished their theological course, under the Professor of the Associate Synod, be taken on trials for license by the presbytery of the bounds. Those of the existing students of said Synod who have commenced, but have not finished their theological studies, shall complete their curriculum with him or in the Divinity Halls of the Scottish Universities; and their sessions of regular attendance on the lectures of the Professor of Theology of the Associate Synod shall be counted as sessions of regular attendance in the Divinity Hall.[15]

Article 7 grants recognition that the Auld Light Burgher hall was very comparable to the halls in the Scottish universities. The methods of teaching and examination were not radically different in each body. The length of the session may have been longer in most of the divinity halls of the Scottish universities, but regular attendance may have been less. Both bodies continued to have extensive presbytery involvement. In essence, there were no radical distinctions. The differences, in all likelihood, centred upon matters of piety and its relation to theology and distinctive Seceder emphasis.

In reviewing the student numbers in the Original Burgher divinity halls, the following is an approximation for select years.[16]

Year	Professor	First Session	Total Number
1800	William Willis	5	5
1802	William Willis	2	5
1804	George Hill	3	6
1812	George Hill	3	8
1817	George Hill	1	12
1820	William Taylor	4	15
1830	William Taylor	2	12
1835	Michael Willis	8	8

The word approximation must be used for total numbers as this assumes a student actually completed all four sessions in the hall. In checking with the student dates of licensure in each case, this gives an accurate point to at least verify that four years had passed from the time of their first session. Thus, the final column is reasonably accurate within one or two students. It should be noted that the synod suspended the divinity hall for the sessions of 1833 and 1834 and placed all responsibility for the students directly with the

---

[15] Scott, *Annals and Statistics of the Original Secession Church*, 70-71. Scott here is quoting directly from Session Eleven, May 25, 1839, Act of the General Assembly of the Church of Scotland, concerning the terms of "Reunion with Seceders".

[16] Scott, *Annals and Statistics of the Original Secession Church*, 478-516.

presbyteries. In 1833 Professor Taylor was seventy-five years old and was unable to carry out all the labours of both a professor and a minister of his charge in Perth.[17]

In previous chapters efforts have been made to note published writings of the divinity hall professors which were first given as lectures in the hall. When this is attempted with the professors of the Original Burgher divinity hall, the results are highly disappointing. The first professor, William Willis, solely published material related to the New Light/Old Light controversy and a collection of sermons in 1822 entitled *A View of Mount Calvary*.[18] It is virtually the same with the second professor, George Hill. The most note-worthy of Hill's published works bears the title *Christian Magistrates Nursing Fathers to the Church*, which was a sermon he preached to the Original Burgher Synod in 1807. His published sermons from 1798, *The Character and Office of the Gospel Ministry*, may possibly have been reworked and used in the hall from 1803 to 1818, but we possess no clear evidence on this point.[19] The third professor, William Taylor, likewise published chiefly on the New Light/Old Light controversy and published various sermons. Taylor's first publication, *Liberty Without Licentiousness* in 1792, was a strong defense of New Light thinking. However, in 1799 he wrote *An Effectual Remedy*, which was a vigorous defense of Old Light principles. He published one work on church polity in 1811, prior to becoming professor of divinity in 1818; and this may have served as the basis for some of the "occasional lectures" in the divinity hall at Perth.[20] Thus we see the writings of these professors were chiefly

---

[17] Scott, *Annals and Statistics of the Original Secession Church*, 514, 474-476; Small, *History of the Congregation of the UP Church*, 1:225-226.

[18] Small, *History of the Congregation of the UP Church*, 2:169-171, 513; Scott, *Annals and Statistics of the Original Secession Church*, 472-473; William Willis, *A Smooth Stone From the Brook or, an Humble Attempt to Prevent Backsliding from the Principles of the Covenanted Church of Scotland, in Some Letters to the Rev. George Lawson* (Glasgow, 1799); *Little Naphthali: or Historical Sketches Concerning the Present Melancholy Apostacy in the Secession with very important expostulations with Apostates* (Glasgow, 1800); *A View of Mount Calvary from the Mount of Transfiguration* (Stirling, 1822); *Ministerial Faithfulness Recommended, Particularly in the Admission of Young Men to the Holy Ministry, in a Sermon preached in the Meeting House in Bristo St., Edinburgh...Together With a Letter, Respecting the Rise, Progress, and Present State of the Mournful Confusion in the Secession...* (Glasgow, 1798).

[19] Small, *History of the Congregation of the UP Church*, 1:671; Scott, *Annals and Statistics of the Original Secession Church*, 473. Scott mentioned George Hill as the author of two other works: *The Character and Office of the Gospel Ministry* (1798) and *Christian Magistrates Nursing Fathers to the Church* (1807). I have been unable to secure either of these two works. Both could provide insight on polity aspects of Hill's professorship. See also George Hill, *The Death of a Faithful Minister in Obedience to the Will of God* (Glasgow, 1811).

[20] Small, *History of the Congregation of the UP Church*, 1:225-226; Scott, *Annals and Statistics of the Original Secession Church*, 474-476. William Taylor, *A Word to the*

absorbed with the New Light/Old Light controversy, and they remain part of that vast sea of pamphlet literature in Scottish Church history of the early nineteenth century. Their writings make no contribution to a fuller understanding of theological education in the Original Burgher hall.

With the fourth professor, Michael Willis, we begin to find some basis for assessing the lectures given in the hall. However, Willis' contribution in Scotland lies not so much with divinity work but in helping to achieve a union with the Church of Scotland, followed by his involvement in the Auld Light Burghers demitting and helping to form the Free Church of Scotland in 1843. Thus Willis' importance in Scotland is more significant in the courts of the church. It was in Toronto where Michael Willis (1799-1879) made a greater contribution to theological education as the first principal of Knox College and as professor of divinity.[21]

Willis began lecturing in divinity at Knox College, Toronto, in 1845 and was made professor in 1847, holding this post until 1870. From 1857 to 1870 he also acted as the principal, making a total of twenty-five years of involvement in theological education in Toronto, versus four or five in Glasgow. It comes as no surprise to learn of Willis' commitment to a theological education based upon "the great prominent revelations of Christianity". He warned his students against the "torrent of wild and licentious criticism, as well as philosophy, which threatened to sap the foundations of Christianity, and even overturn the first principles of all truth".[22] Willis further advocated that ministers must be carefully trained to defend Calvinism and also to possess a careful education in "devout biblical exegesis".[23] Thus it is from materials which Willis gave while at Knox College, Toronto, that we are able to learn more fully how he approached theological education. The writings which were published in Scotland were on polemical issues, either with Roman Catholic emancipation or chiefly on the New Light/Old Light issue; whereas his other published material came from his work in Toronto, and these were

---

Wise, or a Summary Essay in Vindication of the Presbyterian Form of Church Government (1811), may provide further insight into the teaching of polity by Professor Taylor. Taylor's other published work did not have direct bearing on the divinity hall as it likewise was on the New Light-Auld Light controversy. William Taylor, *An Effectual Remedy to the Disputes Presently Existing in the Associate Synod, Respecting the Formula: in a Series of Letters to the Rev. Mr. Lawson* (Glasgow, 1799).

[21] William Gregg, *Short History of the Presbyterian Church in the Dominion of Canada from the Earliest to the Present Time* (Toronto, 1892), 132-135, 160-161; D. C. Masters, *Protestant Church Colleges in Canada: A History* (Toronto, 1966), 45; William Klempa, "History of Presbyterian Theology in Canada to 1875", in *The Burning Bush and a Few Acres of Snow*, ed. William Klempa (Ottawa, 1994), 208-209.

[22] Brian J. Fraser, *Church, College, and Clergy: A History of Theological Education at Knox College, Toronto 1844-1994* (Montreal and Kingston, 1995), 27.

[23] Fraser, *Church, College, and Clergy*, 27.

Collectanea, or Selections from the Greek and Latin Fathers, with Notes and *Pulpit Discourses and College Addresses*.[24]

Willis stressed the proper use of systematic theology as the true handmaid of proper preaching. This was most clearly articulated in his lecture delivered at the close of a session at Knox College, "A Standing Ministry, and the Relation of Systematic Theology to the Work of the Pulpit":

> It is, in our opinion, the *most necessary of all pulpit qualifications*, to be able to assign the proper relation of doctrine to doctrine: no minute knowledge of words will enable, without this, to confute plausible errors.
>
> It is not novices alone who go by the sound rather than the sense of Scripture, while ignoring the logical classification of doctrine.[25]

For Willis, good preaching was doctrinal, with careful exegesis and a practical view "for the strengthening of appeals to the conscience and affections".[26] He believed strongly that preaching had degenerated into a text as "a detached clause" and had become "speculative" and saw as a remedy the promotion of sermons which were based upon a whole verse of Scripture or on various verses – even two to three verses. Likewise, he placed strong emphasis on the conscience and the affections. This was really the old Secession tradition of evangelical theology and piety. In another instance he told the students in Toronto the following:

> My dear friends, we must not rest in simple historical belief, a mental entertainment of the message concerning Christ, though that is very precious and valuable, and nothing good can be got without it. We must not rest in a mere intellectual assent; we must commit our souls to Christ, we must come to Him, we must rest upon Him, we must welcome him to perform in us all that belongs to His office as Saviour, not only as having died for us, but as now teaching by His

---

[24] Scott, *Annals and Statistics of the Original Secession Church*, 494; Michael Willis, *The Religious Question Involved in the Proposed Concessions to Roman Catholics* (Glasgow, 1827); *Discourses on National Establishments of Christianity* (Glasgow, 1833); *National Responsibility and National Covenanting; being the Third Lecture on Church Establishments in Glasgow* (Glasgow, 1835); *Collectanea Graeca et Latina: Selections from the Greek and Latin Fathers with Notes...* (Toronto, 1865); *Pulpit Discourses, Expository and Critical, and College Addresses* (London, 1873). Michael Willis' *Two Brothers: A Biography of John and James More* (1846) cannot be found amongst his works at Knox College, Toronto, nor is it listed in the bibliography by Nicholson in his thesis on Michael Willis.

[25] Michael Willis, "A Standing Ministry, and the Relation of Systematic Theology to the Work of the Pulpit", in *Pulpit Discourses... and College Addresses*, 327.

[26] Willis, *Pulpit Discourses...and College Addresses*, iv-v.

Word and Spirit, that he may reign over us and make us wholly His. That is the faith which gives life.[27]

Piety was never far removed from Willis' student discourses. In addition, the old Marrow theology of the free offer of the gospel was both a prominent note in his lecturing at Knox College and implemented beyond those walls.[28] Willis conducted a mission work in Toronto, where he preached each week; and when the College session was out, he traveled extensively throughout Upper Canada in the backwoods, villages and cities preaching. He recognized the same gospel emphasis in the Evangelical Party of the Church of Scotland and the Free Church as in the Secession. Preaching was to be Christ-centred, "as that around which the whole system of revelation revolves..."[29]; and his theological upbringing and training was maintained in his student work in the Original Burgher hall in Glasgow as well as at Knox College, Toronto. His published closing hall lectures are also in keeping with the traditions in the halls of the Seceders in Scotland. One closing discourse which is different is the one on "New Testament Ethics: Questions Solved", which deals with such matters as slavery, polygamy and violence. It no doubt needs to be read within the context of Willis' active involvement in support of the Buxton Mission in Kent County to the refugee black slaves from the United States. The marks of evangelical theology were a central thrust and must not simply be viewed as social consciousness.[30]

Willis received two honourary degrees, the D.D. from Glasgow University in 1839 and the L.L.D. from Queens' University, Kingston, in 1863.[31] He was a patristics scholar, and his successor at Knox, Principal Caven, wrote that "his knowledge of Patristic Literature far surpassed that of most Presbyterian divines". (As a young man in Scotland he had been encouraged to consider a professorship at St. Andrews University).[32] Of the four Original Burgher professors, Willis was certainly the scholar, and yet he was a Seceder in that evangelical tradition throughout his ministry and conducted his hall in that fashion. The scholarly and the pious were inextricably joined for him.

---

[27] Fraser, *Church, College, and Clergy*, 29, where Fraser is quoting from Richard W. Vaudry, *The Free Church in Victorian Canada, 1844-1861* (Waterloo, 1989) 49.

[28] See Willis, "On the Gospel Call – Its Ground", in *Pulpit Discourses...and College Addresses*, 340-353, which was another of Willis' closing lectures for a session at Knox College.

[29] Willis, "A Standing Ministry, and the Relation of Systematic Theology to the Work of the Pulpit", 335; Scott, *Annals and Statistics of the Original Secession Church*, 495.

[30] Fraser, *Church, College, and Clergy*, 58. Also, David R. Nicholson, "Michael Willis: Missionary Statesman, Social Activist, Christian Educator, and Reformed Theologian" (unpublished Th.M. thesis, Toronto School of Theology, 1973).

[31] Klempa, "History of Presbyterian Theology in Canada to 1875", 208, 209.

[32] Klempa, "History of Presbyterian Theology in Canada to 1875", 209.

In 1839, when the majority of Original Burgher Seceders (Auld Light Burghers) united with the Church of Scotland, the minority portion which did not unite were popularly referred to as the Remnant Synod. Since this remnant was small and lost its professor of divinity, Michael Willis, to the Church of Scotland, this small body appears to have had a crisis in leadership. A new divinity hall was not established by the Remnant Synod, and in 1842 this body united with the Auld Light Antiburghers (the Original Secession Church) to form the United Original Secession Synod.[33]

The Auld Light Antiburghers

Constitutional Associate Divinity Hall (1806)

As with the Burgher Seceders in the late 1790s and early 1800s, the New Light/Old Light controversy emerged in the General Associate Synod. Two divisions occurred amongst the Antiburghers. The first division occurred in 1806 and resulted in the creation of the Constitutional (Antiburgher) Presbytery and the second in 1820 formed the Synod of Protesters (Antiburgher). Both groups were the minority Auld Light Antiburgher factions. The controversy had been festering with the Antiburghers from 1791 and more heatedly from 1796, when a revision of this body's Testimony was presented before the General Associate Synod. This "Narrative and Testimony" was the subject of continual debate from 1796 to 1804. The leading Auld Light party consisted of the Revs. Archibald Bruce, George Whytock, James Aitken, James Hog, Thomas McCrie and Robert Chalmers. The main points of the controversy were virtually identical to the same controversy amongst the Burghers.[34] Scott summarized the differences between the Auld Light and New Light Antiburghers very concisely:

> The chief point of difference betwixt the Old and New Lights, as they were called, related to the connection betwixt Church and State. Whilst the New Lights, or Voluntaries as they have been since designated, denied that civil rulers had anything to do with religion, the Old Lights held that the Church and the State had duties to perform to each other. Civil rulers should recognise the Divine Being as the God of nations, and base their laws upon the decalogue. But whilst the state should thus openly acknowledge the Christian Church, it must on no account interfere in its internal management, since the Lord Jesus is its only King. Respecting Pecuniary Endowments the Old Lights always held it an open question as to whether or not these should be given or received. The Christian people were under solemn obligation to give for the support and spread of the gospel as the Lord had prospered them, and whether or not State funds should also be given for

---

[33] Scott, *Annals and Statistics of the Original Secession Church*, 76, 611.
[34] "Memoir of Rev. James Aitken", in *Sermons by the late Rev. James Aitken* (Edinburgh, 1836), viii-xi; *DSCHT*, 637; McKerrow, *History of the Secession Church*, 430-475.

the support of the Church, was a question, the proper solution of which depended on circumstances. In any case, Old Lights held the Church must not submit to an Erastian yoke. A national recognition and establishment of religion on a scriptural basis they uniformly disinterestedly contended for, as an abstract principle, but the concrete thing as existing in the National Churches of Great Britain and Ireland they repudiated as Erastian, and bringing the Church under subjection to an earthly monarch and government.[35]

The Constitutional Associate Presbytery was constituted on August 28, 1806, and the General Associate Synod proceeded to depose the four ministers who joined to form the new presbytery.

One of the first actions of the Constitutional Associate Presbytery was to appoint the Rev. Archibald Bruce as their professor of divinity, thus the hall continued to meet at Whitburn from 1806 to 1816. The student numbers decreased dramatically, and thus the "Students Barrack" at Whitburn, where the students would lodge during the hall session, was noticeably spacious. There is no need here to review the work of Professor Bruce as this has been done in chapter 12. The fundamental difference from pre-1806 to post-1806 was simply the size of the student body. Beyond this there was no fundamental change as to curriculum, methods of instruction and chief systematic theology texts.

However, the Constitutional Associate Presbytery did undertake one improvement in designating the Rev. John Turnbull of Glasgow to assist with the languages. Turnbull was not a professor of the presbytery, but taught Greek and Hebrew privately in his own classroom on Havannah Street in Glasgow at "three guineas" for the two presbytery students. It appears that Professor Bruce gave his services in gratis, whereas the language teacher, the Rev. Turnbull, charged for his services. It also appears that Turnbull offered his private classes to several University of Glasgow students who found the level of instruction in the university inferior. For example, though several students paid their fees to receive a class ticket for Hebrew, those who wanted to progress went to Turnbull on Havannah Street for instruction; these students included Andrew Dickinson, William Duncan, John "Rabbi" Duncan and William Fleming.[36] Turnbull was the translator of the New Testament into Hebrew for Jewish use and evidently was known for his keen abilities in the Scripture languages. This further reveals that the Constitutionalists made every effort for their small band of divinity students to be well trained and that they were not prepared to lower their standards.

Upon Professor Bruce's death in 1816, the Constitutionalists desired to appoint Thomas McCrie, Sr., as their professor of divinity, but he continually declined. However, McCrie did briefly function as their professor of divinity, yet under protest because he saw his labours in the church as too much to

---

[35] Scott, *Annals and Statistics of the Original Secession Church*, 81.

[36] Scott, *Annals and Statistics of the Original Secession Church*, 93, 536; Small, *History of the Congregation of the UP Church*, 1:406-407.

combine with the professorship.[37] He only served as their professor from 1816 to 1818, after which time the divinity students studied between ministers in the presbytery.

It appears that from 1816 to 1827 (1827 being the year when they united with the Synod of Protesters) the few students which the Constitutionalists had spent some time in Edinburgh with Professor McCrie and then went to Haddington, where the Rev. Robert Chalmers was the Constitutional minister. Students learned how to "command" their discourses, which meant that they were instructed by Chalmers in how to preach without notes and how to properly exercise their voices.[38] In effect, Chalmers served the Constitutional Presbytery as their instructor in homiletics. According to Scott in *Annals of the Original Secession Church*, only three students were trained and licensed by the Constitutional Presbytery after Professor Bruce's death. The other ministers of this presbytery between 1806 and 1827 studied under Professor Bruce of Whitburn or Professor William Moncrieff of Alloa.[39] Thus the chief focus of Professor McCrie's labours among the Constitutional Seceders during this period was not his professorship, and the same can be said for the brief term he taught for the Original Secessionists. McCrie's major influence was through his writings, which clearly commanded attention from several quarters in his generation. He and his son, Thomas McCrie, Jr., were men of note amongst the Auld Light Antiburghers, although it was the son who was more directly involved in the divinity halls than the father.

In briefly reviewing Thomas McCrie Sr.'s life, there are several features that were common to the pattern of many Secession or Kirk ministers of this period. McCrie was born in 1772, and in December, 1788, (age 16) he became a student in the University of Edinburgh and took Latin, Greek, Hebrew, mathematics, logic and moral philosophy for three sessions. In 1791 he became a teacher at a private school in Brechin and taught there for three years. While a teacher he attended the divinity hall at Whitburn during the "harvest months". In 1794 he again returned to the University of Edinburgh and this time took a class ticket in natural philosophy and evidently also had private lessons in elocution. In September, 1795, he was licensed by the General Associates and the next year was ordained to Potterrow Church, Edinburgh.[40] It will be noted

---

[37] *DSCHT*, 506; McKerrow, *History of the Secession Church*, 893.
[38] Scott, *Annals of the Original Secession Church*; Small, *History of the Congregation of the UP Church*, 1:515-516.
[39] Scott, *Annals of the Original Secession Church*, 544. Scott may possibly have missed some students; but in reading his list of ministers in the Constitutional Presbytery, 516-547, I can only find three: John Miller, Thomas McCrie, Jr., and James Beattie. There is a small possibility that Benjamin Laing (543) may have done one session with Thomas McCrie after Professor Bruce's death.
[40] Thomas McCrie, Jr., *Life of Thomas McCrie* (Edinburgh, 1840), 1-24. The article entry in *BDEB*, 2:714, states that McCrie returned to Edinburgh to complete his

that McCrie did not graduate with the M.A. degree from the University of Edinburgh and that while taking his divinity studies, he returned to complete his last arts subject. All of this, coupled with his teaching work, was not in the least unusual in the Secession Churches nor in the Kirk.

McCrie's leadership role in the New Light/Old Light controversy with the Antiburghers has already been stated and does not directly concern our study here.[41] Much of his time beyond his presbytery and pastoral concerns was spent in research and writing. He wrote chiefly on the Reformation and on polemical issues within the Secession churches. A fairly complete list of his published writings is included in the appendix in his biography by his son.[42] There is no systematic theology text, no Church history text, no Bible chronology, no text on casuistry. One must therefore wonder whether any of his writings were used in either the Constitutional Presbytery or the Original Secession divinity halls. The answer is that only a few were used in the halls. In 1833, when Thomas McCrie, Sr., agreed to assist Professor Paxton with the Original Secession divinity hall in Edinburgh, his son stated that "though he delivered no regular course of lectures, but confined himself chiefly to examination and biblical criticism, the preparations for such a task necessarily occupied much of his time".[43] "Examination" probably meant that McCrie examined the students on Marck's *Medulla*, the text Bruce had used and that was still being used by Paxton. The "biblical criticism" was likely a series of three lectures which had originated as essays read to the Society of Edinburgh Ministers, which McCrie had been instrumental in forming in 1814. We have met with such ministerial societies before, namely, that of Stevenson McGill in Glasgow. To this Edinburgh Society McCrie gave a series of lectures on biblical criticism entitled "The Necessity and Advantages of Biblical Interpretation", "The Types of Scripture" and "The Revival of Oriental Literature". The first of these was published and showed his interest in hermeneutics. It was probably also indicative of the assistance he provided to the divinity hall between 1833 to 1835.[44] It would appear that the material from his *Lectures on the Book of Esther* was not used in either the Constitutional Hall or the Original Secession Hall since it was given as lectures in the church in 1825 and "excited general attention, and attracted numbers, of all denominations, to his church".[45] McCrie

---

theological curriculum. He did not; he returned to study natural philosophy in the university. Theology was studied at Whitburn.

[41] MacLeod, *Scottish Theology*, 234-236. MacLeod provided an excellent summary of McCrie's struggles with the matter of the civil magistrate, first setting forth his scruples, then later fully accepting such.

[42] McCrie, Jr., *Life of Thomas McCrie*, 496-497.

[43] McCrie, Jr., *Life of Thomas McCrie*, 384.

[44] McCrie, Jr., *Life of Thomas McCrie*, 291, 497. The essay on "Biblical Interpretation" appeared in *The Presbyterian Review* in 1835.

[45] McCrie, Jr., *Life of Thomas McCrie*, 288-289.

also gave a similar series of lectures on Luke, Kings, Ezra, Nehemiah and Daniel, but all from the pulpit. It is doubtful whether any of these were ever used in either hall.

His major writings were generally biographical studies, with full length ones on John Knox and Andrew Melville; articles on Andrew Rivet, Patrick Hamilton, Francis Lambert and Alexander Henderson; and memoirs of William Veitch and George Brysson.[46] Next to these were his histories of the Reformation in Spain and Italy. We are lacking direct evidence that McCrie lectured on Church history in either hall. He certainly wrote his biographies with a wider than usual historical brush, so the studies would lend themselves to exploring several themes; for example, polity issues with Knox's and Melville's biographies.[47] It was his biography on John Knox which earned him the D.D. from the University of Edinburgh, making McCrie the first Scottish Presbyterian Dissenter to receive such a degree from this university.[48] McCrie was a conscientious Seceder and upheld their evangelical tradition as they understood such, in the manner of what could be called the Marrow tradition. His writings reveal his commitment to this tradition, and we can only assume that he would have influenced his students in this way.[49] Interestingly, Thomas McCrie, Jr., makes no mention of his father's direct involvement with the Constitutional divinity hall and literally relegates his involvement with the Original Secession divinity hall to a footnote. Though it may have deserved more attention than this, the lack of emphasis does appear to be relatively accurate. Therefore, we should not press Thomas McCrie's contribution to these Antiburgher halls too much.

Protesters Divinity Hall (1820)

The Constitutional Associate divinity hall did not educate many ministers, perhaps in part because the presbytery lacked commitment to raising up a professor of divinity. In contrast, it would appear that the Protesters[50] divinity hall under Professor George Paxton was more successful. When the two Auld Light Antiburgher bodies united in 1827, it was Paxton who was unanimously chosen as their professor of divinity, a position he held in the Original Secession divinity hall for nine years. Following his death and the death of his

---

[46] McCrie, Jr., *Life of Thomas McCrie*, 150-151, 497. His biography on Calvin was never completed.

[47] McCrie, Jr., *Life of Thomas McCrie*, 303, 308, 497. McCrie's other noteworthy writing was his critical review of Walter Scott's *Tales of My Landlord* as a "Vindication of the Covenanters" in 1817, 221, 497, which was printed during his professorship with the Constitutional hall. Also, MacLeod, *Scottish Theology*, 256.

[48] *DSCHT*, 506; McKerrow, *History of the Secession Church*, 892.

[49] MacLeod, *Scottish Theology*, 159-161.

[50] In several of the older works, Protesters is spelled "Protestors". For consistency "Protesters" has been adopted here.

assistant, Thomas McCrie, Sr., Thomas McCrie, Jr., was elected to the professorship of divinity in the Original Secession divinity hall from 1836 to 1842, the year of this body's union with the Auld Light Burghers (the Remnant Synod), and was then their Professor from 1842 to 1852. Thus McCrie, Jr., was professor for the Auld Lights for a total of sixteen years.

Original Secession Divinity Hall (1827)/United Original Secession Divinity Hall (1842)

Thomas McCrie, Jr., (1797-1875) began his theological education with Professor Bruce of Whitburn, probably in the 1815 session since he was a student with John (Rabbi) Duncan under Bruce. Following Bruce's death, he continued divinity under his father, Professor McCrie, Edinburgh, and under the Rev. Robert Chalmers, Haddington, who, as has already been noted, was like a tutor of homiletics.[51] In 1836 McCrie, Jr., became the minister of Davie Street Church (Original Secession), Edinburgh, being successor there to his father. On May 13, 1836, he was also made the professor of divinity, combining this with his pastorate.

McCrie's focus in both the Original Secession and the United Original Secession halls was on systematic theology, and from Scott it can be inferred that Marck's *Medulla* continued to be his chief text with the students. Since this was a Latin textbook, it raises the question if the use of Latin prevailed longer in this branch of the Secession than in the main branch, which during this time was the United Secession divinity hall. There is no evidence to show that Professor John Dick or Professor Robert Balmer used Latin textbooks. There is also a possibility that McCrie actually summarized Marck's *Medulla* in English as he kept to the method of Marck, namely, the dialectical approach and the formulation of "accurate distinctions between truth and error".[52] Scott informs us that McCrie did not make any departures in the conduct of the Original or United Original divinity halls and that characteristic of his tenure were lectures which were "highly evangelical, and often accompanied with much unction".[53]

A statistical summary of the numbers of students who attended the Original Secession divinity hall 1827-1836 under Professor Paxton totals thirty-one. Those students who attended the Original Secession and the United Original

---

[51] Scott, *Annals and Statistics of the Original Secession Church*, 544, 542. The article entry on Thomas McCrie, Jr., in *DSCHT*, 507, states that McCrie, Jr., studied in the Original Secession divinity hall, which is inaccurate. He studied at Constitutional Associate divinity hall, Whitburn, with Professor Bruce for one or two sessions. Also, on a personal note, Thomas McCrie, Jr., married a daughter of Rev. Robert Chalmers of Haddington, as did his father Thomas McCrie, Sr., (for his second wife). See Small, *History of the Congregations of the UP Church*, 1:515-516.
[52] Scott, *Annals of the Original Secession Church*, 606-607.
[53] Scott, *Annals of the Original Secession Church*, 606.

divinity halls from 1836 to 1852 under Professor McCrie, Jr., and Professor Laing totals twenty-nine.[54] This makes for a total of twenty-five years and a total of sixty students. If, as a minimum, each student did three sessions in the hall and between two and three students were entering the hall annually, then the number of students attending the hall each year was between seven and eight.[55] This was considerably smaller than in the United Secession (New Light) divinity hall, where the class size was often well over fifty and the total number of students upwards of one hundred.

It is assumed that upon the death of Professor Paxton (who had given his personal library to the hall), the Original Secession divinity hall library was transferred to McCrie, Jr.'s, church (particularly the Session House) on Davie Street or to his home.[56] When the majority portion of the United Original Secession Synod joined the Free Church of Scotland, it is unclear what happened to the divinity hall library. It does not appear to have been a detail mentioned as a term of union. In contrast, it was clearly a term of union that all probationers of the United Original Secession Church were immediately granted status as probationers of the Free Church of Scotland. No questions were raised as to the adequacy of the training of these students, and no further qualifications were placed upon them.[57]

Few details exist concerning Professor McCrie, Jr., and his work in the divinity halls in addition to that stated above. In reviewing his writings for hints as to possible lecture material, we are given little direct evidence of hall lectures. His most famous work was *The Story of the Scottish Church*, a work which began as *Sketches of Scottish Church History* in 1846 and then was reissued and expanded in 1875 under its new title. Though McCrie could have given these as lectures in the halls, we are told that in actuality they were first given as popular lectures to very large audiences in Edinburgh. McCrie wanted Scots, and particularly "the younger members of the Church", to have a deeper interest "in the Church of their fathers". In his preface he set forth some of his historiographic views. For example, he freely told the reader that he was "a Presbyterian of the old school; and he has been at no pains to conceal his sentiments". He also explained, "The author does not attach much value to the high professions of impartiality with which some historians have ushered their productions into the world."[58]

---

[54] This is based upon working through Scott's lists in *Annals of the Original Secession Church*, 562-590, of Original Secession and United Original Secession students and ministers.

[55] These calculations are as accurate as Scott is with his lists. If anything, they may be slightly low.

[56] Scott, *Annals of the Original Secession Church*, 132, 325.

[57] Scott, *Annals of the Original Secession Church*, 220.

[58] Thomas McCrie, Jr., *The Story of the Scottish Church*, original 1875 (Glasgow, 1988), v-vi.

When McCrie went to London in 1856 to the English Presbyterian College, he became the professor of Church history and systematic theology, a post much in keeping with what he had done in the Secession halls of the Original Seceders in Edinburgh. The bulk of his writings were in the field of Church history and included *The Ancient History of the Waldensian Church* and *Annals of English Presbytery*. Next came his writings which were biographical – *Memoirs of Sir Andrew Agnew of Lochnaw*, *Memoir of Rev. J.D. Paxton, of Musselburgh* and *Life of Thomas McCrie*, his father. He also undertook several editing tasks: three volumes for the Wodrow Society, editor for the *British and Foreign Evangelical Review* and editor of the complete works of James Hamilton of London. In addition he translated the *Provincial Letters of Blaise Pascal*. The one work which is more in the field of biblical and systematic theology is his *Lectures on Christian Baptism*.[59]

It would appear that McCrie's gifts, like his father's, lay in the field of Church history. His work does not show the same polemical incisiveness as his father's, and there does not appear to be much original compendium work in systematic theology, as he was content to use the existing compendium.

The second professor in the Original Secession and United Original Secession halls, Professor Benjamin Laing of Colmonell, certainly complemented the curriculum of the halls. It is interesting that, given the relatively small size of these halls, these Original Seceders were willing to expand to two professors. In part it may have been a recognition of McCrie's strengths in certain areas, and it may also have been the unseen pressure to emulate the other Secession divinity halls of the 1830s and 1840s in Scotland, which were increasing the number of professors, particularly in the field of biblical criticism. Benjamin Laing received twelve pounds per year, with which he was to pay for pulpit supply while the hall was in session.[60] It appears that he traveled to Edinburgh and conducted his classes in the Davie Street Church Session House.

Summary

This chapter has attempted to trace the history of theological education and training as practiced by the Auld Light Burghers and Antiburghers. It needs to be acknowledged that numerically they were considerably smaller than the New Light Seceders. Nevertheless, keeping this fact in view, certain parallel practices can be observed and also some unique features noted.

Amongst the Auld Light Burgher professors of divinity (1799-1839), solo professorships combined with a pastorate continued. The hall met in Greenock, Stirling, Cumbernauld, Perth and Glasgow in succession. The only clear evidence of any of the professors leaving printed lecture material was that of

---

[59] Scott, *Annals of the Original Secession Church*, 545.
[60] Scott, *Annals of the Original Secession Church*, 293, 543.

Michael Willis, and that was of a later date. The chief interest of the professor appears to have been that of a defensive polemic for the Auld Light cause. With the Auld Light Antiburghers, the first of these, the Constitutionalists, had two professors who were more widely known, Archibald Bruce and Thomas McCrie, Sr., and this body used additional presbyters to assist their students in specific fields such as biblical languages and homiletics. This was not a move to increase the number of professors, but was more a way of bringing on board tutors to give assistance. Evidence appears to indicate that students, likely only one at a time, may have lived very briefly with the Rev. Robert Chalmers at Haddington for instruction in homiletics. Thus, the sessions in the hall were supplemented by additional tutoring sessions. It also would appear that the Constitutionalists abandoned a hall for a few years and training fell more to a tutorial model. This was likely due to there being so few students. The Auld Light Protestors retained George Paxton as their professor. He then returned to being a professor and a minister of a congregation, a switch from 1806 when he did not pastor a church. When the two Auld Light Antiburgher bodies united in 1827 to form the Original Secession Church, Paxton became this bodies' solo professor of divinity until latterly when he was assisted by Thomas McCrie, Sr. In 1839 the Original Seceders also added a professor of Hebrew and biblical criticism, an interesting move as they had few students in comparison to many of their forefathers who held sole professorships. This addition of a second professor was also a move towards specialization in the Auld Light hall of the late 1830s. In this regard they were moving in a pattern close to that of the United Secessionists (New Lights).

PART THREE

Scottish Patterns and British North America

CHAPTER 15

A Case Study of Theological Education in British North America (1820-1843)

Introduction

This chapter will focus upon the first Presbyterian divinity hall in British North America, the divinity hall of the Presbyterian Church of Nova Scotia, which met in Pictou, then in Halifax between 1820 and 1843. The Presbyterian Church of Nova Scotia was the colonial sister church to the United Secessionists in Scotland and was composed of both Burgher and Antiburgher Secessionists.[1] This hall was conducted from 1820 to 1843 by Professor Thomas McCulloch. By the mid-1840s three other Presbyterian divinity halls had emerged in British North America. The first of these was the divinity hall connected with the new Queen's College in Kingston, Upper Canada. This college opened in 1842 with Principal Liddell and Professor Peter Colin Campbell and was connected with the Church of Scotland. It appears the classes in this divinity hall may not have begun in 1842.[2] The second of these was the divinity hall of the United Secession Church in the Canadas (Missionary Synod), founded in London in 1844.[3] The third such hall was a

---

[1] Both Burgher and Antiburgher Seceders had been ministering in the Lower Provinces of British North America from the late eighteenth century. These two bodies in the New World united in 1817 as a United Secessionist Church and was officially known as the Presbyterian Church of Nova Scotia or sometimes the Presbyterian Church of the Lower Provinces of British North America. Thus, the colonial churches united before the mother churches in Scotland. The colonial church also did not experience a minority group of Auld Lights remaining outside of the union. The colonial situation was thus different from that of Scotland, and these factors explain the colonial results.

[2] John S. Moir, *Enduring Witness: A History of the Presbyterian Church in Canada*, 2d ed. (n.p., 1987), 98; Gregg, *Short History*, 55, 116; *Queen's University Doomsday Book 1831-1924*, a volume of *MSS* relating to the history of Queen's University located in the Douglas Memorial Library, Queen's University, Kingston, Ontario. A matter of interest here is that Peter Colin Campbell became Professor of Greek at King's College, Aberdeen, and in 1855 the principal. *DSCHT*, 130.

[3] Gregg, *Short History*, 70-71. Professor William Proudfoot was the first divinity professor of this hall and had studied in Selkirk with Professor George Lawson. See

direct result of the Disruption in the Church of Scotland and the establishment of the Free Church in 1843. The Free Church hall opened in Toronto in 1844. It was eventually named Knox College.[4] These latter three divinity halls (in Kingston, London and Toronto) would make for an interesting comparative study with those in Scotland in this period. Of particular interest related to the focus of this book on Kirk and Secession halls would be the Kirk hall in Kingston and the second Secession hall in British North America located in London. However, since they are very late in the period covered in this book and also as this is not our primary center of attention, they have been omitted. The selection of the earliest hall by Thomas McCulloch will be sufficient to examine Scottish influence in theological education and training in British North America without taking this book beyond its scope of study. Hence, the Pictou/Halifax hall becomes our singular case study.

This chapter will be divided into two main sections. Section one will commence with a biographical sketch of McCulloch in Scotland. This will be followed by a brief examination of McCulloch's writings, then a concluding look at the operation of the hall, chiefly from student sources. Part two of this chapter will examine the official actions of the Nova Scotian Secession Synod concerning the hall.

Thomas McCulloch: Biographical Sketch, Writings and the Hall

Biographical Sketch

Thomas McCulloch was born in 1776 in Fereneze, Scotland, now part of Barrhead, at that time a distinct area between Neilston and Paisley. His family was connected with the Oakshaw Street (Antiburgher) Church of Paisley. He was a student at the University of Glasgow (1792-1796/7) and, like many, never proceeded to take the M.A. degree. His name first appears as matriculating in Professor Jardine's logic class of 1792, thus making him sixteen when he went to university (assuming this was his first subject).[5]

Stewart D. Gill, *The Reverend William Proudfoot and the United Secession Mission in Canada*, 27, 180.

[4] Gregg, *Short History*, 132-133. The first interim professor of divinity was Andrew King, Glasgow, followed in 1845 by Interim Professor Michael Willis, Glasgow. Church history was first taught by Robert Burns of Paisley. See also Fraser, *Church, College, and Clergy*, 25.

[5] William McCulloch, *Life of Thomas McCulloch, D.D. Pictou*, eds. Isabella and Jean McCulloch ([Truro, Nova Scotia], 1920), 7-8; Marjory Whitelaw, *Thomas McCulloch: His Life and Times* (Halifax, 1985), 4-7; *The Matriculation Albums of the University of Glasgow From 1728 to 1858*, compiler W. Innes Addison (Glasgow, 1913), 167. Matriculation lists prior to 1858 are known to be inaccurate and are really but class lists by subject. Matriculation as we know it did not begin until 1858. In Professor Jardine's 1792 logic class, of twenty-three students, five have been identified as Seceders.

McCulloch's name cannot be found on any class lists at Glasgow for 1793, 1794 or 1795, but this is not conclusive evidence that he was not taking classes. His name is found on a class list for Professor James Jeffrey's 1796 anatomy class.[6] It is assumed that McCulloch took Hebrew at the university because he offered a tutoring class in Hebrew to help support his studies there. Two of his students for Hebrew were Ralph Wardlaw, who became a prominent Congregationalist in Glasgow, and John Waddell, who eventually went to Nova Scotia.[7]

In 1795 McCulloch attended his first session in the divinity hall at Whitburn under Professor Archibald Bruce.[8] It was not unusual for divinity students to return to the Scottish universities between sessions at the Secession divinity halls. McCulloch went back in 1796 to take the anatomy class. Generally speaking, when students went back to the universities, it was to take the natural philosophy class, not anatomy.

Professor Bruce conducted the hall in the harvest season, and it is assumed that McCulloch concluded his fourth session in the divinity hall in 1798, as he was ordained on June 13, 1799, by the Presbytery of Kilmarnock (Antiburgher). He became the minister of the General Associate Church at Stewarton, which was formerly linked with Kilmaurs and had been jointly served by George Paxton.[9] Paxton remained at Kilmaurs, and it was at this time that McCulloch and Paxton established a lasting friendship. Even when Paxton became one of the Protesters at the 1820 Union of New Light Burghers and Antiburghers, McCulloch's esteem for him remained. While in Stewarton McCulloch continued two subjects of study: oriental languages and literature, and British constitutional law and the rights of citizens.[10] It is uncertain whether

---

[6] *Class Catalogue for Anatomy 1790 to 1811*, W. Innes Addison *MS* in the University of Glasgow Archives and *Index to Class Catalogues 1794-1838 University of Glasgow*, in the University of Glasgow Archives.

[7] W. McCulloch, *Life of Thomas McCulloch*, 8; A. E. Betts, *Our Fathers in the Faith: Being an Account of Presbyterian Ministers ordained before 1875 in the Lower Provinces of British North America* (Halifax, 1983), 133. Betts' work is a *Fasti* like volume on the various Presbyterian ministers in the Maritimes up to 1875. There are inaccuracies within it, yet it remains an invaluable resource.

[8] MacKelvie, *Annals and Statistics of the UP Church*, 659.

[9] Small, *History of the Congregations of the UP Church*, 2:312; Betts, *Our Fathers in the Faith*, 65-66; John Ronald, *History of The Cairns United Free Church Stewarton* (Ardrossan, 1926), 9-10.

[10] W. McCulloch, *Life of Thomas McCulloch*, 9. McCulloch appears to have become a master in both of these fields, as can be evidenced in the course of instruction he gave in Pictou Academy, the synod divinity hall and at Dalhousie College. The two texts on law and the rights of men he read were William Blackstone's *Commentaries on the Laws of England* and Charles de Secondat Montesquieu's *Défence de l'esprit des lois*. For helpful editions for today see: William Blackstone, *The Sovereignty of the Law: Selections from Blackstone's Commentaries*, ed. Gareth Jones (London, 1973); Charles

McCulloch taught in the private school which was attached to the Antiburgher Church in Stewarton while he was minister there or if this was staffed by divinity students or others.[11]

In 1803 Thomas McCulloch left Stewarton, accepting the appointment of the General Associate Synod to Prince Edward Island. Arriving late in the year and docking in Pictou, Nova Scotia, McCulloch together with his family was persuaded to remain for the winter in Pictou. The result was that he accepted a call to the vacant Harbour Congregation (Antiburgher) in 1804.[12] While doing catechetical work, he was quickly convinced of the need for a school and proceeded to open one in his home in 1805. Outgrowing this, he built a log schoolhouse on his own property and continued to attract more students, including some from the West Indies. Needing boarding accommodation for some of the students, he added a dormitory wing to his house for sixteen boys. In 1811 he received a government grant for the school, now designated the Pictou Grammar School, of which he was the head teacher. In addition to the school, he continued his ministerial labours at the Harbour Church. McCulloch's long term goal was that the school would raise up men in the Lower Provinces of British North America who would become ministers and thus establish a "native ministry". In order for this to happen, there needed to be a good grammar school, then a college and finally a divinity hall.[13] It was similar to the unified vision on education found in the *First Book of Discipline*.

In 1817 the Pictou Academy (College) opened its doors on the model of the curriculum of the University of Glasgow. A plethora of studies have been done on Thomas McCulloch and the early years of the Pictou Academy, most of which in recent years have come from the pen of Anne Wood.[14] McCulloch's

---

de Secondat Montesquieu, *The Spirit of the Laws*, trans. eds. Anne Cohler, B. C. Miller and H. S. Stone (Cambridge, 1989).

[11] Alastair Barclay, *The Bonnet Town*, (Stewarton, 1989), 16; *Statistical Account of Ayrshire* (Edinburgh, 1842), 739.

[12] W. McCulloch, *Life of Thomas McCulloch*, 18-25.

[13] W. McCulloch, *Life of Thomas McCulloch*, 8, 13-15.

[14] B. Anne Wood, "The Significance of Calvinism in the Educational Vision of Thomas McCulloch", *Vitae Scholasticae* 4 (Spring/Fall, 1985), 15-30; "Thomas McCulloch's Use of Science in Promoting a Liberal Education", *Acadiensis* 17 (Autumn, 1987), 56-73; "Schooling for Presbyterian Leaders: The College Years of Pictou Academy, 1816-1832", in *The Burning Bush and A Few Acres of Snow: The Presbyterian Contribution to Canadian Life and Culture*, ed. William Klempa (Ottawa,1994), 19-37; "Schooling/ Credentials for Professional Advancement: A Case Study of Pictou Presbyterians", in *The Contribution of Presbyterianism to the Maritime Provinces of Canada*, eds. C. H. H. Scobie and G. A. Rawlyk (Montreal/Kingston, 1997), 54-69; *God, Science and Schooling: John William Dawson's Pictou Years, 1820-1855* (Truro, Nova Scotia, 1991); "The Significance of Evangelical Presbyterian Politics in the Construction of State Schooling: A Case Study of the Pictou District, 1817-1866", *Acadiensis* 20 (Spring, 1991), 62-85.

philosophy on a college curriculum can be summarized by quoting from the 1825 *Testimonials* (written to garner support in Scotland for the Pictou Academy):

> The College of Pictou was founded about eight years ago. It is formed upon the model of the Scottish Universities; and like them, is open, in its scientific privileges, to students of all classes in the community, without the interposition of any religious test.[15]

In a letter to Charles Archibald, McCulloch, as the newly appointed President of Dalhousie College, shared with Archibald his curriculum goals: students were to acquire enough language ability (Latin and Greek) to manage "translation specimens" and to have instilled in them the right ideas of the "accuracy of interpretation". If they wanted more than this, they were free to pursue such, but Dalhousie College would not be an Oxford. The college curriculum was also to teach "science and practical intelligence" and in time would require a fourth professor to teach natural history, and specifically geology, mineralogy, zoology and botany.[16] These two, brief selections provide a good summary of McCulloch's vision for a college in British North America and thus uphold the commonly held opinion that McCulloch looked to Glasgow and Edinburgh as his models for emulation.[17] In summary, McCulloch reflected the educational aspirations of the Scottish Enlightenment as accepted by Evangelicals and Moderates at the beginning of the nineteenth century. This is clearly reflected in McCulloch's membership in British learned societies while he lived in Nova Scotia. These societies were The Wernernian Society (of Edinburgh), The Literary and Philosophical Society of Newcastle and The Antiquarian Society of Newcastle.[18] McCulloch's membership, correspondence

---

Other studies include: Stanley E. McMullin, "In Search of the Liberal Mind: Thomas McCulloch and the Impulse to Action", *Journal of Canadian Studies* 23 (1988-89), 68-85; Bruce MacDonald, "Thomas McCulloch: Pioneer Educationalist of Nova Scotia", in *Called to Witness*, ed., W. Stanford Reid (n.p., 1975), 111-127.

[15] "Testimonials in Support of Pictou Academy" (1825), in *The Thomas McCulloch Letters Collection*, Public Archives Nova Scotia (PANS), Halifax, Nova Scotia, *MS* MG1/Vol.551/16.

[16] "Thomas McCulloch to Charles Archibald", dated Pictou, N.S., April 24, 1838, in *Thomas McCulloch Letters Collection*, PANS *MS*, MG1, Vol.553/136.

[17] See also Thomas McCulloch, *The Nature and Uses of a Liberal Education Illustrated, Being a Lecture Delivered at the Opening of the Building, erected for the accommodation of the classes of the Pictou Academical Institution* (Halifax, 1819).

[18] McCulloch's membership in these British societies is listed in Thomas McCulloch, *A Memorial from the Committee of Missions of the Presbyterian Church of Nova Scotia, to the Glasgow Society for Promoting the Religious Interests of the Scottish Settlers in British North America with Observations on the Constitution of that Society, and upon the Proceedings and First Annual Report of the Committee of Directors* (Edinburgh,

and exchanges with these Societies was reflective of a Scottish Enlightened individual.

McCulloch's Writings and the Divinity Hall

We turn now to his writings to follow the chief focus of our study on McCulloch – his role as the synod's professor of divinity. McCulloch held this position for twenty-three years and conducted the divinity hall from 1820 to 1838 in one room of the Pictou Academy in Pictou, Nova Scotia. Upon his move to Halifax to become the first President of Dalhousie College (later University), he conducted the synod's divinity hall in his house on Argyle Street, Halifax. At Dalhousie College McCulloch taught the logic, rhetoric and moral philosophy classes in addition to his presidential duties.[19]

We are fortunate to possess Professor McCulloch's first lecture to the divinity students at the opening of the divinity hall in Pictou in 1820, through which we are able to develop an understanding of McCulloch's vision and conduct for the hall.[20] The lecture should also be viewed as unique since this was the actual opening of the Secession hall in British North America. Taking this into account, the lecture still remains a key source of insight into the hall. Such a lecture as this at the beginning of a session in a divinity hall was commonplace in all of the Scottish Secession halls, as has been cited several times in this book. It was customary with McCulloch's theological professor, Archibald Bruce. This lecture was unique, however, in that McCulloch covered several themes, perhaps because he realized it was a very historic lecture. As would be expected, the lecture combined the marriage of piety with theology, yet it was not excessively pietistic. He reminded the students that the study of divinity was for the purpose of being a minister of the gospel, and, as such, what was preached had to be in harmony with what was studied.[21]

McCulloch began the lecture by recognizing that the men of this first session in the hall had completed their "academical course", were now taking up the "clerical office" and would be taught "under my charge". He then stated that before they began he would "make a few remarks, connected with your choice

---

1826), i; Anon, "Membership List", in *Memoirs of the Wernernian Society* 5 (1823-1824), 583, for McCulloch's membership.

[19] Betts, *Our Fathers in the Faith*, 66; W. McCulloch, *Life of Thomas McCulloch*, 179, 190. He was also very involved with the natural history collection for Dalhousie, 189.

[20] Thomas McCulloch, *Introductory Hints to Theological Students – A Lecture, Delivered at the Opening of the First Theological Class in the Pictou Academical Institution; and Designed to Suggest a Course of Preparation Requisite for the Successful Discharge of Ministerial Duties in the Presbyterian Church of Nova Scotia* (Glasgow, 1821). This lecture was reprinted as Appendix A in W. McCulloch, *Life of Thomas McCulloch*, 197-215. All subsequent references will be to this edition of the lecture.

[21] Appendix A in *Life of Thomas McCulloch*, 215.

of office and your professional studies".[22] McCulloch acknowledged that service in the Presbyterian Church of Nova Scotia presented "few inducements" from a secular perspective, yet he quoted to the students Daniel 12:3 to remind them of the blessings which would flow from their labours. Next he reminded them that they were to be sincere and godly and that "of all the fools who are exalted to honour, there is none more despicable than a pretender to religion…".[23]

That McCulloch was well aware of the historical importance connected to the commencement of the hall is attested throughout the lecture. He reminded them of the reputation of the hall and synod which they bore and that they were but the first fruits "of an abundant harvest", and, as such, they, as the men of the first class, would "give a tone to the character of those who succeed you in education…".[24] Surely this was calculated to make them apply themselves and set a good example. They were exhorted not to "encourage any system of religious opinions which indulges ignorance or inattention to duty; which either permits knowledge to terminate in speculation, or cherishes activity uncombined with intelligence".[25]

He warned the students of becoming diverted from their first labour, "men's souls", by taking up farming or schooling to derive part of their income. McCulloch digressed on this point for several paragraphs in the written text. Basically, he argued that though this may have been necessary in laying the foundations, now that "the same church is founded and enlarged, these are neither consistent with the injunction of Christ, nor with the success of the gospel".[26] Likewise, he stated that it was the responsibility of the Church to provide adequately for her minister, and he made a strong argument of this point to the students.

Following this interlude, McCulloch set forth the value of their philosophical studies "as subservient to theological improvement" and explained that these studies would prove valuable. The students were advised "to review occasionally their former studies; and, to your previous knowledge, to add such acquirements, as may render you esteemed and useful, in the various stations which are within the sphere of your professional choice".[27] McCulloch qualified this in the very next paragraph: "No classical nor scientific acquirements can qualify you to be entrusted with the charge of souls because the principle aim of a Divinity student must be the acquisition of

---

[22] Appendix A in *Life of Thomas McCulloch*, 198.
[23] Appendix A in *Life of Thomas McCulloch*, 199.
[24] Appendix A in *Life of Thomas McCulloch*, 199.
[25] Appendix A in *Life of Thomas McCulloch*, 200.
[26] Appendix A in *Life of Thomas McCulloch*, 200-203.
[27] Appendix A in *Life of Thomas McCulloch*, 204. This point is not far removed from the advice offered by John Stott in his chapter "The Call to Study", in *Between Two Worlds: The Art of Preaching in the Twentieth Century* (Grand Rapids, 1982), 190-210.

religious knowledge."[28] Therefore the students were charged to attend to their divinity studies "as a scientific pursuit" in this regard and thus make the object of their studies the mastery of a system of truth.

McCulloch had very definite views about the indispensable place of systematic theology in a divinity hall. He stated that a minister who cannot see the systematic arrangements is ill qualified to serve in the Church. Connected to this was his belief that "public instructors in the church ought to possess a uniformity of religious views". Error, he said, will not produce the same ends that truth does. Furthermore, in the hall the constitution of the Church was to be taught; that is, "its system of religious principles". McCulloch did not name it, but he was referring to the Westminster Confession of Faith. As in the Church, the school of Christ, so in the hall, the students must study the Bible, and he exhorted them to make this "the subject of [their] rigorous investigation".[29] He reminded them that in the pursuit of truth there is only one "source", the Bible, and so this must be studied with great care and interest.

McCulloch moved from the Confession's system to give advice on how the students were to study the Scriptures. For seven pages of the written text he set before the students several hermeneutical principles; then exhorted them to the right use of the languages in translation work; and finally warned them not to neglect books which dealt with topography, chronology of nations, political systems of the ancient nations, religious life, and customs and habits. (The last point sounds very close to McCulloch's old friend George Paxton's work, *Illustrations of the Holy Scriptures*.) He also told them that commentaries on Scripture would be invaluable and would allow the student to "enjoy the conversation of both the dead and the living". Systematic theology texts, he explained, are invaluable to scriptural study if they prove their system from the Scripture.[30]

In continuing to survey other components of the divinity curriculum in this opening lecture, he then proceeded to briefly (one paragraph of written text) make some comments on "ecclesiastical history". He mentioned its connection to "Christian belief" (historical theology) and "deportment" (practice) and explained that the Scriptures contain the authentic history of the Church, thus providing the student with much Church history. "(F)or a knowledge of succeeding ages, you must apply to the works of the ecclesiastical historian".[31] McCulloch unfortunately did not mention in this introductory lecture which Church history texts he would have the students read, nor did he state such under systematic theology. The only mention of a specific text outside the Scripture was the Constitution of the Church (The Confession) in the field of symbolic theology.

---

[28] Appendix A in *Life of Thomas McCulloch*, 204-205.
[29] Appendix A in *Life of Thomas McCulloch*, 206.
[30] Appendix A in *Life of Thomas McCulloch*, 206-212.
[31] Appendix A in *Life of Thomas McCulloch*, 213.

The final comments concerned what can be referred to as practical theology. Here he gave advice on pulpit eloquence and church polity. He was of the opinion that little regard was given to "communicating". One way to improve, he believed, was for students to be more exacting in composing their sermons with "careful analysis" and to combine this with the study of published sermons for their analysis, doctrine and application ("its practical bearings").[32] McCulloch warned the students to give attention to style and manner in sermons for "the person best qualified to command the attention of an audience, is most likely to promote their improvement. Like the skilful preparer of food, he creates a relish for what he has provided." McCulloch then added this caveat:

> The spirit of God only, it is true, can communicate efficiency to the word of his grace. But the Holy Spirit operates upon the rational mind, by means agreeable to its nature; and, therefore, in religion a pleasing mode of address may be as useful, as in the ordinary intercourse of life.[33]

Concerning polity, McCulloch told the students this was such an important subject that he would "reserve it for the subject of a separate discussion".[34] Here he expressed his concern about ministers and students who applied themselves to sermons, yet could not direct the government of the church. Until this additional lecture on polity was given, McCulloch directed the students to study Paul's "delineations of a Christian bishop" and to "acquire those habits which may qualify you to succeed him in the government of the church".[35]

In conclusion, the lecture reflects a continuity with Scottish patterns in theological education within the Secession. Men entering the hall would have the proper educational background from a university. McCulloch's statements here reflect the ideal of a Scottish Enlightenment university, where the classes encompassed far more than the classics. He recognized that the study of divinity must include the marriage of piety and theology and a commitment to the authority of the Scriptures. McCulloch envisioned the inclusion of confessional or symbolic studies, systematic theology, the proper interpretation of Scripture, and Bible background as all constituting the curriculum to be taught in the divinity hall. Ecclesiastical history, homiletics and polity were "add-ons", much of which he believed could be given to the student more as directed reading. Here McCulloch assumed the presbyteries would take care of ecclesiastical history through assigned chronologies. McCulloch did mention that he would give a lecture on polity. In homiletics it appears that McCulloch

---

[32] Appendix A in *Life of Thomas McCulloch*, 213.
[33] Appendix A in *Life of Thomas McCulloch*, 214.
[34] Appendix A in *Life of Thomas McCulloch*, 214-215.
[35] Appendix A in *Life of Thomas McCulloch*, 215.

assumed that their college courses in rhetoric and logic would have afforded them sufficient background for taking up further sermon analysis.

In reviewing McCulloch's other published writings or *MSS* which were never published, many do not have direct bearing upon his work in the divinity hall. Nevertheless, they do reveal much concerning McCulloch's interests and abilities and the controversies with which he was involved. His two volumes of *Popery Condemned by Scripture and the Fathers* reveal McCulloch to have been a diligent student of Patristic literature.[36] The parallels here are quite striking with McCulloch's own divinity professor, Archibald Bruce, who had acquired an amazing knowledge of Roman Catholic history and the Patristic period. However, these two volumes by McCulloch did not originate as lectures in the divinity hall, and there is no direct evidence showing that McCulloch used these in his lectures. It is possible that students were referred to them in preparing for their ecclesiastical history chronologies. That these two volumes brought a certain fame to McCulloch's name can be seen in the way which William McGavin of Glasgow used them in his serial *The Protestant*.[37] McGavin, in writing to McCulloch after receiving a copy of *Popery Condemned* from the Rev. John Mitchell, wrote:

> I have been very amuzed by it, and have received no small instruction and information upon various points of the popish controversy. It is a subject upon which I would not have thought of reading, had the book not come from a friend,,, My wonder was excited by the great mass of information you had collected from the writings of the ancients, and could not help admiring the patience that carried you through so many ponderous volumes which you must have consulted...[38]

The next major category of McCulloch's writings is of a literary nature. Again, these do not come from lectures in the divinity hall, but rather show McCulloch's range of interest and writing abilities. The most famous of these is his *Stepsure Letters*. This was written as a satire on the political and moral life

---

[36] Thomas McCulloch, *Popery Condemned by Scripture and the Fathers: Being a Refutation of the Principle Popish Doctrines and Assertions maintained in the Remarks on the Rev. Mr. Stanser's Examination of the Rev. Mr. Burke's Letter of Instruction to the Catholic Missionaries of Nova Scotia, and in the Reply to the Rev. Mr. Cochran's Fifth and Last Letter to Mr. Burke, etc.* (Edinburgh, 1808); *Popery Again Condemned by Scripture and the Fathers, Being a Reply to a Part of the Popish Doctrines and Assertions contained in the Remarks on the Refutation, and in the Review of Dr. Cochran's Letters, by the Rev. Edmund Burke* (Edinburgh, 1810).

[37] *DSCHT*, 514. Here the entry article, "McGavin", correctly identifies McCulloch's influence upon William McGavin.

[38] W. McGavin to T. McCulloch, 7 March, 1808, in *Posthumous Works of the Late William McGavin Accompanied with a Memoir; Including Autobiography Extracts from his Correspondence* (Glasgow, 1834), 1:lxxii, lxxiv. And further see W. McGavin to T. McCulloch, 29 March, 1819, in *Posthumous Works*, 1:cccxiii.

of Nova Scotia and is set in the early nineteenth century.[39] Next in distinction would be his *Colonial Gleanings. William, and Melville.* This work is an exploration of the dangers of colonial life to the soul.[40] A significant corpus of McCulloch's literary writings were never published. They have different names — "Tales of the Covenanters" or "Auld Eppie's Tales" – and were written to counter Walter Scott's *The Tale of Old Mortality*. McCulloch wrote his "Tales" with the following purpose:

> I never intended to be an imitator of Sir Walter. I have neither his knowledge nor talents. But on the other hand I conceived that the kind of information and humour which I possess would have enabled me to vindicate where he has misrepresented, and to render contemptible and ludicrous what he has laboured to dignify.[41]

We turn now to McCulloch's other writings, some of which were used in the divinity hall. These works are doctrinal, the most significant being his *Calvinism: The Doctrine of the Scriptures*. It was published posthumously in Glasgow in 1846.[42] From George Patterson, one of McCulloch's students in the divinity hall which met on Argyle Street, Halifax, we learn that "the chief importance was attached to the study of Theology. Orthodoxy was then considered a *sine qua non* in any person looking forward to the Presbyterian ministry. He [Thomas McCulloch] had by this time his lectures on the Calvinistic system written out...."[43] Patterson was in McCulloch's last divinity class (1842 or 1843), and McCulloch's lectures on Calvinism were published shortly after his death. Patterson informed us that this published volume on *Calvinism* was comprised of lectures from the divinity hall. Anne Wood referred to these lectures as "sermons" by McCulloch, but all evidence points to

---

[39] The best edition of this work is the 1990 edited version by Gwendolyn Davies. See Thomas McCulloch, *The Mephibosheth Stepsure Letters*, ed. Gwendolyn Davies (Ottawa, 1990). Many see McCulloch's chief contribution more as "the founder of genuine Canadian humour" than anything else. See Northrop Frye, introduction to *The Stepsure Letters*, by Thomas McCulloch (Toronto, 1960), ix.

[40] Thomas McCulloch, *Colonial Gleanings. William, and Melville* (Edinburgh, 1826).

[41] W. McCulloch, *Life of Thomas McCulloch*, 142. It was Blackwoods, the publisher in Edinburgh, who rejected the *MS* of "Tales". To date I have not found any letters which were exchanged between Thomas McCrie, Sr., and Thomas McCulloch. Thomas McCulloch's biographer only tells us that "friends" encouraged him to write a Covenanter Tale to counter Scott. Unfortunately the biographer does not identify these friends. I assume them to be William McGavin and John Mitchell, but beyond this it is uncertain.

[42] Thomas McCulloch, *Calvinism, The Doctrine of the Scriptures* (Glasgow,[1846]).

[43] George Patterson, "The First Theological Hall in the British Colonies", *The Theologue*, Vol. 3, No. 2 (1892), 38-39. *The Theologue* has been deposited into the Maritime Conference Archives, Sackville, New Brunswick, under "Pine Hill Divinity Hall Collection", Box PHDH-36.

the divinity hall as the venue, not a Sabbath pulpit.[44] This work was subtitled "A Scriptural Account of the Ruin and Recovery of Fallen Man, and a Review of the Principal Objections Which Have Been Advanced Against the Calvinistic System". McCulloch made references to six authors and their works in these lectures:

> John Taylor, *The Scripture Doctrine of Original Sin* (1767),
> Daniel Whitby, *A Discourse Concerning Election and Reprobation* (original, McCulloch uses the 1816 edition),
> George Hill, *Lectures in Divinity* (1825 edition),
> William Magee, *Discourses and Dissertations on the Scriptural Doctrine of Atonement* (1809),
> Jonathan Edwards, *Works* (1817 edition), and
> Benedict Pictet, *Theologie Chretienne* (Genevan edition of 1721).

Pictet was a theologian beloved of Professor Archibald Bruce, but Marck is not in the list of works referred to in these lectures. Hill, though generally classified in the Moderate camp politically, yet Calvinistic in divinity, was widely used by a range of ministers. McCulloch used his lectures to refute and attack the Arminian and Pelagian theology of Taylor and Whitby. Jonathan Edwards had also attacked Taylor. This explains McCulloch's use of Jonathan Edwards' *Works*, since he could see how Edwards defended historic Calvinism.[45] It is not surprising to learn that McCulloch did not deviate from historic orthodox Calvinism.

The other doctrinal writings of McCulloch were on the Holy Spirit, the person of Christ, baptism and the eldership. The first two of these were never published. Again, although it is difficult to determine if his "Dissertation upon the work of the Holy Spirit" and "A Scriptural view of the person and doctrine of Christ" were ever given as lectures in the divinity hall, it is fairly certain that this was the origin of both these studies.[46] Professor John Mitchell wrote to

---

[44] Wood, "The Significance of Calvinism in the Educational Vision of Thomas McCulloch", *Vitae Scholasticae* 4 (Spring/Fall, 1985), 15-30.

[45] For a helpful summary of McCulloch's *Calvinism*, see William Klempa, "History of Presbyterian Theology in Canada to 1875", in *The Burning Bush and A Few Acres of Snow: The Presbyterian Contribution to Canadian Life and Culture*, ed. William Klempa (Ottawa,1994), 201-204. The work of Edwards in which McCulloch was interested was his, *The Great Christian Doctrine of Original Sin Defended; Evidences of its Truth Produced, and Arguments to the Contrary Answered* (1757, 1767, 1819). William Magee's work was also important since it was a refutation of Deism and Rationalism. Magee argues against Thomas Belsham's Unitarianism and the attacks which had been waged against William Wilberforce. See William Magee, *Discourses and Dissertations on the Scriptural Doctrines of Atonement and Sacrifice*, original 1809 (London, 1859), 5.

[46] W. McCulloch, *Life of Thomas McCulloch*, 142-143, 185.

Thomas McCulloch in June, 1843, concerning the *MS* entitled, "A Scriptural view of the person and doctrine of Christ":

> I had it read to me with much care, and cannot but say that the argument for the divinity of Christ, though on a topic which has been frequently handled, seems to me to be discussed in a manner so admirably ingenious and conclusive, that I do not remember to have read any treatise so new, as well as so entirely satisfactory, and I should be extremely sorry, especially in these times of rampant error and infidelity, if the public and Christian religion were deprived of the benefits of it by your declining to publish. Print it, I beseech you.[47]

Four months later McCulloch was dead and this *MS* was never published.

McCulloch represented the conservative side of the Seceders in the 1840s, as is evidenced in a letter he sent to James Mitchell, son of Professor Mitchell, in 1841. It confirms the kind of theology which McCulloch inculcated in the divinity hall in Pictou and Halifax.

> I fear that there is something wrong with the Secession... In my early days had a student in the Secession published against the principles of the church it is not likely that he would have ever published his vagaries from a Secession pulpit. I however rejoice that in the Secession the gospel has still its strenuous defenders. There is need for them I strongly suspect that the doctrine of universal redemption and its concomitant principles lerk extensively where your father and others have no suspicion of its existence. The Secession by its union has added nothing to its orthodoxy.[48]

The Hall

The divinity hall at Pictou began with twelve students in November, 1820, in an upper room of the Pictou Academy. Of these twelve students, six were eventually ordained by the Secession Presbyterians.[49] Like the Secession halls in Scotland, the duration of the whole course was to be covered in four sessions/years. It appears that during the 1820s the hall met on Saturdays, either once a month or twice a month "during the whole four years".[50] All of the students taught school, and the above pattern allowed them to remain in this occupation. We can speculate as to why McCulloch departed from this Scottish practice and did not have them gather for a few weeks in August/September each year. One factor was probably the harvest. Perhaps there were other factors.

---

[47] W. McCulloch, *Life of Thomas McCulloch*, 185-186.

[48] "Thomas McCulloch to James Mitchell, Halifax, N.S., Dec. 2, 1841", in *PANS*, McCulloch Letters File, MG1, Vol.553/122.

[49] Betts, *Pine Hill Divinity Hall*, 10-11.

[50] G. Patterson, "The First Theological Hall in the British Colonies", *The Theologue*, Vol. 3, No. 1(1891), 3.

One of the first students, the Rev. Robert S. Patterson,[51] left a brief description of the conduct of the classes by Professor McCulloch. It reads very similar to various accounts of Scottish Secession halls.

> The most that we received in the way of lectures was remarks on the Confession of Faith. For our knowledge of Divinity, we had to depend in a good measure upon our reading. When we met in the Hall, we delivered discourses on subjects prescribed to us by the Professor. These were criticised by him, and his criticisms were particularly valuable. Although we were obliged to write all our discourses, we were not permitted to read them. The Professor took from us the manuscript, and if we failed to remember it, he told us. This was a kindness to us, as we did not think of reading, when we entered upon the work of preaching. I have never yet read a sermon during my life, either in the Hall or since I left it.[52]

Patterson's comments accord with much in the Scottish Secession halls in that student discourses were the common form of student assignment, followed by critical remarks. Whether or not this ever involved students also giving critical remarks should not be pressed too hard from Robert Patterson's quotation. Also, clearly the Confession lay at the heart of the curriculum, which parallels with what McCulloch stated in his opening lecture to the hall. However, it is difficult to evaluate Patterson's comment on the teaching of divinity (systematic theology). What does "we had to depend in a good measure upon our reading" mean? Did McCulloch never give theology lectures? Evidence shows that he gave some, but we are unclear as to the chief textbook he assigned for readings. Patterson made no mention of exegetical work or of church history, homiletics or polity.

This Patterson went to Scotland in 1824 and was one of three Pictou Academy graduates to be examined by professors at Glasgow University and granted the M.A. degree without further requirement. He was ordained to the Bedeque Church, Prince Edward Island, in 1826 and remained there as minister until 1882.[53] The two other divinity hall students who went to Glasgow for examination were John Murdoch and John McLean. These three men were examined in the Blackstone tradition by Professors Sanford, Jardine, Mylne,

---

[51] In the first class of students in the hall in 1820 were: Angus McGillivray, Michael McCulloch, James McGregor, Duncan MacDonald, John MacDonald, Hugh Ross, Hugh Dunbar, David Fraser, John L. Murdoch, John McLean, Robert S. Patterson and Archibald Patterson. See George Patterson, "The First Theological Hall in the British Colonies", *The Theologue*, Vol. 3, No. 1 (1891), 5-6. The first licentiate died three months after licensure, and Archibald Patterson died in Paisley, Scotland, in 1821. Of the original twelve students, six became ministers in the Lower Provinces, with seven becoming licentiates, but one never receiving a call and eventually taking up farming.

[52] Betts, *Pine Hill Divinity Hall*, 10. Betts is quoting here from George Patterson's "The First Theological Hall in the British Colonies", *The Theologue*, Vol. 3, No. 1 (1891), 5. George Patterson interviewed Robert Patterson shortly before Robert Patterson's death.

[53] Betts, *Our Fathers Faith*, 106-107.

Meikleham, Millard and Walker (or Davidson) in Latin, Greek, logic, moral philosophy, natural philosophy and mathematics.[54] Murdoch was ordained for Windsor, Nova Scotia, and John McLean for Richibucto, New Brunswick. The other three who were ordained from the first class were Hugh Ross to Tatamagouche, Nova Scotia; Hugh Dunbar to Cavendish and New London, Prince Edward Island; and Angus McGillivray to East River, Nova Scotia.[55]

Another Patterson student, George Patterson, attended the hall when it was in Halifax. He stated that Robert Patterson was not very accurate in his comments on the conduct of the hall as it met "once a fortnight, or perhaps sometimes weekly", and Hebrew readings were also done in the hall.[56] This is still difficult to reconcile with the synod directive of 1833, which stated that the sessions in the divinity hall were to be at least four weeks in duration and were to commence the first Wednesday in November.

Originally Dr. McCulloch taught the Hebrew grammar class in the Pictou Academy and the Hebrew translation or exegesis classes in the divinity hall. E. Arthur Betts tentatively postulated that in later years in the Pictou Academy Dr. McCulloch gave the Hebrew grammar class over to his son, Michael, who had completed the academy course. Thus, Dr. McCulloch only retained the divinity

---

[54] G. Patterson, "The First Theological Hall in the British Colonies", *The Theologue*, Vol. 3, No. 2 (1892), 34-35.

[55] Biographical information for the first six men to be ordained who attended the divinity hall in Pictou can be found in the following:

(1) John McLean: A. Blaikie, "Memoir of the Late Rev. J. McLean of Richibucto" I, *Christian Instructor*, Vol. 2, No. 1 (Jan., 1857), 6-13; "Memoir of the Late Rev. J. McLean of Richibucto" II, *Christian Instructor*, Vol. 2, No. 2 (Feb., 1857), 52-59. McLean was likened to be Nova Scotia's Robert Murray McCheyne in piety. He was noted for his enthusiastic distribution of tracts and Brown's Catechism.

(2) John L. Murdoch: Anon., "Obituary – Rev. John L. Murdoch", *The Home and Foreign Record of the Presbyterian Church of the Lower Provinces of British North America*, Vol. 13, No. 9 (1873), 262-265. Comments about Murdoch's time in the hall are found on page 263. His "special licensing" as a Gaelic student was mentioned here and that he was designated as one of "the pioneer native preachers of British America".

(3) Robert Patterson: J.P. MacPhie, *Pictonians at Home and Abroad* (Boston, 1914), 43-45, 62.

(4) Angus McGillivray: Anon., "In Memoriam – Rev. Angus McGillvray", *The Home and Foreign Record of the Presbyterian Church of the Lower Provinces of British North America*, Vol. 9, No. 9 (1869), 234-237.

(5) Hugh Ross: Anon., "Obituary – Hugh Ross", *Christian Instructor*, Vol. 4, No. 1 (Jan., 1859), 30-32.

(6) Hugh Dunbar: Anon., "Obituary – Hugh Dunbar", *Christian Instructor*, Vol. 3, No. 1 (Jan. 1858), 32.

[56] George Patterson, "The First Theological Hall in the British Colonies", *The Theologue*, Vol. 3, No. 1 (1891), 5.

hall Hebrew reading classes and not the grammar portion.[57] Betts' conclusion here is congruent with the development of studies and teaching which was emerging in the academy after its commencement. Likewise, at Dalhousie College, where McCulloch had others to assist him in the teaching, McCulloch was not teaching the entire curriculum. There is conclusive evidence that Michael McCulloch taught Hebrew in Pictou Academy after 1824 to those students who were "looking forward to the ministry". Thus the same model was followed here as in Scotland – students were to have taken Hebrew studies prior to entering the divinity hall, where Hebrew readings would then be undertaken.[58] However, after 1837 Dr. Thomas McCulloch returned to the teaching of all Hebrew grammar lessons and readings in the hall. His Hebrew classes in the divinity hall in Halifax, which met at his house, were not limited to Presbyterians. Charles DeWolfe, a Methodist, also joined McCulloch's Hebrew class. DeWolfe went on to become the professor of theology in Sackville, New Brunswick, at Mount Allison College (University).[59] Another of these students, Alexander McKenzie, went on to teach Hebrew at the divinity hall for the United Presbyterians in London, Upper Canada, 1847 to 1850.

We may glean further details from George Patterson as a student of the hall in Halifax.[60] He stated that there were two classes, one in Hebrew and one in theology. It must be remembered that Patterson attended only one session in the divinity hall with Professor McCulloch, so his comment of "two classes" does not take in view the rotation of subjects possibly covered over four years. Patterson wrote that McCulloch delivered lectures on "the Calvinistic system" and the students were then examined on these lectures. This was standard with all the Scottish halls, both Secession and Kirk. Next, Patterson recorded that the students delivered their discourses *"memoriter"* and "plans of sermons" (skeletons of sermons). The discourses were mainly doctrinal, but sometimes they were also assigned discourses showing the connection of the doctrine with

---

[57] Betts, *Pine Hill Divinity Hall*, 11. Michael McCulloch became professor of classics and mathematics in the Pictou Academy at the conclusion of his studies in the divinity hall, 1824. See G. Patterson, "The First Theological Hall in the British Colonies", *The Theologue*, Vol. 3, No. 1(1891), 7.

[58] G. Patterson, "The First Theological Hall in the British Colonies", *The Theologue*, Vol. 3, No. 2(1892), 36-37.

[59] G. Patterson, "The First Theological Hall in the British Colonies", *The Theologue*, Vol. 3, No. 2(1892), 38; John G. Reid, *Mount Allison University: A History, to 1963* (Toronto, 1984), 1:80, 87-88, 98, 101.

[60] Betts, *Our Fathers Faith*, 106. George Patterson (1824-1897) was ordained in 1849 in Green Hill, Pictou County, and was the author of several books which were historical or doctrinal. See George Patterson, *A History of the County of Pictou, N.S.* (Montreal, 1877); *The Doctrine of the Trinity: Underlying the Revelation of Redemption* (Edinburgh, 1870); *Missionary Life Among the Cannibals: being the life of the Rev. John Geddie, D.D., first missionary to the New Hebrides, with a history of the Nova Scotia Presbyterian Mission on that group* (Toronto, 1882).

the duty. This would have been like an exercise on a text (the doctrine) with the addition attached (the application). Patterson cited three texts in this regard: Titus 2:14, 3:6 and 3:14. These student discourses, exercises and additions were followed by "further elucidation on the part of the Professor". Patterson then clarified this to say that the students were also invited to "state our difficulties or objections". Thus student criticism was not excluded by McCulloch, but clearly he was in charge of these critical discussions. From these criticisms the professor issued some very helpful advice on the art of preaching. Patterson then gave an example which McCulloch used in one of these criticisms: "Give them a good introduction. If you get them with you at the start, it will carry you through the middle of your discourse, then stop when you think they would like a little more...."[61] Understanding the work done through these student discourses begins to shed a proper light on what Patterson said – that they had two classes, Hebrew and theology. He was not counting the discourses which were in the field of applied theology, such as pastoral ministry, homiletics, and also biblical theology or exegesis of Scripture.

It appears that the actual pedagogical style of the divinity hall in both Pictou and Halifax was not unlike the Secession halls in Scotland with a single Professor. The lectures, exercises and conduct of the classes were the same under an Archibald Bruce, a George Lawson or a John Dick. The one main difference was in the actual meeting times of the hall. The Nova Scotia hall appears to have struggled with this issue and moved to a settled pattern of a four week session in November. This was approximately half the length of the session in a Scottish Secession hall, where sessions of six to nine weeks were more the norm. However, the Scottish halls faced a continual struggle in keeping students there for the duration of a whole session, so perhaps in reality there was less of a time difference than it appears.

When the hall was in Pictou, the students resided in their own homes and journeyed for the Saturday meetings to Pictou. It is uncertain where the students resided in later years (1833 to 1837) when they attended the hall in Pictou and in Halifax (1838 to 1843). Since there are no references in his biography to the divinity students during these years, it appears fairly certain that they did not reside with Professor McCulloch.

In the second part of this chapter under synod records, brief discussion will be found on the assistance from Scottish Seceders for the divinity hall library in Pictou. It should also be acknowledged that a society was formed in Scotland which helped both the Pictou Academy and the divinity hall. This society, "The Glasgow Society for Promoting Religion and Liberal Education Among the Settlers in the North American Provinces", was constituted on September 29, 1826. Its chief object was to serve as a defense of liberal education in the Colonies and also to encourage a "native ministry". This society in its inaugural

---

[61] George Patterson, "The First Theological Hall in the British Colonies", *The Theologue*, Vol. 3, No. 2(1891), 38-39.

publication praised Professor McCulloch for his vision and labours in the creation of the Pictou Academy:

> Formed upon the model of the University here, which is so justly regarded by our citizens with partiality, it opens to all without distinction or exception the paths of science, and presents to men of all persuasions in religion, the means of obtaining a complete classical and philosophical education, uncircumscribed by religious disabilities, and untainted by the spirit of party. The theological class, connected with this institution, may be regarded as a *Home Missionary Society*, in which those who are about to be sent forth to preach the gospel to their countrymen, receive an appropriate, and an evangelical education.[62]

The society primarily assisted by sending books for the libraries in the academy and in the hall. Key leaders in this Glasgow Society were William McGavin, Ralph Wardlaw, John Dick and John Mitchell.[63] The society formed shortly after the 1825 "Memorial on Behalf of the Literary and Philosophical Institution at Pictou, Nova Scotia" was circulated in Scotland for the gathering of names. Those who signed this "Memorial" were "recommending it [Pictou Academy] to the public in this country [Scotland]". The list of subscribers included Henry Moncrieff Wellwood, Andrew Thomson, Thomas McCrie, John Jamieson, Robert Jamieson, John Brown, Patrick Neil, James Haldane, Stevenson McGill, George Jardine, William Meikleham, William McGavin, John Dick, James Ewing, Greville Ewing, Ralph Wardlaw and George Baird.[64]

---

[62] *Proceedings in the Formation of the Glasgow Society for Promoting Religion and Liberal Education Among the Settlers in the North American Provinces With an Address by the Committee* (Glasgow, 1827), 12-13.

[63] *Second Report of the Glasgow Society for Promoting Religion and Liberal Education Among the Settlers in the North American Provinces* (Glasgow, 1830), iv, vi. Also in extract form under the article "Institution of Pictou", *Edinburgh Theological Magazine* 4 (1829), 77-86.

[64] "Memorial on Behalf of the Literary and Philosophical Institution at Pictou, Nova Scotia" (n.p., 1825). A copy of this memorial may be found in the Maritime Conference Archives, Sackville, N.B., Box PHDH-1, No. 4. The memorial uses three names for the Pictou Academy: College of Pictou, Pictou Seminary, and The Literary and Philosophical Institution of Pictou. The purpose of the memorial was to appeal "to the generosity of the liberal and enlightened Friends of Science in Britain" and "by the aid of their countrymen, to enable this infant and promising Institution to surmount the adversities with which it has been beset and assailed, and to enlarge its usefulness by multiplying its means of Education; in short, to render it still more efficient as a Scientific and Christian Seminary". (p. 2). The first three subscribers to endorse the memorial were James Hall, George Paxton and John Mitchell, then followed another paragraph of endorsement, after which forty-two subscribers were listed, all of whom constituted leaders in Scottish education, civil government and church.

From the perspective of students in the academy and hall, the Glasgow Colonial Society clearly opposed both institutions. See "Extract of a Letter from a student in

This Memorial of 1825 came at the same time that a second society, Glasgow Colonial Society, was founded, chiefly under the leadership of Robert Burns of Paisley. Since many in its membership were hostile to a non-Kirk college like Pictou, a tremendous friction arose. The Memorial was an effort to overcome this, which failed. Thus, in the mid-1820s two rival societies emerged in Glasgow promoting mission work in British North America. The one mentioned above which was aiding the Secessionists has been virtually ignored by historians.[65] The full list of subscriber names makes for very interesting reading and reveals a degree of complexity historians have often disregarded.

McCulloch was obviously receiving books from this society; and, although today it is difficult to recreate the catalogue list for the divinity hall library in Pictou and Halifax, there are enough hints to lead to the conclusion that a determined effort had been made in its establishment. There are forty-two books in the Atlantic School of Theology Library, Halifax, which bear the seal of "McCulloch's Library". Though there is some uncertainty as to whether they were Professor McCulloch's or the divinity hall's, it appears that these were what students actually consulted, so the question for our purposes is somewhat irrelevant. The two oldest books are Bibles, one printed in Basle in 1556 and the other in Antwerp, 1571, volume five of the *Antwerp Polyglot Bible*. The remainder of the volumes were printed between 1596 and 1818. The majority are from the seventeenth century. Several are patristic writers: Clement of Rome, Eusebius of Caesarea, Lactantius, Athanasius, Gregory of Nazianzus, and Origen of Alexandria, and are all Latin editions. There are several ecclesiastical histories by Allix, du Pin, Bower, Baronius and Alexander Petrie and two gospel harmonies in Latin by Thomas Cartwright and Johann Gerhard. Two interesting volumes are Charles Drelincourt's *La defense de Calvin* (1667)

Theology, Attending the Pictou Academy, To a Clergyman in this Country", dated Pictou, October 8, 1829, *Edinburgh Theological Magazine* 5(1830), 120-121. For encouragement from the "other" Glasgow Society, see "Religious and Philanthropic Intelligence", *Edinburgh Theological Magazine* 5(1830), 182-183.

[65] *DSCHT*, 365. The article on the Glasgow Colonial Society makes no reference to "The Glasgow Society for Promoting Religion and Liberal Education..." and states: "For over a decade the Society was almost solely responsible for providing Presbyterian facilities in Canada...." Also, *Selected Correspondence of the Glasgow Colonial Society 1825-1840*, eds. Elizabeth and Kerr McDougall and John S. Moir (Toronto, The Champlain Society, 1994), xxxviii, xlii. The editors are incorrect to assert that McCulloch was attempting to transform Pictou Academy "into a publically-supported theological college"; a college, yes, to be supported by public support, but not a divinity hall. Other sources are: John S. Moir, "'To Fertilize the Wilderness': Problems and Progress of the Synod of Nova Scotia in its first Quarter Century", *Canadian Society of Presbyterian History, Papers* (1992), 67-86; R. F. Binnington, "The Glasgow Colonial Society and its work in the Development of the Presbyterian Church in British North America 1825-1840" (unpublished Th.D. thesis, Emmanuel College, Toronto, 1960).

and John Forbes' *Instructiones historico - theologicae* (1645).[66] In addition to this collection, there are fifteen more volumes in the Special Collections at Dalhousie University, all bearing this same stamp mark. These sixty volumes in total help us to examine the resources which were available to the divinity students.[67] In addition to the shipments of books from Scotland (culls from the United Secession Divinity Library and from Professor Mitchell), plus money from Scotland for the purchase of books for the divinity library, the Nova Scotian synod often gave a yearly grant. In addition, Dr. McCulloch often used what salary he was given to purchase books, and many congregations in the synod of the Lower Provinces formed "Penny-a-week" Societies.[68] These societies in congregations collected contributions for purchases to be made for the divinity hall library.

One more observation about the theological education under review needs to be made at this point. As was the case in Scotland in both the Secession and Kirk presbyteries, students had several presbytery discourses to complete between each session in the hall. This remained the case with the presbyteries of the Presbyterian Church of Nova Scotia (Secessionist). The normal custom was to give assignments to the students at one presbytery meeting and then to have them present these at subsequent meetings. Student presbytery assignments included homilies (with an assigned text of one verse), Church history chronologies, Greek examinations, Hebrew examination of a prescribed Psalm or text, doctrinal controversies, popular sermons, theses, exegetical

---

[66] "Catalogue of Books from the McCulloch Library" filed with the librarian, *Atlantic School of Theology* (1977), Halifax, Nova Scotia. The books are housed in the Rare Book Room of the library. Though Sheldon MacKenzie also mentions the divinity hall library, he likewise includes no reference to finding a catalogue. See R. Sheldon MacKenzie, *Gathered by the River: The Story of the West River Seminary and Theological Hall, 1848-1858* (Winnipeg, 1998), 57-59.

[67] "Special Collections Card Catalogue", in the Special Collections Library, Dalhousie University, Halifax, Nova Scotia. There is not a separate catalogue of books bearing the Thomas McCulloch stamp; rather, these are within the Special Collections Card Catalogue.

The Special Collections Library at Dalhousie also possesses forty-two volumes of books with the seal of the "Pictou Academy Library". These books were all printed between 1763 to 1816 and, as would be expected, cover the following subjects: natural philosophy, Greek literature, moral philosophy, rhetoric, history and English literature. I have also endeavoured to ascertain where other books from McCulloch's library and from the divinity hall library may have gone. Three were found in the personal library of the Rev. William Campbell, Woodstock, Ontario, namely George Buchanan's *The History of Scotland* [trans. James Aikman] (Glasgow, 1827), volumes 1, 2, and 3 only. The name inside these books is only "Dr. McCulloch", so I conclude they were from his personal library.

[68] G. Patterson, "The First Theological Hall in the British Colonies", *The Theologue*, Vol. 3, No. 1(1891), 4.

exercises and additions.[69] There was nothing in any of these presbytery assignments which deviated from what was being done in Scotland. While it was reflective of the basic approach to theological education and training which was used generally in the divinity halls, it also served to keep the presbyteries heavily involved.

In summary, it appears obvious that Thomas McCulloch's twenty-three years as the Secession professor of divinity in Nova Scotia were patterned upon the models of Scotland. Today his role as a divinity professor has received little attention, while he is more remembered as "the father of Canadian humour" and as one of the pioneering forces of liberal education in Atlantic Canada. His two D.D.'s[70] do not appear to have been related to his work as a divinity professor and, since the divinity hall he served possessed no permanent buildings, its real influence upon British North America has not received the attention it deserves.

Synod Records and Theological Education

In 1817 a union occurred between the Burgher and Antiburgher Secession Churches of Nova Scotia. The result was the formation of the Synod of the Presbyterian Church of Nova Scotia (United Secession), which preceded the same union in Scotland by three years. This united synod was concerned for the state of education in the Maritimes, and thus from its very first meeting we find education was a constant matter before the court. Initially the concern was for college level instruction; then theological instruction was added when the first students completed the college level course of studies. As in Scotland, the Nova Scotian Seceders continued the pattern of having men "complete" a college course before training for the ministry. Since the Seceders were denied access to King's College, Windsor, their only options were to send their young men back to Scotland to study in the Scottish universities or to establish their own college in Nova Scotia. Thomas McCulloch had established a grammar school

---

[69] Sheldon MacKenzie provides in one chapter, "Role of Presbytery in the Curriculum", an excellent overview of the role of presbytery in educating and training divinity students, chiefly between the years 1848 and 1858. These assignments had all been in place during Professor McCulloch's time as well as evidenced by synod's 1843 reminder that all student exercises were to be done before a presbytery transacted other business when they met. See MacKenzie, *Gathered by the River*, 63-77, 98-173.

[70] These D.D.s were from the University of Glasgow and from Union College, Schenectady, New York. The Glasgow D.D. degree was conferred partly "in consideration of the valuable donation of Insects lately presented by him [Thomas McCulloch] to this University". *University of Glasgow Senate Minutes*, MS, University of Glasgow Archives, Glasgow. 1/1/4, 100. Clear evidence is lacking for the reason his American D.D. was conferred, but it was either for his struggle for education in the province of Nova Scotia or his polemical writings on Roman Catholicism.

in Pictou in 1811, and many of these students were ready to advance into college level instruction.

Thus, in 1817 Pictou Academy began as a college level institution, open to Seceders, Kirk students, Baptists, Anglicans and other Dissenters. The institution reflected the open door policy of the Scottish universities and, in particular, the University of Glasgow. The name most often used was "Pictou Academy"; however, various other names have been used. For example, the first reference in the minutes of the newly constituted synod of the Presbyterian Church of Nova Scotia refers to the new institution as the "Presbyterian Academy which is intended to be established in Pictou".[71] The use of the word "Presbyterian" should not imply exclusivity within the student body, but probably was more in reference to the fact that the sponsoring body was (Seceder) Presbyterian. The other word, "Academy", is rather perplexing in its background. There is no direct reference to Calvin's Genevan Academy, though this would be a parallel in certain respects. The term was not being used to describe a secondary school, following elementary school. Academy should simply be taken as synonymous with college, such as Glasgow College, and thus on a few occasions it is not surprising to find it also called Pictou College. There is no concrete evidence to suggest that McCulloch borrowed the word "academy" from that of the English Dissenting academies.

The Secession congregations responded to the call for subscriptions. A report in the 1818 *Minutes* by the Pictou Academy trustees reveals that a collection had been taken in the congregations which helped to purchase a library and "Philosophical Apparatus" (scientific equipment).[72] By the June, 1820, synod meeting, the report on Pictou Academy stated that there were several young men finishing their philosophical studies and ready to enter the study of divinity. A synod committee was appointed to find and recommend the name of someone to become the professor of divinity. Their recommendation was for Thomas McCulloch to assume this task in addition to his pastorate at the Prince Street Church in Pictou and his professorship at Pictou Academy. The synod proceeded to appoint McCulloch as its first professor of divinity at this same meeting and gave twenty pounds from synod funds to purchase more books. It was also agreed to have another collection amongst the congregations

---

[71] *Minutes of the Proceedings of the Synod of the Presbyterian Church of Nova Scotia: 1817*, MS, MF-7, Maritime Conference Archives, Sackville (all subsequent references will be abbreviated and will only give the year and *MS* location code. Since there is an inconsistency in pagination, it cannot be used in the footnotes). Towards the end of the period under examination, printed *Abstracts* of the synod minutes were being produced. Since they are *Abstracts*, the *MS* minutes will be used. The *Abstracts* available can be located on the *Canadian Institute for Historical Microreproductions* (C.I.H.M.) fische for the years 1842, 1843, 1844, and 1845. *Abstract from the Minutes of the Synod of the Presbyterian Church of Nova Scotia 1844-1845*. C.I.H.M. No. 01988.

[72] *Minutes of the Synod of the Presbyterian Church of N.S.:1818*, MS, MF-7

for the purpose of raising money to purchase books for the students of divinity and their library.[73]

The first reference to some kind of theological hall in British North America can be found in the special *Report* issued by the Synod of 1818. This *Report* set forth several ideals or goals for the synod to work towards, such as the securing of a printing press, the exercise of discipline by all the sessions, the increase in meetings for fellowship, etc., the revival of the Presbytery exercise,[74] the congregational full support of ministers and eventually less reliance upon Britain for preachers. With this last point we read:

> all supplies from that quarter must be temporary and precarious... a Church which has no resources for a succession of Clergymen, can neither be extensive nor permanent. The Committee would, therefore, earnestly recommend to the Synod, the establishment of a seminary of education from which Preachers of the Gospel may be procured; and, in the event of attaining this valuable acquisition, it might be also advisable, to afford to young men of piety and talents, every possible encouragement to dedicate themselves to the work of the ministry.[75]

Since the Academy had begun in 1817, we understand the reference here to "a seminary" to broadly mean the Academy and a divinity hall, without which the church could not have a "succession" or a permanence, nor could it be extended. The *Report* of 1818 was truly visionary. Later in the *Report*, the term "seminary" was again used to describe this educational vision in a very broad sense.[76] Clearly the long range goal was for that which was established in Pictou to lead to the securing of ministers.

In reading the synod minutes from 1817 to 1844, the matter of raising funds for collecting books for the academy and divinity libraries figures several times. In 1821 McCulloch declined the salary from the synod for being professor of divinity in order that this money be used to purchase needed books for the use of the divinity students.[77] In 1823 the synod gave £20 from the congregational collections for the library of the divinity hall,[78] and in 1837 £10 were given from which Dr. McCulloch and two others were to select appropriate books.[79] In 1837 the synod also requested that a "Catalogue of the Books in the Divinity Hall Library" be made and presented to the 1838 synod.[80] Turning to the 1838 synod *Minutes,* we discover that the "Catalogue of the

---

[73] *Minutes of the Synod of the Presbyterian Church of N.S., 1820, MS*, MF-7.
[74] *Report... for Promoting Religion*, 3-19, 28.
[75] *Report... for Promoting Religion*, 20-21.
[76] *Report... for Promoting Religion*, 30.
[77] *Minutes of the Synod of the Presbyterian Church of N.S., 1821, MS*, MF-7.
[78] *Minutes of the Synod of the Presbyterian Church of N.S., 1823, MS*, MF-7.
[79] *Minutes of the Synod of the Presbyterian Church of N.S., 1837, MS*, MF-7.
[80] *Minutes of the Synod of the Presbyterian Church of N.S., 1837, MS*, MF-7.

Divinity Hall Library" was completed and duly laid before the synod.[81] Unfortunately, the catalogue itself is not in the *Minutes* and the attempt to locate it has proven unsuccessful to date. It would have been most interesting to have seen what constituted this 1837/38 library catalogue and then to have attempted a full comparison with the United Secession's divinity hall library in Scotland. The divinity library went with Dr. McCulloch's successor, Professor John Keir,[82] to Prince Town, Prince Edward Island, by order of the synod of 1844.[83]

The designation of £10 from synod funds was deemed too little, and in 1838 an extra £20 was added to it from proceeds of the sale of a Mr. Dick's estate. With £30 to purchase books, the committee appears to have been rather slow, because in 1839 they reported having only spent £6 of the £30. They were then directed by the synod to purchase more books.[84]

The synod was not the only means of enlarging the divinity hall library, as there was a stream of correspondence with the mother church in Scotland.[85] Sometimes this was at a formal level between synods, but often it was between professors in Scotland and Nova Scotia, that is, between Professor Mitchell and Professor McCulloch. The correspondence was not restricted to the professors of divinity but was also amongst the divinity students or by McCulloch to the students of divinity in Scotland. Two Nova Scotian divinity students sent a letter to the divinity students in the United Secession hall, Glasgow, in 1827 in

---

[81] *Minutes of the Synod of the Presbyterian Church of N.S., 1838, MS*, MF-7.

[82] Keir likewise studied divinity with Professor Bruce at Whitburn and may have studied for one year with Professor Paxton at Edinburgh. For a brief memoir of Professor Keir, see Anon., "The late Rev. John Keir, D.D.", *Christian Instructor*, Vol. 4, No. 1 (Jan., 1859), 1-8; Vol. 4, No. 2 (Feb., 1859), 33-40; Vol. 4, No. 3 (March, 1859), 65-72; and Vol. 4, No. 4 (April, 1859), 97-110.

[83] *Minutes of the Synod of the Presbyterian Church of N.S., 1844, MS*, MF-7, for the relocation of the divinity library to P.E.I. Personal visit to Montreal, Presbyterian College, to see the "John Keir Library" housed there. There is no catalogue. The collection would be of about five hundred volumes, much of which pre-dates 1844 or McCulloch's death. There is some question if this John Keir Library was really only Keir's personal library or if it may have also been the divinity library. Again, since divinity students used the hall library and the professor's library, it is a mute point for this book. (This library has since been relocated and is now in Toronto at the National Presbyterian Museum.)

[84] *Minutes of the Synod of the Presbyterian Church of N.S, 1838, 1839, MS*, MF-7.

[85] Evidence of this can quickly be found from the Scottish "United Associate Synod Minutes" (April, 1826), 166-168, where full discussion was given to the synod by a report from Professor McCulloch while in Scotland. The synod responded with approval and encouraged congregational offerings to be given to the Pictou Institution. See also "United Associate Synod Minutes" (September, 1826), 176-177, for the report of synod's committee to aid the Nova Scotia Church and its institution.

which they stated the need for assistance with the library.[86] The Scottish students of divinity became patrons for the hall in Pictou, and in 1829/30 they sent £104 for the aid of the hall in Pictou.[87] These exchanges affected more than merely the building of a divinity library in British North America, more of which we will mention at appropriate junctures.

The *Minutes* of synod provide very little evidence of the amount of time divinity students actually spent at the hall and for how many sessions. It appears that for the initial years the divinity hall did not have a regular one month or six week annual session, but rather the divinity students attended a "semi-monthly" divinity class with Professor McCulloch. We learn this from student correspondence between the Pictou hall and the Scottish Secession hall.[88] This was probably due to the fact that Professor McCulloch was engaged in three tasks simultaneously in the early years of the hall – as a minister, academy professor and divinity professor. Also, the initial students were from the Pictou area, hence this schedule would work. However, as time passed there was an obvious switch to a regulated annual session of "four complete weeks every year, commencing on the first Wednesday of November" and "the Professor of Divinity having the power of assembling the students at such other times as he may judge expedient".[89] Though the synod passed this resolution in 1833, it does not necessarily mean that McCulloch had not moved towards an annual session prior to this time. The synod may have been regularizing what he was already doing. From letters and very occasional references in the synod *Minutes*, it would appear that under Thomas McCulloch there were on average ten students in total at each divinity session.[90]

---

[86] "James Waddel and Alexander Blaikie, Divinity Students, Pictou, N. S. to the Students of Theology, United Secession Hall, Glasgow, 19 Nov. 1827", *Letterbook*, National Archives of Scotland, Edinburgh, *MS* CH3/305/2, 183.

[87] "D. Thomas, G. Thomson, Pres. & Sec., United Secession Divinity Hall Society to Rev. McCulloch, Pictou, N. S., 23 September, 1830", *Letterbook*, National Archives of Scotland, Edinburgh, *MS*, CH3/305/2, 226. Also, McCulloch himself describes the Scottish divinity students as providing patronage and that "without your beneficial patronage, so much good could not have been done". See "Thomas McCulloch, Pictou, N. S. to the Theological Students under the inspection of the Rev. Drs. Dick and Mitchell, Glasgow, Scotland, 14 May, 1830", *Letterbook*, National Archives of Scotland, Edinburgh, *MS*, CH3/305/2, 224.

[88] "Waddel and Blaikie, Pictou, N. S. to students of the Secession Hall, Glasgow, 19 Nov., 1828", 180.

[89] *Minutes of the Synod of the Presbyterian Church of N.S., 1833, MS*, MF-7.

[90] Since the synod *Minutes* did not contain student lists, one has to look for other clues. For example, in 1822 McCulloch had eleven students studying divinity, and in 1829 in a letter to the Secession divinity hall we learn he had nine divinity students. Since on average two or three would be licensed each year and ordinarily a student would attend the hall for four years, this allows us to make a fairly accurate statistical average of ten per session. See *Minutes of the Synod of the Presbyterian Church of N.S., 1822, MS*,

Upon McCulloch's death in 1843, the synod of 1844 appointed the Rev. John Keir as professor of divinity. At this time they also stated that each session would last one month and that during the first session the Presbytery of Prince Edward Island would supply the Rev. Keir's pulpit.[91] Under Professor Keir the session began the first Friday of October, and it lasted for one month.[92] We can conclude that the divinity sessions for the Nova Scotian hall were annual one month sessions, not unlike their Scottish counterpart. The "semi-monthly" meetings were only conducted during the initial years of the hall.

As in Scotland, there were obvious attendance problems with some students. We read in the 1833 *Minutes* about some students of divinity who gave "occasional attendance". The synod wanted this to stop and directed that students were to give "constant attendance" during the four week session.[93] It appears that the session did not always begin the first Wednesday of November, as the 1834 synod gave the professor of divinity liberty to alter the meeting time, provided that it was convenient with the students.[94] As in Scotland, attendance at the annual sessions of the divinity hall was not the total extent of the student's education and training. The 1833 synod regulations also stated: "that the presbyteries shall superintend the students who live within their respective bounds, appointing to them courses of reading, assessing them as to their proficiency, and prescribing to them, and receiving from them, such discourses as may be deemed requisite".[95]

The Synod of Nova Scotia maintained the pattern of having students complete a full college course before commencing their theological studies as much as possible. However, as in Scotland, the regulations did not insist upon graduation with a M. A., nor did it preclude doing some of the arts and theology concurrently. There was very little change from the tradition of education in Scotland within the Secession. For example, in the Rev. McCulloch's 1820 report to synod, he stated that several men were finishing their philosophical studies and were ready to enter the study of divinity.[96] This supports the continuity thesis with the Scottish model. We would also expect to

---

MF-7; "Daniel McCurdy and John Baxter, students at the Presbyterian Divinity Hall, Pictou, N. S. to the Students in Glasgow at the Secession Hall, 20 October, 1829", *Letterbook*, National Archives of Scotland, Edinburgh, *MS*, CH3/305/2, 210; and "Thomas McCulloch, Pictou, N. S. to students under the Revs. Dick and Mitchell, 14 May, 1830", *MS* CH3/305/2, 224. Also, the 1843 Minutes state that year two candidates were licensed. See *Minutes of the Synod of the Presbyterian Church of N.S., 1843, MS*, MF-7.

[91] *Minutes of the Synod of the Presbyterian Church of N.S., 1844, MS*, MF-7.

[92] *Abstract from the Minutes of the Synod of the Presbyterian Church of N. S., 1844* (n.p.), 2.

[93] *Minutes of the Synod of the Presbyterian Church of N.S., 1833, MS*, MF-7.

[94] *Minutes of the Synod of the Presbyterian Church of N.S., 1834, MS*, MF-7.

[95] *Minutes of the Synod of the Presbyterian Church of N.S., 1833, MS*, MF-7.

[96] *Minutes of the Synod of the Presbyterian Church of N.S., 1820, MS*, MF-7.

find a synod appointed committee making certain that the arts work was sufficient and of an acceptable standard. Again we find that the synod appointed a five member committee to visit the academy for the purpose of observing and participating in the student examinations in philosophy. These examinations were conducted orally, as was the custom of the day, and in the committee's report back to the synod, they stated that they were "highly pleased". The committee proposed that this good report should be read from all the pulpits.[97] One senses that such committee examinations were not only valuable for guarding orthodoxy, but they promoted the academy's standing in the colonies and served as a challenge to the King's College monopoly.

In 1825 the synod passed a regulation for students of divinity that presbyteries could "if they judge it expedient, admit young men to the study of Divinity though they have not previously attended a course of Natural Philosophy; as condition, however, that they complete their Academical course before they be licensed".[98] This regulation was not far removed from the Secession Church's custom in Scotland, where men often took some of the two courses of study simultaneously. In fact, there is some question as to whether or not this was the case with Thomas McCulloch himself, whereby he undertook some course work at the University of Glasgow while also attending the divinity hall at Whitburn.[99] This was different from lowering the standard by removing the philosophical course altogether. The Presbytery of Truro petitioned the synod about this matter in 1835, and they made it very clear that they disapproved of licensing any student who had not studied natural philosophy.[100] The synod deferred the petition, probably not because of their disapproval but because of the crisis over the future existence of the Pictou Academy. Without an institution of philosophical instruction, the existence of the divinity hall was jeopardized.

The divinity students in Scotland played a vital role in the expansion and mission of the Secession Church, and we find the situation similar for the Synod of Nova Scotia. In fact, one almost senses that the synod had such demands upon it to find home missionary preachers that it kept pressure upon McCulloch to quickly turn out men for licensure trials. In 1823 synod asked McCulloch if any students were ready for licensure because there was a pressing need for "missionary" preachers. McCulloch responded that none of

---

[97] *Minutes of the Synod of the Presbyterian Church of N.S., 1821*, MS, MF-7. See also *Minutes of the Synod of the Presbyterian Church of N.S., 1822*, MS, MF-7, where the Rev. John Keir was appointed to serve on this five member examining committee. These oral examinations were virtually identical to the famous Blackstone examinations conducted at the University of Glasgow.

[98] *Minutes of the Synod of the Presbyterian Church of N.S., 1825*, MS, MF-7.

[99] See earlier in this chapter footnotes 6 and 8.

[100] *Minutes of the Synod of the Presbyterian Church of N.S., 1835*, MS, MF-7.

the men were ready yet for licensure.[101] This not only demonstrates the need for a divinity hall, but it also shows the link to mission work and the extension of the Secession's ministry. Two instances may be cited here as examples. In 1827 and 1828 missionaries were sent to the Bay of Chaleur area of New Brunswick and Quebec and to the area around Richibucto, New Brunswick. The two men who were sent had just completed their course of studies at the divinity hall.[102] The second example again parallels a common theme in Scotland; namely, sending out those students who could preach in Gaelic and encouraging swiftness in licensure. Two students, William Fraser and Alexander McKenzie, both advanced students in the divinity hall and both "acquainted with the Gaelic language", were such students of whom "the commissioners were instructed to take early measures for the licensing of these young men, should they find it to be expedient".[103]

Three were licensed in June, 1824, and George Patterson believed that possibly three others had been licensed in the autumn of 1823 due to the need for Gaelic preachers in Cape Breton. He concludes this from the *Minutes* of Synod, 1822, where "the Presbytery of Pictou was allowed to license such of the young men, who now attend the Divinity Hall and understand the language, as upon examination and trial they shall find qualified, to go for a few weeks to preach the gospel in some of the destitute Gaelic settlements".[104] Patterson believes at least two or three were licensed in 1823 and spent the winter in Cape Breton. If such was the case, it does not necessarily mean that they did not return to the divinity hall to complete their studies. Since a student could not "preach to a congregation" until licensed, an expediency of licensing students for the Gaelic settlements was needed. This was also common in Scotland. However, it appears the Nova Scotian Synod created a special category of "special license" to authorize a student "whose capacity and progress in study they had tested" to preach at a certain place with the understanding that "they should preach only discourses that had been approved either by the Professor or the Presbytery".[105] These Gaelic students thus may have actually been given "special license" for the Gaelic settlements on Cape Breton only. In the 1850s we again find reference to "special license" for the

---

[101] *Minutes of the Synod of the Presbyterian Church of N.S., 1823*, MS, MF-7. The 1818 *Report...for Promoting Religion* stressed the need for all ministers to take their turn in doing missionary work in the colonies. It would appear that once students were forthcoming, the burden fell more upon them to do this. *Report...for Promoting Religion*, 22-23, 30.
[102] *Minutes of the Synod of the Presbyterian Church of N.S., 1828*, MS, MF-7.
[103] *Minutes of the Synod of the Presbyterian Church of N.S., 1832*, MS, MF-7.
[104] George Patterson, "The First Theological Hall in the British Colonies", *The Theologue*, Vol. 3, No. 2(1892), 33.
[105] George Patterson, "The First Theological Hall", 33-34.

third year students to be able to preach, but with the stipulation that they had to complete their fourth year in divinity before ordination.[106]

It appears that the synod annually appointed a committee to oversee the home mission work. This committee then distributed the preachers amongst the presbyteries and "in destitute places as they shall deem most expedient".[107] We unfortunately do not have, in the *Minutes* nor in the *Abstracts*, full lists of names and places assigned.

The final matter of particular note from the *Minutes* of the Synod comes from the 1843 "Report of the Committee on the General State of the Church"; a committee of six, consisting of Professor McCulloch, the Rev. Keir, the Rev. Trotter, Mr. Gammel, Mr. Clarke and Mr. Cameron. The report was adopted and additions were made by the synod. Several items in the report are related to the students of divinity and the presbyteries. There are six sections to the report, with the third point being a general exhortation to greater diligence in preparing students for the office of the minister.[108] It certainly appears that it was not directed to Professor McCulloch but rather to the presbyteries. When presbyteries met, the "Synod further agreed that in all meetings of Pbties at which Students in Divinity are enjoined to give in their prescribed exercises it shall be the order to receive these exercises before the Pbty enters upon the consideration of any other business".[109] Obviously some presbyteries were putting the student exercises later on their docket. This regulation was to correct this and ensure that proper time was given to what should be viewed as a high presbyterial priority – the examination of student discourses. Connected with this resolution was the exhortation to the presbyteries "to enjoin the students in Divinity...to be punctual in their attendance at the Hall, and to come up in due time and duly prepared, so that they may devote their undivided attention to its exercise".[110] This resolution no doubt came from McCulloch's experience with tardy students and a need for better presbyterial involvement.

The other major resolution concerned the actual meeting of the presbytery and its purpose. Though not directly related to students, indirectly it did relate, as students were expected to attend. This fifth resolution states that the meetings of presbytery were to stress the mutual improvement of its members, and the synod added three sub-points here:

---

[106] James McLean, "Our College: – Its History, Its Present Position, and Its Prospects, I – The Pictou and West River Period. 1817-1858", *The Theologue*, Vol. 8, No. 4 (1897), 104.

[107] *Abstract from the Minutes of the Synod of the Presbyterian Church of Nova Scotia, 1843*, (n.p.), 4. This Committee of Missions the following year, 1844, was made the "Board of Domestic Missions". See *Abstract from the Minutes of the Synod of the Presbyterian Church of Nova Scotia, 1844* (n.p.), 2.

[108] *Minutes of the Synod of the Presbyterian Church of N.S., 1843*, MS, MF-7.

[109] *Minutes of the Synod of the Presbyterian Church of N.S., 1843*, MS, MF-7.

[110] *Minutes of the Synod of the Presbyterian Church of N.S., 1843*, MS, MF-7.

1.) The improvement of the members of the Presbytery by the reading and delivery of essays of discourses on some selected or prescribed subject. The essay or discourse may afterwards become the subject of friendly criticism as according to the discretion of the Pbty.
2.) The improvement of the members of the congregation by inviting them to attend such meetings and by communicating to them interesting and important information on the public affairs of the church with the expectation that by these means they may be induced to take a more lively interest in her prosperity.
3.) The personal religious improvement of the members of Presbytery in particular by religious conference and prayer.[111]

All of this was a return to the vision of the old Scottish exercise. To what extent this 1843 synod vision became a reality is beyond comment here, but it did place a greater stress on presbytery as an educational body for on-going ministerial development, "lay-elder" training and student training.

This 1843 resolution can actually be traced back to one of the earliest printed documents of the synod. In 1818 the synod had printed *The Report of a Committee Appointed by the Synod of the Presbyterian Church of Nova Scotia, To Prepare a Statement of Means for Promoting Religion in the Church, Securing the Permanence of the Church, and Enlarging Its Bounds....* This report, amongst other matters, recommended:

the revival of an obsolete practice, from which the Presbyterian Church in other countries has derived much advantage: that is, that the meetings of Presbyteries be as frequent as possible; and be designed for ministerial improvement, as well as for the direction of the affairs of the Church: and, that each Clergyman in rotation, for the exercise of his talents, receive a subject for discussion, which he shall deliver at next ordinary meeting, subject to the critical remarks of his brethren.[112] (Note, later in the report it reads "criticised by the brethren in private".)[113]

The context in the report was the need for ministers to speak with preparation and with skilful rhetoric. It would appear that many were having to farm or teach school in addition to the ministry, and by reading the report, it would appear that this was cause for concern that the standards of preaching would be lowered.[114] Thus the need was felt to return to the presbyterial

---

[111] *Minutes of the Synod of the Presbyterian Church of N.S., 1843*, MS, MF-7.

[112] *The Report of A Committee Appointed by the Synod of the Presbyterian Church of Nova Scotia, to Prepare a Statement of Means for Promoting Religion in the Church, Securing the Permanence of the Church and Enlarging its Bounds*; and *The Subsequent Resolutions and Arrangements of the Synod* (Halifax, 1818), 8-9. [C.I.H.M. #29125]

[113] *Report...for Promoting Religion*, 28.

[114] *Report...for Promoting Religion*, 6-7.

exercise. It is interesting that this was the theme in 1818 and was still the theme in 1843.

The 1843 report moved to improve the Theological Professorship Endowment Fund by encouraging the committee managing those funds to invest them in order to obtain a Bill of Incorporation for the fund.[115] This does show the synod's attempt to seek an adequate fund to pay for its professor of divinity. However, synod had first established the fund in 1832 and set a goal of £2,500.[116] It appears that the fund grew very slowly, as in 1834 it only had £87; in 1836, £162; in 1839, £212; and in 1840, £230.[117]

A reading of the exchange of student letters between the Secession hall in Glasgow and the hall in Pictou highlights two other matters which were important to the development of students for the ministry. One concerns news of the wider church and the world. Waddell and Fraser, writing from Pictou in 1829, told the divinity students under Dick and Mitchell how good it was of them to provide word of missionary news and endeavours.[118] By the 1830s the Pictou academy and hall were keenly aware of missions, perhaps in part as a result of this exchange of letters between the two halls.[119] We also learn from these letters further ways in which the Nova Scotia students had experiences similar to those we have found in Scotland. For example, just as in Scotland probationers or licensed students were constantly sent out itinerating in destitute districts,[120] so were the licentiates in the Synod of Nova Scotia. Also, the students in the Nova Scotia hall formed a society similar to those in the Scottish halls; although it would appear that this society, "The Pictou Students Academical Society", was more inclusive than the Scottish model, perhaps

---

[115] *Minutes of the Synod of the Presbyterian Church of N.S., 1843*, *MS*, MF-7.

[116] *Minutes of the Synod, 1832*, *MS*, MF-7. Part of the reason for the establishment of an Endowment Fund was no doubt due to the fact that in 1830 the synod could only pay Professor McCulloch thirty pounds of the promised forty pounds and thus was in arrears. See *Minutes of the Synod, 1830*, *MS*, MF-7. Betts in *Pinehill Divinity Hall* (p. 12) says it was the synod of 1833 which began the Endowment Fund. The *Minutes* read 1832.

[117] *Minutes of the Synod., 1834, 1836, 1839, and 1840*, *MS*, MF-7. In 1845 the fund had grown to 339 pounds. See *Abstract from the Minutes of the Synod of the Presbyterian Church of Nova Scotia, 1845*, 3.

[118] "Waddel and Fraser, Pictou to the theology students under Dick and Mitchell, Glasgow, 28 Nov., 1829", *MS* CH3/305/2, 215.

[119] On John Geddie, a student of the Pictou Academy and the Divinity Hall and missions, see R. S. Miller, *Misi Gete: John Geddie Pioneer Missionary to the New Hebrides* (Launceston, Tasmania, 1975) and John G. Paton, *John G. Paton, Missionary to the New Hebrides. An Autobiography*, ed. James Paton (New York, 1889), 1:103.

[120] "Students of the United Secession Divinity Hall, Glasgow, to the Students in Divinity under Dr. McCulloch, Pictou College, N. S., 23 Sept., 1830", *Letterbook MS* CH3/305/2, 229.

involving both academy and hall students.[121] Finally, the old Scottish custom of students of divinity teaching in schools or tutoring while pursuing their theological studies continued for some of the divinity students in Nova Scotia. Waddel and Blaikie were both teaching in "country schools" while attending their divinity class.[122]

By way of postscript on what happened to the divinity hall upon Thomas McCulloch's death in 1843, brief mention is here made of his successor Professor John Keir, Princetown, P.E.I. As was previously stated, Keir, like McCulloch, had studied divinity under Professor Archibald Bruce and served as solo professor in the divinity hall. We know that Keir's chief focus was systematic theology. Since we possess Keir's syllabus of lectures, which was published just prior to his death, we are able to see a continuity from the Scottish divinity halls through Thomas McCulloch and to his immediate successor. Keir's published syllabus contains 131 "lectures" on systematic theology, with reference works for the student to consult on each lecture. The overall outline of these lectures follows the structure of Brown and Dick. Dick emerged as a prominent reference for student reading along with Brown, Boston, Calvin, Chalmers, Witsius, etc.[123] No references were found to Marck's *Medulla*, but occasionally reference to Pictet can be found. The syllabus on pastoral theology contains only thirteen lectures together with references, which include Baxter's *Reformed Pastor*, Brown's "Address to His Students", Campbell's *Rhetoric and Lectures on Pulpit Eloquence* and Ostervald's *Lectures on the Sacred Office*.[124] The section on ecclesiastical history amounts to four pages and is prefaced with this introduction:

> In this department a full course of Lectures cannot be given, owing to the shortness of time, and the multiplicity of work required to be done in the other departments. Besides some occasional Lectures on the nature, worth, special importance, ends, etc. of Church History, all that can be accomplished must be by the student's reading, writing essays, and being examined on the subject.

The chief textbook was Edwards' *History of Redemption*, along with reference to Spanheim, Vitringa, Neander, Mosheim and Bogue.[125] It appears that Keir maintained the teaching layout well established in Scotland and also conducted

---

[121] "Waddel and Fraser, Pictou to the theology students under Dick and Mitchell, Glasgow, 28 Nov., 1829", *MS* CH3/305/2, 213.

[122] "Waddel and Blaikie, Pictou to the divinity students of the United Secession Hall, Glasgow, 19 Nov. 1827", *MS* CH3/305/2, 180.

[123] [John Keir], *Course of Study in Systematic and Pastoral Theology and Ecclesiastical History, for Students attending the Theological Seminary of the Presbyterian Church of Nova Scotia* (Charlottetown, P.E.I., 1857), 1-91. This rare work is to be found in the Maritime Conference Archives, Sackville, N.B., Box PHDH-1, No.10.

[124] [Keir], *Course of Study*, 92-99.

[125] [Keir], *Course of Study*, 100-103.

by McCulloch in Nova Scotia. The stress after McCulloch remained on systematic theology as the centre of the curriculum and in the traditional covenantal formulations. Church history was clearly left to student "recess" work under the supervision of the presbyteries, and pastoral theology received lectures, yet of a lesser proportion than that of systematics.

Summary

This single case study of the first Presbyterian divinity hall in British North America shows that the Scottish Secession divinity halls served as models, which Thomas McCulloch transferred to Nova Scotia. Such a hall could only function if the philosophical course was first in place, as was the case in Scotland; then attendance at sessions with a solo professor of divinity could follow. The Nova Scotian hall in the 1820s to 1840s continued with a solo professor, not paralleling the move to specialization in the United Secession Hall, which had begun in the mid-1820s in Scotland. In Nova Scotia this was not so much due to philosophical convictions but because of the pragmatic shortage of ministers and the fact that there was no one to serve as a second professor. However, by the late 1840s this situation was beginning to change and the staffing of the hall was likewise changed.

The pedagogical methods used were the same as in Scotland and over time so was the move to annual sessions, but not initially. There is no evidence to show that McCulloch departed from the traditional theological emphases in the Secession halls. Rather he appears to have followed a consistent and steady course in that regard.

The links with Scotland were strengthened via societies – The Divinity Hall Student Society and The Glasgow Society for Promoting Religion and Liberal Education among the Settlers in the [British] North American Provinces – and well documented student and synod correspondence show that quite an intimate contact was maintained between the two countries. The Nova Scotia Presbyterian Church (Secessionist) Synod minutes reveal very little that is distinctive from the synod involvement in Scotland. The only exception would be that of the Theological Endowment Fund, which for all practical purposes did not have any success. It was established to allow for a professor to be provided for without recourse to having other employment; however, McCulloch combined his work as professor of divinity with his work in the philosophical division of Pictou Academy as well as the Harbour Church. He resigned from the Harbour Church in 1824 and later became the president of Dalhousie College. Pluralities were a way of life for Secession professors of divinity through the 1840s, whether in Scotland, Ireland or Nova Scotia, the only exception being George Paxton. Perhaps this maintained the strong church attachment and created an ethos in these halls as ministerial educational centres rather than simply academic institutes of theology. That model was maintained in Nova Scotia in the period reviewed here, 1820 to 1843.

CHAPTER 16

Conclusion

This book has attempted to uncover the history and development of theological training in both the Kirk and Secession from c.1560-c.1850. At the outset I had expected to find major differences in methodology between these two branches of the Church. This was a false assumption. Beginning on the continent and continuing on through both Kirk and Secession, there was a continuity of both purpose and methodology that is surprisingly uniform.

Perhaps the obvious similarities speak more of the common culture and time period in which both Kirk and Secession were operating. For example, the Seceder halls were for the training of male students for the ministry, like the Kirk halls. All of the halls were ministerial schools only. Like the whole university student population, there were no women in the student body. The students were young and unmarried and had the Church in view. The student body was not there for the purpose of laity training in theology nor for preparation for missionary service, etc. It was a very focused and singular student body. Only in the last period of the Kirk reviewed could it be argued that some were training for missionary service. However, this was not reflected in the curriculum but rather in the informal student gatherings. It was not until 1821 that William Brown, an Associate minister, was appointed the superintendent for the Scottish Missionary Society's new missionary training seminary.[1] All of this tells us that in the halls of our period of study, both Kirk and Secession, a missiological curriculum was absent. This therefore limited the students of divinity in these halls, forcing them to look beyond the traditional halls to gain missions training.[2]

---

[1] William Brown, *The History of the Propagation of Christianity among the Heathen*, 2 vols. (Edinburgh, 1823), 1:vi.

[2] My purpose here was not to write a book on how to do theological education and training in the twenty-first century. I do not believe it is satisfactory to simply be "slaves to the past". Critical historical reflection with contemporary application will be needed. Some direction here might well include the following as a starting point: Manfred W. Kohl, "Theological Education: What Needs to Be Changed", in *Educating for Tomorrow: Theological Leadership for the Asian Context*, eds. Manfred W. Kohl and A. N. Lal Senanayake (Bangalore, India/Indianapolis, IN, 2002), 29-48; "Mission – The Heart of the Church for the New Millennium", *International Congregational Journal* 2 (August, 2001): 87-101. See particularly page 94, the subpoint "Mission Must Develop a

The obvious differences reflect more the circumstances of the time. For example, the locations employed for the halls of the two had clear differences in that the Kirk used the established universities, with their permanent buildings, whereas the Seceders used church buildings and manses. The universities had the advantage of possessing larger libraries, whereas the Seceders had to establish these, and that took several years. By the time of the United Secession hall, considerable libraries were in place for the students. The halls were not modern graduate schools of theology or religious studies.

Other differences, while evident, have proven to be much more subtle than one might have expected. Many of the same key texts can be found in both the Seceder and Kirk halls. When the professors in each produced their own systematic theology texts – Hill and Chalmers and Brown and Dick – the question must be asked, "What were the substantive differences?" Although the curriculum was surprisingly similar between Kirk and Secession, as one probes deeper it is discovered that the emphasis or stress upon various subject areas was different. For example, the Seceders dealt more with polemic theology, or dogmatics, than with apologetics.

> So little did they regard the presence of the enemy at the gates as a menace to the stability of the Christian Confession that their theological interest found its centre of gravity in dogmatic questions which belonged rather to the wranglings of Polemics than to the problems of Apologetics.[3]

The brief study done in this chronological overview has identified the major difference as being the focus by the Secession halls upon the marriage of theology and piety. John Brown of Haddington was reflective of the older Seceder tradition which was still close to the Marrow perspective. Dick moved somewhat away from it, not so much in focus but with the piety of a newer generation of Seceders. Dick was not a Chalmers on natural theology, but he was also not a Brown. An analysis of the Scottish-produced systematic theology textbooks in published or *MS* form of the late eighteenth and early nineteenth centuries needs to be undertaken. These would be those written by Brown, Dick, Hill, Rankin and Hunter.

In order to highlight and contrast similarities and differences, charts have been formulated and included at the end of this chapter. The charts are an effort to bring order to the historical material studied. Headings for these charts have been modified from something which Robert Pazmiño formulated concerning curriculum. It was written in the present tense, but might be understood in the past tense for the purpose of this book. The questions are the following:

Strategic Plan Focusing on Leadership"; and "Radical Transformation in Preparation for the Ministry", *International Congregational Journal* [forthcoming December, 2006]. I thank the author for the privilege of reading the unpublished *MS*. See also my preface, pages xx-xxi, footnote 10.

[3] John MacLeod, "Theology in the Early Days of the Secession", *RSCHS* 8 (1944), 15.

What specifically should be taught, *why* should these areas be taught, *where* is the teaching being done, *when* should various areas be taught, *who* is being taught and who is teaching, and lastly, *what* organizing principles hold it all together?[4]

These seven questions have been broadly followed when constructing the following charts. Pazmiño's sixth question is really two questions, yet this will be treated as one. His seventh question will be limited to the question of degrees, as this matter was addressed in chapter one of this book and has obvious overlap with Pazmiño's first question.

As we examine the six periods of theological education and training in the Church of Scotland (Kirk) as outlined in part one of this book, it becomes apparent that the teaching of Scripture was a central part of the theological curriculum in all six periods. However, this needs to be carefully defined. Generally the biblical languages were studied in the Scottish universities prior to entering the divinity halls. On occasion there may have been further work in Hebrew, but this varied. The Scripture expositional studies which were conducted were not necessarily all within the divinity hall, but were sometimes in the church on Sunday, where a principal or professor also served a plurality. Also, Scripture within the hall was often taught through the student exegetical discourses, etc., thus not always through formal lectures. In Period VI there was a clear change to add more formal biblical instruction to the curriculum, which had not received as much formalized attention through lectures in Period V.

The predominant feature in theological education for all six periods was in the area of dogmatics, which for most of the time-period included catechetical lectures. The texts were by Reformed authors, usually from the continent; for example, Calvin, Wollebius, Ryssen, Essenius, Pictet and Marck. Periods one and two were centred upon Calvin's *Institutes* and early federal theological formulations. The theology of the Covenanter Period was scholastic federalism, yet this time was also a period of intense concern for biblical exposition related to the pulpit, unlike Period V, where the output in biblical exposition decreased. Period VI, following the Scottish Enlightenment, showed the effects of natural theology being grafted into federal theology. Chalmers was an example of such.

The field of Church history moved to become a separate area of study in the halls by Period VI. Previously it had received little attention in the hall and was more the concern of the presbyteries, with their chronological assignments to students. Pastoral theology underwent several changes in the six periods. Yet the relationship between the arts courses in logic, grammar and rhetoric and the divinity training as an aid to learning how to form sermons was recognized throughout all six periods. Thus, the link between arts and the divinity hall must not be ignored. With the Covenanter Period, casuistry became a separate field of study. It then began to decline in the periods of Episcopal Restoration and

---

[4] Pazmiño, *Foundational Issues in Christian Education*, 227.

Revolution Settlement and increased again in Period VI, with lectures on pastoral theology.

The teaching for the Kirk students technically was done in the university divinity halls, but this was not the full extent of the education or training. The arts curriculum was an integral element, as were the presbyteries with their extensive licensure examinations. I have been struck continually how there was an intimate relationship between the arts curriculum and the curriculum of the divinity hall. Students came to divinity with a background which provided many basic tools to study divinity. The theological curriculum in the Kirk and Secession halls demanded an adequate arts background, without which the halls could not have limited their curriculum as narrowly as they did. The students brought a background with them to the hall which was invaluable. Perhaps this explains in part why the divinity sessions were not very long, in addition to the pragmatic reason that the students of divinity were usually school teachers as well.

The arts curriculum still had much continuity with the medieval trivium in the division of studies into grammar, rhetoric and logic. The influence of the trivium could still be discerned in a man such as George Campbell or an educationalist like George Jardine. B. B. Price saw the medieval trivium's grammar as "the study of the use of words and rules for their interconnection. Rhetoric taught of the ways to organize, deliver, express, and evoke words to convey a desired meaning. Logic was the study of the quality of reasoning behind language constructions."[5] Students with backgrounds in these areas came to the divinity halls with a solid foundation to study divinity.

It has been acknowledged that in periods five and six (late eighteenth and early nineteenth centuries), there was a rise of specialized teaching in the arts curriculum. If this thesis were to go beyond 1850, we would see that the arts course continued to broaden with the addition of new fields of study. Therefore it began to undermine the understanding of the traditional arts curriculum as a handmaid to divinity studies. This is beyond the time period of this book, yet would be worthy of further study. One can also sense a move towards specialization in the divinity halls, yet even this was inconsistent. Again, beyond the time period of our book, this would increasingly become a reality. Recent writers are again acknowledging that student background and education prior to coming to a theological college must be evaluated in assessing curriculum.[6]

Several other aspects of divinity training in the Kirk have been noted. The presbytery played a significant role, as did the synod. Since there was no such thing as divinity graduations for the majority of the time during the six periods, the presbytery and the licensure examinations fulfilled this. It was only during

---

[5] B. B. Price, *Medieval Thought: An Introduction* (Oxford, 1992), 199.
[6] J. C. McLellan, "Class Act", *Presbyterian Record*, Vol. 123, No. 5 (May, 1999), 29-30.

the Episcopal Restoration and near the close of Period VI that B.D. degrees were employed. Also, in periods five and six I have included societies as another place where teaching was done. These were supplementary to the presbyterial exercises and did not necessarily include all students, except if the societies met during the hall sessions. Also, the presbytery libraries of the eighteenth century cannot be ignored as a place where theological education occurred outside of hall time. The service of divinity students as family tutors or chaplains, schoolmasters and probationers must also be noted. Since there are no records of field education evaluations or reports, it is extremely difficult to definitively tell what place this had in the formation of students. However, students technically could not preach until they were licensed during most of the periods examined. Therefore, the school work provided field education in catechism, singing, serving as clerks of session, etc. Likewise, the probationary period, often of one to two years or more, was where the student acquired his skills in the pulpit, received congregational evaluations, and became knowledgeable about the realities of the church.

The method of teaching was quite consistent throughout these periods in terms of oral examinations and assigned student discourses, which were followed by evaluation or critique. The latter was the same in the halls and in the presbyteries. From Period I to Period VI, the lectures in the halls went from Latin exclusively to almost entirely English. Likewise, there was a decline in disputation work from Period I to Period VI. The stress was on oral communication and examination as opposed to the submission of written essays for evaluation. The problem of students often only attending to do their discourses and then leaving has been noted earlier in the book.

Part Two in this book on the Secession presented a chronological study on the history and development of theological education and training by the Scottish Seceders. When we examined the curriculum, we found that dogmatics was the first priority in their halls. This is parallel to the Kirk. It was federal theology of a scholastic order, and the main text followed was that of Marck. Both Brown and Dick's handbooks on theology represented federal theology, yet it could be argued that Brown also added biblical theology. When we begin to use such terms as scholastic or federal, we do need to be aware that there are nuances that can be attached to these methodologies. For example, we should see in the Secession professors of divinity a marriage of the scholastic theologian and the experimental theologian. As Beeke wrote of Gisbertus Voetius, so it can be applied to these men: "[They] experienced no tension between detailed scholastic analysis and experimental warmth."[7] Again there is a continuity with medieval scholastic method, but not in its context. Thus, it is accurate to conclude that the Secession professors were not adverse to using the scholastic method provided it was wedded to *theologia practica*.

---

[7] Joel Beeke, *Gisbertus Voetius Toward a Reformed Marriage of Knowledge and Piety*, Guidance from Church History, vol. 2 (Grand Rapids, 1999), 18.

Separate teaching or assignments on the Westminster Confession of Faith appear to have been a standard feature of all the Seceder halls. Generally there was a reliance upon the Scottish universities to provide the basics of grammar in the biblical languages, and added work was done in the hall in the languages, although there was some variance on this point. Likewise, with other biblical studies there was an inconsistency amongst the professors. Some relied mainly on student biblical discourses for this teaching, while others, like a Lawson or a Paxton, devoted more attention to it. It was only with developments in the United Secession hall that a very clear movement to formalize attention to biblical studies occurred. This was the same in the Church of Scotland halls in the universities. Similarly, Church history and pastoral theology formally received more attention in the United Secession hall, as they did in the universities at that time. It would appear that casuistry remained a field of study longer in the Secession halls than in the Scottish universities, yet this too moved to a pastoral theology.

The one factor which stood out with the Seceders, and particularly with the General Associate Synod, was their philosophical class or college. This was a reaction to the skepticism of certain professors within the Scottish universities. However, the General Associate Seceders were not hostile to all aspects of Scottish Common Sense thought; rather it was the scepticism of the Enlightenment and its accompanying de-emphasis on piety which concerned them. They were never able to establish a rival college system to those of the established Scottish universities, nor was the Free Church able to do such in the 1840s and 1850s.

The Seceders conducted their teaching in their own halls with a short annual session and left the students to the care of the presbyteries the rest of the year. Their halls met in their churches and in the manses. The Scottish universities continued to be used by most of the students, and even if students did attend the General Associate philosophical class, this did not exclude their going to the Scottish universities as well. Later some Secession students attended divinity lectures in the Scottish universities between sessions in the Secession hall. The Seceders, like the Kirk, turned to the presbyteries for assistance with the education of their students, for example, with the chronologies and the extensive licensure assignments.

The student body of the Secession halls was very uniform in that all the students were Seceder students for the ministry, chiefly from Scotland, but also from Ireland. This would have been in contrast to the university halls, which in certain periods had a slightly more diverse student body with instances of foreign students also in attendance. However, for several of the periods there were few, if any, foreign students except those from Ireland or England, and latterly Dissenting Presbyterians from Scotland. The Seceders' hall student body was thus more homogeneous than that of the Kirk.

There were defects in the halls and these must be acknowledged. Pleas from Secession professors concerning the workload were found upon more than one occasion. To sit through fifty student discourses in one session was no small task, in addition to conducting lectures and examinations. Similarly, one does wonder how the plurality of offices really worked in the Kirk. It seems evident that sometimes both students and church were served well, sometimes neither.

Numerically, the Auld Lights represented the smallest branch of the Secession. In asking the seven questions concerning their approach to theological education and training, we can make the following observations: the parallels with what was taught by the main Seceders were obvious, bearing in view the exceptions of the distinctives of the Auld Lights. Dogmatic theology was their focus, whether using Brown, Marck or Pictet and the *Westminster Confession*. Church history was not a key focus, yet they did increase in the department of biblical studies, in common with other Seceders and with the Kirk.

The Auld Lights used tutors to offer assistance in the languages, homiletics and philosophy. This was distinct from the other Seceders. Like the main branches of the Secession, the Auld Lights established their own halls for preparing their young men for the ministry, and these comprised their student body. Their professors were ministers with churches (even Paxton returned to looking after a church), which was no different from the New Light Seceders. The Auld Lights continued to use the Scottish universities for languages and arts and held their halls in the manses of the ministers or in the church buildings. Like the Kirk and the other Seceders, the Auld Lights also relied upon the presbyteries to assist in the education and training of the students through presbytery exercises and examinations for the students. There are also no real distinctions as to how teaching was done; that is, it was by lectures which very quickly moved from Latin to English, oral examinations, and student discourses and critiques. Again like the other Seceders, there were no theological degrees.

We have already noted many parallels between the case study of the Secession hall in Nova Scotia, 1820 to 1843, and the Scottish Secession halls and church. The tradition of focusing in the hall upon teaching the Westminster Confession and Calvinism was not unique. Dogmatics was the centre-piece, while Biblical studies and Church history were primarily left to the presbyteries and for student discourses in the hall. All of these patterns were borrowed from Scotland. Again, the Nova Scotia Church's purpose for its hall was to train a native ministry. Thus it was not a hall for the laity or for women. The focus of its student body was purposely narrow. The hall met in a room of the Pictou Academy and then in McCulloch's home in Halifax, and thus never possessed its own building. This was similar to the Secession halls in Scotland. The arts course continued to be critical to the conducting of the hall, as was the presbytery.

One area of difference was the question of when the teaching was done. At first McCulloch held bi-monthly classes, but this was changed to an annual hall session. This does not represent a radical difference, but was more a concession to the students, who were teaching in schools near Pictou. The question of theological degrees was never an issue in the Nova Scotia hall, just as it was not with the Seceders in Scotland. McCulloch also served a plurality of offices – church, academy and hall – for the first few years, then college and hall only. This was again similar to Scotland, where from 1820 to 1843 there were no full-time professors of divinity in the Secession halls. Thus a conclusion becomes obvious: the divinity hall and Secession church in Nova Scotia exhibited no radical departures from the Scottish models in the Secession churches.

Throughout this book an attempt has been made to highlight the contributions of the key professors in both Kirk and Secession. One must never underestimate the influence of a professor upon his students, and it is worthwhile to trace these threads of influence, such as, for instance, that from Geneva or the continent to Scotland. A study of Appendices A and B demonstrates this succession of influence and contribution in Scotland and even beyond to British North America. I draw the obvious observation for the reader that modern, western faculty size would be quite shocking to most of the halls in the time-frame covered in this book for both Kirk and Secession. The fact that theological education and training remained as uniform as it did throughout this three hundred year period is suggestive that imitation rather than innovation was the theme.

I have already stated that further research and writing needs to be undertaken in examining the Scottish produced systematic theology textbooks, particularity those of the late eighteenth and early nineteenth centuries. This should include considerations of the structure, references and their influence upon others and to explore if they were used within Scotland beyond the divinity halls.

Other areas where ongoing research needs to be undertaken are a full treatment of both the Covenanter and Relief approaches to theological education and training prior to 1847. D. D. Ormond's work on the Covenanters and theological education and training[8] is altogether too brief, and Roxburgh's new work will open the door in a fresh way upon the Relief Church. Hopefully this book will continue encourage an appreciation of the Dissenting Presbyterian contributions in Scotland, and a new day of such studies will emerge, perhaps even a small renaissance in this area. Many further avenues for comparison, research and development remain to be explored. For example, the impact and contribution of the Seceders in Ireland and their establishment of a divinity hall under the Rev. John Rogers is worthy of exploration.[9] How was it

---

[8] D. D. Ormond, *A Kirk and a College in the Craigs of Stirling* (Stirling, 1897).
[9] Robert Allen, *The Presbyterian College Belfast 1853-1953* (Belfast, 1954), 38. The Rev. Rogers was appointed the first Burgher professor of divinity in Ireland in 1796 and conducted the hall at Cahans, County Monaghan. Professor Roger's successor in 1815

similar to the Scottish body and how was it different, etc.? Likewise a comparative study needs to be undertaken of the early Secession and Associate Reformed halls in the United States.

Yet it is not only with Dissenting Presbyterians that further work needs to be undertaken. A case study needs to be conducted upon the Kirk hall at Queen's University, Kingston, Upper Canada, which was established in the mid-1840s. Similar questions should be asked, such as was it patterned along the lines of the halls within the Scottish universities? Here one sees the possibility of further research emerging on Peter Colin Campbell.

I believe I would be amiss if I did not at least take observations from this book, which is purely of an historical nature, and set forth certain applications to the contemporary world of Presbyterian, theological education at the beginning of the twenty-first century. Current discussion in higher education concerns itself with distance learning and also the rise of modern technology and its integration into the conveyance of education. I do not claim to be an expert in these matters; however, I do see parallels to some historical practices studied within this book.

When either the Church of Scotland or the Secession presbyteries followed through with the various student assignments, did this not come very close to "distance education"? Many students resided in communities away from their divinity halls yet continued to read extensively and prepare discourses to deliver to their presbyteries and professors when they "went up" to the next session of the hall. The actual time of residency at the hall varied considerably, but quite often it was what would be considered quite brief, a maximum two months for Seceder students and upon occasion longer for those of the Church of Scotland. Therefore it appears to me that a form of distance learning was incorporated into the theological education system. Perhaps we are not as unique as we might think in our modern age.

Though "distance learning" was incorporated into the theological education of students, contact with a professor, or perhaps at most two or three professors, was always at the heart of the system. This raises several critical concerns as to the proper balance between being with the professor and being away employed and working on divinity assignments. It takes discipline to labour on discourses when the professor is not directly with you. Can a divinity course be executed exclusively by distance assignment? This historical study would suggest not because of its heavy reliance upon oral examination. The goal was to prepare men for the pulpits of Kirk and Seceder churches, where the conduct of worship was central. Therefore the tremendous stress on oral assignment and examination was closely related to the final goal. Thus, what should be the place for written versus oral examinations in a theological curriculum today?

---

was Professor Samuel Edgar of Ballynahinch. See also James Seaton Reid, *History of the Presbyterian Church in Ireland*, 2d ed., 1853 (Stoke-on-Trent, 1998), 3:396, 457.

Also, are there balances that need to be maintained between residency and distance learning in today's divinity hall?

Concerning the professors, it is difficult not to become too generalist here, but certain overall points can be asserted. In this study we have seen that professorial writings were not always scholarly but quite often reflected a style which was highly popular with the people in the pew. Does the divinity hall exist chiefly for scholarship or for the educating of ministers? Generally it was found that learning and piety were wedded. The Kirk and Secession halls were not graduate schools for research in religious studies. In the time period under study, the focus was very particular – to educate men for the ministry. Further, is ours an age overly obsessive with degrees? Countless ministers of the Kirk and Secession possessed no degree, others perhaps one. Are we the innovators today?

We have already raised the question of proper educational background prior to coming to the halls. I believe today the matter of pre-requisite and preparatory studies needs to be re-thought. This book has made me keenly aware of this topic, and no doubt divinity colleges in our day, with the great diversity within their student bodies, struggle with this issue. In the time period of this book, students entering the halls exhibited much unity of preparation. This greatly affected the divinity curriculum.

Comparisons from the historical models studied in this book should be made now to our contemporary models. The range for such comparison is wide, but hopefully in these last few paragraphs the door for comparison and for asking critical questions has been opened. Perhaps some will now enter that open door.

Concluding Chart: Kirk Theological Education and Training, c.1560-1860

↑ means – increased; ↓ means – decreased

	What was taught	Why was this taught	Where was teaching done	How was it done	When was it taught	Who did the teaching / Who was being taught	Organizing Principles
Period I *FBD*	Script. exposition, biblical languages, dogmatics – (*Institutes*)	To prepare future Protestant ministers knowledgeable in Scripture and Reformed theology	Arts colleges in the three universities, divinity halls in the universities, exercise	Latin lectures, oral examinations, theses/disputations, assigned exercises	In the arts curriculum (languages & Bible expositions, catechism); in divinity halls, attendance variable; in exercise	- Professors, - Presbytery/exercise - Div. students from Scotland	No divinity degrees
Period II *Nova Erectio*	Script. exposition, biblical languages, dogmatics – (*Institutes* & Catechisms). Rise of Federal theology	To prepare future Protestant ministers knowledgeable in Scripture and Reformed theology	Arts colleges in the six univ. [addition of Marischal, Edinb., Fraserburgh], divinity halls in univ., exercise	Latin lectures, oral examinations, theses/disputations, assigned exercises	In the arts curriculum (languages & Bible expositions, catechism); in divinity halls, attendance variable; in exercise	- Professors, - Presbytery/exercise - Div. students from Scotland, England, Europe	Episcopal reassertion of B.D. & D.D. degrees
Period III *Covenanter*	Script. exposition, Bible chronology, biblical languages, dogmatics – (*Westminster, Dort*) Federal theology, polity, casuistry	To prepare future Protestant ministers knowledgeable in Scripture and Ref. theology; rise of federalism, casuistry important	Arts colleges in the six universities, divinity halls in univ. exercise	Latin lectures, oral examinations, theses/disputations, assigned exercises	In the arts curriculum (languages & Bible expositions, catechism); in divinity halls, attendance variable; in exercise	- Professors, - Presbytery/exercise - Div. students from Scotland, England, Europe	No degrees

Conclusion

	What was taught	Why was this taught	Where was teaching done	How was it done	When was it taught	Who did the teaching / Who was being taught	Organizing Principles
Period IV Episcopal Restoration	Script. exposition, biblical languages; dogmatics– (Wolebius, Heidelberg), Latitudinarian, mystical, casuistry ↓	To prepare future Protestant ministers knowledgeable in Scripture and Reformed theology (?)	Arts colleges in the six universities, divinity halls in univ.. exercises	Latin lectures, oral examinations, theses/disputations, assigned exercises	In the arts curriculum (languages & Bible expositions, catechism); in divinity halls, attendance variable; in exercise	- Professors, - Presbytery/ exercise ———— - Div. students from Scotland, England	D.D. degree for a thesis or common-place
Period V Revolution Settlement	Script. exposition ↑; biblical languages; Catech. – Heidbg.; Federal theology; Scholastic: Ryssen, Pictet, Essenius, Hill, Marck	To prepare future Protestant ministers knowledgeable in Scripture and Reformed theology	Arts colleges in the five universities, presbyteries, divinity halls in univ., rise of societies, presbytery libraries	Latin lectures ↓, oral examinations, theses/disputations, assigned exercises	In the arts curriculum (languages & Bible expositions, catechism); in divinity halls, attendance variable; exercise; presbytery meetings	Professors, Presbytery/ exercise ———— Div. students of the Kirk but also Dissenting Scottish Presbyterians	No B.D. ; D.D. for literary work; Common Sense Philosophy
Period VI Universities' Commission	Script. exposition ↑; Federal theology; Scholastic; Paley, Butler, Hill; Church history ↑; pastoral ↑	To prepare future Protestant ministers knowledgeable in Scripture and Reformed theology	Arts colleges in the five universities, presbyteries. divinity halls in univ.. rise of societies, presbytery libraries	Latin lectures ↓, English ↑, oral examinations, theses/disputations, assigned exercises	In the arts curriculum (languages & Bible expositions, catechism); in divinity halls, attendance variable; exercise; presbytery meetings	- Professors, - Presbytery/ exercise ———— - Div. students of the Kirk but also Dissenting Scottish Presbyterians	Slowly moves toward B.D.; Common Sense Philosophy

Concluding Chart: Secession Theological Education and Training, 1737-1847

↑ means – increased; ↓ means – decreased

	What was taught	Why was this taught	Where was teaching done	How was it done	When was it taught	Who was being taught	Organizing Principles
Associate Church [1737 - 1767] W. Wilson A. Moncrieff E. Erskine J. Fisher J. Swanston	Dogmatics – Federal – Marck, Turretin, *W.C.F.*; Biblical– student discourses; Church history (very little); pastoral – some casuistry, some polity; philosophy class ↑ ↓	To prepare future Seceder ministers who were orthodox and evangelical	Churches, manses; Scottish universities for languages; Seceder philosophy class; presbytery	Latin lectures in hall, student discourses, oral examinations	Language in arts Hall sessions – 2 months	Seceder divinity students	no degrees
Associate Church [1767 - 1820] J. Brown G. Lawson	Dogmatics – Federal/ biblical – Brown, *W.C.F.*; biblical ↑; Church history ↑; pastoral ↑; philosophy class discont.	To prepare future Seceder ministers who were orthodox and evangelical	Scottish universities for languages; hall in churches, manses; presbytery; student societies ↑	English dictates in hall, student discourses, oral examinations, library	Language in arts Hall sessions – 2 months	Seceder divinity students	no degrees
General Associate Church [1748 - 1785] A. Moncrieff G. Paxton	Dogmatics – Federal – Marck, Turretin, *W.C.F.*; biblical studies; philosophy class	To prepare future Seceder ministers who were orthodox and evangelical	Hall in churches, manses; presbytery; Seceder philosophy class	Latin/English in hall, student discourses, oral examinations, library began	Language in arts Hall sessions – 2 months	Seceder divinity students	no degrees

	What was taught	Why was this taught	Where was teaching done	How was it done	When was it taught	Who was being taught	Organizing Principles
General Associate Church [1786-1820] A. Bruce G. Paxton	Dogmatics – Federal – Marck, Pictet, W.C.F.; biblical studies !; Church history !; philosophy class /tutoring	To prepare future Seceder ministers who were orthodox and evangelical	Scottish universities; Hall in churches, manses; presbytery; Seceder philosophy class/tutoring; student debating society	Latin/English in hall, student discourses, oral examinations, sermon skeleton, library began	Language in arts, Hall sessions – 2 months	Seceder divinity students	no degrees
United Secession Hall [1820-1847]	Dogmatics – Federal – Dick; biblical studies !; pastoral theology !; Church history !; more language work	To prepare future Seceder ministers who were orthodox and evangelical [freer]	Languages in Scottish universities; hall in churches in Glasgow & Edinburgh; manse of professor; presbytery !; student societies !	Little Latin, mainly English; some Latin in certain presbyteries; student discourses; more language work; presby. assignments; library !	Language in arts, some also attended divinity in Scottish universities, plus Seceder hall sessions	Seceder divinity students	no degrees

APPENDIX A

A Listing of Theological Professors in the Scottish Universities, c.1560-1860

The Sources
The lists which follow in Appendix A have been compiled by consulting a variety of sources, chief of which was *FES*. Volume seven of *FES* lists the faculty at the universities teaching in the field of theology, and this was compared to volume eight of *FES*, "Addenda and Corrigenda". Upon several occasions the other volumes of *FES* were compared using the presbytery lists. In the event of the *FES* contradicting itself, publications from the universities have been accepted first. The *DNB* was also consulted for a large percentage of the names, for which it served as a means of double checking. Also, where available, the *University Histories*, which often included partial lists, were consulted. Some shorter studies were also consulted, such as Henry Sefton's article "St. Mary's College, St. Andrews, in the eighteenth century", which contains a partial listing of the theological faculty at St. Mary's College. Consultation also includes Peter Bell's current two volume, first draft, *Ministers of the Church of Scotland From 1560-1929: An Index to Fasti Ecclesiae Scotianae*, Volume 1:A-D and Volume 2:E-K. The reader is directed to the bibliography for fuller details.

The Columns
Generally four columns have been used. The first column records the year(s) of service. The second column records the individual's name. Where there are a variety of spellings for the name, the most popular form of the surname has been used. Notes attached to a name have generally been excluded except to show family relationships or a matter of particular importance. The third column is an effort to state if the individual served the university and a parish, chapel or other university appointment at the same time (pluralities). Though efforts have been undertaken to be as accurate as possible here, this column is far from satisfactory. For example, preaching rotas often occurred with a professor and a church, yet the records do not state that the individual was inducted into a charge. Sometimes biographies give us more information to help with this column. Thus, it is difficult to be conclusive in the third column, yet it remains a vital column in terms of the overall study. The last column is an effort to state whether or not the individual studied or spent time abroad. I recognize that there may be still more information to uncover in this fourth column.

GLASGOW UNIVERSITY

Principals & Professors

Year(s)	Principal (Primarius) [1]	If in Conjunction	Time/Study Abroad
1574-1580	Andrew Melville	Govan	Poitiers, Geneva
1580-	Thomas Smeaton	Govan	
1585-	Patrick Sharpe	Govan	
1615-1622	Robert Boyd	Govan	
1622-1623	John Cameron		Bordeaux, Sedan, Geneva, Heidelberg, Saumur
1626-1650	John Strang		
1651	Robert Ramsay		
1653-1660	Patrick Gillespie		
1660-1662	Robert Baillie		Hague
1662-1683	Edward Wright		
1683-1690	James Fall		
1690-1700	William Dunlop		Carolinas
1701-1727	John Stirling		
1728-1761	Neil Campbell		
1761-1785	William Leechman [Leishman]		
1786-1803	Archibald Davidson	Dean of the Thistle	
1803-1823	William Taylor	St. Mungo's	
1823-1857	Duncan MacFarlane	St. Mungo's	
1858-1873	Thomas Barclay		

Chair of Divinity (f.1640)

Year(s)	Professor	If in Conjunction	Time/Study Abroad
1640-1650	1st Chair David Davidson	High Church (minister, then preacher)	
1642-1649	2nd Chair Robert Baillie		
1650-1660	1st Chair Robert Baillie		
1652-1665	2nd Chair John Young		
1669-1674	Gilbert Burnet		
1674-1682	David Liddell	Barony (?)	
1682-1686	Alexander Rose		
1687-1698	James Wemyss		
1688-1692	James Wodrow [2]	Eaglesham	
1692-1707	James Wodrow		
1708-1740(?)	John Simson		

---

[1] May also be referred to as Principal Regent.
[2] Reid tells us that Wodrow served at Eaglesham (1688-1692) while professor at Glasgow. During this period Wodrow was appointed by the Synod of Glasgow and Ayr, then in 1692 it was made a normal professorial appointment and he resigned from Eaglesham Parish Church.

1740-1743	Michael Potter		
1744-1761	William Leechman		
1761-1775	Robert Trail		
1775-1778	James Baillie		
1778-1782	William Wright		
1788-1814	Robert Findlay		
1814-1840	Stevenson MacGill	Dean of Chapel Royal, Middle Quarter	
1840-1862	Alexander Hill		

Hebrew and Oriental Languages (f.1709)

Year(s)	Professor	If in Conjunction	Time/Study Abroad
1709-1744	Charles Northland		
1745-1750	Alexander Dunlop		
1751-1752	William Rowat		
1753-1754	George Muirhead		
1755-1757	John Anderson		
1757-1761	James Buchanan		
1761	Robert Trail		
1761-1814	Patrick Cuming (son of Prof. Cuming, Deinburg)		
1814-1831	Gavin Gibb	St. Andrews (The Wynd)	
1831-1839	William Fleming		
1839-1850	George Gray		
1850-1876	Duncan Harkness Weir		

Ecclesiastical History (f.1716)

Year(s)	Professor	If in Conjunction	Time/Study Abroad
1721-1752	William Anderson		
1752-1762	William Rowat		
1762-1778	William Wright		
1788-1809	Hugh MacLeod		
1797-1841	William McTurk (assistant then prof.)		
1841-1851	James Seaton Reid		
1851-1874	Thomas Thomson Jackson		

ST. MARY'S COLLEGE, ST. ANDREWS

Principals & Professors

Year(s)	Principal (Primarius)	If in Conjunction	Time/Study Abroad
1580-1606[3]	Andrew Melville (uncle)		Poitiers, Geneva
1607-1645	Robert Howie		Rostock, Herborn, Basel

---

[3] See page 27, footnote 10 concerning George Buchanan.

1647-1661	Samuel Rutherford	Colleague of Robert Blair	
1662-1666	Alexander Colville		Sedan
1666-1686	Walter Comrie		
1686-1687	Alexander Rose		
1687-1690	James Lorimer		
1691-1693	William Vilant (Huguenot family)		
1693-1695	Alexander Pitcairn		
1698-1706	Thomas Forester		
1707-1747	James Hadow (father)		
1747-1779	James Murison		
1779-1791	James Gillespie		
1791-1819	George Hill (father-in-law, Cook) Second, First, Thistle, Royal		
1820-1854	Robert Haldane	First Charge, Prof. of Math	
1854-1886	John Tulloch	Dean of Thistle Chapel	

Chair of Divinity and Biblical Criticism (These were the second and third masters until 1707, when the third master was assigned the chair of Church history)

Year(s)	Professor	If in Conjunction	Time/Study Abroad
1579-1593	John Robertson		
1580-1586	James Melville (nephew)		
1588-1599	Patrick Melville (nephew)		
1583-1593	John Caldcleuch		
1593-1611	John Johnston		Heidelberg, Rostock, Helmstedt, Geneva
1617-1636	James Wedderburn		
1627-1634	Patrick Panter		
1639-1640	Samuel Rutherford	Colleague of Robert Blair	
	Vacancy		
1647-1662	Alexander Colville		Sedan
1662-1666	Walter Comrie		
1666- ?	James Tyrie		
1671-1673	Andrew Bruce		
1675-1682	David Falconer		
1682-1685	Alexander Monro		
1686-1687	James Lorimer		
	Vacancy		
1699-1707	James Hadow (father)		
1710-1712	Thomas Halyburton		Rotterdam
1713-1732	Alexander Scrimgeour		
1734-1739	Thomas Tullidelph		
1739-1779	Andrew Shaw		
1779-1788	Harry Spens		
1788-1791	George Hill (father-in-law, Cook)	Second Charge	
1791-1808	Robert Arnot	Kingsbarns	

Appendices

1808-1824	John Cook (son-in-law, Pr. Hill + father John Cook)
1825-1835	John Mitchell
1836-1851	Thomas Thomson Jackson
1851-1868	William Brown

Chair of Hebrew (f.1688) (The Fourth Master from 1560)

Year(s)	Professor	If in Conjunction	Time/Study Abroad
1688-1690	Patrick Gordon		
1695-1718	John Syme (did little teaching)		
1722-1728	Gabriel Johnstone		
1728-1738	Hugh Warrender		
1741-1746	Thomas Craigie		
1748-1780	George Hadow (son)		
1780-1793	Charles Wilson		
1794-1802	John Trotter		
1802-1808	John Cook (son-in-law, Prin. Hill + father)		
1808-1817	Daniel Robertson		
1817-1823	George Buist	Second Charge	
1823-1832	Archibald Baird		
1833-1834	David Scott		
1835-1848	William Tennant		
1848-1868	Alexander F. Mitchell		

Chair of Church History (Third Master) (f.1707)

Year(s)	Professor	If in Conjunction	Time/Study Abroad
1707-1718	Patrick Haldane (cousin)		
1718-1727	James Haldane (cousin)		
1730-1756	Archibald Campbell		
1757-1791	William Brown		Utrecht
1793-1801	Charles Wilson		
1802-1811	John Trotter		
1812-1823	John Lee		
1823-1860	George Buist	Second Charge	
1860-1868	John Cook (son)	St. Leonard's Parish (4 years)	

EDINBURGH UNIVERSITY

Principals & Professors

Year(s)	Principal (Primarius)	If in Conjunction	Time/Study Abroad
1585-1597	Robert Rollock	East Kirk(2yr) East Kirk(1yr)	
1598-1620	Henry Charteris		
1620-1622	Patrick Sands	Second Charge	
1622-1623	Robert Boyd	Second Charge	
1623-1651	John Adamson		
1652	William Colville (not inducted)		
1653-1662	Robert Leighton		Douay
1662-1675	William Colville		
1675-1685	Andrew Cant	Second Charge	
1685-1690	Alexander Monro	Second Charge	
1690-1701	Gilbert Rule	Old Greyfriars	Leiden, France
1703-1715	William Carstares	Second, then High Kirk	Utrecht, Leiden
1716-1729	William Wishart (Sr. -father)	Tron	Utrecht
1730-1732	William Hamilton (father)[4]	Collegiate	
1733-1736	James Smith	West St. Giles	
1737-1753	William Wishart (Jr.-son)[5]	New Greyfriars, Tron	Rotterdam, Leiden
1754-1762	John Gowdie		
1762-1793	William Robertson	Old Greyfriars	
1793-1840	George H. Baird	New Greyfriars, Collegiate, Second	
1840-1859	John Lee[6]	Chair of Divinity, Dean of Chapel Royal	
1859-1868	Sir David Brewster		

Chair of Divinity (f.1620)

Year(s)	Professor	If in Conjunction	Time/Study Abroad
1620-1626	Andrew Ramsay	Old Greyfriars(?)	Saumur
1627-1628	Henry Charteris		
1629-1630	James Fairlie		
1630-1647	John Sharpe		Bordeaux, Die
1648	Alexander Colville (never held office)		Sedan
1649	Samuel Rutherford (never held office)		
1650-1662	David Dickson	Second Charge (St. Giles)	
1662	Patrick Scougal (never held office)		
1664-1675	William Keith	Collegiate	
1675-1681	Lawrence Charteris		
1682	John Menzies (never held office)		

---

[4] *FES*, 7:381 is incorrect on the dates, but *FES*, 1:146 is correct.
[5] Also son-in-law to Thomas Halyburton.
[6] The last minister to hold the position of principal of Edinburgh University.

Appendices

1683-1690	John Strachan	Second Charge of Tron	
1690-1701	George Campbell	Collegiate	Holland
1701-1709	George Meldrum	Second Charge of Tron	
1709-1732	William Hamilton (father)	Collegiate (latter portion)	
1732-1733	James Smith	West St. Giles	
1733-1754	John Gowdie		
1754-1787	Robert Hamilton (son)		
1779-1809	Andrew Hunter (Assistant, then Prof.)	New Greyfriars, Tron	Utrecht
1809-1830	William Ritchie	High Kirk	Continent
1827-1828	John Lee [interim]		
1828-1843	Thomas Chalmers		
1844-1859	John Lee	Dean of Chapel Royal	
1859-1875	Thomas J. Crawford	St. Andrews Second Charge (1yr)	

Chair of Hebrew & Semitic Languages (f.1642)

Year(s)	Professor	If in Conjunction	Time/Study Abroad
1642-1656	Julius Conradus Otto (Jewish) [Naphtali Margolioth]		From Vienna
1656-1679	Alexander Dickson (son)		
1679-1681	Alexander Amedeus (Florentinus)		?
1681-1690	Alexander Douglas		
1692-1694	Patrick Sinclair		
1694-1701	Alexander Rule (son)		
1702-1719	John Goodall		
1719-1732	James Craufurd	Prof. Chemistry + Medicine	Leiden
1732-1753	William Dawson		
1751-1795	James Robertson	Librarian	Leiden
1792-1793	George H. Baird	New Greyfriars	
1793-1812	William Moodie	St. Andrews	
1812-1813	Alexander Murray	Urr	
1813-1847	Alexander Brunton	Tron	
1847	Charles McDowall (never installed since Free Church)		
1848-1880	David Liston		India

Chair of Church History (f.1694)

Year(s)	Professor	If in Conjunction	Time/Study Abroad
1702-1714	John Cumming		Utrecht
1715-1720	William Dunlop (son of Prin. Dunlop, Glasgow)		
1721-1736	Matthew Crauford		
1737-1762	Patrick Cuming (father of Prof.Cuming, Glasgow)	Collegiate	
1762-1788	Robert Cuming (son of Prin.Cuming, Edinburgh)	Evidently became sinecure	
1788-1798	Thomas Hardy	Collegiate	
1799-1831	Hugh Meiklejohn	Aberdeen	
1831-1843	David Welsh		

1844-1860   James Robertson

Chair of Biblical Criticism (f.1846)
Year(s)	Professor	If in Conjunction	Time/Study Abroad
1847-1868	Robert Lee	Old Greyfriars, Dean Chapel Royal	

KING'S COLLEGE, ABERDEEN

Principals & Professors

Year(s)	Principal (Primarius)	If in Conjunction	Time/Study Abroad
1553-1569	Alexander Anderson (deposed 1569 by General Assembly Comm.)		
1569-1582	Alexander Arbuthnot (Ramist)	Old Machar	Bourges
1584-1592	Walter Stuart [Stewart]	Methick	
1592-1632	David Rait	Old Machar	
1632-1640	William Leslie		
1640-1651	William Guild		Holland
1652-1661	John Row	North (Third Charge) & Heb. Lect. Marischal	
1661-1662	William Rait		
1662-1684	Alexander Middleton (father)	Newhills	
1684	George Middleton (son)	briefly also Glamis	
1717-1746	George Chalmers (cousin)	Old Machar (First Charge)	
1746-1800(?)	John Chalmers (cousin)		
1800-1815	Roderick MacLeod		
1815-1854	William Jack		
1855-1860	Peter Colin Campbell		

Chair of Divinity (f.1620)

Year(s)	Professor	If in Conjunction	Time/Study Abroad
1620-1634	John Forbes		Heidelberg, Sedan, etc.
1634-1635	Andrew Strachan		
1635-1641	John Forbes	Greyfriars	
1642	Adam Barclay (Never served)		
1643-1661(?)	William Douglas		
1674-1678	Henry Scougal		
1678-1680	John Menzies	Greyfriars	
1680-1697	James Garden		
1697	Charles Gordon (refused to teach)		
1704-1710	George Anderson		
1711	Thomas Blackwell (may have taught a few months)		
1711-1733	David Anderson		
1735-1770	John Lumsden		
1771-1795	Alexander Gerard (father)	Second Charge	

Appendices

1795-1818	Gilbert Gerard (son)		Amsterdam
1816-1852	Duncan Mearns (father-in-law)		
1852-1867	Robert MacPherson (son-in-law)		

Chair of Hebrew (f.1673)

Year(s)	Professor	If in Conjunction	Time/Study Abroad
1673-1693	Patrick Gordon (grandfather)		
1693-1730	George Gordon (father)		
1730-1767	George Gordon (son)		
1767-1790	John Ross		
1790-1793	Alexander Bell		
1793-1797	Hugh MacPherson		
1798-1846	James Bentley		
1847-1870	Andrew Scott		

Chair of Oriental Languages (f.1727)

Year(s)	Professor	If in Conjunction	Time/Study Abroad
1732-1754	James Donaldson (father)		
1754-1793	Alexander Donaldson (son)	Prof. of Medicine	
1794-1834	James Kidd	Gilcomston	
1832-1837	Robert Simpson (Assistant)		
1835-1860	George G. McLean		

Chair of Church History (f.1843)

Year(s)	Professor	If in Conjunction	Time/Study Abroad
1843-1860	William R. Pirie	Lec. Practical Relig.	
		College Chapel-of-Ease (one year)	
		Prof. of Divinity at Marischal	

Additional

Year(s)	Name and Work		
1669[7]-(?)1672	Paul Shaletti	Taught Hebrew, a converted Jew	Unknown[8] but from Europe
	Then Patrick Gordon, once he was taught assumed the teaching		

---

[7] In *Record of the Exercises of Alford*, 141, 412; and *FES*, 7:368.

[8] Likely from the continent. I have been unable to find out anymore about him.

Murray Lectures on Sunday Mornings[9]

Year(s)	Names	If in Conjunction
1824-1859	Various	Some Prof. often Divinity Probationers who were schoolmasters

MARISCHAL COLLEGE, ABERDEEN

Principals & Professors

Year(s)	Principal (Primarius)	If in Conjunction	Time/Study Abroad
1593-1598	Robert Howie (Ramist)	North (Third Charge)	Rostock, Herborn, Basel
1598-1614	Gilbert Gray		Helmstedt
1616-1619	Andrew Adie		Geneva, Heidelberg, Aldorf, Danzig
1620-1621	William Forbes	North (Third Charge)	
1621-1649	Patrick Duncan		Helmstedt, Heidelberg, Basel
1649-1661	William Moir	Prof. of Mathematics	
1661-1673	James Leslie	M.D., Aberdeen	
1673-1678	Patrick Gordon[10]		
1678-1715	Robert Paterson	Librarian	
1717-1728	Thomas Blackwell (Sr.)	Greyfriars	
1728-1748	John Osborne	North (Third Charge)	
1748-1757	Thomas Blackwell (Jr.)	Prof. of Greek	
1757-1759	Robert Pollock	Greyfriars	
1759-1795	George Campbell	Second Charge, then Greyfriars	
1796-1830	William L. Brown	Greyfriars	Utrecht
1832-1860	Daniel Dewar	Prof. of Church History	

Chair of Divinity (f.1616)

Year(s)	Professor	If in Conjunction	Time/Study Abroad
1625-1639	Robert Barron	Greyfriars	
1649-1678	John Menzies	Greyfriars	
1681-1684	John Menzies	Greyfriars	
1684-1688	Patrick Sibbald	Greyfriars	

---

[9] From 1824 under the Murray bequest – a series of lectures were to be given by "a clergy man to preach a course of lectures in the College Church on Sunday mornings, in the time of the winter sessions, on such subjects as they think fitted to tincture their students with just and liberal notions of pure and undefiled religion and virtue without descending to party distinction and controversies... Two of the lectures I appoint to be printed...." For a listing of the Murray Lectures, see Whytock, "History and Development of Scottish Theological Education and Training", 477-479.

[10] *FES*, 7:358 omits Patrick Gordon.

1697-1711	James Osborne [Osburne]	Greyfriars
1711-1716	Thomas Blackwell (Sr.)	Greyfriars
1717-1728	Thomas Blackwell (Sr.)	Greyfriars & Princ. Marischal
1728-1744	James Chalmers	Greyfriars
1745-1756	Robert Pollock	Greyfriars
1757-1759	Robert Pollock	Greyfriars & Princ. Marischal
1760-1771	Alexander Gerard	Greyfriars
1771-1795	George Campbell	Greyfriars & Princ. Marischal
1795	William L. Brown	Greyfriars
1796-1830	William L. Brown	Greyfriars & Princ. Marischal
1831-1843	Alexander Black	Lecturer in Practical Religion
1843-1860	William R. Pirie	Lecturer in Practical Religion (1844)
		College Chapel-of-Ease (1846-one year)
		Prof. Church History, King's College (1843-1860)

Additional

1841-?	John Row, Lecturer	(Weekly lecturers in Hebrew)

APPENDIX B

A Complete Listing of Theological Professors in the Secession Churches, 1733-1847

The Sources
The lists for Appendix B have chiefly been compiled from MacKelvie, Brown's *MS*, Scott, Smart, and Presbytery and Synod Minutes. Occasionally biographies have also been used to confirm or provide additional information. The reader again is directed to the bibliography for fuller details.

The Columns
Four columns have been used. The first column records the year(s) of service. The second column records the individual's name. Again notes attached to a name have generally been excluded. The third column states the name of the professorship the individual held and the fourth states where the said professor conducted the divinity hall.

The Titles of the Halls
In an effort to organize the various divinity halls within the Secession tradition from 1733 to 1847, main branches, these halls have been kept to Section A. These halls represent the largest statistical grouping of Seceders. Then the following pages identified as Sections B, C and D list the halls in the Auld Light Burgher and Antiburgher traditions from 1799 and 1806 through to their mergers and reunions ending in 1852. The book has adopted a terminus date of 1847 since this was the year the majority of Scottish Seceders joined with the Relief Church, thus ending the Secession tradition in one sense. The smaller branch of post-1852 Original Seceders has not occupied our attention as this study has focussed upon the main Secession branches and has not gone into this small remnant branch in the 1850s and 60s.

Section A
THE SECEDERS (MAIN BRANCHES)

Years	Professor's Name	Title	Location
Divinity Hall of the Associate Presbytery: 1733-1747			
1736(?)1737-1741	William Wilson	Professor of Divinity	Perth
1742-1747	Alexander Moncrieff	Professor of Divinity	Abernethy
Associate Divinity Hall, Associate Synod, 1748-1820			
1748	Ebenezer Erskine	Professor of Divinity	Stirling
1749-1764	James Fisher	Professor of Divinity	Glasgow
1764-1767	John Swanston	Professor of Divinity	Kinross
1767(?)-1787	John Brown	Professor of Divinity	Haddington
1787-1820	George Lawson	Professor of Divinity	Selkirk
General Associate Divinity Hall, General Associate Synod, 1748-1820			
1748-1761	Alexander Moncrieff	Professor of Divinity	Abernethy
1762-1786	William Moncrieff	Professor of Divinity	Alloa
1786-1804	Archibald Bruce	Professor of Divinity	Whitburn
1805-1806	Presbyteries	Professor of Divinity	Various
1807-1820	George Paxton	Professor of Divinity	Edinburgh
United Secession Divinity Hall[2], United Secession Church, 1820-1847			
1820-1825	John Dick	Professor of Divinity	Glasgow
1825-1833	John Dick[3]	Professor of Syst. Theo.	Glasgow
1825-1833	John Mitchell	Professor of Bib. Lit.	Glasgow/Edin.
1834-1842	John Mitchell	Professor of Bib.Lit.	Glasgow/Edin.
1834-1847	John Brown	Professor of Ex. Theo.	Glasgow/Edin.
1834-1844	Robert Balmer	Professor of Syst. Theo.	Glasgow/Edin.
1834-1843[4]	Alexander Duncan	Professor of Past. Theo & Church History	Glasgow/Edin.

---

[2] There are really three stages to the United Secession divinity hall, 1820-1847, in which the hall went from one to two professors, then to four.

[3] John Dick did not do the senior third, fourth and fifth session students in 1833. Rather, they did their studies directly under the oversight of a specially appointed committee, each in the presbytery to which he was attached.

[4] For 1842 only David Duncan gave instruction in pastoral theology and ecclesiastical history by reading his father, Alexander Duncan's, lectures. Dr. John Eadie gave instruction in biblical literature.

1843-1847	James Harper	Professor of Past. Theo.	Edinburgh
1843-1847	John Eadie	Professor of Bib. Lit.	Edinburgh
1843-1847	James Harper [acting then] Professor of Syst. Theo.		Edinburgh
	[plus John Brown Professor of Ex. Theo.]		Edinburgh

Section B

THE AULD LIGHT SECEDERS

Part I: The Auld Light Burghers

Explanation

The original Burgher Synod existed from 1799 to 1839, when the majority entered the Church of Scotland. The minority group were referred to as the Remnant Synod and existed from 1839 to 1842, when they joined the Auld Light Antiburghers (Original Seceders) to form the United Original Synod.

Years	Professor's Name	Title	Location
(I) Original Burgher Synod Divinity Hall: 1799-1839			
1800-1803	William Willis(father)	Professor of Divinity	Greenock, Stirling
1803-1818	George Hill	Professor of Divinity	Cumbernauld
1818-1833	William Taylor	Interim then Prof. of Div.	Perth
1835-1839	Michael Willis(son)	Professor of Divinity	Glasgow

(II) Remnant Synod Divinity Hall: 1839-1842

They do not appear to have ever conducted a separate Hall but rather shared it as presbyters.

Section C

Part II: The Auld Light Antiburghers

Explanation

The first group of Auld Light Antiburghers to emerge as a separate body became known as the Constitutional Associate Presbytery, which was formed in 1806 and lasted until 1827. The second group of Auld Light Antiburghers to emerge were known as the Protesters and lasted from 1820 to 1827, when the Constitutional Presbytery and the Protesters united to form the Synod of Original Seceders in 1827. Thus, this body united the Auld Light Antiburghers into one body until 1842.

Appendices

Years	Professor's Name	Title	Location
(I) Constitutional Associate Divinity Hall: 1806-1827			
1806-1816	Archibald Bruce	Professor of Divinity	Whitburn
1816-1818	Thomas McCrie, Sr.	Professor of Divinity	Edinburgh

Two additional Constitutional Associate ministers provided assistance in theological education but without the designation of professor.

1806-1823	John Turnbull	Instr. in Bib. Languages	Glasgow
1816-1824	Robert Chalmers	Instr. in Homiletics	Haddington

(II) Protesters Divinity Hall: 1820-1827

1820-1827	George Paxton	Professor of Divinity	Edinburgh

(III) Original Secession Divinity Hall: 1827-1842

1827-1836	George Paxton	Professor of Divinity	Edinburgh
1833-1835	Thomas McCrie, Sr.	(Assistant)Prof.of Div.	Edinburgh
1836-1842	Thomas McCrie, Jr.	Professor of Divinity	Edinburgh
1839-1842	Benjamin Laing	Prof. of Heb.& Bib.Crit.	Edinburgh

Section D

Part III: The Auld Light Burghers and Antiburghers – United

Explanation

In 1842 the Remnant of Burgher Auld Lights united with the Original Secession Synod (Auld Light Antiburghers) to form the United Original Secession Synod. This body lasted from 1842 to 1852, at which time the majority joined the Free Church of Scotland. A small minority remained outside of the union and remained a separate body in Scotland until 1954.

Years	Professor's Name	Title	Location
(I) United Original Secession Divinity Hall: 1842-1852			
1842-1852	Thomas McCrie, Jr.	Professor of Divinity	Edinburgh
1842-1852	Benjamin Laing	Prof. of Heb.& Bib.Crit.	Edinburgh

(II) (Continuing) United Original Secession Divinity Hall: 1852-1954
[incomplete list]

1852-1876	Matthew Murray	Professor of Divinity	Glasgow
	William F. Aitken	Prof. of Bib. Crit.	Glasgow
1923-1953	Francis Davidson	Prof. of Bib. Crit.	Paisley

Bibliography

Primary Sources

Abstract from the Minutes of the Synod of the Presbyterian Church of Nova Scotia 1844-1845 [1842-1845]. Canadian Institute for Historical Microreproductions, No. 01988.

Acta Facultatis Artium Universitatis S. Andree 1413-1588. 2 vols. Scottish History Society, Edinburgh, 1964.

Acts of the Associate Presbytery: Act concerning the Doctrine of Grace...Act for renewing the National Covenant of Scotland, and the Solemn League and Covenant.... Edinburgh, 1744.

Acts of the General Assembly of the Church of Scotland 1638 to 1842. Edited by Thomas Pitcairn. Church Law Society, Edinburgh, 1843.

Acts and Proceedings of the Associate Presbytery, Met at Edinburgh, May 1739. Containing their Declinature.... Edinburgh, 1739.

"Acts and Proceedings of the General Associate Synod 1767-1781". National Archives of Scotland, Edinburgh, *MS* CH3/144/1.

"Acts and Proceedings of the General Associate Synod 1781-1794". National Archives of Scotland, Edinburgh, *MS* CH3/144/2.

"Acts and Proceedings of the General Associate Synod 1795-1820". National Archives of Scotland, Edinburgh, *MS* CH3/144/3.

Analysis and Review First Report of Commissioners – Aberdeen Universities. By "a standing committee of graduates and alumni, Kings College". Aberdeen, 1839.

Anon. "Extract of a Letter from a Student in Theology, Attending the Pictou Academy, To a Clergyman in this Country". Dated Pictou, October 8, 1829. *Edinburgh Theological Magazine* 5 (1830): 120-121.

Anon. "Membership List". *Memoirs of the Wernernian Society* 5 (1823-1824): 583.

— "Religious and Philanthropic Intelligence". *Edinburgh Theological Magazine* 5 (1830): 182-183.

— "Two Glasgow Society Minute Books" [1796-1831]. Book 1. "The Gaelic Chapel Students' Society". *RSCHS* 5 (1935): 175-181.

— "Two Glasgow Society Minute Books" [1826-1839]. Book 2. "The Clerical Literary Society". *RSCHS* 5 (1935), 181-184.

Balmer, Robert. *Academical Lectures and Pulpit Discourses*. 2 vols. Edinburgh, 1845.

Beattie, James. *Essay on Truth*. Edinburgh, 1770.

The Booke of the Universall Kirk of Scotland. Edited by Alexander Peterkin. Edinburgh, 1839.

Boston, Thomas. *The Art of Man-Fishing*. Original 1773, *MS* 1699. Fearn, Ross-shire, 1998.

— *The Complete Works of Thomas Boston*. Edited by Samuel McMillan. Original 1853. 12 vols. Wheaton, Illinois, 1980.

— *A General Account of My Life*. Edited by George D. Low. London, 1908.

— *Human Nature in its Fourfold State*. Edinburgh, 1720.

— *Memoirs of Thomas Boston*. New ed. Edited by George Morrison, 1899. Edinburgh, 1988.
Brown, John (of Broughton Place). *Analytical Exposition of the Epistle of Paul the Apostle to the Romans*. Edinburgh, 1857.
— *Discourses and Sayings of our Lord Jesus Christ*. Original 1850. 2d. ed. 1852, enlarged. 3 vols. Edinburgh, 1990.
— *An Exposition of the Epistle of the Apostle Paul to the Hebrews*. Edited by David Smith. 2 vols. Edinburgh, 1862.
— *An Exposition of the Epistle of Paul the Apostle to the Galatians*. Edinburgh, 1853.
— *The Sufferings and Glories of the Messiah: an Exposition of Psalm XVIII, and Isaiah LII:13-LIII:12*. Edinburgh, 1853.
Brown, John (of Haddington). *Address to Students of Divinity*. Edited by John Brown (Broughton Place). Reprint with notes. Edinburgh, 1859.
— *The Absurdity and Perfidy of all Authoritative Toleration of Gross Heresy, Blasphemy, Idolatry, and Popery in Britain*. Glasgow, 1780.
— *A Brief Dissertation on Christ's Righteousness Shewing In what Extent and Proportion it is imputed to us in Justification; Together with the Sentiments of orthodox Divines upon this important question*. Edinburgh, 1759.
— *The Christian, the Student, and Pastor Exemplified in the Lives of Nine Ministers*. Edinburgh, 1781.
— *A Compendious History of the British Churches in England, Scotland, Ireland, and America. Giving An Account of the Most Material Transactions since the introduction of Christianity to the Present Time. With an Introductory Sketch of the History of the Waldenses*. Glasgow, 1784. With appendix, 2 vols., Edinburgh, 1789.
— *A Compendious View of Natural and Revealed Religion*. MS annotations in an interleaved copy, Glasgow, 1782. Plus *MS* annotations by John Brown (Broughton Place) to the "Address to Students of Divinity", which prefaces the *Compendious View*; plus notes on "Textual Difficulties" and "Textual Difficulties Solved". New College Library, Edinburgh, BRO 59.
— *A Compendious View of Natural and Revealed Religion*. Original 1782. London, 1817.
— *A Concordance to the Holy Scriptures of the Old and New Testaments*. New York, 1871.
— *A Dictionary of the Holy Bible*. Edited by John Brown Patterson. London and Edinburgh, 1845.
— "An evangelical and practical view of Old Testament types". New College Library, Edinburgh, *MS* BRO 55, 576 pp.
— *The Family and Church Psalm Book, with Notes and Illustrations, designed to explain the sense, and to aid in the exercise of Christian Devotion by John Brown. B With an Appendix, Containing the whole of the Author's Commentary on the Book of Revelation...*. Editor not identified. Edinburgh, 1835.
— *General History of the Christian Church from the Birth of our Saviour to the Present Time Containing A succinct Account of external Events...and the Disputes, Heresies, and Sects...with An Appendix, containing the History of Philosophers, Deists, Socinians...to which is subjoined A List of Errors, especially since the Reformation*. 2 vols. Edinburgh, 1771.
— *Harmony of Scripture Prophecies, and History of Their Fulfilment*. Glasgow, 1784.

Bibliography 413

— *An Historical Account of the Rise and Progress of the Secession*. 5th ed. Glasgow, 1788.
— *Letters on the Exemplary Behaviour of Ministers: Originally Composed for the Use of His Students*. Edited by John Brown (Whitburn). Edinburgh, 1827.
— *Letters on the Constitution of the Christian Church*. Original 1767. Edinburgh, 1799.
— *Memoir and Select Remains of John Brown of Haddington*. Edited by William Brown. Edinburgh, 1856.
— "Memoirs of the Secession". New College Library, Edinburgh, *MS* BRO 70.
— "On the Composition of Pulpit Discourses". *Christian Repository*. Nov. 1817, 661-671.
— *The Posthumous Works of the Late Rev. Mr. John Brown of Haddington with Short Memoirs*. Edited by John Brown (Whitburn) and Ebenezer Brown. Perth, 1797.
— *Practical Piety Exemplified in the Lives of Thirteen eminent Christians...and Illustrated in Casuistical Hints or Cases of Conscience*. Glasgow, 1783. [This work can also be found in *MS* form in the New College Library, Edinburgh, *MS* BRO 44. It was transcribed by William Falkirk in 1781 and is 348 pages of hand-written text.]
— *The Psalms of David in Metre with Notes, Exhibiting the Connection, Explaining the Sense, and for Directing and Animating the Devotion*. Dallas, Texas, 1991.
— *Sacred Typology or A Brief View of the Figures and Explication of the Metaphors contained in Scripture*. Middlebury, Vermont, 1812.
— *Self-Interpreting Bible*. 2 vols. London, 1791.
— "Skeletons of Sermons by the Rev. John Brown of Haddington". Historic Collections, Special Libraries and Archives King's College, University of Aberdeen, *MS* 3245/9 (undated).
— *Select Remains of John Brown*. Edited by John and Ebenezer Brown. London, 1789.
— *Two Short Catechisms Mutually Connected*. Original 1764. Edinburgh, 1818.
Brown, John (of Wamphray). *An Exposition of the Epistle of Paul to the Romans with Large Practical Observations; delivered in Several Lectures*. Editor not named. Edinburgh, 1766.
Brown, William L. *Essays on the Existence of a Supreme Creator*. Aberdeen, 1816.
Brown, William. *The History of the Propagation of Christianity among the Heathen*. 2d ed. 2 vols. Edinburgh, 1823.
Bruce, Archibald. *Collected Works of Archibald Bruce*. 1774-1817. [9 vols., housed in New College Library, Edinburgh].
— "Draft Sermons and Lecture Notes". [1775-1789], New College Library, *MS* BRU 1.
— *Introductory and Occasional Lectures, for Forming the Minds of Young Men, Intending the Holy Ministry*. Original 1797 and reprint 1817. [Vol. I, 1797 and 1817; Vol. II, 1817]. Edinburgh.
Bucer, Martin. *De Regno Christi* in *Melanchthon and Bucer*. Edited by Wilhelm Pauck. Library of Christian Classics. Vol. 19. London, 1969. 174-394.
Burnet, Gilbert. *History of His Own Times*. 2 vols. London, 1838.
— *History of His Own Times*. Abridged by Thomas Stackhouse. London, 1986.
Calvin, John. *Commentary on I Corinthians*. Translated by John Pringle. Vol. 1. Calvin Translation Society, Edinburgh, 1848.
Campbell, George. *Address to the People of Scotland*. Aberdeen, 1779.
— *Dissertation on Miracles*. Edinburgh,1762.
— *Lectures on Ecclesiastical History*. London, 1800.
— *The Works of George Campbell*. 6 vols. London, 1840.

"Catalogue of Books from the McCulloch Library". Filed with the Librarian, Atlantic School of Theology, Halifax, Nova Scotia, 1977.

A Catalogue of the Graduates in the Faculties of Arts, Divinity, and Law, of the University of Edinburgh. The Bannatyne Club, Edinburgh, 1858.

"Catalogue of the Library of the Rev. John Brown, D. D. March, 1847", to which is added "Index of Pamphlets: 1-150; 151-267". Historic Collections, Special Libraries and Archives King's College, University of Aberdeen, *MS*. (No library numbers had been assigned to this *MS* as of July 3, 2000.) [1847 plus some later editions].

Certain Papers of Robert Burnet, Gilbert Burnet, and Robert Leighton. Edited by H. C. Foxcroft. Scottish History Society, Edinburgh, 1904. 315-370.

Chalmers, Thomas. *Posthumous Works*. Edited by William Hanna. Vol. 9. Edinburgh, 1849.

Class Catalogue for Anatomy 1790 to 1811. Compiled and transcribed by W. Innes Addison. *MS* in the University of Glasgow Archives, Glasgow.

Collected Works of Archibald Bruce. 9 vols. Whitburn, and Edinburgh, 1774-1820.

"Correspondence of the Secession Hall Students". In Letterbook II, 1829. Bound in *United Secession Divinity Hall Society Correspondence: 1820-1843*. National Archives of Scotland, Edinburgh, *MS* CH3/305/2 .

Dewar, Daniel. *Elements of Systematic Theology*. 3 vols. Glasgow, 1867.

Dick, John. *The Conduct and Doom of False Teachers*. Edinburgh, 1788.

— *Confessions of Faith Shown to be Necessary, and the Duty of Churches with Respect to them Explained*. Edinburgh, 1796.

— *An Essay on the Inspiration of the Holy Scriptures of the Old and New Testaments*. Original 1800. Edinburgh, 1810.

— *Lectures on the Acts of the Apostles*. 2d ed. Glasgow, 1822.

— *Lectures on Theology*. Edited by Andrew C. Dick. 2 vols. Edinburgh, 1834.

— *Lectures on Theology*. Edited by Andrew C. Dick and [J.F.]. 2 vols. Philadelphia, 1841.

— *Sermons*. Glasgow, 1816.

— *A Sermon on the Qualifications and the Call of Missionaries*. Edinburgh, 1801.

Dickson, David. *Therapeutica Sacra: Shewing Briefly the Method of Healing the Diseases of the Conscience Concerning Regeneration*. Edinburgh, 1664.

— *Truth's Victory over Error....* (Original in Latin, 1684.) Glasgow, 1725.

Duncan, John. *Rich Gleanings from Rabbi Duncan*. Edited by J. S. Sinclair. Original 1925. Glasgow, 1984.

Edwards, Jonathan. *The Great Christian Doctrine of Original Sin Defended; Evidences of its Truth Produced, and Arguments to the Contrary Answered*. Glasgow, 1819.

Erskine, Ebenezer. *The Stone Rejected by the Builders, Exalted as the Head-Stone of the Corner*. Edinburgh, 1732.

— *The True State of the Question*. Edinburgh, 1747.

— *The Whole Works of Ebenezer Erskine Consisting of Sermons and Discourses*. Edited by James Fisher. Original 1761. Edinburgh, 1871.

Erskine, Ebenezer, William Wilson, Alexander Moncrieff, and James Fisher. *Reasons by Ebenezer Erskine, William Wilson, Alexander Moncrieff, and James Fisher, why they have not aceded to the judicatories of the Established Church*. Edinburgh, 1735.

Erskine, Ralph. *Fancy no Faith: or, A Seasonable Admonition....* Glasgow, 1747.

— *The Sermons and Other Practical Works of Ralph Erskine*. Original 1764-1765. 7 vols. London, 1865.

Ferguson, Alexander. *A Display of the Act and Testimony published by Mr. Ebenezer Erskine and his associates who separated from the Church of Scotland in the year 1734, and were deposed by the General Assembly in the year 1740*....Glasgow, 1761.

Ferme, Charles. *A Logical Analysis of the Epistle of Paul to the Romans*. Edited by W. Alexander. Wodrow Society, Edinburgh, 1850.

The First Book of Discipline. Edited by James K. Cameron. Edinburgh, 1972.

Fisher, James. *The Assembly's Shorter Catechism Explained*. Glasgow, 1753.

— *Christ the Sole and Wonderful Doer in the Work of Man's Redemption; an action Sermon...to which is subjoined The Doers of the Heart summoned to open to the King of Glory; an action sermon....* Glasgow, 1755.

— "Fisher's Register of the Divinity Hall, 1750-1763". As Appendix 3 in *Memorial of Rev. James Fisher*, edited by John Brown (of Broughton Place). Edinburgh, 1849.

— *A Review of a Pamphlet entitled "A Serious Enquiry into the Burgess Oaths of Edinburgh, Perth, and Glasgow"; wherein the most material arguments against the Burgess Oath are impartially weighed and examined*. Glasgow, 1747.

— *A Review of the Preface to a Narrative of the Extraordinary Work at Kilsyth and other Congregations in the Neighbourhood, written by the Rev. Mr. James Robe, Minister of Kilsyth....* Glasgow, 1742.

— "Sacramental Sermons by Mr. James Fisher... and Sundry others, Ralph Erskine, Ebenezer Erskine,... all at Sacramentall occasions". [1730's and undated] Historic Collections, Special Libraries and Archives, King's College University of Aberdeen, *MS* 3245/7.

— "Two Sermons by Rev. Mr. James Fisher of Glasgow: Isaiah 22:11, 12 and Ephesians 1:14" [1747 and 1749] Historic Collections, Special Libraries and Archives King's College, University of Aberdeen, *MS* 3245/8.

Fraser, William. "Book K – Sermons by William Fraser, written A.D.1816, 1817, and 1818". Also contains "Statistics of Students in the Burgher Divinity Hall, Selkirk 1798, when Fraser was a student there, under Prof. George Lawson, and their situation in 1818". New College Library, Edinburgh, *MS* FRA 5.

The Geneva Bible (The Annotated New Testament 1602 Edition). Edited by Gerald T. Sheppard. New York, 1989.

Gerard, Alexander. *Dissertations on Subjects Relating to the Genius and Evidences of Christianity*. Edinburgh, 1766.

— *The Influence of the Pastoral Office*. Aberdeen, 1760.

— *Pastoral Care*. Edited by Gilbert Gerard. London/Aberdeen, 1799.

— "A Plan of Education in the Marischal College and University of Aberdeen, with the Reasons of it". Aberdeen, 1755.

Gib, Adam. *The Present Truth: A Display of the Secession Testimony*. 2 vols. Edinburgh, 1774.

The Graduation Roll 1413-1579 and The Matriculation Roll 1473-1579 in *Early Records of the University of St. Andrews*. Edited by James M. Anderson. Scottish History Society, Edinburgh, 1926.

Guild, William. *Anti-christ in his true Colours, or the Pope of Rome proven to bee that Man of Sinne,....* Aberdeen, 1655.

— *Love's Entercours between the Lamb and his Bride, or A Clear Explication...of the Song of Solomon*. London, 1658.

— *Moses Unveiled: or those figures pointing out Christ Jesus whereunto is added the Harmony of All the Prophets*. London, 1620.

— *The Noveltie of Poperie discovered and chieflie proved by Romanists out of themselves.* Aberdeen, 1656.
— *The Only Way to Salvation, or the Life and Soul of True Religion.* London, 1608.
— *The Sealed Book Opened, being an explication of the Revelations.* Aberdeen, 1656.
— *Three Rare Monuments of Antiquita, or Bertram, a Frenchman, Aelfricus, an Englishman, and Maurus, a Scotsman: all stronglie convincing that grosse error of transubstantiation.* Aberdeen, 1624.
— *The Throne of David, an Exposition of II Samuel.* Oxford, 1659.
Hall, Archibald. *Impartial Survey of the Religious Clause in some Burgess-Oaths.* Edinburgh, 1771.
Halyburton, Thomas. *Memoirs of the Rev. Thomas Halyburton, With an Introductory essay by the Rev. D. Young.* Glasgow, 1824.
— *Memoirs of the Rev. Thomas Halyburton.* Edited by Joel R. Beeke. Grand Rapids, 1996.
— *Natural Religion Insufficient.* Edinburgh, 1714.
— *The Works of the Rev. Thomas Halyburton.* Edited by Robert Burns. Glasgow, 1837.
Hamilton, William. *The Truth and Excellency of the Christian Religion.* Edinburgh, 1732.
Hill, George. *The Death of a Faithful Minister in Obedience to the Will of God.* Glasgow, 1811.
— *Lectures in Divinity.* Edited by Alexander Hill. Original 1821. Philadelphia, 1844.
— *Lectures upon Portions of the Old Testament.* Edinburgh, 1812.
Hunter, Andrew. "Theological Lectures". Edinburgh University Library, *MS* Dc. 3.22-7.
Jardine, George. *Outlines of Philosophical Education.* 2d ed. Glasgow, 1825.
[Keir, John]. *Course of Study in Systematic and Pastoral Theology and Ecclesiastical History, for Students attending the Theological Seminary of the Presbyterian Church of Nova Scotia* . Charlottetown, P.E.I., 1857.
Knox, John. *The Works of John Knox.* Edited by D. Laing. 6 vols. Edinburgh, 1846-1864.
Lawson, George. *Considerations on the overture lying before the Associate Synod, respecting some alterations in the Formula concerning the power of the Civil magistrate in matters of religion, and the obligation of our Covenants, National and Solemn League, on posterity.* Edinburgh, 1797.
— *Discourses on the History of David and on the Introduction of Christianity into Britain.* Berwick, 1833.
— *Discourses on the whole book of Esther. To which are added, sermons, on parental duties, duties on military courage, and on the improvement to be made of the alarm of war.* Original 1804. Edinburgh, 1809.
— *Exposition of the Book of Proverbs.* 2 vols. Edinburgh, 1821.
— *Lectures on the history of Joseph.* 2 vols. Edinburgh, 1807.
— *Lectures on the whole book of Ruth: to which are added, discourses on the condition and duty of unconverted sinners, on the sovereignty of grace in the conversion of sinners, and, on the means to be used in the conversion of our neighbours.* Edinburgh, 1805.
— "On the Popery of Protestants; Notes on various Biblical passages; Essay on the faults into which ministers are in danger of falling in preaching". [undated] Historic Collections, Special Libraries and Archives King's College, University of Aberdeen, *MSS* 3245/11.

Bibliography 417

— *Reflections on the illness and death of a beloved daughter*. Edinburgh, 1805.
— *Sermons: On the Death of Faithful Ministers, On Wars and Revolutions, To the Aged*. Hawick, 1810.
— *Sermons on Various Relative Duties*. Edinburgh, 1809.
Leechman, William. *The Temper, Character, and Duty of a Minister*. Glasgow, 1755.
Leighton, Robert. *A Practical Commentary on the First Epistle of Peter*. Original 1693-1694. London, 1870.
The Letters and Journals of Robert Baillie. Edited by David Laing. Edinburgh, 1841.
Letters of Samuel Rutherford With a Sketch of His Life. Edited by Andrew Bonar. (Original edited by McWard, 1664.) Edinburgh, 1984.
McCulloch, Thomas. *Calvinism, The Doctrine of the Scripture*. Glasgow, [1846].
— *Colonial Gleanings. William, and Melville*. Edinburgh, 1826.
— *Introductory Hints to Theological Students – A Lecture, Delivered at the opening of the First Theological Class in the Pictou Academical Institution; and Designed to Suggest a Course of Preparation Requisite for the Successful Discharge of Ministerial Duties in the Presbyterian Church of Nova Scotia*. Glasgow, 1821.
— *A Memorial from the Committee of Missions of the Presbyterian Church of Nova Scotia, to the Glasgow Society for Promoting the Religious Interests of the Scottish Settlers in British North America with Observations on the Constitution of that Society, and upon the Proceedings and First Annual Report of the Committee of Directors*. Edinburgh, 1826.
— *The Mephibosheth Stepsure Letters*. Edited by Gwendolyn Davies. Ottawa, 1990.
— *The Nature and Uses of a Liberal Education, Being a Lecture Delivered at the Opening of the Building, erected for the accommodation of the classes of the Pictou Academical Institution*. Halifax, 1819.
— *Popery Again Condemned by Scripture and the Fathers* Edinburgh, 1810.
— *Popery Condemned by Scripture and the Fathers*. Edinburgh, 1808.
— "Thomas McCulloch to Charles Archibald". Dated Pictou, N.S., April 24, 1838. *Thomas McCulloch Letters Collection*. PANS, Halifax, N.S. *MS*, McCulloch Letter File, MG1, Vol.553/136.
— "Thomas McCulloch to James Mitchell". Dated Dec.2, 1841, Halifax, N. S. *Thomas McCulloch's Letter Collection*. PANS, Halifax, N.S. *MS*, McCulloch Letter File, MG1, Vol. 553/122.
— "Thomas McCulloch, Pictou, N.S. to the Theological Students under the inspection of the Rev. Drs. Dick and Mitchell, Glasgow, Scotland, 14 May, 1830". *Letterbook*. [United Secession Hall] National Archives of Scotland, Edinburgh, *MS* CH3/305/2 .
McCurdy, Daniel, and John Baxter. "Daniel McCurdy and John Baxter, students at the Presbyterian Divinity Hall, Pictou, N.S. to the Students in Glasgow at the Secession Hall, 20 October, 1829". *Letterbook*. [United Secession Hall] National Archives of Scotland, Edinburgh, *MS* CH3/305/2.
MacGill, Stevenson. *Considerations Addressed to a Young Minister*. Glasgow, 1809.
— *Lectures on Rhetoric and Criticism*. Edinburgh, 1838.
MacKnight, James. *A New and Literal Translation from the Original Greek, of all the Apostolical Epistles, with a Commentary and Notes Philological, Critical, Explanatory and Practical*. 4 vols. Edinburgh, 1795.
McLerie, David. *The Clergy-man Corrected by the Weaver; in a letter from David McLerie, Weaver in Paisley, to the Rev. Mr. Alexander Ferguson, Minister of the Gospel at Kilwinning*. Glasgow, 1761.

The Matriculation Albums of the University of Glasgow From 1728 to 1858. Edited by W. Innes Addison. Glasgow, 1913.
Melville, James. *Autobiography and Diary of Mr. James Melville 1556-1610.* Edited by R. Pitcairn. Wodrow Society, Edinburgh, 1842.
"Memorial on Behalf of the Literary and Philosophical Institution at Pictou, Nova Scotia". n.p., 1825. Maritime Conference Archives, Sackville, N.B., Box PHDH-1, No. 4.
"Minutes of the Associate Presbytery,1733-1740". National Archives of Scotland, Edinburgh, *MS* CH3/27/1.
"Minutes of the Associate Presbytery (and Synod),1741-1747". National Archives of Scotland, Edinburgh, *MS* CH3/28/1.
"Minutes of the Associate Presbytery and General Associate Presbytery,1745-1752". National Archives of Scotland, Edinburgh, *MS* CH3/144/4.
"Minutes of the General Associate Synod,1752-1763". National Archives of Scotland, Edinburgh, *MS* CH3/144/5.
"Minutes of the General Associate Synod,1763-1775". National Archives of Scotland, Edinburgh, *MS* CH3/144/6.
"Minutes of the Proceedings of the Associate Synod,1747-1766" . National Archives of Scotland, Edinburgh, *MS* CH3/28/2 .
"Minutes of the Proceedings of the Associate Synod,1766-1787" . National Archives of Scotland, Edinburgh, *MS* CH3/28/3.
"Minutes of the Proceedings of the Associate Synod,1787-1820" . National Archives of Scotland, Edinburgh, *MS* CH3/28/4.
Minutes of the Proceedings of the Synod of the Presbyterian Church of Nova Scotia: 1817 [to 1844]. Maritime Conference Archives, Sackville, New Brunswick, *MS* 11F-7.
Moncrieff, Alexander. *Practical Works of Alexander Moncrieff.* Edinburgh, 1779.
Munimenta Alme Universitatis Glasguensis, Records of the University of Glasgow From its Foundation Till 1727. Edited by C. Innes. 3 vols. Maitland Club, Glasgow, 1854.
The New Foundation. Translated by G. Patrick Edwards. In *King's College, Aberdeen, 1560-1641,* by David Stevenson. Aberdeen, 1990. 149-166.
Nisbet, Alexander. *An Exposition With Practical Observations Upon the Book of Ecclesiastes.* Edinburgh, 1694.
Officers and Graduates of University and King's College Aberdeen. Edited by P. J. Anderson. New Spalding Club, Aberdeen, 1893.
The Order of the College of Geneva. Translated by W. Stanford Reid. Original 1559. English translation in the appendix to "Calvin and the Founding of the Academy of Geneva". *Westminster Theological Journal* 18 (1955): 22-23.
Paxton, George. *An Inquiry into the obligation of religious covenants upon posterity.* Edinburgh, 1801.
— *The Duty of the Church to her Rulers. A Sermon....* Glasgow, 1796.
— *Illustrations of the Holy Scriptures*: in three parts. I, From the geography of the East. II, From the Natural history of the East. III, From the customs of ancient and modern nations. 3d ed. 2 vols. Edinburgh, 1819.
— *Letters to the Rev. William Taylor; concerning healing Divisions of the Church.* Glasgow, 1802.
— *The Sin and Danger of circulating the Apocrypha in connection with the Holy Scriptures; with a brief statement of what is known concerning the Authors of the*

Apocryphal books; the Time of their Publication, and their Introduction into the Canon. Edinburgh, 1828.

— *The Villager and Other Poems.* Edinburgh, 1813.

Pictet, Benedict. *Christian Theology.* Translated by F. Reyroux. London, 1834.

—— *True and False Religion Examined and the Protestant Reformation Vindicated.* Translated by Archibald Bruce. Whitburn, 1797.

Polhill, Edward. *Essay on the Extent of the Death of Christ.* Berwick, 1842.

Porteous, William. *The Doctrine of Toleration & Applied to Present Times: in a sermon, preached in the Wynd Church of Glasgow, 10th December, 1778. Being a Public Feast, appointed by the Provisional Synod of Glasgow and Ayr.* Glasgow, 1778.

Posthumous Works of the Late William McGavin Accompanied with a Memoir; Including Autobiography Extracts from his Correspondence. Glasgow, 1834.

The Principal Acts of the General Assembly of the Church of Scotland, 1843. Edinburgh, 1843.

The Principal Acts of the General Assembly of the Church of Scotland, 1845. Edinburgh, 1845.

The Principal Acts of the General Assembly of the Church of Scotland, 1846. Edinburgh, 1846.

The Principal Acts of the General Assembly of the Church of Scotland, 1849. Edinburgh, 1849.

The Principal Acts of the General Assembly of the Church of Scotland, 1850. Edinburgh, 1850.

The Principal Acts of the General Assembly of the Church of Scotland, 1863. Edinburgh, 1863.

Proceedings in the Formation of the Glasgow Society for Promoting Religion and Liberal Education Among the Settlers in the North American Provinces With an Address by the Committee. Glasgow, 1827.

Rankin, Alexander. *Institutes of Theology; or, A Concise System of Divinity.* 1822.

Records of the Dioceses of Argyll and the Isles 1560-1860. Edited by J. B. Craven. Kirkwall, 1907.

Records of the Meeting of the Exercise of Alford 1662-1668. Edited by Thomas Bell. New Spalding Club, Aberdeen, 1897.

The Register of the Company of Pastors of Geneva in the Time of Calvin. Edited and translated by P. E. Hughes. Grand Rapids, 1966.

Register of the Diocesan Synod of Dunblane 1662-1668. Edited by John Wilson. Edinburgh, 1927.

Register of Ministers, Exhorters and Readers and of their Stipends after the Period of the Reformation. Maitland Club, Edinburgh, 1820.

Report Made to His Majesty by a Royal Commission of Inquiry into the State of the Universities of Scotland. Great Britain, House of Commons, 1831.

Report of a Committee Appointed by the Synod of the Presbyterian Church of Nova Scotia, to Prepare a Statement of Means for Promoting Religion in the Church, Securing the Permanence of the Church, and Enlarging its Bounds, and also, the Subsequent Resolutions and Arrangements of the Synod. Halifax, 1818.

Richardinus, Robert. *Commentary on the Rule of St. Augustine.* Original 1530. Scottish History Society, Edinburgh, 1935.

A Roll of the Graduate of the University of Glasgow 1727 to 1897. Edited by W. Innes Addison. Glasgow, 1898.

Rollock, Robert. *Select Works of Robert Rollock*. Edited by W. M. Gunn. Wodrow Society, Edinburgh, 1849.

Ross, John. *The Present State of the Edinburgh Divinity Hall*. Edinburgh, 1813.

Row, John (Sr. & Jr.). *The History of the Kirk of Scotland*. Edited by David Laing. Original *MS* 1650. Wodrow Society, Edinburgh, 1842.

"Rules to be observed in the Theological Society, instituted February 16th at Kinross, 1765". (Associate Burgher Synod Divinity Hall – Kinross, Haddington and while in part at Selkirk.) New College Library, Edinburgh, *MS* ASS.B unpaginated.

Rutherford, Samuel. *Christ Dying and Drawing Sinners to Himself*. London, 1647.

— *Trial and Triumph of Faith*. London, 1645.

The School of Faith. Edited and translated by Thomas Torrance. London, 1959.

Scott, David. *Annals and Statistics of the Original Secession Church*. Edinburgh, 1886.

Scottish Universities Commission: General Report of The Commissioners under The Universities (Scotland) Act, 1858. With an Appendix, Containing Ordinances, Minutes, Reports on Special Subjects, and Other Documents. Great Britain, House of Commons; Edinburgh: Murray and Gibb, 1863.

The Second Book of Discipline. Edited by James Kirk. Edinburgh, 1980.

Second Report of the Glasgow Society for Promoting Religion and Liberal Education Among the Settlers in the North American Provinces. Glasgow, 1830.

Selected Correspondence of the Glasgow Colonial Society 1825-1840. Edited by Elizabeth and Kerr McDougall, John S. Moir. Toronto, The Champlain Society, 1994.

Selections from the Records of the Kirk Session, Presbytery, and Synod of Aberdeen. Edited by John Stuart. Spalding Club, Aberdeen, 1846.

Somerville, Thomas. *My Own Life and Times 1741-1814*. Edinburgh, 1861.

Statistical Account of Ayrshire. Edinburgh, 1842.

Stirling Presbytery Records 1581-1587. Edited by James Kirk. Scottish History Society, Edinburgh, 1981.

A Supplement to Burnet's History of My Own Time derived from His Original Memoirs, etc. Edited by H. C. Foxcroft. Oxford, 1902.

Swanston, John. *Sermons on Several Important Subjects*. Glasgow, 1773.

Taylor, John. *The Scripture-Doctrine of Original Sin*. London, 1746.

Taylor, William. *An Effectual Remedy to the Disputes Presently Existing in the Associate Synod, respecting the Formula: in a Series of Letters to the Rev. Lawson from William Taylor*. Glasgow, 1799.

— "Student *MS* of John Brown of Haddington's 'Cases of Conscience relative to temptations of Satan; indwelling sin... and scandalous offences'". 1781. New College Library, Edinburgh, *MS* BRO 44, 348 pp. [This is an accurate handwritten student transcription of what was printed in Brown's *Practical Piety*. Glasgow, 1783].

"Testimonials in Support of Pictou Academy" (1825). *The Thomas McCulloch Letters Collection*. PANS, Halifax, Nova Scotia, *MS* MG1/Vol.551/16.

"D. Thomas, G. Thomson, Pres. & Sec., United Secession Divinity Hall Society to Rev. McCulloch, Pictou, N.S. 23 September, 1830". *Letterbook*. [United Secession Hall] National Archives of Scotland, Edinburgh, *MS* CH3/305/2.

Turretin, Francis. *Institutes of Elenctic Theology*. Edited by James T. Dennison and translated by G. M. Giger. 3 vols. Phillipsburg, New Jersey, 1992-1997.

Bibliography 421

"United Associate Synod Minutes, Sept. 8, 1820 - Sept. 17, 1834". United Church of Canada Archives, Victoria University, University of Toronto, Toronto, *MS* (Microfilm) Mic.D.7.2.#22 [CH3/298/1].

"United Associate Synod Minutes, April 20, 1835 - May 13, 1847", United Church of Canada Archives, Victoria University, University of Toronto, Toronto, *MS* (Microfilm) Mic.D.7.2.#23 [CH3/298/1,2].

University of Glasgow Senate Minutes. University of Glasgow Archives, Glasgow, *MS* 1/1/4.

"James Waddel and Alexander Blaikie, Divinity Students, Pictou, N.S. to the Students of Theology, United Secession Hall, Glasgow, 19 Nov. 1827". *Letterbook.* [United Secession Hall] National Archives of Scotland, Edinburgh, *MS* CH3/305/2.

"Waddel and Fraser, Divinity Students, Pictou, N.S. to the Students of Theology, United Secession Hall, Glasgow, 28 Nov. 1829". *Letterbook.* [United Secession Hall] National Archives of Scotland, Edinburgh, *MS* CH3/305/2.

Westminster Confession of Faith. Original 1646. Glasgow, 1958.

Willcock, John. *A Shetland Minister of the Eighteenth Century.* Kirkwall, 1897.

Willis, Michael. *Collectanea Graeca et Latina: Selections from the Greek and Latin Fathers with Notes....* Toronto, 1865.

— *Discourses on National Establishments of Christianity.* Glasgow, 1833.

— *National Responsibility and National Covenanting, being the Third Lecture on Church Establishments in Glasgow.* Glasgow, 1835.

— *Pulpit Discourses, Expository and Critical, and College Addresses.* London, 1873.

— *The Religious Question Involved in the Proposed Concessions to Roman Catholics.* Glasgow, 1827.

Willis, William. *A Smooth Stone from the Brook. or, An Humble Attempt to Prevent Backsliding from Covenanted Church of Scotland, in Some Letters to the Rev. George Lawson.* Glasgow, 1799.

— *Little Naphthali: or Historical Sketches Concerning the Present Melancholy Apostacy in the Secession with very important expostulations with Apostates.* Glasgow, 1800.

— *Ministerial Faithfulness Recommended, Particularly in the Admission of Young Men to the Holy Ministry, in a Sermon preached in the Meeting House in Bristo St., Edinburgh...Together With a Letter, Respecting the Rise, Progress, and Present State of the Mournful Confusion in the Secession....* Glasgow, 1798.

— *A View of Mount Calvary from the Mount of Transfiguration.* Stirling, 1822.

Wilson, William. "Abbreviated notes on sermons by William Wilson" [1731-1735]. Historic Collections, Special Libraries and Archives King's College, University of Aberdeen, *MS* 3245/4.

— *A Defence of the Reformation-Principles of the Church of Scotland. Wherein the Exceptions that are laid against the Conduct of the Associate Presbytery, as also against their judicial Act and Testimony, by the Reverend Mr. Currie in his Essay on Separation, are examined;....* Edinburgh, 1739.

— *The Evening-Time of the Church of Christ issuing in Light. A Sermon preached at Orwell, June 11, 1739. being Monday after the Celebration of the Sacrament of the Lord's Supper there; upon Zechariah xiv.7.* Edinburgh, 1743.

— *Sermons by the Rev. and Learned Mr. William Wilson, late Minister of the Gospel at Perth.* Edinburgh, 1748.

— *The Testimony deserted: a plain discovery of the defections and self-inconsistences that Mr. John McMillan, and the people in communion with him, are guilty of,... in a letter to a friend.* Glasgow, 1743.

— *A vindication and defence of the Christian peoples divine right to choose their own ministers.* Edinburgh, 1739.

The Works of the Rev. Thomas Halyburton. Edited by Robert Burns. Glasgow, 1837.

Witsius, Herman. *On the Character of a True Theologian.* Edited by J. Ligon Duncan. Greenville, South Carolina, 1994.

— *Sacred Dissertations on the Apostles' Creed.* Translated by Donald Fraser. Original Latin 1681, original English 1823. Escondido, California, 1993.

Secondary Sources and Theses

Alexander, William L. *Memoirs of the Life and Writings of Ralph Wardlaw.* Edinburgh, 1856.

Allen, Robert. *The Presbyterian College Belfast 1853-1953.* Belfast, 1954.

Anderson, Michael D. "Bishop Gilbert Burnet, 1643-1715; a critical account of his conception of the Christian ministry". Unpublished Ph.D. thesis, University of Edinburgh, New College, 1966.

Atkinson, D. W. "Zachary Boyd as Minister of the Barony Parish". *RSCHS* 24. (1990-1992): 22.

Anon. *Annals of Moncrieff United Free Church, Alloa, 1747-1904.* Alloa, 1904.

— "Ecclesiastical Intelligence". *Edinburgh Theological Magazine* 3 (1828): 500-501.

— "Evangelical Beauties, selected from the Works of Archbishop Leighton with a Short Account of his Life by John Brown, Whitburn". A review in *Edinburgh Theological Magazine* 2 (1827): 264.

— "Is it Expedient to Require Students of Divinity in the Secession to Pay Fees to Their Professors?". *Edinburgh Theological Magazine* 5 (1830): 505-506.

— "In Memoriam – Rev. Angus MacGillivray". *The Home and Foreign Record of the Presbyterian Church of the Lower Provinces of British North America.* Vol. 9, No. 9 (1869): 234-237.

— "The Late Rev. John Keir, D.D.". *Christian Instructor.* Vol. 4, No. 1 (Jan.1859): 1-8; Vol. 4, No. 2 (Feb., 1859): 33-40; Vol. 4, No. 3 (Mar.1859): 65-72; and Vol. 4, No. 4 (April, 1859): 97-110.

— "Life of George Buchanan". In *The History of Scotland*, by George Buchanan. Translated by James Aikman. Vol. 1. Glasgow, 1827.

— "Memoir of the Rev. Alexander Moncrieff of Culfargie, Minister of the Gospel at Abernethy". *The Christian Magazine* (1804): 89-96, 133-140.

— [J.F.] "Memoir of the Rev. John Dick, D. D.". In *Lectures on Theology*, by John Dick. Vol. 1. American ed. Philadelphia, 1841.

— "Obituary – Hugh Dunbar". *Christian Instructor* Vol. 3, No. 1 (Jan., 1858): 32.

— "Obituary – Hugh Ross". *Christian Instructor* Vol. 4, No. 1 (Jan., 1859): 30-32.

— "Obituary – Rev. John L. Murdoch". *The Home and Foreign Record of the Presbyterian Church of the Lower Provinces of British North America.* Vol. 13, No. 9 (1873): 262-265.

— [R.W.] Preface to *Truth's Victory Over Error*, by David Dickson. Glasgow, 1725.

—— "Review of Adam Thomson's, *A Comparative View of the English and Scottish Dissenters*". *Edinburgh Theological Magazine* 6 (1831): 323-324.
—— "Theological Discourses of the Students in the Secession Church". *Edinburgh Theological Magazine* 3 (1828): 205-206.
Armour, Eric. "The Rev. Samuel Armour, 1785-1853". *RSCHS* 5 (1935): 85-90.
Baird, H. M. "Notes on Theological Education in the Reformed Churches of France and French Switzerland". *Presbyterian Review* 1 (1880): 85-103.
Bannerman, Douglas. *Worship, Order, and Polity of the Presbyterian Church*. Edinburgh, 1894.
Bannerman, James. *Inspiration: The Infallible Truth and Divine Authority of Holy Scriptures*. Edinburgh, 1865.
Barber, Cyril J. Foreword to *Proverbs*, by George Lawson. Original 1821. Grand Rapids, 1984.
Barclay, Alastair. *The Bonnet Town*. Stewarton, 1989.
Bardgett, F. D. "'Four Parische Kirkis to Ane Preicheir'". *RSCHS* 22 (1986): 195-209.
Barker, William S. "John H. Leith, Crisis in the Church". A review in *WTJ* 61 (1999): 140-143.
Barnet, John G. *Life and Complete Works of Michael Bruce*. London, 1926.
Barrie, J. M. *The Little Minister*. Original 1891. Cleveland, 1933.
Baxter, David B. *The Parish of Largs*. Edited by Mary Hall. Largs, 1992.
Baxter, J. H. "The Theological Society 1760-1960". *St. Mary's College Bulletin* 3 (1961): 11-18.
Baxter, Richard. *The Practical Works of Richard Baxter: A Christian Directory*. 1846 edition. Vol. 1. Morgan, Pennsylvania, 2000.
Bebbington, D. W., ed. *The Baptists in Scotland*. Glasgow, 1988.
Bebbington, D. W. *Evangelism in Modern Britain: A History from the 1730's to the 1980's*. Original 1989. Grand Rapids, 1992.
Beeke, Joel. "Ebenezer and Ralph Erskine: Dissenters with a Cause (1)". *Banner of Sovereign Grace Truth* (November, 1999): 229-231.
—— "Ebenezer and Ralph Erskine: Dissenters with a Cause (2)". *Banner of Sovereign Grace Truth* (December, 1999): 262-264.
—— *Gisbertus Voetius Toward a Reformed Marriage of Knowledge and Piety*. Guidance from Church History. Vol. 2. Grand Rapids, 1999.
—— "Gisbertus Voetius, Toward a Reformed Marriage of Knowledge and Piety". In *Protestant Scholasticism: Essays in Reassessment*. Edited by Carl R. Trueman and R. S. Clark. Carlisle, 1999. 227-243.
Belfrage, Henry. "A Short Account of Dr. Lawson and His Writings". In *Discourses on the History of David*, by George Lawson. Berwick, 1833.
Bell, Peter. *Ministers of the Church of Scotland From 1560 to 1929: An Index to Fasti Ecclesiae Scoticanae, First Draft* [A-D and E-K]. 2 vols. Edinburgh, 1997 and 1999.
Benton, Woodrow W. "The Ecclesiology of George Hill, 1750-1819". Unpublished Ph.D. thesis, University of Edinburgh, New College, 1969.
Berkof, Louis. *Introductory Volume to Systematic Theology*. Rev. ed. Grand Rapids, 1932.
Betts, E. Arthur. *Our Fathers in the Faith: Being an Account of Presbyterian ministers ordained before 1875 in the Lower Provinces of British North America*. Halifax, 1983.
—— *Pine Hill Divinity Hall: 1820-1970*. Truro, N.S., 1970.

Bierma, Lyle D. *German Calvinism in the Confessional Age: The Covenant Theology of Casper Olevianus*. Grand Rapids, 1996.
Binnington, R. F. "The Glasgow Colonial Society and its work in the Development of the Presbyterian Church in British North America 1825-1840". Unpublished Th.D. thesis, Emmanuel College, Toronto, 1960.
Blaikie, A. "Memoir of the Late Rev. J. McLean of Richibucto" I. *Christian Instructor*. Vol. 2, No. I (Jan., 1857): 6-13; Vol.2, No. 2 (Feb., 1857): 52-59.
Blomberg, Craig L. *Interpreting the Parables*. Downers Grove, Illinois, 1990.
Bolton, J. S. *The Old West Kirk 1591-1991*. Greenock, 1991.
Bower, A. *The History of the University of Edinburgh*. Vol. 3. Edinburgh, 1830.
Briggs, C. A. *History of the Study of Theology*. 2 vols. London, 1916.
Brown, A. L., and Michael Moss. *The University of Glasgow: 1451-1996*. Edinburgh, 1996.
— *The University of Glasgow: 1451-2001*. Edinburgh, 2001.
Brown, Colin. *Christianity and Western Thought: A History of Philosophers, Ideas and Movements*. Vol. 1. Leicester, 1990.
Brown, C. G. *The Social History of Religion in Scotland since 1730*. London, 1987.
Brown, David. *Life of the Late John Duncan*. Edinburgh, 1872.
Brown, George. "Alphabetical List of the Students of Divinity of the United Secession Church, from the Rise of the Secession, till the year 1840". New College Library, Edinburgh, *MS* USC 5-11, unpaginated.
— "Annals of the Divinity Hall of the Secession Church of Scotland Containing Both Chronological and Alphabetical Lists of all who have been enrolled as Students...also an account of all the congregations of the United Presbyterian Church...". New College Library, Edinburgh, *MS* BRO55, 576 pp.
Brown, James. *The Life of a Scottish Probationer: Being a Memoir of Thomas Davidson with his poems and extracts from his letters*. 4th ed. Glasgow, 1908.
Brown, John (of Broughton Place). *Memorials of the Rev. James Fisher*. In *Fathers of the United Presbyterian Church*. Edinburgh, 1849.
— "Review of Archibald Bruce's 'A Critical Account of the Life, Character, and Discourses of Mr. Alexander Morus'". *The Edinburgh Christian Instructor* 8 (March, 1814): 182-195.
Brown, John (of Whitburn). "The Life of Ralph Erskine". In *The Sermons and Other Practical Works of Ralph Erskine*. Vol. 7. Original 1764-65. London, 1865.
— *Memoirs of Private Christians*. Glasgow, n.d.
Brown, Stewart J. *Thomas Chalmers and the Godly Commonwealth in Scotland*. Oxford, 1982.
Brown, William Adams. *The Education of American Ministers*. Vol. 1. New York, 1934.
Bruce, Michael. *Works of Michael Bruce*. Edited by A. B. Grosart. Edinburgh, 1865.
Bulloch, J. M. *A History of the University of Aberdeen, 1495-1895*. London, 1895.
Burleigh, J. H. S. *A Church History of Scotland*. London, 1960.
Burnet, George B. *The Holy Communion in the Reformed Church of Scotland 1560-1960*. Edinburgh, 1960.
Burns, Robert. *Memoir of the Rev. Stevenson MacGill*. Edinburgh, 1842.
Butler, D. *The Life and Letters of Robert Leighton*. London, 1903.
Button, C. N. "Scottish Mysticism in the 17th Century, with special reference to Samuel Rutherford". Unpublished Ph.D. thesis, University of Edinburgh, 1927.
Calhoun, David. *Princeton Seminary*. 2 vols. Edinburgh, 1994-1996.

Cameron, J. K. "The Piety of Samuel Rutherford (c.1600-61): a neglected feature of seventeenth-century Scottish Calvinism", *Nederlands Archief voor Kerkgeschiedenis* 65 (1985): 153-159.
— "Some Aberdeen Students on the Continent in the Late Sixteenth and Early Seventeenth Centuries". In *The Universities of Aberdeen and Europe: The First Three Centuries*, edited by Paul Dukes. Quincentennial Studies. Aberdeen, 1995. 57-78.
Cameron, N. M. de S., organ. ed.; D. F. Wright, D. C. Lachman and D. E. Meek, gen. eds. *Dictionary of Scottish Church History and Theology*. Edinburgh, 1993.
Campbell, William M. "Lex Rex and Its Author". *RSCHS* 7 (1941): 204-228.
— "Robert Boyd of Trochrigg". *RSCHS* 12 (1954-56): 220-234.
Cant, Robert Gordon. *The University of St. Andrews*. Rev. ed. Edinburgh, 1970.
— *The University of St. Andrews, A Short History*. 3d ed. St. Andrews, 1992.
Carlyle, Alexander. *The Autobiography of Dr. Alexander Carlyle of Inveresk 1722-1805*. Edited by J. H. Burton. London/Edinburgh, 1910.
Carter, Jennifer and J. H. Pittock, eds. *Aberdeen and the Enlightenment*. Aberdeen, 1987.
Carter, Jennifer and Donald Witherington, eds. *Scottish Universities: Distinctiveness and Diversity*. Edinburgh, 1992.
Cheyne, A. C. "John Caird (1820-1898) Preacher, Professor, Principal". In *Traditions of Theology in Glasgow 1450-1900. A Miscellany*. Edited by W. I. P. Hazlett. Edinburgh, 1993. 43-58.
— *Studies in Scottish Church History*. Edinburgh, 1999.
Christie, George. "Scripture Exposition in Scotland in the Seventeenth Century". *RSCHS* 1 (1926): 97-111.
Clark, Ian D. L. "The Reverend Andrew Lothian 1763-1831 United Secession Minister". *RSCHS* 20 (1980): 143-162.
Clarke, T. E. S. and H. C. Foxcroft. *A Life of Gilbert Burnet*. Cambridge, 1907.
Clarke, Tristram. "The Williamite Episcopalians and the Glorious Revolution in Scotland". *RSCHS* 24 (1992): 33-51.
Coffey, John. *Politics, Religion and the British Revolutions: The Mind of Samuel Rutherford*. Cambridge, 1997.
Conn, Harvie M., and Samuel Rowen, eds. *Missions and Theological Education in World Perspective*. Urbanus, Michigan, 1984.
Copleston, Frederick. *A History of Philosophy: Volume V Hobbes to Hume*. The Bellarmine Series, vol. 16. London, 1964.
Coutts, James. *A History of the University of Glasgow 1451-1909*. Glasgow, 1909.
Dabney, Robert L. *Syllabus and Notes of the Course of Systematic and Polemic Theology*. 2d ed. 1878. Edinburgh, 1985.
Daiches, David. "The Scottish Enlightenment". In *The Scottish Enlightenment 1730-1790 A Hotbed of Genius*, edited by David Daiches, Peter Jones and Jean Jones. Original 1986. Saltire Society, Edinburgh, 1996. 1-41.
Dalzel, Andrew. *History of the University of Edinburgh*. 2 vols. Edinburgh, 1862.
Dargan, Edwin C. *A History of Preaching*. Original 1905. 2 vols. Grand Rapids, 1970.
Davies, Gareth, and Lionel A. Ritchie. "Dr. Chalmers and the University of Glasgow". *RSCHS* 12 (1958): 185-201.
d'Aubigne, J. H. M. *History of the Reformation in Europe*. Vol. 7. London, 1876.

de Greef, W. *The Writings of John Calvin: An Introductory Guide*. Translated by Lyle D. Biersma. Grand Rapids, 1993.

Dennison, James T. "The Life and Career of Francis Turretin". Vol. 3, *Institutes of Elenctic Theology*, by Francis Turretin. Phillipsburg, NJ, 1977.

de Ridder-Symoens, H. and J. M. Fletcher, eds. *Academic Relations Between the Low Countries and the British Isles, 1450-1700*. Ghent, 1989.

Dick, Andrew C. "Memoir of the Rev. John Dick". In *Lectures on Theology*, by John Dick. Edinburgh, 1834.

Dictionary of National Biography. Edited by Leslie Stephen and S. Lee. London,1885 –.

Donaldson, Gordon. "Scottish Presbyterian Exiles in England, 1584-1588". *RSCHS* 14 (1960-1962): 67-80.

Drelincourt, Charles. *Les visites charitables, ou les consolations chretiennes, pour toutes sortes de personnes afligées*. Genève, 1666.

Drummond, Andrew L. *The Kirk and the Continent*. Edinburgh, 1956.

Drummond, A. L. and James Bulloch. *The Scottish Church 1688-1843: The Age of the Moderates*. Edinburgh, 1973.

Drummond, A. L. "Witherspoon of Gifford and American Presbyterianism". *RSCHS* 12 (1958): 185-201.

Dunbar, Linda J. "Synods and Superintendence: John Winram and Fife, 1561-1572". *RSCHS* 27 (1997): 97-125.

Duncan, J. Ligon. "Owning the Confession: Subscription in the Scottish Presbyterian Tradition". In *The Practice of Confessional Subscription*, edited by David W. Hall. Lanham, Maryland, 1995. 77-91.

Dunlop, A. Ian. *The Kirks of Edinburgh: The Congregations, Churches and Ministers of the Presbytery of Edinburgh Church of Scotland 1560-1984*. Scottish Record Society, New Series, vols. 15 & 16. Edinburgh, 1988.

–— *William Carstares and the Kirk by Law Established*. Edinburgh, 1967.

Durkan, John, and James Kirk. *The University of Glasgow 1451-1577*. Glasgow, 1977.

Drysdale, A. H. *History of the Presbyterians in England: Their Rise Decline and Revival*. London, 1889

Eadie, John. *Life and Times of the Rev. William Wilson in Fathers of the United Presbyterian Church*. Edinburgh, 1849.

Edwards, Jonathan. *The Works of Jonathan Edwards*. Edited by Edward Hickman. Original 1834. Edinburgh, 1974.

Eells, Hastings. *Martin Bucer*. Original 1931. Reprint New York, 1971.

Elshout, Bartel. *The Pastoral and Practical Theology of Wilhelmus à Brakel*. Grand Rapids, 1997.

Emerson, Roger L. *Professors, Patronage and Politics: The Aberdeen Universities in the Eighteenth Century*. Quincentennial Studies. Aberdeen, 1992.

Evans, William B. "Imputation and Impartation: The Problem of Union with Christ in Nineteenth-Century American Reformed Theology". Unpublished Ph.D. thesis, Vanderbilt University, 1996.

Fairbairn, Patrick. *Typology and Scripture*. Original 1845-1847. Grand Rapids, 1989.

Fagg, Jane B. "'Complaints and Clamours', the ministry of Adam Fergusson, 1700-1754". *RSCHS* 25 (1995): 288-308.

Farley, Edward. "The Reform of Theological Education As a Theological Task". *Theological Education* 17 (1981): 93-117.

Fasti Ecclesiae Scoticanae. Compiled by Hew Scott. Original 1866. Rev. ed. Vols. 1-7. Edinburgh, 1915 to 1928.
Fasti Ecclesiae Scoticanae. Compiled by Hew Scott. Original 1866. Vol. 8, by Comm. of General Assembly (Edinburgh, 1914 to 1929), and *Addenda and Corigenda 1560-1949* (Edinburgh, 1950).
Ferguson, Alexander. *A Display of the Act and Testimony published by Mr. Ebenezer Erskine and his Associates who separated from the Church of Scotland in the year 1734, and were deposed by the General Assembly in the year 1740....* Glasgow, 1761.
Ferrier, Andrew. *Memoirs of the Rev. William Wilson.* Glasgow, 1830.
Flavel, John. "A Familiar Conference Between a Minister and a Doubting Christian Concerning the Sacrament of the Lord's Supper". In *The Works of John Flavel*, vol. 6. Original 1820. London, 1968.
Forrester, David M. "Adam Gib, The Anti-Burgher". *RSCHS* 7 (1941): 141-169.
Foster, Walter R. *The Church Before the Covenants.* Edinburgh, 1975.
Fraser, Brian J. *Church, College, and Clergy: A History of Theological Education at Knox College, Toronto, 1844-1994.* Montreal/Kingston, 1995.
Fraser, Donald. *The Life and Diary of Ebenezer Erskine.* Edinburgh, 1831.
Fratt, Steven Douglas. "Scottish Theological Trends in the Eighteenth Century: Tensions between 'Head' and 'Heart'". Unpublished Ph.D. thesis, University of California, Santa Barbara, 1987.
Frye, Northrop. Introduction to *The Stepsure Letters*, by Thomas McCulloch. Toronto, 1960.
Gerstner, Jonathan Neil. *The Thousand Generation Covenant Dutch Reformed Covenant Theology and Group Identity in Colonial South Africa, 1652-1814.* Studies in the History of Christian Thought, vol. 44. Leiden, 1991.
Gill, Stewart D. *The Reverend William Proudfoot and the United Secession Mission in Canada.* Lewiston/Queenston/Lampeter, 1991.
— "'We Are Too Scotch': The Rev. William Proudfoot and the United Secession Mission to Canada". *RSCHS* 22 (1985): 175-194.
Good, James I. *History of the Swiss Reformed Church Since the Reformation.* Philadelphia, 1913.
Graham, William D. "Training for the Future". In *Proceedings of the International Conference of Reformed Churches – African Region.* Cape Town, 1995. 70-89.
Grant, Alexander. *The Story of the University of Edinburgh.* 2 vols. London, 1884.
Gregg, William. *History of the Presbyterian Church in the Dominion of Canada, from the Earliest Times to 1834....* Toronto, 1885.
— *Short History of the Presbyterian Church in the Dominion of Canada, from the Earliest Times to the Present Time.* Toronto, 1892.
Grell, Ole Peter. *Calvinist Exiles in Tudor and Stuart England.* See "The Attraction of Leiden University for English Students of medicine and theology, 1590-1642". Aldershot, Hunts, 1996. 221-240.
Grenz, Stanley J. *The Millennial Maze.* Downers Grove, Illinois, 1992.
Grudem, Wayne. *Systematic Theology: An Introduction to Biblical Doctrine.* Leicester/Grand Rapids, 1994.
A Guide to the Major Collections in the Department of Special Collections. 3d ed. Glasgow University Library, Glasgow, 1995.

Guignet, Marguerite. "Mark Duncan, Professor at Saumer, 1606-1640". *RSCHS* 5 (1935): 73-80.
Hall, Robert G. "Archibald Bruce at Whitburn (1746-1816) with a special reference to his view of church and state". Unpublished Ph.D. thesis, University of Edinburgh, New College, 1954.
Hamilton, Ian. *The Erosion of Calvinist Orthodoxy: Seceders and Subscription in Scottish Presbyterianism.* Rutherford Studies in Historical Theology, edited by N. M. de S. Cameron, D. MacLeod and D. F. Wright. Edinburgh,1990.
— "Samuel Rutherford (ca 1600-1661)". *Banner of Truth* 443-444 (August-September, 2000): 9-18.
Hart, D. G., and Albert R. Mohler, eds. *Theological Education in the Evangelical Tradition.* Grand Rapids, 1996.
Haskins, C. A. *The Rise of Universities.* Original 1923. Ithaca and London, 1957.
Haws, Charles H. *Scottish Parish Clergy at the Reformation 1540-1574.* Scottish Record Society, Edinburgh, 1972.
Hay, James and Henry Belfrage. *Memoir of the Rev. Alexander Waugh.* 3d ed. Edinburgh, 1839.
Hazlett, Wm. Ian P. "Ebbs and Flows of Theology in Glasgow 1451-1843". In *Traditions of Theology in Glasgow 1450-1980*, edited by Wm. Ian P. Hazlett. Edinburgh, 1993. 1-26.
— "The Scots Confession of 1560: Context, Complexion and Critique". *ARG* 78 (1987): 287-320.
Henderson, G. D. "Aberdeen Divines: being a History of the Chair of Divinity in King's College, Aberdeen". Typescript *MS* in Historic Collections, Special Libraries and Archives King's College, University of Aberdeen.
— *The Burning Bush: Studies in Scottish Church History.* Edinburgh, 1957.
— "The Exercise". *RSCHS* 7 (1941): 13-29.
— *The Founding of Marischal College Aberdeen.* Aberdeen, 1947.
— *Religious Life Seventeenth Century Scotland.* Cambridge, 1937.
Heppe, Heinrich. *Reformed Dogmatics Set Out and Illustrated from the Sources.* Edited by Ernst Bizer. Translated by G. T. Thomson. London, 1950.
Heron, Alastair. *Kirk by Divine Right.* Edinburgh, 1985.
Heyer, Henri. *L'Eglise de Genève 1535-1909.* Original 1909. Niewkoop, 1974.
Hill, Alexander. "Preface by the Editor". In *Lectures in Divinity*, by George Hill. Original 1821. Philadelphia, 1844.
Hillerbrand, Hans J., editor-in-chief. *The Oxford Encyclopedia of the Reformation.* 4 vols. New York/Oxford, 1996.
Hobart, R. R. "Archibald Bruce of Whitburn". *Original Secession Magazine* (4th series), 1, (1903): 486.
Hoffecker, Andrew. *Piety and the Princeton Theologians.* Phillipsburg, New Jersey, 1981.
Hope, Nicholas. *German and Scandinavian Protestantism 1700 to 1918.* Oxford, 1995.
Horn, D. B. *A Short History of the University of Edinburgh 1556-1889.* Edinburgh, 1967.
Howell, Wilber Samuel. *Eighteenth-Century British Logic and Rhetoric.* Princeton, 1971.

Index to the Acts and Proceedings of the General Assembly of the Church of Scotland From the Revolution to the Present Time. Edited by John Wilson. 2d ed. Edinburgh, 1871.

"Index to the Minutes of the Associate Presbytery and Synod, 1733-1820". National Archives of Scotland, Edinburgh, *MS* CH3/28/5.

Jacob, W. M. "Libraries for the parish: individual donors and charitable societies". In *The Cambridge History of Libraries in Britain and Ireland.* Vol. 3. [forthcoming].

— "Provision of Books for Poor Clergy Parochial Libraries in the British Isles and the North American Colonies, 1680-1720". In *The Church and The Book*, edited by R. N. Swanson. Studies in Church History, vol. 38. Ecclesiastical History Society, 2005.

Johnson, William S., and John Leith, eds. *Colonial Beginnings, 1519-1799*. Reformed Reader: A Sourcebook in Christian Theology, vol. 1. Louisville, 1993.

Julian, John, ed. *A Dictionary of Hymnology.* Rev. ed. London, 1907.

Kearney, Hugh. *Scholars and Gentlemen: Universities and Society in Pre-Industrial Britain, 1500-1700.* London, 1970.

Kingdon, Robert. *Geneva and the Coming of the Wars of Religion in France, 1555-1563.* Geneva, 1956.

— "Geneva and the Coming of the Wars of Religion in France, 1555-1563". Unpublished Ph.D. thesis, University of Columbia, 1955.

— *Geneva and the Consolidation of the French Protestant Movement, 1564-1572.* Geneva, 1967.

Kirk, James. "The Influence of Calvinism on the Scottish Reformation". *RSCHS* 18 (1974): 157-179.

— Introduction to *Stirling Presbytery Records 1581 to 1587.* Scottish History Society, Edinburgh, 1981.

— *Patterns of Reformation.* Edinburgh, 1989.

Klauber, Martin I. "Continuity and Discontinuity in Post-Reformation Reformed Theology: An Evaluation of the Muller Thesis". *Journal of the Evangelical Theological Society* 33, No.4 (1990): 467-475.

Klempa, William. "History of Presbyterian Theology in Canada to 1875". In *Burning Bush and A few Acres of Snow: The Presbyterian Contribution to Canadian Life and Culture.* Edited by William Klempa. Ottawa, 1994. 193-218.

Knox, E. A. *Robert Leighton, Archbishop of Glasgow.* London, 1930.

Kohl, Manfred W. "Theological Education: What Needs to Be Changed". In *Educating for Tomorrow: Theological Leadership for the Asian Context.* Edited by Manfred W. Kohl and A. N. Lal Senanayake. Bangalore, India/Indianapolis, IN, 2002. 29-48.

— "Mission – The Heart of the Church for the New Millennium". *International Congregational Journal* 2 (August, 2001). 87-101.

— "Radical Transformation in Preparation for the Ministry". *International Congregational Journal* [forthcoming December, 2006].

Kurtz, Johann Heinrich. *Church History.* Translated by John MacPherson. 3 vols. New York and London 1898

Lachman, David C. *The Marrow Controversy.* Rutherford Studies in Historical Theology, edited by N. M. de S. Cameron, D. MacLeod and D. F. Wright. Edinburgh, 1988.

Laing, David. "Life and Writings of John Row, Principal of King's College, Aberdeen". In *History of the Kirk of Scotland*, by John Row, edited by David Laing. Original *MS* 1650. Wodrow Society, Edinburgh, 1842.

Landreth, P. *The United Presbyterian Divinity Hall, in its Changes and Enlargements for 140 Years*. Edinburgh, 1876.
Lane, Anthony N. S. *John Calvin Student of the Church Fathers*. Grand Rapids, 1999.
Lathan, Robert. *History of the Associate Reformed Synod of the South*. Original 1882. Charlotte, N. C., 1982.
Lee, Francis Nigel. *The Covenantal Sabbath*. Lord's Day Observance Society, London, 1969.
Leith, John. *Crisis in the Church: The Plight of Theological Education*. Louisville, 1997.
Lewis, Donald M., ed. *The Blackwell Dictionary of Evangelical Biography 1730-1860*. 2 vols. Oxford, 1995.
Lewis, Gillian. "The Geneva Academy". In *Calvinism in Europe, 1540-1620*, edited by Andrew Pettegree, Alastair Duke and Gillian Lewis. Cambridge, 1996.
Lindsay, T. M. "The Covenant Theology". *British and Foreign Evangelical Review* 28 (1879): 521-537.
Lippe, R. *Selections from Wodrows Biographical Collections*. New Spalding Club, Aberdeen, 1890.
Livingston, James C. *Modern Christian Thought: Volume I, The Enlightenment and the Nineteenth Century*. Upper Saddle River, New Jersey, 1997.
Lloyd-Jones, Martyn. *Sermon on the Mount*. Vol. 1. Grand Rapids, 1959.
Lyall, David. "Theological Education in a clinical setting". Unpublished Ph.D. thesis, University of Edinburgh, New College, 1979.
Lyby, Thorkild, and Peter Ole Grell, "The consolidation of Lutheranism in Denmark and Norway". In *The Scandinavian Reformation: from evangelical movement to institutionization of reform*, edited by Peter Ole Grell. Cambridge, 1995. 114-143.
Lynn, Robert Wood. "Notes Toward a History: Theological Encyclopedia and the Evolution of Protestant Seminary Education, 1808-1868". *Theological Education* 17 (1981): 118-144.
McCallum, Donald P. "George Hill, D.D.: Moderate or Evangelical Erastian?". Unpublished M.A. thesis, University of Western Ontario, London, 1989.
McCloy, Frank Dixon. "John Mitchell Mason: Pioneer in American Theological Education". *Journal of Presbyterian History* 44 (1966): 141-155.
McCoy, F. N. *Robert Baillie and the Second Scots Reformation*. Berkeley, 1974.
McCoy, Wayne Livingston. "John Brown of Edinburgh (1784-1858), Churchman and Theologian". Unpublished Ph.D. thesis, New College, University Of Edinburgh, 1956.
McCrie, C. G. *The Confessions of the Church of Scotland*. Edinburgh, 1907.
McCrie, Thomas (Sr.). *The Life of Andrew Melville*. 2 vols. Edinburgh, 1819.
— *The Life of Melville*. Reprint. 2 vols. n.p., 1985.
McCrie, Thomas (Jr.). *Life of Thomas McCrie* [Senior]. Edinburgh, 1840.
— *The Story of the Scottish Church*. Original 1875. Glasgow, 1988.
McCulloch, William. *Life of Thomas McCulloch D. D.* Edited by Isabella and Jean McCulloch. Truro, N.S., 1920.
McDonald, Bruce. "Thomas McCulloch: Pioneer Educationalist of Nova Scotia". In *Called to Witness*, edited by W. Stanford Reid. n.p., 1975. 111-127.
McElroy, Davis D. *Scotland's Age of Improvement: A Survey of Eighteenth-Century Literary Clubs and Societies*. Washington, D.C., 1969.

--- "The Literary Clubs and Societies of Eighteenth Century Scotland". Unpublished Ph.D. thesis, University of Edinburgh, 1952.
MacEwen, A. R. *The Erskines*. Famous Scots Series. Edinburgh, 1900.
MacFarlane, John. *The Life and Times of George Lawson, D. D., Selkirk, Professor of Theology to the Associate Synod*. Original 1862. Edinburgh, 1880.
McGowan, A. T. B. *The Federal Theology of Thomas Boston*. Rutherford Studies in Historical Theology, edited by D. F. Wright and D. MacLeod. Carlisle and Edinburgh, 1997.
MacGregor, Janet G. *The Scottish Presbyterian Polity*. Edinburgh, 1926.
McGrath, Alister E. *Christian Theology: An Introduction*. 2d ed. Oxford, 1997.
--- *Historical Theology: An Introduction to the History of Christian Thought*. Oxford, 1998.
--- *The Intellectual Origins of the European Reformation*. Oxford, 1987.
--- *Reformation Thought: An Introduction*. 3d ed. Oxford, 1999.
McIntosh, John R. *Church and Theology in Enlightenment Scotland: The Popular Party, 1740-1800*. East Linton, East Lothian, 1998.
MacIver, Iain F. "'I did not seek...but was sought after': The Election of Thomas Chalmers to the Chair of Divinity at Edinburgh University, October, 1827". *RSCHS* 20 (1980): 223-229.
McKay, W. D. J. *An Ecclesiastical Republic: Church Government in the Writings of George Gillespie*. Rutherford Studies in Historical Theology, edited by David F. Wright and Donald MacLeod. Carlisle and Edinburgh, 1997.
MacKelvie, William. *Annals and Statistics of the United Presbyterian Church*. Edinburgh, 1873.
MacKenzie, James. *Life of Michael Bruce: Poet of Loch Leven*. Edinburgh, 1908.
MacKenzie, Robert. *John Brown of Haddington*. London, 1918.
--- *John Brown of Haddington*. Abridged ed. London, 1964.
MacKenzie, R. Sheldon. *Gathered by the River: The Story of the West River Seminary and Theological Hall, 1848-1858*. Winnipeg, 1998.
McKerrow, John. *History of the Secession Church*. Glasgow, 1841.
McKim, Donald K., ed. *Historical Handbook of Major Biblical Interpreters*. Downers Grove, Illinois/Leicester, England, 1998.
--- *Ramism in William Perkins' Theology*. New York, 1987.
McLachlan, H. *English Education Under the Test Acts: Being the History of the Non-Conformist Academies 1662-1820*. Manchester, 1931.
MacLean, Donald. "Highland Libraries in the Eighteenth Century". *Transactions of the Gaelic Society of Inverness* 3 (1922-1924): 92-94.
MacLean, James. "Our College: - Its History, Its Present Position, and Its Prospects" I.
--- "The Pictou and West River Period, 1818-1858". *The Theologue*, Vol. 8, No. 4 (1897): 101-106.
Maclehose, James. *The Glasgow University Press 1638-1931*. Glasgow, 1931.
McLellan, J. C. "Class Act". *Presbyterian Record*, Vol. 123, No. 5 (May, 1999): 29-30.
MacLeod, John. *Scottish Theology in Relation to Church History Since the Reformation*. 3d ed. Edinburgh, 1974.
--- "Theology in the Early Days of the Secession". *RSCHS* 8 (1944): 1-15.
McLerie, David. *The Clergyman Corrected by the Weaver; in a letter from David McLerie, Weaver in Paisley, to the Rev. Mr. Alexander Ferguson, Minister of the Gospel at Kilwinning*. Glasgow, 1761.

MacMeeken, J. W. *History of the Scottish Metrical Psalms with an Account of the Paraphrases and Hymns*. Glasgow, 1872.

MacMillan, D. *The Aberdeen Doctors*. London, 1909.

McMillan, William. *The Worship of the Scottish Reformed Church, 1550-1638*. London, 1931.

McMullin, Stanley E. "In Search of the Liberal Mind: Thomas McCulloch and the Impulse to Action". *Journal of Canadian Studies* 23 (1988-1989): 68-45.

— "Thomas McCulloch: The Evolution of a Liberal Mind". Unpublished Ph.D. thesis, Dalhousie University, Halifax, 1975.

McNeill, John T. *The History and Character of Calvinism*. New York, 1954.

McPherson, A., ed. *History of the Free Presbyterian Church of Scotland (1898-1970)*. Inverness, n.d.

MacPhie, J. P. *Pictonians at Home and Abroad*. Boston, 1914.

MacWhirter, A. "The Last Anti-Burghers A Footnote to Secession History". *RSCHS* 8 (1944): 255-291.

Maag, Karen. "Education and Training for the Calvinist ministry: the Academy of Geneva,1559-1620". In *The Reformation of the Parishes*, edited by Andrew Pettegree. Manchester, 1993.

— *Seminary or University? The Genevan Academy and Reformed Higher Education, 1560-1620*. Aldershot, Hants, 1995.

Mackie, J. D. *The University of Glasgow 1451-1951*. Glasgow, 1954.

Magee, William. *Discourses and Dissertations on the Scriptural Doctrines of Atonement and Sacrifice*. Original 1809. London, 1859.

Marshall, James S. *North Leith Parish Church: The First 500 Years*. Edinburgh, 1992.

Masters, D. C. *Protestant Church Colleges in Canada: A History*. Toronto, 1966.

Maxwell, Thomas. "The Scotch Presbyterian Eloquence – A Post-Revolution Pamphlet". *RSCHS* 8 (1944): 225-253.

Maxwell, William D. *A History of Worship in the Church of Scotland*. London, 1955.

Mechie, Stewart "Education for the Ministry in Scotland Since the Reformation", 1 and 2. *RSCHS* 14 (1963):115-133; 161-178.

— "Education for the Ministry in Scotland Since the Reformation", 3. *RSCHS* 15 (1966): 1-20.

Meek, Donald E. "Scottish Highlanders, North American Indians and the SSPCK: Some Cultural Perspectives". *RSCHS* 23 (1989): 378-396.

Miller, Glenn T. *Piety and Intellect: The Aims and Purpose of Ante-Bellum Theological Education*. Atlanta, 1990.

Miller, R. S. *Misi Gete: John Geddie Pioneer Missionary to the New Hebrides*. Launceston, Tasmania, 1975.

Miller, Samuel. *An Able and Faithful Ministry*. Original 1812. Reprint edited by Kevin Reed. Dallas, 1984.

— *Letters on Clerical Manners and Habits, Addressed to a Student in the Theological Seminary at Princeton, N.J.* New York, 1827.

Mitchell, John. "Biographical Memoir" [of George Paxton]. In *Illustrations of Scripture: From the Geography, Natural History, and Manners and Customs of the East*, by George Paxton. 3d ed., edited by Robert Jamieson. Vol 1. Edinburgh, 1842.

Moffat, Charles L. "James Hog of Carnock, 1658-1734; Leaders in the Evangelical Party in early eighteenth-century Scotland". Unpublished Ph.D. thesis, University of Edinburgh, New College, 1961.

Moir, John S. *The Church in the British Era*. A History of the Christian Church in Canada, vol. 2. Toronto, 1972.
— *Enduring Witness: A History of the Presbyterian Church in Canada*. 2d ed. n.p., 1987.
— "'To Fertilize the Wilderness': Problems and Progress of the Synod of Nova Scotia in its first Quarter Century". *Canadian Society of Presbyterian History, Papers* (1992): 67-86.
Monter, E. William. *Calvin's Geneva*. New York, 1967.
Moore, T. M. "Some Observations Concerning the Educational Philosophy of John Calvin". *WTJ* 46 (1984): 140-155.
Moss, Michael, Moira Rankin and Lesley Richmond, comps. *Who, Where and When: The History and Constitution of the University of Glasgow*. Glasgow, 2001.
Muller, Richard A. "The Era of Protestant Orthodoxy". In *Theological Education in the Evangelical Tradition*, edited by D. G. Hart and R. Albert Mohler, Jr. Grand Rapids, 1996. 103-128.
— "Calvin and the 'Calvinists': Assessing Continuities and Discontinuities between the Reformation and Orthodoxy" (2). *Calvin Theological Journal* 31 (1996): 125-160.
— *Dictionary of Latin and Greek Theological Terms*. Grand Rapids, 1985.
— "*Institutes of Elentic Theology* Vol. 2 by F. Turretin, trans. G. Geiger, ed. J. Dennison". A review in *Calvin Theological Journal* 29 (1994): 614-615.
— *Post-Reformation Reformed Dogmatics*. 2 vols. Grand Rapids, 1987 and 1993.
— *The Study of Theology: From Biblical Interpretation to Contemporary Formulation*. Foundations of Contemporary Interpretation, edited by Moisés Silva. Grand Rapids, 1991.
Murison, W. *Sir David Lindsay*. Cambridge, 1938.
Murray, Douglas. "Disruption to Union". In *Studies in the History of Worship in Scotland*, edited by D. Forrester and D. Murray. 2d ed. Edinburgh, 1996.
Murray, Iain. "Ministerial Training: A Sketch of Theological Education". *Banner of Truth* 15 (1963):12-21.
Naphy, Wiliam G. "The Renovation of the Ministry in Calvin's Geneva". In *The Reformation of the Parishes*, edited by Andrew Pettigree. Manchester, 1993. 113-132.
Needham, N. R. *2000 Years of Christ's Power Part Two: The Middle Ages*. London, 2000.
Nicholson, David R. "Michael Willis: Missionary Statesman, Social Activist, Christian Educator, and Reformed Theologian". Unpublished Th.M. thesis, Toronto School of Theology, 1973.
Noll, Mark A. "The Earliest Protestants and the Reformation of Education". *WTJ* 43 (1980): 97-131.
Nuttall, Geoffrey F. *The Significance of Trevecca College 1768-1791*. London, 1969.
Ong, Walter J. "Ramus, Peter". In *The Encyclopedia of Philosophy*, edited by Paul Edwards, vol. 7. New York, 1967. 66-68.
Ormond, D. D. *A Kirk and a College in the Craigs of Stirling*. Stirling, 1897.
Osborn, Ronald E. *Folly of God: The Rise of Christian Preaching*. St. Louis, Missouri, 1999.
Owen, John *Biblical Theology*. Translated by Stephen P. Westcott. Original 1661. Morgan, PA, 1994.

— *The Works of John Owen*. Edited by William Goold. Original 1850-1853. Vols. 3, 4, 6, 7. London, 1965-1967.
Oxford Dictionary of the Christian Church. Edited by F. L. Cross. Original 1957. 3d ed., edited by E. A. Livingstone. Oxford, 1997.
Packer, J. I. *A Quest for Godliness*. Wheaton, Illinois, 1990.
Pannier, Jacques. "Scots in Saumur in the Seventeenth Century". Translated by W. J. Couper, *RSCHS* 5 (1935):140-143.
Park, Trevor. "Theological Education and Ministerial Training for the Ordained Ministry of the Church of England,1800-1850". Unpublished Ph.D. thesis, Open University, 1990.
Parker, T. H. L. *Calvin's Preaching*. Edinburgh, 1992.
— *The Oracles of God: An Introduction to the Preaching of John Calvin*. London,1947.
Paton, John G. *John G. Paton, Missionary to the New Hebrides, An Autobiography*. Edited by James Paton. New York, 1889.
Patrick, Millar. *Four Centuries of Scottish Psalmody*. London, 1949.
Patterson, George. *A History of the County of Pictou, N. S.* Montreal, 1877.
— "The First Theological Hall in the British Colonies". *The Theologue*, Vol. 3, No. 1 (1891): 1-7.
— "The First Theological Hall in the British Colonies". *The Theologue*, Vol. 3, No. 2 (1892): 33-40.
Pazmiño, Robert W. *Foundational Issues in Christian Education: An Introduction in Evangelical Perspective*. 2d ed. Grand Rapids, 1997.
Pettegree, Andrew. *Emden and the Dutch Revolt: Exile and Development of Reformed Protestantism*. Oxford, 1992.
Philip, Adam. *The Devotional Literature of Scotland*. Dunfermline, n.d.
Philip, R. G. "Scottish Scholars at Geneva". *RSCHS* 6 (1938): 216-231.
Piggin, Stuart, and John Roxborogh. *The St. Andrews Seven*. Edinburgh, 1985.
Price, B. B. *Medieval Thought: An Introduction*. Oxford, 1992.
Rait, R. S. *The Universities of Aberdeen: A History*. Aberdeen, 1895.
Reardon, Bernard M. G. *Religious Thought in the Reformation*. London, 1981.
Reid, H. M. B. *The Divinity Principals in the University of Glasgow 1545-1654*. Glasgow, 1917.
— *The Divinity Professors in the University of Glasgow 1640-1903*. Glasgow, 1923.
Reid, James Seaton. *History of the Presbyterian Church in Ireland*. Original 1st ed., 1833; 2d ed., 1853. 3 vols. Stoke-on-Staffordshire, 1998.
Reid, John G. *Mount Allison University: A History, to 1963*. Vol. 1. Toronto, 1984.
Reid, W. Stanford. "Calvin and the Founding of the Academy of Geneva". *Westminster Theological Journal* 18 (1955): 1-33.
— "Reformation in France and Scotland: A Case Study in Sixteenth-Century Communication". In *Later Calvinism: International Perspectives*, edited by W. Fred Graham. Vol. 22 in Sixteenth Century Essays and Studies. Kirksville, Mo., 1994. 195-214.
— *Trumpeter of God: A Biography of John Knox*. New York, 1974.
Reymond, Robert L. *A New Systematic Theology of the Christian Faith*. Nashville, 1998.
Riddell, J. G. "Divinity". In *Fortuna Domus. A series of lectures delivered in the University of Glasgow in commemoration of the fifth century of its foundation*, edited by J. B. Neilson. Glasgow, 1952. 1-20.

Ronald, John. *History of the Cairns United Free Church Stewarton*. Ardrossan, 1926.
Rothwell, Malcolm A. "The Selection of Candidates for the Church of Scotland Ministry". Unpublished Ph.D. thesis, University of Edinburgh, 1975.
Roxborogh, John. *Thomas Chalmers: Enthusiast for Mission*. Rutherford Studies in Historical Theology, edited by David F. Wright and Donald MacLeod. Carlisle and Edinburgh, 1999.
Roxburgh, Kenneth B. E. *Thomas Gillespie and the Origins of the Relief Church in 18th Century Scotland*. Bern, 1999.
Ryken, Philip G. "Scottish Reformed Scholasticism". In *Protestant Scholasticism: Essays in Reassessment*, edited by Carl R. Trueman and R. Scott Clark. Carlisle, 1999. 196-210.
— *Thomas Boston as the Preacher of the Fourfold State*. Rutherford Studies in Historical Theology, edited by David F. Wright and Donald MacLeod. Carlisle and Edinburgh, 1999.
Sanderson, Margaret. *Ayrshire and the Reformation: People and Change, 1490-1600*. East Linton, 1997.
Schaeffer, Francis A. *A Christian Manifesto*. In *The Complete Works of Francis A. Schaeffer: A Christian Worldview*. Original 1981. Westchester, Illinois, 1982.
Schaff, Philip. *Germany; Its Universities, Theology, and Religion*. Edinburgh, 1857.
— *Theological Propaedeutic: A General Introduction to the Study of Theology, Exegetical, Historical, Systematic, and Practical*. New York, 1894.
Schlenther, Boyd Stanley. *Queen of the Methodists: The Countess Of Huntingdon and the Eighteenth-Century Crisis of Faith and Society*. Durham, 1997.
— "Scottish Influences, Especially Religious, in Colonial America". *RSCHS* 19 (1977): 133-154.
Scott, David. *Annals and Statistics of the Original Secession Church: Till its Disruption and Union with the Free Church of Scotland in 1852*. Edinburgh, 1886.
Sefton, Henry. "St. Mary's College, St. Andrews, in the eighteenth century". *RSCHS* 24 (1991): 161-179.
Selles, Otto H. "A Case of Hidden Identity: Antoine Court, Benedict Pictet, and Geneva's Aid to France's Desert Churches (1715-1724)". In *The Identity of Geneva: The Christian Commonwealth, 1564-1864*, edited by John B. Roney and Martin I. Klauber. Westport, Connecticut, 1998. 93-109.
Sermons and Life of Mr. Robert Bruce. Compiled by Robert Wodrow. Edinburgh, 1843.
[Seymour, Aaron]. *The Life and Times of Selina Countess of Huntingdon*. Original 1839-1844. 2 vols. Stoke-on-Trent, 2000.
Shaw, Duncan. "Zwinglian Influence on the Scottish Reformation". *RSCHS* 22 (1985): 119-139.
Sheppard, Gerald T. "The Genevan Bible (The Annotated New Testament 1602 Edition)". In *The Geneva Bible (The Annotated New Testament 1602 Edition)*, edited by Gerald T. Sheppard. New York, 1989. 1-4.
Sher, Richard. "The Book in the Scottish Enlightenment". In *The Culture of the Book in the Scottish Enlightenment*, edited by Paul Wood. Toronto, 2000. 40-60.
— *Church and University in the Scottish Enlightenment: The Moderate Literati of Edinburgh*. Edinburgh, 1985.
Small, R. *History of the Congregations of the United Presbyterian Church*. 2 vols. Edinburgh, 1904.

Sprunger, Keith L. *Dutch Puritanism: A History of English and Scottish Churches of the Netherlands in the Sixteenth and Seventeenth Centuries*. Studies in the History of Christian Thought, vol. 31. Leiden, 1982.
Steinmetz, David. "The Scholastic Calvin". In *Protestant Scholasticism: Essays in Reassessment*, edited by Carl R. Trueman and R. Scott Clark. Carlisle, 1999. 16-30.
Steven, William. *The History of the Scottish Church, Rotterdam*. Edinburgh, 1832.
Stevenson, David. *King's College, Aberdeen, 1560-1641: From Protestant Reformation to Covenanting Revolution*. Aberdeen, 1990.
Stewart, David. "The 'Aberdeen Doctors' and the Covenanters". *RSCHS* 22 (1984): 35-44.
Still, William. *Theological Studies in Genesis and Romans*. Vol. 3 in *Collected Writings of William Still*, edited by David C. Searle and Sinclair B. Ferguson. Edinburgh/Fearn, 2000.
Story, R. H. *Life and Remains of Robert Lee*. 2 vols. London, 1870.
Strand, Kenneth. "John Calvin and the Brethren of the Common Life". *Andrews University Seminary Studies* 13 (1975): 67-78.
—— "John Calvin and the Brethren of the Common Life: The Role of Strasbourg". *Andrews University Seminary Studies* 15 (1977): 43-50.
Strickland, D. R. "Union with Christ in the Theology of Samuel Rutherford". Unpublished Ph.D. thesis, University of Edinburgh, 1972.
Strong, A. H. *Systematic Theology*. Burlington, Ontario, 1907.
Suderman, Jeffrey M. "Orthodoxy and Enlightenment: George Campbell (1719-1796) and the Aberdeen Enlightenment". Unpublished Ph.D. thesis, University of Western Ontario, 1995.
Tait, Robert S. *The Universities of Scotland*. Aberdeen, 1895.
Tamburello, Dennis E. *Union with Christ: John Calvin and the Mysticism of St. Bernard*. Louisville, 1994.
Torrance, Thomas F. *Scottish Theology From John Knox to John MacLeod Campbell*. Edinburgh, 1996.
University of Glasgow: History and Constitution 1977-1978. Glasgow, 1977.
Valentine, J. *An Aberdeen Principal of Last Century*. Aberdeen, 1856.
Van Harten, Pieter Hendrick. *De Prediking van Ebenezer en Ralph Erskine: Evangelieverkondiging in het spanningsveld van verkiezing en belofte (with a summary in English – The Preaching of Ebenezer and Ralph Erskine: Preaching of the Gospel in the Tension between Election and Promise)*. Gravenhage, Netherlands, 1986.
Van Vechten, Jacob. *Memoirs of John M. Mason, D. D., S.T.P. with Portions of His Correspondence*. New York, 1856.
Venema, Hermann. *Institutes of Theology*. Translated by Alexander W. Brown. Edinburgh, 1850.
Voges, Friedhelm. "Moderate and Evangelical Thinking in the later Eighteenth Century: Differences and Shared Attitudes" . *RSCHS* 22 (1985): 141-157.
Von Mosheim, Johann Lorenz. *Institutes of Ecclesiastical History, Ancient and Modern*. Translated by James Murdock, revised by James Seaton Reid. 6th ed. London, 1868.
Walker, J. *Theology and Theologians of Scotland 1560-1750*. Original 1872. Reprint Edinburgh, 1982.
Wallace, Ronald. *Calvin, Geneva and the Reformation*. Edinburgh/Grand Rapids, 1988.
Watt, Hugh, comp. *New College Edinburgh A Centenary History*. Edinburgh, 1946.

Weir, Mullo. "Oriental and Old Testament Studies". In *Fortuna Domus. A series of lectures delivered in the University of Glasgow in commemoration of the fifth century of its foundation*, edited by J. B. Neilson. Glasgow, 1952. 133-155.

Weir, Thomas E. "Pastoral Care in the Church of Scotland in the Seventeenth Century". Unpublished Ph.D. thesis, Edinburgh University, New College, 1961.

Welch, Edwin. *Spiritual Pilgrim: A Reassessment of the life of the Countess of Huntingdon*. Cardiff, 1995.

Wendel, François. *Calvin: Origins and Developments of His Religious Thought*. Translated by Philip Mairet. Original 1950. Grand Rapids, 1997.

The Westminster Directory. Edited and notes by Thomas Leishman. Church Service Society, Edinburgh, 1901.

Whitelaw, Marjory. *Thomas McCulloch His Life and Times*. Halifax, 1985.

Whytock, Jack C. "The History and Development of Scottish Theological Education and Training, Kirk and Secession (c. 1560-c.1850)". Unpublished Ph.D. thesis, University of Wales, Lampeter, 2001.

— "The Influence of Continental Models of Church Discipline on the Scottish First Book of Discipline". Unpublished M.Th. thesis, University of Glasgow, 1988.

— "Thomas McCulloch and the Rhetoric of Piety". *The Canadian Society of Presbyterian History, Papers* (2003): 81-93.

— "A Case Study of Presbyterian Theological Education in British North America (1820-1843)". *The Canadian Society of Presbyterian History, Papers* (2002): 43-66.

Wilson, John E. Jr. "Covenanters, Seceders, Moderates and Evangelicals: The Scottish Origins of American Presbyterianism". In *Ever a Frontier*, edited by J. A. Walther. Grand Rapids, 1994. 1-32.

Wilson, J. Stewart. "The Story of the Scottish Metrical Version of the Psalm". *British and Foreign Evangelical Review* 28 (1879): 61-64.

Witt, , Ronald G. "The Humanist Movement". In *Handbook of European History, 1400-1600*, edited by Thomas A., Brady, Jr., Heiko A. Oberman and James D. Tracy. Vol.2. Grand Rapids/Leiden, 1995. 93-125.

Wodrow, Robert. *The History of the Sufferings of the Church of Scotland from the Restoration to the Revolution*. Original 1721-1722. New edition, edited by R. Burns. 4 vols. Glasgow, 1828.

— *Life of James Wodrow*. Edinburgh, 1828.

Wood, B. Anne. *God, Science and Schooling: John William Dawson's Pictou Years, 1820-1855*. Truro, Nova Scotia, 1991.

— "Schooling/Credentials for Professional Advancement: A Case Study of Pictou Presbyterians". In *The Contribution of Presbyterianism to the Maritime Provinces of Canada*, edited by C. H. H. Scobie and G. A. Rawlyk. Montreal/Kingston, 1997. 54-69.

— "Schooling for Presbyterian Leaders: The College Years of Pictou Academy, 1816-1832". In *The Burning Bush and A Few Acres of Snow: The Presbyterian Contribution to Canadian Life and Culture*, edited by William Klempa. Ottawa, 1994. 19-37.

— "The Significance of Calvinism in the Educated Vision of Thomas McCulloch". *Vitae Scholasticae* 4 (Spring/Fall, 1985): 15-30.

— "Thomas McCulloch's Use of Science in Promoting a Liberal Education". *Acadiensis* 17 (Autumn, 1987): 56-73.

— "The Significance of Evangelical Presbyterian Politics in the Constitution of State Schooling: A Case Study of the Pictou District, 1817-1866". *Acadiensis* 20 (Spring, 1991): 62-85.

Wood, Paul B. *The Aberdeen Enlightenment: The Arts Curriculum in the Eighteenth Century*. Quincentennial Studies. Aberdeen, 1993.

— "Aberdeen and Europe in the Enlightenment". In *The Universities of Aberdeen and Europe: The First Three Centuries,* edited by Paul Dukes. Quincentennial Studies. Aberdeen, 1995. 119-142.

Woodruff, Stephen A. "The Pastoral Ministry in the Church of Scotland in the eighteenth century, with special reference to Thomas Boston, John Willison and John Erskine". Unpublished Ph.D. thesis, University of Edinburgh, New College, 1966.

Woolsey, Andrew. "Unity and Continuity in Covenantal Thought". 2 vols. Unpublished Ph.D. thesis, University of Glasgow, 1988.

Wright, David F. "Andrew Hunter of Barjarg (1744-1809): Evangelical Divine in an Age of Improvement". *RSCHS* 26 (1996): 135-168.

Wright, David F. and Gary D. Badcock, eds. *Disruption to Diversity Edinburgh Divinity 1846-1996*. Edinburgh, 1996.

Young, B. W. *Religion and Enlightenment in Eighteenth-Century England: Theological Debate from Locke to Burke*. Oxford, 1998.

Young, David and John Brown (of Broughton Place). *Memorials of Alexander Moncrieff and James Fisher*. Edinburgh, 1849.

Young, James. *Life of John Welsh*. Edinburgh, 1866.

Young, William G. *The Parish of Urquhart and Logie Wester*. n.p., 1984.

Index

à Kempis, Thomas, 59, 71
à Lasco, John, 29, 30
Aberdeen, 28, 37, 44, 45, 57, 58, 66, 68, 69, 78, 93, 141, 153, 162, 291, 292, 401, 404
Aberdeen Doctors, 21, 51, 53
Aberdeen University, xxv, 153
Abernethy, 171, 181, 182, 207, 407
Academy
   English Dissenting, 94, 129, 308, 368
   Geneva, ix, xv, 4, 5, 6, 7, 8, 13, 14, 15, 16, 17, 18, 19, 20, 23, 27, 39, 41, 43, 76, 107, 158, 368
   Herborn, 45
   Homerton, 279
   Lausanne, 13
   Loudun, 23
   Montauban, 23
   Montpellier, 23
   Nimes, 23
   Orthez, 22, 23
   Pictou. *See* Pictou Academy/Divinity Hall
   Saumur, 23, 53
   Sedan, 22, 23
   Utrecht, 20
   Warrington, 129
Acominatus, 99
ad fontes, 6, 7
Adamson, John, 70, 71, 400
Adie, Andrew, 404
Aitken, James, 336
Aitken, William F., 409
Aldorf, 404
Alexander, William L., 117
Alford Exercise, 82, 84
Alleine, Joseph, 242

Allen, Robert, 387
Alloa, xii, 185, 199, 201, 203, 204, 206, 273, 274, 275, 285, 318, 338, 407
Althusius, Johannes, 45
Altingius, 126
Ambrose, 99
Amedeus, Alexander, 401
Amsterdam, 53, 57, 61, 228, 403
Amyraldian, 271, 283, 316, 319
Amyraldianism, 23, 53, 243, 283
Amyraut, Moise, 23, 316, 317
Anabaptists, 66
Anatomy, 39, 112, 118, 349
Anderson, Alexander, 402
Anderson, David, 402
Anderson, George, 402
Anderson, John, 196, 397
Anderson, William, 397
Anselem, 7
Apocrypha, 254, 289
Apocrypha Controversy, 310
Apologetics, 116, 133, 165, 381
Aquinas, 58
Arbuthnot, Alexander, 402
Archibald, Robert, 184, 204
Arminian(s), 53, 57, 58, 66, 87, 122, 140, 319, 328, 358
Arminianism, 126, 141, 325
Arnot, Robert, 398
Arts, xxiii, 4, 14, 18, 19, 22, 24, 26, 27, 28, 33, 36, 38, 39, 40, 41, 42, 43, 45, 52, 54, 55, 57, 61, 69, 70, 71, 74, 75, 76, 77, 78, 79, 80, 86, 89, 101, 104, 106, 110, 111, 115, 116, 117, 118, 133, 139, 142, 144, 145, 146, 148, 149, 150, 151, 153, 159, 160, 198, 208, 213, 243, 273, 276, 286,

289, 292, 308, 330, 339, 372, 373, 382, 383, 386, 390, 391, 392, 393
Associate Church (Burgher), xiii, 94, 184, 188, 190, 192, 200, 209, 210, 211, 212, 223, 252, 253, 258, 260, 263, 269, 271, 273, 286, 288, 291, 292, 293, 299, 301, 303, 310, 317, 318, 328, 329, 347, 367, 387, 392, 408
Associate Presbytery, 179
Associate Reformed Church, 325
Atkinson, D. W., 66
Atonement, 94, 237, 271, 310, 316, 319, 321, 323, 358
Atonement Controversy, 310, 319, 323
Aubeterre, 15
Augustine, 7, 26, 59, 99, 267, 313
Auld Light Antiburghers. *See* General Associate Church (Antiburgher)
Auld Light Divinity Halls, xiii, 327
Auld/Old Light Burghers, xiii, 327, 328, 329, 330, 333, 336, 341, 343, 408, 409
Auld/Old Lights, 286, 292, 323, 327, 329, 332, 344

Baconian, 113, 114
Badcock, Gary D., xxi
Baillie, James, 397
Baillie, Robert, 53, 56, 57, 60, 61, 66, 67, 68, 69, 88, 396
Baird, Archibald, 399
Baird, George, 144, 364, 400, 401
Baird, H. M., 11
Balmer, Robert, xiii, 309, 310, 311, 316, 318, 319, 320, 321, 323, 324, 341, 407
Bannerman, James, 141
Baptism, 228, 232, 254, 358
Baptists, xx, 368
Barber, Cyril J., 266
Barclay, Adam, 402
Barclay, Alastair, 350
Barclay, Thomas, 163, 396
Bardgett, F. D., 33
Barker, William S., xxi
Barnet, John G., 200

Barony, 66, 396
Barrie, J. M., 327
Barron, Robert, 404
Basel, 45, 46, 53, 397, 404
Baxter, J. H., 93
Baxter, John, 372
Baxter, Richard, xii, 99, 227, 237, 242, 243, 280, 317, 378
Beattie, James, 214, 338
Bebbington, David, xx
Beeke, Joel, xxi, 20, 105, 190, 384
Belfrage, Henry, 212, 213, 214, 215, 222, 265, 268, 269
Bell, Alexander, 403
Bengel, 142, 313, 316
Bentley, James, 403
Berkof, Louis, 218
Betts, A. E., 349, 352, 359, 360, 361, 362, 377
Beza, Theodore, 4, 5, 13, 14, 17, 18, 34, 36, 40, 41, 47, 52, 99, 250, 313
Bierma, Lyle D., 10, 40
Binnington, R. F., 365
Black, Alexander, 405
Blackstone (examination chair), 360, 373
Blackstone, William, 349
Blackwell, Thomas Jr., 404
Blackwell, Thomas Sr., 130, 402, 404, 405
Blaikie, Alexander, 361, 371, 378
Blair, Hugh, 131
Blair, Robert, 57, 398
Blomberg, Craig L., 315
Bogue, David, 378
Book of Common Prayer, 56
Bordeaux, 396, 400
Boston, Thomas, 21, 39, 41, 103, 104, 176, 209, 216, 229, 236, 251, 317
Botany, 112, 288, 351
Bourges, 402
Bourignon, Antoinette, 88
Bower, A., 107
Boyd, Robert, 23, 41, 52, 53, 55, 56, 60, 396, 400

Index

Breach of 1747, xi, 176, 184, 185, 187, 188, 198, 200, 201, 207, 264
Brewster, 313
Brewster, Sir David, 400
Briggs, C. A., 14, 21, 22, 23, 128
British North America, xiv, xx, xxii, xxiii, 3, 272, 274, 276, 325, 345, 347, 349, 350, 351, 352, 365, 367, 369, 371, 379, 387
Brown, A. L., xxi, 101, 112, 113, 114
Brown, Colin, 133
Brown, David, 276
Brown, Ebenezer, 212, 223, 235, 242
Brown, George, 177, 253
Brown, James, 258
Brown, John (Broughton Place/Edinburgh), xiii, 182, 189, 193, 210, 215, 216, 217, 251, 265, 271, 282, 283, 309, 310, 311, 312, 313, 314, 315, 316, 317, 318, 323, 324, 407
Brown, John (Haddington), xii, 128, 132, 133, 134, 135, 137, 138, 139, 140, 164, 175, 176, 178, 184, 185, 187, 190, 197, 200, 208–56, 257, 259, 260, 261, 262, 265, 269, 270, 271, 274, 280, 284, 288, 292, 293, 299, 300, 301, 302, 310, 315, 322, 329, 330, 378, 381, 384, 386, 392, 407
Brown, John (Wamphray), 217, 243, 244, 251
Brown, John (Whitburn), 84, 191, 212, 223, 230, 238, 273, 310
Brown, Stewart J., 125
Brown, William, 213, 225, 235, 243, 380
Brown, William (St. Mary's College), 399
Brown, William Adams, 222
Brown, William L., 124, 125, 131, 165, 404, 405
Bruce, Andrew, 398
Bruce, Archibald, xii, 60, 109, 132, 138, 176, 197, 201, 258, 263, 272–85, 272, 273, 276, 278, 279, 282, 285, 286, 287, 288, 289, 321, 336, 337, 338, 339, 341, 344, 349, 352, 356, 358, 363, 378, 393, 407, 409
Bruce, Michael, 185, 199, 200, 257
Bruce, Robert, 38
Brunton, Alexander, 401
Bucer, Martin, 7, 26, 99
Buchanan, George, 27, 59, 366, 397
Buchanan, James, 397
Buist, George, 399
Bullinger, 17, 217
Bulloch, J. M., 33, 43, 44, 45, 125, 133, 251
Burgess Oath, 183, 187, 188, 194
Burgess, Anthony, 99, 216
Burleigh, J. H. S., 3
Burnet, George B., 3
Burnet, Gilbert, x, 71, 85, 86, 87, 88, 99, 178, 396
Burns, Robert, 87, 96, 105, 120, 122, 123, 124, 125, 126, 150, 151, 152, 348, 365
Bursar(s), x, 42, 44, 45, 54, 72, 73, 74, 78, 82, 84, 86, 97, 98
Bursary, 44, 74, 78, 82, 84, 86, 90, 97, 98, 151, 291
Butler, D., 71, 108, 159, 165, 391
Button, C. N., 59

Caldcleuch, John, 398
Calhoun, David, 256, 325
Calmet, Augustine, 247
Calvin, John, xv, 4, 5, 6, 7, 8, 9, 10, 11, 12, 13, 14, 17, 18, 19, 21, 25, 26, 30, 34, 36, 37, 47, 51, 71, 76, 99, 126, 158, 165, 217, 265, 280, 313, 340, 365, 368, 378, 382
Calvinism, 4, 10, 16, 21, 22, 23, 40, 45, 59, 67, 87, 115, 116, 130, 140, 333, 350, 357, 358, 386
Cambridge University, xxv, 121
Cameron, James K., 5, 26, 38, 41, 45, 46, 53, 59
Cameron, John, 53, 396
Cameron, N. M. de S., xx
Campbell, Archibald, 171, 183, 399
Campbell, George, 104, 106, 189, 401

Campbell, George (Principal), xi, 91, 93, 109, 113, 114, 115, 128, 130, 131, 132, 133, 134, 135, 136, 137, 138, 132–38, 142, 162, 212, 214, 215, 246, 264, 276, 313, 378, 383, 404, 405
Campbell, Neil, 396
Campbell, Peter Colin, 347, 388, 402
Campbell, William M., 59
Cant, Andrew, 400
Cant, Robert G., 33, 38, 77, 90, 113
Cape Breton, 374
Carlyle, Alexander, 96, 108, 129, 131, 138
Carolinas, 396
Carstares, William, 110, 400
Cartwright Thomas, 38, 365
Casuistry, xii, 76, 79, 80, 87, 88, 137, 223, 227, 228, 231, 233, 242, 255, 323, 339, 382, 385, 390, 391, 392
Catecheticks, 105
Catechise, xii, 228, 230, 234, 242
Catholicism (Roman), 64, 109, 188, 367
Celibacy, 33
Chair of Divinity, xix, 50, 57, 62, 122, 144, 164, 396, 398, 400, 402, 404
Chaldee, 37, 101, 148, 161
Chalmers, George, 402
Chalmers, James, 405
Chalmers, John, 402
Chalmers, Robert, 336, 341, 344, 409
Chalmers, Thomas, 125, 126, 130, 140, 141, 144, 145, 159, 163, 164, 165, 378, 381, 382, 401
Chamier, Daniel, 126
Chamies, Daniel, 23
Chapel Royal, 139, 162, 397, 400, 401, 402
Chapel-of-Ease, 405
Charles I, 70
Charnock, 130
Charteris, Henry, 400
Charteris, Lawrence, 400
Cheyne, A. C., 130, 131, 141, 271, 319
Cheyne, Robert, 82
Christ's College, Aberdeen, 209, 317
Christie, George, 62, 63

Chronology, 61, 75, 80, 88, 98, 103, 104, 135, 157, 159, 161, 179, 180, 242, 249, 302, 305, 322, 339, 354, 390
Chrysostom, 7, 99, 264, 313
Church Fathers, 7, 8, 40, 99, 134, 140, 218, 264, 270, 280, 315, 322
Church government. *See* Polity/church government
Church of Scotland, xv, xix, xx, xxi, xxiii, 3, 34, 55, 65, 70, 71, 72, 87, 88, 91, 94, 95, 98, 99, 101, 103, 113, 115, 116, 117, 124, 129, 132, 139, 140, 141, 142, 148, 149, 150, 151, 152, 153, 154, 155, 156, 157, 162, 163, 164, 165, 169, 170, 171, 175, 176, 177, 180, 181, 184, 188, 193, 202, 215, 219, 240, 243, 260, 269, 277, 282, 284, 292, 302, 309, 316, 328, 330, 331, 332, 333, 335, 336, 342, 347, 382, 385, 388, 395, 408. *See also* Kirk
Cicero, 14, 131
Clarke, T. E. S., 86, 92, 375
Clerical Literary Society, 96, 124
Clerk, presbytery, 180
Clerk, session, 103, 384
Clerk, synod, 227
Cocceius, 67, 216, 217, 218, 248, 251, 316
Cock, Daniel, 190
Coffey, John, 59
Collegium Sapientiae, 21
Colloquy, 12, 13, 26, 29
Colonies, xx, xxii, 152, 204, 357, 359, 360, 361, 362, 363, 366, 373, 374
Colville, Alexander, 398, 400
Colville, William, 400
Common Sense (philosophy), 116, 133, 165, 186, 325, 385, 391
Company of Pastors, ix, xv, 5, 6, 10, 12, 13, 15, 16, 19, 21
Comrie, Walter, 398
Conn, Harvie M., xxii
Constitutional Associate Divinity Hall, 336, 409

Index

Continent, 5, 20, 21, 22, 23, 26, 29, 40, 45, 46, 52, 54, 57, 67, 73, 87, 127, 152, 270, 276, 380, 382, 387, 401, 403
Cook, John (father), 399
Cook, John (son), 399
Copleston, Frederick, 116
Count John VI of Nassau, 45
Court, Antoine, 23, 24
Coutts, James, 33, 36
Covenant Theology. *See* Federal Theology
Covenanter Expository Series, x, 57, 63
Covenanter Period, x, 42, 52, 56, 67, 70, 72, 77, 382
Covenanters, 45, 51, 69, 70, 81, 87, 129, 151, 193, 236, 244, 265, 269, 340, 357, 387
Craigie, Thomas, 399
Crakanthorpe, 99
Crauford, Matthew, 401
Craufurd, James, 401
Crawford, Thomas, 70
Crawford, Thomas J., 401
Crichton, Mrs. John, 149
Cromwell, Oliver, 68, 69
Cumbernauld, 329, 343, 408
Cuming, Patrick (father), 401
Cuming, Patrick (son), 397
Cuming, Robert, 401
Cumming, John, 401
Cunningham, William, 140
Currie, John, 175

d'Aubigne, J. H. M., 10
Dabney, Robert, 130, 217
Daiches, David, 94, 112
Dalhousie College/University, xxv, 349, 351, 352, 362, 366, 379
Dalzel, Andrew, 39, 50, 71, 78, 79
Daneau, Lambert, 16, 23
Danzig, 404
Dargan, Edwin C., 131
Davidson, Archibald, 396
Davidson, David, 396
Davidson, Francis, 409

Davies, Gareth, 144
Dawson, William, 401
de Greef, W., 10
Deacon, 233, 289
Debating Society, 214, 255, 278, 330
Degrees
  B.A., xvii, 34, 113
  B.D., 34, 51, 76, 90, 101, 149, 153, 154, 163, 384, 390, 391
  D.D., 51, 52, 76, 90, 125, 129, 149, 204, 212, 259, 270, 286, 287, 291, 293, 301, 305, 317, 318, 324, 335, 340, 348, 362, 367, 370, 390, 391
  L.L.D., 335
  M.A., 28, 34, 37, 39, 40, 42, 43, 47, 54, 55, 57, 68, 76, 81, 82, 90, 101, 104, 105, 106, 110, 111, 113, 139, 149, 151, 153, 155, 163, 173, 181, 189, 208, 212, 213, 285, 291, 339, 348, 360
Deism, 105, 129, 141, 325, 358
Delitzsch, F., 162
Dennison, James T., 217, 283
Dennyloanhead, 272
Devil, 222
Dewar, Daniel, 141, 164, 165, 404
DeWolfe, Charles, 362
Dick, Andrew C., 291, 292, 293, 294, 297, 302, 303
Dick, John, 128, 131, 141, 253, 257, 291, 292, 293, 294, 296, 297, 298, 301, 302, 303, 304, 305, 309, 320, 324, 341, 363, 364, 370, 377, 378, 381, 384, 393, 407
Dickson, Alexander, 64, 71, 401
Dickson, David, x, 52, 56, 57, 61, 62, 63, 64, 65, 66, 69, 70, 71, 77, 78, 87, 224, 227, 244, 302, 400
Dictates, 42, 61, 64, 65, 74, 128, 392
Die, 22, 23, 400
Diocesan Synod, x, 82
Directory for the Publick Worship of God, 75, 76
Disruption, xx, xxi, 94, 154, 155, 158, 162, 164, 348

Dissenters, xx, xxi, 94, 151, 190, 280, 308, 309, 368
Dissenting Presbyterians, xx, 95, 327, 385, 388
Divinity Controversy, 102
Divinity Halls. *See* particular location
Doddridge, Philip, 131, 236, 280
Dogmatics, 43, 87, 89, 139, 218, 255, 290, 381, 382, 384, 390, 391
Donaldson, Alexander, 403
Donaldson, Gordon, 38
Donaldson, James, 403
Doolittel, 100
Dort, 5, 87
Dort, Canons of, 60, 390
Dort, Synod of, 22, 99
Douay, 400
Douglas, Alexander, 401
Douglas, William, 402
Drelincourt, Charles, 227, 228, 365
Drummond, Andrew L., 21, 22, 23, 115, 125, 127, 133, 251
Duisburg, 20
DuJon, François, 21, 99
Dumfries University, 149
Dunbar, Hugh, 360, 361
Dunbar, Linda J., 31
Dunblane, 56, 84
Dunblane Register, 84
Duncan, Alexander, 309, 310, 318, 320, 321, 322, 323, 324, 407
Duncan, David, 324, 407
Duncan, J. Ligon, 92, 280
Duncan, John "Rabbi", 276, 285, 337, 341
Duncan, Patrick, 404
Dunfermline, 188
Dunlop, A. Ian, 25, 110
Dunlop, Alexander, 193, 397
Dunlop, William, 396, 401
Durkan, John, 36, 37, 43, 44, 47
Dury, Robert, 38

Eadie, John, 173, 174, 175, 176, 304, 323, 324, 407, 408

Eaglesham, 396
Ecclesiastical Ordinances, 9, 12
Ecclesiastical/Church History (study of), xiii, xix, xxii, xxv, 3, 20, 38, 61, 75, 80, 99, 103, 106, 107, 108, 112, 121, 130, 131, 132, 134, 135, 137, 140, 141, 143, 148, 149, 151, 152, 157, 159, 161, 164, 175, 183, 194, 196, 197, 212, 213, 223, 240, 241, 242, 251, 255, 277, 282, 309, 310, 319, 321, 322, 324, 325, 339, 340, 342, 343, 354, 355, 356, 360, 366, 378, 379, 382, 384, 385, 386, 391, 392, 393, 398, 399, 401, 403, 404, 405, 407
Edict of Toleration, 23
Edinburgh, xx, 31, 51, 52, 67, 73, 78, 93, 108, 131, 179, 187, 204, 205, 214, 259, 285, 286, 287, 289, 290, 305, 310, 318, 324, 338, 339, 341, 342, 343, 351, 393, 401, 407, 408, 409
Edinburgh College/University, ix, xxv, 4, 18, 39, 41, 42, 43, 45, 47, 48, 49, 50, 51, 53, 54, 56, 57, 60, 61, 63, 64, 65, 68, 70, 71, 79, 90, 96, 97, 104, 106, 107, 108, 109, 110, 111, 114, 115, 125, 127, 128, 129, 130, 131, 138, 139, 144, 145, 146, 147, 148, 153, 158, 159, 162, 163, 164, 176, 185, 189, 193, 198, 199, 202, 207, 212, 213, 257, 258, 285, 318, 338, 339, 340, 351, 390, 400
Edinburgh Exercise, 31
Edinburgh Missionary Society, 128, 261, 293
Edinburgh Theological Magazine, 84, 165, 306, 307, 308, 364, 365
Edwards, Jonathan, 129, 236, 242, 250, 264, 358, 378
Elder, 29, 30, 60, 92, 170, 226, 233, 358, 376
Elshout, Bartel, 251
England, xxii, 38, 42, 51, 66, 70, 98, 117, 121, 122, 129, 236, 240, 241, 246, 260, 279, 311, 314, 349, 385, 390
English Presbyterian College, 343

Enlightenment, 94, 95, 114, 116, 143, 190, 193, 281, 385
Episcopal Restoration, x, 81, 86, 90, 382, 384
Erasmus, 7, 8, 11, 99, 105, 313
Erastianism, 60, 327
Erskine, Ebenezer, xxi, 104, 110, 170, 171, 172, 176, 187, 188, 189, 190, 191, 192, 193, 194, 198, 200, 201, 208, 209, 211, 217, 227, 229, 248, 255, 407
Erskine, Henry, 122
Erskine, Ralph, xxi, 59, 104, 175, 176, 177, 188, 190, 191, 194, 198, 200, 209, 217, 229, 265, 274, 414
Essay, 38, 63, 95, 96, 117, 119, 120, 121, 123, 131, 133, 146, 214, 219, 255, 263, 287, 293, 302, 303, 305, 307, 311, 318, 319, 322, 323, 324, 333, 339, 376, 378, 384
Essenius, 104, 126, 128, 382, 391
Europe, 4, 5, 10, 16, 19, 24, 45, 403
Eusebius, 99, 365
Evans, William B., 301
Exegesis, 7, 10, 13, 14, 15, 18, 19, 22, 29, 43, 49, 66, 86, 88, 102, 103, 109, 116, 131, 136, 142, 156, 157, 175, 176, 179, 206, 211, 243, 246, 248, 251, 261, 262, 268, 271, 277, 278, 311, 312, 313, 314, 315, 333, 334, 361, 363
Exercise, ix, x, xvii, 25, 26, 29, 30, 31, 33, 34, 38, 47, 48, 54, 55, 60, 82, 83, 90, 92, 93, 96, 98, 100, 103, 104, 105, 106, 136, 148, 157, 181, 192, 195, 196, 198, 211, 253, 278, 325, 363, 367, 369, 375, 376, 377, 384, 386, 390, 391
Experimental religion, 84, 151, 205, 219, 325

Fagg, Jane B., 109, 110
Fairbairn, Patrick, 246, 248, 251
Fairlie, James, 400
Falconer, David, 398
Fall, James, 92, 396
Farley, Edward, xxii

Federal Theology, 40, 41, 46, 52, 53, 67, 79, 87, 90, 140, 176, 216, 218, 270, 289, 301, 322, 325, 382, 384
Ferguson, Alexander, 171
Ferme, Charles, 41, 48, 49
Ferrier, Andrew, 172, 173, 174, 175, 176, 236
Findlay, Robert, 121, 124, 397
First Book of Discipline, ix, xxiii, 4, 25, 26, 27, 28, 29, 30, 31, 32, 34, 35, 38, 44, 50, 54, 68, 350
Fisher, James, 170, 171, 180, 182, 188, 189, 191, 193, 194, 195, 196, 197, 198, 200, 201, 208, 209, 248, 255, 392, 407
Five Articles of Perth, 53
Flavel, John, 99, 225, 265
Flavel, William, 216
Fleming, William, 337, 397
Forbes, John, 21, 50, 51, 53, 366, 402
Forbes, William, 51, 404
Forester, Thomas, 398
Form of Presbyterial Church-Government, 74, 75, 76
Forrester, David M., 162, 176
Foster, Walter R., 55
Four Brethren, 170, 172, 181
Foxcroft, H. Cl, 86
France, ix, 4, 5, 6, 10, 11, 14, 15, 16, 19, 22, 23, 24, 38, 52, 53, 162, 282, 327, 400
Franecker, 21
Frankfurt-on-the-Oder, 20
Fraser, Brian J., 333, 335, 348
Fraser, David, 360
Fraser, Donald, 189, 190, 192, 194, 236, 280
Fraser, James, 235, 236, 237
Fraser, Sir Alexander, 48
Fraser, William, 193, 194, 262, 263, 374
Fraserburgh, x, 48, 49, 55, 390
Free Church of Scotland, xx, xxi, xxiii, xxv, 94, 153, 163, 210, 323, 325, 333, 335, 342, 348, 385, 401, 409
Free Presbyterian Church, xvi

French, 4, 10, 11, 13, 16, 18, 21, 22, 23, 24, 55, 134, 160, 207, 264, 273, 284, 315
Frye, Northrop, 357
Fuller, 313

Gaelic Chapel Students' Society (Glasgow), 94, 95
Gairney Bridge, Kinross, 170
Garden, James, 88, 142, 402
Garrioch, William, 82
General Assembly, x, xi, 25, 28, 30, 32, 34, 36, 49, 54, 56, 57, 69, 70, 72, 73, 74, 76, 77, 78, 79, 91, 92, 93, 97, 98, 100, 101, 103, 115, 125, 129, 147, 151, 152, 153, 154, 155, 156, 157, 158, 165, 169, 170, 171, 302, 309, 331, 402
General Assembly, Glasgow, 56, 61, 72
General Associate Church (Antiburgher), xiii, 129, 138, 176, 184, 185, 187, 188, 201, 202, 204, 206, 207, 257, 263, 264, 272, 285, 286, 287, 288, 289, 291, 293, 303, 304, 317, 321, 327, 328, 336, 338, 339, 340, 343, 344, 347, 348, 349, 350, 367, 392, 393, 406, 408, 409
Geneva, 4, 5, 9, 10, 11, 12, 13, 14, 15, 16, 17, 19, 20, 21, 22, 23, 24, 25, 26, 36, 38, 43, 45, 71, 107, 250, 276, 283, 387, 396, 397, 398, 404
Gerard, Alexander, 93, 113, 118, 131, 132, 133, 138, 212, 402, 405
Gerard, Gilbert, 133, 142, 403
German Higher Critical (thought), 313
Gib, Adam, 176, 177, 180, 188, 201, 289
Gibb, Gavin, 397
Gilcomston, 403
Gill, Stewart D., 328, 348
Gillespie, George, 60, 67
Gillespie, James, 398
Gillespie, Patrick, x, 56, 57, 67, 396
Gillespie, Thomas, xx
Glamis, 402
Glasgow, xi, xx, xxi, 61, 78, 94, 96, 124, 129, 173, 182, 187, 189, 193, 194, 209, 228, 248, 257, 264, 266, 292, 297, 302, 304, 305, 310, 317, 318, 323, 333, 335, 337, 339, 343, 349, 356, 357, 365, 370, 377, 393, 401, 407, 408, 409
Glasgow College/University, ix, xxi, xxv, 28, 33, 34, 36, 37, 38, 42, 43, 44, 45, 47, 48, 50, 52, 53, 54, 57, 60, 61, 63, 64, 65, 67, 68, 71, 78, 85, 86, 87, 90, 92, 99, 104, 110, 112, 113, 114, 116, 117, 119, 121, 122, 124, 125, 126, 127, 129, 144, 145, 146, 147, 148, 153, 158, 159, 163, 171, 173, 174, 178, 185, 193, 202, 252, 273, 310, 318, 335, 337, 348, 350, 351, 360, 368, 373, 396
Glasgow Society for Promoting Religion and Liberal Education..., 363, 364, 365, 379
Gomar, Francis, 22
Good, James I., 283
Goodall, John, 401
Goodwin, Thomas, 265
Gordon Lectures, 161
Gordon, Charles, 402
Gordon, George (father), 403
Gordon, George (son), 403
Gordon, Patrick, 399, 403, 404
Gouge, 99, 100
Govan, 37, 52, 396
Gowdie, John, 400, 401
Grant, Alexander, 5, 39, 42, 71
Gray, George, 397
Gray, Gilbert, 404
Greek, 7, 8, 11, 14, 16, 18, 22, 23, 27, 34, 36, 39, 45, 53, 66, 68, 71, 75, 76, 77, 83, 86, 90, 99, 101, 102, 103, 104, 106, 109, 110, 112, 113, 118, 134, 136, 139, 140, 142, 145, 146, 155, 157, 161, 174, 178, 179, 184, 193, 200, 206, 207, 208, 209, 212, 214, 243, 254, 262, 264, 265, 267, 273, 277, 278, 284, 285, 287, 291, 305, 307, 312, 315, 317, 321, 325, 330, 334, 337, 338, 347, 351, 361, 366, 404
Greenock, 81, 329, 343, 408
Gregg, William, 333, 347, 348
Grenz, Stanley J., 250

Index 447

Greyfriars, 44, 52, 56, 162, 292, 400, 401, 402, 404, 405
Groningen, 21
Grotius, Hugo, 185, 265, 313
Grudem, Wayne, 221
Guignet, Marguerite, 23
Guild, William, 63, 64, 68, 402
Gymnasium, 17, 22, 24, 45

Haddington, xii, 138, 184, 209, 211, 214, 258, 259, 261, 330, 338, 341, 344, 407, 409
Hadow, George, 399
Hadow, James, 130, 181, 182, 398
Hague, 396
Haldane, James, 364, 399
Haldane, Patrick, 399
Haldane, Robert, 398
Halifax, xxv, 347, 348, 349, 351, 352, 357, 359, 361, 362, 363, 365, 366, 376, 386
Hall, Archibald, 188
Hall, Robert G., 273, 276, 278
Halyburton, Thomas, 105, 106, 131, 219, 228, 235, 236, 237, 240, 398, 400
Hamilton, Ian, xx, 60, 316
Hamilton, Robert, 107, 128, 401
Hamilton, William, 131, 193, 400, 401
Hardy, Thomas, 401
Harper, James, 324, 408
Hart, D. G., xxi, 3
Haws, Charles H., 33
Hay, James, 212, 213, 214, 215, 222
Hazlett, Wm. Ian P., xix, 5, 25, 37, 52, 61, 185, 186, 271
Hebrew, 4, 8, 11, 14, 18, 22, 23, 27, 28, 34, 36, 37, 42, 43, 44, 50, 53, 54, 61, 64, 68, 69, 71, 75, 76, 78, 83, 85, 86, 90, 101, 102, 103, 104, 105, 106, 108, 109, 110, 121, 125, 136, 143, 147, 148, 151, 152, 153, 157, 159, 160, 161, 164, 174, 176, 178, 179, 189, 193, 200, 206, 208, 209, 212, 243, 254, 257, 262, 265, 268, 286, 292, 305, 307, 308, 312, 315, 321, 325, 330, 337, 338, 344, 349, 361, 362, 366, 382, 397, 399, 401, 403, 405
Heidelberg, ix, xv, 5, 19, 20, 21, 40, 46, 50, 396, 398, 402, 404
Heidelberg Catechism, 5, 21, 40, 71, 86, 87, 104, 391
Helmstedt, 241, 398, 404
Henderson, G. D., xix, 4, 30, 42, 44, 50, 51, 69, 88, 89, 199, 257, 258, 340
Henry, Matthew, 236, 237, 244, 245, 313
Herborn, 5, 20, 22, 45, 46, 53, 397, 404
Hermeneutics, 13, 162, 245, 255, 305, 313, 339
Heron, Alastair, 328
Heyer, Henri, 12
Hill, Alexander, 139, 397
Hill, George, 125, 128, 130, 131, 139, 140, 141, 161, 302, 329, 330, 331, 332, 358, 381, 391, 398, 408
Hobart, R. R., 273, 282
Hodge, Charles, 222, 301
Hoffecker, Andrew, 222, 223
Hogg, James, 235, 236, 237, 245
Holland, 23, 110, 162, 173, 182, 279, 401, 402
Homiletics, xii, 13, 109, 127, 130, 131, 183, 228, 229, 230, 231, 232, 238, 244, 255, 323, 338, 341, 344, 355, 360, 363, 386, 409
Homily, 102, 103, 105, 109, 136, 157, 196, 214, 261, 278, 306, 307, 325
Hope, Nicholas, 20
Horn, D. B., 42, 110, 111, 112
Howell, Wilber Samuel, 134
Howie, Robert, 41, 45, 46, 53, 54, 72, 397, 404
Huguenot, 22, 42, 282, 398
Humanities, 9, 14, 16, 36
Hume, David, 115, 116, 131, 133, 138, 214, 217, 240, 248
Hunter, Andrew, 107, 108, 128, 401
Hunter, Andrew (of Barjarg), 96, 128
Hunter, John, 176, 177, 178, 179, 180
Hymns, 70, 199, 269

Hyperius, Andreas, 17

India, 130, 152, 305, 380, 401
Infralapsarian, 87
Infralapsarianism, 283
Ireland, xxii, 94, 100, 129, 164, 172, 181, 190, 195, 197, 201, 202, 203, 236, 240, 241, 260, 294, 328, 337, 379, 385, 387
Irvine, 62, 66, 227
Irving, John, 83

Jack, William, 402
Jackson, Thomas Thomson, 397, 399
Jacob, W. M., 100
Jardine, George, 112, 117, 118, 119, 120, 121, 122, 125, 152, 348, 360, 364, 383
Jenkyn, 99
Johnson, William S., 217
Johnston, John, 46, 398
Johnstone, Gabriel, 399
Josephus, 134, 313
Julian, John, 199, 204

Kearney, Hugh, 44, 53
Keir, John, 370, 372, 373, 375, 378
Keith, George (Earl Marischal), 4
Keith, William, 400
Kennedy, Herbert, 104
Kidd, James, 165, 403
Kinclaven, 171, 193, 194
King's College, x, 34, 35, 37, 38, 39, 42, 43, 44, 45, 48, 50, 51, 53, 54, 63, 64, 68, 69, 70, 71, 76, 83, 88, 89, 90, 109, 113, 114, 118, 137, 138, 145, 147, 148, 150, 158, 160, 161, 212, 276, 291, 347, 405
King's College, Windsor, 367, 373
Kingdon, Robert, 10, 15, 16
Kingsbarns, 398
Kinross, xi, xii, 170, 178, 198, 199, 252, 253, 254, 255, 257, 407
Kirk, xv, xvi, xxiii, 28, 33, 68, 72, 73, 77, 91, 128, 131, 133, 138, 142, 144, 159, 170, 183, 186, 191, 192, 208, 240, 275, 276, 303, 322, 325, 338, 348, 362, 366, 368, 380, 381, 383, 384, 385, 386, 387, 388, 389, 390, 391. *See also* Church of Scotland
Kirk, James, 4, 25, 30, 32, 33, 36, 37, 47
Kirkcaldy, 68, 204, 205
Klauber, Martin I., 24, 284
Klempa, William, 333, 335, 350, 358
Knox College (Toronto), xxv, 333, 334, 335, 348
Knox, E. A., 71
Knox, John, xvi, xix, 4, 10, 25, 30, 31, 33, 43, 57, 68, 71, 124, 333, 334, 335, 340
Kohl, Manfred W., 380
Kuinoel, 313
Kurtz, Johann Heinrich, 20
Kuyper, Abraham, 165

Lachman, David, xxi, 98, 127
Laing, Benjamin, 338, 342, 343, 409
Laing, David, 30, 61, 68, 69
Laity, 380, 386
Landreth, P., xx, xxi, 172, 177, 178, 182, 183, 184, 188, 189, 190, 191, 194, 199, 201, 203, 204, 252, 260, 261, 262, 305
Lane, Anthony N. S., 7
Lathan, Robert, 188
Latimer, 267
Latin, 11, 13, 16, 18, 27, 28, 29, 33, 34, 36, 37, 39, 42, 45, 50, 52, 53, 57, 62, 64, 65, 66, 68, 71, 75, 76, 77, 83, 85, 86, 93, 99, 101, 102, 103, 104, 105, 106, 107, 110, 111, 112, 113, 118, 126, 134, 136, 145, 146, 155, 156, 157, 173, 174, 182, 184, 190, 196, 200, 206, 207, 208, 209, 212, 273, 277, 278, 280, 284, 285, 288, 291, 301, 307, 313, 315, 325, 334, 338, 341, 351, 361, 365, 384, 386, 390, 391, 392, 393
Latitudinarian, 87, 88, 136, 391
Law (study of), 14, 28, 34, 36, 43, 45, 46, 52, 112, 117, 145, 146, 149, 349
Lawson, George, xii, 142, 200, 252, 253, 257–71, 257, 264, 266, 267, 268, 269,

Index 449

290, 293, 299, 302, 310, 313, 318, 329, 330, 332, 347, 363, 385, 407
Lecturer(s), 158, 405
Lee, Francis Nigel, 217
Lee, John, 164, 264, 399, 400, 401
Lee, Robert, 162, 163, 164, 402
Leechman, William, 127, 128, 129, 131, 185, 273, 396, 397
Leiden, ix, xv, 4, 5, 8, 19, 20, 21, 22, 24, 70, 182, 400, 401
Leighton, Robert, 56, 57, 64, 66, 70, 71, 84, 87, 99, 400
Leith, John, xxi, 79, 80, 109, 124, 217
Leslie, James, 404
Leslie, William, 402
Leusden, 110
Lewis, Gillian, 16
Libertines, 66
Licensing of Probationers, 100, 156
Licentiate, 177, 258, 360
Liddell, David, 86, 396
Limborch, 126
Lindsay, T. M., 67
Lippe, R., 49
Liston, David, 401
Literary and Philosophical Society of Newcastle, 351
Lithuanian students, 97
Liturgy, 4, 9, 70, 163, 164, 282, 323
Lloyd-Jones, Martin, 109
Logic, 7, 18, 34, 37, 39, 40, 43, 46, 49, 54, 106, 112, 113, 114, 117, 118, 134, 145, 146, 152, 155, 200, 202, 206, 212, 273, 277, 281, 325, 338, 348, 352, 356, 361, 382, 383
Lombard, 7, 33, 99
London (Canada), 347, 348, 362
London (England), 51, 58, 67, 70, 76, 139, 212, 343
London Missionary Society, 212, 261
London, Tower of, 49
Londonderry (Nova Scotia), 190
Lord's Supper, 99, 225, 231, 232, 239, 323
Lorimer, James, 398

Lothian, Andrew, 261, 297
Lumsden, John, 402
Luther, Martin, 3, 7, 135, 313
Lynn, Robert Wood, xxii

Maag, Karen, 10, 14, 15, 16, 17, 21, 43
Maccovius, 126
MacDonald, Duncan, 360
MacDonald, John, 360
MacEwen, A. R., 209
MacFarlane, Duncan, 125, 396
MacFarlane, John, 257, 258, 260, 261, 262, 264, 265, 266, 267, 268, 269, 270, 271
MacGill, Stevenson, 92, 96, 119, 120, 121, 122, 123, 124, 125, 126, 131, 142, 150, 151, 152, 159, 164, 397
MacGregor, Janet G., 30
MacIver, Iain F., 144
MacKelvie, William, 171, 172, 177, 182, 189, 190, 194, 198, 199, 201, 205, 212, 223, 248, 253, 261, 262, 263, 285, 286, 287, 294, 305, 318, 321, 324, 349, 406
MacKenzie, James, 185, 199
MacKenzie, Robert, 178, 190, 191, 197, 208, 209, 210, 211, 212, 217, 218, 233, 235, 240, 241, 243, 246, 247, 248
MacKenzie, Sheldon, xxii, 366, 367
Mackie, J. D., 33
MacKnight, James, 142
MacLean, Donald, 98
Maclehose, James, 69
MacLeod, Donald, 39, 41, 139, 141, 165, 229
MacLeod, Hugh, 397
MacLeod, John, 57, 58, 59, 60, 66, 67, 70, 87, 88, 139, 140, 141, 165, 243, 244, 248, 269, 270, 283, 319, 339, 340, 381
MacLeod, Roderick, 402
MacMeeken, J. W., 70
MacMillan, D., 53
MacPherson, Hugh, 403
MacPherson, Robert, 403
MacPhie, J. P., 361
MacWhirter, A., 327

Magee, William, 358
Mair, John, 82
Manton, 99, 100, 265
Marburg, 20
Marck, Johannes, 22, 127, 143, 176, 182, 194, 199, 202, 211, 217, 218, 257, 265, 278, 279, 287, 339, 341, 358, 378, 382, 384, 386, 392, 393
Maresius, Samuel, 126
Marischal College, x, 4, 5, 39, 42, 44, 45, 46, 48, 49, 50, 51, 53, 54, 69, 70, 89, 109, 113, 114, 115, 118, 124, 132, 134, 135, 137, 138, 145, 147, 148, 150, 160, 161, 212, 214, 215, 246, 259, 270, 276, 390, 402, 403, 405
Marrow, xxi, 98, 127, 130, 171, 175, 176, 181, 182, 183, 190, 191, 192, 193, 242, 272, 282, 335, 340, 381
Marrowmen, 174, 191, 229
Marshall, Andrew, 94, 319, 323
Mason, John, 201, 204, 206, 207
Mason, John Jr., 269
Massillon, 264
Masters, D. C., 333
Mastricht, 217, 218
Mathematics, 18, 37, 70, 106, 113, 145, 155, 206, 273, 277, 338, 361, 362, 404
Mather, Cotton, 52, 236
Maxwell, Thomas, 130
Maxwell, William D., 3
McCallum, Donald, 125, 139, 140, 141
McCloy, Frank Dixon, 207
McCoy, F. N., 60, 61
McCoy, Wayne Livingston, 310, 311, 312, 313, 314, 317, 318
McCrie, C. G., 65, 71, 88, 316
McCrie, Thomas Jr., 92, 169, 170, 338, 339, 340, 341, 342, 343, 409
McCrie, Thomas Sr., 4, 46, 47, 49, 51, 265, 269, 273, 284, 285, 336, 337, 338, 339, 340, 341, 343, 344, 357, 364, 409
McCulloch, Michael, 360, 362
McCulloch, Thomas, xiv, xxii, 96, 130, 272, 273, 282, 285, 286, 287, 289, 308, 347, 348, 349, 350, 351, 352, 353, 354, 355, 356, 357, 358, 359, 360, 361, 362, 363, 364, 365, 366, 367, 368, 369, 370, 371, 372, 373, 375, 377, 378, 379, 386, 387
McCulloch, William, 286, 348, 349, 350, 352, 357, 358, 359
McCurdy, Daniel, 372
McDowall, Charles, 401
McElroy, Davis D., 93, 96
McEwen, William, 190, 248
McGavin, William, 356, 357, 364
McGill William, 292
McGill, Hugh, 190
McGillivray, Angus, 360, 361
McGowan, A. T. B., xvii, xxv, 41
McGrath, Alister E., 6, 8, 115, 242
McGregor, James, 360
McIntosh, John R., 115, 116, 133, 282
McKerrow, John, 170, 171, 172, 173, 183, 184, 188, 190, 198, 201, 202, 203, 204, 205, 209, 211, 261, 262, 269, 273, 277, 278, 279, 303, 304, 306, 309, 311, 317, 319, 320, 321, 322, 323, 325, 328, 336, 338, 340
McKim, Donald K., 40, 246
McLachlan, H., 129
McLean, George G., 403
McLean, John, 360, 361
McLellan, J. C., 383
McLerie, David, 171
McMillan, William, 30, 31, 32, 48, 104
McMullin, Stanley E., 351
McNeill, John T., 10
McTurk, William, 397
Mearns, Duncan, 165, 403
Mechie, Stewart, xix, xx, 26, 50, 74, 81, 85, 106, 127, 129, 152, 153, 154, 158, 272, 311
Medicine, 14, 43, 45, 110, 111, 112, 117, 142, 145, 146, 149, 401, 403
Meiklejohn, Hugh, 401
Meldrum, George, 401

Index 451

Melville, Andrew, xvi, 4, 33, 34, 36, 44, 36-55, 56, 73, 76, 114, 280, 340, 396, 397
Melville, James, 33, 34, 398
Melville, Patrick, 398
Memoriter, 258, 311, 362
Menzies, John, 69, 88, 400, 402, 404
Methick, 402
Methodist(s), 157, 210, 362
Middleton, Alexander, 402
Middleton, George, 402
Miller, Glenn, xxiii, 6, 13, 14, 314
Miller, R. S., 377
Miller, Samuel, 73, 240
Miller,Glenn, 314
Missions, xxii, 124, 128, 269, 277, 278, 293, 351, 375, 377, 380
Mitchell, Alexander F., 164, 399
Mitchell, James, 359
Mitchell, John, 161, 204, 285, 286, 287, 288, 294, 296, 304, 305, 307, 309, 323, 356, 357, 358, 359, 364, 399, 407
Moderate (party), 91, 108, 116, 121, 125, 129, 131, 133, 138, 139, 140, 141, 142, 191, 192, 193, 215, 228, 276, 358
Moir, John S., 347, 365
Moir, William, 404
Moncrieff, Alexander, xi, xii, 170, 171, 172, 181, 182, 183, 184, 185, 188, 191, 200, 201, 392, 407
Moncrieff, William, 201, 202, 203, 273, 274, 275, 285, 338, 407
Monro, Alexander, 129, 398, 400
Montauban, 22, 23, 126
Monter, William E., 14
Moodie, William, 401
Moore, T. M., 9
Morus, Alexander, 282, 283, 317
Mosheim, J., 134, 164, 241, 317, 322, 378
Mosheim. J., 140
Moss, Michael, xxi, 101, 112, 113, 114
Muirhead, George, 397
Muller, Richard A., xxii, 3, 4, 17, 87, 104, 107, 126, 284

Murdoch, John L., 360, 361
Murison, James, 398
Murison, W., 26, 28
Murray, Alexander, 125, 401
Murray, Alexander (Bequest and Lectures), 160, 161, 404
Murray, Douglas, 162
Murray, Iain, 58
Murray, Matthew, 409
Musical instruments, 34, 288

Naphy, William G., 9, 12
National Covenant, 70, 72, 171
Natural Religion, 122, 131, 319
Neander, 313, 378
Needham, N. R., xxv
Neuenhaus, J., 7
Nevin, John W., 301
New Brunswick, 357, 361, 362, 374
New College, xxi, xxv, 130, 177, 185, 194, 200, 215, 224, 246, 252, 263, 272, 273, 279, 310
New Light Burghers, 349
New Light/Old Light controversy, 332, 333, 336, 339
New Lights, 269, 279, 289, 291, 318, 327, 329, 332, 336, 343, 344, 386
New York, 201, 367
Newhills, 402
Newman, John Henry, xvii
Newtonian, 112, 114, 115
Nicholson, David R., 334, 335
Nisbet, Alexander, 52, 63, 244
Noll, Mark A., 6
North (Third Charge), 402, 404
Northland, Charles, 397
Nova Erectio, ix, 4, 36, 37, 38, 48, 49, 54
Nova Scotia, 130, 190, 201, 286, 347, 348, 349, 350, 351, 352, 353, 356, 357, 361, 362, 363, 364, 365, 366, 367, 368, 370, 372, 373, 375, 376, 377, 378, 379, 386, 387
Nuttall, Geoffrey F., 210

Old Machar, 402
Olevianus, 40, 45, 46, 53
Olshausen, 313, 315
Ong, Walter J., 39
Oriental Languages, 61, 112, 147, 149, 247, 349, 397, 403
Origin, 99
Original Secession Divinity Hall, xiii, 341, 409
Orkney, 81, 99, 103
Ormond, D. D., 387
Osborne, James, 405
Osborne, John, 404
Ostervald, 127, 128, 378
Otto, Julius Conradus, 71, 78, 401
Owen, John, 64, 67, 211, 216, 217, 219, 220, 225, 235, 264, 265, 280, 317
Oxford, 64
Oxford University, 121

Paisley, 171, 348, 360, 365, 409
Paley, 159, 161, 391
Pannier, Jacques, 23
Panter, Patrick, 398
Papist, 66
Paraeus, 126
Paraphrases, 199
Pareus, 21, 104
Park, Trevor, 121
Parker, T. H. L., 10
Parochial libraries
  Aberlour, 99
  Abernethy, 99
  Alford, 99
  Auchterarder, 99
  Caithness, 99
  Dumbarton, 22, 99, 100
  Dunblane, 99
  Dunkeld, 99
  Inverness, 99
  Kincardine, 99
  Orkney, 99
  Ross, 99
  Shetland, 99
  Sutherland, 99
  Synod of Argyle, 99
  Synods of Angus and Mearns, 99
Pastoral Theology, xiii, 158, 160, 165, 309, 310, 321, 322, 323, 324, 378, 379, 383, 385, 393, 407
Paterson, Robert, 404
Paton, John G., 377
Patrick, Millar, 70
Patronage, 143, 169, 170, 171, 283, 328, 371
Patterson, Archibald, 360
Patterson, George, 357, 359, 360, 361, 362, 363, 366, 374
Patterson, J. Brown, 313
Patterson, Robert, 360, 361
Paxton, George, 272, 285–89, 285, 286, 287, 288, 289, 304, 305, 306, 339, 340, 341, 342, 344, 349, 354, 364, 370, 379, 385, 386, 407, 409
Pazmiño, Robert W., 8, 9, 381, 382
Pedagogical, xxiii, 114, 270, 289, 291, 298, 363, 379
Penny-a-week Societies, 366
Perth, 48, 68, 72, 171, 172, 175, 176, 177, 178, 181, 187, 198, 202, 332, 343, 407, 408
Pettegree, Andrew, 9, 10, 16, 29
Philip, Adam, 66
Philip, R. G., 4
Philosophical class, Secession, xi, xii, 184, 185, 186, 200, 204, 205, 206, 207, 276, 385, 392
Philosophy, xvi, 9, 16, 23, 34, 36, 39, 70, 75, 95, 101, 102, 106, 110, 112, 113, 114, 115, 116, 117, 118, 131, 132, 133, 146, 151, 184, 185, 201, 202, 204, 205, 206, 208, 213, 214, 219, 273, 276, 277, 281, 285, 286, 291, 300, 325, 333, 351, 373, 386, 392, 393
Philosophy, moral, 28, 37, 106, 109, 111, 112, 113, 114, 115, 116, 145, 155, 165,

Index 453

185, 200, 212, 214, 273, 277, 325, 338, 352, 361, 366
Philosophy, natural, 106, 110, 112, 113, 145, 155, 174, 200, 206, 212, 273, 277, 281, 295, 325, 338, 339, 349, 361, 366, 373
Pictet, Benedict, 24, 107, 127, 128, 143, 211, 217, 218, 265, 283, 317, 358, 378, 382, 386, 391, 393
Pictou, 347, 350, 352, 362, 364, 368, 369, 371, 377, 387
Pictou Academy/Divinity Hall, 308, 348, 349, 350, 351, 352, 359, 360, 361, 362, 363, 364, 365, 368, 370, 371, 373, 377, 379, 386
Pictou Grammar School, 350, 368
Piety, xii, xxiii, 6, 13, 17, 19, 20, 36, 58, 59, 73, 76, 79, 84, 88, 89, 100, 127, 131, 133, 138, 140, 141, 142, 174, 181, 183, 214, 215, 216, 219, 220, 221, 222, 223, 224, 225, 226, 227, 228, 233, 236, 237, 255, 267, 270, 279, 280, 281, 282, 288, 289, 293, 296, 298, 299, 300, 302, 312, 324, 330, 331, 334, 335, 352, 355, 361, 369, 381, 384, 385, 389
Pirie, Alexander, 204
Pirie, William R., 403, 405
Piscator, 45, 46
Pitcairn, Alexander, 398
Plato, 17, 207
Pluralities, xi, 121, 124, 125, 126, 139, 154, 379, 395
Poitiers, 36, 396, 397
Poland, 38
Polity/church government, xii, 15, 26, 30, 36, 60, 61, 67, 101, 130, 135, 136, 148, 175, 233, 234, 255, 289, 323, 332, 333, 340, 355, 360, 390, 392
Pollock, Robert, 404, 405
Poole, 100
Popular sermon, 102, 103, 106, 109, 127, 136, 157, 175, 178, 179, 180, 181, 193, 196, 211, 214, 260, 261, 278, 307, 320, 325, 330, 366

Popular/Evangelical (party), 91, 96, 108, 116, 122, 124, 125, 128, 133, 140, 141, 142, 165, 192, 282, 335
Porteous, William, 282
Potter, Michael, 397
Practical Divinity, xii, 66, 99, 137, 183, 194, 196, 197, 223, 224, 225, 227
Practical Religion, 161, 405
Predestination, 23, 48, 53, 57
Presbyterian Church of the Lower Provinces of British North America, 347, 361
Presbyterianism, xix, xx, xxiv, 38, 53, 55, 56, 69, 79, 89, 91, 92, 129, 234, 350
Presbyteries, xvi, xxiii, 47, 54, 55, 60, 73, 74, 76, 78, 79, 80, 82, 84, 88, 90, 91, 92, 97, 98, 99, 100, 101, 102, 103, 104, 136, 147, 152, 154, 155, 156, 158, 170, 180, 181, 198, 200, 207, 210, 234, 259, 260, 277, 279, 283, 295, 296, 303, 307, 308, 309, 322, 325, 332, 355, 366, 367, 372, 373, 375, 376, 379, 382, 383, 384, 385, 386, 388, 391, 393, 407
Presbytery
  Aberdeen, 47
  Associate, xi, 170, 171, 172, 173, 175, 177, 178, 179, 180, 181, 182, 184, 192, 200, 204, 337, 407, 408
  Associate of Glasgow, 192
  Caithness, 98
  Constitutional, 273, 279, 286
  Dumbarton, 22, 98, 99, 100
  Dunblane, 98
  Dunfermline, 174
  Dunkeld, 48, 98
  Edinburgh, 47, 115, 258, 325
  Glasgow, 47, 60, 174
  Irvine, 175
  Kilmarnock (Antiburgher), 349
  Kinclaven, 193
  Kirkcaldy, 105, 184
  Lewis, 98
  Moray, 98
  Orkney, 98

Perth, 48, 182
Pictou, 374
Prince Edward Island, 372
Ross, 98
Shetland (Zetland), 98
St. Andrews, 47
Stirling, 104
Sutherland, 98
United Associate of Stirling, 306
United Associate of Stirling and Falkirk, 308, 325
Price, B. B., 383
Prideaux, 134
Prince Edward Island, 350, 360, 361, 370, 372
Princeton College, 116, 293, 301, 305, 324
Princeton Seminary, 73, 216, 222, 223, 240, 256, 325
Pringle, Alexander, 201, 202
Probationer(s), xxiii, 91, 92, 93, 103, 105, 156, 175, 179, 180, 181, 255, 258, 260, 262, 285, 292, 295, 296, 307, 325, 330, 342, 377, 384, 404
Prophesying, 25, 27, 29
Protesters Divinity Hall, xiii, 340, 409
Protestors, 68, 286, 287, 288, 340, 344
Proudfoot, William, 328, 347, 348

Quaker(s), 66
Quakerism, 66, 89
Quebec, 94, 374
Queen's College/University, 347, 388
Quesnel, 313

Rait, David, 50, 51, 402
Rait, R. S., 40, 43, 45, 46, 49, 50, 51, 71, 113, 114
Rait, William, 402
Ramsay, Andrew, 400
Ramsay, Robert, 396
Ramus, 36, 39, 40
Rankin, Moira, xxi
Reader, 27, 31, 32
Reardon, R. S., 6, 7, 8, 11, 12

Reflections, 140, 220, 221, 236, 248, 300, 302
Regent/regenting, 4, 13, 17, 22, 27, 28, 33, 34, 35, 36, 37, 38, 39, 42, 43, 44, 45, 48, 49, 53, 54, 57, 60, 70, 77, 86, 89, 104, 110, 111, 112, 113, 114, 146, 186, 189, 207, 255, 291, 396
Reid, H. M. B., xix, 34, 36, 53, 61, 62, 63, 64, 66, 68, 87, 88, 121, 125, 126, 127
Reid, James Seaton, 164, 241, 388, 396, 397
Reid, John G., 362
Reid, Thomas, 114, 115, 116
Reid, W. Stanford, 4, 5, 6, 13, 14, 17, 18, 351
Relief Church, xx, xxiv, 94, 387, 406
Remnant Synod, 328, 336, 341, 408
Resolutioner, 68
Revival, 66
Revolution Settlement, x, 42, 91, 126, 383
Reymond, Robert L., 221
Reynolds, 99
Rhetoric, 8, 18, 46, 112, 117, 124, 131, 132, 133, 134, 145, 146, 152, 200, 352, 356, 366, 376, 378, 382, 383
Richmond, Leslie, xxi
Riddell, J. G., 36, 66, 86
Ritchie, Lionel A., 144
Ritchie, William, 144, 145, 159, 401
Robertson, Daniel, 399
Robertson, James, 108, 212, 257, 324, 401
Robertson, James (2), 402
Robertson, John, 398
Robertson, William, 106, 130, 138, 139, 240, 400
Robertsonian Library, 296, 297, 317
Rogers, John, 387
Rollock, Robert, 39, 40, 41, 45, 46, 48, 52, 53, 54, 67, 317, 400
Ronald, John, 349
Rose, Alexander, 86, 396, 398
Ross, Hugh, 360, 361
Ross, James, 83
Ross, John, 111

Index 455

Ross, John (Professor), 403
Rostock, 397, 398, 404
Rotterdam, 5, 53, 105, 398, 400
Row, John, 41, 51, 56, 57, 68, 69, 70, 402
Row, John (2), 405
Rowat, William, 397
Rowen, Samuel, xxii
Roxburgh, Kenneth B. E., xx, 387
Royal College of Surgeons, 325
Royal Commission on Universities, xi, 111, 126, 145, 146, 147, 148, 149, 150, 152, 153, 156, 158, 159, 160, 161, 162, 165
Rule, Alexander, 104, 189, 401
Rule, Gilbert, 129, 189, 400
Rutherford, Samuel, x, xx, xxv, 39, 41, 56, 57, 58, 59, 60, 66, 67, 68, 69, 77, 104, 217, 229, 236, 244, 398, 400, 420, 428, 429, 431, 435
Ryken, Philip G., 39, 104, 209, 229, 317

Sanderson, Margaret, 32
Sands, Patrick, 400
Saumur, 22, 23, 283, 396, 400
Saurin, 264
Scandinavia, 38
Schaeffer, Francis A., 59
Schleiermacher, Freidrich, 314
Schlenther, Boyd S., 116, 210
Schola privata, 13, 18, 36
Schola publica, 13, 14, 17, 18, 20, 21, 26
Scholastic theology, 4, 14, 57, 58, 217, 218, 270, 284, 382, 384
Scholasticism, 20, 57, 60, 115, 284
School, 6, 165, 207, 225
Schoolmaster, 16, 27, 69, 85, 209, 257, 292
Schools, ix, x, xxv, 6, 9, 10, 11, 12, 13, 14, 17, 19, 20, 22, 23, 25, 26, 27, 28, 43, 45, 47, 58, 68, 72, 77, 79, 83, 87, 88, 89, 90, 97, 100, 105, 108, 109, 115, 116, 128, 142, 146, 158, 199, 202, 217, 248, 258, 273, 275, 277, 284, 299, 307, 330, 335, 338, 342, 350, 354, 359, 365, 366, 367, 368, 376, 378, 380, 381, 383, 387, 389

Science, 18, 110, 112, 114, 115, 117, 118, 185, 245, 351, 364
Scots Confession, 25, 33
Scott, Andrew, 403
Scott, David, 284, 287, 289, 328, 329, 330, 331, 332, 334, 335, 336, 337, 338, 341, 342, 343, 399
Scott, Sir Walter, 265, 269
Scottish Enlightenment, xi, 91, 94, 96, 112, 114, 115, 116, 117, 129, 132, 133, 138, 185, 186, 200, 282, 288, 351, 352, 355, 382
Scottish Missionary Society, 380
Scottish Paraphrases, 70, 199, 269
Scottish Psalter 1650, 68, 70
Scottish Society for Propagating the Christian Religion, 124
Scotus, 58, 99
Scougal, Henry, 83, 88, 89, 402
Scougal, Patrick, 400
Scrimgeour, Alexander, 398
Secession, xi, xiv, xv, xvi, xix, xx, xxiii, 6, 108, 128, 132, 140, 165, 169, 170, 171, 172, 175, 176, 179, 182, 183, 184, 185, 186, 187, 188, 191, 192, 193, 194, 198, 200, 202, 207, 212, 223, 226, 234, 241, 242, 244, 248, 251, 258, 259, 262, 264, 270, 271, 275, 276, 279, 288, 289, 327, 330, 334, 335, 338, 339, 348, 349, 352, 355, 359, 360, 362, 363, 366, 367, 368, 371, 372, 373, 374, 377, 379, 380, 381, 383, 384, 385, 386, 387, 388, 389, 392, 406
Second Book of Discipline, 25, 33, 34
Sedan, 22, 23, 50, 396, 398, 400, 402
Sefton, Henry, xix, 63, 93, 130, 139, 193, 395
Selina, Countess of Huntingdon, 210
Selkirk, xii, 40, 94, 252, 257, 258, 259, 260, 261, 262, 263, 264, 265, 268, 271, 310, 318, 329, 347, 407
Selles, Otto H., 24
Semi-Arminians, 276
Seneca, 6

Seymour, Aaron, 210
Shaletti, Paul, 403
Sharpe, John, 400
Sharpe, Patrick, 396
Shaw, Andrew, 398
Shaw, Duncan, 30, 40
Shaw, Robert, 65
Shepard, 99
Shepherd, Thomas, 236
Sheppard, Gerald T., 250
Sher, Richard, 115, 129, 138
Shorter Catechism, 129, 191, 194, 301
Sibbald, Patrick, 404
Simeon, Charles, 151
Simprin, 105
Simpson, Robert, 403
Simson, John, 127, 129, 130, 143, 171, 173, 174, 175, 182, 396
Sinclair, Patrick, 401
Skeletons, 287, 362
Small, R., 190, 204, 206, 209, 212, 244, 257, 258, 304, 321, 332, 337, 338, 341, 349
Smeaton, Thomas, 396
Smith, Adam, 110, 112, 115
Smith, James, 400, 401
Smith, Pye, 313
Societies, 93, 94, 95, 96, 100, 116, 127, 172, 173, 179, 256, 261, 278, 288, 309, 339, 351, 365, 366, 379, 384, 391, 392, 393
Societies, praying, 171, 172, 178
Society for Propagating Christian Knowledge (England), 98
Socinian(s), 66, 122, 140, 292, 328
Socinianism, 92, 141, 163, 325
Solo professor, xiii, 186, 257, 270, 289, 291, 321, 343, 344, 378, 379
Somerville, Thomas, 93, 106, 107, 108, 127, 128
Southern Presbyterians, 325
Spens, Harry, 398
Sprunger, Keith L., 20

St. Andrews, xix, 27, 28, 31, 33, 34, 36, 37, 38, 39, 42, 48, 51, 57, 58, 60, 68, 77, 78, 90, 93, 105, 109, 113, 114, 130, 139, 145, 146, 148, 153, 158, 161, 171, 181, 183, 193, 240, 287, 335, 395, 401
St. Andrews (The Wynd), 397
St. Leonard's College, 27, 33, 38, 109, 113
St. Leonard's Parish, 399
St. Mary's, ix, 37, 38, 46, 47, 48, 50, 53, 54, 57, 68, 72, 77, 84, 89, 93, 105, 130, 139, 141, 158, 161, 162, 163, 164, 182, 395
St. Mungo's, 125, 396
St. Salvator's College, 38, 113
States College, 22
Steven, William, 5
Stevenson, David, 35, 43
Stewart, Dugald, 115
Stewarton, 66, 285, 286, 349, 350
Still, William, 268
Stipend, 27, 273
Stirling, xi, 47, 67, 187, 189, 190, 192, 206, 209, 248, 323, 329, 343, 407, 408
Stirling, John, 173, 396
Story, R. H., 162, 163, 164
Strachan, Andrew, 402
Strachan, John, 401
Strand, Kenneth, 13
Strang, John, 53, 57, 61, 396
Strickland, D. R., 59
Strong, A. H., 249
Stuart, Walter, 402
Students Barrack at Whitburn, 337
Sturm, Jacob, 9, 13, 18, 22, 26
Subscription, x, xx, 72, 75, 91, 92
Suderman, Jeffrey M., 93, 113, 114, 132, 135, 136, 137
Supralapsarian, 57
Supralapsarianism, 283
Swanston, John, 198, 199, 200, 210, 252, 255, 257, 258, 407
Syme, John, 399
Synod
    Aberdeen, 84
    Argyle, 98

Diocesan Synod of Dunblane, 84, 85
Perth and Stirling, 170, 171
Syntagma, Polant, 126
Syriac, 37, 44, 54, 61, 101, 148, 161, 207
Systematic theology, 126, 132, 137, 139, 140, 141, 147, 149, 161, 165, 176, 202, 215, 218, 287, 294, 297, 298, 299, 300, 301, 304, 309, 310, 318, 319, 322, 325, 329, 330, 334, 337, 339, 341, 343, 354, 355, 360, 378, 379, 381, 387

Tait, Robert S., 33
Tamburello, Dennis E., 13
Taylor, John, 129, 358
Taylor, William, 223, 269, 313, 329, 330, 331, 332, 333, 396, 408, 420
Tennant, William, 399
Theological Club (Aberdeen), 93
Theological Society (Associate Hall), 252
Thirteen Colonies, 201
Thirty-Nine Articles, 87
Thistle Chapel, 139, 398
Tholuck, 313, 316
Thomson, Andrew, 122, 308, 364, 371
Tischendorf, 162
Toronto, xxv, 333, 334, 335, 348
Torrance, Thomas F., 57, 65, 71, 77, 87
Trail, Robert, 397
Traill, 264
Trevecca, 210
Trivium, 383
Tron, 61, 96, 400, 401
Trotter, John, 399
Tullidelph, Thomas, 398
Tulloch, John, 398
Turnbull, John, 337, 409
Turretin, Alphonse, 128
Turretin, Francis, 5, 104, 126, 190, 191, 194, 202, 209, 211, 216, 217, 218, 265, 278, 279, 283, 301, 317, 392
Tutor, xvi, 13, 15, 28, 33, 38, 98, 104, 109, 114, 118, 119, 122, 139, 158, 183, 184, 189, 257, 258, 275, 307, 341, 344, 349, 378, 384, 386, 393

Tyrie, James, 398

Unitarian, 129
Unitarianism, 129, 358
United Free Church, 203, 209, 275, 349
United Original Secession Divinity Hall, 409
United Original Secession Divinity Hall (Continuing), 409
United Original Secession Synod, 336, 342, 409
United Presbyterian Church, xxiv, 171, 173, 189, 193, 263, 317, 324
United Secession Church, 177, 279, 293, 297, 308, 315, 319, 323, 326, 328, 347, 407
United States, 325, 335, 388
Urr, 125, 401
Ursinus, 46, 87, 104, 217, 265, 317
Utrecht, 21, 57, 104, 110, 182, 399, 400, 401, 404

Valentine, J., 132
Valeton, Jean, 16
Valla, Lorenzo, 7
van Ryssen, Leonard, 104, 128
Van Vechten, Jacob, 204, 206
Venema, Hermann, 301, 302, 317
Vienna, 71, 401
Vilant, William, 398
Vitringa, 248, 249, 251, 265, 316, 378
Voetius, Gisbert, 20, 57, 126, 217, 316, 384
Voges, Friedhelm, 116, 133, 142
Voluntarist, 270
Voluntary Controversy, 310
Vulgate, 7, 11

Waddel, James, 371, 377, 378
Waddell, John, 349, 377
Waldensians, 241
Wales, xxii, xxv, 100, 210
Waleus, Antonius, 126
Walker, J., 57, 58, 59, 62, 66, 67, 244
Wallace, Robert, 162

Wallace, Ronald, 14
Walloon College, 22
Wardlaw, Ralph, 117, 261, 264, 349, 364
Warfield, Benjamin, 222
Warrender, Hugh, 399
Watson, Robert, 240
Watson, Thomas, 100
Watts, Isaac, 280
Waugh, Alexander, 212, 213, 214, 215, 221, 222, 269
Wedderburn, James, 398
Weir, Duncan Harkness, 397
Weir, Thomas E, 437
Welch, Edwin, 210
Wellwood, Sir Henry Moncrieff, 122, 123, 127, 133, 364
Welsh, David, 163, 401
Wemyss, James, 86, 396
Wendel, François, 7
Wendelin, Marcus Friedrich, 126
Wernernian Society, 351, 352
West Indies, 350
West Linton, Peebleshire, 257, 258
West St. Giles, 400, 401
Westminster Assembly, 57, 58, 60, 67, 75, 87, 129, 164
Westminster Confession, 60, 64, 88, 146, 202, 216, 236, 269, 278, 292, 301, 327, 330, 354, 385, 386, 390
Westminster Divines, 87
Westminster Standards, x, 74
Wetstein, 313
Whitburn, 203, 223, 263, 273, 275, 279, 281, 282, 283, 285, 310, 321, 337, 338, 339, 341, 349, 370, 373, 407, 409
Whitby, Daniel, 358
Whitefield, George, 108, 176, 177, 183
Whitelaw, Marjory, 348
Whytock, Jack C., xv, xvi, xvii, xxiv, 4, 99, 192, 404
Whytock, George, 336

Willet, 99
William of Orange, 21
Willis, Michael, 323, 328, 329, 330, 331, 333, 334, 335, 336, 344, 348, 408
Willis, William, 269, 329, 330, 331, 332, 408
Wilson, Charles, 399
Wilson, J. Stewart, 70
Wilson, John, 150
Wilson, William, xi, 170, 171, 172, 173, 174, 175, 176, 177, 180, 181, 182, 184, 191, 198, 407
Wishart, William Jr., 115, 116, 400
Wishart, William Sr., 130, 400
Witherspoon, John, 116, 186
Witsius, Herman, 67, 110, 216, 217, 251, 265, 280, 316, 378
Witt, Ronald G., 8
Wittenburg, 3
Wodrow Society, 49, 68, 343
Wodrow, James, 126, 127, 143, 396
Wodrow, Robert, 87, 126, 127
Wollebius, 86, 87, 217, 382
Women, 37, 239, 254, 380, 386
Wood, B. Anne, 350, 357, 358
Woolsey, Andrew, 40, 41, 46, 49, 67
Wotherspoon, Laurence, 204
Wright, David F., xix, xx, xxi, 29, 39, 41, 49, 77, 96, 107, 108, 128, 229
Wright, Edward, 396
Wright, William, 397

York, 94
Young, David, 182
Young, James, 5, 41
Young, John, 68, 396
Young, John (Antiburgher), 206
Young, William G., 27

Zanchi, 99, 317
Zurich, 25, 29

Studies in Christian History and Thought

(All titles uniform with this volume)
Dates in bold are of projected publication

David Bebbington
Holiness in Nineteenth-Century England
David Bebbington stresses the relationship of movements of spirituality to changes in their cultural setting, especially the legacies of the Enlightenment and Romanticism. He shows that these broad shifts in ideological mood had a profound effect on the ways in which piety was conceptualized and practised. Holiness was intimately bound up with the spirit of the age.
2000 / 0-85364-981-2 / viii + 98pp

J. William Black
Reformation Pastors
Richard Baxter and the Ideal of the Reformed Pastor
This work examines Richard Baxter's *Gildas Salvianus, The Reformed Pastor* (1656) and explores each aspect of his pastoral strategy in light of his own concern for 'reformation' and in the broader context of Edwardian, Elizabethan and early Stuart pastoral ideals and practice.
2003 / 1-84227-190-3 / xxii + 308pp

James Bruce
Prophecy, Miracles, Angels, *and* Heavenly Light?
The Eschatology, Pneumatology and Missiology of Adomnán's Life of Columba
This book surveys approaches to the marvellous in hagiography, providing the first critique of Plummer's hypothesis of Irish saga origin. It then analyses the uniquely systematized phenomena in the *Life of Columba* from Adomnán's seventh-century theological perspective, identifying the coming of the eschatological Kingdom as the key to understanding.
2004 / 1-84227-227-6 / xviii + 286pp

Colin J. Bulley
The Priesthood of Some Believers
Developments from the General to the Special Priesthood in the Christian Literature of the First Three Centuries
The first in-depth treatment of early Christian texts on the priesthood of all believers shows that the developing priesthood of the ordained related closely to the division between laity and clergy and had deleterious effects on the practice of the general priesthood.
2000 / 1-84227-034-6 / xii + 336pp

Anthony R. Cross (ed.)
Ecumenism and History
Studies in Honour of John H.Y. Briggs
This collection of essays examines the inter-relationships between the two fields in which Professor Briggs has contributed so much: history—particularly Baptist and Nonconformist—and the ecumenical movement. With contributions from colleagues and former research students from Britain, Europe and North America, *Ecumenism and History* provides wide-ranging studies in important aspects of Christian history, theology and ecumenical studies.
2002 / 1-84227-135-0 / xx + 362pp

Maggi Dawn
Confessions of an Inquiring Spirit
Form as Constitutive of Meaning in S.T. Coleridge's Theological Writing
This study of Coleridge's *Confessions* focuses on its confessional, epistolary and fragmentary form, suggesting that attention to these features significantly affects its interpretation. Bringing a close study of these three literary forms, the author suggests ways in which they nuance the text with particular understandings of the Trinity, and of a kenotic christology. Some parallels are drawn between Romantic and postmodern dilemmas concerning the authority of the biblical text.
2006 / 1-84227-255-1 / approx. 224 pp

Ruth Gouldbourne
The Flesh and the Feminine
Gender and Theology in the Writings of Caspar Schwenckfeld
Caspar Schwenckfeld and his movement exemplify one of the radical communities of the sixteenth century. Challenging theological and liturgical norms, they also found themselves challenging social and particularly gender assumptions. In this book, the issues of the relationship between radical theology and the understanding of gender are considered.
2005 / 1-84227-048-6 / approx. 304pp

Crawford Gribben
Puritan Millennialism
Literature and Theology, 1550–1682
Puritan Millennialism surveys the growth, impact and eventual decline of puritan millennialism throughout England, Scotland and Ireland, arguing that it was much more diverse than has frequently been suggested. This Paternoster edition is revised and extended from the original 2000 text.
2007 / 1-84227-372-8 / approx. 320pp

Galen K. Johnson
Prisoner of Conscience
John Bunyan on Self, Community and Christian Faith
This is an interdisciplinary study of John Bunyan's understanding of conscience across his autobiographical, theological and fictional writings, investigating whether conscience always deserves fidelity, and how Bunyan's view of conscience affects his relationship both to modern Western individualism and historic Christianity.

2003 / 1-84227-223-3 / xvi + 236pp

R.T. Kendall
Calvin and English Calvinism to 1649
The author's thesis is that those who formed the Westminster Confession of Faith, which is regarded as Calvinism, in fact departed from John Calvin on two points: (1) the extent of the atonement and (2) the ground of assurance of salvation.

1997 / 0-85364-827-1 / xii + 264pp

Timothy Larsen
Friends of Religious Equality
Nonconformist Politics in Mid-Victorian England
During the middle decades of the nineteenth century the English Nonconformist community developed a coherent political philosophy of its own, of which a central tenet was the principle of religious equality (in contrast to the stereotype of Evangelical Dissenters). The Dissenting community fought for the civil rights of Roman Catholics, non-Christians and even atheists on an issue of principle which had its flowering in the enthusiastic and undivided support which Nonconformity gave to the campaign for Jewish emancipation. This reissued study examines the political efforts and ideas of English Nonconformists during the period, covering the whole range of national issues raised, from state education to the Crimean War. It offers a case study of a theologically conservative group defending religious pluralism in the civic sphere, showing that the concept of religious equality was a grand vision at the centre of the political philosophy of the Dissenters.

2007 / 1-84227-402-3 / x + 300pp

Byung-Ho Moon
Christ the Mediator of the Law
Calvin's Christological Understanding of the Law as the Rule of Living and Life-Giving

This book explores the coherence between Christology and soteriology in Calvin's theology of the law, examining its intellectual origins and his position on the concept and extent of Christ's mediation of the law. A comparative study between Calvin and contemporary Reformers—Luther, Bucer, Melancthon and Bullinger—and his opponent Michael Servetus is made for the purpose of pointing out the unique feature of Calvin's Christological understanding of the law.

2005 / 1-84227-318-3 / approx. 370pp

John Eifion Morgan-Wynne
Holy Spirit and Religious Experience in Christian Writings, c.AD 90–200

This study examines how far Christians in the third to fifth generations (c.AD 90–200) attributed their sense of encounter with the divine presence, their sense of illumination in the truth or guidance in decision-making, and their sense of ethical empowerment to the activity of the Holy Spirit in their lives.

2005 / 1-84227-319-1 / approx. 350pp

James I. Packer
The Redemption and Restoration of Man in the Thought of Richard Baxter

James I. Packer provides a full and sympathetic exposition of Richard Baxter's doctrine of humanity, created and fallen; its redemption by Christ Jesus; and its restoration in the image of God through the obedience of faith by the power of the Holy Spirit.

2002 / 1-84227-147-4 / 432pp

Andrew Partington,
Church and State
The Contribution of the Church of England Bishops to the House of Lords during the Thatcher Years

In *Church and State*, Andrew Partington argues that the contribution of the Church of England bishops to the House of Lords during the Thatcher years was overwhelmingly critical of the government; failed to have a significant influence in the public realm; was inefficient, being undertaken by a minority of those eligible to sit on the Bench of Bishops; and was insufficiently moral and spiritual in its content to be distinctive. On the basis of this, and the likely reduction of the number of places available for Church of England bishops in a fully reformed Second Chamber, the author argues for an evolution in the Church of England's approach to the service of its bishops in the House of Lords. He proposes the Church of England works to overcome the genuine obstacles which hinder busy diocesan bishops from contributing to the debates of the House of Lords and to its life more informally.

2005 / 1-84227-334-5 / approx. 324pp

Michael Pasquarello III
God's Ploughman
Hugh Latimer: A 'Preaching Life' (1490–1555)

This construction of a 'preaching life' situates Hugh Latimer within the larger religious, political and intellectual world of late medieval England. Neither biography, intellectual history, nor analysis of discrete sermon texts, this book is a work of homiletic history which draws from the details of Latimer's milieu to construct an interpretive framework for the preaching performances that formed the core of his identity as a religious reformer. Its goal is to illumine the practical wisdom embodied in the content, form and style of Latimer's preaching, and to recapture a sense of its overarching purpose, movement, and transforming force during the reform of sixteenth-century England.

2006 / 1-84227-336-1 / approx. 250pp

Alan P.F. Sell
Enlightenment, Ecumenism, Evangel
Theological Themes and Thinkers 1550–2000

This book consists of papers in which such interlocking topics as the Enlightenment, the problem of authority, the development of doctrine, spirituality, ecumenism, theological method and the heart of the gospel are discussed. Issues of significance to the church at large are explored with special reference to writers from the Reformed and Dissenting traditions.

2005 / 1-84227-330-2 / xviii + 422pp

Alan P.F. Sell
Hinterland Theology
Some Reformed and Dissenting Adjustments
Many books have been written on theology's 'giants' and significant trends, but what of those lesser-known writers who adjusted to them? In this book some hinterland theologians of the British Reformed and Dissenting traditions, who followed in the wake of toleration, the Evangelical Revival, the rise of modern biblical criticism and Karl Barth, are allowed to have their say. They include Thomas Ridgley, Ralph Wardlaw, T.V. Tymms and N.H.G. Robinson.
2006 / 1-84227-331-0 / approx. 350pp

Alan P.F. Sell and Anthony R. Cross (eds)
Protestant Nonconformity in the Twentieth Century
In this collection of essays scholars representative of a number of Nonconformist traditions reflect thematically on Nonconformists' life and witness during the twentieth century. Among the subjects reviewed are biblical studies, theology, worship, evangelism and spirituality, and ecumenism. Over and above its immediate interest, this collection provides a marker to future scholars and others wishing to know how some of their forebears assessed Nonconformity's contribution to a variety of fields during the century leading up to Christianity's third millennium.
2003 / 1-84227-221-7 / x + 398pp

Mark Smith
Religion in Industrial Society
Oldham and Saddleworth 1740–1865
This book analyses the way British churches sought to meet the challenge of industrialization and urbanization during the period 1740–1865. Working from a case-study of Oldham and Saddleworth, Mark Smith challenges the received view that the Anglican Church in the eighteenth century was characterized by complacency and inertia, and reveals Anglicanism's vigorous and creative response to the new conditions. He reassesses the significance of the centrally directed church reforms of the mid-nineteenth century, and emphasizes the importance of local energy and enthusiasm. Charting the growth of denominational pluralism in Oldham and Saddleworth, Dr Smith compares the strengths and weaknesses of the various Anglican and Nonconformist approaches to promoting church growth. He also demonstrates the extent to which all the churches participated in a common culture shaped by the influence of evangelicalism, and shows that active co-operation between the churches rather than denominational conflict dominated. This revised and updated edition of Dr Smith's challenging and original study makes an important contribution both to the social history of religion and to urban studies.
2006 / 1-84227-335-3 / approx. 300pp

Martin Sutherland
Peace, Toleration and Decay
The Ecclesiology of Later Stuart Dissent

This fresh analysis brings to light the complexity and fragility of the later Stuart Nonconformist consensus. Recent findings on wider seventeenth-century thought are incorporated into a new picture of the dynamics of Dissent and the roots of evangelicalism.

2003 / 1-84227-152-0 / xxii + 216pp

G. Michael Thomas
The Extent of the Atonement
A Dilemma for Reformed Theology from Calvin to the Consensus

A study of the way Reformed theology addressed the question, 'Did Christ die for all, or for the elect only?', commencing with John Calvin, and including debates with Lutheranism, the Synod of Dort and the teaching of Moïse Amyraut.

1997 / 0-85364-828-X / x + 278pp

David M. Thompson
Baptism, Church and Society in Britain from the Evangelical Revival to *Baptism, Eucharist and Ministry*

The theology and practice of baptism have not received the attention they deserve. How important is faith? What does baptismal regeneration mean? Is baptism a bond of unity between Christians? This book discusses the theology of baptism and popular belief and practice in England and Wales from the Evangelical Revival to the publication of the World Council of Churches' consensus statement on *Baptism, Eucharist and Ministry* (1982).

2005 / 1-84227-393-0 / approx. 224pp

Mark D. Thompson
A Sure Ground on Which to Stand
The Relation of Authority and Interpretive Method of Luther's Approach to Scripture

The best interpreter of Luther is Luther himself. Unfortunately many modern studies have superimposed contemporary agendas upon this sixteenth-century Reformer's writings. This fresh study examines Luther's own words to find an explanation for his robust confidence in the Scriptures, a confidence that generated the famous 'stand' at Worms in 1521.

2004 / 1-84227-145-8 / xvi + 322pp

Carl R. Trueman and R.S. Clark (eds)
Protestant Scholasticism
Essays in Reassessment

Traditionally Protestant theology, between Luther's early reforming career and the dawn of the Enlightenment, has been seen in terms of decline and fall into the wastelands of rationalism and scholastic speculation. In this volume a number of scholars question such an interpretation. The editors argue that the development of post-Reformation Protestantism can only be understood when a proper historical model of doctrinal change is adopted. This historical concern underlies the subsequent studies of theologians such as Calvin, Beza, Olevian, Baxter, and the two Turrentini. The result is a significantly different reading of the development of Protestant Orthodoxy, one which both challenges the older scholarly interpretations and clichés about the relationship of Protestantism to, among other things, scholasticism and rationalism, and which demonstrates the fruitfulness of the new, historical approach.

1999 / 0-85364-853-0 / xx + 344pp

Shawn D. Wright
Our Sovereign Refuge
The Pastoral Theology of Theodore Beza

Our Sovereign Refuge is a study of the pastoral theology of the Protestant reformer who inherited the mantle of leadership in the Reformed church from John Calvin. Countering a common view of Beza as supremely a 'scholastic' theologian who deviated from Calvin's biblical focus, Wright uncovers a new portrait. He was not a cold and rigid academic theologian obsessed with probing the eternal decrees of God. Rather, by placing him in his pastoral context and by noting his concerns in his pastoral and biblical treatises, Wright shows that Beza was fundamentally a committed Christian who was troubled by the vicissitudes of life in the second half of the sixteenth century. He believed that the biblical truth of the supreme sovereignty of God alone could support Christians on their earthly pilgrimage to heaven. This pastoral and personal portrait forms the heart of Wright's argument.

2004 / 1-84227-252-7 / xviii + 308pp

Paternoster
9 Holdom Avenue,
Bletchley,
Milton Keynes MK1 1QR,
United Kingdom
Web: www.authenticmedia.co.uk/paternoster

www.ingramcontent.com/pod-product-compliance
Lightning Source LLC
Chambersburg PA
CBHW052046290426
44111CB00011B/1641